7250

8/9
346 11: 2, 8, 9, 13
394 12. 2, 3, 4, 5

8/23
4313: 2, 5, 6, 8
4714: 5, 6, 7, 9

501
T 13:30
W 07:30
560

13   12

Microeconomics

AND BEHAVIOR

Microeconomics
AND BEHAVIOR

Fourth Edition

Robert H. Frank
Cornell University

with the assistance of
Amy J. Glass
The Ohio State University

Boston   Burr Ridge, IL   Dubuque, IA   Madison, WI   New York   San Francisco   St. Louis
Bangkok   Bogotá   Caracas   Lisbon   London   Madrid
Mexico City   Milan   New Delhi   Seoul   Singapore   Sydney   Taipei   Toronto

McGraw-Hill Higher Education

*A Division of The **McGraw-Hill** Companies*

MICROECONOMICS AND BEHAVIOR

This book is printed on acid-free paper.

1 2 3 4 5 6 7 8 9 0   DOC DOC   0 9 8 7 6 5 4 3 2 1 0

ISBN 0-07-366083-3

Editorial director: *Michael Junior*
Publisher: *Gary Burke*
Executive editor: *Lucille Sutton*
Development editor: *Thomas Thompson*
Marketing manager: *Nelson Black*
Project manager: *Eva Strock*
Production supervisor: *Rich DeVitto*
Supplements coordinators: *Louis Swaim, Florence Fong, Becky Szura*
Designer: *Carol Barr*
Cover designer: *Nicole Leong*
Typeface: *Palatino*
Compositor and prepress: *GTS Graphics, Inc.*
Printer: *RR Donnelley & Sons*

Cover photographs by PhotoDisc®

Library of Congress Cataloging-in-Publication Data

Frank, Robert H.
   Microeconomics and behavior/Robert H. Frank; with the assistance of Amy J. Glass.—4th ed.
      p.   cm.
   Includes index.
   ISBN 0-07-366083-3 (alk. paper)
   1. Microeconomics.   2. Economic man.   3. Self-interest.
4. Consumer behavior.   5. Microeconomics Examinations, questions, etc.   6. Economic man Examinations, questions, etc.   7. Self-interest Examinations, questions, etc.   8. Consumer behavior Examinations, questions, etc.   9. Self-interest Examinations, questions, etc.   I. Glass, Amy Jocelyn.   II. Title.
HB171.5.F733   1999
338.5—dc21

INTERNATIONAL EDITION ISBN 0-07-116947-4
Copyright © 2000. Exclusive rights by The McGraw-Hill Companies, Inc. for manufacture and export. This book cannot be re-exported from the country to which it is consigned by McGraw-Hill. The International Edition is not available in North America.

http://www.mhhe.com

FOR DAVID, JASON,
CHRISTOPHER, AND HAYDEN

ABOUT THE AUTHOR

Robert H. Frank received his B.S. in mathematics from Georgia Tech in 1966, then taught math and science for two years as a Peace Corps Volunteer in rural Nepal. He received his M.A. in statistics from the University of California at Berkeley in 1971, and his Ph.D. in economics in 1972, also from U.C. Berkeley. He is the Goldwin Smith Professor of Economics at Cornell University, where he has taught since 1972 and where he currently holds a joint appointment in the department of economics and the Johnson Graduate School of Management. During leaves of absence from Cornell, he served as chief economist for the Civil Aeronautics Board from 1978 to 1980 and was a Fellow at the Center for Advanced Study in the Behavioral Sciences in 1992–93. He has published on a variety of subjects, including price and wage discrimination, public utility pricing, the measurement of unemployment spell lengths, and the distributional consequences of direct foreign investment. For the past several years, his research has focused on rivalry and cooperation in economic and social behavior. His books on these themes include *Choosing the Right Pond: Human Behavior and the Quest for Status* (Oxford University Press, 1985) and *Passions Within Reason: The Strategic Role of the Emotions* (W. W. Norton, 1988). He and Philip Cook are co-authors of *The Winner-Take-All Society* (The Free Press, 1995), which received a Critic's Choice Award and appeared on both the *New York Times* Notable Books list and *Business Week* Ten Best list for 1995. His most recent general interest publication is *Luxury Fever* (The Free Press, 1999). Professor Frank's books have been translated into eight languages. He has been awarded an Andrew W. Mellon Professorship (1987–1990), a Kenan Enterprise Award (1993), and a Merrill Scholars Program Outstanding Educator Citation (1991).

CONTENTS

Appendixes (on Web site: see www.mhhe.com/economics/frank4)
  3. The Utility Function Approach to the Consumer Budgeting Problem
  4. Additional Topics in Demand Theory
  5. Additional Topics in Supply Theory
  6. Search Theory and the Winner's Curse
  9. Mathematical Extensions of Production Theory
 10. Mathematical Extensions of the Theory of Costs
 13. Additional Models of Monopolistic Competition
 14. Labor
 15. A More Detailed Look at Exhaustible Resource Allocation

Preface

My goal in writing *Microeconomics and Behavior* was to produce an intellectually challenging text that at the same time would be accessible and engaging to students. The more common approach in this market has been to emphasize one or the other of these dimensions. Some texts have done well by sacrificing rigor in the name of user-friendliness. But although such books sometimes keep students happy, they often fail to prepare them for upper-division courses in the major. Other texts have succeeded by sacrificing accessibility in the name of rigor, where rigor is all too often taken to mean mathematical density. These courses overwhelm many undergraduates, and even those few who become adept at solving well-posed mathematical optimization problems are often baffled by questions drawn from everyday contexts. I have always believed that a text could at once be rigorous *and* user-friendly. And to judge by the breadth of *Microeconomics and Behavior*'s adoption list, many of you apparently agree.

I wrote *Microeconomics and Behavior* in the conviction that the teaching of intuition and the teaching of technical tools are complements, not substitutes. Students who learn only technical tools rarely seem to develop any real affection for our discipline, and even more rarely do they acquire that distinctive mindset we call "thinking like an economist." By contrast, students who develop economic intuition are stimulated to think more deeply about the technical tools they learn and to find more interesting ways to apply them. Most important, they usually end up *liking* economics.

Microeconomics and Behavior develops the core analytical tools with great patience and attention to detail. At the same time, it embeds these tools in a uniquely diverse collection of examples and applications to illuminate the power and versatility of the economic way of thinking.

Economic Naturalism

In more than thirty years of teaching, I have found that the most effective device for developing intuition is to train students to become "economic naturalists." Studying biology enables people to observe and marvel at many details of life that would otherwise escape notice. In much the same way, studying microeconomics can enable students to see the mundane details of ordinary existence in a sharp new light. Throughout the text, I develop intuition by means of examples and applications drawn from everyday experience. *Microeconomics and Behavior* teaches students to see each feature of the man made landscape as the reflection of an implicit or explicit cost-benefit calculation.

An economic naturalist is someone who wonders why the business manager of the economics department was delighted when I began putting the lecture notes for my course on the university's Intranet server, whereas the business manager in the management school (where I also teach) was upset. About a week into the term, I got an urgent letter from the management school's business manager telling me that henceforth I should instruct the copy center to make hard-copies of my lecture notes for distribution to students free of charge. No similar instruction came from the business manager of the economics department. When I asked for clarification, the management school's manager told me that students had been downloading my notes and printing them out in the school's computer labs at a cost of 5 cents a page, which was far more than the 1.25 cents the school's copy center charges for duplication. Fair enough. But then why was the economics department's administrator not worried about the same problem? (When I then asked whether he wanted me to distribute hardcopies of my notes, he said "Don't you dare!")

I soon discovered that their different viewpoints had nothing to do with the very different cultures of the two units; instead, they were a consequence of a small but important difference in economic incentives: Whereas in the business school the same administrator pays for printing in both the computer labs and the copy center, the economics department administrator pays only for printing on the department copier. When economics students print my lecture notes off the web in various campus computer laboratories in the Arts College, the bills go directly to the college. So from the economics department's point of view, these copies were free.

Year in and year out, the most valuable assignments in my course are the two brief papers in which I ask students to report their efforts to become economic naturalists. Their specific charge is to use microeconomic principles to answer a question prompted by a personal observation. In recent terms, students have grappled with questions such as these: Why do they put Braille dots on the keypads of drive-up ATM machines? Why do top female models earn more than top male models? Why do brides spend so much money on wedding dresses while grooms often rent cheap tuxedos (even though grooms could potentially wear their tuxedos on many other occasions and brides will never wear their dresses again)? Why is coffee so much more expensive in Japan than in the United States? Why are child safety seats required in cars but not in airplanes? Why aren't NFL kickers paid the same as leading scorers in other sports? The beauty of this assignment is not only that students enjoy writing these papers, but also that few manage to complete them without becoming lifelong economic naturalists.

Focus on Problem Solving

Most economists agree that a critical step in learning price theory is to solve problems. More than any other text currently available in the marketplace, *Microeconomics and Behavior* prepares students for its end-of-chapter problems by taking them through a sequence of carefully crafted examples and exercises within each chapter. Because most of these examples and exercises are drawn from familiar contexts, and because students engage more readily with the concrete than with the abstract, this approach has proven effective. By contrast, my experience with many current texts is that students often reach the end-of-chapter problems with little or no idea how to proceed.

Optimal Topic Coverage

A guiding principle in the evolution of *Microeconomics and Behavior* has been that topics should be emphasized in proportion to both their importance and the difficulty that students have in mastering them. Because the basic rational choice model is the building block for much of what comes later in the course, I have devoted considerably more attention to its development than competing texts do. I have also allocated extra space for elasticity and its applications in demand theory and for the average-marginal distinction in production theory.

As an additional means of identifying topics most difficult to master, I used recent research showing that people often systematically violate the prescriptions of the rational choice model. For example, whereas the model says that rational persons will ignore sunk costs, many people are in fact strongly influenced by them. (Someone who receives an expensive but painfully tight pair of shoes as a gift is much less likely to wear them than someone who spent $200 out of his own pocket for those same shoes.) Especially in the chapters on consumer behavior, I call students' attention to situations in which they themselves are likely to make irrational choices. Because students' resources are limited, it makes sense to focus on precisely those issues for which knowing price theory is most likely to be helpful.

It may seem natural to wonder whether discussing examples of irrational choices might confuse students who are struggling to master the details of the rational choice model. Ironically, however, my experience has been exactly to the contrary. Such examples actually underscore the normative message of the traditional theory. Students who are exposed to them invariably gain a deeper understanding of the basic theoretical principles at issue. Indeed, they often seem to take an almost conspiratorial pride in being able to see through the errors of judgment that many consumers make. For instructors who want to pursue how cognitive limitations affect consumer behavior in greater detail, a supplementary chapter on this topic is included.

A Broader Conception of Self-Interest

Another goal in *Microeconomics and Behavior* has been to incorporate a broader conception of preferences into models of individual choice. Most texts mention at the outset that our rational choice model takes people's tastes as given. They may be altruists, sadists, or masochists; or they may be concerned solely with advancing their own material interests. But having said that, most texts then proceed to ignore all motives other than material self-interest. It is easy to see why, because economic research has scored its most impressive gains on the strength of this portrayal of human motivation. It tells us, for example, why car pools form in the wake of gasoline price increases and why thermostats are generally set lower in apartments that have separately metered utilities.

And yet, as students are keenly aware, our *homo economicus* caricature is patently at odds with much of what we know about human behavior. People vote in presidential elections. They give anonymously to public television stations and private charities. They donate bone marrow to strangers with leukemia. They endure great trouble and expense to see justice done, even when it will not undo the original injury. At great risk to themselves, they pull people from burning buildings and jump into icy rivers to rescue people who are about to drown. Soldiers throw their bodies atop live grenades to save their comrades. Seen through the lens of the self-interest theory emphasized in current microeconomics textbooks, such behavior is the human equivalent of planets traveling in square orbits. Indeed, many students are strongly alienated by our self-interest model, which they perceive as narrow and mean-spirited.

Microeconomics and Behavior freely concedes the importance of the self-interest motive in many contexts, but also contains a supplementary chapter on the role of unselfish motives in social and economic transactions. Using elementary game theory, this chapter identifies circumstances in which people who hold such motives have a competitive advantage over pure opportunists. For example, the chapter shows that people known to have cooperative predispositions can solve prisoner's dilemmas and other commitment problems in a way that purely self-interested persons cannot.

Our theoretical models of human nature are important, not least because they mold our expectations about how others will behave. Economics is the social science most closely identified with the self-interest model of human behavior. Does this model color our expectations of others, and perhaps even our own behavior? In a recent study, Tom Gilovich, Dennis Regan, and I found numerous indications that economists are much more likely than others to behave opportunistically in social dilemmas.[1] For example, academic economists were more than twice as likely as the members of any other discipline we surveyed to report that they give no money at all to any private charity. In an experiment, we also found that economics majors were more than twice as likely as nonmajors to cheat when playing one-shot prisoner's dilemmas with strangers.

This difference was not merely a reflection of the fact that people who chose to major in economics were more opportunistic to begin with. We found, for example, that the difference in cheating grew larger the longer a student had studied economics. Questionnaire responses also indicated that freshmen in their first microeconomics course were more likely at the end of the term to expect opportunistic behavior from others than they were at the beginning.

There are thus at least some grounds for concern that, by stressing only the self-interest motive, economists may have undermined our students' propensities for cooperative behavior. The irony, as I show in Chapter 7, is that the internal logic of the economic model never predicted such narrowly self-interested behavior in the first place.

Additional Pedagogical Features

Unlike most intermediate texts, *Microeconomics and Behavior* contains no boxed applications, which tend to distract students from the thread of argument being developed. Instead, applications and examples are integrated fully into the text. Many of these have the added advantage of being drawn from experiences to which students can personally relate.

The chapter introductions and summaries are other innovative features of *Microeconomics and Behavior*. Most chapters begin with an anecdote that poses a problem or question that the material developed in the chapter will enable the student to answer. These introductions have proved especially helpful for the many students who find that getting started is often the hardest step. The chapter summaries in most current texts consist of brief annotated lists of the topics covered. The chapter summaries in *Microeconomics and Behavior*, by contrast, are written in a narrative form that carefully synthesizes the material covered in the chapters.

---

[1] See R. H. Frank, T. D. Gilovich, and D. T. Regan, "Does Studying Economics Inhibit Coorperation?", *Journal of Economic Perspectives*, Spring 1993.

Each chapter concludes with a selection of problems that range in difficulty from routine to highly challenging. These problems have all been class-tested to ensure their accuracy and effectiveness in helping students master the most important concepts in the chapters.

Answers to all in-text exercises appear at the end of the chapter in which they occur. Variations and extensions of these exercises are echoed in the end-of-chapter problems; this approach enables students to approach these problem sets with greater confidence. Detailed answers to all end-of-chapter problems are included in the Instructor's Manual.

Core and Supplementary Chapters

As the table of contents makes clear, *Microeconomics and Behavior* includes the standard microeconomics text core chapters, in the order in which they are most commonly presented. It also includes four supplementary chapters that explore new developments and other material not generally included in the core chapters. With the time constraints of the single-term course in mind, the supplementary chapters have been written in a more discursive style than the core chapters, which makes them accessible to students with little or no faculty supervision. Thus, with virtually no disruption of established single-term lecture plans, these chapters can be assigned as supplementary readings.

Changes in the Fourth Edition

Most college textbooks are far too long. And since almost everyone seems to agree that this is a problem, the natural solution would seem to be to publish shorter ones. Yet a short book usually fails because too many potential adopters cannot find their favorite topics in it. Successful books are usually big to begin with, and almost invariably they grow longer with each edition. New developments have to be covered, after all, and it is almost impossible to delete existing material that adopters have grown accustomed to using.

Recent developments in technology, however, provide grounds for hope. In this edition of *Microeconomics and Behavior*, my aim has been to create a much more compact printed textbook—one whose length is manageable for the standard single-term course in intermediate microeconomics—while at the same time keeping the more detailed coverage of previous editions within easy reach of all who care to use it. To this end, I transferred all eight appendixes from the third edition onto the *Microeconomics and Behavior*, Fourth Edition, Web site (www. mhhe.com/economics/frank4). This material is listed clearly in the table of contents, and you'll also find additional references to it in the text itself.

The entire text has also gone through another round of thorough editing. The result is a leaner book with a sharper focus on core principles and on basic microeconomic models, which allows students to focus on those concepts crucial to a fuller understanding of the models. This has been done while retaining the essential character of the earlier editions that attracted such a loyal group of users.

The text retains its focus on problem solving, but the end-of-chapter materials are now linked more closely to specific chapter topics and examples, helping students improve retention and streamline studying. The worked examples and exercises in each chapter offer students the opportunity to teach themselves and to learn promptly from their mistakes. And many new problems and exercises have been added.

The Ancillaries

The supplements package has been expanded and improved. It now consists of the following materials:

INSTRUCTOR'S MANUAL AND TEST BANK

Each chapter contains a Chapter Summary, a Chapter Outline, Teaching Suggestions, a list of Stumbling Blocks for Students, Answers to Text Questions for Review, Problems, and Study Guide Homework Assignments. Problems, multiple-choice questions, and essay questions are also included.

COMPUTERIZED TEST BANK (WINDOWS)

The Brownstone Diploma 97 software contains a test-generation program (Exam for Windows), a grade-book program, and an on-line testing program. It can create a wide array of paper tests, self-grading HTML tests (administered over a campus intranet or the Internet), and network-based tests (administered over a campus network in a computer lab). Network-based tests can be automatically graded, and their results can be pulled directly into the grade-book program.

OVERHEAD TRANSPARENCIES

Two hundred transparencies reproduce key figures in the text.

STUDY GUIDE

For each chapter, the Guide provides these sections: Boiling Down (the chapter), Chapter Outline, Important Terms, A Case to Consider, Multiple-Choice Questions, Problems, and Homework Assignments.

GrafTool (WINDOWS)

Developed by Mark Reiman of Pacific Lutheran University, this Windows software contains 12 full-length tutorials, extensive graphical and numerical exercises, along with a hyperlink glossary and a bibliography.

WEB SITE

The Website contains a great many features for both students and instructors, including the eight appendixes that appeared in the third edition of the textbook (see www.mhhe.com/economics/frank4).

Acknowledgments

In preparing the fourth edition of *Microeconomics and Behavior*, I benefited enormously from the assistance of Professor Amy Jocelyn Glass of The Ohio State University. As a long-time user of earlier editions, Amy provided a fresh perspective on how different elements of the book work in the classroom. And because she was not swayed by proprietary sentiments about the text as it stood, she was often much better able to identify candidates for trimming than I could. My sincere thanks to her.

I also thank the many reviewers involved in the project. Their insights and critiques led to many improvements, and I hope they are as pleased as I am with their influence on the final product. Reviewers involved in the preparation of this edition are as follows:

Anita M. Benvignati	*George Washington University*
Philip J. Grossman	*University of Texas, Arlington*
Geoffrey A. Jehle	*Vassar College*
Sumit Joshi	*George Washington University*
Philip King	*San Francisco State University*
Janet Koscianski	*Shippensburg University*
Norman P. Obst	*Michigan State University*
Dorothy Siden	*Salem State College*
Rohini Somanathan	*Emory University*
Kenneth R. Troske	*University of Missouri, Columbia*

Reviewers of earlier editions:

Jack Adams	*University of Arkansas–Little Rock*
Robert F. Allen	*Creighton University*
Ted Amato	*University of North Carolina–Charlotte*
Bruce Benson	*Florida State University*
Swati Bhatt	*New York University*
Scott Bierman	*Carleton College*
Michael R. Butler	*Texas Christian University*
Robert Carbaugh	*Central Washington University*
Anthony M. Carilli	*Hampden–Sydney College*
Philip J. Cook	*Duke University*
James L. Dietz	*California State University–Fullerton*
Maxim Engers	*University of Virginia*
Mickey Falkson	*Cornell University*

Paul Farnham	*Georgia State University*
Robert M. Feinberg	*American University*
Randall Filer	*City University of New York–Hunter College*
Raymond Fishe	*University of Miami*
Roger Frantz	*San Diego State University*
Gary Gigliotti	*Rutgers University*
Lorraine Glover	*California State University–Northridge*
Devra Goldbe	*City University of New York–Hunter College*
Thomas A. Gresik	*Pennsylvania State University*
Loren Guffey	*University of Central Arkansas*
Harish Gupta	*University of Nebraska–Lincoln*
Simon Hakim	*Temple University*
Karen Hallows	*University of Missouri*
Jim Halteman	*Wheaton College*
Clifford B. Hawley	*West Virginia University*
Dean Hiebert	*Illinois State University*
Harold M. Hochman	*Baruch College*
Laurence R. Iannaccone	*Santa Clara University*
Julie Iskow	*University of Vermont*
Donald Keenan	*University of Georgia*
Herbert Kessell	*St. Michael's College*
Philip King	*San Francisco State University*
John Klock	*Brandeis Univeristy*
Kenneth Koford	*University of Delaware*
Anthony Krautmann	*DePaul University*
Alan J. MacFadyen	*University of Calgary*
Craig MacPhee	*University of Nebraska–Lincoln*
John D. Mason	*Gordon College*
Thomas E. Merz	*Michigan Technological University*
Robert E. Moore	*Georgia State University*
Michael A. Murphy	*Tufts University*
Clark Nardinelli	*Clemson University*
Robert H. Nicholson	*University of Richmond*
Charles Noussair	*Purdue University*
Diane S. Owen	*The College of William and Mary*
Michael T. Peddle	*Northern Illinois University*
John Pomery	*Purdue University*
Joseph M. Prinzinger	*Lynchburg College*
Dagmar Rajagopal	*Ryerson Polytechnical Institute*
J. David Richardson	*Syracuse University*
Sheldon Sax	*Middlebury College*
John Schnell	*University of Alabama–Huntsville*
Bruce Seaman	*Georgia State University*
Larry G. Sgontz	*University of Iowa*
William Shaffer	*Georgia Tech*

Jason Shogren	*Iowa State University*
Dorothy Ryan Siden	*Salem State College*
Henry Thompson	*Auburn University*
Steven Tomlinson	*University of Texas–Austin*
Nicholas S. Vonortas	*George Washington University*
Don Waldman	*Colgate University*
Charles E. White	*Framingham State College*

As usual, I welcome further comments and suggestions.

Robert H. Frank

Microeconomics
AND BEHAVIOR

PART ONE

Introduction

In these first two chapters we review material from the introductory microeconomics course. Chapter 1 applies the principles of cost-benefit analysis to a variety of choices familiar from experience. Its goal is to give you an intuitive feel for what it means to "think like an economist."

Chapter 2 develops basic supply and demand analysis, our analytical tool for explaining the prices and quantities of goods traded in markets. We will see that although unregulated markets may not always yield outcomes we like, they often produce the best results attainable under the circumstances. By contrast, governmental efforts to help the poor by regulating prices and quantities often produce undesired side effects. We will see that a better way to assist the poor is with programs that enlarge their incomes.

CHAPTER 1

Thinking Like an Economist

Microeconomics is the study of how people choose under conditions of scarcity. Hearing this definition for the first time, many people react by saying that the subject is of little real relevance to most citizens of developed countries, for whom, after all, material scarcity is largely a thing of the past.

This reaction, however, takes too narrow a view of scarcity. Even when material resources are abundant, other important resources are certain not to be. At his death, Aristotle Onassis was worth several billion dollars. He had more money than he could possibly spend and used it for such things as finely crafted whale ivory footrests for the barstools on his yacht. And yet, in an important sense, he confronted the problem of scarcity much more than most of us will ever have to. Onassis was the victim of *myasthenia gravis,* a debilitating and progressive neurological disease. For him, the scarcity that mattered was not money but time, energy, and the physical skill needed to carry out ordinary activities.

Time is a scarce resource for everyone, not just the terminally ill. In deciding which movies to see, for example, it is time, not the price of admission, that constrains most of us. With only a few free nights available each month, seeing one movie means not being able to see another, or not being able to have dinner with friends.

Time and money are not the only important scarce resources. Consider the economic choice you confront when a friend brings you along as his guest to a buffet brunch. It is an all-you-can-eat affair, and you must decide how to fill your

*"Oh, it's great here, all right, but I sort of feel uncomfortable
in a place with no budget at all."*

Drawing by D. Reilly; © 1976 The New Yorker Magazine, Inc.

plate. Even if you are not rich, money would be no object, since you can eat as much as you want for free. Nor is time an obstacle, since you have all afternoon and would rather spend it in the company of your friend than be anywhere else. The important scarce resource here is the capacity of your stomach. A smorgasbord of your favorite foods lies before you, and you must decide which to eat and in what quantities. Eating another waffle necessarily means having less room for more scrambled eggs. The fact that no money changes hands here does not make your choice any less an economic one.

Every choice involves important elements of scarcity. Sometimes the most relevant scarcity will be of monetary resources, but in many of our most pressing decisions it will not. Coping with scarcity in one form or another is the essence of the human condition. Indeed, were it not for the problem of scarcity, life would be stripped of much of its intensity. For someone with an infinite lifetime and limitless material resources, hardly a single decision would ever matter.

In this chapter we examine some basic principles of microeconomic theory and see how an economist might apply them to a wide variety of choices involving scarcity. Later chapters more formally develop the theory. For now, our only goal is to get an intuitive feel for that distinctive mindset known as "thinking like an economist." And the best way to do that is to work through a series of problems familiar from actual experience.

The Cost-Benefit Approach to Decisions

Many of the choices economists study can be posed in the form of the following question:

Should I do activity x?

For the choice confronting a moviegoer, ". . . do activity x?" might be, for example, ". . . see *Casablanca* tonight?" For the person attending the buffet brunch, it might be ". . . eat another waffle?" Economists answer such questions by comparing the costs and benefits of doing the activity in question. The decision rule we use is disarmingly simple. If $C(x)$ denotes the costs of doing x and $B(x)$ the benefits, it is:

If $B(x) > C(x)$, do x; otherwise don't.

To apply this rule, we need some way to define and measure costs and benefits. Monetary values are a useful common denominator for this purpose, even when the activity has nothing directly to do with money. We define $B(x)$ as the maximum dollar amount you would be willing to pay to do x. Often $B(x)$ will be a hypothetical magnitude, the amount of money you would be willing to pay if you had to, even though no money will actually change hands. $C(x)$, in turn, is the value of all the resources you must give up in order to do x. Here too $C(x)$ need not involve an explicit transfer of money to anyone.

For most decisions, at least some of the benefits or costs will not be readily available in monetary terms. To see how we proceed in such cases, consider the following simple decision.

EXAMPLE 1-1   *Should I turn down my stereo?*

You have settled into a comfortable chair and are listening to your stereo when you realize that the next two tracks on the album are ones you dislike. If you had a compact disc player, you would have programmed it not to play them. But you don't, and so you must decide whether to get up and turn the music down or to stay put and wait it out.

The benefit of turning it down is not having the songs you don't like blare away at you. The cost, in turn, is the inconvenience of getting out of your chair. If you are extremely comfortable and the music is only mildly annoying, you will probably stay put. But if you haven't been settled for long or if the music is really bothersome, you are more likely to get up.

Even for simple decisions like this one, it is possible to translate the relevant costs and benefits into a monetary framework. Consider first

**Reservation price
of activity** x The
price at which a
person would be
indifferent be-
tween doing x
and not doing x.

the cost of getting out of your chair. If someone offered you 1 cent to get up out of a comfortable chair and there were no reason other than the penny to do it, would you take the offer? If you are like most people, you would not. But if someone offered you $1000, you would be on your feet in an instant. Somewhere between 1 cent and $1000 lies your *reservation price,* the minimum amount it would take to get you out of the chair.

To see where the threshold lies, imagine a mental auction with yourself in which you keep boosting the offer by small increments from 1 cent until you reach the point where it is barely worthwhile to get up. Where this point occurs will obviously depend on circumstance. If you are rich, it will tend to be higher than if you are poor because a given amount of money will seem less important; if you feel energetic, it will be lower than if you feel tired; and so on. For the sake of discussion, suppose your reservation price for getting out of the chair turns out to be $1. You can conduct a similar mental auction to determine the maximum sum you would be willing to pay someone to turn the music down. This reservation price measures the benefits of turning the music down; let us suppose it turns out to be 75 cents.

In terms of our formal decision rule, we then have x = "turn my stereo down," with $B(x)$ = $.75 < $C(x)$ = $1, which means that you should remain in your chair. Listening to the next two songs will be unpleasant, but less so than getting up would be. A reversal of these cost and benefit figures would imply a decision to get up and turn the music down. If $B(x)$ and $C(x)$ happened to be equal, you would be indifferent between the two alternatives.

A Note on the Role of Economic Theory

The idea that anyone might actually calculate the costs and benefits of turning down a stereo may sound a little strange, not to say absurd. Economists have come under heavy criticism for making unrealistic assumptions about how people behave, and outsiders are quick to wonder what purpose is served by the image of a person trying to decide how much he would pay to avoid getting up out of his chair.

There are two responses to this criticism. The first is that economists don't assume that people make explicit calculations of this sort at all. Rather, many economists argue, we can make useful predictions if we assume that people act *as if* they made such calculations. This view is forcefully expressed by Nobel laureate Milton Friedman, who illustrates his point by looking at the techniques expert pool players use. He argues that the shots they choose, and the specific ways they attempt to make them, can be predicted extremely well by someone who assumes that the players take careful account of all the relevant laws of

Newtonian physics. Of course, very few expert pool players have had formal training in physics, and hardly any can recite such laws as "the angle of incidence equals the angle of reflection." Nor are they likely to know the definitions of "elastic collisions" and "angular momentum." Even so, Friedman argues, they would never have become expert players in the first place *unless* they played as dictated by the laws of physics. Our theory of pool player behavior assumes, unrealistically, that pool players know the laws of physics. Friedman urges us to judge this theory not by how accurate its central assumption is but by how well it predicts behavior. And on this score, it performs very well indeed.

Like pool players, the rest of us too must develop skills for coping with our environments. Many economists, Friedman among them, believe that useful insights into our behavior can be gained by assuming that we act as if governed by the rules of rational decision making. He feels that by trial and error we eventually absorb these rules, just as pool players absorb the laws of physics.

A second response to the charge that economists make unrealistic assumptions is to concede that actual behavior does often differ from the predictions of economic models. Thus, as economist Richard Thaler puts it, we often behave more like novice than expert pool players—ignoring bank shots and having no idea about putting the proper spin on the cue ball to position it for the next shot. We will see considerable evidence in support of this second view.

But even where economic models fail on descriptive grounds, they often provide very useful guidance for making better decisions. That is, even if they don't always predict how we *do* behave, they may often give useful insights into how to achieve our goals more efficiently. If novice pool players have not yet internalized the relevant physical laws, they may nonetheless consult them for guidance about how to improve. Economic models often play an analogous role with respect to ordinary consumer and business decisions. Indeed, this role alone provides a compelling reason for learning economics.

Common Pitfalls in Decision Making

Some economists are embarrassed if an outsider points out that much of what they do boils down to an application of the principle that we should perform an action if and only if its benefits exceed its costs. That just doesn't sound like enough to keep a person with a Ph.D. busy all day! There is more to it, however, than meets the eye. People who study economics quickly discover that measuring costs and benefits is a tricky business. Indeed, it is as much an art as a science. Some costs seem almost deliberately hidden from view. Others may seem relevant but, on a closer look, turn out not to be.

Economics teaches us how to identify the costs and benefits that really matter. The principles we use are simple and commonsensical, but they are ones that many people ignore in everyday life. An important goal of this book is to teach you how to become a better decision maker. One of the best ways to do this is to examine the kinds of decisions that many people make incorrectly.

PITFALL 1. IGNORING IMPLICIT COSTS

One pitfall involves activities not all of whose costs are explicit. If doing activity x means not being able to do activity y, then the value to you of doing y is an *opportunity cost* of doing x. Many people make bad decisions because they tend to ignore the value of such forgone opportunities. This insight suggests that it will almost always be instructive to translate questions such as "Should I do x?" into ones such as "Should I do x or y?" In the latter question, y is simply the most highly valued alternative to doing x. The following example helps drive this important point home.

EXAMPLE 1-2   *Should I go skiing today or work as a research assistant?*

There is a ski area near your campus, and you often go skiing there. From experience you can confidently say that a day on the slopes is worth $60 to you. The charge for the day is $40 (which includes bus fare, lift ticket, and equipment). But this is not the only cost of going skiing. You must also take into account the value of the most attractive alternative you will forgo by heading for the slopes. Suppose that if you don't go skiing, you will work at your new job as a research assistant for one of your professors. The job pays $45 per day, and you like it just well enough to have been willing to do it for free. So the question you face is, "Should I go skiing or stay and work as a research assistant?"

Here the cost of skiing is not only the explicit cost of the ski package ($40) but also the opportunity cost of the lost earnings ($45). The total costs are therefore $85, which exceeds the benefits of $60. Since $C(x) > B(x)$, you should stay on campus and work for your professor. Someone who ignored the opportunity cost of the forgone earnings, however, would have decided incorrectly to go skiing.

Note in Example 1-2 the role of your feelings about the job. The fact that you liked it just well enough to have been willing to do it for free is another way of saying that there are no psychic costs associated with doing it. This is important because it means that by not doing the job you would not be escaping something unpleasant. Of course, not all jobs fall into this category. Suppose instead that your job had been to scrape plates in the dining hall for the same pay, $45/day, and that the job was so unpleasant that you would be unwilling to do it for less than $30/day. Assuming your manager at the dining hall permits you to take a day off whenever you want, let us now reconsider your decision about whether to go skiing.

EXAMPLE 1-3   *Should I go skiing today or scrape plates (same as Example 1-2 except for the alternative)?*

There are two equivalent ways to look at this decision. One is to say that one benefit of going skiing is not having to scrape plates. Since you would never be willing to scrape plates for less than $30/day, avoiding that task is worth that amount to you. Going skiing thus carries with it the indirect benefit of not scraping plates. When we add that indirect benefit to the $60 direct benefit of the skiing, we get $B(x) = \$90$. In this view of the problem, $C(x)$ is the same as before, namely, the $40 ski charge plus the $45 opportunity cost of the lost earnings, or $85. So now $B(x) > C(x)$, which means you should go skiing.

Alternatively, we could have viewed the unpleasantness of the plate-scraping job as an offset against its salary. By this approach, we would subtract the $30/day of unpleasantness of the job from its $45/day earnings and say that the opportunity cost of not working in the dining hall is only $15/day. Then $C(x) = \$40 + \$15 = \$55 < B(x) = \$60$, and again the conclusion is that you should go skiing.

It makes no difference which of these two ways you handle the valuation of the unpleasantness of scraping plates. It is critically important, however, that you do it either one way or the other. Don't count it twice!

Example 1-3 makes clear that there is a reciprocal relationship between costs and benefits. Not incurring a cost is the same as getting a benefit. By the same token, not getting a benefit is the same as incurring a cost.

Obvious as this sounds, it is often overlooked. Consider, for example, the case of a foreign graduate student who got his degree a few years ago and was about to return to his home country. The trade regulations of his nation permitted people returning from abroad to bring back a new automobile without having to pay the normal 50 percent tariff. The student's father-in-law asked him to bring him back a new $10,000 Chevrolet and sent him a check for exactly that amount. This put the student in a quandary. He had been planning to bring back a Chevrolet and sell it in his home country. Because, as noted, new cars normally face a 50 percent import tax, such a car would sell at a dealership there for $15,000. The student estimated that he could easily sell it privately for $14,000, which would net him a $4000 profit. Thus the opportunity cost of giving the car to his father-in-law for $10,000 was going to be $4000! Not getting this big benefit was a big cost. In the end, it was one the student elected to bear because he valued keeping peace in the family even more. Even from a strictly economic point of view, the best decision is not always the one that leaves you with the most money in your pocket.

*E*XAMPLE *1-4* *Should I work first or go to college first?*

The costs of going to college are not limited to tuition, fees, housing, food, books, supplies, and the like. They also include the opportunity cost of the earnings forgone while studying. The amount you earn increases with the amount of experience you have. The more experience you have, the larger the earnings you must forgo to attend college. This opportunity cost of attending college is therefore lowest when you are right out of high school.

On the benefit side, one big gain of a college education is that it leads to sharply higher earnings. The sooner you go to college, the longer you will be able to take advantage of this benefit. Another benefit is the pleasantness of going to college as opposed to working. In general, the kinds of jobs people hold tend to be less unpleasant (or more pleasant) the more education and experience they have. By going to college right away, you thus avoid having to work at the least pleasant jobs. For most people, then, it makes sense to go to college first and work afterward. Certainly it makes more sense to attend college at age 20 than at age 50.

A common exception to this general rule involves people who are too immature right out of high school to reap the benefits of college work. For them, it will often be sensible to work for a year or two and then go to college.

The college example is a perfect illustration of Friedman's argument about how to evaluate a theory. No one would pretend that high school seniors make their decisions about when to attend college on the basis of sophisticated calculations involving opportunity costs. On the contrary, most students go to college right out of high school simply because that is what most of their peers do. It is the thing to do.

But this begs the question of how it got to *be* the thing to do. Customs such as going to college right out of high school do not originate out of thin air. A host of different societies have had centuries to experiment with this issue. If there were a significantly better way of arranging the learning and working periods of life, some society ought to have long since discovered it. Our current custom has probably survived because it is so efficient. People may not make explicit calculations about the opportunity cost of forgone earnings, but they often behave *as if* they do.[1]

---

[1]This does not mean that all customs necessarily promote efficiency. For example, circumstances may have changed in such a way that a custom that promoted efficiency in the past no longer does so. In time, such a custom might change. Yet many habits and customs, once firmly entrenched, are very slow to change.

As the following example makes clear, failure to take opportunity costs into account often causes people to misjudge what fairness requires of certain transactions.

EXAMPLE *1-5*   *Is it fair to charge interest when lending a friend or relative some money?*

> Suppose a friend lends you $10,000, and her primary concern in deciding whether to charge interest is to decide if it would be "fair" to do so. She could have put that same money in the bank, where it would have earned, say, 5 percent interest, or $500, each year. If she charges you $500 interest for each year the loan is out, she is merely recovering the opportunity cost of her money. If she didn't charge you any interest, it would be the same as making you a gift of $500 a year. Now, she might well wish to make you a yearly gift of that amount, or indeed even a much larger amount. But no one would say it was unfair if she didn't give you a large cash gift each year. And it makes no more sense to say that her recovery of the opportunity cost of lending you money is unfair.

Yet the impression remains among many in society that the lending of money at interest is somehow an unsavory practice. Witness the following exchange that appeared in an Ann Landers column.[2]

Dear Ann Landers:

I have four children who are successful in their marriages and careers. I have always tried to treat them in an even-handed way when it comes to matters such as college tuition and loans for home purchases. It has been my policy to charge a modest rate of interest for the loans in order not to favor one child over another.

Recently my oldest daughter asked for a two-year loan to help finance a larger home. Both she and her husband have good jobs, but they wanted to avoid using nonliquid assets. . . . As in the past, I mailed her a check accompanied by a note to sign and return to me. The note was an agreement to pay interest. I included a repayment schedule. To my surprise, she cashed the check and returned the note with the reference to interest crossed out. Subsequently, she has been making her monthly payments to me on principal only.

In a recent visit to her home, my daughter and I discussed the situation but we were unable to resolve the issue. . . . Is my loan policy unreasonable? How would you handle this?

Carl in Akron

---

[2]*Ithaca Journal*, July 7, 1992, p. 9B.

Ann Landers' response begins,

Dear Carl:

For openers, I would never charge a child of mine interest on a loan. Since it is your money, however, you have every right to do with it whatever you wish. . . .

Had Carl not charged his daughter interest, he would, in effect, have given her a gift, three-quarters of which was financed out of the future inheritances of his other three children. And yet Ann Landers and many others are apparently not reassured when an economist tells them that the interest is merely the lender's opportunity cost of not having deposited the money in a bank. Perhaps they believe the economist's response begs the question asked in the next example.

EXAMPLE 1-6   *Why do banks pay interest in the first place?*

> Suppose you owned a bank and someone deposited $10,000 in it on January 1 without your having to pay him interest. You could then take the money and buy a productive asset, such as a stand of trees. Suppose that each year trees grow at the rate of 6 percent and that the price of a tree is proportional to the amount of lumber in it. At the end of the year, you could then sell the trees for $10,600 and have $600 more than before.
>
> But that same option was available to the person who put his money in your bank. Why should he give *you* the $600 he could have earned? He will be willing to let you use his money only if you compensate him for the opportunity cost of not using it himself. If you pay him 5 percent interest, he will get $500, which will probably be acceptable to him because he won't have to go to the trouble of tending the trees himself (or of lending the money to someone who will tend them). You get to keep the remaining $100 for taking care of that.

If interest is really a reimbursement for the opportunity cost of money, why are so many people hostile to moneylenders? Perhaps the answer is that people who borrow are often poor, while those who lend are often rich. This is not always the case. Former billionaire Donald Trump borrowed to finance his real estate developments, and sometimes the money came from the pension funds of low-wage workers. But more commonly, interest payments involve transfers of money from people who seem desperately to need it to those who seem to have more than they can spend. Note, though, that even here it is the differences in wealth, not the interest payments themselves, that are a more logical focus of concern. The well-being of poor people can be improved if some way can be

FIGURE 1-1
Money can be used to buy a productive asset, like a tree, that grows more valuable with the passage of time. To lend someone money is to forgo the opportunity to reap the gain from such an investment. The interest paid on loans merely reflects this opportunity cost.

INTEREST REFLECTS THE OPPORTUNITY COST OF MONEY

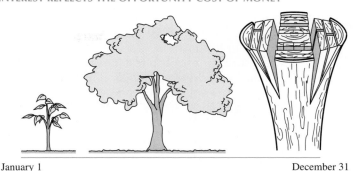

January 1   December 31

found to increase their wealth. They are not necessarily helped, however, by laws and customs that make it difficult to borrow money.

As simple as the opportunity cost concept is, it is one of the most important in microeconomics. The art in applying the concept correctly lies in being able to recognize the most valuable alternative that is sacrificed by the pursuit of a given activity.

PITFALL 2. FAILING TO IGNORE SUNK COSTS

An opportunity cost will often not seem like a relevant cost when in reality it is. Another pitfall in decision making is that sometimes expenditure will seem like a relevant cost when in reality it is not. Such is often the case with *sunk costs*, costs that are beyond recovery at the moment a decision is made. Unlike opportunity costs, these costs should be ignored. The principle of ignoring sunk costs emerges clearly in the following example.

*E*XAMPLE *1-7*   *Should I drive to Boston or take the bus?*

You are planning a 250-mile trip to Boston. Except for the cost, you are completely indifferent between driving and taking the bus. Bus fare is $100. You don't know how much it would cost to drive your car, so you call Hertz for an estimate. The Hertz representative tells you that for your make of car the costs of a typical 10,000-mile driving year are as follows:

Insurance	$1000
Interest	2000
Fuel & oil	1000
Maintenance	1000
Total	$5000

Suppose you calculate that these costs come to $0.50/mile and use this figure to compute that the 250-mile trip will cost you $125 by car. And since this is more than the $100 bus fare, you decide to take the bus.

If you decide in this fashion, you commit the error of counting sunk costs. Your insurance and interest payments do not vary with the number of miles you drive each year. Both are sunk costs and will be the same whether or not you drive to Boston. Of the costs listed, fuel and oil and maintenance are the only ones that vary with miles driven. These come to $2000 for each 10,000 miles you drive, or $0.20/mile. At $0.20/mile, it costs you only $50 to drive to Boston, and since this is much less than the bus fare, you should drive.

In Example 1-7, note the role of the assumption that, costs aside, you are indifferent between the two modes of transport. This lets us say that the only comparison that matters is the actual cost of the two modes. If you had preferred one mode to the other, however, we would also have had to weigh that preference. For example, if you were willing to pay $60 to avoid the hassle of driving, the real cost of driving would be $110, not $50, and you should take the bus.

Exercises such as the one below are sprinkled throughout the text to help you make sure that you understand important analytical concepts. You will master microeconomics more effectively if you do these exercises as you go along.

EXERCISE 1-1

How, if at all, would your answer to the question in Example 1-7 be different if the hassle of driving is $20 and you average one $28 traffic ticket for every 200 miles you drive?

As a check, the answers to the in-chapter exercises are at the end of each chapter. Naturally, the exercises will be much more useful if you work through them before consulting the answers.

EXAMPLE 1-8 *The pizza experiment*

A local pizza parlor offers an all-you-can-eat lunch for $3. You pay at the door, and then the waiter brings you as many slices of pizza as you like. One of my colleagues performed this experiment: He had an assistant serve as the waiter for one group of tables.[3] The "waiter"

---

[3]See Richard Thaler, "Toward a Positive Theory of Consumer Choice," *Journal of Economic Behavior and Organization*, 1, 1980.

selected half the tables at random and gave everyone at those tables a $3 refund before taking orders. The remaining half of his tables got no refund. He then kept careful count of the number of slices of pizza each diner ate. What difference, if any, do you predict in the amounts eaten by these two groups?

Diners in each group confront the question "Should I eat another slice of pizza?" Here, the activity x consists of eating one more slice. For both groups, $C(x)$ is exactly zero: even members of the group that did not get a refund can get as many additional slices as they want at no extra charge. Because the refund group was chosen at random, there is no reason to suppose that its members like pizza any more or less than the others. For everyone, the decision rule says keep eating until there is no longer any extra pleasure in eating another slice. Thus, $B(x)$ should be the same for each group, and people from both groups should keep eating until $B(x)$ falls to zero.

By this reasoning, the two groups should eat the same amount of pizza, on the average. The $3 admission fee is a sunk cost and should have no influence on the amount of pizza one eats. *In fact, however, the group that did not get the refund consumed substantially more pizza.*

Although our cost-benefit decision rule fails the test of prediction in this experiment, its message for the rational decision maker stands unchallenged. The two groups logically *should* have behaved the same. The only difference between them, after all, is that patrons in the refund group have lifetime incomes that are $3 higher than the others'. Surely no one believes that such a trivial difference should have any effect on pizza consumption. Members of the no-refund group seemed to want to make sure they "got their money's worth." In all likelihood, however, this motive merely led them to overeat.[4]

What's wrong with being motivated to "get your money's worth"? Absolutely nothing, as long as the force of this motive operates *before* you enter into transactions. Thus it makes perfectly good sense to be led by this motive to choose one restaurant over an otherwise identical competitor that happens to cost more. Once the price of your lunch has been determined, however, the get-your-money's-worth motive should be abandoned. The satisfaction you get from eating another slice of pizza should then depend only on how hungry you are and on how much you like pizza, not on how much you paid for the privilege of eating all you can eat. Yet people often seem not to behave in this fashion. The difficulty may be that we are not creatures of complete flexibility. Perhaps motives that it makes sense to hold in one context are not easily abandoned in another.

---

[4]An alternative to the "get-your-money's-worth" explanation is that $3 is a significant fraction of the amount of cash many diners have available to spend *in the short run*. Thus members of the refund group might have held back in order to save room for the dessert they could now afford to buy. To test this alternative explanation, the experimenter could give members of the no-refund group a $3 cash gift earlier in the day and then see if the amount of pizza consumed by the two groups still differed.

EXERCISE 1-2

Jim wins a ticket from a radio station to see a jazz band perform at an outdoor concert. Mike has paid $18 for a ticket to the same concert. On the evening of the concert there is a tremendous thunderstorm. If Jim and Mike have the same tastes, which of them will be more likely to attend the concert, assuming that each decides whether to attend the concert on the basis of a standard benefit-cost comparison?

PITFALL 3. FOCUSING ON ONLY SOME OF THE RELEVANT COSTS

The decision maker who falls victim to the sunk-cost pitfall takes into account a cost that he or she ought to have ignored. The implicit-cost pitfall was to do just the opposite: to ignore costs that ought to be taken into account. But as the following example makes clear, implicit costs are not the only costs that people tend to ignore.

EXAMPLE 1-9

If I am an energy-conservation-minded consumer who can't afford to rent a new car, should I rent a 10-year-old Buick ($100/yr, 20 miles per gallon) or a 10-year-old Toyota ($300/yr, 40 mpg)?

The impulse of many conservation-minded consumers is immediately to choose the Toyota because of its better gas mileage. But there are only so many used Toyotas to go around. Suppose there are a total of 1000 Buicks and 1000 Toyotas. If I rent a Toyota instead of a Buick, someone else will have to rent a Buick instead of a Toyota. If my goal is to save energy, I should take the Toyota only if the person who will end up with the extra Buick is someone who drives fewer miles each year than I do.

But how can anyone possibly know whether that would happen? If the rental rates of the two cars are determined in the open marketplace, and people generally pick the kind of car that minimizes their total driving expenses, we can say this: My choosing the Toyota will reduce society's energy consumption if and only if the Toyota is cheaper for me than the Buick. To see why, first note that if gasoline costs $1 per gallon, the yearly cost of the Buick is given by

$$C_b = \$100 + \frac{\$M}{20}, \tag{1.1}$$

where M is the number of miles I drive each year. The corresponding cost for the Toyota is

$$C_t = \$300 + \frac{\$M}{40}. \tag{1.2}$$

These two costs will be exactly the same if I happen to drive exactly 8000 miles a year, as illustrated in Figure 1-2. (To get this number, equate the right-hand sides of Equations 1.1 and 1.2 and solve for M.) If I drive any more than 8000 miles, the Toyota will be cheaper; if less, the Buick will be cheaper. For example, if I drive 4000 miles a year, I should choose the Buick even if energy conservation is the only thing I care about.

But how do I know that the person who rents the Toyota I could have rented won't be someone who drives even less than I do? If everyone follows the rule "drive the cheapest car," this clearly cannot happen at the given rental rates. (If the Buick is cheaper for me, it will also be cheaper for someone who drives fewer miles per year than I do.) But what if half the drivers, including me, drive 4000 miles a year while everyone else drives only 3000? If that were the case, then *everyone* would find the Buick cheaper at the current rental rates. No one would want to rent a Toyota. Rental companies would then discover that they could boost the prices on their Buicks substantially and still manage to rent them all. By the same token, they would have a strong incentive to cut the rental rates on their Toyotas, rather than watch them gather dust in their parking lots. In the end, the rental rates of the two cars would adjust so that the Toyotas are cheaper overall for the heavy-mileage drivers, the Buicks cheaper for the light-mileage drivers.

FIGURE 1-2
The Buick is cheaper if driven less than 8000 miles each year. Otherwise, the Toyota is cheaper.

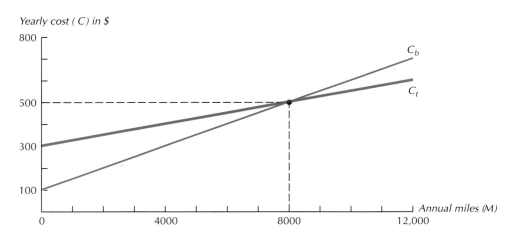

EXERCISE 1-3

If the rental charge for Buicks rises from $100/yr to $200/yr in Example 1-9, how many miles would you have to drive each year to make the Toyota cheaper than the Buick?

The Invisible Hand

One of the most important insights of economic analysis is that the individual pursuit of self-interest is often not only *consistent* with broader social objectives, but actually even *required* by them. In Example 1-9, for instance, we saw that purely self-interested consumers would choose cars in such a way that the energy consumption of society as a whole would be minimized. No one was *trying* to save scarce fossil fuels for future generations. People were simply trying to keep their own costs to a minimum. Indeed, if people had consciously tried to reduce total energy consumption by renting Toyotas, no matter how little they drove, the result would have been greater total energy consumption.

Wholly unaware of the effects of their actions, self-interested consumers often act as if driven by what Adam Smith called an *invisible hand* to produce the greatest social good. In perhaps the most widely quoted passage from *The Wealth of Nations,* Smith wrote:

It is not from the benevolence of the butcher, the brewer, or the baker that we expect our dinner, but from their regard of their own interest. We address ourselves not to their humanity, but to their self-love, and never talk to them of our necessities, but of their advantage.

Modern economists sometimes lose sight of the fact that Smith did not believe that *only* selfish motives are important. In his earlier treatise, *The Theory of Moral Sentiments,* for example, he wrote movingly about the compassion we feel for others:

How selfish soever man may be supposed, there are evidently some principles in his nature, which interest him in the fortune of others, and render their happiness necessary to him, though he derives nothing from it, except the pleasure of seeing it. Of this kind is pity or compassion, the emotion which we feel for the misery of others, when we either see it, or are made to conceive it in a very lively manner. That we often derive sorrow from the sorrow of others, is a matter of fact too obvious to require any instances to prove it; for this sentiment, like all the other original passions of human nature, is by no means confined to the virtuous and humane, though they perhaps may feel it with the most exquisite sensibility. The greatest ruffian, the most hardened violator of the laws of society, is not altogether without it.

Smith was well aware, moreover, that the outcome of unbridled pursuit of self-interest is sometimes far from socially benign. As the following example illustrates, the invisible hand mechanism breaks down when important costs or benefits accrue to people other than the decision makers themselves.

*E*XAMPLE *1-10* *Should I burn my leaves or haul them into the woods?*

External cost of an activity A cost that is generated by an activity and that falls on people who are not directly involved in the activity.

Suppose the cost of hauling the leaves is $20 and the cost to the homeowner of burning them is only $1. If the homeowner cares only about costs that accrue directly to herself, she will burn her leaves. The difficulty is that burning leaves entails an important *external cost,* which means a cost borne by people who are not directly involved in the decision. This external cost is the damage done by the smoke from the fire. That cost accrues not to the homeowner who makes the decision about burning the leaves but to the people who live downwind. Suppose the smoke damage amounts to $25. The good of the community then requires that the leaves be hauled, not burned. From the perspective of the self-interested homeowner, however, it seems best to burn them.[5]

External costs and benefits are often the underlying reason for laws that limit individual discretion. Most communities, for example, now have laws prohibiting the burning of leaves within city limits. Such laws may be viewed as a way of making the costs and benefits seen by individuals more nearly resemble the costs and benefits experienced by the community as a whole. With a law against burning leaves in effect, the potential leaf burner weighs the penalty of breaking the law against the cost of hauling the leaves. Most people conclude it is cheaper to haul them.

Rationality and Self-Interest

Self-interest standard of rationality A theory that says rational people consider only costs and benefits that accrue directly to themselves.

To be rational means to make decisions according to the cost-benefit criterion—that is, to take an action if and only if its benefits exceed its costs. There are two important refinements of this definition of rationality. One is the *self-interest standard of rationality*, which says that rational persons assign significant weight to only those costs and benefits that accrue directly to themselves. This standard explicitly sets aside such motives as trying to make other people happy, trying to do the right thing, and so on.

[5]Of course, if the homeowner interacts frequently with the people downwind, self-interest may still dictate hauling the leaves, to preserve goodwill for future interactions. But where the people downwind are anonymous strangers, this motive will operate with much less force.

Present-aim standard of rationality A theory that says rational people act efficiently in pursuit of whatever objectives they hold at the moment of choice.

The alternative definition is the so-called ***present-aim standard of rationality.*** Its only requirement is that persons act efficiently in the pursuit of whatever aims or objectives they happen to hold at the moment of action. The attraction of this broader standard is that it encompasses such benign motives as charity, duty, and the like. We know, after all, that many people hold such motives, and our theory becomes more descriptively accurate if it incorporates them explicitly. The difficulty is that the present-aim standard of rationality often appears too broad. For example, if the overriding desire of an obese person is to stuff himself with a huge chocolate cake, the present-aim standard calls this behavior rational provided only that the person does not pay more for the cake than necessary. The fact that eating the cake might later be a cause of deep regret, or even of the person's premature death, is simply not relevant under the present-aim standard. The self-interest standard, by contrast, would call eating the cake irrational under these circumstances.

The formal theory of rational choice can be developed under either standard of rationality. If we employ the self-interest standard, we begin with the implicit assumption that people are basically selfish. Use of the present-aim standard, by contrast, requires us to make alternative assumptions about people's goals. Ironically, the difficulty with the present-aim standard is that it allows us to explain too much—even the most bizarre forms of behavior can be "accounted for" by simply assuming that people have tastes for them. Suppose, for example, that we see someone drink a gallon of used crankcase oil and keel over dead. The present-aim approach can "explain" this behavior by saying that the person must have really *liked* crankcase oil.

Both the present-aim and self-interest standards of rationality find widespread application in economic analysis. Whichever standard we employ entails an inevitable compromise. The self-interest standard is a compromise because we know that unselfish motives are often important. The present-aim standard is a compromise because it is often vague and open-ended. Chapter 7 discusses how to impose reasonable restrictions on the use of the present-aim standard. But for now let us focus on the self-interest standard and see what sorts of behavior it predicts.

*E*XAMPLE *1-11*   *Should I vote in the next presidential election?*

A purely self-interested person is almost sure to answer no. To see why, look first at the benefits for such a person when she votes. Even if she believes that one party will serve her interests much better than the other, her vote will not matter unless it tips the outcome of the election. Given the millions of votes in presidential elections, however, the likelihood of casting a decisive vote is virtually nil. The costs of voting, by contrast, are clearly positive. It takes time and effort to get to the polls, and national elections are held in November, when the weather is often nasty. Since the costs of voting are positive and the

> benefits essentially zero, the cost-benefit model predicts that a purely self-interested person will not vote.

Several important points must be made about Example 1-11. First, the standard rejoinder—"What if *everyone* who favors your candidate stayed home?"—fails to acknowledge the fundamental incentive problem. The likelihood that other people will vote is unaffected by any one person's decision to vote. They will either turn out or not, no matter what any one of us does.

Note also the irony that the self-interest prediction holds only if a large number of people violate it by casting their ballots. Thus, if *everyone* followed the self-interest calculus, no one would vote, in which case it *would* pay a self-interested person to vote. (As Yogi Berra once said of a St. Louis restaurant, "It's so crowded, no one goes there.") But, of course, millions of people do vote in each presidential election, and it is unlikely that many of them do so in the expectation that almost everyone else will stay home.

The voting example is another opportunity to consider what standards ought to apply when we assess the predictive performance of a theory. On one hand, critics of the self-interest model would emphasize that it clearly performs badly here since it is contradicted by millions of voters each election. Something besides the simple self-interest model must be driving the behavior of these voters. Supporters of the self-interest model, on the other hand, would emphasize that even though large numbers of people do vote, most do not. They would also insist, correctly, that the self-interest model helps us understand *why* they don't. In particular, it challenges the common interpretation that nonvoters are people who simply don't care about the outcome of the election. They may care very much indeed but be discouraged by the near certainty that their votes will make no difference. On purely descriptive grounds, then, the self-interest model gets mixed reviews with respect to voting behavior. It seems to explain some people's behavior but cannot account for others'.

The voting example also drives home an important point about the role of the self-interest model. When the self-interest model predicts that a person will not vote, it does not mean that it would be morally wrong to vote. Rather, it means only that voting will not promote the decision maker's material interests. By calling attention to the material forces that act on people, the self-interest model thus actually helps explain why democratic societies encourage people to take the responsibilities of citizenship seriously. After all, it is in the interest of society as a whole to have an active, participatory, well-informed electorate, and if material rewards do not favor such a posture, society can employ moral and cultural pressures on its behalf. Virtually every democratic society teaches its citizens that they have a duty to vote.

Someone who takes these teachings to heart will not behave in strict accordance with the self-interest model. In weighing her decision to vote, there will now be an additional factor, namely, her desire to avoid the bad feelings that would result from failure to do her duty. If we take account of this additional factor, we can do a much better job of predicting her behavior. The costs of voting will still be measured much as before. But now the benefits will not be zero but the amount she would be willing to pay to avoid the bad feeling she would experience by not voting. A theory built along these lines does not predict that she will vote no matter what. As before, costs will matter. Thus, if it is snowing hard enough, or if she has pressing alternative demands on her time, she may well decide to stay home despite her feelings of duty.

Would Parents Want Their Daughter or Son to Marry Homo Economicus?

Many economists and other behavioral scientists remain skeptical about the importance of duty and other unselfish motives. They feel that the larger material payoffs associated with selfish behavior so strongly dominate other motives that, as a first approximation, we may safely ignore nonegoistic motives.

With this view in mind, the stereotypical decision maker in the self-interest model is often given the label *Homo economicus,* or "economic man." *Homo economicus* does not experience the sorts of sentiments that motivate people to vote, or to return lost wallets to their owners with the cash intact. On the contrary, personal material costs and benefits are the only things he cares about. He does not contribute voluntarily to private charities or public television stations. He keeps his promises only when it pays to do so. If the pollution laws are not carefully enforced, he disconnects the catalytic converter on his car to save on fuel. And so on.

Obviously, many people do not fit the me-first caricature of the self-interest model. They donate bone marrow to strangers with leukemia. They endure great trouble and expense to see justice done, even when it will not undo the original injury. At great risk to themselves, they pull people from burning buildings and jump into icy rivers to rescue people who are about to drown. Soldiers throw their bodies atop live grenades to save their comrades.

This is not to say that selfish motives are unimportant. They obviously account for a great deal. When a detective investigates a murder, for example, her first question is, "Who stood to benefit from the victim's death?" When an economist studies a government regulation, he wants to know whose incomes it enhances. When a senator proposes a new spending project, the political scientist tries to discover which of his constituents will be its primary beneficiaries.

Our goal in much of this text is to understand the kinds of behaviors to which selfish motives give rise in specific situations. But throughout this process, it is critical to remember that the self-interest model is not intended as a prescription for how to conduct your own affairs. On the contrary, we will see in later chapters that *Homo economicus* is woefully ill suited to the demands of social existence as we know it. Each of us probably knows people who more or less fit the *Homo economicus* caricature. And our first priority, most of the time, is to steer clear of them.

The irony here is that to be a purely self-interested person carries with it a degree of social isolation that is not only bad for the soul but also harmful to the pocketbook. To succeed in life, even in purely material terms, people must be able to work together, to form alliances and relationships of trust. But what sensible person would be willing to trust *Homo economicus*? Later chapters present specific examples of how unselfish motives confer material rewards on the people who hold them. For the present, however, bear in mind that the self-interest model is intended only to capture one part of human behavior, albeit an important one.

The Concept of Marginal Analysis

One of the keys to thinking like an economist is to realize that the costs and benefits that really matter are those that occur *at the margin*. Thus, as we saw in the all-you-can-eat pizza example (Example 1-8), when deciding whether to eat another slice of pizza, the relevant costs and benefits are the respective costs and benefits of consuming an additional slice of pizza—that is, *the marginal costs* and *marginal benefits*. Since in that example you could eat as much as you wanted for a fixed fee (and you do not value the time necessary to eat the pizza), the marginal cost of an extra slice of pizza was exactly zero. The marginal benefit of an extra slice is the maximum amount you would be willing to pay for that slice. Typically, the hungrier you are, the more you would be willing to pay for an extra slice of pizza. This means that the marginal benefit of an additional slice of pizza starts out relatively high and then declines steadily as you eat more slices.

For a hypothetical customer, suppose the value of additional slices of pizza declines as shown by the marginal benefit curve in Figure 1-3. He values pizza at \$2/slice when he has eaten one slice, at 60 cents/slice when he has eaten two

FIGURE 1-3
When a restaurant offers all the pizza you can eat for a fixed fee, the marginal cost of pizza is zero. The customer should keep eating pizza as long as the marginal benefit is positive. In this example, he should stop at three slices.

THE OPTIMAL AMOUNT OF PIZZA AT AN ALL-YOU-CAN-EAT LUNCH

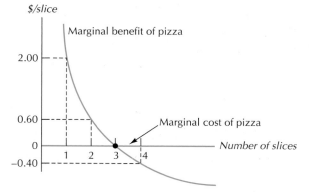

slices, and at zero per slice when he has eaten three slices. As the marginal benefit curve in Figure 1-3 shows, the value of additional slices of pizza may even be negative beyond some point. Thus the curve tells us that once four slices have been eaten, this customer would actually be willing to pay 40 cents/slice to *avoid* eating additional pizza.

The marginal cost of pizza under the terms of the all-you-can-eat lunch is exactly zero, plotted as the horizontal line shown in Figure 1-3. The logic of marginal analysis tells us that the customer's optimal decision rule is to keep eating more pizza as long as the marginal benefit exceeds the marginal cost. The optimal pizza consumption thus occurs when his marginal benefit and marginal cost curves cross—at three slices in this example.

Similar reasoning enables us to answer the question posed in the following exercise.

EXERCISE 1-4

How many slices of pizza should you consume if you value the time needed to eat a slice of pizza at $0.60?

EXAMPLE 1-12 *How much memory should your computer have?*

Suppose random access memory can be added to your computer at a cost of $5 per megabyte. Suppose also that the value to you, measured in terms of your willingness to pay, of an additional megabyte of memory is as shown by the curve labeled *B* in Figure 1-4. How many megabytes of memory should you purchase?

In Figure 1-4, the curve *B* is the relevant marginal benefit curve. Its downward slope reflects the fact that the value of an additional megabyte to you falls with each megabyte you add. (As we will see in Chapter 3, it is a common pattern that the more someone has of a good, the less value he assigns to having additional units of it.) Curve *C* in the diagram measures the cost of each additional megabyte, assumed constant at $5. This is the relevant marginal cost curve. The optimal quantity of memory for you is the quantity at which these two curves cross—namely, 4 megabytes. With any less memory than that, the benefits of adding more will exceed the costs, and so you should expand. With any more than 40 megabytes, what you would save by contracting exceeds what you would give up, so you should contract.

FIGURE 1-4
The optimal amount of memory to purchase is the quantity for which the marginal benefit of an additional megabyte is just equal to its marginal cost.

THE OPTIMAL QUANTITY OF COMPUTER MEMORY

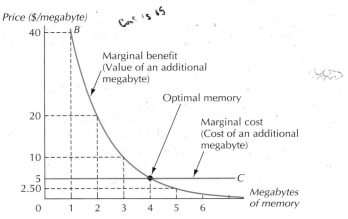

Note that the question in the computer memory example was not of the form "Should I do x?" that was used in our original cost-benefit decision rule. Note also that in answering this question we first translated it into that original format. Thus, what began as a question of the form "How much x should I buy?" was easily translated to one of the form "Should I buy an additional unit of x?" The answer, not surprisingly, is that you should buy an additional unit if and only if the marginal benefits exceed the marginal costs.

The Economic Naturalist

Studying biology enables people to observe and marvel at many details of life that would otherwise escape them. For the naturalist, a walk in a quiet woods becomes an adventure. In much the same way, studying microeconomics enables someone to become an "economic naturalist," a person who sees the mundane details of ordinary existence in a sharp new light. Each feature of the manmade landscape is no longer an amorphous mass but the result of an implicit cost-benefit calculation. Following are examples of economic naturalism.

EXAMPLE 1-13 *Why is airline food so bad?*

Everyone complains about airline food. Indeed, if any serious restaurant dared to serve such food, it would go bankrupt in short order. Our complaints seem to take for granted that airline meals should be just as good as the ones we eat in restaurants. But why should they? The cost-benefit perspective makes clear that airlines should increase the quality of their meals if and only if the benefits would outweigh the costs of doing so. The benefits of better food are probably well measured by what passengers would be willing to pay for it, in the form of higher ticket prices. If a restaurant-quality meal could be had for, say, a mere $5 increase in costs, most people would probably be delighted to pay it. The difficulty, however, is that it would be much more costly than that to prepare significantly better meals at 39,000 feet in a tiny galley with virtually no time. It could be done, of course. An airline could remove 20 seats from the plane, install a modern, well-equipped kitchen, hire extra staff, spend more on ingredients, and so on. But these extra costs would be more like $50 per passenger than $5. For all our complaints about the low quality of airline food, few of us would be willing to bear this extra burden. The sad result is that airline food is destined to remain unpalatable because the costs of making it better outweigh the benefits.

Many of us respond warmly to the maxim "Anything worth doing is worth doing well." After all, it encourages a certain pride of workmanship that is often sadly lacking. Example 1-13 makes clear, however, that if the maxim is interpreted literally, it does not make any sense. It is completely unmindful of the need to weigh costs against benefits. To do something well means to devote time, effort, and expense to it. But time, effort, and expense are scarce. To devote them to one activity makes them unavailable for another. Increasing the quality of one of the things we do thus necessarily means to reduce the quality of others—yet another application of the concept of opportunity cost. Every intelligent decision must be mindful of this tradeoff.

Everything we see in life is the result of some such compromise. For Steffi Graf to play tennis as well as she does means that she cannot become a concert pianist. And yet this obviously does not mean that she shouldn't spend any time playing the piano. It just means that she should hold herself to a lower standard there than in the tennis arena.

EXAMPLE 1-14 Why do manual transmissions have five forward speeds, automatics only four?

The more forward speeds a car's transmission has, the better its fuel economy will be. The additional gears act like the "overdrive" of cars of the 1940s, conserving fuel by allowing cars to cruise at highway speeds at lower engine speeds. Most cars in current production offer five forward speeds on their manual transmissions, only three or four on their automatics. Since fuel economy is obviously a good thing, why limit the number of speeds on automatics? The reason is that fuel economy is not our only objective. We also want to keep the price of the car within limits. Automatic transmissions are much more complex than manual ones, and the cost of adding an extra speed is accordingly much greater in automatics. The benefits of adding an extra speed, by contrast, are the same in both cases. If carmakers follow the rule "Add an extra speed if its benefits outweigh its costs," then automatics will have fewer speeds than manuals.

The reasoning in Example 1-14 also helps make clear why many manual transmissions now have five forward speeds when 40 years ago most had only three (and many automatic transmissions only two). The benefit of adding an extra speed, again, is that it increases fuel economy. The value of this benefit, in dollar terms, thus depends directly on the price of fuel. The price of gasoline relative to other goods doubled during the 1970s, which helps explain why transmissions have more speeds than they used to.

EXAMPLE 1-15 *Why have paper towels replaced hot-air hand dryers in public restrooms?*

In the 1950s and 1960s, paper towel dispensers were replaced by electric hot-air hand dryers in many public restrooms. More recently, however, it is the hot-air dryers themselves that are being replaced by paper towel dispensers. The explanation for these movements naturally has to do with the costs and benefits of the different methods of drying hands. The hot-air dryers made their original appearance on the heels of a steady decline in the price of electricity. When power became cheap, as it did in the 1950s and 1960s, electric dryers became less expensive to operate and maintain than the traditional paper towel dispensers. With the Arab oil embargoes of the 1970s, however, the price of energy rose dramatically, making paper towels once again the hand-drying method of choice.

Some economic naturalists may also find it amusing to speculate about why the paper towel dispensers of today are so different from the earlier ones. Most current designs feature a continuous hand crank. The paper is inside on a roll; and the longer you turn the crank, the longer the sheet of paper towel you get. Older designs also had a roll of paper inside, but you had to pull the paper out by hand. Most of the older models would also release only a limited amount of paper with each pull. To get more, you had to reset the release mechanism by pushing a button on the front of the dispenser.

The advantage of the older design, from the establishment's point of view, was that it induced people to use less paper. Indeed, if your hands were wet enough, it was difficult to get any paper at all because, when you pulled, the wet paper would simply tear away in your hands.

But if establishments saved on paper with the old design, why have they switched to the new one? The answer is that saving on paper is not their only objective. They also want satisfied customers. Incomes are higher now than they were 30 years ago, and customers are willing to pay more for a more convenient way of drying their hands. The current design may use a little more paper, but it is so much less frustrating that customers seem happy to pay more for their meals or their gasoline in order to cover the extra costs.

Some people may respond that the old design, infuriating though it was, was better because of its paper-saving property. These people feel that it is wrong to waste paper and that we ought to be willing to tolerate plenty of inconvenience to avoid doing so. The same people also often lament the thousands of trees that must be cut down in order to print each Sunday's *New York Times*. But trees are a renewable resource, which means there is no reason to treat them differently from any other scarce but renewable resource. When the demand for paper is high, we cut down more trees, to be sure. But the market also provides a strong incentive to plant new ones. The irony here is that the more paper we use, the more trees we have. If every metropolitan newspaper were to cease publication tomorrow, we would ultimately have *fewer* acres of forest, not more.

This is not to say, however, that private markets always provide the correct incentives to conserve important resources. In the Pacific Northwest, for example, logging companies are currently cutting down the few remaining stands of virgin redwoods to supply contractors with timber to build homes. Many of these trees are more than 2000 years old, a national treasure we can never hope to replace. To the logging companies, however, they are worth more as lumber than as monuments to the past.

Many of us feel such anguish at the thought of these trees being cut down that we would gladly make a donation to someone who could prevent it. And yet it is probably impractical for the lumber companies to realize the true value we place on these trees. It wouldn't work, for example, to wall off their land and charge admission to see them. The invisible hand breaks down when the incentives in private markets do not lead us to protect nonreproducible resources that society wants to see preserved. In such cases, it is the responsibility of government to protect them. But where reproducible resources are concerned, we do not confront the same difficulty.

Positive Questions and Normative Questions

Normative question A question about what policies or institutional arrangements lead to the best outcomes.

Whether the remaining stands of virgin redwoods ought to be protected is in the end a ***normative question***—a question involving our values. A normative question is a question about what *ought* to be or *should* be. By itself, economic analysis cannot answer such questions. A society that reveres nature and antiquity may well decide the fate of the redwoods differently from one that holds other values, even though members of both societies are in complete agreement about all the relevant economic facts and theories. Economic analysis is on firmer

Positive question
A question about the consequences of specific policies or institutional arrangements.

ground when it comes to answering *positive questions*—questions about what the consequences of specific policies or institutional arrangements will be. If we ban the cutting of virgin redwoods, what will happen to the price of lumber? What substitute building materials are likely to be developed, and at what cost? How will employment in the logging and housing industries be affected? These are all positive economic questions, and the answers to them are clearly relevant to our thinking about the underlying normative question.

Microeconomics and Macroeconomics

Our focus in this chapter is on issues confronting the individual decision maker. As we proceed, we'll also consider economic models of groups of individuals—for example, the group of all buyers or all sellers in a market. The study of individual choices and the study of group behavior in individual markets both come under the rubric of microeconomics. Macroeconomics, by contrast, is the study of broader aggregations of markets. For example, it tries to explain the national unemployment rate, the overall price level, and the total value of national output.

Economists are much better at predicting and explaining what goes on in individual markets than what happens in the economy as a whole. When prominent economists disagree in the press or on television, the subject is much more likely to be one from macroeconomics than from microeconomics. But even though economists are still not very good at answering macroeconomic questions, there is no denying the importance of macroeconomic analysis. After all, recessions and inflation disrupt the lives of millions of people.

Modern economists increasingly believe that the key to progress in macroeconomics lies in more careful analysis of the individual markets that make up broader aggregates. As a result, the distinction between micro and macro has become less clear in recent years. The graduate training of all economists, micro and macro alike, is increasingly focused on microeconomic analysis.

Summary

Microeconomics is the science of choice under scarcity. Scarcity is ever present, even when material resources are abundant. There are always important limitations on time, energy, and the other things we need to pursue our goals.

Much of the economist's task is to try to answer questions of the form "Should I do activity *x*?" The approach to answering them is disarmingly simple. It is to do *x* if and only if its costs are smaller than its benefits. Not incurring a cost is the same as getting a benefit.

We saw that the cost-benefit model sometimes fails to predict how people behave when confronted with everyday choices. The art of cost-benefit analysis lies in being able to specify and measure the relevant costs and benefits, a skill that many decision makers conspicuously lack. Some costs, like sunk costs, will often seem relevant but turn out not to be. Others, like implicit costs, are sometimes ignored, even though they are of central importance. Benefits too are often difficult to conceptualize and measure. Experience has taught that becoming aware of the most common pitfalls helps most people become better decision makers.

The principles of rational choice are by no means limited to formal markets for goods and services. Indeed, some form of implicit or explicit cost-benefit calculation lies behind almost every human action, object, and behavior. Knowledge of the underlying principles casts our world in a sharp new light, not always flattering, but ever a source of stimulating insight.

Questions for Review

1. What is the opportunity cost of your reading a novel this evening?

2. Distinguish between the present-aim and self-interest standards of rationality.

3. Give three examples of activities that are accompanied by external costs or benefits.

4. How does the self-interest model help us understand why children in most democratic countries are brought up to believe that it is their duty to vote?

5. Why should sunk costs be irrelevant for current decisions?

6. How can the self-interest model be useful for studying the behavior of people who do not think explicitly in terms of costs and benefits?

Problems

1. Jamal has a very flexible summer job. He works every day but is allowed to take a day off anytime he wants. His friend Don suggests they take off work on Tuesday and go to the amusement park. The admission charge for the amusement park is $15 per person, and it will cost them $5 each for gasoline and parking. Jamal loves amusement parks and a day at the park is worth $45 to him. However, Jamal also enjoys his job so much that he would actually be willing to pay $10 per day to do it.

   a. If Jamal earns $10 if he works, should he go to the amusement park?
   b. If Jamal earns $15 . . . ?
   c. If Jamal earns $20 . . . ?

2. Tom is a mushroom farmer. He invests all his spare cash in additional mushrooms, which grow on otherwise useless land behind his barn. The mushrooms double in size during their first year, after which time they are harvested and sold at a constant price per pound. Tom's friend Dick asks Tom for a loan of $200, which he promises to repay after 1 year. How much interest will Dick have to pay Tom in order for Tom to be no worse off than if he had not made the loan?

3. The meal plan at University A lets students eat as much as they like for a fixed fee of $500 per semester. The average student there eats 250 lb of food per semester. Uni-

versity B charges students $500 for a book of meal tickets that entitles the student to eat 250 lb of food per semester. If the student eats more than 250 lb, he or she pays extra; if the student eats less, he or she gets a refund. If students are rational, at which university will average food consumption be higher?

4. You are planning a 1000-mile trip to Florida. Except for the matter of cost, you are completely indifferent between driving and taking the bus. Bus fare is $260. The costs of operating your car during a typical 10,000-mile driving year are as follows:

Insurance	$1000
Interest	2000
Fuel & oil	1200
Tires	200
License & registration	50
Maintenance	1100
Total	$5550

Should you drive or take the bus?

5. Al and Jane have rented a banquet hall to host a party in celebration of their wedding anniversary. Fifty people have already accepted their invitation. Given that number, the caterers will charge $400 for food and $100 for drinks. The band will cost $300 for the evening, and the hall costs $200. Now Al and Jane are considering inviting 10 more people. By how much will these extra guests increase the cost of their party?

6. You drive 5000 miles a year and buy gasoline at the price of $1/gal. Except for differences in annual costs, you are indifferent between driving a 10-year-old Buick ($200/yr, 20 mpg) or a 10-year-old Toyota ($400/yr, 50 mpg). Which one should you drive?

7. Bill and Joe live in Ithaca. At 2 P.M., Bill goes to the local Ticketron outlet and buys a $30 ticket to a basketball game to be played that night in Syracuse (50 miles north). Joe plans to attend the same game, but doesn't purchase his ticket in advance because he knows from experience that it is always possible to buy just as good a seat at the arena. At 4 P.M., a heavy, unexpected snowstorm begins, making the prospect of the drive to Syracuse much less attractive than before. If both Bill and Joe have the same tastes and are rational, is one of them more likely to attend the game than the other? If so, say who and explain why. If not, explain why not.

8. Two types of radar weather-detection devices are available for commercial passenger aircraft: the "state-of-the-art" machine and another that is significantly less costly, but also less effective. The Federal Aviation Administration (FAA) has hired you for advice on whether all passenger planes should be required to use the state-of-the-art machine. After careful study, your recommendation is to require the more expensive machine only in passenger aircraft with more than 200 seats. How would you justify such a recommendation to an FAA member who complains that all passengers, irrespective of the number of seats in the aircraft in which they happen to find themselves, have a right to the best weather-detecting radar currently available?

9. A group has chartered a bus to New York City. The driver costs $100, the bus costs $500, and tolls will cost $75. The driver's fee is nonrefundable, but the bus may be canceled a week in advance at a charge of only $50. At $18 per ticket, how many people must buy tickets so that the trip need not be canceled?

10. Residents of your city are charged a fixed weekly fee of $6 for refuse collection. They are allowed to put out as many cans as they wish. The average household disposes of three cans per week in this way.

   Now, suppose that your city changes to a "tag" system. Each can of refuse to be collected must have a tag affixed to it. The tags cost $2 each.

   What effect do you think the introduction of the tag system will have on the total quantity of trash collected in your city?

11. Suppose that random access memory (RAM) can be added to your computer at a cost of $50 per megabyte. Suppose also that the value to you, measured in terms of your willingness to pay, of an additional megabyte of memory is $200 for the first megabyte, and then falls by one-half for each additional megabyte. Draw a graph of marginal cost and marginal benefit. How many megabytes of memory should you purchase?

12. As in Problem 11, but suppose the cost of RAM falls to $25 per megabyte. How many megabytes of memory should you purchase now? Suppose additionally that your benefit for an additional megabyte of memory rises to $400 for the first megabyte, also falling by one-half for each additional megabyte. How many megabytes of memory should you purchase now, with both the lower price and the larger benefit?

*13. Dana has purchased a $40 ticket to a rock concert. On the day of the concert she is invited to a welcome-home party for a friend returning from abroad. She cannot attend both the concert and the party. If she had known about the party before buying the ticket, she would have chosen the party over the concert. *True or false:* It follows that if she is rational, she will go to the party anyway. Explain.

*14. Yesterday you were unexpectedly given a free ticket to a Rolling Stones concert scheduled for April 1. The market price of this ticket is $75, but the most you could sell it for is only $50. Today you discover that Pearl Jam will be giving a concert that same evening. Tickets for the Pearl Jam concert are still available at $75. Had you known before receiving your Stones ticket yesterday that Pearl Jam would be coming, you definitely would have bought a ticket to see them, not the Rolling Stones. *True or false:* From what we are told of your preferences, it follows that if you are a rational utility maximizer, you should attend the Pearl Jam concert. Explain.

*15. Mr. Smith recently faced a choice between being (*a*) an economics professor, which pays $60,000/yr, or (*b*) a safari leader, which pays $50,000/yr. After careful deliberation, Smith took the safari job, but it was a close call. "For a dollar more," he said, "I'd have gone the other way."

   Now Smith's brother-in-law approaches him with a business proposition. The terms are as follows:

   - Smith must resign his safari job to work full-time in his brother-in-law's business.
   - Smith must give his brother-in-law an interest-free loan of $100,000, which will be repaid in full if and when Smith leaves the business. (Smith currently has much more than $100,000 in the bank.)
   - The business will pay Smith a salary of $70,000/yr. He will receive no other payment from the business.

---

*Problems marked with an asterisk are more difficult.

The interest rate is 10 percent per year. Apart from salary considerations, Smith feels that working in the business would be just as enjoyable as being an economics professor. For simplicity, assume there is no uncertainty regarding either Smith's salary in the proposed business or the security of his monetary investment in it. Should Smith join his brother-in-law and, if so, how small would Smith's salary from the business have to be to make it NOT worthwhile for him to join? If not, how large would Smith's salary from the business have to be to make it worthwhile for him to join?

*16. You have just purchased a new Ford Taurus for $20,000, but the most you could get for it if you sold it privately is $15,000. Now you learn that Toyota is offering its Camry, which normally sells for $25,000, at a special sale price of $20,000. If you had known before buying the Taurus that you could buy a Camry at the same price, you would have definitely chosen the Camry. *True or false:* From what we are told of your preferences, it follows that if you are a rational utility maximizer, you should definitely not sell the Taurus and buy the Camry. Explain.

Answers to In-Chapter Exercises

1-1. Someone who gets a $28 traffic ticket every 200 miles driven will pay $35 in fines, on the average, for every 250 miles driven. Adding that figure to the $20 hassle cost of driving, and then adding the $50 fuel, oil, and maintenance cost, we have $105. This is more than the $100 bus fare, which means taking the bus is best.

1-2. The $18 Mike paid for his ticket is a sunk cost at the moment he must decide whether to attend the concert. For both Jim and Mike, therefore, the costs and benefits should be the same. If the benefit of seeing the concert outweighs the cost of sitting in the rain, they should go. Otherwise they should stay home.

1-3. Let M^* be the annual mileage for which the total costs of the two types of cars are the same. That is, $200 + M^*/20 = 300 + M^*/40$, which solves for $M^* = 4000$ miles/yr. If you drive more than 4000 miles/yr, the Toyota will be cheaper.

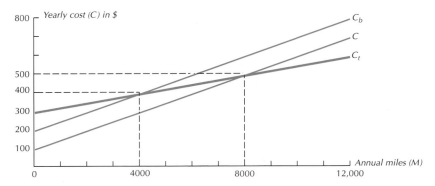

1-4. You should eat three slices because the third slice is the last slice for which the marginal benefit of eating the pizza exceeds its marginal cost (in terms of the value of your time).

CHAPTER

2

Supply and Demand

n 1979 I was working for the federal government and living in Washington, D.C. Outside my apartment window stood a gas station. With 16 pumps, it was larger than most, but otherwise typical of the modern urban self-serve station.

In April of that year, a major oil supply interruption occurred in the Mideast, which sent gasoline prices skyrocketing. To keep prices from rising still further, the Carter administration implemented a complex system of fuel allocations and

price controls. One result of this program was that in many urban markets there was substantially less gasoline available than motorists wanted to buy at the regulated prices. At the gas station outside my apartment window, this showed up as a line of cars that stretched for several blocks.

Quarrels over position in such queues were common during the summer of 1979, and many motorists got into fistfights and shouting matches with one another. One motorist was shot and killed for butting into line. Tensions continued until the gasoline lines dwindled with the passing of the heavy-travel months.

The government's system of price controls and allocations tried to accomplish a task that we usually relegate to private market forces. The Washington experience was typical of similar interventions in other times and places. It is the rule, not the exception, for these programs to produce confusion and conflict. Of course, the unfettered market can itself produce outcomes we do not like. But rarely does it fail to allocate available supplies in a smooth, efficient manner.

Chapter Preview

In this chapter we explore why markets function so smoothly most of the time and why attempts at direct allocation are so often problematic. The early part of the chapter looks at basic supply and demand analysis. First, we review the usual descriptive features of supply and demand analysis covered in the introductory course. Next, we'll see that, for given attributes of buyers and sellers, the unregulated competitive market yields the best attainable outcome, in the sense that any other combination of price and quantity would be worse for at least some buyers or sellers.

We'll also see that despite this attractive feature, market outcomes often do not command society's approval. Concern for the well-being of the poor has motivated the governments of every Western society to intervene in a variety of ways—for instance, by adopting laws that peg prices above or below their equilibrium levels. Such laws, we will see, almost always generate harmful, if unintended, consequences.

We will also see that a generally more efficient solution to the problems of the poor is to boost their incomes directly. The law of supply and demand cannot be repealed by the legislature. But legislatures can alter the underlying forces that govern the shape and position of supply and demand schedules.

Finally, we explore supply and demand analysis as a useful device for understanding how taxes affect equilibrium prices and quantities. In particular, it helps dispel the myth that a tax is paid primarily by the party on whom it is directly levied; rather, the burden of a tax falls on whichever side of the market is least able to avoid it.

Supply and Demand Analysis

Our basic tool for analyzing market outcomes is supply and demand analysis, already familiar to most of you from your introductory course. Let us begin with the following working definition of a market.

Definition: A market consists of the buyers and sellers of a good or service.

Some markets are confined to a single specific time and location. For example, all the participating buyers and sellers (or at least their designated representatives) gather together in the same place for an antiques auction. Other markets span vast geographic territory, and most participants in them never meet or even see one another. The New York Stock Exchange is such a market. The Internet is becoming another such market for many goods.

Sometimes the choice of market definition will depend on the bias of the observer. In antitrust cases, for example, current policy prohibits mergers between companies whose combined share of the market would exceed a given threshold. Accordingly, government prosecutors who oppose a merger will often try to define markets as narrowly as possible, thereby making the combined market share as large as possible. The merging companies, by contrast, tend to view their markets in much broader terms, which naturally makes their combined market share smaller. The Stouffer's Corporation, when it wanted to merge with Nestlé, told the court that both firms were in the business of selling "frozen dinners." The Justice Department argued to the same court that the two companies were in the business of selling "high-priced ethnic entrees." In general, as in this particular instance, the best market definition will depend on the purpose at hand.

Over the years, economists have increasingly recognized that even subtle product differences matter a great deal to some consumers, and the trend in analysis has been toward ever narrower definitions of goods and markets. Two otherwise identical products are often classified as separate if they differ only with respect to the times or places they are available. An umbrella on a sunny day, for example, is in this sense a very different product from an umbrella during a downpour. And the markets for these two products behave very differently indeed. (My editor tells me that low-quality umbrellas in Manhattan sell for $6 on rainy days, only $3 on sunny days.)

To make our discussion concrete, let us consider the workings of a specific market—say, the one for $1\frac{1}{2}$-pound lobsters in Hyannis, Massachusetts, on July 20, 2000. For this market, the task of analysis is to explain both the price of lobsters and the quantity traded. To do this, we begin with the basic *demand curve*, a simple mathematical relationship that tells how many lobsters buyers wish to purchase at various possible prices (holding all else constant). The curve *DD* depicted in Figure 2-1, for example, tells us that 4000 lobsters will be demanded at a price of $4 each, 1000 at a price of $10, and so on.

If a visitor from Mars were told only that lobsters sell for $4 each, he would have no way of knowing whether they were cheap or expensive. In 1900, a $4 lobster would have been out of reach of all but the wealthiest consumers. In 2000, by contrast, lobsters would have been considered an incredible bargain at that price. Unless otherwise stated, the price on the vertical axis of the demand curve diagram will refer to the **real price** of the good, which means its price relative to the prices of all other goods and services. Thus, the prices on the vertical axis of Figure 2-1 represent lobster prices on July 20, 2000, and the context within which those prices are interpreted by buyers is the set of prices of all other goods on that same date.

Real price of a product Its price relative to the prices of other goods and services.

The demand curve shown in Figure 2-1 happens to be linear, but demand curves in general need not be. The key property assumed of them is that they are downward sloping: the quantity demanded rises as the price of the product falls. This property is often called the **law of demand.** Although we will see in Chapter 4 that it is theoretically possible for a demand curve to be upward sloping, such exceptions are virtually never encountered in practice. To be sure, the negative slope of the demand curve accords in every way with our intuitions about how people respond to rising prices.

Law of demand The empirical observation that when the price of a product falls, people demand more of it.

As we will see in more detail in Chapter 4, there are normally two independent reasons for the quantity demanded to fall when the price rises. One is that many people will switch to a close substitute. Thus, when lobster gets more expensive, some consumers may switch to crab, others to meat or poultry. A second reason people buy less when the price rises is that they are not *able* to buy as much as before. Incomes, after all, go only so far. When the price of a product goes up, it is not possible to buy as much as before unless we at the same time purchase less of something else.

The demand curve for a good is a summary of the various cost-benefit calculations that buyers make with respect to the good, as we will see in greater

FIGURE 2-1
The demand curve tells the quantities buyers will wish to purchase at various prices. Its key property is its downward slope; when price falls, the quantity demanded increases. This property is called the law of demand.

THE DEMAND CURVE FOR LOBSTERS IN HYANNIS, MASS., JULY 20, 2000

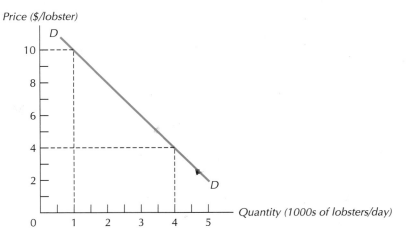

detail in the next chapter. The question each person faces is, "Should I buy the product?" (and usually, "If so, how much of it?"). The cost side of the calculation is simply the price of the product (and implicitly, the other goods or services that could be bought with the same money). The benefit side is the satisfaction provided by the product. The negative slope of the demand schedule tells us that the cost-benefit criterion will be met for fewer and fewer potential buyers as the price of the product rises.

On the seller's side of the market, the corresponding analytical tool is the supply schedule. A hypothetical schedule for our lobster market is shown as line *SS* in Figure 2-2. Again, the linear form of this particular schedule is not a characteristic feature of supply schedules generally. What these schedules do tend to have in common is their upward slope: The quantity supplied rises as the price of a product rises. This property can be called the *law of supply.* For a supplier to be willing to sell a product, its price must cover the cost of producing or acquiring it. As we will see in detail in Chapter 9, the cost of producing additional units often tends to rise as more units are produced, especially in the short run. When this is the case, increased production is profitable only at higher prices.

In our lobster market, the reasons for this are clear. Suppliers harvest the lobsters closest to shore first, and then work their way farther off shore as they try to enlarge their catch. The more lobsters they try to harvest, the farther they have to go, and hence the more it costs.

An alternative way of describing the supply schedule is to call it the set of price-quantity pairs for which suppliers are satisfied. The term "satisfied" has a technical meaning here, which is that any point on the supply schedule represents the quantity that suppliers want to sell, *given the price they face.* They would obviously be happy to get even higher prices for their offerings. But for any given price, suppliers would consider themselves worse off if forced to sell either

Law of supply
The empirical observation that when the price of a product rises, firms offer more of it for sale.

FIGURE 2-2
The upward slope of the supply schedule reflects the fact that costs tend to rise when producers expand production in the short run.

A SUPPLY SCHEDULE FOR LOBSTERS IN HYANNIS, MASS., JULY 20, 2000

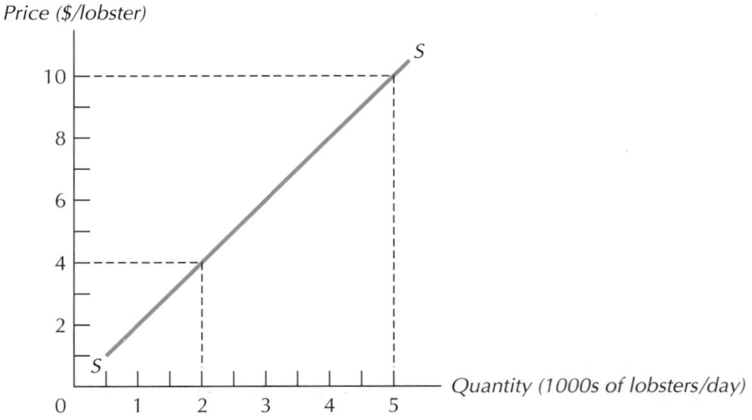

Price ($/lobster)

Quantity (1000s of lobsters/day)

more or less than the corresponding quantity on the supply schedule. If, for example, the price of lobsters in Figure 2-2 were $4, suppliers would not be satisfied selling either more or fewer than 2000 lobsters a day.

The demand schedule may be given a parallel description. It is the set of price-quantity pairs for which buyers are satisfied in precisely the same sense. At any given price, they would consider themselves worse off if forced to purchase either more or less than the corresponding quantity on the demand schedule.

Equilibrium Quantity and Price

With both the supply and demand schedules in hand, we can describe the *equilibrium quantity and price* of lobsters. It is the price-quantity pair at which both buyers and sellers are satisfied. Put another way, it is the price-quantity pair at which the supply and demand schedules intersect. Figure 2-3 depicts the equilibrium in our lobster market, at which a total of 3000 lobsters is traded at a price of $6 each.

If we were at any price-quantity pair other than the one in Figure 2-3, either buyers or sellers, or both, would be dissatisfied in the sense described above. If the price happened for some reason to lie above the $6 equilibrium level, sellers would tend to be the ones who are frustrated. At a price of $8, for example, buyers would purchase only 2000 lobsters, whereas sellers would offer 4000. (See Figure 2-4.) Buyers would be satisfied at a price of $8, but sellers would not. A situation in which price exceeds its equilibrium value is called one of *excess supply*, or *surplus*. At $8, there is an excess supply of 2000 lobsters.

If, by contrast, the price happened to lie below the equilibrium price of $6, then buyers would be the ones dissatisfied. At a price of $4, for example, they would want to purchase 4000 lobsters, whereas suppliers would be willing to

Excess supply
The amount by which quantity supplied exceeds quantity demanded.

FIGURE 2-3
The intersection of the supply and demand curves represents the price-quantity pair at which all participants in the market are "satisfied": Buyers are buying the amount they want to buy at that price, and sellers are selling the amount they want to sell.

EQUILIBRIUM IN THE LOBSTER MARKET

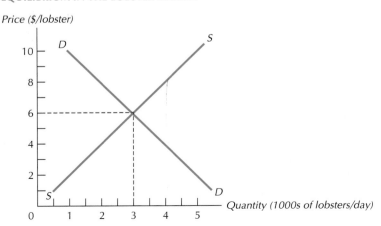

FIGURE 2-4
When price exceeds
the equilibrium
level, there is excess
supply, or surplus.
When price is below
the equilibrium
level, there is excess
demand, or
shortage.

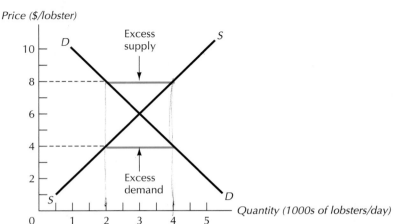

EXCESS SUPPLY AND EXCESS DEMAND

Excess demand
The amount by
which quantity
demanded ex-
ceeds quantity
supplied.

sell only 2000. A situation in which price lies below its equilibrium value is referred to as one of *excess demand*, or *shortage*. At a price of $4 in this lobster market, there is an excess demand of 2000 lobsters. At the market equilibrium price of $6, both excess demand and excess supply are exactly zero.

EXERCISE 2-1

At a price of $2 in this hypothetical lobster market, how much excess demand for lobsters will there be? How much excess supply will there be at a price of $10?

Adjustment to Equilibrium

When price differs from the equilibrium price, trading in the marketplace will be constrained—by the behavior of buyers if the price lies above equilibrium, by the behavior of sellers if below. At any price other than the equilibrium price, one side or the other of the market is dissatisfied. At prices above equilibrium, for example, sellers are not selling as much as they want to. The impulse of a dissatisfied seller is to reduce the price. In the seafood business, after all, the rule of thumb is "sell it or smell it." At a price of $8 each, 2000 lobsters are being sold, but another 2000 go unclaimed. Each seller reasons, correctly, that if he were to cut his price slightly, while other sellers remained at $8, he could move all his unsold lobsters. Buyers will abandon sellers who charge $8 in favor of those who charge only $7.95. But then the deserted sellers themselves have a motive for cutting price. And if all sellers cut price to $7.95, each will again have a large quantity of unsold lobsters. Downward pressure on price will persist so long as there remain any dissatisfied sellers—that is, until price falls to its equilibrium value.

When price is below $6, buyers are dissatisfied. Under these conditions, sellers will realize that they can increase their prices and still sell as much as they wish to. This upward pressure on price will persist until price reaches its equilibrium value. Put another way, consumers will start bidding against each other in the hope of seeing their demands satisfied.

An extraordinary feature of this equilibrating process is that no one consciously plans or directs it. The actual steps that consumers and producers must take to move toward equilibrium are often indescribably complex. Suppliers looking to expand their operations, for example, must choose from a bewilderingly large menu of equipment options. Buyers, for their part, face literally millions of choices about how to spend their money. And yet the adjustment toward equilibrium results more or less automatically from the natural reactions of self-interested individuals facing either surpluses or shortages.

Some Welfare Properties of Equilibrium

Given the attributes—tastes, abilities, knowledge, incomes, and so on—of buyers and sellers, the equilibrium outcome has some attractive properties. Specifically, we can say that no reallocation can improve some people's position without harming the position of at least some others. *If price and quantity take anything other than their equilibrium values, however, it will always be possible to reallocate so as to make at least some people better off without harming others.*

Sticking with the lobster example, suppose that the price is $4 and that suppliers therefore offer only 2000 lobsters. As indicated in Figure 2-5 (next page), when only 2000 lobsters are available, buyers are willing to pay $8 apiece for them. Here, the value to the buyer of the last lobster caught ($8) is higher than the cost of harvesting it ($4), which means that there is room to cut a deal.

Suppose, for example, a dissatisfied buyer were to offer a supplier $5 for a lobster. The supplier would gladly sell an additional lobster at this price (since, at 2000 lobsters, additional lobsters cost only $4 each to harvest). This transaction would improve the buyer's position by $3 (the difference between the $8 value he attaches to the lobster and the $5 he paid for it). It would also improve the seller's position by $1 (the difference between the $5 she got and the $4 cost of harvesting the extra lobster). No one suffers any harm from this transaction (except the extra lobster!), and the two participants reap a total of $4 additional benefit from it ($3 for the buyer, $1 for the seller). A similar argument can be made concerning any price that is below the equilibrium value. For any such price, it will always be possible to make some people better off without hurting others.

What if the price had been higher than the equilibrium price to begin with? Suppose that price is $8 and that trading is therefore limited by buyers' demands

FIGURE 2-5
When the quantity traded in the market is below (or above) the equilibrium quantity, it is always possible to reallocate resources in such a way that some people are made better off without harming others. Here, a dissatisfied buyer can pay a seller $5 for an additional lobster, thus making both parties better off.

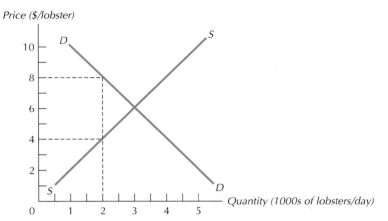

AN OPPORTUNITY FOR IMPROVEMENT IN THE LOBSTER MARKET

for 2000 lobsters. (Again, see Figure 2-5.) Now a dissatisfied seller can propose a transaction that will make both the seller and some buyers better off. Suppose, for example, a seller offers an additional lobster for sale for $7. Since buyers value additional lobsters at $8, whoever buys it will be better off by $1. And since lobsters cost only $4 to harvest, the seller will be better off by $3. Again, no one is injured by this transaction, and again the two parties gain a total of $4.

Thus, no matter whether price starts out above or below its equilibrium value, it will always be possible to put together a transaction that benefits all participants. We'll examine the welfare properties of the market system in much greater detail in Chapter 16. But for now, we may observe that the equilibrium price and quantity constitute the best outcome attainable, given the initial attributes and endowments of buyers and sellers.

Free Markets and the Poor

The fact that market equilibrium outcomes are efficient in the sense described above does not mean that they are necessarily desirable in any absolute sense. All markets may be in perfect equilibrium, for example, and yet many people may lack sufficient incomes to purchase even the bare necessities of life. The claim that market equilibrium is efficient does not challenge the notion that it is difficult, often even painful, to be poor. Efficiency says merely that, *given the low incomes of the poor,* free exchange enables them to do the best they can. One can hold this view and yet still believe that it is desirable to provide public assistance to people who are unable to earn adequate incomes in the marketplace.

Concern for the well-being of the poor motivates most societies to try to alter market outcomes, as in the gasoline price control example mentioned earlier. The difficulty, as in that example, is that many of our direct interventions in markets produce unintended and often harmful consequences. Indeed, some of them clearly do much more harm than good. As we will see, a more thorough understanding of the workings of the market mechanism would prevent many of the most costly consequences of our current approach.

EXAMPLE 2-1 *Denied boarding compensation. What are the efficiency and distributional implications of handling excess demand for airline travel through a first-come, first-served policy as opposed to an auction mechanism?*

It has always been a common practice for commercial airlines to issue more reservations than there are seats on a flight. Because many reservation holders fail to show up for their flights, this practice seldom causes difficulty. Occasionally, however, 160 passengers will show up for a flight on which there are only, say, 150 seats. Before the late 1970s, airlines dealt with overbooked flights by boarding passengers on a first-come, first-served basis.

The difficulty with this solution is that it gives insufficient weight to the interests of passengers with pressing needs to arrive at their destinations on time. With this problem clearly in mind, the Civil Aeronautics Board (CAB), the government agency that used to regulate the commercial aviation industry, proposed a simple regulation. When too many people showed up for a flight, the airline would be required to call for volunteers to abandon their seats in return for a cash payment (which could also be supplemented by an in-kind payment, such as a free air ticket). The airline would be required to keep increasing its offer until it got enough volunteers.

The advantage of the CAB proposal was that it would allow passengers to decide for themselves how pressing their schedules were. People with important meetings could simply refuse to volunteer. Others with time on their hands could agree to wait a few hours, often in return for several hundred dollars and a free trip to Hawaii. By comparison with the first-come, first-served solution, the CAB proposal promised a better outcome for all passengers.

Or at any rate, so it seemed. A consumer-action group immediately objected to the CAB's proposal on the grounds that it was unfair to low-income passengers. The group's complaint was that the auction method of soliciting volunteers would almost always result in the poorest ticket holders being the ones to wait for the next flight.

Now, a poor person will surely be more likely to find a cash payment a compelling reason to volunteer. But by the act of volunteering, a person says that the cash payment is *worth* the wait. It is one thing to say that the world would be a better place if poor people had higher incomes and were not tempted by their poverty to give up their seats on airplanes. But the consumer group was not proposing to give the poor higher incomes. Rather, it wanted to see the industry stick with the system that bumped passengers from overbooked flights irrespective of the value they attached to remaining on board.

It is hard to see how poor people would feel their interests well served by a consumer-action group that prevented them from earning extra cash by volunteering to wait for the next flight. And in the end, the CAB adopted its denied-boarding-compensation proposal, to the benefit of air travelers of all incomes.

Many critics of the market system complain that it is unfair to ration goods and services by asking how much people are willing to pay for them. This criterion, they point out, gives short shrift to the interests of the poor. But as Example 2-1 clearly illustrates, serious contradictions are inherent in alternative schemes of allocation. Consider again our hypothetical lobster market. Suppose we are concerned that the equilibrium price of $6 will exclude many deserving poor persons from ever being able to know the pleasure of a lobster dinner. And suppose that, with this in mind, we adopt a system that periodically gives free lobsters to the poor. Wouldn't such a system represent a clear improvement in the eyes of any person who feels compassion for the poor?

The answer, as in Example 2-1, is that for the same cost we can do even better. When a poor person, or indeed even a rich person, does not buy lobster because the price is too high, she is saying, in effect, that she would prefer to spend her money on other things. If we gave such a person a lobster, what would she want to do with it? In an ideal world, she would immediately sell it to someone willing to pay the $6 equilibrium price for it. We know there will be such persons because some of the lobsters that would have been bought for $6 were instead given to the poor. The poor person's sale of the lobster to one of these people will bring about a clear improvement for both parties—for the buyer, or else he would not have bought it, and for the seller because the lobster is worth less than $6 to her.

The practical difficulty, as we will see in detail in later chapters, is that it would take time and effort for our hypothetical poor person to find a buyer for the lobster. In the end, she would probably eat it herself. True enough, she might enjoy her lobster dinner. But by her own reckoning, she would have enjoyed the $6 even more.

The structure of the problem is much the same in the gasoline price controls example. The controls were implemented in the sincere belief that they were needed to protect the poor from the economic burden of sharply higher gasoline prices. Their effect, however, was to induce a host of behaviors that helped neither the rich nor the poor.

Despite statements to the contrary by critics of the market system, people are highly responsive to energy prices when they make decisions about how to spend their incomes. If gasoline costs $1.50/gal, for example, many people will

form car pools or purchase fuel-efficient cars, even though they would do neither of these things if gasoline prices were only $0.85/gal. Whether a long trip
is considered worth taking will also clearly depend on the price of gasoline.

Whether or not fuel is in unusually short supply, it is in everyone's interest—
rich or poor—to restrict its uses to the ones people value most. But the costs of
a policy that does not do this are particularly high when fuel is scarce. Selling
gasoline for less than the equilibrium price is just such a policy. It encourages
people to use gasoline in grossly wasteful ways.

RENT CONTROLS

It has been said that the surest way to destroy a city, short of dropping a nuclear
bomb on it, is to pass a rent control law. Such laws, like so many others, are
motivated by an honest concern for the well-being of low-income citizens. But
their economic consequences are no less damaging for being unintended.

Basic supply and demand analysis is again all we need to see clearly the
nature of the difficulties. Figure 2-6 depicts the supply and demand schedules
for a hypothetical urban apartment market. The equilibrium rent in this market
would be $600/month, and at this level there would be 60,000 apartments
traded. The city council, however, has passed a law that holds rents at $R_c =$
$400/month, or $200 below the market-clearing value. At $400/month, buyers
would like to rent 80,000 apartments, but suppliers are willing to offer only
40,000. There is an excess demand of 40,000 units. And if the rent control level
remains fixed at $400/month, excess demand will tend to grow over time as pop-
ulation grows and inflation reduces the value of money.

In an unregulated market, the immediate response to such a high level of
excess demand would be for rents to rise sharply. But here the law prevents them

FIGURE 2-6
With the rent control
level set at $400 a
month, there is an
excess demand of
40,000 apartments a
month.

RENT CONTROLS

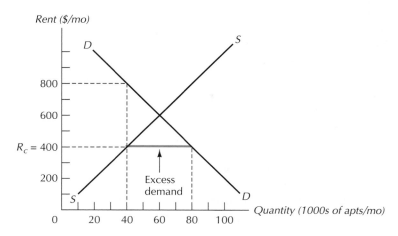

from rising above R_c. Yet there are other ways the pressures of excess demand can make themselves felt. One is for owners to spend less on maintaining the quality of their rental units. After all, if there are two renters knocking at the door of each vacant apartment, a landlord has considerable room to maneuver. Clogged drains, peeling paint, broken thermostats, and the like are not apt to receive prompt attention when rents are set well below market-clearing levels.

Nor are these the most serious difficulties. With an offering of only 40,000 apartments per month, we see in Figure 2-6 that renters would be willing to pay as much as $800/month for an apartment. This pressure almost always finds ways, legal or illegal, of expressing itself. In New York City, for example, it is not uncommon to see "finder's fees" or "key deposits" as high as several thousand dollars. Owners who cannot charge a market-clearing rent for an apartment also have the option of converting it to a condominium or co-op, which enables them to sell their asset for a price much closer to its true economic value.

Even when rent controlled apartment owners do not hike their prices in these various ways, serious misallocations result. A widow steadfastly remains in her seven-room apartment even after her children have left home because it is much cheaper than alternative dwellings not covered by rent control. It would be much better for all concerned if she relinquished that space to a larger family. But under rent controls, she has every economic incentive not to do so.

*E*XAMPLE 2-2   *Suppose the rent control is lowered (strengthened) to $200/month. What is the excess demand, and how does it compare to the excess demand when rents were limited (more loosely) to $400/month?*

> At $200/month, buyers would like to rent 100,000 apartments, but suppliers are willing to offer only 20,000. Thus there is an excess demand of 80,000 units. The excess demand is greater than the excess demand of 40,000 units at the $400/month rent control.

*E*XERCISE 2-2

> In the market for apartments described in Figure 2-6, what would happen if the rent control level were set at $625/mo?

There are much more effective ways to help poor people than to give them cheap gasoline, rent controlled apartments, or free lobsters. One would be to give them additional income and let them decide for themselves how to spend it. Chapter 18 examines some of the practical difficulties involved in transferring additional purchasing power into the hands of the poor. In brief, the most pressing problem is that it is hard to target cash to the genuinely needy without attracting others who could fend for themselves. But as we will see, economic reasoning also suggests practical ways to overcome this difficulty. There are no simple or easy solutions. But given the enormous losses caused by policies that keep prices below their equilibrium levels, these issues surely deserve our most serious attention.

Price Supports

The rent control example considered a case in which the government imposed a price ceiling to prevent the price from rising to its equilibrium level. For many agricultural products, the government's policy has been to impose not price controls but *price supports,* or *price floors,* whose effect is to keep prices above their equilibrium levels. By contrast to the price ceiling case, which required merely the announcement of a level beyond which prices were not permitted to rise, price supports require the government to become an active buyer in the market.

Figure 2-7, for example, depicts a price support level of P_s in the market for soybeans. Because P_s is above the equilibrium price, there is an excess supply of 200,000 tons/yr. To maintain the price at $P_s = \$400$/ton, the government must purchase 200,000 tons/yr of soybeans. Otherwise farmers would face powerful incentives to cut their prices.

An important purpose of farm price supports is to ensure prices sufficiently high to provide adequate incomes for farm families. In practice, however, the supports have proved an extremely costly and inefficient instrument for that task. One problem is the disposition of the surplus bought by the government each year. To produce this surplus requires valuable labor, capital, fertilizer, and other inputs. Yet often it is simply left to decay in government storage bins. Another

FIGURE 2-7
For a price support to have any impact, it must be set above the market-clearing price. Its effect is to create excess supply, which the government then purchases.

A PRICE SUPPORT IN THE SOYBEAN MARKET

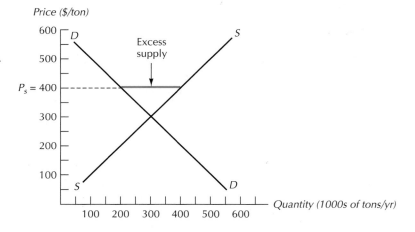

difficulty is that much of the surplus is produced by large corporate farms, whose owners are in no need of support. For every extra dollar that price supports put into the hands of a needy family farmer, several more go into the coffers of prosperous agribusinesses. Price supports also raise the food bills of all families, and often even raise prices for goods that are not directly supported. (See Example 2-4.) If society wants to subsidize small family farms, there are much more efficient and direct means of doing so than with agricultural price supports.

The Rationing and Allocative Functions of Prices

Prices serve two important and distinct functions. First, they ration existing supplies of goods. Scarcity is the universal feature of economic life. People want more of virtually everything than could be supplied at a price of zero. Equilibrium prices serve to curtail these excessive claims by rationing scarce supplies to the users who place the highest value on them. This is the *rationing function of price.*

Rationing function of price The process whereby price directs existing supplies of a product to the users who value it most highly.

The second function of price is that of a signal to direct productive resources among the different sectors of the economy. In industries in which there is excess demand, firms are able to charge more than they need to cover their costs of production. The resulting profits act as a carrot that lures additional resources into these industries. The other side of this coin is that losses act as the stick that drives resources out of those industries in which there is excess supply. This is the so-called *allocative function of price,* the driving force behind Adam Smith's invisible hand.

Allocative function of price The process whereby price acts as a signal that guides resources away from the production of goods whose prices lie below cost toward the production of goods whose prices exceed cost.

Rent controls subvert both critical functions of the price mechanism. The rationing function is undercut by the alternative mechanisms that distribute housing with little regard to the value people place on it. The underlying needs of renters are relegated to secondary status. Both luck and the people you happen to know are often decisive. Artificially low rents undercut the allocative function of price by sending a false signal to investors about the need for additional housing. With rent controls in effect, apartment builders earn less than they could by investing their money in other industries. And it is hardly surprising, therefore, that many of them do precisely that. The cruel irony is that the pressing need in many communities with rent controls is for more low-income housing units, not fewer—which is precisely what the market would produce on its own if the poor were given more money.

Determinants of Supply and Demand

Supply and demand analysis is useful not only for the normative insight it offers into questions of public policy but also for a rich variety of descriptive purposes. Most important, it helps us to predict how equilibrium prices and quantities will respond to changes in market forces. Because supply and demand curves intersect to determine equilibrium prices and quantities, anything that shifts these curves will tend to alter equilibrium values in a predictable way. In the next several chapters, we investigate in detail the forces that determine the shape and position of market demand curves. For the moment, let's discuss a few whose roles are intuitively clear.

DETERMINANTS OF DEMAND

Incomes. It is obvious that income will influence the amount of most goods and services people will purchase at any given price. For most goods, the quantity demanded at any price will rise with income. Goods that have this property are called *normal goods*. So-called *inferior goods* (such as ground beef with high fat content) are the exception to this general pattern. For such goods, the quantity demanded at any price will fall with income. The idea is that consumers abandon these goods in favor of higher-quality substitutes (such as leaner grades of meat in the ground beef case) as soon as they can afford to.

Tastes. Not all people share the same tastes. Nor do tastes always remain fixed over time. In Western societies, culture instills a taste for sitting on padded furniture, whereas in many Eastern societies, people are conditioned to favor sitting cross-legged on the floor. The demand for armchairs thus tends to be larger in the West than in the East. By the same token, the demand for skirts with hemlines above the knee tends to vary sharply from one decade to another.

Prices of Substitutes and Complements. Bacon and eggs play a complementary role in the diets of some people. For such people, a sharp increase in the price of bacon would lead not only to a reduction in the quantity of bacon demanded but also to a reduction in the demand for eggs. Such goods are considered complements: An increase in the price of one good decreases demand for the other good. In the case of close substitutes, such as coffee and tea, an increase in the price of one will tend to increase the demand for the other.

Expectations. People's expectations about future income and price levels also affect their current purchase decisions. For example, someone who expects sharply higher income in the future is likely to spend more today than an otherwise identical person who expects a much smaller income in the future. (After all, with a higher expected income, the need to save for the future diminishes.) Similarly, people will often accelerate their current purchases of goods whose prices are expected to rise sharply in the months to come.

Population. In general, the larger a market, the more a good or service at any given price will be purchased. Thus, in cities with growing populations, the demand for housing increases from year to year, whereas it tends to fall in cities with declining populations.

Figure 2-8 graphically displays some factors that shift demand curves.

FIGURE 2-8
Prices of substitutes and complements, incomes, population, expectation of future price and income changes, and tastes all influence the position of the current demand curve for a product.

FACTORS THAT SHIFT DEMAND CURVES

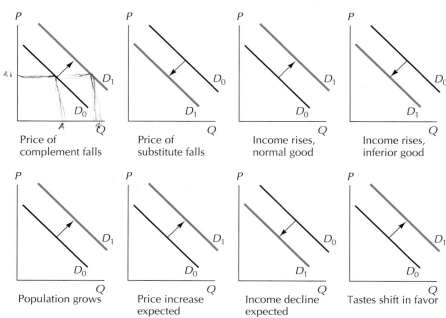

Price of complement falls

Price of substitute falls

Income rises, normal good

Income rises, inferior good

Population grows

Price increase expected

Income decline expected

Tastes shift in favor

DETERMINANTS OF SUPPLY

Technology. The amount suppliers are willing to offer at any price depends first and foremost on their costs of production. These costs, in turn, are closely linked to technology. For instance, the discovery of a more efficient lobster trap will reduce the cost of harvesting lobsters, which results in a rightward shift in the supply schedule.

Factor Prices. Another important determinant of a supplier's costs is the payment it must make to its factors of production: labor, capital, and so on. If the price of lobster boats rises, or if the wage paid to lobstermen goes up, the supply schedule for lobsters will shift to the left.

The Number of Suppliers. The more firms there are that can supply any product, the greater will be the quantity supplied of that product at any given price. The supply schedule of personal computers has shifted sharply to the right as more and more companies have begun producing them.

Expectations. Suppliers too will take expected changes in prices into account in their current production decisions. For example, if ranchers expect beef prices to rise sharply in the future because of an epidemic affecting young cattle, they are likely to withhold current supplies of mature livestock to take advantage of the higher future prices.[1]

Weather. For some products, particularly agricultural ones, nature has a great deal to say about the placement of the supply schedule. In years of drought, for example, the supply schedule for many foodstuffs will be shifted sharply to the left.

Figure 2-9 shows the effects of some factors that shift supply schedules.

Neither of the above lists of supply and demand shifters is meant to be exhaustive.

CHANGES IN DEMAND VERSUS CHANGES IN THE QUANTITY DEMANDED

When economists use the expression *change in demand,* they mean a shift in the entire demand curve. Thus, when the average income level of buyers changes, the demand curve shifts—there is a change in demand. When we say *change in the quantity demanded,* we mean a movement along the demand curve. When the price of a good falls, for example, the result is an increase in the quantity demanded, not an increase in demand.

FIGURE 2-9
Technology, input prices, the number of firms, expectations about future prices, and the weather all affect the position of the supply schedule for a given product.

FACTORS THAT SHIFT SUPPLY SCHEDULES

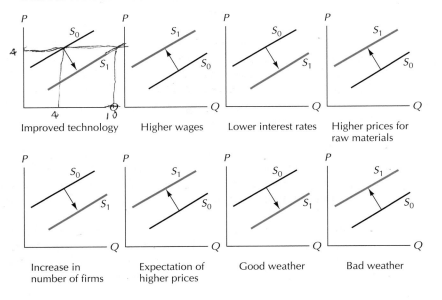

Improved technology Higher wages Lower interest rates Higher prices for raw materials

Increase in number of firms Expectation of higher prices Good weather Bad weather

[1]Note that supply is the quantity offered for sale at various prices, not necessarily production (when able to store inventory). Hence, the ranchers reduce sales of cattle in the current period, since they can sell them in a later period when prices are higher.

Analogous interpretations attach to the expressions *change in supply* and *change in the quantity supplied.* These terminological distinctions are important for clear communication both in classroom discussion and on exams. And if the experience of previous generations of students is any guide, it requires effort to keep them straight.

Predicting and Explaining Changes in Price and Quantity

To predict or explain changes in equilibrium prices and quantities, we must be able to predict or account for the shifts in the relevant supply and/or demand schedules. When supply and demand curves have the conventional slopes, the following propositions about equilibrium prices and quantities will hold:

- An increase in demand will lead to an increase in both the equilibrium price and quantity.
- A decrease in demand will lead to a decrease in both the equilibrium price and quantity.
- An increase in supply will lead to a decrease in the equilibrium price and an increase in the equilibrium quantity.
- A decrease in supply will lead to an increase in the equilibrium price and a decrease in the equilibrium quantity.

These simple propositions permit us to answer a variety of questions.

EXAMPLE 2-3 *Why do the prices of some goods, like apples, go down during the months of heaviest consumption while others, like beachfront cottages, go up?*

The answer is that the seasonal consumption increase is the result of a supply increase in the case of apples, a demand increase in the case of cottages. As shown in Figure 2-10, these shifts produce the observed seasonal relationships between equilibrium prices and quantities. (The subscripts *w* and *s* in Figure 2-10 are used to denote winter and summer values, respectively.) When demand increases (as for cottages), the increase in the equilibrium quantity occurs concurrently with an increase in the equilibrium price. When supply increases (as for apples), the increase in the equilibrium quantity occurs concurrently with a decrease in the equilibrium price.

FIGURE 2-10
The quantities con-
sumed of both ap-
ples and beachfront
cottages are highest
in the summer
months. (*a*) Apple
prices are at their
lowest during the
summer because the
quantity increase is
the result of in-
creased supply. (The
subscripts *w* and *s*
denote winter and
summer values, re-
spectively.) (*b*) Cot-
tage prices are at
their highest in sum-
mer because the
quantity increase is
the result of an in-
crease in demand.

TWO SOURCES OF SEASONAL VARIATION

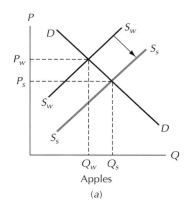

Apples

(*a*)

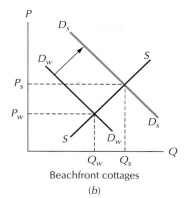

Beachfront cottages

(*b*)

EXERCISE 2-3

What will happen to the equilibrium price and quantity in the fresh
seafood market if each of the following events occurs: (1) a scientific
report is issued saying that fish contains mercury, which is toxic to
humans, and (2) the price of diesel fuel (used to operate fishing boats)
falls significantly?

EXAMPLE 2-4 *If soybeans are one of the ingredients in cattle feed, how does a price support program in the
soybean market affect the equilibrium price and quantity of beef?*

The price support program raises the price of cattle feed, which causes
a leftward shift in the supply schedule for beef. (See Figure 2-11.) This,
in turn, results in an increase in the equilibrium price and a reduction
in the equilibrium quantity of beef.

The Algebra of Supply and Demand

The examples thus far have focused on a geometric approach to market equilibrium. This approach is fine for illustrating the basic principles of the theory.
But for actually computing numerical values, it usually is more convenient to
find equilibrium prices and quantities algebraically. Suppose, for example, the
supply schedule for a product is given by

THE EFFECT OF SOYBEAN PRICE SUPPORTS ON THE EQUILIBRIUM PRICE AND QUANTITY OF BEEF

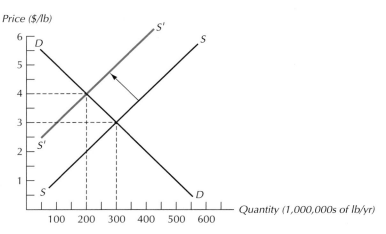

$$P = 2 + 3Q^s, \qquad (2.1)$$

and that its demand schedule is given by

$$P = 10 - Q^d, \qquad (2.2)$$

where P is the product price and Q^s and Q^d stand for the quantity supplied and the quantity demanded, respectively. In equilibrium, we know that $Q^s = Q^d$. Denoting this common value as Q^*, we may then equate the right-hand sides of Equations 2.1 and 2.2 and solve:

$$2 + 3Q^* = 10 - Q^*, \qquad (2.3)$$

which gives $Q^* = 2$. Substituting $Q^* = 2$ back into either the supply or demand equation gives the equilibrium price, $P^* = 8$.

Needless to say, we could have graphed Equations 2.1 and 2.2 to arrive at precisely the same solution (see Figure 2-12). The advantage of the algebraic approach is that it is much less painstaking than having to produce accurate drawings of the supply and demand schedules.

EXERCISE 2-4

Find the equilibrium price and quantity in a market whose supply and demand curves are given by $P = 4Q^s$ and $P = 12 - 2Q^d$, respectively.

FIGURE 2-12
The algebraic and geometric approaches lead to exactly the same equilibrium prices and quantities. The advantage of the algebraic approach is that exact numerical solutions can be achieved more easily. The geometric approach is useful because it gives a more intuitively clear description of the supply and demand curves.

GRAPHS OF EQUATIONS 2.1 AND 2.2

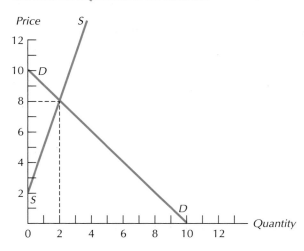

Taxes

Supply and demand analysis is also a useful tool for analyzing the effects of various taxes. In this section we consider a constant tax per unit of output. How will the equilibrium price and quantity of a product be affected if a tax of $T = 10$ is levied on each unit sold by the producer? There are two equivalent ways to approach this question. The first is to suppose that the tax is levied on the seller. In Figure 2-13, the line SS denotes the original supply schedule. At a price of $P_0 = 25$, sellers were willing to supply Q_0 units of output. When a tax $T = 10$ is levied on sellers, the market price would have to be $P_0 + 10 = 35$ for them to get the same net payment that they used to receive when the price was $P_0 = 25$. At a price of 35, then, suppliers will offer the same amount of output they used to offer at a price of 25. The resulting after-tax supply schedule is the original supply schedule shifted upward by $T = 10$.

In Figure 2-14, DD represents the demand curve facing the sellers who have been taxed $T = 10$ per unit of output. The effect of the tax is to cause the equilibrium quantity to fall from Q^* to Q_1^*. The price paid by the buyer rises from P^* to P_1^*; and the price, net of the tax, received by the seller falls to $P_1^* - 10$.

Note in Figure 2-14 that even though the seller pays a tax of T on each product purchased, the total amount the seller receives per unit lies less than T below the old equilibrium price. Note also that even though the tax is collected from the seller, its effect is to increase the price paid by buyers. The burden of the tax is thus divided between the buyer and the seller.

Algebraically, the seller's share of the tax, denoted t_s, is the reduction in the price the seller receives, divided by the tax:

$$t_s = \frac{P^* - (P_1^* - T)}{T}.$$ (2.4)

FIGURE 2-13
The original supply schedule tells us what price suppliers must charge in order to cover their costs at any given level of output. From the seller's perspective, a tax of $T = 10$ units is the same as a unit-cost increase of 10 units. The new supply curve thus lies 10 units above the old one.

A TAX OF $T = 10$ LEVIED ON THE SELLER SHIFTS THE SUPPLY SCHEDULE UPWARD BY T UNITS

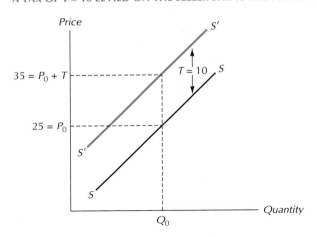

FIGURE 2-14
The tax causes a re-duction in equilib-rium quantity from Q^* to Q_1^*. The new price paid by the buyer rises from P^* to P_1^*. The new price received by the seller falls from P^* to $P_1^* - 10$.

EQUILIBRIUM PRICES AND QUANTITIES WHEN A TAX OF $T = 10$ IS LEVIED ON THE SELLER

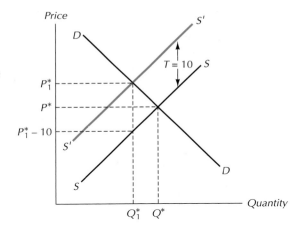

Similarily, the buyer's share of the tax, t_b, is the increase in price (including tax) divided by the tax:

$$t_b = \frac{P_1^* - P^*}{T}.$$ (2.5)

EXERCISE 2-5

Verify that $t_s + t_b = 1$.

In general, t_b and t_s depend on the shapes of the supply and demand schedules. If, for example, supply is highly unresponsive to changes in price, t_b will be close to zero, t_s close to 1. Conversely, if demand is highly unresponsive to price, t_b will be close to 1, t_s close to zero. These claims amount to a statement that a tax tends to fall most heavily on the side of the market that can least escape it. If buyers have no substitute products to which they are prepared to turn, the lion's share of the tax will be passed on to them by suppliers. But if suppliers have no alternative other than to go on supplying a product, most of the burden of a tax will fall on them. As long as the supply curve is positively sloped and the demand curve is negatively sloped, however, both t_s and t_b will be positive.

The second way of analyzing the effect of a tax of $T = 10$ per unit of output is to imagine that the tax is collected directly from the buyer and to analyze how that would affect the demand curve for the product. In Figure 2-15, the demand curve before the imposition of the tax is denoted by the line DD. At a price of P_1, buyers would demand a quantity of Q_1. After the imposition of the tax, the total amount that buyers have to pay if the product price is P_1 will be $P_1 + 10$. Accordingly, the quantity they demand falls from Q_1 to Q_2. In like fashion, we can reckon the quantity demanded at any other price after imposition of the tax. The resulting after-tax demand curve will be the line $D'D'$ in Figure 2-15. It is simply the original demand curve translated downward by 10 units.

If line SS in Figure 2-16 denotes the supply schedule for this market, we can easily trace out the effects of the tax on the equilibrium price and quantity. The equilibrium quantity falls from Q^* to Q_2^*, and the equilibrium price falls from P^* to P_2^*. The total price paid by the buyer after imposition of the tax rises to $P_2^* + 10$.

Is the effect of a tax on the seller any different from the effect of a tax levied on the buyer? Not at all. To illustrate, suppose the supply and demand curves

FIGURE 2-15
Before the tax, buyers would buy Q_1 units at a price of P_1. After the tax, a price of P_1 becomes $P_1 + 10$, which means buyers will buy only Q_2. The effect of the tax is to shift the demand curve downward by 10 units.

THE EFFECT OF A TAX OF $T = 10$ LEVIED ON THE BUYER

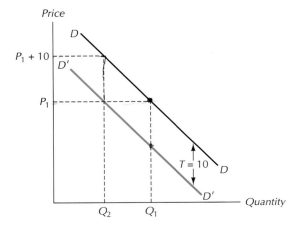

EQUILIBRIUM PRICES AND QUANTITIES AFTER IMPOSITION OF A TAX OF $T = 10$ PAID BY THE BUYER

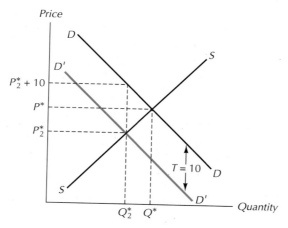

for a market are given by $P = Q^s$ and $P = 10 - Q^d$, respectively, and consider first the effect of a tax of 2 per unit of output imposed on the seller. Figure 2-17a shows the original supply and demand curves and the new after-tax supply curve, $S'S'$. The original equilibrium price and quantity are both equal to 5. The new equilibrium price to the buyer (inclusive of tax) and quantity are 6 and 4, respectively. The price received by sellers, net of the tax, is 4.

Now, consider a tax of 2 per unit of output imposed on the buyers. Figure 2-17b shows the original supply and demand curves and the new after-tax demand curve, $D'D'$. Note that the effects on price and quantity are exactly the same as in the case of the tax levied on sellers shown in panel a.

A TAX ON THE BUYER LEADS TO THE SAME OUTCOME AS A TAX ON THE SELLER

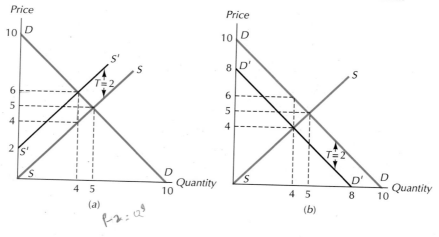

EXERCISE 2-6

Consider a market whose supply and demand curves are given by $P = 4Q^s$ and $P = 12 - 2Q^d$, respectively. How will the equilibrium price and quantity in this market be affected if a tax of 6 per unit of output is imposed on sellers? If the same tax is imposed on buyers?

When tax revenues have to be raised, many political leaders find it expedient to propose a sales tax on corporations because "they can best afford to pay it." But careful analysis of the effects of a sales tax shows that its burden will be the same whether it is imposed on buyers or sellers. The *legal incidence of the tax* (whether it is imposed on buyers or on sellers) has no effect on the *economic incidence* of the tax (the respective shares of the tax burden borne by buyers and sellers). Economically speaking, the entity from which the tax is actually collected is thus a matter of complete indifference.

A word of caution: When we say that the economic burden of the tax does not depend on the party from whom the tax is directly collected, this does not mean that buyers and sellers always share the burden of taxes equally. Their respective shares may, as noted, be highly unequal. The independence of legal incidence and economic incidence simply means that the burden will be shared in the same way no matter where the tax is placed.

Summary

The supply curve is generally an upward-sloping line that tells what quantity sellers will offer at any given price. The demand curve is a downward-sloping line that tells what quantity buyers will demand at any given price. In an unregulated market, the equilibrium price and quantity are determined by the intersection of these two curves.

If price is above its equilibrium, there will be dissatisfied sellers, or excess supply. This condition motivates sellers to cut their prices. By contrast, when prices are below equilibrium, there will be dissatisfied buyers, or excess demand. This condition motivates sellers to charge higher prices. The only stable outcome is the one in which excess demand and excess supply are exactly zero.

Given the attributes of buyers and sellers, the equilibrium price and quantity represent the best attainable outcome, in the sense that any other price-quantity pair would be worse for at least some buyers or sellers.

The fact that market outcomes are efficient in this sense does not mean they necessarily command society's approval. On the contrary, we often lament the fact that many buyers enter the market with so little income. Concern for the well-being of the poor has motivated the governments of every Western society to intervene in a variety of ways to alter the outcomes of market forces.

Sometimes these interventions take the form of laws that peg prices above or below their equilibrium levels. Such laws often generate harmful, if unintended, consequences. Programs such as rent control, for example, interfere with both the rationing and allocative functions of the price mechanism. They lead to black marketeering and a rapid deterioration of the stock of rental housing. By the same token, price support laws in agriculture tend to enrich large corporate farms while doing little to ease the plight of the small family farm. In almost every instance, it is possible to design an alternative intervention that is better in every respect.

If the difficulty is that the poor have too little money, the solution is to discover ways of boosting their incomes directly. Legislatures cannot repeal the law of supply and demand. But legislatures do have the capacity to alter the underlying forces that govern the shape and position of supply and demand schedules.

Supply and demand analysis is the economist's basic tool for predicting how equilibrium prices and quantities will change in response to changes in market forces. Four simple propositions guide this task: (1) an increase in demand will lead to an increase in both the equilibrium price and quantity; (2) a decrease in demand will lead to a decrease in both the equilibrium price and quantity; (3) an increase in supply will lead to a decrease in the equilibrium price and an increase in the equilibrium quantity; and (4) a decrease in supply will lead to an increase in the equilibrium price and a decrease in the equilibrium quantity.

Incomes, tastes, the prices of substitutes and complements, expectations, and population are among the factors that shift demand schedules. Supply schedules, in turn, are governed by such factors as technology, input prices, the number of suppliers, expectations, and, for agricultural products, the weather.

Supply and demand analysis is a useful device for understanding how taxes affect equilibrium prices and quantities. In particular, it helps dispel the myth that a tax is paid primarily by the party on whom it is directly levied. In practice, the burden of a tax falls on whichever side of the market is least able to avoid it.

Questions for Review

1. What is the difference between "scarcity" and "shortage"?

2. What would the supply curve look like for a good that is not scarce? Assuming the good is useful, what would its demand curve look like? Explain why a positive price for a commodity implies that it is scarce.

3. Give two examples of actions taken by the administration of your college or university whose effect is to prevent specific markets from reaching equilibrium. What evidence of excess supply or excess demand can you cite in these examples?

4. What is the difference between "a reduction in supply" and "a reduction in the quantity supplied"?

5. Identify each of the following as (1) a change in demand or (2) a change in the quantity demanded.

a. Grape consumption falls because of a consumer boycott.
b. Grape consumption falls because of a tax on grape producers.
c. Grape consumption rises because of a good harvest.
d. Grape consumption rises because of a change in tastes.

6. When there is excess supply, why is any single seller able to sell all she wants to by offering only a small reduction below the current market price?

7. Give an example of a market in which the allocative function of price is not very important.

8. The steeper the demand curve for some good relative to the supply curve for that good, the greater the proportion of a tax on that good that will fall on buyers. True or false? Explain.

9. Suppose you are a government official and need to collect revenue by taxing a product. For political reasons, you want the burden of the tax to fall mostly on consumers, not firms (who have been substantial contributors to your campaign fund). What should you look for when picking a product to tax?

10. Which would a poor person be more likely to accept and why?

a. A $50,000 Mercedes (immediate resale value = $30,000)
b. $35,000 cash

Problems

1. The government, fearful that a titanium shortage could jeopardize national security, imposes a tax of $2/oz on the retail price of this rare metal. It collects the tax from titanium sellers. The original supply and demand schedules for titanium are as shown in the diagram. Show, in the same diagram, how the short-run equilibrium price and quantity of titanium will be affected by the tax. Label all important points clearly.

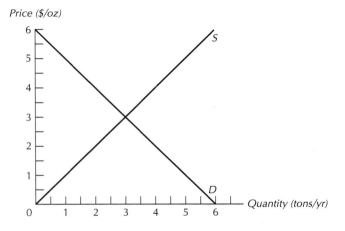

2. In the market for titanium described in Problem 1 (with no tax), suppose that a price floor of $4/oz results in sales of only 2 tons/yr (with no tax). Describe a transaction that will make some buyers and sellers better off without harming others.

3. Suppose the titanium market in Problem 1, with a tax of $2/oz, experiences growth in the demand for titanium because of new-found medical uses. The new demand curve is $P = 8 - Q$. Find the change in government tax revenue due to the heightened demand for titanium.

4. Suppose instead the titanium market in Problem 2, with no tax but a price floor at $4/oz, suffers a reduction in supply because of dwindling titanium reserves. The new supply curve is $P = 2 + Q$. How does excess supply change due to the reduction in supply? Is the price floor still binding (does it cause price to rise from its equilibrium level)?

5. Assume that tea and lemons are complements and that coffee and tea are substitutes.

   a. How, if at all, will the imposition of an effective ceiling price on tea affect the price of lemons? Explain.
   b. How, if at all, will the imposition of an effective ceiling price on tea affect the price of coffee? Explain.

6. The market for digital video disks (DVDs) has supply and demand curves given by $P = 2Q^s$ and $P = 42 - Q^d$, respectively.

   a. How many units will be traded at a price of $35? At a price of $14? Which participants will be dissatisfied at these prices?
   b. What quantity of DVDs at what price will be sold in equilibrium?
   c. What is the total revenue from DVD sales?

7. Suppose state government levies a tax of $9 on each DVD sold, collected from sellers.

   a. What quantity of DVDs will be sold in equilibrium?
   b. What price do buyers pay?
   c. How much do buyers now spend in total?
   d. How much money goes to the government?
   e. Show the above results graphically.

8. For the tax described in Problem 7,

   a. What fraction of the tax does the seller bear?
   b. What fraction of the tax does the buyer bear?

9. President Reagan negotiated a "voluntary" import quota on Japanese cars sold in the United States in the early 1980s. Some of his advisers had recommended that he impose a higher import tax (tariff) instead. Assuming the tariff was in the form of a constant tax T per Japanese car sold in the United States and that T was chosen to produce the same quantity reduction as the quota, how will the prices paid for Japanese cars by U.S. consumers compare under the two policies?

10. Hardware and software for computers are complements. Discuss the effects on the equilibrium price and quantity

a. In the software market, when the price of computer hardware falls.

b. In the hardware market, when the price of computer software rises.

11. Suppose a newly released study shows that battery-powered toys harm a child's development and recommends that parents adjust their purchasing behavior accordingly. Use diagrams to show the effect on price and quantity in each of the following markets:

    a. The market for battery-powered toys

    b. The market for D batteries

    c. The market for yo-yos (which do not require batteries)

12. Using diagrams, show what changes in price and quantity would be expected in the following markets under the scenarios given:

    a. *Crude oil:* As petroleum reserves decrease, it becomes more difficult to find and recover crude oil.

    b. *Air travel:* Worries about air safety cause travelers to shy away from air travel.

    c. *Rail travel:* Worries about air safety cause travelers to shy away from air travel.

    d. *Hotel rooms in Hawaii:* Worries about air safety cause travelers to shy away from air travel.

    e. *Milk:* A genetically engineered hormone enables large milk producers to cut production costs.

13. For each scenario in Problem 12, state whether the effect is a change in demand or just a change in quantity demanded.

14. Many studies on rats and mice have established that charred meat grilled over hot coals causes cancer. Since the government cannot easily regulate home cooking methods, an alternative method has been proposed to discourage the consumption of barbecued meat. The proposal is to place a 100 percent tax at the retail level on charcoal briquets. Suppose the daily demand for charcoal was $P = 120 - 2Q$ and the supply was $P = 30 + Q$, where P is in dollars and Q is the number of 20-lb bags of charcoal sold weekly.

    a. What is the before- and after-tax price of charcoal?

    b. What is the before- and after-tax quantity of charcoal?

    c. How is the tax divided among sellers and buyers?

15. Supply is $P = 4Q$, while demand is $P = 20$, where P is price in dollars and Q is units of output per week.

    a. Find the equilibrium price and quantity (using both algebra and a graph).

    b. If sellers must pay a tax of $T = \$4/$unit, what happens to the quantity exchanged, the price buyers pay, and the price sellers receive (net of the tax)?

    c. How is the burden of the tax distributed across buyers and sellers and why?

16. Repeat Problem 15, but instead suppose the buyer pays the tax, demand is $P = 28 - Q$, and supply is $P = 20$.

17. Suppose demand for football games is $P = 1900 - (1/50)Q$ and supply is fixed at $Q = 90,000$ seats.

     a. Find the equilibrium price and quantity of seats for a football game (using algebra and a graph).

     b. Suppose the government prohibits tickets scalping (selling tickets above their face value), and the face value of tickets is $50 (this policy places a price ceiling at $50). How many consumers will be dissatisfied (how large is excess demand)?

     c. Suppose the next game is a major rivalry, and so demand jumps to $P = 2100 - (1/50)Q$. How many consumers will be dissatisfied for the big game?

     d. How do the distortions of this price ceiling differ from the more typical case of upward-sloping supply?

18. Suppose the supply of a good is $P = Q$ and demand is fixed at $Q = 12$ units per week.

     a. Find the equilibrium price and quantity.

     b. Suppose the government levies a tax equal to $4 on sellers of the good. Find the equilibrium quantity, price paid by buyers, and price received by the sellers (net of taxes).

     c. How is the tax burden distributed and why?

19. The demand for apartments is $P = 1200 - Q$ while the supply is $P = Q$ units. The government imposes rent control at $P = \$300/\text{month}$. Suppose demand grows in the market to $P = 1400 - Q$.

     a. How is excess demand affected by the growth in demand for apartments?

     b. At what price would the government have to set the rent control to keep excess demand at the same level as prior to the growth in demand?

20. Suppose demand is $P = 600 - Q$ and supply is $P = Q$ in the soybean market, where Q is tons of soybeans per year. The government sets a price support at $P = \$500/\text{ton}$ and purchases any excess supply at this price. In response, as a long-run adjustment, farmers switch their crops from corn to soybeans, expanding supply to $P = (1/2)Q$.

     a. How does excess supply with the larger supply compare to excess supply prior to the farmers switching crops?

     b. How much more does the government have to spend to buy up the excess supply?

Answers to In-Chapter Exercises

2-1. At a price of $2/lobster, the quantity demanded is 5000 lobsters/day and the quantity supplied is 1000 lobsters/day, making excess demand equal to 4000 lobsters/day. At a price of $10/lobster, excess supply is 4000 lobsters/day.

2-2. A rent control level set above the equilibrium price has no effect. The rent will settle at its equilibrium value of $600/mo.

2-3. The fall in the price of diesel fuel shifts the supply curve to the right. The report on mercury shifts the demand curve to the left. As shown in the following diagrams, the equilibrium price will go down (both panels) but the equilibrium quantity may go either up (panel *b*) or down (panel *a*).

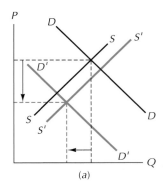

(a)

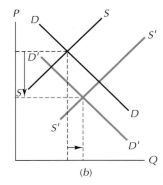

(b)

2-4. $4Q^* = 12 - 2Q^*$, which yields $Q^* = 2$ and $P^* = 4Q^* = 8$.

2-5. $t_s + t_b = [(P^* - P_1^* + T) + (P_1^* - P^*)]/T = T/T = 1$.

2-6. The original price and quantity are given by $P^* = 8$ and $Q^* = 2$, respectively. The supply curve with the tax is given by $P = 6 + 4Q^s$. Letting P' and Q' denote the new equilibrium values of price and quantity, we now have $6 + 4Q' = 12 - 2Q'$, which yields $Q' = 1$, $P' = 10$, where P' is the price paid by buyers. $P' - 6 = 4$ is the price received by sellers. Alternatively, the demand curve with a tax of 6 levied on buyers is given by $P = 6 - 2Q^d$, and we have $4Q' = 6 - 2Q'$, which again yields $Q' = 1$. $P'' = 4$, where P'' is the price received by sellers. $P'' + T = P'' + 6 = 10$ is the price paid by buyers.

PART TWO 2

The Theory of Consumer Behavior

These chapters develop the theory of consumer behavior. Chapter 3 is of special importance, for it lays out the economic theory of how people with limited resources choose between competing alternatives. The methods and tools developed in this chapter recur throughout the remainder of the book, and indeed throughout all of economics. Chapter 4 shows how the theory of rational individual choice can be used to derive individual and market demand curves. Chapter 5 explores numerous applications of rational choice and demand theories, including the theory of choices that involve future consequences.

Chapter 6 shows how the rational choice model can be extended to cover choices that involve uncertainty or incomplete information. Chapter 7 examines the role of unselfish motives in economic and social behavior and shows why honest people often have an economic advantage over people who cheat. Finally, Chapter 8 looks at a variety of circumstances in which ordinary people have a tendency to make irrational choices. Experience shows that being aware of these tendencies helps people make better decisions.

CHAPTER 3

Rational Consumer Choice

ou have just cashed your monthly allowance check and are on your way to the local music store to buy an Eric Clapton CD you've been wanting. The price of the disc is $10. In scenario 1 you lose $10 on your way to the store. In scenario 2 you buy the disc and then trip and fall on your way out of the store; the disc shatters as it hits the sidewalk. Try to imagine your frame of mind in each scenario.

a. Would you proceed to buy the disc in scenario 1?
b. Would you return to buy the disc in scenario 2?

These questions[1] were recently put to a large class of undergraduates who had never taken an economics course. In response to the first question, 54 percent answered yes, saying they would buy the disc after losing the $10 bill. But only 32 percent answered yes to the second question—68 percent said they would *not* buy the disc after having broken the first one. There is, of course, no "correct" answer to either question. The events described will have more of an impact, for example, on a poor consumer than on a rich one. Yet a moment's reflection reveals that your behavior in one scenario logically should be exactly the same

---

[1]These questions are patterned after similar questions posed by decision theorists Daniel Kahneman and Amos Tversky (see Chapter 8).

as in the other. After all, in both scenarios, the only economically relevant change is that you now have $10 less to spend than before. This might well mean that you will want to give up having the disc; or it could mean saving less or giving up some other good or service that you would have bought instead. But your choice should not be affected by the particular way you happened to become $10 poorer. In both scenarios, the cost of the disc is $10, and the benefits you will receive from listening to it are also the same. You should either buy the disc in both scenarios or not buy it in both scenarios. And yet, as noted, many people said they would behave differently in the two scenarios.

Chapter Preview

Our task in this chapter is to set forth the economist's basic model for answering questions such as the ones asked above. This model is known as the theory of *rational consumer choice*. It underlies all individual purchase decisions, which in turn add up to the demand curves we worked with in the preceding chapter.

Rational choice theory begins with the assumption that consumers enter the marketplace with well-defined preferences. Taking prices as given, their task is to allocate their incomes to best serve these preferences. Two steps are required to carry out this task. Step 1 is to describe the various combinations of goods the consumer is *able* to buy. We will see that these combinations depend on both her income level and the prices of the goods. Step 2 then is to select from among the feasible combinations the particular one that she *prefers* to all others. Analysis of step 2 requires some means of describing her preferences, in particular, a summary of the rank ordering she assigns to all feasible combinations. Formal development of these two elements of the theory occupy our attention throughout this chapter. Because the first element—describing the set of possibilities—is much less abstract than the second, let us begin with it.

The Opportunity Set or Budget Constraint

Bundle A particular combination of two or more goods.

For simplicity, let us begin by considering a world with only two goods,[2] food and shelter. A **bundle** of goods is the term used to describe a particular combination of food, measured in pounds per week, and shelter, measured in square yards per week. Thus, in Figure 3-1, one bundle (bundle A) might consist of 5 sq yd/wk of shelter and 7 lb/wk of food, while another (bundle B) consists of 3 sq yd/wk of shelter and 8 lb/wk of food. For brevity's sake, we may use the notation (5, 7) to denote bundle A and the notation (3, 8) to denote bundle B. More generally, (S_0, F_0) will denote the bundle with S_0 sq yd/wk of shelter and F_0 lb/wk of food. By convention, the first number of the pair in any bundle represents the good measured along the horizontal axis.

---

[2]As economists use the term, a "good" may refer to either a product or a service.

FIGURE 3-1
A bundle is a specific combination of goods. Bundle *A* has 5 units of shelter and 7 units of food. Bundle *B* has 3 units of shelter and 8 units of food.

TWO BUNDLES OF GOODS

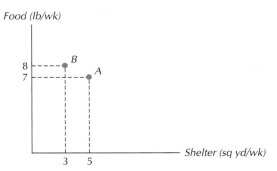

Note that the units on both axes are *flows*, which means physical quantities per unit of time—pounds per week, square yards per week. Consumption is always measured as a flow. It is important to keep track of the time dimension because without it there would be no way to evaluate whether a given quantity of consumption was large or small. (Suppose all you know is that your food consumption is 4 lb. If that's how much you eat each day, it's a lot. But if that's all you eat in a month, you're not likely to survive for long.)[3]

Suppose the consumer's income is $M = \$100/\text{wk}$, all of which she spends on some combination of food and shelter. (Note that income is also a flow.) Suppose further that the prices of shelter and food are $P_S = \$5/\text{sq yd}$ and $P_F = \$10/\text{lb}$, respectively. If the consumer spent all her income on shelter, she could buy $M/P_s = (\$100/\text{wk}) \div (\$5/\text{sq yd}) = 20$ sq yd/wk. That is, she could buy the bundle consisting of 20 sq yd/wk of shelter and 0 lb/wk of food, denoted (20, 0). Alternatively, suppose the consumer spent all her income on food. She would then get the bundle consisting of $M/P_F = (\$100/\text{wk}) \div (\$10/\text{lb})$, which is 10 lb/wk of food and 0 sq yd/wk of shelter, denoted (0, 10).

In Figure 3-2 these polar cases are labeled *K* and *L*, respectively. The consumer is also able to purchase any other bundle that lies along the straight line that joins points *K* and *L*. [Verify, for example, that the bundle (12, 4) lies on this same line.] This line is called the *budget constraint* and is labeled *B* in the diagram.

Budget constraint The set of all bundles that are affordable with given income and prices. Also called the *opportunity set.*

Recall the maxim from high school algebra that the slope of a straight line is its "rise" over its "run" (the change in its vertical position divided by the corresponding change in its horizontal position). Here, note that the slope of the budget constraint is its vertical intercept (the rise) divided by its horizontal intercept (the corresponding run): $-(10 \text{ lb/wk})/(20 \text{ sq yd/wk}) = -\frac{1}{2} \text{ lb/sq yd}$. The minus sign signifies that the budget line falls as it moves to the right—that it has a negative slope. More generally, if M denotes the consumer's weekly income, and P_S

---

[3]The flow aspect of consumption helps us alleviate any concern about goods not being divisible. If you consume 1.5 lb/mo, then you consume 18 lb/yr, which is a whole number.

THE BUDGET CONSTRAINT, OR OPPORTUNITY SET

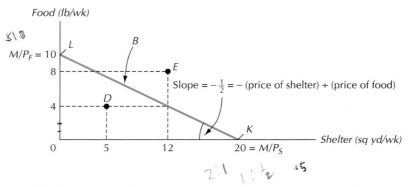

and P_F denote the prices of shelter and food, respectively, the horizontal and vertical intercepts will be given by (M/P_S) and (M/P_F), respectively. Thus the general formula for the slope of the budget constraint is given by $-(M/P_F)/(M/P_S)$
$= -P_S/P_F$, which is simply the negative of the price ratio of the two goods.
Given their respective prices, it is the rate at which food can be exchanged for
shelter. Thus, in Figure 3-2, 1 lb of food can be exchanged for 2 sq yd of shelter.
In the language of opportunity cost from Chapter 1, we would say that the
opportunity cost of an additional square yard of shelter is $P_S/P_F = \frac{1}{2}$ lb of food.

In addition to being able to buy any of the bundles along her budget constraint, the consumer is also able to purchase any bundle that lies within the *budget triangle* bounded by it and the two axes. *D* is one such bundle in Figure 3-2.
Bundle *D* costs \$65/wk, which is well below the consumer's income of \$100/wk.
The bundles on or within the budget triangle are also referred to as the *feasible*

set, or **affordable set.** Bundles like *E* that lie outside the budget triangle are said
to be *infeasible,* or *unaffordable.* At a cost of \$140/wk, *E* is simply beyond the con-
sumer's reach.

If *S* and *F* denote the quantities of shelter and food, respectively, the budget
constraint must satisfy the following equation:

$$P_S S + P_F F = M,$$ (3.1)

which says simply that the consumer's weekly expenditure on shelter ($P_S S$)
plus her weekly expenditure on food ($P_F F$) must add up to her weekly income
(M). To express the budget constraint in the manner conventionally used to
represent the formula for a straight line, we solve Equation 3.1 for F in terms
of S, which yields

$$F = \frac{M}{P_F} - \frac{P_S}{P_F} S.$$ (3.2)

Equation 3.2 is another way of seeing that the vertical intercept of the budget constraint is given by M/P_F and its slope by $-(P_S/P_F)$. The equation for the budget constraint in Figure 3-2 is $F = 10 - \frac{1}{2}S$.

BUDGET SHIFTS DUE TO PRICE OR INCOME CHANGES

Price Changes.   The slope and position of the budget constraint are fully determined by the consumer's income and the prices of the respective goods. Change any one of these factors and we have a new budget constraint. Figure 3-3 shows the effect of an increase in the price of shelter from $P_{S1} = \$5/\text{sq yd}$ to $P_{S2} = \$10$. Since both weekly income and the price of food are unchanged, the vertical intercept of the consumer's budget constraint stays the same. The rise in the price of shelter rotates the budget constraint inward about this intercept, as shown in the diagram.

Note in Figure 3-3 that even though the price of food has not changed, the new budget constraint, B_2, curtails not only the amount of shelter the consumer can buy but also the amount of food.[4]

EXERCISE 3-1

Show the effect on the budget constraint B_1 in Figure 3-3 of a fall in the price of shelter from \$5/sq yd to \$4/sq yd.

In Exercise 3-1, you saw that a fall in the price of shelter again leaves the vertical intercept of the budget constraint unchanged. This time the budget constraint rotates outward. Note also in Exercise 3-1 that although the price of food remains unchanged, the new budget constraint enables the consumer to buy bundles that contain not only more shelter but also more food than she could afford on the original budget constraint.

EXERCISE 3-2

Show the effect on the budget constraint B_1 in Figure 3-3 of a rise in the price of food from \$10/lb to \$20/lb.

Exercise 3-2 demonstrates that when the price of food changes, the budget constraint rotates about its horizontal intercept. Note also that even though income

---

[4]The single exception to this statement involves the vertical intercept (0, 10), which lies on both the original and the new budget constraints.

FIGURE 3-3
When shelter goes
up in price, the ver-
tical intercept of the
budget constraint re-
mains the same. The
original budget con-
straint rotates in-
ward about this
intercept.

THE EFFECT OF A RISE IN THE PRICE OF SHELTER

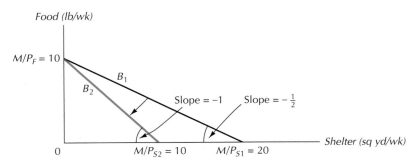

and the price of shelter remain the same, the new budget constraint curtails not only the amount of food the consumer can buy but also the amount of shelter.

When we change the price of only one good, we necessarily change the slope of the budget constraint, $-P_S/P_F$. The same is true if we change both prices by different proportions. But as Exercise 3-3 will illustrate, changing both prices by exactly the same proportion gives rise to a new budget constraint with the same slope as before.

EXERCISE 3-3

Show the effect on the budget constraint B_1 in Figure 3-3 of a rise in the price of food from \$10/lb to \$20/lb and a rise in the price of shelter from \$5/sq yd to \$10/sq yd.

Note from Exercise 3-3 that the effect of doubling the prices of both food and shelter is to shift the budget constraint inward and parallel to the original budget constraint. The important lesson of this exercise is that the slope of a budget constraint tells us only about *relative prices*, nothing about how high prices are in absolute terms. When the prices of food and shelter change in the same proportion, the opportunity cost of shelter in terms of food remains the same as before.

Income Changes.   The effect of a change in income is much like the effect of an equal proportional change in all prices. Suppose, for example, that our hypothetical consumer's income is cut by half, from \$100/wk to \$50/wk. The horizontal intercept of the consumer's budget constraint then falls from 20 sq yd/wk to 10 sq yd/wk, and the vertical intercept falls from 10 lb/wk to 5 lb/wk, as shown in Figure 3-4. Thus the new budget, B_2, is parallel to the old, B_1, each with a slope of $-\frac{1}{2}$. In terms of its effect on what the consumer can buy, cutting income by one-half is thus no different from doubling each price. Precisely the same budget constraint results from both changes.

*E*XERCISE 3-4

Show the effect on the budget constraint B_1 in Figure 3-4 of an increase in income from $100/wk to $120/wk.

Exercise 3-4 illustrates that an increase in income shifts the budget constraint parallel outward. As in the case of an income reduction, the slope of the budget constraint remains the same.

BUDGETS INVOLVING MORE THAN TWO GOODS

The examples discussed so far have all been ones in which the consumer is faced with the opportunity to buy only two different goods. Needless to say, not many consumers have such narrow options. In its most general form, the consumer budgeting problem can be posed as a choice between not two but N different goods, where N can be an indefinitely large number. With only two goods ($N = 2$), the budget constraint is a straight line, as we just saw. With three goods ($N = 3$), it is a plane. When we have more than three goods, the budget constraint becomes what mathematicians call a *hyperplane*, or *multidimensional plane*. The only real difficulty is in representing this multidimensional case geometrically. We are just not very good at visualizing surfaces that have more than three dimensions.

The nineteenth-century economist Alfred Marshall proposed a disarmingly simple solution to this problem. It is to view the consumer's choice as being one between a particular good—call it X—and an amalgam of other goods, denoted

FIGURE 3-4
Both horizontal and vertical intercepts fall by half. The new budget constraint has the same slope as the old but is closer to the origin.

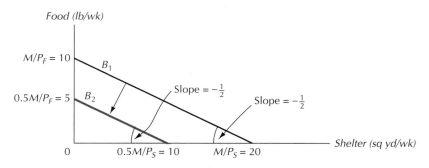

THE EFFECT OF CUTTING INCOME BY HALF

FIGURE 3-5
The vertical axis measures the amount of money spent each month on all goods other than X.

THE BUDGET CONSTRAINT WITH THE COMPOSITE GOOD

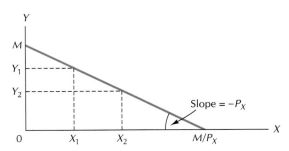

Y. This amalgam is generally called the *composite good*. We may think of the composite good as the amount of income the consumer has left over after buying the good X. Equivalently, it is the amount of money the consumer spends on goods other than X.

To illustrate how this concept is used, suppose the consumer has an income level of $\$M$/wk, and the price of X is given by P_X. The consumer's budget constraint may then be represented as a straight line in the X, Y plane, as shown in Figure 3-5. For simplicity, the price of a unit of the composite good is taken to be 1, so that if the consumer devotes none of his income to X, he will be able to buy M units of the composite good. All this means is that he will have $\$M$ available to spend on other goods if he buys no X. Alternatively, if he spends all his income on X, he will be able to purchase the bundle $(M/P_X, 0)$. Since the price of Y is assumed to be $\$1$/unit, the slope of the budget constraint is simply $-P_X$.

As before, the budget constraint summarizes the various combinations of bundles that are affordable. Thus, the consumer can have X_1 units of X and Y_1 units of the composite good in Figure 3-5, or X_2 and Y_2, or any other combination that lies on the budget constraint.

KINKED BUDGET CONSTRAINTS

The budget constraints we have seen so far have all been straight lines. When relative prices are constant, the opportunity cost of one good in terms of any other is the same, no matter what bundle of goods we already have. But sometimes the budget constraints we encounter in practice are kinked lines. By way of illustration, consider the following example of quantity discounts.

*E*XAMPLE 3-1 *The Gigawatt Power Company charges $0.10 per kilowatt-hour (kWh) for the first 1000 kWh of power purchased by a residential customer each month, but only $0.05/kWh for all additional kWh. For a residential customer with a monthly income of $400, graph the budget constraint for electric power and the composite good.*

> If the consumer buys no electric power at all, he will have \$400/mo available for the purchase of other goods. Thus the vertical intercept of his budget constraint is the point (0, 400). As shown in Figure 3-6, for each of the first 1000 kWh he buys, he must give up \$0.10, which means that the slope of his budget constraint starts out at $-\frac{1}{10}$. Then at 1000 kWh/mo, the price falls to \$0.05/kWh, which means that the slope of his budget constraint from that point rightward is only $-\frac{1}{20}$.

Note that along the budget constraint shown in Figure 3-6, the opportunity cost of electricity depends on how much electricity the consumer has already purchased. Consider a consumer who now uses 1020 kWh each month and is trying to decide whether to leave his front porch light on all night, which would result in an additional consumption of 20 kWh/mo. Leaving his light on will cost him an extra \$1/mo. Had his usual consumption level been only 980 kWh/mo, however, the cost of leaving the front porch light on would have been \$2/mo. On the basis of this difference in the opportunity cost of additional electricity, we can predict that people who already use a lot of electricity (more than 1000 kWh/mo) should be more likely than others to leave their porch lights burning at night.

EXERCISE 3-5

> Suppose instead Amperage Electric Power charged \$0.05/kWh for the first 1000 kWh of power purchased by a residential consumer each month, but \$0.10/kWh each for all additional kilowatt-hours. For a residential consumer with a monthly income of \$400, graph the budget constraint for electric power and the composite good. What if the rate jumps to \$0.10/kWh for *all* kilowatt-hours if power consumption in a month exceeds 1000 kWh (where the higher rate applies to all, not just the additional, kilowatt-hours)?

IF THE BUDGET CONSTRAINT IS THE SAME, THE DECISION SHOULD BE THE SAME

Even without knowing anything about the consumer's preferences, we can use budgetary information to make certain inferences about how a rational consumer will behave. Suppose, for example, that the consumer's tastes do not change over time and that he is confronted with exactly the same budget constraint in each of two different situations. If he is rational, he should make exactly the same choice in both cases. As the following example makes clear, however, it may not always be immediately apparent that the budget constraints are in fact the same.

FIGURE 3-6
Once electric power
consumption
reaches 1000
kWh/mo, the oppor-
tunity cost of addi-
tional power falls
from $0.10/kWh to
$0.05/kWh.

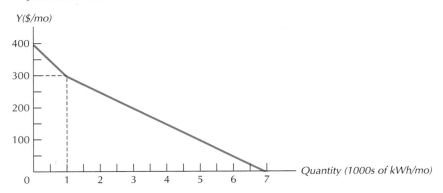

A QUANTITY DISCOUNT GIVES RISE TO A NONLINEAR BUDGET CONSTRAINT

EXAMPLE 3-2 *On one occasion, Gowdy fills his car's tank with gasoline on the evening before his departure on a fishing trip. He awakens to discover that a thief has siphoned out all but 1 gallon from his 21-gallon tank. On another occasion, he plans to stop for gas on his way out the next morning before he goes fishing. He awakens to discover that he has lost $20 from his wallet. If gasoline sells for $1/gal and the round-trip will consume 5 gallons, how, if at all, should Gowdy's decision about whether to take the fishing trip differ in the two cases? (Assume that, monetary costs aside, the inconvenience of having to refill his tank is negligible.)*

> Suppose Gowdy's income is $M/mo. Before his loss, his budget constraint is line B_1 in Figure 3-7. In both instances described, his budget constraint at the moment he discovers his loss will shift inward to B_2. If he does not take the trip, he will have $M − \$20$ available to spend on other goods in both cases. And if he does take the trip, he will have to purchase the required gasoline at $1/gal in both cases. No matter what the source of the loss, the remaining opportunities are exactly the same. If Gowdy's budget is tight, he may decide to cancel his trip. Otherwise, he may go despite the loss. But because his budget constraint and tastes are the same in the lost-cash case as in the stolen-gas case, it would not be rational for him to take the trip in one instance but not in the other.

Note that the situation described in Example 3-2 has the same structure as the one described in the broken-disc example with which we began this chapter. It too is one in which the decision should be the same in both instances because the budget constraint and preferences are the same in each.

Although the rational choice model makes clear that the decisions *should* be the same if the budget constraints and preferences are the same, people sometimes choose differently. The difficulty is often that the way the different situations are described sometimes causes people to overlook the essential

FIGURE 3-7
A theft of $20 worth of gasoline has exactly the same effect on the budget constraint as the loss of $20 in cash. The bundle chosen should therefore be the same, irrespective of the source of the loss.

BUDGET CONSTRAINTS FOLLOWING THEFT OF GASOLINE, LOSS OF CASH

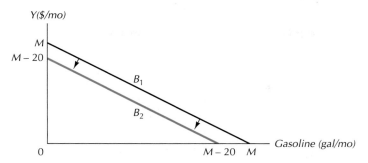

similarities between them. For instance, in Example 3-2, many people erroneously conclude that the cost of taking the trip is higher in the stolen-gas case than in the lost-money case, and so they are less likely to take the trip in the former instance. Similarly, many people were less inclined to buy the disc after having broken the first one than after having lost $10 because they thought, incorrectly, that the disc would cost more under the broken-disc scenario. As we have seen, however, the amount that will be saved by not buying the disc, or by not taking the trip, is exactly the same under each scenario.

To recapitulate briefly, the budget constraint or opportunity set summarizes the combinations of bundles that the consumer is able to buy. Its position is determined jointly by income and prices. From the set of feasible bundles, the consumer's task is to pick the particular one she likes best. To identify this bundle, we need some means of summarizing the consumer's preferences over all possible bundles she might consume; we now turn to this task.

Consumer Preferences

Preference ordering A scheme whereby the consumer ranks all possible consumption bundles in order of preference.

For simplicity, let us again begin by considering a world with only two goods: shelter and food. A *preference ordering* is a scheme that enables the consumer to rank different bundles of goods in terms of their desirability, or order of preference. Consider two bundles, A and B. For concreteness, suppose that A contains 4 sq yd/wk of shelter and 2 lb/wk of food, while B has 3 sq yd/wk of shelter and 3 lb/wk of food. Knowing nothing about a consumer's preferences, we can say nothing about which of these bundles he will prefer. A has more shelter, but less food, than B. Someone who spends a lot of time at home would probably choose A, while someone with a rapid metabolism would be more likely to choose B.

In general, we can say that for any two such bundles, the consumer is able to make one of three possible statements: (1) A is preferred to B, (2) B is preferred to A, or (3) A and B are equally preferred. The preference ordering enables the consumer to rank different bundles but not to make more precise quantitative statements about their relative desirability. Thus, the consumer might be able to say that he prefers A to B but not that A provides twice as much satisfaction as B.

Preference orderings often differ widely among consumers. One person will like Rachmaninoff, another the Rolling Stones. Despite these differences, however, most preference orderings share several important features. More specifically, economists generally assume four simple properties of preference orderings. These properties allow us to construct the concise analytical representation of preferences we need for the budget allocation problem.

1. Completeness.   A preference ordering is *complete* if it enables the consumer to rank all possible combinations of goods and services. Taken literally, the completeness assumption is virtually always false, for there are many goods we know too little about to be able to evaluate decisively. It is nonetheless a useful simplifying assumption for the analysis of choices among bundles of goods with which consumers are familiar. Its real intent is to rule out instances like the one portrayed in the fable of Buridan's ass. The hungry animal was unable to choose between two bales of hay in front of him and starved to death as a result.

2. More-Is-Better.   The more-is-better property of preference orderings means simply that, other things equal, more of a good is preferred to less. We can, of course, think of examples where more of something makes us worse off rather than better (as with someone who has overeaten). But these examples usually contemplate some sort of practical difficulty, such as having a self-control problem or being unable to store a good for future use. As long as people can freely dispose of goods they don't want, having more of something can't make them worse off.

As an example of the application of the more-is-better assumption, consider the two bundles A, which has 12 sq yd/wk of shelter and 10 lb/wk of food, and B, which has 12 sq yd/wk of shelter and 11 lb/wk of food. The assumption tells us that B is preferred to A, because it has more food and no less shelter.

3. Transitivity.   If you like steak better than hamburger, and you like hamburger better than hot dogs, then you are probably someone who likes steak better than hot dogs. To say that a consumer's preference ordering is *transitive* means that, for any three bundles A, B, and C, if he prefers A to B and prefers B to C, then he always prefers A to C. For example, suppose A is (4, 2), B is (3, 3), and C is (2, 4). If you prefer (4, 2) over (3, 3) and you prefer (3, 3) over (2, 4), then you must prefer (4, 2) over (2, 4). The preference relationship is thus assumed to be like the relationship used to compare heights of people. If O'Neal is taller than Pippen and Pippen is taller than Bogues, we know that O'Neal must be taller than Bogues.

Not all comparative relationships are transitive. The relationship "half sibling," for example, is not. I have a half sister who, in turn, has three half sisters of her own. But her half sisters are not my half sisters. A similar nontransitivity is shown by the relationship "defeats in football." Some seasons, Ohio State defeats Michigan, and Michigan defeats Michigan State, but that doesn't tell us that Ohio State will necessarily defeat Michigan State.

Transitivity is a simple consistency property and applies as well to the relation "equally preferred to" and to any combination of it and the "preferred to" relation. For example, if A is equally preferred to B and B is equally preferred to C, it follows that A is equally preferred to C. Similarly, if A is preferred to B and B is equally preferred to C, it follows that A is preferred to C.

The transitivity assumption can be justified as eliminating the potential for a "money pump" problem. To illustrate, suppose you prefer A to B and B to C, but now suppose you actually prefer C over A, so that your preferences are intransitive. If you start with C, you would trade C for B, trade B for A, and then trade A for C. This cycle could continue forever. If in each stage you were charged a tiny fee for the trade, you would spend all your money on trading and make the other trader very rich. Clearly, preferences that permit you to be drained of all your money are not rational.

As reasonable as the transitivity property sounds, we will see examples in later chapters of behavior that seems inconsistent with it. But it is an accurate description of preferences in most instances, and unless otherwise stated, we will adopt it throughout as a working assumption.

4. Convexity.   Mixtures of goods are preferable to extremes. If you are indifferent between two bundles A and B, your preferences are convex if you prefer a bundle that contains half of A and half of B (or any other mixture) to either of the original bundles. For example, suppose you are indifferent between $A = (4, 0)$ and $B = (0, 4)$. If your preferences are convex, you will prefer the bundle $(2, 2)$ to each of the more extreme bundles. This property conveys the sense that we dislike having too little of most things.

INDIFFERENCE CURVES

Let us consider some implications of these assumptions about preference orderings. Most important, they enable us to generate a graphical description of the consumer's preferences. To see how, consider first the bundle A in Figure 3-8, which has 12 sq yd/wk of shelter and 10 lb/wk of food. The more-is-better assumption tells us that all bundles to the northeast of A are preferred to A, and that A, in turn, is preferred to all those to the southwest of A. Thus, the more-is-better assumption tells us that Z, which has 28 sq yd/wk of shelter and 12 lb/wk of food, is preferred to A and that A, in turn, is preferred to W, which has only 6 sq yd/wk of shelter and 4 lb/wk of food.

Now consider the set of bundles that lie along the line joining W and Z. Because Z is preferred to A and A is preferred to W, it follows that as we move from Z to W we must encounter a bundle that is equally preferred to A. (The intuition behind this claim is the same as the intuition that tells us that if we climb on any continuous path on a mountainside from one point at 1000 feet above sea level to another at 2000 feet, we must pass through every intermediate altitude along the way.) Let B denote the bundle that is equally preferred to A, and suppose it contains 17 sq yd/wk of shelter and 8 lb/wk of food. (The

FIGURE 3-8
Z is preferred to *A* because it has more of each good than *A* has. For the same reason, *A* is preferred to *W*. It follows that on the line joining *W* and *Z* there must be a bundle *B* that is equally preferred to *A*. In similar fashion, we can find a bundle *C* that is equally preferred to *B*.

GENERATING EQUALLY PREFERRED BUNDLES

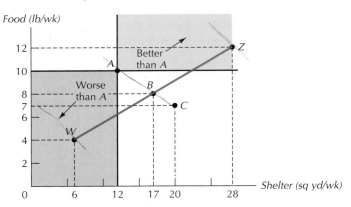

Indifference curve A set of bundles among which the consumer is indifferent.

exact amounts of each good in *B* will of course depend on the specific consumer whose preferences we are talking about.) The more-is-better assumption also tells us that there will be only one such bundle on the straight line between *W* and *Z*. Points on that line to the northeast of *B* are all better than *B*; those to the southwest of *B* are all worse.

In precisely the same fashion, we can find another point—call it *C*—that is equally preferred to *B*. *C* is shown as the bundle (20, 7), where the specific quantities in *C* again depend on the preferences of the consumer under consideration. By the transitivity assumption, we know that *C* is also equally preferred to *A* (since *C* is equally preferred to *B*, which is equally preferred to *A*).

We can repeat this process as often as we like, and the end result will be an *indifference curve*, a set of bundles all of which are equally preferred to the original bundle *A*, and hence also equally preferred to one another. This set is shown as the curve labeled *I* in Figure 3-9. It is called an indifference curve because the consumer is indifferent among all the bundles that lie along it.

An indifference curve also permits us to compare the satisfaction implicit in bundles that lie along it with those that lie either above or below it. It permits us, for example, to compare bundle *C* (20, 7) to bundle *K* (23, 4), which has less food and more shelter than *C* has. We know that *C* is equally preferred to *D* (25, 6) because both bundles lie along the same indifference curve. *D*, in turn, is preferred to *K* because of the more-is-better assumption: it has 2 sq yd/wk more shelter and 2 lb/wk more food than *K* has. Transitivity, finally, tells us that since *C* is equally preferred to *D* and *D* is preferred to *K*, *C* must be preferred to *K*.

By analogous reasoning, we can say that bundle *L* is preferred to *A*. *In general, bundles that lie above an indifference curve are all preferred to the bundles that lie on it. Similarity, bundles that lie on an indifference curve are all preferred to those that lie below it.*

FIGURE 3-9
An indifference curve is a set of bundles that the consumer prefers equally. Any bundle, such as *L*, that lies above an indifference curve is preferred to any bundle on the indifference curve. Any bundle on the indifference curve, in turn, is preferred to any bundle, such as *K*, that lies below the indifference curve.

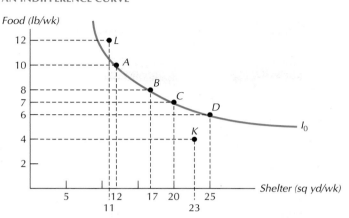

AN INDIFFERENCE CURVE

The completeness property of preferences implies that there is an indifference curve that passes through every possible bundle. That being so, we can represent a consumer's preferences with an *indifference map,* an example of which is shown in Figure 3-10. This indifference map shows just four of the infinitely many indifference curves that, taken together, yield a complete description of the consumer's preferences.

The numbers $I_1, \ldots, I_4$ in Figure 3-10 are index values used to denote the order of preference that corresponds to the respective indifference curves. Any index numbers would do equally well provided they satisfied the property $I_1 < I_2 < I_3 < I_4$. In representing the consumer's preferences, what really counts is the *ranking* of the indifference curves, not the particular numerical values we assign to them.[5]

Indifference map
A representative sample of the set of a consumer's indifference curves, used as a graphical summary of her preference ordering.

FIGURE 3-10
The entire set of a consumer's indifference curves is called the consumer's indifference map. Bundles on any indifference curve are less preferred than bundles on a higher indifference curve, and more preferred than bundles on a lower indifference curve.

PART OF AN INDIFFERENCE MAP

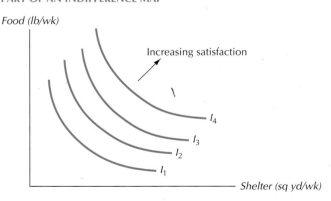

[5]For a more complete discussion of this issue, see the appendix to this chapter in the "For the Instructor" section at our Web site www.mhhe.com/economics/frank4.

FIGURE 3-11
If indifference curves were to cross, they would have to violate at least one of the assumed properties of preference orderings.

WHY TWO INDIFFERENCE CURVES DO NOT CROSS

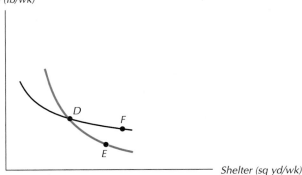

The four properties of preference orderings imply four important properties of indifference curves and indifference maps:

1. Indifference curves are ubiquitous. Any bundle has an indifference curve passing through it. This property is assured by the completeness property of preferences.
2. Indifference curves are downward-sloping. An upward-sloping indifference curve would violate the more-is-better property by saying a bundle with more of both goods is equivalent to a bundle with less of both.
3. Indifference curves (from the same indifference map) cannot cross. To see why, suppose that two indifference curves did, in fact, cross as in Figure 3-11. The following statements must then be true:

   E is equally preferred to *D* (because they each lie on the same indifference curve).
   D is equally preferred to *F* (because they each lie on the same indifference curve).
   E is equally preferred to *F* (by the transitivity assumption).

   But we also know that

   F is preferred to *E* (because more is better).

   Because it is not possible for the statements *E is equally preferred to F* and *F is preferred to E* to be true simultaneously, the assumption that two indifference curves cross thus implies a contradiction. The conclusion is that the original proposition must be true, namely, two indifference curves cannot cross.
4. Indifference curves become less steep as we move downward and to the right along them. As discussed below, this property is implied by convexity property of preferences.

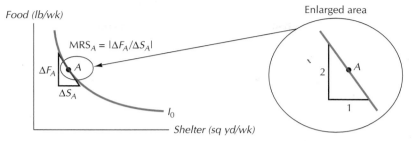

FIGURE 3-12
MRS at any point along an indifference curve is defined as the absolute value of the slope of the indifference curve at that point. It is the amount of food the consumer must be given to compensate for the loss of 1 unit of shelter.

TRADE-OFFS BETWEEN GOODS

Marginal rate of substitution (MRS) At any point on an indifference curve, the rate at which the consumer is willing to exchange the good measured along the vertical axis for the good measured along the horizontal axis; equal to the absolute value of the slope of the indifference curve.

An important property of a consumer's preferences is the rate at which he is willing to exchange, or "trade off," one good for another. This rate is represented at any point on an indifference curve by the *marginal rate of substitution (MRS),* which is defined as the absolute value of the slope of the indifference curve at that point. In the left panel of Figure 3-12, for example, the marginal rate of substitution at point A is given by the absolute value of the slope of the tangent to the indifference curve at A, which is the ratio $\Delta F_A / \Delta S_A$.[6] (The notation ΔF_A means "small change in food from the amount at point A.") If we take ΔF_A units of food away from the consumer at point A, we have to give him ΔS_A additional units of shelter to make him just as well off as before. The right panel of the figure shows an enlargement of the region surrounding bundle A. If the marginal rate of substitution at A is 2, this means that the consumer must be given 2 lb/wk of food to make up for the loss of 1 sq yd/wk of shelter.

Whereas the slope of the budget constraint tells us the rate at which we can substitute food for shelter without changing total expenditure, the MRS tells us the rate at which we can substitute food for shelter without changing total satisfaction. Put another way, the slope of the budget constraint is the marginal cost of shelter in terms of food, and the MRS is the marginal benefit of shelter in terms of food.

The convexity property of preferences tells us that along any indifference curve, the more a consumer has of one good, the more she must be given of that good before she will be willing to give up a unit of the other good. Stated differently, MRS declines as we move downward to the right along an indifference curve. Indifference curves with diminishing rates of marginal substitution are thus convex—or bowed outward—when viewed from the origin. The indifference curves shown in Figures 3-9, 3-10, and 3-12 all have this property, as does the curve shown in Figure 3-13.

In Figure 3-13, note that at bundle A food is relatively plentiful and the consumer would be willing to sacrifice 3 lb/wk of it in order to obtain an additional

---

[6]More formally, the indifference curve may be expressed as a function $Y = Y(X)$ and the MRS at point A is defined as the absolute value of the derivative of the indifference curve at that point: $\text{MRS} = |dY(X)/dX|$.

FIGURE 3-13
The more food the consumer has, the more she is willing to give up to obtain an additional unit of shelter. The marginal rates of substitution at bundles *A, C,* and *D* are 3, 1, and 1/5, respectively.

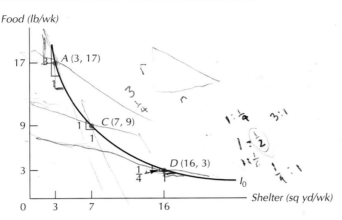

DIMINISHING MARGINAL RATE OF SUBSTITUTION

square yard of shelter. Her MRS at *A* is 3. At *C*, the quantities of food and shelter are more balanced, and there she would be willing to give up only 1 lb/wk to obtain an additional square yard of shelter. Her MRS at *C* is 1. Finally, note that food is relatively scarce at *D*, and there she would be willing to give up only $\frac{1}{4}$ lb/wk of food to obtain an additional unit of shelter. Her MRS at *D* is $\frac{1}{4}$.

Intuitively, diminishing MRS means that consumers like variety. We are usually willing to give up goods we already have a lot of to obtain more of those goods we now have only a little of.

USING INDIFFERENCE CURVES TO DESCRIBE PREFERENCES

To get a feel for how indifference maps describe a consumer's preferences, let us see how indifference maps can be used to portray differences in preferences between two consumers. Suppose, for example, that both Tex and Mahatma like potatoes but that Mahatma likes rice much more than Tex does. This difference in their tastes is captured by the differing slopes of their indifference curves in Figure 3-14. Note in Figure 3-14*a*, which shows Tex's indifference map, that Tex would be willing to exchange 1 lb of potatoes for 1 lb of rice at bundle *A*. But at the corresponding bundle in Figure 3-14*b*, which shows Mahatma's indifference map, we see that Mahatma would trade 2 lb of potatoes for only 1 lb of rice. Their difference in preferences shows up clearly in this difference in their marginal rates of substitution of potatoes for rice.

The Best Feasible Bundle

We now have all the tools we need to determine how the consumer should allocate his income between two goods. The indifference map tells us how the various bundles are ranked in order of preference. The budget constraint, in turn, tells us which bundles are affordable. The consumer's task is to put the two

FIGURE 3-14
Relatively speaking, Tex is a potato lover; Mahatma, a rice lover. This difference shows up in the fact that at any given bundle Tex's marginal rate of substitution of potatoes for rice is smaller than Mahatma's.

PEOPLE WITH DIFFERENT TASTES

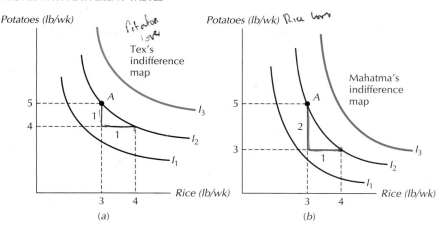

(a)

(b)

Best affordable bundle The most preferred bundle of those that are affordable.

together and to choose the most preferred or ***best affordable bundle.*** (Recall from Chapter 1 that we need not suppose that consumers think explicitly about budget constraints and indifference maps when deciding what to buy. It is sufficient to assume that people make decisions *as if* they were thinking in these terms, just as expert pool players choose between shots as if they knew all the relevant laws of Newtonian physics.)

For the sake of concreteness, let us again consider the choice between food and shelter that confronts a consumer with an income of $M = \$100/wk$ facing prices of $P_F = \$10/lb$ and $P_S = \$5/sq\ yd$. Figure 3-15 shows this consumer's budget constraint and part of his indifference map. Of the five labeled bundles—A, D, E, F, and G—in the diagram, G is the most preferred because it lies on the highest indifference curve. G, however, is not affordable, nor is any other bundle that lies beyond the budget constraint. The more-is-better assumption implies that the best affordable bundle must lie *on* the budget constraint, not inside it.

FIGURE 3-15
The best the consumer can do is to choose the bundle on the budget constraint that lies on the highest attainable indifference curve. Here, that is bundle *F*, which lies at a tangency between the indifference curve and the budget constraint.

THE BEST AFFORDABLE BUNDLE

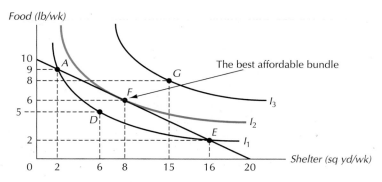

(Any bundle inside the budget constraint would be less preferred than one just slightly to the northeast, which would also be affordable.)

Where exactly is the best affordable bundle located along the budget constraint? We know that it cannot be on an indifference curve that lies partly inside the budget constraint. On the indifference curve I_1, for example, the only points that are even candidates for the best affordable bundle are the two that lie on the budget constraint, namely, A and E. But A cannot be the best affordable bundle because it is equally preferred to D, which in turn is less desirable than F by the more-is-better assumption. So by transitivity, A is less desirable than F. For the same reason, E cannot be the best affordable bundle.

Since the best affordable bundle cannot lie on an indifference curve that lies partly inside the budget constraint, and since it must lie on the budget constraint itself, we know it has to lie on an indifference curve that intersects the budget constraint only once. In Figure 3-15, that indifference curve is the one labeled I_2, and the best affordable bundle is F, which lies at the point of tangency between I_2 and the budget constraint. With an income of \$100/wk and facing prices of \$5/sq yd for shelter and \$10/lb for food, the best this consumer can do is to buy 6 lb/wk of food and 8 sq yd/wk of shelter.

The choice of bundle F makes perfect sense on intuitive grounds. The consumer's goal, after all, is to reach the highest indifference curve he can, given his budget constraint. His strategy is to keep moving to higher and higher indifference curves until he reaches the highest one that is still affordable. For indifference maps for which a tangency point exists, as in Figure 3-15, the best bundle will always lie at the point of tangency.

In Figure 3-14, note that the marginal rate of substitution at F is exactly the same as the absolute value of the slope of the budget constraint. This will always be so when the best affordable bundle occurs at a point of tangency. The condition that must be satisfied in such cases is therefore

$$\text{MRS} = \frac{P_S}{P_F}. \tag{3.3}$$

The right-hand side of Equation 3.3 represents the opportunity cost of shelter in terms of food. Thus, with $P_S = \$5/\text{sq yd}$ and $P_F = \$10/\text{lb}$, the opportunity cost of an additional square yard of shelter is $\frac{1}{2}$ lb of food. The left-hand side of Equation 3.3 is $|\Delta F/\Delta S|$, the absolute value of the slope of the indifference curve at the point of tangency. It is the amount of additional food the consumer must be given in order to compensate him fully for the loss of 1 sq yd of shelter. In the language of cost-benefit analysis discussed in Chapter 1, the slope of the budget constraint represents the opportunity cost of shelter in terms of food, while the slope of the indifference curve represents the benefits of consuming shelter as compared with consuming food. Since the slope of the budget constraint is $-\frac{1}{2}$ in this example, the tangency condition tells us that $\frac{1}{2}$ lb of food would be required to compensate for the benefits given up with the loss of 1 sq yd of shelter.

If the consumer were at some bundle on the budget line for which the two slopes are not the same, then it would always be possible for him to purchase a better bundle. To see why, suppose he were at a point where the slope of the indifference curve (in absolute value) is less than the slope of the budget constraint, as at point E in Figure 3-15. Suppose, for instance, that the MRS at E is only $\frac{1}{4}$. This tells us that the consumer can be compensated for the loss of 1 sq yd of shelter by being given an additional $\frac{1}{4}$ lb of food. But the slope of the budget constraint tells us that by giving up 1 sq yd of shelter, he can purchase an additional $\frac{1}{2}$ lb of food. Since this is $\frac{1}{4}$ lb more than he needs to remain equally satisfied, he will clearly be better off if he purchases more food and less shelter than at point E. The opportunity cost of an additional pound of food is less than the benefit it confers.

Exercise 3-6

Suppose that the marginal rate of substitution at point A in Figure 3-15 is 1.0. Show that this means the consumer will be better off if he purchases less food and more shelter than at A.

CORNER SOLUTIONS

Corner solution
In a choice between two goods, a case in which the consumer does not consume one of the goods.

The best affordable bundle need not always occur at a point of tangency. In some cases, there may simply *be* no point of tangency—the MRS may be everywhere greater, or less, than the slope of the budget constraint. In this case we get a *corner solution,* like the one shown in Figure 3-16, where M, P_F, and P_S are again given by \$100/wk, \$10/lb, and \$5/sq yd, respectively. The best affordable bundle is the one labeled A, and it lies at the upper end of the budget constraint. At A the MRS is less than the absolute value of the slope of the budget constraint. For the sake of illustration, suppose the MRS at $A = 0.25$, which means that this consumer

FIGURE 3-16
When the MRS of food for shelter is always less than the slope of the budget constraint, the best the consumer can do is to spend all his income on food.

A CORNER SOLUTION

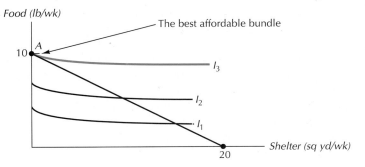

would be willing to give up 0.25 lb of food to get an additional square yard of shelter. But at market prices the opportunity cost of an additional square yard of shelter is 0.5 lb of food. He increases his satisfaction by continuing to give up shelter for more food until it is no longer possible to do so. Even though this consumer regards shelter as a desirable commodity, the best he can do is to spend all his income on food. Market prices are such that he would have to give up too much food to make the purchase of even a single unit of shelter worthwhile.

The indifference map in Figure 3-16 satisfies the property of diminishing marginal rate of substitution—moving to the right along any indifference curve, the slope becomes smaller in absolute terms. But because the slopes of the indifference curves start out smaller than the slope of the budget constraint here, the two never reach equality.

Indifference curves that are not strongly convex are characteristic of goods that are easily substituted for one another. Corner solutions are more likely to occur for such goods, and indeed are almost certain to occur when goods are perfect substitutes. For such goods, the MRS does not diminish at all; rather, it is everywhere the same. With perfect substitutes, indifference curves are straight lines. If they happen to be steeper than the budget constraint, we get a corner solution on the horizontal axis; if less steep, we get a corner solution on the vertical axis.

EXAMPLE 3-3   *Consider the case of Mattingly, a caffeinated cola drinker. He spends all his soft drink budget on Coca-Cola and Jolt cola and cares only about the total caffeine content of what he drinks. If Jolt has twice the caffeine of Coke, and if Jolt costs $1/pint and Coke costs $0.75/pint, how will Mattingly spend his soft drink budget of $15/wk?*

For Mattingly, Jolt and Coke are *perfect substitutes*, which means that his indifference curves will not have the usual convex shape but will instead be linear. The top line in Figure 3-17 is the set of all possible Coke-Jolt combinations that provide the same satisfaction as the bundle consisting of 0 pints of Jolt per day and 30 pints of Coke per day. Since each pint of Jolt has twice the caffeine of a pint of Coke, all bundles along this line contain precisely the same amount of caffeine. The next blue line down is the indifference curve for bundles equivalent to bundle (0, 20); and the third blue line down is the indifference curve corresponding to (0, 10). Along each of these indifference curves, the marginal rate of substitution of Coke for Jolt is always $\frac{2}{1}$, that is, 2 pints of Coke for every pint of Jolt.

In the same diagram, Mattingly's budget constraint is shown as line B. The slope of his indifference curves is -2; of his budget constraint, $-\frac{4}{3}$. The best affordable bundle is the one labeled A, a corner solution in which he spends all his budget on Jolt. This makes intuitive sense in the light of Mattingly's peculiar preferences: he cares only about total caffeine content, and at the given prices, Jolt provides more caffeine per dollar than Coke does. If the Jolt-Coke price ratio, P_J/P_C had been $\frac{3}{1}$ (or any other amount greater than $\frac{2}{1}$), Mattingly would have spent all his income on Coke. That is, we would again have had a corner solution, only this time on the vertical axis. Only if the price ratio had been exactly $\frac{2}{1}$ might we have seen Mattingly spend part of his income on each good. In that case, any combination of Coke and Jolt on his budget constraint would have served him equally well.

Most of the time we will deal with problems that have not corner but *interior solutions*—that is, with problems where the best affordable bundle will lie at a point of tangency. An interior solution, again, is one where the MRS is exactly the same as the slope of the budget constraint.

EXERCISE 3-7

Suppose Albert uses exactly two pats of butter on each piece of toast. If toast costs $0.10/slice and butter costs $0.20/pat, find Albert's best affordable bundle if he has $12/mo to spend on toast and butter. Suppose Albert starts to watch his cholesterol and therefore alters his preference to using exactly one pat of butter on each piece of toast. How much toast and butter would Albert then consume each month?

FIGURE 3-17
Here, the MRS of Coke for Jolt is 2 at every point. Whenever the price ratio P_J/P_C is less than 2, a corner solution results in which the consumer buys only Jolt. On the budget constraint *B*, the consumer does best to buy bundle *A*.

EQUILIBRIUM WITH PERFECT SUBSTITUTES

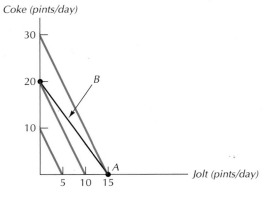

INDIFFERENCE CURVES WHEN THERE ARE MORE THAN TWO GOODS

In the examples discussed so far, the consumer cares about only two goods. Where there are more than two, we can construct indifference curves by using the same device we used earlier to represent multigood budget constraints. We simply view the consumer's choice as being one between a particular good X and an amalgam of other goods Y, which is again called the composite good. As before, the composite good is the amount of income the consumer has left over after buying the good X.

In the multigood case, we may thus continue to represent the consumer's preferences with an indifference map in the XY plane. Here, the indifference curve tells not the rate at which the consumer will exchange some particular good Y for a good X, but the rate at which he will exchange the composite good for X. Just as in the two-good case, equilibrium occurs when the consumer reaches the highest indifference curve attainable on his budget constraint.

An Application of the Rational Choice Model

As the following example makes clear, the composite good construct enables us to deal with more general questions than we could in the simple two-good case.

Example 3-4 *Is it better to give poor people cash or food stamps?*

One objective of the food stamp program is to alleviate hunger among poor people. Under the terms of the program, people whose incomes fall below a certain level are eligible to receive a specified quantity of food stamps. For example, a person with an income of $400/mo might be eligible for $100/mo worth of stamps. These stamps can then be used to buy $100/mo worth of food. Any food he buys in excess of $100/mo he must pay for in cash. Stamps cannot be used to purchase cigarettes, alcohol, and various other items. The government gives food retailers cash for the stamps they accept in exchange for food.

The cost to the government for the consumer in the example given was $100—the amount it had to reimburse the store for the stamps. Would the consumer have been better off had he instead been given $100 directly in cash? We can try to answer this question by investigating which alternative would get him to a higher indifference curve.

Suppose Y denotes the composite good, X denotes food. If the consumer's income is $400/mo and P_x is the price of food, his initial equilibrium is the bundle J in Figure 3-18 (page 94). The effect of the food stamp program is to increase the total amount of food he can buy each month from $400/P_X$ to $500/P_X$. In terms of the *maximum* amount of food he can buy, the food stamp program is thus exactly the same as a cash grant of $100.

Where the two alternatives differ is in terms of the maximum amounts of other goods he can buy. With a cash grant of $100, he has a total monthly income of $500, and this is, of course, the maximum amount of nonfood goods (the composite good) he can buy. His budget constraint in this case is thus the line labeled *AE* in Figure 3-18.

With the food stamp program, by contrast, the consumer is not able to buy $500/mo of nonfood goods because his $100 in food stamps can be used only for food. The maximum amount of nonfood goods he can purchase is $400. In Figure 3-18, his budget constraint under the food stamp program is labeled *ADF*. For values of *Y* less than $400, it is thus exactly the same as his budget constraint under the cash grant program. For values of *Y* larger than $400, however, his budget constraint under the food stamp program is completely flat.

Note that the consumer whose indifference curves are shown in Figure 3-18 buys exactly the same bundle, namely, bundle *K*, under both programs. The effect of the food stamp program here is precisely the same as the effect of the cash grant. In general, this will be true whenever the consumer with a cash grant would have spent more on food anyway than the amount of food stamps he would have received under the food stamp program.

Figure 3-19 (page 94) depicts a consumer for whom this is *not* the case. With a cash grant, he would choose the bundle *L*, which would put him on a higher indifference curve than he could attain under the food stamp program, which would lead him to buy bundle *D*. Note that bundle *D* contains exactly $100 worth of food, the amount of food stamps he received. Bundle *L*, by contrast, contains less than $100 worth of food. Here, the effect of the food stamp program is to cause the recipient to spend more on food than he would have if he had instead been given cash.

The face value of the food stamps most participants receive is smaller than what they would spend on food. For these people, the food stamp program leads, as noted, to exactly the same behavior as a pure cash grant program.

The analysis in Example 3-4 raises the question of why Congress did not just give poor people cash grants in the first place. The ostensible reason is that Congress wanted to help poor people buy food, not luxury items or even cigarettes and alcohol. And yet if most participants would have spent at least as much on food as they received in stamps, not being able to use stamps to buy other things is a meaningless restriction. For instance, if someone would have spent $150 on food anyway, getting $100 in food stamps simply lets him take

FIGURE 3-18
By comparison with the budget constraint under a cash grant (*AE*), the budget constraint under food stamps (*ADF*) limits the amount that can be spent on nonfood goods. But for the consumer whose indifference map is shown, the equilibrium bundles are the same under both programs.

FOOD STAMP PROGRAM VS. CASH GRANT PROGRAM

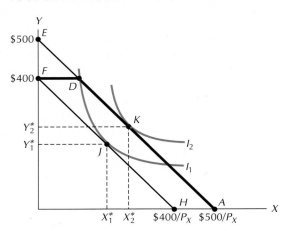

some of the money he would have spent on food and spend it instead on whatever else he chooses.

On purely economic grounds, there is thus a strong case for replacing the food stamp program with a much simpler program of cash grants to the poor. At the very least, this would eliminate the cumbersome step of requiring grocers to redeem their stamps for cash.

As a political matter, however, it is easy to see why Congress might have set things up the way it did. Many of the taxpayers who sponsor antipoverty programs would be distressed to see their tax dollars used to buy illicit substances. If the food stamp program prevents even a tiny minority of participants from spending more on such goods, it spares many political difficulties.

FIGURE 3-19
For the consumer whose indifference map is shown, a cash grant would be preferred to food stamps, which force him to devote more to food than he would choose to spend on his own.

WHERE FOOD STAMPS AND CASH GRANTS YIELD DIFFERENT OUTCOMES

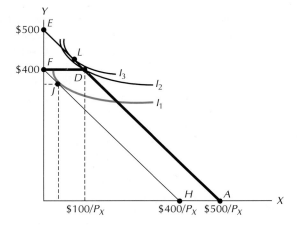

THE PUZZLE OF GIFT GIVING

Example 3-4 calls our attention to a problem that applies not just to the food stamp program but to all other forms of in-kind transfers as well: Although the two forms of transfer are sometimes equivalent, gifts in cash seem clearly superior on those occasions when they differ. Consider, for example, the phenomenon of gift giving. Occasionally someone receives a gift that is exactly what he would have purchased for himself had he been given an equivalent amount of money. But we are all far too familiar with gifts that miss the mark. Who has never been given an article of clothing that he was embarrassed to wear? The logic of the economic choice model seems to state unequivocally that we could avoid the problem of useless gifts if we followed the simple expedient of giving cash. And yet virtually every society continues to engage in ritualized gift giving.

The fact that this custom has persisted should not be taken as evidence that people are stupid. Rather, it suggests that there may be something about gift giving that the rational choice model fails to capture. One purpose of giving a gift is to express affection for the recipient. A thoughtfully chosen gift accomplishes this in a way that a gift of cash cannot. Or it may be that some people have difficulty indulging themselves with even small luxuries and would feel compelled to spend cash gifts on purely practical items. For these people, a gift provides a way of enjoying a small luxury without having to feel guilty about it.[7] This interpretation is supported by the observation that we rarely give purely practical gifts like plain cotton underwear or laundry detergent.

Whatever the real reasons people may have for giving in kind rather than in cash, it seems safe to assume that we do not do it because it never occurred to us to give cash. On the contrary, occasionally we do give cash gifts, especially to young relatives with low incomes. But even though there are advantages to gifts in cash, people seem clearly reluctant to abandon the practice of giving in kind.

Summary

Our task in this chapter was to set forth the basic model of rational consumer choice. In all its variants, this model retains certain common features; in particular, it takes consumers' preferences as given and assumes they will try to satisfy them in the most efficient way.

The first step in solving the budgeting problem is to identify the set of bundles of goods that the consumer is able to buy. The consumer is assumed to have an income level given in advance and to face fixed prices. Prices and income together define the consumer's budget constraint, which, in the simple two-good case, is a downward-sloping line whose slope, in absolute value, is the ratio of the two prices. It is the set of all possible bundles that the consumer might purchase if he spends his entire income.

---

[7]For a discussion of this interpretation, see R. Thaler, "Mental Accounting and Consumer Choice," *Marketing Science, 4,* Summer 1985.

The second step in solving the consumer budgeting problem is to summarize the consumer's preferences. Here, we begin with a preference ordering by which the consumer is able to rank all possible bundles of goods. This ranking scheme is assumed to be complete and transitive and to exhibit the more-is-better property. Preference orderings that satisfy these restrictions give rise to indifference maps, or collections of indifference curves, each of which represents combinations of bundles among which the consumer is indifferent. Preference orderings are also assumed to exhibit a diminishing marginal rate of substitution, which means that, along any indifference curve, the more of a good a consumer has, the more he must be given to induce him to part with a unit of some other good. The diminishing MRS property is what accounts for the characteristic convex shape of indifference curves.

The budget constraint tells us what combinations of goods the consumer can afford to buy. To summarize the consumer's preferences over various bundles, we may use either an indifference map or a utility function. In the indifference-curve framework, the best affordable bundle occurs at a point of tangency between an indifference curve and the budget constraint. At that point, the marginal rate of substitution is exactly equal to the rate at which the goods can be exchanged for one another at market prices.

An appendix to this chapter (see the "For the Instructor" section at our Web site www.mhhe.com/economics/frank4) develops the utility function approach to the consumer budgeting problem. Topics covered include cardinal versus ordinal utility, algebraic construction of indifference curves, and the use of calculus to maximize utility.

Questions for Review

1. If the prices of all products are rising at 20 percent per year and your employer gives you a 20 percent salary increase, are you better off, worse off, or equally well off in comparison with your situation a year ago?

2. *True or false:* If you know the slope of the budget constraint (for two goods), you know the prices of the two goods. Explain.

3. *True or false:* The downward slope of indifference curves is a consequence of the diminishing marginal rate of substitution.

4. Construct an example of a preference ordering over Coke, Diet Coke, and Diet Pepsi that violates the transitivity assumption.

5. Explain in your own words how the slope of an indifference curve provides information about how much a consumer likes one good relative to another.

6. Explain why a consumer will often buy one bundle of goods even though he prefers another.

7. Why are corner solutions especially likely in the case of perfect substitutes?

8. *True or false:* If the indifference curve map is concave to the origin, then the optimal commodity basket must occur at a corner equilibrium, except possibly when there are quantity discounts.

9. If Ralph were given $10, he would spend none of it on tuna fish. But when asked, he claims to be indifferent between receiving $10 worth of tuna fish and a $10 bill. How could this be?

Problems

1. The Acme Seed Company charges $2/lb for the first 10 lb you buy of marigold seeds each week and $1/lb for every pound you buy thereafter. If your income is $100/wk, draw your budget constraint for the composite good and marigold seeds.

2. Same as Problem 1, except now the price for every pound after 10 lb/wk is $4/lb.

3. Smith likes cashews better than almonds and likes almonds better than walnuts. He likes pecans equally well as macadamia nuts and prefers macadamia nuts to almonds. Assuming his preferences are transitive, which does he prefer:

   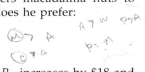

   a. Pecans or walnuts?
   b. Macadamia nuts or cashews?

4. Originally P_X is worth $120 and P_Y is $80. *True or false:* If P_X increases by $18 and P_Y increases by $12, the new budget line will be shifted inward and parallel to the old budget line. Explain.

5. Martha has $150 of disposable income to spend each week and cannot borrow money. She buys Malted Milk Balls and the composite good. Suppose that Malted Milk Balls cost $2.50 per bag and the composite good costs $1 per unit.

   a. Sketch Martha's budget constraint.
   b. What is the opportunity cost, in terms of bags of Malted Milk Balls, of an additional unit of the composite good?

6. In Problem 5, suppose that in an inflationary period the cost of the composite good increases to $1.50 per unit, but the cost of Malted Milk Balls remains the same.

   a. Sketch the new budget constraint.
   b. What is the opportunity cost of an additional unit of the composite good?

7. In Problem 6, suppose that Martha demands a pay raise to fight the inflation. Her boss submits and raises her salary so that her disposable income is now $225/wk.

   a. Sketch the new budget constraint.
   b. What is the opportunity cost of an additional unit of the composite good?

8. Picabo, an aggressive skier, spends her entire income on skis and bindings. She wears out one pair of skis for every pair of bindings she wears out.

   a. Graph Picabo's indifference curves for skis and bindings.
   b. Now draw her indifference curves on the assumption that she is such an

aggressive skier that she wears out two pairs of skis for every pair of bindings she wears out.

9. Suppose Picabo in Problem 8 has $3600 in income to spend on skis and bindings each year. Find Picabo's best affordable bundle of skis and bindings under both of the preferences described in the previous problem. Skis are $480/pr and bindings are $240/pr.

10. For Alexi, coffee and tea are perfect substitutes: One cup of coffee is equivalent to one cup of tea. Suppose Alexi has $90/mo to spend on these beverages, and coffee costs $0.90/cup while tea costs $1.20/cup. Find Alexi's best affordable bundle of tea and coffee. How much could the price of a cup of coffee rise without harming her standard of living?

11. Eve likes apples but doesn't care about pears. If apples and pears are the only two goods available, draw her indifference curves.

12. Koop likes food but dislikes cigarette smoke. The more food he has, the more he would be willing to give up to achieve a given reduction in cigarette smoke. If food and cigarette smoke are the only two goods, draw Koop's indifference curves.

13. If you were president of a conservation organization, which rate structure would you prefer the Gigawatt Power Company to use: the one described in Example 3-1, or one in which all power sold for $0.08/kWh? (Assume that each rate structure would exactly cover the company's costs.)

14. Paula, a former actress, spends all her income attending plays and movies and likes plays exactly three times as much as she likes movies.

    a. Draw her indifference map.
    b. Paula earns $120/wk. If play tickets cost $12 each and movie tickets cost $4 each, show her budget line and highest attainable indifference curve. How many plays will she see?
    c. If play tickets are $12, movie tickets $5, how many plays will she attend?

15. For each of the following, sketch:

    a. A typical person's indifference curves between garbage and the composite good.
    b. Indifference curves for the same two commodities for Oscar the Grouch on *Sesame Street,* who loves garbage and has no use for the composite good.

16. Boris budgets $9/wk for his morning coffee with milk. He likes it only if it is prepared with 4 parts coffee, 1 part milk. Coffee costs $1/oz, milk $0.50/oz. How much coffee and how much milk will Boris buy per week? How will your answers change if the price of coffee rises to $3.25/oz? Show your answers graphically.

17. The federal government wants to support education but must not support religion. To this end, it gives the University of Notre Dame $2 million with the stipulation that this money be used for secular purposes only. The accompanying graph shows Notre Dame's pre-federal-gift budget constraint and best attainable indifference curve over secular and nonsecular expenditures. How would the university's welfare differ if the gift came without the secular-use restriction?

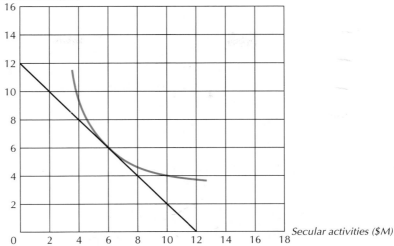

Nonsecular activities ($M)

Secular activities ($M)

18. Continental Long Distance Telephone Service offers an optional package for in-state calling whereby each month the subscriber gets the first 50 min of in-state calls free, the next 100 min at $0.25/min, and any additional time at the normal rate of $0.50/min. Draw the budget constraint for in-state phone calls and the composite good for a subscriber with an income of $400/mo.

19. For the Continental Long Distance subscriber in Problem 18, what is the opportunity cost of making an additional 20 min of calls if he currently makes

    a. 40 min of calls each month?
    b. 140 min of calls each month?

20. You have the option of renting a car on a daily basis for $40/day or on a weekly basis for $200/wk. Draw your budget constraint for a budget of $360/trip.

    a. Find your best affordable bundle if your travel preferences are such that you require exactly $140 worth of other goods for each day of rental car consumption.
    b. Alternatively, suppose you view a day of rental car consumption as a perfect substitute for $35 worth of other goods.

21. Howard said that he was exactly indifferent between consuming four slices of pizza and one beer versus consuming three slices of pizza and two beers. He also said that he prefers a bundle consisting of one slice of pizza and three beers to either of the first two bundles. Do Howard's preferences exhibit diminishing marginal rates of substitution?

22. Your local telephone company has offered you a choice between the following billing plans:

    Plan A: Pay $0.05 per call.

Plan B: Pay an initial $2/wk, which allows you up to 30 calls per week at no charge. Any calls over 30/wk cost $0.05 per call.

If your income is $12/wk and the composite good costs $1, graph your budget constraints for the composite good and calls under the two plans.

*23. At your school's fund-raising picnic, you pay for soft drinks not with cash but with tickets purchased in advance—one ticket per bottle of soft drink. Tickets are available in sets of three types:

Small: $3 for 3 tickets
Medium: $4 for 5 tickets
Large: $5 for 8 tickets

If the total amount you have to spend is $12 and fractional sets of tickets cannot be bought, graph your budget constraint for soft drinks and the composite good.

*24. Consider two Italian restaurants located in identical towns 200 miles apart. The restaurants are identical in every respect but their tipping policies. At one, there is a flat $15 service charge, but no other tips are accepted. At the other, a 15 percent tip is added to the bill. The average food bill at the first restaurant, exclusive of the service charge, is $100. How, if at all, do you expect the amount of food eaten in the two restaurants to differ?

*25. Mr. R. Plane, retired college administrator, consumes only grapes and the composite good Y ($P_Y = \$1$). His income consists of $10,000/yr from social security, plus the proceeds from whatever he sells of the 2000 bushels of grapes he harvests annually from his vineyard. Last year, grapes sold for $2/bushel, and Plane consumed all 2000 bushels of his grapes in addition to 10,000 units of Y. This year the price of grapes is $3/bushel, while P_Y remains $1. If his indifference curves have the conventional shape, will this year's consumption of grapes be greater than, smaller than, or the same as last year's? Will this year's consumption of Y be greater than, smaller than, or the same as last year's? Explain.

Answers to In-Chapter Exercises

3-1. *Food (lb/wk)*

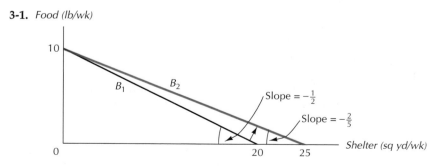

Problems marked with an asterisk (*) are more difficult.

3-2. *Food (lb/wk)*

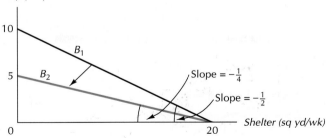

3-3. *Food (lb/wk)*

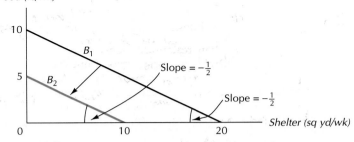

3-4. *Food (lb/wk)*

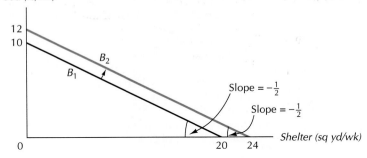

3-5. The budget constraint for a residential consumer with Amperage Electric Power would be kinked outward, as the initial rate for the first 1000 kWh/mo is lower. For power consumption X up to 1000 kWh/mo, the budget constraint has a slope of the lower rate \$0.05/kWh.

$$Y = 400 - 0.05X \qquad 0 \le X \le 1000 \text{ kWh/mo}$$

For power consumption X above 1000 kWh/mo, the budget constraint has a slope of the higher rate \$0.10/kWh.

$$Y = 450 - 0.10X \qquad X > 1000 \text{ kWh/mo}$$

The kink occurs where the level of consumption of other goods when $X = 1000$ kWh/mo is $Y = 400 - 0.05X = 400 - 50 = 350$, or equivalently, $Y = 450 - 0.10X = 450 - 100 = 350$. If the rate were instead \$0.10/kWh for all kWh that exceeded 1000 kWh/mo, then the budget constraint for $X > 1000$ kWh/mo would be

$$Y = 400 - 0.10X \qquad X > 1000 \text{ kWh/mo}$$

and would have a discrete jump from $Y = 350$ to $Y = 300$ at $X = 1000$ kWh/mo.

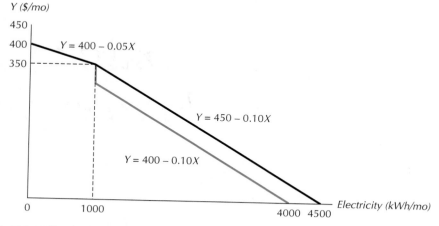

3-6. At bundle A, the consumer is willing to give up 1 lb of food to get an additional square yard of shelter. But the market prices it is necessary to give up only $\frac{1}{2}$ lb of food to buy an additional square yard of shelter. It follows that the consumer will be better off than at bundle A if he buys 1 lb less of food and 2 sq yd more of shelter.

3-7. Albert's budget constraint is $T = 120 - 2B$. Albert's initial preferences are for two pats of butter for every slice of toast $B = 2T$. Substituting this equation into his budget constraint yields $T = 120 - 4T$, or $5T = 120$, which solves for $T = 24$ slices of toast, and thus $B = 48$ pats of butter each month. Albert's new preferences are for one pat of butter for every slice of toast $B = T$. Substituting this equation into his budget constraint yields $T = 120 - 2T$, or $3T = 120$, which solves for $T = 40$ slices of toast, and thus $B = 40$ pats of butter each month. Not only has Albert cut the fat, but he is consuming more fiber too!

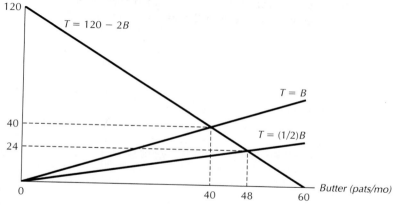

CHAPTER
4

Individual and Market Demand

A pound of salt costs 30 cents at the grocery store where I shop. My family and I use the same amount of salt at that price as we would if it instead sold for 5 cents/lb or even $10/lb. I also consume about the same amount of salt now as I did as a graduate student, when my income was less than one-tenth as large as it is today.

Salt is an unusual case. The amounts we buy of many other goods are much more sensitive to prices and incomes. Sometimes, for example, my family and I consider spending a sabbatical year in New York City, where housing prices are more than triple what they are in Ithaca. If we ever do go there, we will probably live in an apartment that is less than one-fourth the size of our current house.

Chapter Preview*

Viewed within the framework of the rational choice model, my behavior with respect to salt and housing purchases is perfectly intelligible. Our focus in this chapter is to use the tools from Chapter 3 to shed additional light on why, exactly, the responses of various purchase decisions to changes in income and price differ so widely. In Chapter 3, we saw how changes in prices and incomes affect the budget constraint. Here we will see how changes in the budget constraint affect actual purchase decisions. More specifically, we will use the rational choice model to generate an individual consumer's demand curve for a product and employ our model to construct a relationship that summarizes how individual demands vary with income.

We will see how the total effect of a price change can be decomposed into two separate effects: (1) the substitution effect, which denotes the change in the quantity demanded that results because the price change makes substitute goods seem either more or less attractive; and (2) the income effect, which denotes the change in quantity demanded that results from the change in purchasing power caused by the price change.

Next on our agenda, we will show how individual demand curves can be added to yield the demand curve for the market as a whole. A central analytical concept we will develop in this chapter is the price elasticity of demand, a measure of the responsiveness of purchase decisions to small changes in price. We will also consider the income elasticity of demand, a measure of the responsiveness of purchase decisions to small changes in income. And we will see that, for some goods, the distribution of income, not just its average value, is an important determinant of market demand.

A final elasticity concept in this chapter is the cross-price elasticity of demand, which is a measure of the responsiveness of the quantity demanded of one good to small changes in the prices of another good. Cross-price elasticity is the criterion by which pairs of goods are classified as being either substitutes or complements.

These analytical constructs provide a deeper understanding of a variety of market behaviors as well as a stronger foundation for intelligent decision and policy analysis.

The Effects of Changes in Price

THE PRICE-CONSUMPTION CURVE

Recall from Chapter 2 that a market demand curve is a relationship that tells how much of a good the market as a whole wants to purchase at various prices. Suppose we want to generate a demand schedule for a good—say, shelter—not for the market as a whole but for only a single consumer. Holding income, preferences, and the prices of all other goods constant, how will a change in the price of shelter affect the amount of shelter the consumer buys? To answer this question, we begin with this consumer's indifference map, plotting shelter on the horizontal axis and the composite good Y on the vertical axis. Suppose the consumer's income is $120/wk, and the price of the composite good is again 1. The vertical intercept of her budget constraint will then be 120. The horizontal intercept will be $120/P_S$, where P_S denotes the price of shelter. Figure 4-1 shows four budget constraints that correspond to four different prices of shelter, namely, $24/sq yd, $12/sq yd, $6/sq yd, and $4/sq yd. The corresponding best affordable bundles contain 2.5, 7, 15, and 20 sq yd/wk of shelter, respectively. If we were to repeat this procedure for indef-

FIGURE 4-1
Holding income and the price of Y fixed, we vary the price of shelter. The set of optimal bundles traced out by the various budget lines is called the price-consumption curve, or PCC.

THE PRICE-CONSUMPTION CURVE

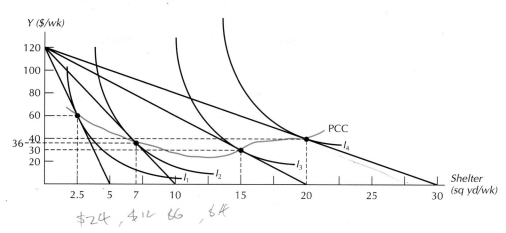

Price-consumption curve (PCC)
Holding income and the price of Y constant, the PCC for a good X is the set of optimal bundles traced on an indifference map as the price of X varies.

initely many prices, the resulting points of tangency would trace out the line labeled PCC in Figure 4-1. This line is called the *price-consumption curve,* or **PCC**.

For the particular consumer whose indifference map is shown in Figure 4-1, note that each time the price of shelter falls, the budget constraint rotates outward, enabling the consumer to purchase not only more shelter but more of the composite good as well. And each time the price of shelter falls, this consumer chooses a bundle that contains more shelter than in the bundle chosen previously. Note, however, that the amount of money spent on the composite good may either rise or fall when the price of shelter falls. Thus, the amount spent on other goods falls when the price of shelter falls from \$24/sq yd to \$12/sq yd but rises when the price of shelter falls from \$6/sq yd to \$4/sq yd. Below, we will see why this is a relatively common purchase pattern.

THE INDIVIDUAL CONSUMER'S DEMAND CURVE

An individual consumer's demand curve is like the market demand curve in that it tells the quantities the consumer will buy at various prices. All the information we need to construct the individual demand curve is contained in the price-consumption curve. The first step in going from the PCC to the individual demand curve is to record the relevant price-quantity combinations from the PCC in Figure 4-1, as in Table 4-1. (Recall from Chapter 3 that the price of shelter along any budget constraint is given by income divided by the horizontal intercept of that budget constraint.)

The next step is to plot the price-quantity pairs from Table 4-1, with the price of shelter on the vertical axis and the quantity of shelter on the horizontal. With sufficiently many price-quantity pairs, we generate the individual's demand curve, shown as the line DD in Figure 4-2. Note carefully that in moving from the PCC to the individual demand curve, we are moving from a graph in which both axes measure quantities to one in which price is plotted against quantity.

To derive the indi-
vidual's demand
curve for shelter
from the PCC in Fig-
ure 4-1, begin by
recording the quan-
tities of shelter that
correspond to the
shelter prices on
each budget con-
straint.

TABLE 4-1   **A DEMAND SCHEDULE**

Price of shelter ($/sq yd)	Quantity of shelter demanded (sq yd/wk)
24	2.5
12	7
6	15
4	20

The Effects of Changes in Income

THE INCOME-CONSUMPTION CURVE

**Income-con-
sumption curve
(ICC)** Holding
the prices of X
and Y constant,
the ICC for a
good X is the set
of optimal bun-
dles traced on an
indifference map
as income varies.

The PCC and the individual demand schedule are two different ways of summarizing how a consumer's purchase decisions respond to variations in prices.
Analogous devices exist to summarize responses to variations in income. The
income analog to the PCC is the *income-consumption curve*, or *ICC*. To generate the PCC for shelter, we held preferences, income, and the price of the composite good constant while tracing out the effects of a change in the price of
shelter. In the case of the ICC, we hold preferences and relative prices constant
and trace out the effects of changes in income.

In Figure 4-3, for example, we hold the price of the composite good constant
at 1 and the price of shelter constant at $10/sq yd and examine what happens
when income takes the values $40/wk, $60/wk, $100/wk, and $120/wk. Recall
from Chapter 3 that a change in income shifts the budget constraint parallel to

FIGURE 4-2
Like the market de-
mand curve, the in-
dividual demand
curve is a relation-
ship that tells how
much the consumer
wants to purchase at
different prices.

AN INDIVIDUAL CONSUMER'S DEMAND CURVE

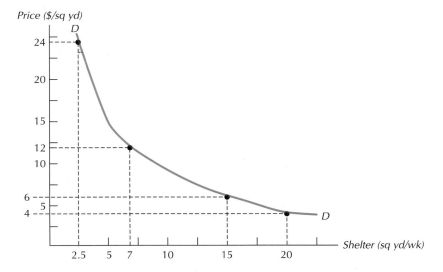

FIGURE 4-3
As income in-
creases, the budget
constraint moves
outward. Holding
preferences and rel-
ative prices con-
stant, the ICC traces
out how these
changes in income
affect consumption.
It is the set of all tan-
gencies as the bud-
get line moves
outward.

AN INCOME-CONSUMPTION CURVE

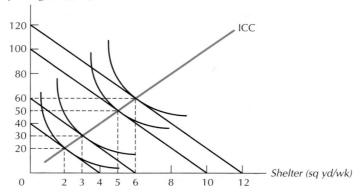

itself. As before, to each budget there corresponds a best affordable bundle. The
set of best affordable bundles is denoted as ICC in Figure 4-3. For the consumer
whose indifference map is shown, the ICC happens to be a straight line, but this
need not always be the case.

THE ENGEL CURVE

Engel curve A
curve that plots
the relationship
between the
quantity of X
consumed and
income.

The analog to the individual demand curve in the income domain is the individual *Engel curve*. It takes the quantities of shelter demanded from the ICC and
plots them against the corresponding values of income. If we do this for indefinitely many income-consumption pairs for the consumer shown in Figure 4-3,
we trace out the line *EE* shown in Figure 4-4. The Engel curve shown in Figure
4-4 happens to be linear, but Engel curves in general need not be.

Note carefully the distinction between what we measure on the vertical axis
of the ICC and what we measure on the vertical axis of the Engel curve. On the
vertical axis of the ICC, we measure the amount the consumer spends each week
on all goods other than shelter. On the vertical axis of the Engel curve, by contrast, we measure the consumer's total weekly income.

TABLE 4-2   **INCOME AND QUANTITY OF SHELTER
            DEMANDED**

Income ($/wk)	Quantity of shelter demanded (sq yd/wk)
40	2
60	3
100	5
120	6

FIGURE 4-4
Holding preferences and relative prices constant, the Engel curve tells how much shelter the consumer will purchase at various levels of income.

AN INDIVIDUAL CONSUMER'S ENGEL CURVE

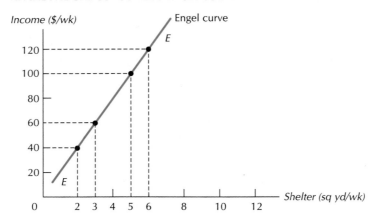

Note also that, as was true with the PCC and individual demand curves, the ICC and Engel curves contain essentially the same information. The advantage of the Engel curve is that it allows us to see at a glance how the quantity demanded varies with income.

NORMAL AND INFERIOR GOODS

Note that the Engel curve in Figure 4-5a is upward-sloping, implying that the more income a consumer has, the more tenderloin steak he will buy each week. Most things we buy have this property, which is the defining characteristic of a *normal good*. Goods that do not have this property are called *inferior goods*. For such goods, an increase in income leads to a reduction in the quantity demanded. Figure 4-5b is an example of an Engel curve for an inferior good. The more income a person has, the less hamburger he will buy each week.

Why would someone buy less of a good following an increase in his income?

FIGURE 4-5
(a) This Engel curve is for a normal good. The quantity demanded increases with income. (b) This Engel curve for hamburger has the negative slope characteristic of inferior goods. As the consumer's income grows, he switches from hamburger to more desirable cuts of meat.

THE ENGEL CURVES FOR NORMAL AND INFERIOR GOODS

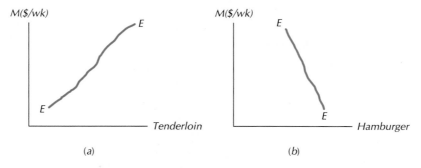

The prototypical inferior good is one for which there are several strongly preferred, but more expensive, substitutes. Supermarkets, for example, generally carry several different grades of ground beef, ranging from hamburger, which has the highest fat content, to ground sirloin, which has the lowest. A consumer who is trying to restrict the amount of fat in his diet will tend to switch to a leaner grade of meat as soon as he is able to afford it. For such a consumer, hamburger will be an inferior good.

For any consumer who spends all her income, it is a matter of simple arithmetic that not all goods can be inferior. After all, when income rises, it is mathematically impossible to spend less on all goods at once. From this observation, it follows that the more broadly a good is defined, the less likely it is to be inferior. Thus, while hamburger is an inferior good for many consumers, there are probably very few people for whom the good "meat" is inferior, and fewer still for whom "food" is inferior.[1]

THE INCOME AND SUBSTITUTION EFFECTS OF A PRICE CHANGE

Substitution effect That component of the total effect of a price change that results from the associated change in the relative attractiveness of other goods.

Income effect That component of the total effect of a price change that results from the associated change in real purchasing power.

In Chapter 2 we saw that a change in the price of a good affects purchase decisions for two reasons. For concreteness, we will consider the effects of a price increase. (The effects of a price reduction will be in the opposite direction from those of a price increase.) One effect of a price increase is to make close substitutes of the good more attractive than before. For example, when the price of rice increases, wheat becomes more attractive. This is the so-called *substitution effect* of a price increase.

The second effect of a price increase is to reduce the consumer's purchasing power. For a normal good, this effect too will tend to reduce the amount purchased. But for an inferior good, the effect is just the opposite. The loss in purchasing power, taken by itself, tends to increase the quantity purchased of an inferior good. The change in the quantity purchased attributable to the change in purchasing power is called the *income effect* of the price change.

The *total effect* of the price increase is the sum of the substitution and income effects. The substitution effect always causes the quantity purchased to move in the opposite direction from the change in price—when price goes up, the quantity demanded goes down; and conversely, when price goes down, the quantity demanded goes up. The direction of the income effect depends on whether the good is normal or inferior. For normal goods, the income effect works in the same direction as the substitution effect—when price goes up [down], the fall [rise] in purchasing power causes the quantity demanded to fall [rise]. For inferior goods, by contrast, the income and substitution effects work against one another.

[1]Another useful way to partition the set of consumer goods is between so-called *necessities* and *luxuries*. A good is defined as a luxury for a person if he spends a larger proportion of his income on it when his income rises. A necessity, by contrast, is one for which he spends a smaller proportion of his income when his income rises. (More on this distinction follows.)

The substitution and income effects of a price increase can be seen most clearly when they are displayed graphically. Let us begin by depicting the total effect of a price increase. In Figure 4-6, the consumer has an initial income of $120/wk and the initial price of shelter is $6/sq yd. This gives rise to the budget constraint labeled B_0, and the optimal bundle on that budget is denoted by A, which contains 10 sq yd/wk of shelter. Now let the price of shelter increase from $6/sq yd to $24/sq yd, resulting in the budget labeled B_1. The new optimal bundle is D, which contains 2 sq yd/wk of shelter. The movement from A to D is called the total effect of the price increase. Naturally, the price increase causes the consumer to end up on a lower indifference curve (I_1) than the one he was able to attain on his original budget (I_0).

To decompose the total effect into the income and substitution effects, we begin by asking the following question: How much income would the consumer need to reach his original indifference curve (I_0) after the increase in the price of shelter? Note in Figure 4-7 that the answer is $240/wk. If the consumer were given a total income of that amount, it would undo the injury caused by the loss in purchasing power resulting from the increase in the price of shelter. The budget constraint labeled B' is purely hypothetical, a device constructed for the purpose at hand. It has the same slope as the new budget constraint (B_1)—namely, -24—and it is just far enough out from the origin to be tangent to the original indifference curve, I_0. With the budget constraint B', the optimal bundle is C, which contains 6 sq yd/wk of shelter. The movement from A to C gives rise to the substitution effect of the price change—which here involves a reduction of 4 sq yd/wk of shelter and an increase of $36/wk of the composite good.

The hypothetical budget constraint B' tells us that even if the consumer had enough income to reach the same indifference curve as before, the increase in the price of shelter would cause him to reduce his consumption of it in favor of

FIGURE 4-6
With an income of $120/wk and a price of shelter of $6/sq yd, the consumer chooses bundle A on the budget constraint B_0. When the price of shelter rises to $24/sq yd, with income held constant at $120/wk, the best affordable bundle becomes D. The movement from 10 to 2 sq yd/wk of shelter is called the total effect of the price increase.

THE TOTAL EFFECT OF A PRICE INCREASE

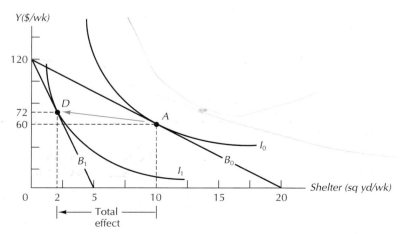

FIGURE 4-7

To get the substitution effect, slide the new budget B_1 outward parallel to itself until it becomes tangent to the original indifference curve, I_0. The movement from A to C gives rise to the substitution effect, the reduction in shelter due solely to the fact that shelter is now more expensive relative to other goods. The movement from C to D gives rise to the income effect. It is the reduction in shelter that results from the loss in purchasing power implicit in the price increase.

THE SUBSTITUTION AND INCOME EFFECTS OF A PRICE CHANGE

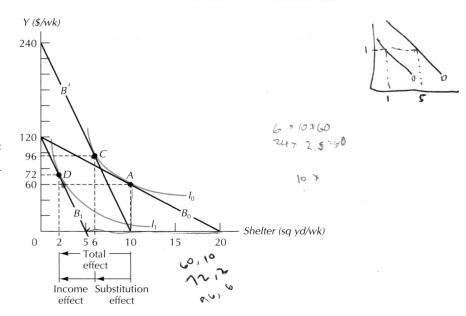

other goods and services. *For consumers whose indifference curves have the conventional convex shape, the substitution effect of a price increase will always be to reduce consumption of the good whose price increased.*

The income effect of the price increase stems from the movement from C to D. The particular good shown in Figure 4-7 happens to be a normal good. The hypothetical movement of the consumer's income from \$240/wk to \$120/wk serves to accentuate the reduction of his consumption of shelter, causing it to fall from 6 sq yd/wk to 2 sq yd/wk.

Whereas the income effect reinforces the substitution effect in the case of a normal good, the two effects tend to offset one another in the case of an inferior good. In Figure 4-8, the line B_0 depicts the budget constraint for a consumer with an income of \$24/wk who faces a price of hamburger of \$1/lb. On B_0 the best affordable bundle is A, which contains 12 lb/wk of hamburger. When the price of hamburger rises to \$2/lb, the resulting budget constraint is B_1 and the best affordable bundle is now D, which contains 9 lb/wk of hamburger. The total effect of the price increase is thus to reduce the quantity of hamburger consumed by 3 lb/wk. Budget constraint B' once again is the hypothetical budget constraint that enables the consumer to reach the original indifference curve at the new price ratio. Note in this case that the substitution effect of the price change (the change in hamburger consumption associated with movement from A to C in Figure 4-8) is to reduce the quantity of hamburger consumed by 4 lb/wk—that is, to reduce it by more than the value of the total effect. The income effect by

FIGURE 4-8
By contrast to the
case of a normal
good, the income ef-
fect acts to offset the
substitution effect
for an inferior good.

INCOME AND SUBSTITUTION EFFECTS FOR AN INFERIOR GOOD

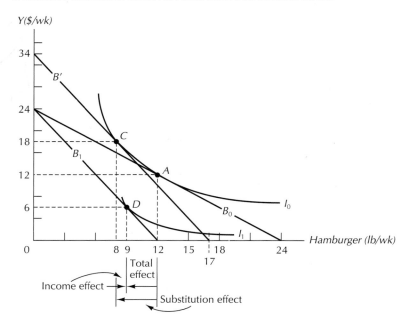

itself (the change in hamburger consumption associated with the movement from
C to D) actually serves to increase hamburger consumption by 1 lb/wk. The
income effect thus works in the opposite direction from the substitution for an
inferior good like hamburger.

*E*XAMPLE 4-1 *Income and substitution effects for perfect complements. Suppose skis and bindings are perfect, one-for-one complements and Paula spends all her equipment budget of $1200/yr on
these two goods. Skis and bindings each cost $200. What will be the income and substitu-
tion effects of an increase in the price of bindings to $400 per pair?*

> Since our goal here is to examine the effect on two specific goods (skis
> and bindings), we proceed by devoting one axis to each good and dis-
> pense with the composite good. On the original budget constraint, B_0,
> the optimal bundle is denoted A in Figure 4-9. Paula buys three pairs
> of skis per year and three pairs of bindings. When the price of bind-
> ings rises from $200 per pair to $400 per pair, we get the new budget
> constraint, B_1, and the resulting optimal bundle D, which contains two
> pairs of skis per year and two pairs of bindings. An equipment budget
> of $1800/yr is what the consumer would need at the new price to attain
> the same indifference curve she did originally (I_0). (To get this figure,

slide B_1 out until it hits I_0, then calculate the cost of buying the bundle at the vertical intercept—here, nine pairs of skis per year at $200 per pair.) Note that because perfect complements have right-angled indifference curves, the budget B' results in an optimal bundle C that is exactly the same as the original bundle A. For perfect complements, the substitution effect is zero. So for this case, the total effect of the price increase is exactly the same as the income effect of the price increase.

Example 4-1 tells us that if the price of ski bindings goes up relative to the price of skis, people will not alter the proportion of skis and bindings they purchase. But because the price increase lowers their real purchasing power (that is, because it limits the quantities of both goods that they can buy), they will respond by buying fewer units of ski equipment. The income effect will thus cause them to lower their consumption of both skis and bindings by the same proportion.

*E*XERCISE 4-1

Repeat Example 4-1 with the assumption that pairs of skis and pairs of bindings are perfect two-for-one complements. (That is, assume that Paula wears out two pairs of skis for every pair of bindings she wears out.)

FIGURE 4-9
For perfect complements, the substitution effect of an increase in the price of bindings (the movement from A to C) is equal to zero. The income effect (the movement from A to D) and the total effect are one and the same.

INCOME AND SUBSTITUTION EFFECTS FOR PERFECT COMPLEMENTS

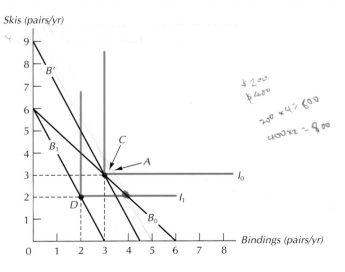

EXAMPLE 4-2 Income and substitution effects for perfect substitutes. Suppose Pam considers tea and coffee to be perfect one-for-one substitutes and spends her budget of $12/wk on these two beverages. Coffee costs $1/cup, while tea costs $1.20/cup. What will be the income and substitution effects of an increase in the price of coffee to $1.50/cup?

Pam will demand 12 cups of coffee per week and no cups of tea (point *A* in Figure 4-10) as they contribute equally to her utility but tea is more expensive. When the price of coffee rises, Pam switches to consuming only tea, buying 10 cups of tea per week and no coffee (point *D*). Pam would need a budget of $14.40/wk to afford 12 cups of tea (point *C*), which she likes as well as the 12 cups of coffee she originally consumed. The substitution effect is from (12,0) to (0,12) and the income effect from (0,12) to (0,10), with the total effect from (12,0) to (0,10). With perfect substitutes, the substitution effect can be very large: For small price changes (near MRS), consumers may switch from consuming all one good to consuming only the other good.

EXERCISE 4-2

Starting from the original price, what will be the income and substitution effects of an increase in the price of tea to $1.50/cup?

Consumer Responsiveness to Changes in Price

We began this chapter with the observation that for certain goods, such as salt, consumption is highly insensitive to changes in price while for others, such as housing, it is much more sensitive. The principal reason for studying income and substitution effects is that these devices help us understand such differences.

FIGURE 4-10
For perfect substitutes, the substitution effect of an increase in the price of coffee (the movement from *A* to *C*) can be very large.

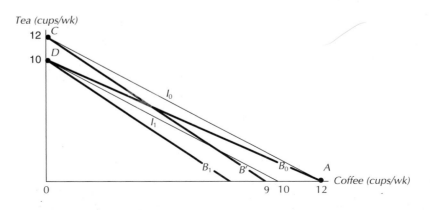

Let us consider first the case of salt. When analyzing substitution and income effects, there are two salient features to note about salt. First, for most consumers, it has no close substitutes. If someone were forbidden to shake salt onto his steak, he might respond by shaking a little extra pepper, or even by squeezing some lemon juice onto it. But for most people, these alternatives would fall considerably short of the real thing. The second prominent feature of salt is that it occupies an almost imperceptibly small share of total expenditures. An extremely heavy user of salt might consume a pound every month. If this person's income were $1200/mo, a doubling of the price of salt—say, from $0.30/lb to $0.60/lb—would increase the share of his budget accounted for by salt from 0.00025 to 0.0005. For all practical purposes, therefore, the income effect of a price increase of salt is negligible.

It is instructive to represent these two properties of salt diagrammatically. In Figure 4-11, the fact that salt has no close substitutes is represented by indifference curves with a nearly right-angled shape. Salt's negligible budget share is captured by the fact that the cusps of these indifference curves occur at extremely small quantities of salt.

Suppose, as in Figure 4-11, the price of salt is originally $0.30/lb, resulting in an equilibrium bundle labeled A in the enlarged region, which contains 1.0002 lb/mo of salt. A price increase to $0.60/lb results in a new equilibrium bundle D with 1 lb/mo of salt. The income and substitution effects are measured in terms of the intermediate bundle C. Geometrically, the income effect is small because the original tangency occurred so near the vertical intercept of the budget constraint. When we are near the pivot point of the budget

FIGURE 4-11
The total effect of a price change will be very small when (1) the original equilibrium bundle lies near the vertical intercept of the budget constraint and (2) the indifference curves have a nearly right-angled shape. The first factor causes the income effect (the reduction in salt consumption associated with the movement from C to D) to be small; the second factor causes the substitution effect (the reduction in salt consumption associated with the movement from A to C) to be small.

INCOME AND SUBSTITUTION EFFECTS OF A PRICE INCREASE FOR SALT

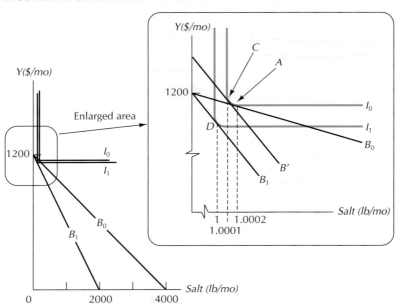

constraint, even a very large rotation produces only a small movement. The substitution effect, in turn, is small because of the nearly right-angled shape of the indifference curves.

Let us now contrast the salt case with the housing example. With housing, the two salient facts are that (1) it accounts for a substantial share of total expenditures (roughly 30 percent for many people), and (2) most people have considerable latitude to substitute between housing and other goods. The second assertion may not appear obvious at first glance, but on reflection, its plausibility becomes clear. Indeed, there are many ways to substitute away from housing expenditures. The most obvious is to switch from a larger to a smaller dwelling. Many Manhattanites, for example, can afford to live in apartments larger than the ones they now occupy, yet they prefer to spend what they save in rent on restaurant meals, theater performances, and the like. Another substitution possibility is to consume less conveniently located housing. Someone who works in Manhattan can live near her job and pay extremely high rent; alternatively, she can live in New Jersey or Long Island and pay considerably less. Or she can choose an apartment in a less fashionable neighborhood, or one not quite as close to a convenient subway stop. The point is that there are many different options for housing, and the choice among them will depend strongly on income and relative prices.

In Figure 4-12, the consumer's income is $120/wk and the initial price of shelter is $0.60/sq yd. The resulting budget constraint is labeled B_0, and the best affordable bundle on it is A, which contains 100 sq yd/wk of shelter. An increase in the price of shelter to $2.40/sq yd causes the quantity demanded to fall to 20 sq yd/wk. The smooth convex shape of the indifference curves represents the high degree of substitution possibilities between housing and other goods and accounts for the relatively large substitution effect (the fall in shelter consumption associated with the movement from A to C). Note also that the original equilibrium bundle, A, was a tangency far from the vertical pivot point of the budget constraint. By contrast to the case of salt, here the rotation in the budget constraint caused by the price increase produces a large movement in the location of the relevant segment of the new budget constraint. Accordingly, the income effect for shelter (the fall in shelter consumption associated with the movement from C to D) is much larger than in the case of salt. With both a large substitution and a large income effect working together, the total effect of an increase in the price of shelter (the fall in shelter consumption associated with the movement from A to D) is very large.

EXAMPLE 4-3 *Deriving individual demand curve for perfect complements. James views car washes and gasoline as perfect complements in a 1-to-10 ratio, requiring one car wash for every 10 gallons of gas. Gas costs $1/gal, and James has $48/mo to spend on gas and car washes. (See Figure 4-13, page 118.) Construct James's demand curve for car washes by considering his quantity demanded of car washes at various prices (such as 2, 6, 14; see Figure 4-14).*

FIGURE 4-12
Because shelter occupies a large share of the budget, its income effect tends to be large. And because it is practical to substitute away from shelter, the substitution effect also tends to be large. The quantities demanded of goods with both large substitution and large income effects are highly responsive to changes in price.

INCOME AND SUBSTITUTION EFFECTS FOR A PRICE-SENSITIVE GOOD

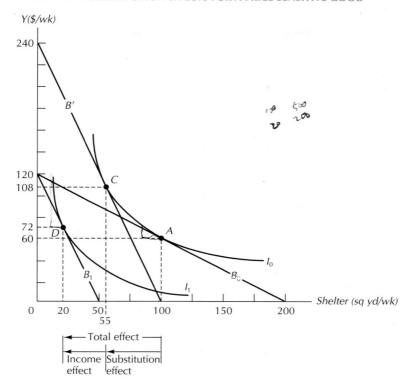

James's preferences dictate that his optimal bundle must satisfy $G = 10W$, as his indifference curves are L-shaped. James's budget constraint is $G + P_WW = 48$, or $G = 48 - P_WW$. Substituting $G = 10W$, his budget constraint is $10W + P_WW - 48$, which implies $(10 + P_W)W = 48$. At $P_W = 2$, $W = 4$; at $P_W = 6$, $W = 3$; at $P_W = 14$, $W = 2$, as summarized in Table 4-3.

TABLE 4-3   A DEMAND SCHEDULE FOR CAR WASHES

Price of car wash ($/wash)	Quantity of car washes demanded (washes/mo)
2	4
6	3
14	2
38	1

FIGURE 4-13
With $48/mo, James buys 4 washes/mo when the price is $2/wash (budget constraint *B*), 3 washes/mo when the price is $6/wash (budget constraint *B'*), and 2 washes/mo when the price is $14/wash (budget constraint *B''*).

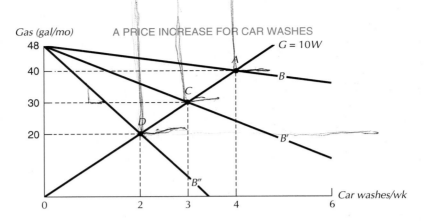

FIGURE 4-14
The quantity of car washes James demands at various prices forms his demand curve for car washes.

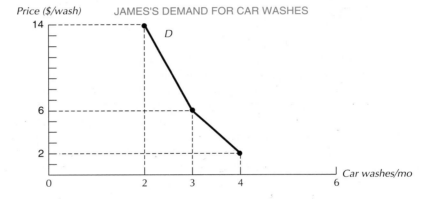

Market Demand: Aggregating Individual Demand Curves

Having seen where individual demand curves come from, we are now in a position to see how individual demand curves may be aggregated to form the market demand curve. For simplicity, let us consider a market for a good—for the sake of concreteness, again shelter—that consists of only two potential consumers. Given the demand curves for each of these consumers, how do we generate the market demand curve for shelter? In Figure 4-15, D_1 and D_2 represent the individual demand curves for consumers 1 and 2, respectively. To get the market demand curve, we begin by calling out a price—say, $4/sq yd—and adding the quantities demanded by each consumer at that price. This sum, 6 sq yd/wk + 2 sq yd/wk = 8 sq yd/wk, is the total quantity of shelter demanded in the market at the price $4/sq yd. We then plot the point (8, 4) as one of the quantity-price pairs on the market demand curve *D* in the right panel of Figure 4-15. To generate additional points on the market demand curve, we simply repeat this process for other prices. Thus, the price $8/sq yd corresponds to a quantity of 4 + 0 = 4 sq yd/wk on the market demand curve for shelter. Pro-

FIGURE 4-15
The market demand curve (*D* in the right panel) is the horizontal sum of the individual demand curves, D_1 (left panel) and D_2 (center panel).

GENERATING MARKET DEMAND FROM INDIVIDUAL DEMANDS

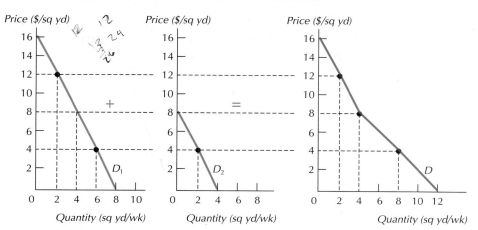

ceeding in like fashion for additional prices, we trace out the entire market demand curve for shelter. Note that for prices above $8/sq yd, consumer 2 demands no shelter at all, and so the market demand curve for prices above $8 is identical to the demand curve for consumer 1.

The procedure of announcing a price and adding the individual quantities demanded at that price is called *horizontal summation*. It is carried out the same way whether there are only two consumers in the market or many millions. In both large and small markets, the market demand curve is the horizontal summation of the individual demand curves.

In Chapter 2 we saw that it is often easier to generate numerical solutions when demand and supply curves are expressed algebraically rather than geometrically. Similarly, it will often be convenient to aggregate individual demand curves algebraically rather than graphically. When using the algebraic approach, a common error is to add individual demand curves vertically instead of horizontally. A simple example makes this danger clear.

EXAMPLE 4-4 Smith and Jones are the only consumers in the market for beech saplings in a small town in Vermont. Their demand curves are given by $P = 30 - 2Q_J$ and $P = 30 - 3Q_S$, where Q_J and Q_S are the quantities demanded by Jones and Smith, respectively. What is the market demand curve for beech saplings in their town?

> When we add demand curves horizontally, we are adding quantities, not prices. Thus it is necessary first to solve the individual demand equations for the respective quantities in terms of price. This yields $Q_J = 15 - (P/2)$ for Jones, and $Q_S = 10 - (P/3)$ for Smith. If the quantity demanded in the market is denoted by Q, we have $Q = Q_J + Q_S = 15 - (P/2) + 10 - (P/3) = 25 - (5P/6)$.

Solving back for P, we get the equation for the market demand curve: $P = 30 - (6Q/5)$. We can easily verify that this is the correct market demand curve by adding the individual demand curves graphically, as in Figure 4-16 below.

The common pitfall is to add the demand functions as originally stated and then solve for P in terms of Q. Here, this would yield $P = 30 - (5Q/2)$, which is obviously not the market demand curve we are looking for.

EXERCISE 4-3

Write the individual demand curves for shelter in Figure 4-17 in algebraic form, then add them algebraically to generate the market demand curve for shelter. (*Caution:* Note that the formula for quantity along D_2 is valid only for prices between 0 and 8.)

The horizontal summation of individual consumers' demands into market demand has a simple form when the consumers in the market are all identical. Suppose n consumers each have the demand curve $P = a - bQ_i$. To add up the quantities for the n consumers into market demand, we rearrange the consumer demand curve $P = a - bQ_i$ to express quantity alone on one side $Q_i = a/b - (1/b) P$. Then market demand is the sum of the quantities demanded Q_i by each of the n consumers.

$$Q = nQ_i = n\left(\frac{a}{b} - \frac{1}{b}P\right) = \frac{na}{b} - \frac{n}{b}P.$$

We can then rearrange market demand $Q = na/b - (n/b)P$ to get back in the

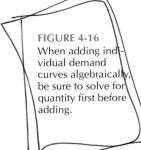

FIGURE 4-16
When adding individual demand curves algebraically, be sure to solve for quantity first before adding.

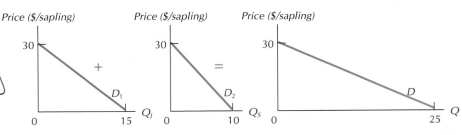

THE MARKET DEMAND CURVE FOR BEECH SAPLINGS

FIGURE 4-17
With respect to
price, the demand
for a good is elastic
if its price elasticity
is less than −1, in-
elastic if its price
elasticity exceeds
−1, and unit elastic
if its price elasticity
is equal to −1.

THREE CATEGORIES OF PRICE ELASTICITY

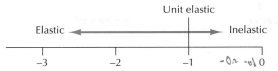

form of price alone on one side $P = a - (b/n)Q$. The intuition is that each one unit demanded by the market is $1/n$ unit for each consumer to demand. These calculations suggest a general rule for constructing the market demand curve when consumers are identical. If we have n individual consumer demand curves $P = a - bQ_i$, then the market demand curve is $P = a - (b/n)Q$.

EXAMPLE 4-5 *Suppose a market has 10 consumers, each with demand curve $P = 10 - 5Q_i$, where P is the price in dollars per unit and Q_i is the number of units demanded per week by the ith consumer (Figure 4-18). Find the market demand curve.*

First, we need to rearrange the representative consumer demand curve $P = 10 - 5Q_i$ to have quantity alone on one side:

$$Q_i = 2 - \tfrac{1}{5}P.$$

Then we multiply by the number of consumers, $n = 10$:

$$Q = nQ_i = 10Q_i = 10(2 - \tfrac{1}{5}P) = 20 - 2P.$$

Finally, we rearrange the market demand curve $Q = 20 - 2P$ to have price alone on one side, $P = 10 - (\tfrac{1}{2})Q$, to return to the slope-intercept form.

FIGURE 4-18
When 10 consumers
each have demand
curve $P = 10 - 5Q_i$
the market demand
curve is the horizon-
tal summation $P = 10 - (\tfrac{1}{2})Q$, with the
same price intercept
and $\tfrac{1}{10}$ the slope.

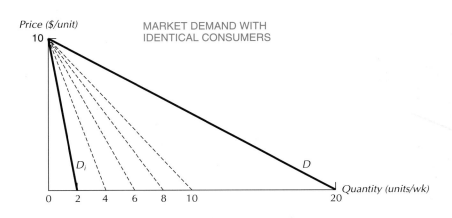

EXERCISE 4-4

Suppose a market has 30 consumers, each with demand curve $P = 120 - 60Q_i$, where P is price in dollars per unit and Q_i is the number of units demanded per week by the ith consumer. Find the market demand curve.

Price Elasticity of Demand

Price elasticity of demand The percentage change in the quantity of a good demanded that results from a 1 percent change in its price.

An analytical tool of central importance is the ***price elasticity of demand***. It is a quantitative measure of the responsiveness of purchase decisions to variations in price, and as we will see in both this and later chapters, it is useful for a variety of practical problems. *Price elasticity of demand is defined as the percentage change in the quantity of a good demanded that results from a 1 percent change in price.* For example, if a 1 percent rise in the price of shelter caused a 2 percent reduction in the quantity of shelter demanded, then the price elasticity of demand for shelter would be -2. The price elasticity of demand will always be negative (or zero) because price changes always move in the opposite direction from changes in quantity demanded.

The demand for a good is said to be *elastic* with respect to price if its price elasticity is less than -1. The good shelter mentioned in the preceding paragraph would thus be one for which demand is elastic with respect to price. The demand for a good is *inelastic* with respect to price if its price elasticity is greater than -1 and *unit elastic* with respect to price if its price elasticity is equal to -1. These definitions are portrayed graphically in Figure 4-17 on page 121.

When interpreting actual demand data, it is often useful to have a more general definition of price elasticity that can accommodate cases where the observed change in price does not happen to be 1 percent. Let P be the current price of a good and let Q be the quantity demanded at that price. And let ΔQ be the change in the quantity demanded that occurs in response to a very small change in price, ΔP. The price elasticity of demand at the current price and quantity will then be given by

$$\eta = \frac{\Delta Q/Q}{\Delta P/P}.$$
(4.1)

The numerator on the right side of Equation 4.1 is the proportional change in quantity. The denominator is the proportional change in price. Equation 4.1 is exactly the same as our earlier definition when ΔP happens to be a 1 percent change in current price. The advantage is that the more general definition also works when ΔP is any other small percentage change in current price.

GEOMETRIC INTERPETATIONS OF PRICE ELASTICITY

Another way to interpret Equation 4.1 is to rewrite it as

$$\eta = \frac{\Delta Q}{\Delta P} \frac{P}{Q}. \tag{4.2}$$

Equation 4.2 suggests a simple interpretaion in terms of the geometry of the market demand curve. When ΔP is small, the ratio $\Delta P/\Delta Q$ is the slope of the demand curve, which means that the ratio $\Delta Q/\Delta P$ is the reciprocal of that slope. Thus the price elasticity of demand may be interpreted as the product of the ratio of price to quantity and the reciprocal of the slope of the demand curve:[2]

$$\eta = \frac{P}{Q} \frac{1}{slope}. \tag{4.3}$$

Equation 4.3 is called the *point-slope method* of calculating price elasticity of demand. By way of illustration, consider the demand curve for shelter shown in Figure 4-19. Because this demand curve is linear, its slope is the same at every point, namely, -2. The reciprocal of this slope is $-\frac{1}{2}$. The price elasticity of demand at point A is therefore given by the ratio of price to quantity at A ($\frac{12}{2}$) multiplied by the reciprocal of the slope at A ($-\frac{1}{2}$), so we have $\eta_A = (\frac{12}{2})(-\frac{1}{2}) = -3$.

When the market demand curve is linear, as in Figure 4-19, several properties of price elasticity quickly become apparent from this interpretation. The first is that the price elasticity is different at every point along the demand curve. More

FIGURE 4-19
The price elasticity of demand at any point is the product of the price-quantity ratio at that point and the reciprocal of the slope of the demand curve at that point. The price elasticity at A is thus $(\frac{12}{2})(-\frac{1}{2}) = -3$.

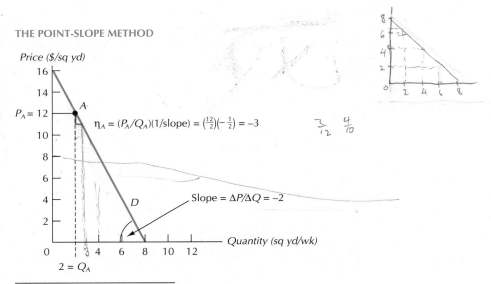

THE POINT-SLOPE METHOD

$\eta_A = (P_A/Q_A)(1/slope) = (\frac{12}{2})(-\frac{1}{2}) = -3$

Slope $= \Delta P/\Delta Q = -2$

[2]In calculus terms, price elasticity is defined as $\eta = (P/Q)[dQ(P)/dP]$.

specifically, we know that the slope of a linear demand curve is constant throughout, which means that the reciprocal of its slope is also constant. The ratio of price to quantity, by contrast, takes a different value at every point along the demand curve. As we approach the vertical intercept, it approaches infinity. It declines steadily as we move downward along the demand curve, finally reaching a value of zero at the horizontal intercept.

A second property of demand elasticity it that it is never positive. As noted earlier, because the slope of the demand curve is always negative, its reciprocal must also be negative; and because the ratio P/Q is always positve, it follows that the price elasticity of demand—which is the product of these two—must always be a negative number (except at the horizontal intercept of the demand curve, where P/Q, and hence elasticity, is zero). For the sake of convenience, however, economists often ignore the negative sign of price elasticity and refer simply to its absolute value. When a good is said to have a "high" price elasticity of demand, this will always mean that its price elasticity is large in absolute value, indicating that the quantity demanded is highly responsive to changes in price. Similarly, a good whose price elasticity is said to be "low" is one for which the absolute value of elasticity is small, indicating that the quantity demanded is relatively unresponsive to changes in price.

A third property of price elasticity at any point along a straight-line demand curve is that it will be inversely related to the slope of the demand curve. The steeper the demand curve, the less elastic is demand at any point along it. This follows from the fact that the reciprocal of the slope of the demand curve is one of the factors used to compute price elasticity.

EXERCISE 4-5

Use the point-slope method (Equation 4.3) to determine the elasticity of the demand curve $P = 32 - Q$ at the point where $P = 24$.

Two polar cases of demand elasticity are shown in Figure 4-20. In Figure 4-20a, the horizontal demand curve, with its slope of zero, has an infinitely high price elasticity at every point. Such demand curves are often called *perfectly elastic* and, as we will see, are especially important in the study of competitive firm behavior. In Figure 4-20b, the vertical demand curve has a price elasticity everywhere equal to zero. Such curves are called *perfectly inelastic.*

As a practical matter, it would be impossible for any demand curve to be perfectly inelastic at all prices. Beyond some sufficiently high price, income effects must curtail consumption of the good. This will be true even for a seemingly essential good with no substitutes, such as surgery for certain malignant tumors. Even so, the demand curve for many such goods and services will be perfectly inelastic over an extremely broad range of prices (recall the salt example discussed earlier in this chapter).

FIGURE 4-20
(*a*) The price elastic-
ity of the demand
curve is equal to $-\infty$
at every point. Such
demand curves are
said to be perfectly
elastic. (*b*) The price
elasticity of the de-
mand curve is equal
to 0 at every point.
Such demand curves
are said to be per-
fectly inelastic.

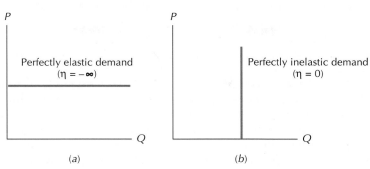

TWO IMPORTANT POLAR CASES

THE UNIT-FREE PROPERTY OF ELASTICITY

Another way of measuring responsiveness to changes in price is to use the slope
of the demand curve. Other things equal, for example, we know that the quantity demanded of a good with a steep demand curve will be less responsive to
changes in price than will one with a less steep demand curve.

Since the slope of a demand curve is much simpler to calculate than its elasticity, it may seem natural to ask, "Why bother with elasticity at all?" One
important reason is that the slope of the demand curve is very sensitive to the
units we use to measure price and quantity, while elasticity is not. By way of
illustration, notice in Figure 4-21*a* that when the price of gasoline is measured
in \$/gal, the slope of the demand curve at point *C* is -0.02. By contrast, in Fig-
ure 4-21*b*, where price is measured in \$/oz, the slope at *C* is -0.00015625. In
both cases, however, note that the price elasticity of demand at *C* is -3. This
will be true no matter how we measure price and quantity. And most people

FIGURE 4-21
The slope of the de-
mand curve at any
point depends on
the units in which
we measure price
and quantity. The
slope at point *C*
when we measure
the price of gasoline
in dollars per gallon
(*a*) is much larger
than when we mea-
sure the price in dol-
lars per ounce (*b*).
The price elasticity
at any point, by con-
trast, is completely
independent of units
of measure.

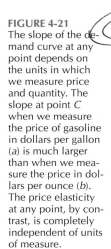

ELASTICITY IS UNIT-FREE

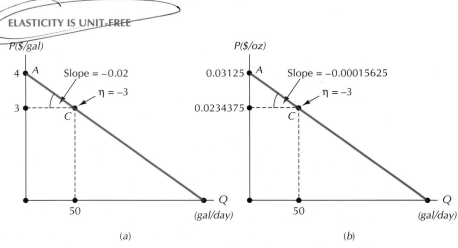

find it much more informative to know that a 1 percent cut in price will lead to a 3 percent increase in the quantity demanded than to know that the slope of the demand curve is −0.00015625.

SOME REPRESENTATIVE ELASTICITY ESTIMATES

As the entries in Table 4-4 show, the price elasticities of demand for different products often differ substantially. The low elasticity for theater and opera performances probably reflects the fact that buyers in this market have much larger than average incomes, so that income effects of price variations are likely to be small. Income effects for green peas are also likely to be small even for low-income consumers, yet the price elasticity of demand for green peas is more than 14 times larger than for theater and opera performances. The difference is that there are many more close substitutes for green peas than there are for theater and opera performances. Later in this chapter we investigate in greater detail the factors that affect the price elasticity of demand for a product.

ELASTICITY AND TOTAL EXPENDITURE

Suppose you are the administrator in charge of setting tolls for the Golden Gate Bridge, which links San Francisco to Marin County. At the current toll of $1/trip, 100,000 trips/hr are taken across the bridge. If the price elasticity of demand for trips is −2.0, what will happen to the number of trips taken per hour if you raise the toll by 10 percent? With an elasticity of −2.0, a 10 percent increase in price will produce a 20 percent reduction in quantity. Thus the number of trips will

TABLE 4-4   **PRICE ELASTICITY ESTIMATES FOR SELECTED PRODUCTS***

Good or service	Price elasticity
Green peas	−2.8
Electricity	−1.2
Beer	−1.19
Movies	−0.87
Air travel (foreign)	−0.77
Shoes	−0.70
Theater, opera	−0.18

*These short-run elasticity estimates are taken from the following sources: H. S. Houthakker and Lester Taylor, *Consumer Demand in the United States: Analyses and Projections*, 2d ed., Cambridge, MA: Harvard University Press, 1970; L. Taylor, "The Demand for Electricity: A Survey," *Bell Journal of Economics*, Spring 1975; K. Elzinga, "The Beer Industry," in Walter Adams (ed.), *The Structure of American Industry*, New York: Macmillan, 1977.

fall to 80,000/hr. Total expenditure at the higher toll will be (80,000 trips/hr)($1.10/trip) = $88,000/hr. Note that this is smaller than the total expenditure of $100,000/hr that occurred under the $1 toll.

Now suppose that the price elasticity had been not −2.0 but −0.5. How would the number of trips and total expenditure then be affected by a 10 percent increase in the toll? This time the number of trips will fall by 5 percent, to 95,000/hr, which means that total expenditure will rise to (95,000 trips/hr) ($1.10/trip) = $104,500/hr. If your goal as an administrator is to increase the total revenue collected from the bridge toll, you will need to know something about the price elasticity of demand for trips before deciding whether to raise the toll or to lower it.

This example illustrates one of the most important relationships in all of economics, namely, the one between price elasticity and total expenditure. The questions we want to be able to answer are of the form, "If the price of a product changes, how will the total amount spent on the product be affected?" and "Will more be spent on the product if we sell more units at a lower price or fewer units at a higher price?" In Figure 4-22, for example, we might want to know how total expenditures for shelter are affected when the price falls from $12/sq yd to $10/sq yd.

The total expenditure, R, at any quantity-price pair (Q, P) is given by the product

$$R = PQ. \qquad (4.4)$$

In Figure 4-22, the total expenditure at the original quantity-price pair is thus ($12/sq yd)(4 sq yd/wk) = $48/wk. Geometrically, it is the sum of the two shaded areas E and F. Following the price reduction, the new total expenditure is ($10/sq yd)(6 sq yd/wk) = $60/wk, which is the sum of the shaded areas F and G. These two total expenditures have in common the shaded area F. The

FIGURE 4-22
When price falls, people spend less on existing units (E). But they also buy more units (G). Here, G is larger than E, which means that total expenditure rises.

THE EFFECT ON TOTAL EXPENDITURE OF A REDUCTION IN PRICE

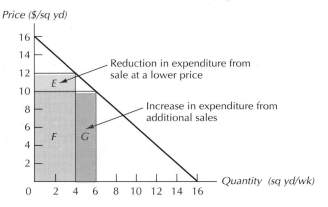

change in total expenditure is thus the difference in the two shaded areas E and G. The area E, which is ($2/sq yd)(4 sq yd/wk) = $8/wk, may be interpreted as the reduction in expenditure caused by selling the original 4 sq yd/wk at the new, lower price. G, in turn, is the increase in expenditure caused by the additional 2 sq yd/wk of sales. This area is given by ($10/sq yd)(2 sq yd/wk) = $20/wk. Whether total expenditure rises or falls thus boils down to whether the gain from additional sales exceeds the loss from lower prices. Here, the gain exceeds the loss by $12, so total expenditure rises by that amount following the price reduction.

If the change in price is small, we can say how total expenditure will move if we know the initial price elasticity of demand. Recall that one way of expressing price elasticity is the percentage change in quantity divided by the corresponding percentage change in price. If the absolute value of that quotient exceeds 1, we know that the percentage change in quantity is larger than the percentage change in price. And when that happens, the increase in expenditure from additional sales will always exceed the reduction from sales of existing units at the lower price. In Figure 4-22, note that the elasticity at the original price of $12 is 3.0, which confirms our earlier observation that the price reduction led to an increase in total expenditure. Suppose, on the contrary, that price elasticity is less than unity. Then the percentage change in quantity will be smaller than the corresponding percentage change in price, and the additional sales will not compensate for the reduction in expenditure from sales at a lower price. Here, a price reduction will lead to a reduction in total expenditure.

EXERCISE 4-6

For the demand curve in Figure 4-22, what is the price elasticity of demand when $P = \$4/sq$ yd? What will happen to total expenditure on shelter when price falls from $4/sq yd to $3/sq yd?

The general rule for small price reductions, then, is this: *A price reduction will increase total revenue if and only if the absolute value of the price elasticity of demand is greater than 1.* Parallel reasoning leads to an analogous rule for small price increases: *An increase in price will increase total revenue if and only if the absolute value of the price elasticity is less than 1.* These rules are summarized in the top panel of Figure 4-23, where the point M is the midpoint of the demand curve.

The relationship between elasticity and total expenditure is spelled out in greater detail in the relationship between the top and bottom panels of Figure 4-23. The top panel shows a straight-line demand curve. For each quantity, the bottom panel shows the corresponding total expenditure. As indicated in the bottom panel, total expenditure starts at zero when Q is zero and increases to its maximum value at the quantity corresponding to the midpoint of the demand curve (point M in the top panel). At that same quantity, price elasticity is unity. Beyond

FIGURE 4-23
When demand is elastic, total expenditure changes in the opposite direction from a change in price. When demand is inelastic, total expenditure and price both move in the same direction. At the midpoint of the demand curve (M), total expenditure is at a maximum.

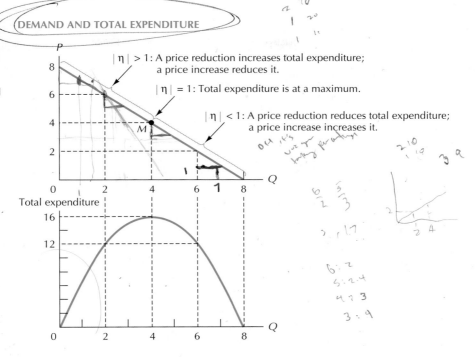

DEMAND AND TOTAL EXPENDITURE

$|\eta| > 1$: A price reduction increases total expenditure; a price increase reduces it.

$|\eta| = 1$: Total expenditure is at a maximum.

$|\eta| < 1$: A price reduction reduces total expenditure; a price increase increases it.

Total expenditure

that quantity, total expenditure declines with output, reaching zero at the quantity corresponding to the horizontal intercept of the demand curve.

*E*XAMPLE 4-6 *The market demand curve for bus rides in a small community is given by $P = 100 - (Q/10)$, where P is the fare per ride in cents and Q is the number of rides purchased each day. If the price is 50 cents/ride, how much revenue will the transit system collect each day? What is the price elasticity of demand for bus rides? If the system needs more revenue, should it raise or lower its price? How would your answers have differed if the initial price had been not 50 cents/ride but 75 cents?*

Total revenue for the bus system is equal to total expenditure by riders, which is the product PQ. First we solve for Q from the demand curve and get $Q = 1000 - 10P$. When P is 50 cents/ride, Q will be 500 rides/day and the resulting total revenue will be \$250/day. To compute the price elasticity of demand, we can use the formula $\eta = (P/Q)(1/\text{slope})$. Here the slope is $-\frac{1}{10}$, so $1/\text{slope} = -10$ (see footnote 3). P/Q takes the value $50/500 = \frac{1}{10}$. Price elasticity is thus the product $(-\frac{1}{10})(10) = -1$. With a price elasticity of unity, total revenue

[3]The slope here is from the formula $P = 100 - (Q/10)$.

attains its maximum value. If the bus company either raises or lowers its price, it will earn less than it does at the current price.

At a price of 50 cents, the company was operating at the midpoint of its demand curve. If the current price had instead been 75 cents, it would be operating above the midpoint. More precisely, it would be halfway between the midpoint and the vertical intercept (point K in Figure 4-24). Quantity would be only 250 rides/day, and price elasticity would have been −3 (computed, for example, by using the ratio of the line segments EK and KA). Operating at an elastic point on its demand curve, the company could increase total revenue by cutting its price.

Determinants of Price Elasticity of Demand

What factors govern the size of the price elasticity of demand for a product? To answer this question, it is useful to draw first on our earlier discussion of substitution and income effects, which suggests primary roles for the following factors:

- **Substitution possibilities.** The substitution effect of a price change tends to be small for goods for which there are no close substitutes. Consider, for example, the vaccine against rabies. People who have been bitten by rabid animals have nothing to substitute for this vaccine, and the demand for the vaccine will tend to be highly inelastic. We saw that the same was true for a good such as salt. But consider now the demand for a particular brand of salt, say, Morton's. Despite the advertising claims of salt manufacturers, one brand of salt is a more-or-less perfect substitute for any other. Because the substitution effect between specific brands of salt will be large, a rise in the price of one brand should sharply curtail the quantity of it demanded. In

FIGURE 4-24
At a price of 50 cents/ride, the bus company is maximizing its total revenues. At a price of 75 cents/ride, demand is elastic with respect to price, and so the company can increase its total revenues by cutting its price.

THE DEMAND FOR BUS RIDES

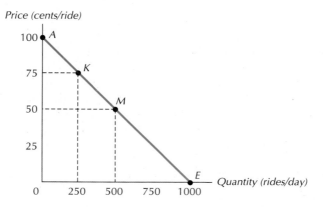

general, the absolute value of price elasticity will rise with the availability of attractive substitutes.

- **Budget share.** The larger the share of total expenditures accounted for by the product, the more important will be the income effect of a price change. Goods such as salt, rubber bands, cellophane wrap, and a host of others account for such small shares of total expenditures that, for most people, the income effects of a price change are likely to be negligible for these goods. For goods like housing and higher education, by contrast, the income effect of a price increase is likely to be large indeed. In general, the smaller the share of total expenditure accounted for by a good, the less elastic the demand will be.

- **Direction of income effect.** A factor closely related to the budget share is the direction—positive or negative—of its income effect. While the budget share tells us whether the income effect of a price change is likely to be large or small, the direction of the income effect tells us whether it will offset or reinforce the substitution effect. Thus, a normal good will tend to have a higher price elasticity than an inferior good, other things equal, because the income effect reinforces the substitution effect for a normal good but offsets it for an inferior good.

- **Time.** Our analysis of individual demand did not focus explicitly on the role of time. But it too has an important effect on people's responses to changes in prices. Consider again the oil price increases of the 1970s. One response of a consumer confronted with a higher price of gasoline is simply to drive less. But many auto trips are part of a larger pattern and cannot be abandoned, or even altered, very quickly. A person cannot simply stop going to work, for example. He can cut down on his daily commute by joining a car pool or by purchasing a house closer to where he works. He can also curtail his gasoline consumption by trading in his current car for one that gets better mileage. But all these steps take time, and as a result, the demand for gasoline will be much more elastic in the long run than in the short run.

The short- and long-run effects of a supply shift in the market for gasoline are contrasted in Figure 4-25. The initial equilibrium at *A* is disturbed by a supply reduction from *S* to *S'*. In the short run, the effect is for price to rise to $P_{SR} = \$1.40/\text{gal}$ and for quantity to fall to $Q_{SR} = 5$ million gal/day. The long-run demand curve is more elastic than the short-run demand curve. As consumers have more time to adjust, therefore, price effects tend to moderate while quantity effects tend to become more pronounced. Thus the new long-run equilibrium in Figure 4-25 occurs at a price of $P_{LR} = \$1.20/\text{gal}$ and a quantity of $Q_{LR} = 4$ million gal/day.

We see an extreme illustration of the difference between short- and long-run price elasticity values in the case of natural gas used in households. The price elasticity for this product is only -0.1 in the short run but a whopping -10.7 in

FIGURE 4-25
The more time people have, the more easily they can switch to substitute products. The price effects of supply alterations are therefore always more extreme in the short run than in the long run.

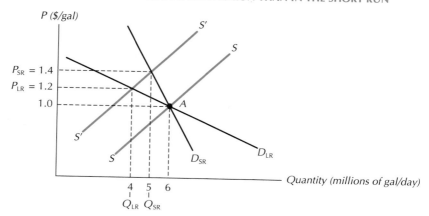

PRICE ELASTICITY IS GREATER IN THE LONG RUN THAN IN THE SHORT RUN

the long run![4] This difference reflects the fact that once a consumer has chosen appliances to heat and cook with, he or she is virtually locked in for the short run. People aren't going to cook their rice for only 10 minutes just because the price of natural gas has gone up. In the long run, however, consumers can and do switch between fuels when there are significant changes in relative prices.

The Dependence of Market Demand on Income

As we have seen, the quantity of a good demanded by any person depends not only on its price but also on the person's income. Since the market demand curve is the horizontal sum of individual demand curves, it too will naturally be influenced by consumer incomes. In some cases, the effect of income on market demand can be accounted for completely if we know only the average income level in the market. This would be the case, for example, if all consumers in the market were alike in terms of preference and all had the same incomes.

In practice, however, a given level of average income in a market will sometimes give rise to different market demands depending on how income is distributed among persons. A simple example helps make this point clear.

EXAMPLE 4-7 *Two consumers, A and B, are in a market for food. Their tastes are identical, and each has the same initial income level, $120/wk. If their individual Engel curves for food are as given by the locus EE in Figure 4-26, how will the market demand curve for food be affected if A's income goes down by 50 percent while B's goes up by 50 percent?*

---

[4]H. S. Houthakker and Lester Taylor, *Consumer Demand in the United States: Analyses and Projections,* 2d ed., Cambridge, MA: Harvard University Press, 1970.

FIGURE 4-26
When individual En-
gel curves take the
nonlinear form
shown, the increase
in food consumption
that results from a
given increase in in-
come will be smaller
than the reduction
in food consumption
that results from an
income reduction of
the same amount.

THE ENGEL CURVE FOR FOOD OF _A_ AND _B_

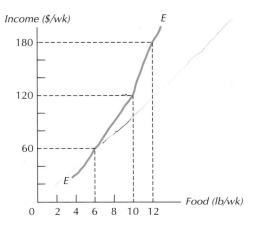

The nonlinear shape of the Engel curve pictured in Figure 4-26 is plausible considering that a consumer can eat only so much food. Beyond some point, increases in income should have no appreciable effect on the amount of food consumed. The implication of this relationship is that _B_'s new income ($180/wk) will produce an increase in his consumption (2 lb/wk) that is smaller than the reduction in _A_'s consumption (4 lb/wk) caused by _A_'s new income ($60/wk).

What does all this say about the corresponding individual and market demand curves for food? Identical incomes and tastes give rise to identical individual demand curves, denoted D_A and D_B in Figure 4-27. Adding D_A and D_B horizontally, we get the initial market demand curve, denoted D. The nature of the individual Engel curves tells us that _B_'s increase in demand will be smaller than _A_'s reduction in demand following the shift in income distribution. Thus, when we add the new individual demand curves (D'_A and D'_B), we get a new market demand for food (D') that lies to the left of the original demand curve.

The dependence of market demands on the distribution of income are important to bear in mind when the government considers policies to redistribute income. A policy that redistributes income from rich to poor, for example, is likely to increase demand for goods like food and reduce demand for luxury items, such as jewelry and foreign travel.

Demand in many other markets is relatively insensitive to variations in the distribution of income. In particular, the distribution of income is not likely to matter much in markets in which individual demands tend to move roughly in proportion to changes in income.

FIGURE 4-27
A given increase in income produces a small demand increase for *B* (*b*); an income reduction of the same size produces a larger demand reduction for *A* (*a*). The redistribution from *A* to *B* leaves average income unchanged but reduces market demand (*c*).

MARKET DEMAND SOMETIMES DEPENDS ON THE DISTRIBUTION OF INCOME

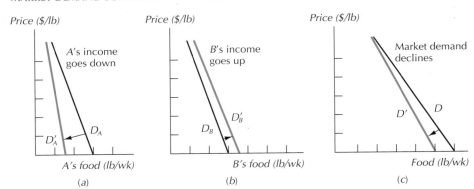

Income elasticity of demand The percentage change in the quantity of a good demanded that results from a 1 percent change in income.

Engel curves at the market level are schedules that relate the quantity demanded to the average income level in the market. The existence of a stable relationship between average income and quantity demanded is by no means assured for any given product because of the distributional complication just discussed. In particular, note that we cannot construct Engel curves at the market level by simply adding individual Engel curves horizontally. Horizontal summation works as a way of generating market demand curves from individual demand curves because all consumers in the market face the same market price for the product. But when incomes differ widely from one consumer to another, it makes no sense to hold income constant and add quantities across consumers.

As a practical matter, however, reasonably stable relationships between various aggregate income measures and quantities demanded in the market may nonetheless exist. Suppose such a relationship exists for the good *X* and is as pictured by the locus *EE* in Figure 4-28, where *Y* denotes the average income level of consumers in the market for *X*, and *Q* denotes the quantity of *X*. This locus is the market analog of the individual Engel curves discussed earlier.

If a good exhibits a stable Engel curve, we may then define its **income elasticity of demand**, a formal measure of the responsiveness of purchase decisions to variations in the average market income. Denoted ϵ, it is given by a formula analogous to the one for price elasticity:[5]

$$\epsilon = \frac{\Delta Q/Q}{\Delta Y/Y} \tag{4.5}$$

where *Y* denotes average market income and Δ*Y* is a small change therein.

Goods like food, for which a change in income produces a less than proportional change in the quantity demanded at any price, thus have an income elasticity less than 1. Such goods are called *necessities*, and their income elasticities

---

[5]In calculus terms, the corresponding formula is ϵ = (Y/Q) [dQ(Y)/dY].

FIGURE 4-28
The market Engel curve tells what quantities will be demanded at various average levels of income.

AN ENGEL CURVE AT THE MARKET LEVEL

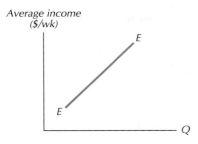

must lie in the interval $0 < \epsilon < 1$. Food is a commonly cited example. *Luxuries* are those goods for which $\epsilon > 1$. Common examples are expensive jewelry and foreign travel. Inferior goods are those for which $\epsilon < 0$. Goods for which $\epsilon = 1$ will have Engel curves that are straight lines through the origin, as pictured by the locus EE in Figure 4-29a. The market Engel curves for luxuries, necessities, and inferior goods, where these exist and are stable, are pictured in Figure 4-29b.

The income elasticity formula in Equation 4.5 is easier to interpret geometrically if we rewrite it as

FIGURE 4-29
(a) The good whose Engel curve is shown has an income elasticity of 1. For such goods, a given proportional change in income will produce the same proportional change in quantity demanded. Thus when average income doubles, from M_0 to $2M_0$, the quantity demanded also doubles, from Q_0 to $2Q_0$. (b) The Engel curves show that consumption increases more than in proportion to income for a luxury and less than in proportion to income for a necessity, and it falls with income for an inferior good.

ENGEL CURVES FOR DIFFERENT TYPES OF GOODS

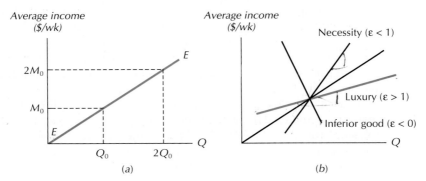

$$\epsilon = \frac{Y}{Q} \frac{\Delta Q}{\Delta Y}. \qquad (4.6)$$

The first factor on the right side of Equation 4.6 is simply the ratio of income to quantity at a point along the Engel curve. It is the slope of the line from the origin (a ray) to that point. The second factor is the reciprocal of the slope of the Engel curve at that point. If the slope of the ray exceeds the slope of the Engel curve, the product of these two factors must be greater than 1 (the luxury case). If the ray is less steep, ϵ will be less than 1 but still positive, provided the slope of the Engel curve is positive (the necessity case). Thus, in distinguishing between the Engel curves for necessities and luxuries, what counts is not the slopes of the Engel curves themselves but how they compare to the slopes of the corresponding rays. Finally, if the slope of the Engel curve is negative, ϵ must be less than zero (the inferior case).[6]

APPLICATION: FORECASTING ECONOMIC TRENDS

If the income elasticity of demand for every good and service were 1, the composition of GNP would be completely stable over time (assuming technology and relative prices remain unchanged). The same proportion would be devoted to food, travel, clothing, and indeed to every other consumption category.

As the entries in Table 4-5 show, however, the income elasticities of different consumption categories differ markedly. And therein lies one of the most important applications of the income elasticity concept, namely, forecasting the composition of future purchase patterns. Ever since the industrial revolution in the West, real purchasing power per capita has grown at roughly 2 percent per year. Our knowledge of income elasticity differences enables us to predict how consumption patterns in the next century will differ from the ones we see today.

Thus, a growing share of the consumer's budget will be devoted to goods like restaurant meals and automobiles, whereas ever smaller shares will go to tobacco, fuel, and electricity. And if the elasticity estimates are correct, the absolute amounts spent per person on margarine, pork products, and public transportation will be considerably smaller in the next century than they are today.

Cross-Price Elasticities of Demand

The quantity of a good purchased in the market depends not only on its price and consumer incomes but also on the prices of related goods. **Cross-price elasticity of demand** is the percentage change in the quantity demanded of

---

[6]Note that an inferior good also satisfies the definition of a necessity.

TABLE 4-5 INCOME ELASTICITIES OF DEMAND FOR SELECTED PRODUCTS*

Good or service	Income elasticity
Automobiles	2.46
Furniture	1.48
Restaurant meals	1.40
Water	1.02
Tobacco	0.64
Gasoline and oil	0.48
Electricity	0.20
Margarine	−0.20
Pork products	−0.20
Public transportation	−0.36

*These estimates come from H. S. Houthakker and Lester Taylor, *Consumer Demand in the United States: Analyses and Projections,* 2d ed., Cambridge, MA: Harvard University Press, 1970; L. Taylor and R. Halvorsen, "Energy Substitution in U.S. Manufacturing," *Review of Economics and Statistics,* November 1977; H. Wold and L. Jureen, *Demand Analysis,* New York: Wiley, 1953.

Cross-price elasticity of demand
The percentage change in the quantity of one good demanded that results from a 1 percent change in the price of the other good.

one good caused by a 1 percent change in the price of the other. More generally, for any two goods, X and Z, the cross-price elasticity of demand may be defined as follows:[7]

$$\eta_{XZ} = \frac{\Delta Q_X / Q_X}{\Delta P_Z / P_Z},$$ (4.7)

where ΔQ_X is a small change in Q_X, the quantity of X, and ΔP_Z is a small change in P_Z, the price of Z. η_{XZ} measures how the quantity demanded of X responds to a small change in the price of Z.

Unlike the elasticity of demand with respect to a good's own price (the *own-price elasticity*), which is never greater than zero, the cross-price elasticity may be either positive or negative. X and Z are defined as *complements* if $\eta_{XZ} < 0$. If $\eta_{XZ} > 0$, they are *substitutes*. Thus, a rise in the price of ham will reduce not only the quantity of ham demanded, but also, because ham and eggs are complements, the demand for eggs. A rise in the price of coffee, by contrast, will tend to increase the demand for tea. Estimates of the cross-price elasticity of demand for selected pairs of products are shown in Table 4-6 on the following page.

---

[7]In calculus terms, the corresponding expression is given by $\eta_{XZ} = (P_Z/Q_X)\,(dQ_X/dP_Z)$.

TABLE 4-6   **CROSS-PRICE ELASTICITIES FOR SELECTED PAIRS OF PRODUCTS***

Good or service	Good or service with price change	Cross-price elasticity
Butter	Margarine	+0.81
Margarine	Butter	+0.67
Natural gas	Fuel oil	+0.44
Beef	Pork	+0.28
Electricity	Natural gas	+0.20
Entertainment	Food	−0.72
Cereals	Fresh fish	−0.87

*From H. Wold and L. Jureen, *Demand Analysis*, New York: Wiley, 1953; L. Taylor and R. Halvorsen, "Energy Substitution in U.S. Manufacturing," *Review of Economics and Statistics,* November 1977; E. T. Fujii et al., "An Almost Ideal Demand System for Visitor Expenditures," *Journal of Transport Economics and Policy*, 19, May 1985, 161–171; and A. Deaton, "Estimation of Own- and Cross-Price Elasticities from Household Survey Data," *Journal of Econometrics*, 36, 1987: 7–30.

Exercise 4-7

Would the cross-price elasticity of demand be positive or negative for the following pairs of goods: (*a*) apples and oranges, (*b*) airline tickets and automobile tires, (*c*) computer hardware and software, (*d*) pens and paper, (*e*) pens and pencils?

Summary

Our focus in this chapter was on how individual and market demands respond to variations in prices and incomes. To generate a demand curve for an individual consumer for a specific good *X*, we first trace out the price-consumption curve in the standard indifference curve diagram. The PCC is the line of optimal bundles observed when the price of *X* varies, with both income and preferences held constant. We then take the relevant price-quantity pairs from the PCC and plot them in a separate diagram to get the individual demand curve.

The income analog to the PCC is the income-consumption curve, or ICC. It too is constructed using the standard indifference curve diagram. The ICC is the line of optimal bundles traced out when we vary the consumer's income, holding preferences and relative prices constant. The Engel curve is the income analog to the individual demand curve. We generate it by retrieving the relevant income-quantity pairs from the ICC and plotting them in a separate diagram.

Normal goods are those the consumer buys more of when income increases and inferior goods are those she buys less of as income rises.

The total effect of a price change can be decomposed into two separate effects: (1) the substitution effect, which denotes the change in the quantity demanded that results because the price change makes substitute goods seem either more or less attractive, and (2) the income effect, which denotes the change in quantity demanded that results from the change in real purchasing power caused by the price change. The substitution effect always moves in the opposite direction from the movement in price: price increases [reductions] always reduce [increase] the quantity demanded. For normal goods, the income effect also moves in the opposite direction from the price change, and thus tends to reinforce the substitution effect. For inferior goods, the income effect moves in the same direction as the price change, and thus tends to undercut the substitution effect.

The fact that the income and substitution effects move in opposite directions for inferior goods suggests the theoretical possibility of a Giffen good, one for which the total effect of a price increase is to increase the quantity demanded. There have been no documented examples of the existence of Giffen goods, and in this text we adopt the convention that all goods, unless otherwise stated, are demanded in smaller quantities at higher prices.

Goods for which purchase decisions respond most strongly to price tend to be ones that have large income and substitution effects that work in the same direction. For example, a normal good that occupies a large share of total expenditures and for which there are many direct or indirect substitutes will tend to respond sharply to changes in price. For many consumers, housing is a prime example of such a good. The goods least responsive to price changes will be those that account for very small budget shares and for which substitution possibilities are very limited. For most people, salt has both of these properties.

There are two equivalent techniques for generating market demand curves from individual demand curves. The first is to display the individual curves graphically and then add them horizontally. The second method is algebraic and proceeds by first solving the individual demand curves for the respective Q values, then adding those values, and finally solving the resulting sum for P.

A central analytical concept in demand theory is the price elasticity of demand, a measure of the responsiveness of purchase decisions to small changes in price. Formally, it is defined as the percentage change in quantity demanded that is caused by a 1 percent change in price. Goods for which the absolute value of elasticity exceeds 1 are said to be elastic; those for which it is less than 1, inelastic; and those for which it is equal to 1, unit elastic.

Another important relationship is the one between price elasticity and the effect of a price change on total expenditure. When demand is elastic, a price reduction will increase total expenditure; when inelastic, total expenditure falls when the price goes down. When demand is unit elastic, total expenditure is at a maximum.

The value of the price elasticity of demand for a good depends largely on four factors: substitutability, budget share, direction of income effect, and time. (1) *Substitutability.* The more easily consumers may switch to other goods, the more elastic demand will be. (2) *Budget share.* Goods that account for a large share of total expenditures will tend to have higher price elasticity. (3) *Direction of income effect.* Other factors the same, inferior goods will tend to be less elastic with respect to price than are normal goods. (4) *Time.* Habits and existing commitments limit the extent to which consumers can respond to price changes in the short run. Price elasticity of demand will tend to be larger, the more time consumers have to adapt.

Changes in the average income level in a market will generally shift the market demand curve. The income elasticity of demand for a good X is defined analogously to its price elasticity. It is the percentage change in quantity that results from a 1 percent change in income. Goods whose income elasticity of demand exceeds zero are called normal goods; those for which it is less than zero are called inferior; those for which it exceeds 1 are called luxuries; and those for which it is less than 1 are called necessities. For normal goods, an increase in income will shift market demand to the right; and for inferior goods, an increase in income will shift demand to the left. For some goods, the distribution of income, not just its average value, is an important determinant of market demand.

The cross-price elasticity of demand is a measure of the responsiveness of the quantity demanded of one good to a small change in the price of another. Formally, it is defined as the percentage change in the quantity demanded of one good that results from a 1 percent change in the price of the other. If the cross-price elasticity of demand for X with respect to the price of Z is positive, X and Z are substitutes; and if negative, they are complements. In remembering the formulas for the various elasticities—own price, cross-price, and income—many people find it helpful to note that each is the percentage change in an effect divided by the percentage change in the associated causal factor.

An appendix to this chapter (see the "For the Instructor" section at our Web site www.mhhe.com/economics/frank4) examines additional topics in demand theory, including the constant elasticity demand curve, arc elasticity, and the income-compensated demand curve.

Questions for Review

1. Why does the quantity of salt demanded tend to be unresponsive to changes in its price?

2. Why is the quantity of education demanded in private universities much more responsive than salt is to changes in price?

3. Draw Engel curves for both a normal good and an inferior good.

4. Give two examples of what are, for most students, inferior goods.

5. Can the price-consumption curve for a normal good ever be downward-sloping?

6. To get the market demand curve for a product, why do we add individual demand curves horizontally rather than vertically?

7. Summarize the relationship between price elasticity, changes in price, and changes in total expenditure.

8. Why don't we measure the responsiveness of demand to price changes by the slope of the demand curve instead of using the more complicated expression for elasticity?

9. For a straight-line demand curve, what is the price elasticity at the revenue maximizing point?

10. Do you think a college education at a specific school has a high or low price (tuition) elasticity of demand?

11. How can changes in the distribution of income across consumers affect the market demand for a product?

12. If you expected a long period of declining GNP, what kinds of companies would you choose to invest in?

13. *True or false:* For a budget spent entirely on two goods, an increase in the price of one will necessarily decrease the consumption of both, unless at least one of the goods is inferior. Explain.

14. Mike spends all his income on tennis balls and basketball tickets. His demand curve for tennis balls is elastic. *True or false:* If the price of tennis balls rises, he consumes more tickets. Explain.

15. *True or false:* If each individual in a market has a straight-line demand curve for a good, then the market demand curve for that good must also be a straight line. Explain.

16. Suppose your budget is spent entirely on two goods: bread and butter. If bread is an inferior good, can butter be inferior as well?

Problems

1. Sam spends $6/wk on orange juice and apple juice. Orange juice costs $2/cup while apple juice costs $1/cup. Sam views 1 cup of orange juice as a perfect substitute for 3 cups of apple juice. Find Sam's optimal consumption bundle of orange juice and apple juice each week. Suppose the price of apple juice rises to $2/cup, while the price of orange juice remains constant. How much additional income would Sam need to afford his original consumption bundle?

2. Bruce has the same income and faces the same prices as Sam, but he views 1 cup of orange juice as a perfect substitute for 1 cup of apple juice. Find Bruce's optimal consumption bundle. How much additional income would Bruce need to afford his original consumption bundle when the price of apple juice doubles?

3. Maureen has the same income and faces the same prices as Sam and Bruce, but Maureen views 1 cup of orange juice and 1 cup of apple juice as perfect complements. Find Maureen's optimal consumption bundle. How much additional income would Maureen need to afford her original consumption bundle when the price of apple juice doubles?

4. The market for lemonade has 10 potential consumers, each having an individual demand curve $P = 101 - 10Q_i$, where P is price in dollars per cup and Q_i is the number of cups demanded per week by the ith consumer. Find the market demand curve using algebra. Draw an individual demand curve and the market demand curve.

What is the quantity demanded by each consumer and in the market as a whole when lemonade is priced at $P = \$1/\text{cup}$?

5.   **a.** For a demand curve $P = 60 - 0.5Q$, find the elasticity at $P = 10$.
         b. If the demand curve shifts parallel to the right, what happens to the elasticity at $P = 10$?

6. Consider the demand curve $Q = 100 - 50P$.

   a. Draw the demand curve and indicate which portion of the curve is elastic, which portion is inelastic, and which portion is unit elastic.
   b. Without doing any additional calculation, state at which point of the curve expenditures on the goods are maximized, and then explain the logic behind your answer.

7. Suppose the demand for crossing the Golden Gate Bridge is given by $Q = 10{,}000 - 1000P$.

   a. If the toll (P) is $2, how much revenue is collected?
   b. What is the price elasticity of demand at this point?
   c. Could the bridge authorities increase their revenues by changing their price?
   d. The Red and White Lines, a ferry service that competes with the Golden Gate Bridge, began operating hovercrafts that made commuting by ferry much more convenient. How would this affect the elasticity of demand for trips across the Golden Gate Bridge?

8. Consumer expenditures on safety are thought to have a positive income elasticity. For example, as incomes rise, people tend to buy safer cars (large cars with side air bags), they are more likely to fly on trips rather than drive, they are more likely to get regular health tests, and they are more likely to get medical care for any health problems the tests reveal. Is safety a luxury or a necessity?

9. Professors Adams and Brown make up the entire demand side of the market for summer research assistants in the economics department. If Adams's demand curve is $P = 50 - 2Q_A$ and Brown's is $P = 50 - Q_B$, where Q_A and Q_B are the hours demanded by Adams and Brown, respectively, what is the market demand for research hours in the economics department?

10. Suppose that at a price of $400, 300 tickets are demanded to fly from Ithaca, New York, to Los Angeles, California. Now the price rises to $600, and 280 tickets are still demanded. Assuming the demand for tickets is linear, find the price elasticities at the quantity-price pairs (300, 400) and (280, 600).

11. The monthly market demand curve for calculators among engineering students is given by $P = 100 - Q$, where P is the price per calculator in dollars and Q is the number of calculators purchased per month. If the price is $30, how much revenue will calculator makers get each month? Find the price elasticity of demand for calculators. What should calculator makers do to increase revenue?

12. What price maximizes total expenditure along the demand curve $P = 27 - Q^2$?

13. A hot dog vendor faces a daily demand curve of $Q = 1800 - 15P$, where P is the price of a hot dog in cents and Q is the number of hot dogs purchased each day.

    a. If the vendor has been selling 300 hot dogs each day, how much revenue has he been collecting?

    b. What is the price elasticity of demand for hot dogs?

    c. The vendor decides that he wants to generate more revenue. Should he raise or lower the price of his hot dogs?

    d. At what price would he achieve maximum total revenue?

14. Rank the absolute values of the price elasticities of demand at the points A, B, C, D, and E on the following three demand curves.

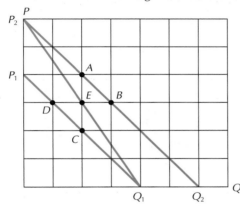

15. Draw the Engel curves for the following goods: food, Hawaiian vacations, cashews, Kmart brand sneakers ($4.99/pr).

16. Is the cross-price elasticity of demand positive or negative for the following pairs of items?

    a. Tennis rackets and tennis balls

    b. Peanut butter and jelly

    c. Hot dogs and hamburgers

complements are negative

subs are positive

*17. In 1981, X cost $3 and sold 400 units. That same year, a related good Y cost $10 and sold 200 units. In 1982, X still cost $3 but sold only 300 units, while Y rose in price to $12 and sold only 150 units. Other things the same, and assuming that the demand for X is a linear function of the price of Y, what was the cross-price elasticity of demand for X with respect to Y in 1981?

*18. Smith cannot tell the difference between rice and wheat and spends all her food budget of $24/wk on these foodstuffs. If rice costs $3/lb, draw Smith's price-consumption curve for wheat and the corresponding demand curve.

---

*Problems marked with an asterisk (*) are more difficult.

*19. Repeat the preceding problem on the assumption that rice and wheat are perfect, one-for-one complements.

*20. Suppose your local espresso bar makes the following offer: People who supply their own half-pint carton of milk get to buy a cup of cappuccino for only $1.50 instead of $2.50. Half-pint cartons of milk can be purchased in the adjacent convenience store for $0.50. In the wake of this offer, the quantity of cappuccino sold goes up by 60 percent and the convenience store's total revenue from sales of milk exactly doubles.

    a.   *True or false:* If there is a small, but significant, amount of hassle involved in supplying one's own milk, it follows that absolute value of the price elasticity of demand for cappuccino is 3. Explain.

    b.   *True or false:* It follows that demand for the convenience store's milk is elastic with respect to price. Explain.

Answers to In-Chapter Exercises

4-1. On Paula's original budget, B_0, she consumes at bundle A. On the new budget, B_1, she consumes at bundle D. (To say that D has 1.5 pr of bindings per year means that she consumes 3 pr of bindings every 2 yr.) The substitution effect of the price increase (the movement from A to C) is zero.

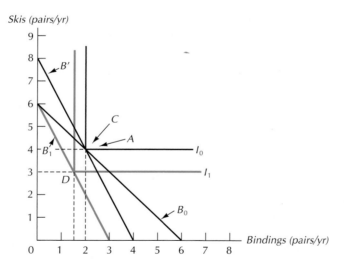

4-2. The income effect, substitution effect, and total effects are all zero because the price change does not alter Pam's optimal consumption bundle.

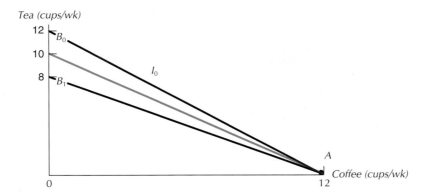

4-3. The formulas for D_1 and D_2 are $P = 16 - 2Q_1$ and $P = 8 - 2Q_2$, respectively. For the region in which $0 \leq P \leq 8$, we have $Q_1 = 8 - (P/2)$ and $Q_2 = 4 - (P/2)$. Adding, we get $Q_1 + Q_2 = Q = 12 - P$, for $0 \leq P \leq 8$. For $8 < P \leq 16$, the market demand curve is the same as D_1, namely, $P = 16 - 2Q$.

4-4. First, we need to rearrange the representative consumer demand curve $P = 120 - 60Q_i$ to have quantity alone on one side:

$$Q_i = 2 - \tfrac{1}{60}P.$$

Then we multiply by the number of consumers, $n = 30$,

$$Q = nQ_i = 30Q_i = 30 \left(2 - \tfrac{1}{60}P\right) = 60 - \tfrac{1}{2}P.$$

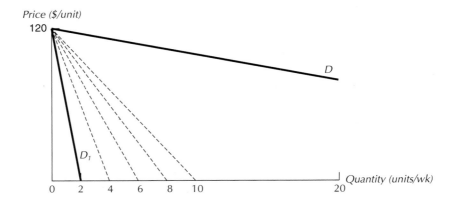

Finally, we rearrange the market demand curve $Q = 60 - \frac{1}{2}P$ to have price alone on one side, $P = 120 - 2Q$, to return to the slope-intercept form.

4-5. Since the slope of the demand curve is -1, we have $\eta = -P/Q$. At $P = 24$, $Q = 8$, and so $\eta = -P/Q = -\frac{24}{8} = -3$.

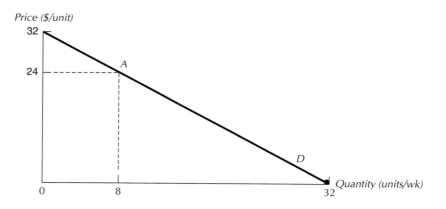

4-6. Elasticity when $P = \$4/\text{sq yd}$ is $\frac{1}{3}$, so a price reduction will reduce total expenditure. At $P = 4$, total expenditure is $\$48/\text{wk}$, which is more than the $\$39/\text{wk}$ of total expenditure at $P = 3$.

4-7. Substitutes, such as a, b, and e, have positive cross-price elasticity (an increase in price of one good raises quantity demanded of the other good). Complements, such as c and d, have negative cross-price elasticity (an increase in price of one good lowers quantity demanded of the other good).

CHAPTER

5

Applications of Rational Choice and Demand Theories

*I*n the 1996–1997 academic year, annual tuition and fees at Cornell University passed the $21,000 level. The university has a special policy whereby children of its faculty who attend Cornell are required to pay only fees, which come to approximately $2000/yr. Needless to say, this policy provides a strong financial incentive for faculty children to attend Cornell.

The faculty committee on compensation argued for many years that the university should extend the same tuition benefits to faculty children who attend universities other than Cornell. The traditional response of the university was that it could not afford to make such an offer. Under prodding by economists on the committee, however, the administration eventually took a tentative step in this direction by offering to pay one-third of tuition and fees at other universities. To its surprise, this new policy not only did not cost the university any money, it actually saved a great deal because the number of faculty children attending Cornell went down significantly once the new policy was in effect. This drop opened up an equivalent number of new positions in the freshman class, and because most of these were filled by tuition-paying students, Cornell came out ahead. Faculty families who received the new financial aid also came out ahead, and so did the new students who otherwise would have been unable to attend Cornell. The university had overlooked the opportunity cost of allocating positions to faculty children and had failed to anticipate that so many of them would be vacated because of the new offer.

Chapter Preview

Cornell's tuition policy provides yet another lesson that prices affect behavior. In this chapter we take up a variety of applications and examples involving the rational choice and demand theories developed in Chapters 3 and 4. We begin with two examples—a gasoline tax and school vouchers—that illustrate how the rational choice model can be used to shed light on important economic policy questions. Next we consider the concept of consumer surplus, a measure of how much the consumer benefits from being able to buy a given product at a given price. And we will see how the rational choice model can be used to examine how price and income changes affect welfare.

Next on our agenda is a sequence of case studies that illustrate the role of price elasticity in policy analysis. Here we examine the effect of a fare increase implemented by the Metropolitan Atlanta Rapid Transit Authority, the effect of liquor taxes on alcohol consumption by heavy drinkers, and the question of why National Football League tickets are priced so much higher than major league baseball tickets.

Finally, we consider how the rational choice model can be adapted to consider choices that have future consequences.

Using the Rational Choice Model to Answer Policy Questions

Many government policies affect not only the incomes that people receive but also the prices they pay for specific goods and services. Sometimes these effects are the deliberate aim of government policy, but on other occasions they are the unintended consequence of policies directed toward other ends. In either case, both common sense and our analysis of the rational choice model tell us that changes in incomes and prices can normally be expected to alter the ways in which consumers spend their money. And as we will see, the rational choice model can yield crucial insights not always available to policy analysts armed with only common sense.

APPLICATION: A GASOLINE TAX AND REBATE POLICY

As an interesting historical case in point, consider a policy proposal made during the Carter administration to use gasoline taxes to help limit the quantity demanded of gasoline, thereby making the United States less dependent on foreign sources of oil. One immediate objection to this proposal was that the resulting rise in gasoline prices would impose economic hardship on the poor. Anticipating this objection, the Carter administration proposed to ease the burden on the poor by using the proceeds of the gasoline tax to reduce the payroll tax (the tax used to finance Social Security). Critics immediately responded that to return the proceeds of the tax in this fashion would defeat its purpose. These critics believed that if consumers got the gas tax back in the form of higher paychecks, they would go on buying just as much gasoline as before. But as we will see, these critics were woefully in need of instruction in the basic principles of rational choice.

Let's consider an illustrative example. Suppose the current price of gasoline is $1.00/gal and a tax of $0.50/gal is imposed that results in a $0.50 rise in the price of gasoline.[1] Suppose also that a representative consumer is then given a lump-sum payroll tax rebate that happens to be exactly equal to the amount of gasoline tax he pays. (Here, the term "lump-sum" means that the rebate does not vary with the amount of gasoline he consumes.) True or false: This policy will have no effect on the amount of gasoline this consumer buys. Critics of the Carter proposal would of course answer "true," but once we translate the effects of the proposal into the familiar rational choice framework, we quickly see that the correct response is "false."

To analyze the tax-and-rebate combination, let's consider a consumer whose income is $150/wk. This consumer's budget constraint before the imposition of the tax is shown as B_1 in Figure 5-1.[2] On this budget constraint, he chooses bundle C, which contains 58 gal/wk of gasoline. His budget constraint with a

FIGURE 5-1
The tax rotates the original budget constraint from B_1 to B_2. The rebate shifts B_2 out to B_3. The rebate does not alter the fact that the tax makes gasoline 50% more expensive relative to all other goods. The consumer shown in the diagram responds by consuming 22 gal/wk less gasoline.

A GASOLINE TAX AND REBATE

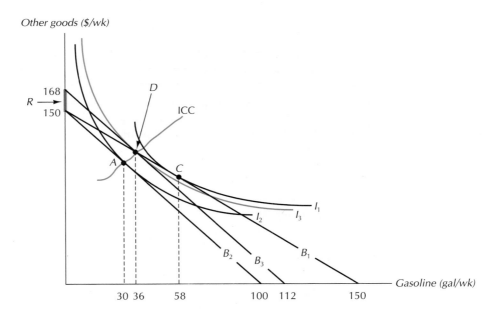

[1]Recall from Chapter 2 that the rise in equilibrium price will be exactly the same as the tax when the supply curve for gasoline is perfectly horizontal.
[2]The equation for B_1 is $Y = 150 - G$, for B_2 is $Y = 150 - 1.5G$, and for B_3 is $Y = 168 - 1.5G$, where G is gasoline (gal/wk) and Y is all other goods ($/wk).

$1.50/gal price of gasoline would be B_2 if he received no rebate. On this budget constraint, he would consume bundle A, which contains only 30 gal/wk of gasoline. But how do we find the budget constraint that corresponds to a rebate equal to the amount collected from him in gasoline taxes?

The first step is to note that for any given quantity of gasoline consumed, the vertical distance between budget constraints B_1 and B_2 corresponds to the total amount of tax paid on that amount of gasoline. Thus, at 1 gal/wk of gasoline, the vertical distance between B_1 and B_2 would be $0.50; at 2 gal/wk, it would be $1.00; and so on.

Our next step is to trace out how the consumer's consumption will vary as a function of the size of the rebate. To do this, note that a rebate is like income from any other source, so what we really want to do is to trace out how the consumer responds to changes in income. As we saw in Chapter 4, the appropriate tool for this task is the income-consumption curve, or ICC. Accordingly, we construct the ICC through bundle A, as shown in Figure 5-1.

Now look at bundle D, the point where the ICC through A intersects the original budget constraint B_1. D is the equilibrium bundle on the budget constraint labeled B_3, where the price of gasoline is $1.50/gal and the consumer has $(150 + R)/wk = $168/wk of income. This means that if we give the consumer a rebate of $R = $18/wk, he will consume bundle D and pay exactly $18/wk in gasoline taxes. Note, however, that D lies well to the left of the original bundle C, which means that, despite the rebate, the consumer substantially curtails his gasoline consumption. If gasoline is a normal good, the effect of the rebate is to offset partially the income effect of the price increase. It does nothing to alter the substitution effect.

In the end, the Carter administration's tax-and-rebate proposal was never implemented, largely because of the objections of critics who lacked the economic knowledge to understand it. And as a result, the United States remains dangerously dependent on foreign oil more than 25 years after Carter left office.

APPLICATION: SCHOOL VOUCHERS

In recent years, there has been much discussion of the need to improve the quality of elementary and secondary education in the United States. Many policy analysts have recommended that this improvement be accomplished by introducing more competition into the market for educational services. To this end there have been proposals that each family be given a voucher that could be used toward the tuition at any school of the family's choosing.

Such proposals contrast with the current system in most school districts, under which all families are required to pay school taxes and are then entitled to "free" tuition at the nearest public school. Under the current system, families who choose to go to private schools do not receive a refund on their school taxes. Critics of the current system complain that because tuition-charging private schools are unable to compete effectively with free public schools, public schools face little pressure to perform.

Setting aside the question of whether a voucher system would lead ultimately to higher educational quality, let us examine the likely effect of vouchers on the overall level of resources devoted to education. We can use the rational choice model to examine the educational choice confronting a representative family.

For simplicity, suppose that the quantity of education measured in terms of classroom-hours per year is fixed, and that when we speak of spending more on education, we mean not buying more hours of education but buying education of higher quality. Suppose the current tax system charges each family P_e of tax for 1 unit of public education, whether or not the family uses it, where "1 unit" is defined as a year's worth of education of the quality currently offered in the public schools. If it does not send its child to public school, the family has the option to purchase 1 or more units of education at a private school, also at the price of P_e per unit. For example, to buy 1.2 units of education at a private school would mean to purchase education of 20 percent higher quality than is currently offered in the public schools. Families are required by law to provide their child with at least 1 unit of education, public or private.

Given these values, we can now derive the current budget constraint for education and other goods for a representative family whose pretax income is Y. If there were no taxes and no public schools, the family's budget constraint would be the line labeled ABD in Figure 5-2. But because each family must pay P_e in school taxes, the vertical intercept of the current budget constraint is not Y but $Y - P_e$. Since 1 unit of public education is free, the family's budget constraint is horizontal out to 1 unit. If the family then wants to buy more than 1 unit of education under the current system, it must withdraw its child from the public school and enroll her in a private school at an additional cost of P_e per unit. This explains why the current budget constraint drops vertically by P_e at 1 unit of education. Thereafter the budget constraint continues to slope downward at the rate of P_e per unit. Thus the budget constraint for a family considering how much education to purchase is denoted by $A'BCE$ in Figure 5-2.

FIGURE 5-2
The family has a pretax income of Y, out of which it must pay P_e in school taxes. It is entitled to 1 unit of tuition-free public education. In lieu of public education, it may purchase at least 1 unit of private education at the price of P_e per unit. Its budget constraint is thus $A'BCE$, and its optimal bundle is B, which contains 1 unit of public education.

EDUCATIONAL CHOICE UNDER THE CURRENT SYSTEM

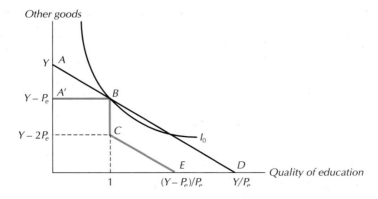

Note in Figure 5-2 that the nonlinear budget constraint makes a tangency solution unlikely for a family with indifference curves like the one shown. For such a family, the optimal bundle is, in effect, a corner solution in which exactly 1 unit of public education is chosen.

Let us now contrast this result with what would happen under a voucher system. Under that system, families again pay P_e in school tax, then get a voucher worth P_e, which may be used toward the purchase of either public or private education. Under the voucher system, the law still requires that families provide at least 1 unit of education for their children. The budget constraint under the voucher system will thus be given by $A'BD$ in Figure 5-3.

Compare Figures 5-2 and 5-3. Note that the principal difference produced by the voucher system is to eliminate the discontinuity at point B of the budget constraint. Parents no longer have to forfeit their school taxes when they switch from public to private schools; they can purchase small increments in education beyond 1 unit without essentially having to "pay double." And indeed, the family in Figure 5-3 responds by choosing bundle G, which contains more than 1 unit of education. The analysis thus suggests that one effect of switching to a voucher system will be to increase the level of resources spent on educational services.

In times of budgetary stress, many people will be tempted to conclude that we should avoid any policy that will require additional resources. For these people, several cautionary notes should be stressed. First, our analysis did not take into account the possibility that competition among schools might make schools more efficient in their production of educational services. Thus, while parents might indeed choose to purchase more units of education under a voucher scheme, competition might drive the cost per unit down, making the net effect on expenditures hard to determine. Second, any additional resources devoted to education as a result of the voucher system would come from parents directly, not from governments. And it is by no means clear that a goal of public policy should be to prevent parents from spending more on education and less on other goods. Finally, a more complete analysis should consider the effect of additional

FIGURE 5-3
Unlike the current system, the voucher system allows parents to provide small increases above 1 unit of education at the price of P_e per unit. The budget constraint is now $A'BD$, and the family shown now chooses bundle G, which contains more than 1 unit of education.

EDUCATIONAL CHOICE UNDER A VOUCHER SYSTEM

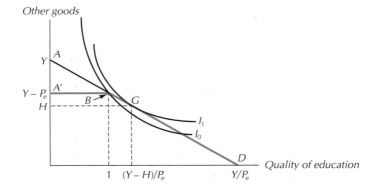

education on economic productivity. After all, any increase in productivity that results from additional education could of course be used to offset the cost of the resources used to produce that education. In sum, our analysis in this example focuses on only one part of a much larger picture. But it is an important part, one that policymakers cannot afford to neglect.

Consumer Surplus

Consumer surplus A dollar measure of the extent to which a consumer benefits from participating in a transaction.

When exchange takes places voluntarily, economists generally assume that it makes all participants better off. Otherwise they would not have engaged in the exchange. It is often useful to have a dollar measure of the extent to which people benefit from a transaction. Such a measure, called *consumer surplus,* is particularly important for the purpose of evaluating potential government programs. It is relatively straightforward to measure the costs of, say, building a new road. But an intelligent decision about whether to build the road cannot be made without a reliable estimate of the extent to which consumers will benefit from it.

USING DEMAND CURVES TO MEASURE CONSUMER SURPLUS

The easiest way to measure consumer surplus involves the consumer's demand curve for the product. In both panels in Figure 5-4, the line labeled D represents an individual's demand curve for shelter, which sells for a market price of $3/sq yd. In panel (*a*), note that the most the consumer would have been willing

FIGURE 5-4
(a) The height of the demand curve at any quantity measures the most the consumer would be willing to pay for an extra unit of shelter. That amount minus the market price is the surplus he gets from consuming the last unit. (b) The total consumer surplus is the shaded area between the demand curve and the market price.

THE DEMAND CURVE MEASURE OF CONSUMER SURPLUS

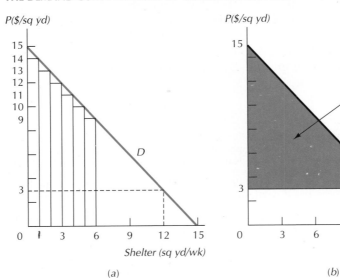

(a)

(b)

to pay for the first square yard of shelter is $14. Since shelter costs only $3/sq yd, this means that he obtains a surplus of $11 from his purchase of the first square yard of shelter each week. The most he would be willing to pay for the second square yard of shelter is $13, so his surplus from the purchase of that unit will be smaller, only $10. His surplus from the third unit is smaller still, at $9. For shelter or any other perfectly divisible good, the height of the individual's demand curve at any quantity represents the most the consumer would pay for an additional unit of it.[3] In this example, if we subtract the purchase price of $3/sq yd from that value and sum the resulting differences for every quantity out to 12 sq yd/wk, we get roughly the shaded area shown in panel (b). (If we use infinitesimal increments along the horizontal axis, we get exactly the shaded area.) This shaded area represents the individual's consumer surplus from the purchase of 12 sq yd/wk of shelter.

EXAMPLE 5-1   *An individual's demand curve for gasoline is given by P = 10 − Q, where P is the price of gasoline ($/gal), and Q is the quantity she consumes (gal/wk). If the individual's weekly income is $1000 and the current price of gasoline is $2/gal, by how much will her consumer surplus decline if an oil import restriction raises the price to $3/gal?*

At a price of $2/gal, she consumes only 8 gallons of gasoline per week, which amounts to less than 2 percent of her income. The income effect of the price increase is therefore likely to be insignificant, so we can use the demand curve approximation to measure her consumer surplus before and after the price increase. (See footnote 3.) Figure 5-5 displays her demand curve. Her consumer surplus at the price of $2/gal is given by the area of the triangle AEF in Figure 5-5, $CS = \frac{1}{2}(10 − 2)8 = \$32/wk$. Following the price increase, her consumption falls from 8 to 7 gal/wk, and her surplus shrinks to the area of the triangle ACD, $CS' = \frac{1}{2}(10 − 3)7 = \$24.50/wk$. Her loss in consumer surplus is the difference between these two areas, which is the area of the trapezoid $DCEF$, the shaded region in Figure 5-5. This area is equal to $CS − CS' = 32 − 24.5 = \$7.50/wk$.

---

[3]These statements about willingness-to-pay are literally true only if the demand curve we are talking about is an income-compensated demand curve like the one discussed in the appendix to Chapter 4 (see the "For the Instructor" section at our Web site www.mhhe.com/economics/frank4). If the demand curve shown were an ordinary demand curve of the sort we have been using, it would tell us that the consumer would be willing to buy 1 unit at a price of $14, 2 units at a price of $13, and so on. From this it would not be strictly correct to conclude that, having already paid $14 for the first unit, the consumer would then be willing to spend an *additional* $13 for the second unit. If the income effect of the demand for the good is positive, the fact that the consumer is now $14 poorer than before means that he would be willing to pay somewhat less than $13 for the second unit. But since income effects for most goods are small, it will generally be an acceptable approximation to measure consumer surplus using the ordinary demand curve. In a widely cited article, Robert Willig has argued that the demand curve method will almost always yield an acceptable approximation of the true value of consumer benefits. See R. Willig, "Consumer Surplus without Apology," *American Economic Review*, 66, 1976: 589–597.

FIGURE 5-5
At a price of $2/gal, consumer surplus is given by the area of triangle *AEF*. At a price of $3/gal, consumer surplus shrinks to the area of triangle *ACD*. The loss in consumer surplus is the difference in these two areas, which is the area of the shaded region.

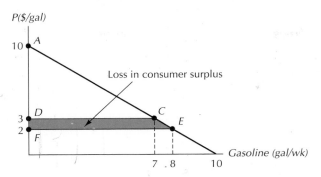

THE LOSS IN CONSUMER SURPLUS FROM AN OIL PRICE INCREASE

EXERCISE 5-1

By how much would consumer surplus shrink in Example 5-1 if the price of gasoline rose from $3/gal to $4/gal?

APPLICATION: TWO-PART PRICING

Economic reasoning suggests that a voluntary exchange will take place between a buyer and a seller if and only if that exchange makes both parties better off. On the buyer's side, we may say that willingness to exchange depends on the buyer's expectation of receiving consumer surplus from the transaction.

Economic theory does not tell us very much about how the gains from exchange will be divided between the buyer and the seller. Sometimes the buyer will be in an advantageous bargaining position, enabling her to capture most of the benefits. Other times the buyer's options will be more limited, and in these cases, her consumer surplus is likely to be smaller. Indeed, as the following example illustrates, the seller can sometimes design a pricing strategy that captures *all* the consumer surplus.

EXAMPLE 5-2 *Why do some tennis clubs have an annual membership charge in addition to their hourly court fees?*

A suburban tennis club rents its courts for $25 per person per hour. John's demand curve for court time, $P = 50 - \frac{1}{4}Q$, measured in hours per year, is given in Figure 5-6. Assuming there were no other tennis clubs in town, what is the maximum annual membership fee John would be willing to pay for the right to buy court time for $25/hr?

FIGURE 5-6
At a price of $25/hr,
John receives
$1250/yr (the
shaded area) of con-
sumer surplus from
renting court time.
The maximum an-
nual membership
fee the club can
charge is $1250.

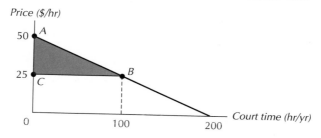

AN INDIVIDUAL DEMAND CURVE FOR TENNIS COURT TIME

The answer to this question is the consumer surplus John receives from being able to buy as much court time as he wants at the $25/hr price. This is equal to the area of triangle *ABC* in Figure 5-6, which is $CS = \frac{1}{2}(50 - 25)100 = \$1250/\text{yr}$. If the club charged a fee higher than that, John would be better off not renting any court time at all.

EXERCISE 5-2

In Example 5-2, how much would the maximum annual membership fee be if the club charged only $20/hr for court time?

Example 5-2 sheds light on many of the pricing practices we observe throughout the economy. Many amusement parks, for example, charge a fixed admission fee in addition to a charge for each ride. Many telephone companies charge a fixed monthly fee in addition to charges based on actual calls made. And some shopping clubs charge a fixed membership fee for the right to buy items carried in their stores or catalogs. Pricing schemes such as these are often called *two-part pricing*. Their effect is to transfer a portion of the consumer surplus from the buyer of the product to the seller.

Overall Welfare Comparisons

The concept of consumer surplus helps us identify the benefits (or costs) of changes that occur in particular markets. Often we will want to assess whether consumers are better or worse off as a result of changes not just in one market but in many. Here too our model of rational choice lets us draw a variety of useful inferences. Consider the following example.

EXAMPLE 5-3 *Jones spends all his income on two goods: X and Y. The prices he paid and the quantities he consumed last year are as follows: $P_X = 10$, $X = 50$, $P_Y = 20$, and $Y = 25$. This year P_X and P_Y are both 10, and Jones's income is \$750. Assuming his tastes do not change, in which year was Jones better off, last year or this?*

assume!

To answer this question, it is helpful to begin by comparing Jones's budget constraints for the 2 years. To do this, we note first that his income last year was equal to what he spent, namely, $P_X X + P_Y Y = 1000$. For the prices given, we thus have the budget constraints shown in Figure 5-7a.

In Figure 5-7a, we see that Jones's budget constraint for this year contains the very same bundle he bought last year. Since his tastes have not changed, this tells us he cannot be worse off this year than last. After all, he can still afford to buy the same bundle as before. But our standard assumptions about preference orderings enable us to draw an even stronger inference. In particular, if his indifference curves have the usual convex shape, we know that an indifference curve—call it I_0—was tangent to last year's budget constraint at the point A in Figure 5-7b. We also know that this year's budget constraint is steeper than last year's, which tells us that part of I_0 must lie inside this year's budget triangle. On I_0, bundle A is equally preferred to bundle C. And because more is better, we know that D is preferred to C. It thus follows that D is preferred to A, and so we know that Jones was able to purchase a bundle of goods this year that he likes better than the one he bought last year. It follows that Jones was better off this year than last.

FIGURE 5-7
(a) If the consumer's budget constraint for this year contains the same bundle he bought last year (bundle A), he will be at least as well off this year as last. (b) If, in addition, relative prices are different in the two years, he will necessarily be able to buy a better bundle this year (bundle D).

BUDGET CONSTRAINTS FOR 2 YEARS

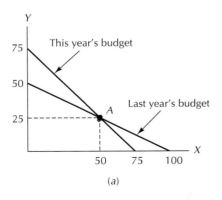

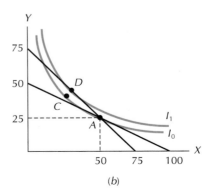

EXERCISE 5-3

Jones spends all his income on two goods: X and Y. The prices he paid and the quantities he consumed last year are as follows: $Px = 15$, $X = 20$, $P_y = 25$, and $Y = 30$. This year the prices have changed ($Px = 15$ and $P_y = 20$), and Jones's income is now $900. Assuming his tastes have not changed, in which year was Jones better off, last year or this?

APPLICATION: THE WELFARE EFFECTS OF CHANGES IN HOUSING PRICES

Consider the following two scenarios:

1. You have just purchased a house for $200,000. The very next day, the prices of all houses, including the one you just bought, double.
2. You have just purchased a house for $200,000. The very next day, the prices of all houses, including the one you just bought, fall by half.

In each case, how does the price change affect your welfare? (Are you better off before the price change or after?)

I recently asked a class of first-year graduate students in economics these questions. The overwhelming majority responded that you are better off as a result of the price increase in scenario 1, but worse off as a result of the price drop in scenario 2. Although most students seemed very confident about these two responses, only one turns out to be correct.

To see why, let us first consider the case in which all housing prices double. Suppose your total wealth just before purchasing your house was $400,000. Let the size of your current house correspond to 1 unit of housing and let the price of other goods (the composite good) be 1. Your original budget constraint under scenario 1 will then correspond to the line labeled B_1 in Figure 5-8. Its vertical intercept, $400,000, is the maximum amount you could have spent on other goods. Its horizontal intercept, 2 units of housing, corresponds to the maximum quantity of housing you could have bought (that is, a house twice as large as your current house). On B_1, the equilibrium at A represents your original purchase. At A, you have 1 unit of housing and $200,000 left for other goods.

After the price of your house doubles, your budget constraint becomes the line labeled B_2 in Figure 5-8. To calculate the vertical intercept of B_2, note that your current house can now be sold for $400,000, which, when added to the $200,000 you had left over after buying your house, yields a maximum of $600,000 available for other goods. The horizontal intercept of B_2 tells us that when the price of housing doubles to $400,000/unit, your $600,000 will buy a maximum of only 1.5 units of housing. Note finally that on B_2 your optimal bun-

FIGURE 5-8
When the price of
housing doubles,
your budget con-
straint becomes B_2,
which also contains
your original bundle
A. Because C, the
optimal bundle on
B_2, lies on a higher
indifference curve
than A, the effect of
the housing price in-
crease is to make
you better off.

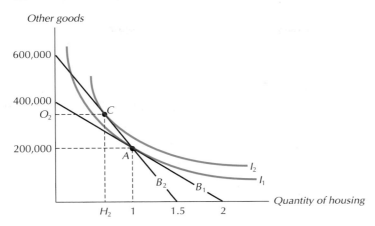

RISING HOUSING PRICES AND THE WELFARE OF HOMEOWNERS

dle is C, which contains $H_2 < 1$ units of housing and $O_2 > \$200,000$ worth of other goods. And since bundle C lies on a higher indifference curve than bundle A, you are better off than before the price increase.

Not surprisingly, when the price of housing goes up, your best response is to buy fewer units of housing and more units of other goods. Note that you are insulated from the harm of the income effect of the price increase because the price increase makes the house you own more valuable.

So far, so good. Now let us consider what for many students was the more troubling case—namely, scenario 2, in which housing prices fall by half. Again adopting the units of measure used in scenario 1, your budget constraint following the fall in housing prices is the line labeled B_3 in Figure 5-9. To get its vertical intercept, note that sale of your current house will now yield only $\$100,000$, which, when added to the $\$200,000$ you already have, makes a maximum of $\$300,000$ available for the purchase of other goods. To calculate the horizontal intercept of B_3, note that when the price of housing falls to $\$100,000$, your $\$300,000$ will now buy a maximum of 3 units of housing. Given the budget constraint B_3, the best affordable bundle is the one labeled D, which contains $H_3 > 1$ units of housing and $O_3 < 200,000$ units of other goods. As in scenario 1, the effect of the relative price change is again to move you to a higher indifference curve. This time, however, your direction of substitution is the opposite of the one in scenario 1: Because housing is now cheaper than before, you respond by purchasing more units of housing and fewer units of other goods.

In each scenario, note that your new budget constraint contains your original bundle, which means that you have to be at least as well off after the price change as before. Note also that in each case the change in relative prices means that your new budget constraint contains bundles which lie beyond your original indifference curve, making it possible to achieve a better outcome in each scenario.

FIGURE 5-9
When the price of
housing falls by half,
your budget con-
straint becomes B_3,
which also contains
your original bundle
A. Because D, the
optimal bundle on
B_3, lies on a higher
indifference curve
than A, the effect of
the housing price
drop is to make you
better off.

FALLING HOUSING PRICES AND THE WELFARE OF HOMEOWNERS

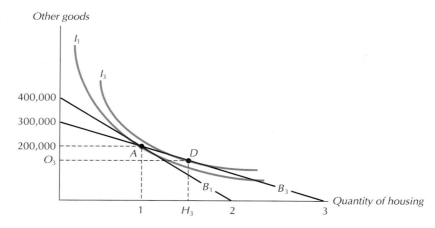

APPLICATION: A BIAS IN THE CONSUMER PRICE INDEX

The consumer price index (CPI) measures changes in the "cost of living," the amount a consumer must spend to maintain a given standard of living. Published each month by the Bureau of Labor Statistics, the CPI is calculated by first computing the cost of a representative bundle of goods and services during a reference period and then dividing that cost into the current cost of the same bundle. Thus, if it cost $100 to buy the representative bundle in the reference period and $150 to buy the same bundle today, the CPI would be 1.5. Announcing this figure, government spokespersons would explain that it meant the cost of living had increased by 50 percent compared to the reference period.

What the CPI fails to take into account, however, is that when the prices of different goods rise by different proportions, consumers do not generally buy the same bundle of goods they used to buy. Instead, the typical pattern is to substitute away from those goods whose prices have risen the most. By reallocating their budgets in this fashion, consumers are able to escape at least part of the harmful effects of price increases. Because the CPI fails to take substitution into account, it tends to overstate increases in the cost of living.

A simple example using the rational choice model makes this point unmistakably clear. Suppose the only goods in the economy were rice and wheat and that the representative consumer consumed 20 lb/mo of each in the reference period. If rice and wheat each cost $1/lb in the reference period, what will be the CPI in the current period if rice now costs $2/lb and wheat costs $3/lb? The cost of the reference period bundle at reference period prices was $40, while at current prices the same bundle now costs $100. The CPI thus takes the value of

FIGURE 5-10
For this consumer, rice and wheat are perfect substitutes. When the price of each was $1/lb, she bought 20 lb/mo of each in the reference period, for a total expenditure of $40/mo. If the current prices of rice and wheat are $2/lb and $3/lb, respectively, the expenditure required to buy the original bundle is $100/mo. The CPI is the ratio of these two expenditures, $100/$40 = 2.5. But the consumer can attain her original indifference curve, I_0, by buying bundle C, which costs only $80 at current prices. The cost of maintaining the original level of satisfaction has thus risen by a factor of only 2.0.

THE BIAS INHERENT IN THE CONSUMER PRICE INDEX

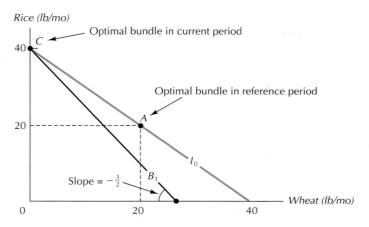

$100/$40 = 2.5. But is it really correct to say that the cost of living is now 2.5 times what it was?

To consider an extreme case, suppose our representative consumer regarded rice and wheat as perfect one-for-one substitutes, meaning that her indifference curves are negatively sloped 45° lines. In Figure 5-10, her original bundle is denoted as *A* and her original indifference curve (which coincides exactly with her original budget constraint) is labeled I_0. Now suppose we ask, how much income would she need in the current period to achieve the same level of satisfaction she achieved in the reference period? At the new prices, the slope of her budget constraint is no longer −1, but −3/2. With a budget constraint with this new slope, she could reach her original indifference curve most cheaply by buying the bundle labeled *C* in Figure 5-10. And since the cost of *C* at current prices is only $80, we can say that the cost of maintaining the original level of satisfaction has gone up by a factor of only 2.0, not 2.5.

In general, we can say that the extent to which the CPI overstates the cost of living will go up as substitution possibilities increase. The bias will also be larger when there are greater differences in the rates of increase of different prices.

QUALITY CHANGE: ANOTHER BIAS IN THE CPI?

Gathering data on the prices of goods and services might seem like a straightforward task. In practice, however, it is complicated by the existence of discounts, rebates, and other promotional offers in which the actual transaction price may be substantially different from the official list price.

Yet important as they are, accurate price data are not sufficient for estimating changes in the cost of living. We must also account for changes in the quality of what we buy. And this, unfortunately, turns out to be a far more complicated task than measuring changes in prices.

A brief look at the automobile industry illustrates the difficulty. The U.S. Department of Commerce reported that the average price paid for a new vehicle in 1994 was $19,675, a 5.1 percent increase over 1993, and a 72.8 percent increase since 1984.[4] During that same 10-year span, the CPI rose only 42.6 percent. Does this mean that the prices of cars have risen much more rapidly than those of other goods and services? Not necessarily. After all, recently produced cars contain many features not found on earlier models. For example, whereas approximately 90 percent of cars sold in the United States in 1994 came equipped with air bags and about 40 percent with antilock brakes, virtually none had these features in 1984. Convenience items like rear window defrosters and power windows, once confined to luxury cars, rose more than 50 percent during the same decade.

The Department of Commerce now calculates a special automotive CPI, which deducts the cost of such additional features in an effort to measure changes in the prices of comparably equipped cars. This index rose only 32.2 percent between 1984 and 1994—or about 10 percent *less* than the overall CPI.

Although these adjustments obviously help, they capture only a small part of the automobile quality changes that have been occurring in recent years. For example, the automotive CPI made no allowance for the fact that 1995 cars had achieved a 40 percent reduction in hydrocarbon emissions and a 60 percent reduction in oxides of nitrogen relative to 1984 cars. Nor did the index allow for the fact that cars are much more reliable, crashworthy, and corrosion resistant than they were a decade ago.

The pace of auto quality improvement is vividly illustrated by a comparison of the 1995 Honda Civic DX sedan—one of the company's smallest and cheapest cars during that model year—to Honda's top-of-the-line Accord sedan from 1982. Besides having a bevy of safety features not found on the older Accord, the '95 Civic had a larger interior; a quieter, cleaner-burning, yet more powerful engine (102 horsepower versus 75); better tires and brakes; and a much more sophisticated suspension. The '95 Civic accelerated from 0 to 60 mph in 9.1 seconds, compared to 12.2 seconds for the '82 Accord; the '95 Civic got 40 miles per gallon on the highway, while the '82 Accord got only 32. Whereas the '95 Civic's finish will survive six northern winters in near-showroom condition, similar exposure left the '82 Accord riddled with rust. The '82 Accord had a sticker price of $8995, but since it was in short supply, many dealers sold it for about $10,000. The '95 Civic had a sticker price of $12,360, and most dealers sold it at a substantial discount. So even with the passage of 13 years, the nominal dollar trans-

---

[4]The data in this section are drawn from Csaba Csere, "Do Cars Cost Too Much, Or Do We Just Like Costly Cars?," *Car and Driver,* June 1995, p. 9.

action price was not much higher for the Civic than for the older Accord. The '95 Civic's sticker price, adjusted for changes in the overall CPI, translates into $8852 in 1982 dollars—in effect, a much better car for less money.

If the Civic-Accord comparison is representative, it seems that the government's attempts to adjust for automobile quality improvements have fallen short. With the growth of global competition, quality has been improving rapidly not just in automobiles but in other goods and services as well. And we may be sure that, as in the auto industry, many of the relevant changes will have escaped the Department of Commerce's notice.

Failure to account fully for quality of improvements has the same effect as failure to account for substitution. Both cause the official cost-of-living index to overstate the true increase in prices.

The CPI has extremely important implications for the federal budget deficit, for this is the index used to determine the cost-of-living adjustments received by Social Security recipients and beneficiaries of a host of other government programs. Even a slight upward bias in the CPI can swell the budget deficit by many billions of dollars. For those who wish to pursue this topic further, price indexes are taken up in greater detail in the appendix to this chapter, which can be found in the "For the Instructor" section at our Web site www.mhhe.com/ecomomics/frank4.

Using Price Elasticity of Demand

In the sphere of applied economic analysis, few tools are more important than the concept of price elasticity of demand. In this section we examine applications of this concept in three very different settings.

APPLICATION: THE MARTA FARE INCREASE

To cover a rising budget deficit in 1987, the Metropolitan Atlanta Rapid Transport Authority raised its basic fare from 60 to 75 cents/ride. In the 2 months following the fare increase, total system revenues rose 18.3 percent in comparison with the same period a year earlier.[5] Assuming a linear demand curve and that the observed changes in ridership are the result of the fare increase, what do these figures tell us about the original price elasticity of demand for rides on the MARTA system? If Q_1 denotes the original quantity of riders and ΔQ the change in riders due to the fare increase, and if ΔP and P_1 denote the price change and original price, respectively, we want to use the information given to calculate the expression $\eta = (\Delta Q/Q_1)/(\Delta P/P_1)$. Suppose the demand curve

---

[5]See Bert Roughton, Jr., "MARTA Sees Ridership Dip with Fare Hike," *The Atlanta Constitution*, October 8, 1987, p. 7.

for rides on MARTA is as shown by the curve labeled D in Figure 5-11. The fact that total revenues went up by 18.3 percent may be expressed as follows:

$$\frac{75(Q_1 + \Delta Q) - 60Q_1}{60Q_1} = 0.183, \tag{5.1}$$

where $\Delta Q < 0$ is the fall in ridership. Equation 5.1 reduces to

$$\frac{15Q_1 + 75\Delta Q}{60Q_1} = 0.183, \tag{5.2}$$

which, in turn, solves for

$$\frac{\Delta Q}{Q_1} = -0.0536. \tag{5.3}$$

Since we know that $\Delta P/P_1 = \frac{15}{60} = 0.25$, this tells us that $\eta = -0.0536/0.25 = -0.2144$. The demand for MARTA rides thus turns out to be highly inelastic with respect to price, which is consistent with the fact that the fare increase led to a substantial increase in total expenditure.

APPLICATION: THE PRICE ELASTICITY OF DEMAND FOR ALCOHOL

How does the consumption of alcoholic beverages respond to changes in their price? For many decades, the conventional wisdom on this subject responded, "not very much." Unfortunately, however, estimates of the price elasticity of demand for alcohol tend to be highly unreliable. The problem is that liquor prices

FIGURE 5-11
Knowing the percentage change in total expenditure and the percentage change in price enables us to calculate the price elasticity of demand.

THE MARTA FARE INCREASE

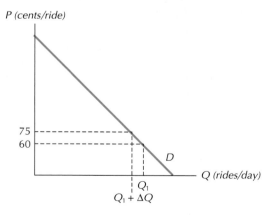

usually don't vary sufficiently to permit an accurate estimate of their effects.

In a careful study,[6] Philip Cook made use of some previously unexploited data on significant changes in alcohol prices. He suggested that the price elasticity of demand for alcohol may be much higher than we thought.

Cook's method was to examine changes in alcohol consumption that occur in response to changes in state liquor taxes. Of the 48 contiguous states, 30 license and tax the private sale of liquor. Periodically, most of these states increase their nominal liquor taxes to compensate for the effects of inflation. The pattern is for the real value of a state's liquor tax to be highest right after one of these tax increases, then to erode steadily as the cost of living rises over the next several years. The fact that taxes are not adjusted continuously to keep their real value constant provides the real price variability we need to estimate the responsiveness of alcohol purchases to price changes.

There were 39 liquor tax increases in Cook's 30-state sample during the period 1960–1975. In 30 of these 39 cases, he found that liquor consumption declined relative to the national trend in the year following the tax increase. His estimate of the price elasticity of demand was −1.8, a substantially higher value than had been found in previous studies.

Cook's interpretation of his findings provides an interesting case study in the factors that govern price elasticity. One salient fact about the alcohol market, he noted, is that heavy drinkers, though a small fraction of the total population, account for a large fraction of the total alcohol consumed. This fact has led many people to expect that alcohol consumption would be unresponsive to variations in price. The common view of heavy drinkers, after all, is that they drink primarily out of habit, not because of rational deliberations about price. Stated another way, analysts always expected the substitution effect to be small for these people. But even if the substitution effect were zero for heavy drinkers, there would remain the income effect to consider. The budget share devoted to alcohol tends to be large among heavy drinkers for two reasons. The obvious one is that heavy drinkers buy a lot of liquor. Less obvious, perhaps, is that their incomes tend to be significantly smaller than average. Many heavy drinkers have difficulty holding steady jobs and often cannot work productively in the jobs they do hold. The result is that the income effect of a substantial increase in the price of liquor forces many heavy drinkers to consume less. In support of this interpretation, Cook observed that mortality from cirrhosis of the liver declines sharply in the years following significant liquor tax increases. This is a disease that for the most part afflicts only people with protracted histories of alcohol abuse, and clinical experience reveals that curtailed drinking can delay or prevent its onset in long-term heavy drinkers.

---

[6]Philip J. Cook, "The Effect of Liquor Taxes on Drinking, Cirrhosis, and Auto Accidents," in *Alcohol and Public Policy*, Mark Moore and Dean Gerstein (eds.), Washington, DC: National Academy Press, 1982.

APPLICATION: WHY DO NATIONAL FOOTBALL LEAGUE GAMES COST SO MUCH MORE THAN MAJOR LEAGUE BASEBALL GAMES?

The New York Giants charge $65 for the best seats at their home games, whereas the New York Yankees charge only $18 for theirs. Some fans believe that this difference is the result of football having eclipsed baseball as America's national pastime—that football prices are so much higher simply because people like football games better. But this judgment is at best premature, for there is a simple economic reason for the price difference, one that has nothing to do with the intrinsic merits of the two sports. It is that the regular major league baseball season has 162 games, the National Football League season only 16. If the two sports charged the same prices, the ticket bill for a regular fan would be more than 10 times higher in baseball than in football. Even at current prices, serious baseball fans spend a much larger share of their incomes on tickets than serious football fans do. This higher budget share means the price elasticity of demand will be larger for baseball tickets; and this, in turn, will lead owners to charge less for them.

Knowledgeable sports fans realize that baseball is still very much America's pastime, even though its ticket prices are considerably lower than football's.

The Intertemporal Choice Model

The choices we have considered thus far have involved trade-offs between alternatives in the present—the choice between food now and clothing now, between travel now and stereo equipment now, and so on. There was no hint in any of these choices that the alternative chosen today might affect the menu of alternatives available in the future.

Yet such effects are a prominent feature of many of our most important decisions. Our task in this section is to enlarge the basic consumer choice model in Chapter 3 to accommodate them.

INTERTEMPORAL CONSUMPTION BUNDLES

When deciding what to do with their incomes, people may either consume them all now or save part for the future. The question we want to be able to answer is, "How would rational consumers distribute their consumption over time?" To keep the analysis manageable, it is helpful to begin by supposing that there are only two time periods, namely, *current* and *future*. In the standard, or *atemporal*, choice model in Chapter 3, the alternatives were different goods that could be consumed in the current period—apples now versus oranges now, etc. In our simple *intertemporal choice model*, the alternatives instead will be *current consumption* (denoted C_1) versus *future consumption* (denoted C_2). Each of these is an amalgam—the functional equivalent of the composite good (see Chapter 3). For the sake of simplicity, we set aside the question of how to apportion current and future consumption among the various specific consumption goods.

In the atemporal choice model, any bundle of goods can be represented as a point in a simple two-dimensional diagram. We use an analogous procedure in the intertemporal choice model. In Figure 5-12, for example, current consumption of $6000 combined with future consumption of $6000 is represented by the bundle E. Bundle D represents current consumption of $3000 and future consumption of $9000.

THE INTERTEMPORAL BUDGET CONSTRAINT

Suppose you receive $50,000 income in the current period and $60,000 income in the future period. Suppose also that if you deposit some of your income from the current period in a bank, you can receive your principal plus 20 percent in the future period. Similarly, if you wish to borrow against your future income, you may receive $1 in the current period for every $1.20 you must repay in the future period. (See Figure 5-13.) To construct your intertemporal budget constraint, first note that you can always merely consume your income in each period, so C_1 = $50,000 and C_2 = $60,000 must be a point on your intertemporal budget constraint. Another option is to deposit all $50,000 (maximum lending) and thus receive 1.2(50,000) = $60,000 in addition to your $60,000 future income for C_2 = $120,000 future consumption with no current consumption (C_1 = 0). Yet another option is to borrow 60,000/1.2 = $50,000 (maximum borrowing) in addition to your $50,000 current income for C_1 = $100,000 current consumption with no future consumption (C_2 = 0). The equation for your intertemporal budget constraint is C_2 = 120,000 − 1.2C_1, or, equivalently, 1.2C_1 + C_2 = $120,000.

In general, suppose you receive M_1 of your income in the first period and M_2 in the second, and can either borrow or lend at the interest rate r. Under these circumstances, what is the most you can consume in the future period? Maximum future consumption occurs when you set all your current income aside for future use. Setting aside M_1 in the current period at the interest rate r means

FIGURE 5-12
Alternative combinations of current and future consumption are represented as points in the C_1, C_2 plane. By convention, the horizontal axis measures current consumption; the vertical axis, future consumption.

INTERTEMPORAL CONSUMPTION BUNDLES

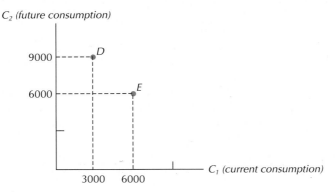

FIGURE 5-13
For every dollar by
which current con-
sumption is reduced,
it is possible to in-
crease future con-
sumption by $1.2.

THE INTERTEMPORAL BUDGET CONSTRAINT

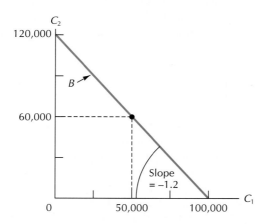

your deposit will grow to $M_1(1 + r)$ by the future period. So the most you can possibly consume in the future is that amount plus your future income, or $M_1(1 + r) + M_2$.

What is the most you could consume in the current period? The answer is your current income plus the maximum amount you can borrow against your future income. The most you can borrow against a future income of M_2 is called the ***present value*** of M_2, denoted $PV(M_2)$. It is the amount that, if deposited today at the interest rate r, would be worth exactly M_2 in the future period. Accordingly, we can find the present value of M_2 by solving $PV(M_2)(1 + r) = M_2$ for $PV(M_2)$:

Present value
The present value
of a payment of X
dollars T years
from now is
$X/(1 + r)^T$, where
r is the annual
rate of interest.

$$PV(M_2) = \frac{M_2}{1 + r}.$$ (5.4)

For example, if M_2 were $110,000 and the interest rate were 10 percent (that is, $r = 0.10$), the present value of M_2 would be $110,000/1.1 = $100,000. Present value is a simple equivalence relationship between sums of money that are payable at different points in time. If $r = 0.10$, then $100,000 today will be worth $110,000 in the future. By the same token, $110,000 in the future is worth $100,000 today when the interest rate is 10 percent.

It is not necessary, of course, to borrow or save the maximum amounts possible. The consumer who wishes to shift some of her future income into the current period can borrow any amount up to the maximum at the rate of $1/(1 + r)$ dollars today for every dollar given up in the future. Or, she can save any amount of her current income and get back $(1 + r)$ dollars in the future for every dollar not consumed today. The intertemporal budget constraint, shown as the

FIGURE 5-14
The opportunity cost of $1 of present consumption is $(1 + r)$ dollars of future consumption. The horizontal intercept of the intertemporal budget constraint is the present value of lifetime income, $M_1 + M_2/(1 + r)$.

INTERTEMPORAL BUDGET CONSTRAINT WITH INCOME IN BOTH PERIODS, AND BORROWING OR LENDING AT THE RATE r

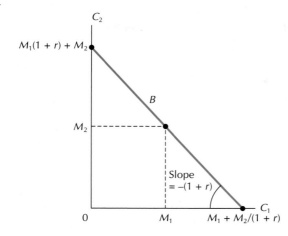

locus B in Figure 5-14, is thus again the straight line that joins the maximum current consumption and maximum future consumption points. And its slope will again be $-(1 + r)$. As in the atemporal model, here too the slope of the budget constraint may be interpreted as a relative price ratio. This time it is the ratio of the prices of current and future consumption. Current consumption has a higher price than future consumption because of the opportunity cost of the interest forgone when money is spent rather than saved. It is conventional to refer to the horizontal intercept of the intertemporal budget constraint as the *present value of lifetime income*.

EXERCISE 5-4

You have $50,000 of current income and $42,000 of future income. If the interest rate between the current and future period is 5 percent, what is the present value of your lifetime income? What is the maximum amount you could consume in the future? What is the equation describing your intertemporal budget constraint?

As in the atemporal case considered in Chapter 3, the intertemporal budget constraint is a convenient way of summarizing the consumption bundles that someone is *able* to buy. And again as before, it tells us nothing about which particular combination a person will *choose* to buy.

INTERTEMPORAL INDIFFERENCE CURVES

To discover which bundle the consumer will select from those that are feasible, we need some convenient way of representing the consumer's preferences over current and future consumption. Here again the analytical device is completely analogous to one we used in the atemporal case. Just as a consumer's preferences over two current consumption goods may be captured by an indifference map, so too may his preferences over current and future goods be represented in this fashion. In Figure 5-15, the consumer is indifferent between the bundles that lie on the locus I_1, each of which is less desirable than the bundles on I_2, and so on.

The absolute value of the slope of the intertemporal indifference curve at any point is the marginal rate of substitution between future and current consumption. At point A in Figure 5-15, it is given by $|\Delta C_2/\Delta C_1|$, and this ratio is also referred to as the ***marginal rate of time preference (MRTP)*** at A (see footnote 7). If $|\Delta C_2/\Delta C_1| > 1$ at A, the consumer is said to exhibit *positive time preference* at that point. This means that he requires more than 1 unit of future consumption to compensate him for the loss of a unit of current consumption. If $|\Delta C_2/\Delta C_1| < 1$ at a point, he is said to exhibit *negative time preference* at that point. Such a person is willing to forego 1 unit of current consumption in return for less than 1 unit of future consumption. Finally, if $|\Delta C_2/\Delta C_1| = 1$ at a point, the consumer is said to have *neutral time preference* at that point. With neutral time preference, present and future consumption trade off against one another at the rate of 1 to 1.

As in the atemporal case, it appears justified to assume that the marginal rate of time preference declines as one moves downward along an indifference curve. The more current consumption a person already has, the more she will be will-

> **Marginal rate of time preference** The number of units of consumption in the future a consumer would exchange for 1 unit of consumption in the present.

FIGURE 5-15
As in the atemporal model, movements to the northeast represent increasing satisfaction. The absolute value of the slope of an indifference curve at a point is called the marginal rate of time preference (MRTP) at that point. The MRTP at A is $|\Delta C_2/\Delta C_1|$.

AN INTERTEMPORAL INDIFFERENCE MAP

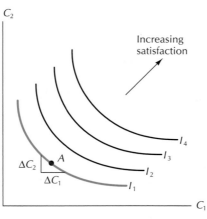

[7]In calculus terms, the marginal rate of time preference is given by $|dC_2/dC_1|$.

ing to give up in order to obtain an additional unit of future consumption. For most of us then, the question of whether time preference is positive, negative, or neutral will be a matter of where we happen to be on our indifference maps. The scion of a wealthy family who is unable to borrow against the $5 billion he is due to inherit in 2 years very likely has strongly positive time preference. By contrast, the primitive farmer whose food stocks are perishable is likely to have negative time preference in the wake of having harvested a bumper crop.[1]

The optimal allocation between current and future consumption is determined exactly as in the atemporal model. The consumer selects the point along his budget constraint that corresponds to the highest attainable indifference curve. If the intertemporal indifference curves have the conventional convex shape, we ordinarily get a tangency solution like the one shown in Figure 5-16. If the MRTP is everywhere larger than (or everywhere smaller than) the slope of the budget constraint, corner solutions result, just as in the atemporal case.

Note in Figure 5-16 that the marginal rate of time preference at the optimal bundle (C^*_1, C^*_2) is positive, because the absolute value of the slope of the budget constraint is $1 + r > 1$. In the example pictured in the diagram, the consumer has the same income in each time period, but consumes slightly more in period 2.

The optimal allocation will of course be different for different consumers. The optimum shown in Figure 5-17a, for example, is for a consumer whose preferences are much more heavily tilted in favor of future consumption. The one shown in Figure 5-17b, by contrast, is for a consumer who cares much more about present consumption. But in each case, note that the slope of the indifference curve at the optimal point is the same. As long as consumers can borrow and lend at the interest rate r, the marginal rate of time preference at the optimal bundle will be $(1 + r)$ (except, of course, in the case of corner solutions). For interior solutions, positive time preference is the rule, regardless of the consumer's preferences.

It is conventional to assume that both current and future consumption are normal goods. Thus an increase in the present value of lifetime income, all other factors constant, will cause both current and future consumption to rise.

FIGURE 5-16
As in the atemporal model, the optimal intertemporal consumption bundle (bundle *A*) lies on the highest attainable indifference curve. Here, that occurs at a point of tangency.

THE OPTIMAL INTERTEMPORAL ALLOCATION

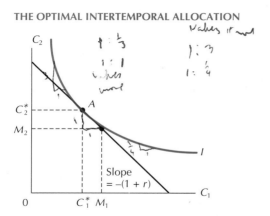

FIGURE 5-17
(*a*) The patient consumer postpones the bulk of consumption until the future period. (*b*) The impatient consumer consumes much more heavily in the current period. But in equilibrium, the marginal rate of time preference $(1 + r)$ is the same for both types of consumers.

PATIENCE AND IMPATIENCE

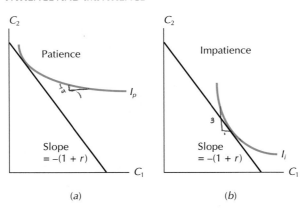

(*a*)   (*b*)

EXAMPLE 5-4 *You have current income of $100,000 and future income of $154,000, and can borrow and lend at the rate $r = 0.1$. Under these conditions, you consume exactly your income in each period. True or false: An increase in r to $r = 0.4$ will cause you to save some of your current income.*

Line *B* in Figure 5-18 is the original budget constraint. Its horizontal intercept is the present value of lifetime income when $r = 0.1$: $100,000 + $154,000/1.1 = $240,000. Its vertical intercept is future income plus $(1 + r)$ times current income: $154,000 + (1.1)($100,000) = $264,000. The optimal bundle occurs at *A*, by assumption, which implies that the MRTP at *A* is 1.1. When the interest rate rises to 0.4, the intertemporal budget constraint becomes *B'*. Its horizontal intercept is $100,000 + $154,000/1.4 = $210,000. Its vertical intercept is $154,000 + (1.4)($100,000) = $294,000. Because the MRTP at *A* is less than the absolute value of the slope of the budget constraint *B'*, it follows that the consumer will be better off by consuming less in the present and more in the future than he did at *A*. The new bundle is shown at *D* in Figure 5-18.

APPLICATION: THE PERMANENT INCOME AND LIFE-CYCLE HYPOTHESES

Economists once assumed that a person's current consumption depends primarily on her current income. Thus if a consumer received a windfall roughly equal to her current income, the prediction was that her consumption would roughly double.

In the 1950s, however, Milton Friedman, Franco Modigliani, Richard Brum-

FIGURE 5-18
When the interest rate goes up, the intertemporal budget constraint rotates about the current endowment point. If the current endowment point (A) was optimal at the lower interest rate, the new optimal bundle (D) will have less current consumption and more future consumption.

THE EFFECT OF A RISE IN THE INTEREST RATE

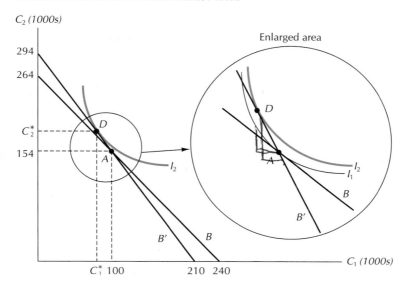

berg, and others argued that the intertemporal choice model suggests otherwise.[8] To illustrate, consider a consumer with current and future incomes both equal to 120, who can borrow and lend at the rate $r = 0.2$. The locus labeled B in Figure 5-19 is the consumer's intertemporal budget constraint, and the optimal bundle along it is denoted by A. Note that the horizontal intercept of B is the present value of lifetime income, namely, $120 + (120/1.2) = 220$.

Notice what happens when this consumer's current income rises from 120 to 240. His budget constraint is now the locus labeled B', and the optimal bundle is D. The effect of increasing current income is thus to increase not only current consumption (from 80 to 150) but future consumption as well (from 168 to 228). Because intertemporal indifference curves exhibit <u>diminishing marginal rates</u> of <u>time preference,</u>[9] the consumer generally does best not to concentrate too much of his consumption in any one period. By spreading his windfall over both periods, he is able to achieve a better outcome.

Friedman's *permanent income hypothesis* says that the primary determinant of current consumption is not current income but what he called ***permanent income.*** In terms of our simple intertemporal choice model, permanent income is simply the present value of lifetime income. (Following the increase in current income

Permanent income The present value of lifetime income.

---

[8]See Franco Modigliani and R. Brumberg, "Utility Analysis and the Consumption Function: An Interpretation of Cross-Section Data," in K. Kurihara (ed.), *Post Keynesian Economics,* London: Allen & Unwin, 1955; and Milton Friedman, *A Theory of the Consumption Function,* Princeton, NJ: Princeton University Press, 1957.

[9]Diminishing marginal rate of time preference is the intertemporal analog of diminishing marginal rate of substitution in the atemporal model.

FIGURE 5-19
The effect of a rise in current income (from 120 to 240) will be felt as an increase not only in current consumption (from 80 to 150), but also in future consumption (from 168 to 228).

PERMANENT INCOME, NOT CURRENT INCOME, IS THE PRIMARY DETERMINANT OF CURRENT CONSUMPTION

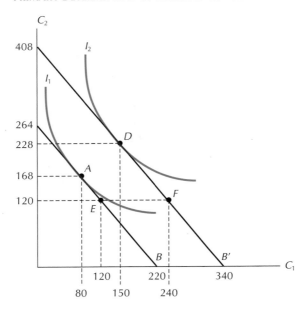

in Figure 5-19, permanent income is $240 + 120/1.2 = 340$.) When we consider that in reality the future consists of not just one but many additional periods, it becomes clear that current income constitutes only a small fraction of permanent income. (If there were 10 future periods we were concerned about, for example, then a 10 percent increase in current income would cause permanent income to increase by just over 2 percent.)[10] Accordingly, Friedman argued, a given proportional change in current income should give rise to a much smaller proportional change in current consumption, just as we saw in Figure 5-19. (The *life-cycle hypothesis* of Modigliani and Brumberg tells essentially the same story.)

FACTORS ACCOUNTING FOR DIFFERENCES IN TIME PREFERENCE

Uncertainty regarding the future is one reason to prefer current to future consumption. In countries at war, for example, people often live as though there were no tomorrow, as indeed for many of them there will not be. By contrast, a peaceful international climate, secure employment, stable social networks, good health, and a variety of similar factors tend to reduce uncertainty about the future, in the process justifying greater weight on future as opposed to current consumption.

---

[10]Again, we assume an interest rate of $r = 0.2$.

Intertemporal indifference maps, like the atemporal variety, will also vary according to the disposition of the individual. My first son, for example, has strongly positive time preferences in most situations. (His indifference curves are very steep with respect to the current consumption axis.) Ever since he was a small boy, he always ate his favorite part of his meal first, then worked his way through to his least favored items. Only with pressure would he eat his vegetables at all, and even then he always ate them last. My second son is the polar opposite case. He always starts with the foods he likes least, carefully husbanding his favorite items for the end of his meal. This contrast in their behavior at the dinner table pervades virtually every other aspect of their lives.

Time preference depends also on the specific circumstances of the choice at hand. Experimental studies have isolated certain situations in which most people have strongly positive time preference, others in which they show strongly negative time preference. Carnegie-Mellon University economist George Loewenstein, for example, told experimental subjects to imagine they had won a kiss from their favorite movie star and then asked them when they would most like to receive it. Even though getting it right away was one of the options, most subjects elected to wait an average of several days. These choices imply negative time preference, and Loewenstein explained that most subjects simply wanted a little while to savor the anticipation of the kiss.[11]

Loewenstein also told a group of subjects to imagine that they were going to receive a painful electric shock and then asked them when they would like to receive it. This time most subjects chose to get it right away. They apparently wanted to spend as little time as possible dreading the shock. But since an electric shock is a "bad" rather than a "good," these choices too imply negative time preference.

While negative time preferences are occasionally observed in individual cases and can be invoked among many people by suitably chosen experiments, by far the more common case is for a general preference for present over future consumption. We can be sure, for example, that if we put a can of honey-roasted cashews in front of Loewenstein's experimental subjects, not many of them would want to wait a few days to anticipate the pleasure of eating them. On the contrary, the nuts would probably disappear in short order, even if that meant spoiling dinner an hour away.

Nineteenth-century economist Eugen von Böhm-Bawerk suggested that one reason for such behavior is that current consumption opportunities confront our senses directly, whereas future ones can only be imagined. The pleasure of eating the roasted nuts, for example, is both intense and immediate. Even those people who would strongly prefer the meal to the nuts often lack the self-control to wait. Böhm-Bawerk believed that our "faulty telescopic faculty" was no good reason to assign greater weight to current than to future pleasures. Uncertainty aside, he felt that people would reap greater satisfaction from their lives if they weighed the present and the future equally.

---

[11]See George Loewenstein, "Anticipation and the Valuation of Delayed Consumption," *Economic Journal, 97,* September 1987: 666–684.

OTHER FACTORS THAT AFFECT INTERTEMPORAL CHOICE

Preference for a Rising Consumption Standard.   Evidence suggests that most people seem to prefer a consumption pattern that gives even more weight to future than to current consumption because satisfaction depends not only on the level of consumption but also on its rate of change. There is evidence, for example, that an improving standard of living can often bring greater satisfaction than a static one at a higher level.

At the most fundamental level, support for this idea comes from our knowledge of how the human nervous system perceives and processes information. As psychologists and biologists explain it, we are much less sensitive to the absolute level of any sensory stimulus than to deviations from norms or reference standards we adopt from experience. The pedestrian in New York City, for example, often fails to notice the horns that blare at him, whereas upstate villagers are often startled by much fainter sounds. Like the din of the metropolis, consumption at any constant level becomes a norm. As such, it is at least partly taken for granted, serving as the standard against which future consumption levels are measured.

Voter behavior is further evidence of the importance of an improving consumption standard. The average performance of the U.S. economy was little different during Ronald Reagan's first term of office than it was during Jimmy Carter's. Yet it is widely believed that a worsening economy helped defeat Carter in 1980, just as an improving economy helped reelect Reagan in 1984.

To test your own intuition about the importance of a rising consumption profile, imagine yourself living on a deserted island faced with a once-and-for-all choice between the two consumption profiles shown in Figure 5-20. Which one would you pick?

In a sample of 112 undergraduates who were asked to make a choice similar to the one portrayed in Figure 5-20, 87 (78 percent) chose the rising profile (panel b).[12] This pattern seems strongly at odds with Böhm-Bawerk's notion that

FIGURE 5-20
Many people declare a strong preference for a growing consumption profile (panel b) over a static profile (panel a).

LEVEL VERSUS GROWING CONSUMPTION PROFILES

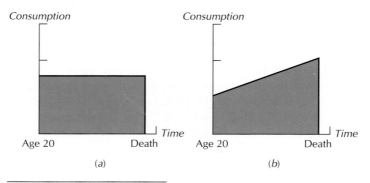

[12]See R. Frank and R. Hutchens, "Wages, Seniority, and the Demand for Rising Consumption Profiles," *Journal of Economic Behavior and Organization, 21,* 1993: 251–276.

people generally put too much weight on current consumption. There are at least two reasons for the apparent discrepancy. One is that the savings incentives we face individually are very different from the ones we face as whole societies. Indeed, as we see in the next section, individuals face strong incentives to concentrate their consumption in the present, even though they might wish that everyone would save more for the future.

Positional Concerns and Intertemporal Choice. The definition of a "fast" swimmer is inescapably relative. Swimmer Mark Spitz won seven gold medals in the 1972 Olympics, and yet his winning times in each event would have been too slow even to qualify for the 1996 U.S. team. To be a fast swimmer means simply to be faster than the other swimmers against whom you compete.

Positional good
A good whose value depends strongly on how it compares with similar goods consumed by others; also called a *status good*.

The late British economist Fred Hirsch coined the term ***positional goods*** to refer to goods and services whose value is strongly influenced by their *relative quality*.[13] Luxury goods like diamonds are a quintessential example. A "good" diamond, like a fast swimmer, is one that compares favorably with the diamonds that others own. A good job, similarly, is one that is better than most other jobs. The standards that define a good job in the twentieth century are very different from those that applied in the fifteenth century. Education is likewise something with a strong positional component. Whether society considers you well educated, and thus qualified for a good job, depends to a large extent on how your education compares with the education received by your peers.

The central feature of a positional good is its inherent scarcity. Although it is possible to imagine an environment in which people had more food than they could possibly consume, the same cannot be said of a positional good.

Drawing by William Walter Haefeli. Copyright © 1979 Saturday Review, Inc.

*"I admit it **does** look very impressive. But you see, nowadays **everyone** graduates in the top ten per cent of his class."*

---

[13]See Fred Hirsch, *Social Limits to Growth*, Cambridge, MA: Harvard University Press, 1976.

This feature of positional goods shapes a variety of important decisions, including the one of how much to save. At any moment, a family can save more of its income for retirement, or spend more now for, say, a house in a better school district. For most parents, the lure of providing relative educational advantages for their children is powerful. Yet the laws of simple arithmetic tell us that no matter how much each family spends on housing, only 10 percent of the children can occupy seats in the top decile of the educational quality distribution. In the aggregate, saving less and spending more for houses in better school districts serves only to bid up the prices of those houses. It does nothing to alter the relative distribution of educational opportunities.[14]

Spending on positional goods is thus very much like a military arms race. Each side spends more in an effort not to fall behind, but in the end, their efforts merely offset one another. Positional concerns cause the individual payoff from spending to appear spuriously large, the payoff from saving spuriously small. These concerns are thus in direct competition with the desire to have a rising consumption profile. To provide the best possible education for your children, you must spend heavily during the early years of the life cycle. By contrast, to achieve a rising consumption profile, you must save a lot during the early years. Given the strength of positional concerns, it is easy to see why even people who strongly value a rising consumption profile might nonetheless save very little. Indeed, most families would have grossly inadequate incomes for retirement were it not for the Social Security system and private forced-savings programs. These programs may be interpreted as collective actions to shelter part of our incomes from spending on positional goods, in the process helping achieve a more preferred lifetime consumption profile.[15]

The importance of positional concerns suggests an important amendment to the life-cycle and permanent income models of savings. If positional concerns are important, people in the lower part of the income distribution will naturally have more difficulty than others in keeping up with community consumption standards. The clear prediction is that the savings rate will rise with position in the income distribution. By contrast, the life-cycle and permanent income models predict that the savings rates will be independent of position in the income distribution. As an empirical matter, the latter prediction is strongly contradicted: In every country for which the relevant data are available, savings rates rise sharply with income.

The Self-Control Pitfall.   Another reason for low savings rates coexisting with a preference for a rising consumption profile is that people often seem to have

---

[14]Nor, for that matter, does it alter the absolute value of educational services consumed by each student.

[15]For a detailed argument in support of this interpretation, see R. Frank, *Choosing the Right Pond: Human Behavior and the Quest for Status*, New York: Oxford University Press, 1985.

difficulty carrying out plans they believe to be in their own interests. Thomas Schelling notes, for example, that most cigarette smokers say they want to quit.[16] Many of them, with great effort, have done so. (Both Schelling and I are members of this group and can testify to the difficulty.) Many more, however, have tried to quit and failed.

One way of solving the self-control problem is captured by the example of Homer's Ulysses, who was faced with having to sail past dangerous reefs where the sirens lay. Ulysses realized that once he was within earshot of the sirens' cries, he would be drawn irresistibly toward them and sail to his doom on the reefs. Able to foresee this temporary change in his preferences, he came up with an effective ***commitment device:*** He instructed his crewmen to strap him tightly to the mast and not to release him, even though he might beg them to, until they had sailed safely past.

Similar sorts of commitment devices are familiar in modern life. Fearing they will be tempted to spend their savings, people join "Christmas clubs," special accounts that prohibit withdrawals until late autumn; they buy whole-life insurance policies, which impose substantial penalties on withdrawals before retirement. Fearing they will spoil their dinners, they put the salted nuts out of easy reach. Fearing they will gamble too much, they limit the amount of cash they take to Atlantic City. Fearing they will stay up too late watching TV, they move the television out of the bedroom.

The moral of the burgeoning self-control literature is that *devising* a rational intertemporal consumption plan is only part of the problem. There is also the task of *implementing* it. But here too, rational deliberation can help us avoid some of the most important pitfalls. The consumer who has just given up smoking, for example, can predict that he will desperately want a cigarette if he goes out drinking with his friends on Friday nights. And he can also insulate himself from that temptation by committing himself to alternative weekend activities for the next month or so. By the same token, the person who wants to shield herself from the temptation to spend too much may have part of her pay diverted automatically into a savings account, and this is precisely what millions of people do.

These issues once again highlight the distinction between the positive and normative roles of the rational choice model discussed in Chapter 1. Thus, because the rational choice model takes no account of self-control problems and the like, it will sometimes fail to predict how people actually behave. But note carefully that this does not mean that the model, even in its narrowest form, is wrong or useless. For here, as in other instances, it can play the important normative role of guiding people toward better decisions, ones that accord more fully with their real objectives.

Commitment device A device that commits a person to behave in a certain way in the future, even though he may wish to behave otherwise when the time comes.

---

[16]See Thomas Schelling, *Choice and Consequence*, Cambridge, MA: Harvard University Press, 1984.

Summary

In this chapter our primary focus was on applications of the rational choice and demand theories developed in Chapters 3 and 4. We also considered the concept of consumer surplus, which measures the amount by which a consumer benefits by being able to buy a given product at a given price. We saw that consumer surplus is well approximated by the area bounded above by the individual demand curve and below by the market price. Two-part pricing structures are a device by which a portion of consumer surplus is transferred from the buyer to the seller.

The rational choice model is also useful for evaluating the welfare effects of price and income changes. It suggests why the consumer price index, the government's measure of changes in the cost of living, may often overstate the true cost of achieving a given level of satisfaction.

The intertemporal choice model is, in every essential respect, analogous to the atemporal choice model in Chapter 3. In the two-dimensional case, it begins with a commodity graph that depicts current and future consumption levels of a composite good. The consumer's initial endowment is the point, (M_1, M_2), that corresponds to current and future income. If the consumer can borrow and lend at the rate r, his intertemporal budget constraint is then the line passing through the endowment point with a slope of $-(1 + r)$. The opportunity cost of a unit of current consumption is $1 + r$ units of future consumption. The horizontal intercept of the intertemporal budget constraint is the present value of all current and future income, which is also called the present value of lifetime wealth.

The consumer's intertemporal preferences are represented with an indifference map with essentially the same properties as in the atemporal case. A consumer is said to exhibit positive, neutral, or negative time preference at a point if his marginal rate of time preference (the absolute value of the slope of his indifference curve) at that point is greater than 1, equal to 1, or less than 1, respectively. In the case of interior solutions, equilibrium occurs at a tangency between the intertemporal budget constraint and an indifference curve. Because the slope of the intertemporal budget constraint exceeds 1 when $r > 0$, consumers will exhibit positive time preference in equilibrium, irrespective of the shape of their indifference curves.

An important application of the intertemporal choice model is to the study of decisions about how much to save. The permanent income and life-cycle hypotheses employ the model to demonstrate that it is the present value of lifetime wealth, not current income alone, that governs current consumption (and hence current savings).

An appendix to this chapter (see the "For the Instructor" section at our Web site www.mhhe.com/economics/frank4) discusses additional applications of rational choice and demand theories, including cost-of-living indices and the use of indifference curves to measure consumer surplus.

Questions for Review

1. Explain in your own words why a gasoline tax whose proceeds are refunded to the consumer in a lump-sum amount will nonetheless reduce the consumption of gasoline.

2. Explain in your own words what a two-part pricing scheme is and why sellers might use one.

3. Do you think a college education has a high- or low-price (tuition) elasticity of demand?

4. Explain in your own words why even long-term heavy drinkers might be highly responsive to increases in the price of alcohol.

5. Explain why 1 plus the interest rate in the intertemporal choice model is analogous to the relative price ratio in the consumer choice model discussed in Chapter 3.

6. Bus services are generally more energy efficient than individuals using cars to commute to work. However, the trend over the past 30 years has been a decline in the proportion of commuters taking buses despite an increase in real energy prices. Why?

7. Jennifer, who earns an annual salary of $20,000, wins $25,000 in the lottery. Explain why she most likely will not spend all her winnings during the next year.

Problems

1. Using a diagram like Figure 5-2, explain why, under our current method of educational finance, a rich family is much more likely than a poor family to send its children to a private school.

2. When the price of gasoline is $1/gal, you consume 1000 gal/yr. Then two things happen: (1) The price of gasoline rises to $2/gal and (2) a distant uncle dies, with the instruction to his executor to send you a check for $1000/yr. If no other changes in prices or income occur, do these two changes leave you better off than before?

3. Larry demands strawberries according to the schedule $P = 4 - (Q/2)$, where P is the price of strawberries ($/pint) and Q is the quantity (pint/wk). Assuming that the income effect is negligible, how much will he be hurt if the price of strawberries goes from $1/pint to $2/pint?

4. The only video rental club available to you charges $4 per movie per day. If your demand curve for movie rentals is given by $P = 20 = 2Q$, where P is the rental price ($/day) and Q is the quantity demanded (movies per year), what is the annual maximum membership fee you would be willing to pay to join this club?

5. Jane spends all her income on hot dogs and caviar. Her demand curve for caviar is inelastic at all prices for caviar. Unfortunately, the accident at Chernobyl has caused the supply of caviar to fall and the price to rise. What has happened to Jane's consumption of hot dogs? Explain. (*Note:* You should assume that the accident at Chernobyl had no effect on the price of hot dogs or Jane's preference for caviar.)

6. Jones spends all his income on two goods, X and Y. The prices he paid and the quantities he consumed last year are as follows: $P_X = 15$, $X = 20$, $P_Y = 25$, and $Y = 30$. If the

prices next year are $P_X = 6$ and $P_Y = 30$, and Jones's income is 1020, will he be better or worse off than he was in the previous year? (Assume that his tastes do not change.)

7. Smith lives in a world with two time periods, this period and the next period. His income in each period, which he receives at the beginning of each period, is $210. If the interest rate, expressed as a fraction, is 0.05 per time period, what is the present value of his lifetime income? Draw his intertemporal budget constraint. On the same axes, draw Smith's intertemporal budget constraint when $r = 0.20$.

8. Suppose Smith from Problem 7 views current and future consumption as perfect, one-for-one substitutes for one another. Find his optimal consumption bundle.

9. Suppose Smith from Problem 7 views current and future consumption as one-to-one complements. Find his optimal consumption bundle.

10. Karen earns $75,000 in the current period and will earn $75,000 in the future

   a. Assuming that these are the only two periods, and that banks in her country borrow and lend but at an interest rate $r = 0$, draw her intertemporal budget constraint.
   b. Now suppose banks offer 10 percent interest on funds deposited during the current period, and offer loans at this same rate. Draw her new intertemporal budget constraint.

11. Find the present value of $50,000 to be received after 1 year if the rate of interest for 1 year is

   a. 8 percent
   b. 10 percent
   c. 12 percent

12. Crusoe will live this period and the next period as the lone inhabitant of his island. His only income is a crop of 100 coconuts that he harvests at the beginning of each period. Coconuts not consumed in the current period spoil at the rate of 10 percent per period.

   a. Draw Crusoe's intertemporal budget constraint. What will be his consumption in each period if he regards future consumption as a perfect, one-for-one substitute for current consumption?
   b. What will he consume each period if he regards 0.8 unit of future consumption as being worth 1 unit of current consumption?

13. In the fall, Crusoe puts 50 coconuts from his harvest into a cave just before a family of bears goes in to hibernate. As a result, he is unable to get the coconuts out before the bears emerge the following spring. Coconuts spoil at the same rate no matter where he stores them, and yet he continues this practice each year. Why might he do this?

14. Kathy earns $55,000 in the current period and will earn $60,000 in the future period. What is the maximum interest rate that would allow her to spend $105,000 in the current period? What is the minimum interest rate that would allow her to spend $120,500 in the future period?

15. Smith receives $100 of income this period and $100 next period. At an interest rate of 10 percent, he consumes all his current income in each period. He has a diminishing marginal rate of time preference between consumption next period and consumption

this period. *True or false:* If the interest rate rises to 20 percent, Smith will save some of his income this period. Explain.

16. At current prices, housing costs $50 per unit and the composite good has a price of 1 per unit. A wealthy benefactor has given Joe, a penniless person, 1 unit of housing and 50 units of the composite good. Now the price of housing falls by half. *True or false:* Joe is better off as a result of the price change. Explain.

*17. Tom and Karen are economists. In an attempt to limit their son Harry's use of the family car, they charge him a user fee of 20 cents/mile. At that price he still uses the car more than they would like, but they are reluctant to antagonize him by simply raising the price further. So Tom and Karen ask him the following question: What is the minimum increase in your weekly allowance you would accept in return for having the fee raised to 40 cents/mile? Harry, who is a known truth-teller and has conventional preferences, answers $10/wk.

    a. If Tom and Karen increase Harry's allowance by $10/wk and charge him 40 cents/mile, will he drive less than before? Explain.

    b. Will the revenue from the additional mileage charges be more than, less than, or equal to $10/wk? Explain.

*18. All book buyers have the same preferences, and under current arrangements, those who buy used books at $22 receive the same utility as those who buy new books at $50. The annual interest rate is 10 percent, and there are no transaction costs involved in the buying and selling of used books. Each new textbook costs m to produce and lasts for 2 yr.

    a. What is the buyer's reservation price for the use of a new book for 1 yr?

    b. How low would m have to be before a publisher would find it worthwhile to print books with disappearing ink—ink that vanishes 1 yr from the point of sale of a new book, thus eliminating the used-book market? (Assume that eliminating the used-book market will exactly double the publisher's sales.)

*19. Herb wants to work exactly 12 hr/wk to supplement his graduate fellowship. He can either work as a clerk in the library at $6/hr or tutor first-year graduate students in economics. Pay differences aside, he is indifferent between these two jobs. Each of three first-year students has a demand curve for tutoring given by $P = 10 - Q$, where P is the price in dollars per hour, and Q is the number of hours per week. If Herb has the option of setting a two-part tariff for his tutoring services, how many hours per week should he tutor and how many hours should he work in the library? If he does any tutoring, what should his rate structure be?

†20. Cornell is committed to its current policy of allowing the children of its faculty to attend the university without paying tuition. Suppose the demand curve of Cornell faculty children (CFCs) for slots in other universities is given by $P = 10 - 5Q_0$, where P is the tuition price charged by other universities (in thousands of dollars) and Q_0 is the number of CFCs who attend those universities. Cornell is now considering a

---

*Problems marked with an asterisk (*) are more difficult.

†Problems marked with a dagger (†) are most easily solved using calculus.

proposal to subsidize some proportion k of the tuition charged to CFCs who attend other universities. Suppose Cornell knows that it can fill all its available slots with non-CFCs who pay tuition at the rate of $15,000/yr. Assuming that all CFCs who do not attend other universities will go to Cornell, what value of k will maximize Cornell's tuition revenues, net of outside subsidies, if the tuition price at all other universities is $8000/yr?

[†]21. How will your answer to the preceding problem differ if the tuition charged by outside universities is $4000/yr? What is the economic interpretation of a value of k greater than 1?

*22. Harry runs a small movie theater, whose customers all have identical tastes. Each customer's reservation price for the movie is $5, and each customer's demand curve for popcorn at his concession stand is given by $P_c = 4 - Q_c$, where P_c is the price of popcorn in dollars and Q_c is the amount of popcorn in quarts. If the marginal cost of allowing another patron to watch the movie is zero, and the marginal cost of popcorn is $1, at what price should Harry sell tickets and popcorn if his goal is to maximize his profits? (Assume that Harry is able to costlessly advertise his price structure to potential patrons.)

Answers to In-Chapter Exercises

5-1. Initial consumer surplus at $P = 3 (and $Q = 7$ gal/wk) is $CS = \frac{1}{2}(10 - 3)7 = 24.50/wk. Consumer surplus at the higher price $P' = 4 (and $Q' = 6$ gal/wk) is $CS' = \frac{1}{2}(10 - 4)6 = 18/wk. The loss in consumer surplus is given by the area of $DCEF$, which equals $24.5 - 18 = 6.50/wk.

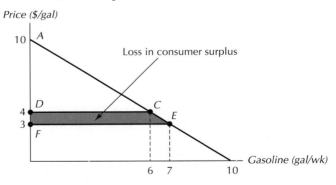

5-2. The maximum membership fee is now given by the area of triangle $AB'C'$, which is $CS = \frac{1}{2}(50 - 20)120 = $1800/yr.

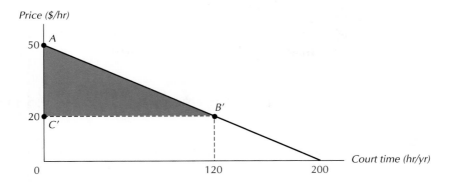

5-3. The two budget lines and last year's optimal bundle are shown in the diagram. A closer look at the tangency point (enlarged area) shows that this year Jones can now afford to purchase a bundle he prefers to the one he bought last year.

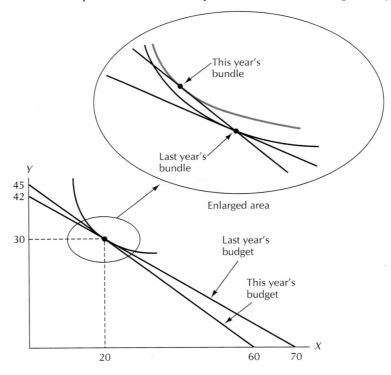

5-4. PV = \$50,000 + \$42,000/1.05 = \$90,000. Maximum future consumption = \$50,000(1.05) + \$42,000 = \$94,500. The equation for your intertemporal budget constraint is $C_2 = 194,500 - 1.05C_1$.

CHAPTER

6

The Economics of Information and Choice Under Uncertainty

*W*hen a toad and his rival vie for the same mate, each faces an important strategic decision. Should he fight for her or set off in search of another? To fight is to risk injury, but to continue searching has costs as well. At the very least, it will consume time. And there is no guarantee that the next potential mate will not herself be the object of some other toad's affections.

In deciding between these alternatives, each toad's assessment of the other's fighting capabilities plays an important role. If one's rival is considerably larger, the likelihood of prevailing will be low and the likelihood of injury high, so it will be prudent to continue searching. Otherwise, it may pay to fight.

Many of these decisions must be made at night, when it is hard to see. Toads have therefore found it expedient to rely on various nonvisual clues; the most reliable is the pitch of the rival's croak. In general, the larger a toad is, the longer and thicker are its vocal cords, and hence the deeper its croak. Hearing a deep croak in the night, a toad may reasonably infer that a big toad made it. Indeed, experiments have shown that the common toad is much more likely to be intimidated by a deep croak than by a high-pitched one.[1]

---

[1]See John Krebs and Richard Dawkins, "Animal Signals: Mind Reading and Manipulation," in J. Krebs and N. Davies (eds.), *Behavioral Ecology: An Evolutionary Approach*, 2d ed., Sunderland, MA: Sinauer Associates, 1984.

Chapter Preview

Information is an important input for decision making, not only for toads, but for consumers and firms as well. Our models in previous chapters assumed perfect information. In practice, however, we are often woefully ill informed. Our concern in the first part of this chapter is with the question of how we gather and evaluate relevant information. Because many of the issues that will concern us arise in simple form in the context of the toad's problem, it provides a convenient starting point for our discussion. We see that the principles that govern communication between toads help us understand such diverse issues as product warranties, hiring practices, and even how people choose partners in personal relationships. We also examine statistical discrimination, the process by which people use group characteristics to help estimate the characteristics of specific individuals.

Although the quality of decisions can often be improved by the intelligent gathering of information, it is almost impossible to acquire all potentially relevant information. Our task in the second part of this chapter is to expand the consumer choice model in Chapter 3 to accommodate decisions made under uncertainty.

The Economics of Information

COMMUNICATION BETWEEN POTENTIAL ADVERSARIES

The problems of communication between parties whose goals are potentially in conflict are fundamentally different from those involving parties with common goals. Toads searching for mates obviously fall into the former category, as in general will any two parties to an economic exchange. The seller, for example, sometimes has an incentive to overstate the quality of his product. The buyer, likewise, often has an incentive to understate the amount she is willing to pay for it. And the potential employee may be tempted to misrepresent his qualifications for the job.

Bridge partners, by contrast, clearly share common goals. When a bridge player uses the standard bidding conventions to tell his partner something, there is no reason for his partner not to take the message at face value. Neither player has anything to gain by deceiving the other. Communication here is a pure problem of information transfer. A message need only be decipherable. Error aside, its credibility is not in question.

A very different logic applies, however, when the interests of would-be communicators are in conflict, or even potentially so. Suppose, for example, the bridge player whispers to the opponent on her left, "I always bid conservatively." What is the opponent to make of such a remark? It is perfectly intelligible. Yet if all parties are believed to be rational, the relationship between them is such that the statement can convey no real information. If being known as a conservative bidder would be an advantage, that would be reason enough for a player to call himself one, true or not. The statement is neither credible nor incredible; it simply contains no information.

The streetwise shopper knows to be wary of inflated claims about product quality. But how exactly does she distinguish a good product from a bad one? How, similarly, does a producer persuade a potential rival that he will cut his price sharply if the rival enters his market? Statements like "I will cut my price" are problematic in the same sense discussed for the opposing bridge players. Since the producer has an incentive to utter such statements whether true or not, they should convey no information.

We do know, however, that adversaries can communicate information that has strategic value. Toads, after all, are able to broadcast information of this sort. But they do not do it merely by saying "I am a big toad." The big toad's implicit claim is credible only because of the physical barriers that prevent the small toad from uttering a deep croak. The toad's croak is an example of a signal: a means of conveying information.

Signaling Communication that conveys information.

The toad example illustrates two important properties of *signaling* between potential adversaries: (1) signals must be costly to fake; and (2) if some individuals use signals that convey favorable information about themselves, others will be forced to reveal information even when it is considerably less favorable. Each principle is important for understanding how economic agents gather and interpret information. Let's begin by stating each principle in terms of its application in the toad example and then examining its application in a variety of economic contexts.

THE COSTLY-TO-FAKE PRINCIPLE

For a signal between adversaries to be credible, it must be costly (or, more generally, difficult) to fake. If small toads could costlessly imitate the deep croak that is characteristic of big toads, a deep croak would no longer *be* characteristic of big toads. But they cannot. Big toads have a natural advantage, and it is that fact alone that enables deepness of croak to emerge as a reliable signal.

Costly-to-fake principle For a signal to an adversary to be credible, it must be costly to fake.

This *costly-to-fake principle* has clear application to signals between people. It is at work, for example, in the following episode from Joe McGinnis's *Fatal Vision*. Captain Jeffrey MacDonald, an Army Green Beret physician, has been told he is suspected of having killed his wife and daughters. The Army has assigned him a military defense attorney. Meanwhile, however, MacDonald's mother recruits Bernard Segal, a renowned private attorney from Philadelphia, to defend her son. When Segal calls MacDonald in Fort Bragg, North Carolina, to introduce himself, his first question is about MacDonald's Army attorney:

"Are his shoes shined?"

"What?!" MacDonald sounded incredulous. Here he was, all but accused of having murdered his own wife and children, and in his very first conversation with the Philadelphia lawyer who presumably had been hired to set things right, the first question the lawyer asks is about the condition of the other lawyer's shoes.

Segal repeated the question. "And this time," he said later, "I could almost hear Jeff smiling over the phone. That was when I first knew I had a client who was not only intelligent but who caught on very quickly. He said, no, as a matter of fact, the lawyer's shoes were kind of scruffy. I said, 'Okay in that case, trust him. Cooperate with him until I can get down there myself.' The point being, you see, that if an Army lawyer keeps his shoes shined, it means he's trying to impress the system. And if he was trying to impress the system in that situation—the system being one which had already declared a vested interest, just by public announcement of suspicion, in seeing his client convicted—then he wasn't going to do Jeff any good. The unshined shoes meant maybe he cared more about being a lawyer."

The condition of the attorney's shoes was obviously not a perfect indication of his priorities in life. Yet they did provide at least *some* reason to suspect that he was not just an Army lackey. Any attorney who wore scruffy shoes merely to convey the impression that he was not looking to get ahead in the Army actually *wouldn't* get ahead. So the only people who can *safely* send such a signal are those who really do care more about their roles as attorneys.

Some economic applications of the costly-to-fake principle:

Product Quality Assurance.   Many products are so complex that consumers cannot inspect their quality directly. In such cases, firms that offer high quality need some means of communicating this fact to potential buyers. Otherwise, they will not be able to charge high enough prices to cover their added costs.

One way to solve this problem is for the firm to develop a reputation for delivering high quality.[2] But conditions will not always allow a firm to do this. Consider the case of sidewalk vendors who sell wristwatches on the streets of any large city. If such a "firm" decides to go out of business, it can do so with virtually no losses. It has no headquarters, no costly capital equipment, no loyal customers to worry about—indeed, no sunk costs of any kind. Even if a vendor had supplied quality products on the same street corner for years, that would provide no assurance that he would still be in business tomorrow. And if he *were* planning to go out of business, his incentive would be to sell the lowest quality merchandise he could pass off. In short, a firm with no obvious stake in the future has an inherently difficult time persuading potential customers it will make good on its promises.

The incentives are different for a firm with extensive sunk costs. If such a firm goes out of business, it loses the value of substantial investments that cannot be liquidated. Accordingly, the material interests of these firms favor doing everything they can to remain in business. And if buyers know that, they can place much greater trust in the promise of a high-quality product. If such a firm charged a price commensurate with high quality and then delivered shoddy merchandise, it would get too little repeat business to survive, and would thus have incurred its sunk costs in vain.

---

[2]This illustration is based on Benjamin Klein and Keith Leffler, "The Role of Market Forces in Assuring Contractual Performance," *Journal of Political Economy,* August 1981.

These observations suggest a reason for believing that heavily advertised products will in fact turn out to have higher quality, just as their slogans proclaim. An extensive national advertising campaign is a sunk cost, its value lost forever if the firm goes out of business. Having made such an investment, the firm then has every incentive to deliver. That firms believe many consumers have spotted this pattern is evidenced by the fact that they often say ". . . as seen on national TV . . ." in their magazine ads.

Choosing a Trustworthy Employee.   In many situations employees have an opportunity to cheat their employers. Many productive activities would have to be abandoned if firms were unable to hire employees who would not cheat in these situations. The firm needs a signal that identifies a prospective employee as trustworthy. One basis for such a signal might be the relationship between a person's character and the costs or benefits of membership in specific groups. For example, perhaps trustworthy people generally enjoy working in volunteer charitable organizations, which untrustworthy people instead tend to consider highly burdensome. In such cases, the groups people decide to join will convey statistically reliable information about their character.

This notion seems borne out in the practice whereby many professional couples in New York City recruit governesses for their children. The care of children is one of those tasks in which trustworthiness is of obvious importance since it is difficult to monitor the caretaker's performance directly. The very reason for needing someone else to look after them, after all, is that you are not there to do so yourself. Bitter experience has apparently persuaded many New Yorkers that the local labor market is not a good place to recruit people who perform reliably without supervision.

The solution many of these couples have adopted is to advertise for governesses in Salt Lake City newspapers. The couples have discovered that persons raised in the Mormon tradition are trustworthy to a degree that the average New Yorker is not. The signal works because someone who merely wanted to *appear* trustworthy would find it unpalatable, if not impossible, to have remained in the Mormon tradition. The tradition involves continuing, intensive moral indoctrination, an experience most purely opportunistic persons would find too taxing to endure. Like the deepness of a toad's croak as a signal of its size, membership in the Mormon tradition is a good signal of trustworthiness because it would be so costly for an opportunistic person to simulate.

Choosing a Hard-Working, Smart Employee.   As a final illustration of the costly-to-fake principle, consider a degree with honors from an elite university. Employers are looking for people who are smart and willing to work hard. There are obviously a great many people in the world who have both these traits yet do not have an elite degree. Even so, employers are reasonably safe in assuming that a person who has such a degree is both smart and hard-working, for it is not obvious how anyone without that combination of traits could go about getting an elite degree with honors.

No one really questions the fact that the graduates of elite institutions generally turn out to be productive employees. But there is a lively debate indeed about the extent to which attendance at these institutions actually *causes* high productivity. People who think it does point to the fact that the graduates of elite institutions earn significantly higher salaries. Skeptics caution, however, that the entire differential cannot be attributed to the quality of their education. The problem is that the students at the best institutions were undoubtedly more productive to begin with. These institutions, after all, screen their applicants carefully and accept only those with the strongest records of achievement.

THE FULL-DISCLOSURE PRINCIPLE

Full-disclosure principle Individuals must disclose even unfavorable qualities about themselves, lest their silence be taken to mean that they have something even worse to hide.

A second important principle illustrated by the toad example can be called the *full-disclosure principle*, which says that if some individuals stand to benefit by revealing a favorable value of some trait, others will be forced to disclose their less favorable values. This principle helps answer the initially puzzling question of why the smaller toads bother to croak at all.[3] By croaking, they tell other toads how small they are. Why not just remain silent and let them wonder?

Suppose all toads with croaks pitched higher than some threshold did, in fact, remain silent. Imagine an index from 0 to 10 that measures the pitch of a toad's croak, with 10 being the highest and 0 the lowest; and suppose, arbitrarily, that toads with an index value above 6 kept quiet (see Figure 6-1).

It is easy to see why any such pattern would be inherently unstable. Consider a toad with an index of 6.1, just above the cutoff. If he remains silent, what will other toads think? From experience, they will know that *because* he is silent, his croak must be pitched higher than 6. But how much higher?

Lacking information about this particular toad, they cannot say exactly. It generally will be possible, however, to make a statistical guess. Suppose toads were uniformly scattered along the pitch scale. This means that if we picked a toad at random from the entire population of toads, the pitch of its croak would be equally likely to take any value along the pitch scale. With the croaking threshold at 6, however, a toad who remained silent would be systematically different

FIGURE 6-1
If only those toads with a pitch below 6.0 bother to croak, toads who remain silent reveal that their pitch is, on the average, significantly higher than 6.0.

THE INFORMATION IMPLICIT IN SILENCE

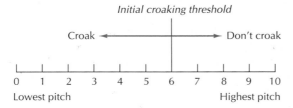

---

[3]See Krebs and Dawkins, 1984.

from a randomly selected toad. In particular, experience would tell that the average index for toads who remain silent is 8 (halfway between 6 and 10). Any toad with an index less than 8 would, by the fact of his silence, create the impression that he is smaller than he really is. Our toad with an index of 6.1 would therefore do far better to croak than not.

Thus, if the threshold for remaining silent were 6, it would pay all toads with an index less than 8 to croak. If they do, of course, the threshold will not remain at 6. It will shift to 8. But a threshold of 8 will not be stable either. With the cutoff at that level, it will pay all toads with an index less than 9 to croak. *Any* threshold less than 10 is for similar reasons destined to unravel. This process happens not because the small toads want to call attention to their smallness by croaking. Rather, they are forced to do so in order to keep from appearing smaller than they really are.

The full-disclosure principle derives from the fact that potential adversaries do not all have access to the same information. In the toad case, the asymmetry is that the silent toad knows exactly how big he is, while his rival can make only an informed guess. As the following illustrations demonstrate, similar asymmetries give rise to important signals between economic agents.

Product Warranties.   Information asymmetries help explain, for example, why the producer of a low-quality product might disclose that fact by offering only very limited warranty coverage. The asymmetry here is that producers know much more than consumers about how good their products are. The firm that knows it has the best product has a strong incentive to disclose that information to consumers. A credible means of doing so is to provide a liberal guarantee against product defects. (This device is credible because of the costly-to-fake principle—a low-quality product would break down frequently, making it too costly to offer a liberal guarantee.)

Once this product appears with its liberal guarantee, consumers immediately know more than before, not only about *its* quality, but about the quality of all remaining products as well. In particular, they know that the ones without guarantees cannot be of the highest quality. Lacking any other information about an unguaranteed product, a prudent consumer would estimate its quality as the average level for such products. But this means consumers will underestimate the quality of those products that are just slightly inferior to the best product.

Consider the situation confronting the producer of the second-best product. If it continues to offer no guarantee, consumers will think its product is worse than it really is. Accordingly, this producer will do better to offer a guarantee of its own. But because of its product's slightly lower quality, the terms of its guarantee cannot be quite so liberal as those for the best product.

With the second-best product now guaranteed, the class of remaining unguaranteed products is of still lower average quality than before. The unraveling process is set in motion, and in the end, all producers must either offer guarantees or live with the knowledge that consumers rank their products lowest in quality. The terms of the guarantees will in general be less liberal the lower a product's quality. Producers clearly do not want to announce their low quality levels by offering stingy warranty coverage. Their problem is that failure to do so would make consumers peg their quality levels even lower than they really are.

When Chrysler declares, "We back them better because we build them better," we cannot be 100 percent sure it is telling the literal truth. But if the claim were grossly misleading—that is, if Chrysler cars were significantly more likely to break down than others—it would be a costly lie indeed. And therein lies a rational motive for consumers to credit Chrysler's statement.

Regulating the Employment Interviewer.   Another illuminating application of the full-disclosure principle is the difficulty that principle predicts for government policies that try to restrict the amount of information corporations can demand of job applicants. Consider, for example, the legislation that prohibits employers from asking about marital status and plans for having children. Before the enactment of this legislation, employers routinely solicited such information, particularly from female job candidates. The information is correlated with the likelihood of withdrawal from the labor force, and the employer's motive in asking for it was to avoid investing in the hiring and training of workers who would not stay long. Since the demographic information is costly to fake (few people would refrain from marrying in order to appear less likely to drop out of the labor force), it can be a signal between parties whose interests might be in conflict. The purpose of the legislation was to prevent employers from favoring job candidates on the basis of demographic status.

To achieve this, however, it is not sufficient merely to prohibit employers from asking about demographic categories. For if a woman realizes that her own particular categories place her in the most favored hiring category, she has every incentive to *volunteer* information about them. This sets up the familiar unraveling process whereby all but the least favorable information will eventually be volunteered freely by job candidates. The candidate who fails to volunteer information, however unfavorable, is simply assumed to be in the least favorable category. If the legislation were to achieve its desired intent, it would somehow have to prohibit job candidates from volunteering the information at issue.

People and things belong to categories. Categories, in turn, often exist in hierarchies. Some categories are, by consensus, better than others. To be trustworthy is better than to be untrustworthy, hard-working better than lazy, and so on. The general message of the full-disclosure principle is that lack of evidence that something resides in a favored category will often suggest that it belongs to a less favored one. Stated in this form, the principle seems transparently simple. And yet its implications are sometimes far from obvious.

The Lemons Principle.   For example, the full-disclosure principle helps resolve the long-standing paradox of why new cars usually lose a large fraction of their market value the moment they are driven from the showroom. How is it, exactly, that a new car purchased for $15,000 on Wednesday could command a price of only $12,000 in the used-car market on Thursday? Clearly the car does not lose 20 percent of its value within 24 hours merely because of physical depreciation.

Economists struggled for years to make sense out of this curious pattern of events. In an uncomfortable departure from their characteristic professional posture, some even speculated that consumers held irrational prejudices against used cars. Berkeley economist George Akerlof, however, suggested that mysterious superstitions might not be necessary. In his "The Market for 'Lemons,'" one of the most widely cited economics papers in the past several decades, he offered an ingenious alternative explanation (which became the first clear statement of the full-disclosure principle).[4]

Akerlof began with the assumption that new cars are, roughly speaking, of two basic types: good ones and "lemons." The two types look alike. But the owner of any given car knows from experience which type hers is. Since prospective buyers cannot tell which type is which, good cars and lemons must sell for the same price. We are tempted to think the common price will be a weighted average of the respective values of the two types, with the weights being the proportions accounted for by each type. In the new-car market, in fact, this intuition proves roughly correct.

In the used-car market, however, things work out differently. Since good cars are worth more to their owners than lemons are to theirs, a much larger fraction of the lemons finds its way quickly into the used-car market. As used-car buyers notice the pattern, the price of used cars begins to fall. This fall in price then reinforces the original tendency of owners of good cars not to sell. In extreme cases, the *only* used cars for sale will be lemons.

Akerlof's insight was to realize that the mere fact that a car was for sale constituted important information about its quality. This is not to say that having a lemon is the only reason that prompts people to sell their cars. Even if it were just a minor reason, however, it would still keep the owner of a good car from getting full value for it in the secondhand market. And that may be all that is needed to initiate the by now familiar unraveling process. Indeed, trouble-free cars rarely find their way into the used-car market except as a result of heavy pressure from external circumstances. ("Going overseas, must sell my Volvo station wagon" or "Injured hand, must sell stick shift.")

Akerlof's explanation thus vindicates our intuition that physical depreciation is an insufficient reason for the sharp price differential between new and used cars. The gap is much more plausibly understood as a reflection of the fact that cars offered for sale, taken as a group, are simply of lower average quality than cars not offered for sale.

The Stigma of the Newcomer.   The full-disclosure principle also suggests why it might once have been more difficult than it is now to escape the effects of a bad reputation by moving. In the current environment, where mobility is high, a

---

[4]George Akerlof, "The Market for 'Lemons,'" *Quarterly Journal of Economics*, 1970.

dishonest person would be attracted to the strategy of moving to a new location each time he got caught cheating. But in less mobile times, this strategy would have been much less effective, for when societies were more stable, trustworthy people had much more to gain by staying put and reaping the harvest of the good reputation they worked to develop. In the same sense that it is not in the interests of the owner of a good car to sell, it was not in the interests of an honest person to move. In generally stable environments, movers, like used cars, were suspect. Nowadays, however, there are so many *external* pressures to move that the mere fact of being a newcomer carries almost no such presumption.

CHOOSING A RELATIONSHIP

Most people want mates who are kind, caring, healthy, intelligent, physically attractive, and so on. Information about physical attractiveness may be gathered at a glance. But many of the other traits people seek in a mate are difficult to observe, and people often rely on behavioral signals that reveal them. To be effective, such signals must be costly to fake. Someone who is looking for, say, a highly disciplined partner might thus do well to take special interest in people who run marathons in less than $2\frac{1}{2}$ hours.

Even the degree of interest a person shows in a prospective partner will sometimes reveal a lot. Groucho Marx once said he wouldn't join any club that would have him as a member. To follow a similar strategy in the search for a relationship would obviously result in frustration. And yet Groucho was clearly onto something. There may be good reasons for avoiding a seemingly attractive searcher who is too eager. If this person is as attractive as he or she seems, why such eagerness? Such a posture will often suggest unfavorable values for traits that are difficult to observe. The properties of effective signals thus make it clear why coyness, within limits, is so adaptive. It is very difficult, apparently, for eager persons to disguise their eagerness.

The same properties also have implications for the institutional arrangements under which people search for partners. An often decried difficulty of modern urban life is that heavy work schedules make it hard for people to meet one another. In response, commercial dating services offer to match people with ostensibly similar interests and tastes. Participants in these services are thus spared the time and expense of getting to know people with whom they have few interests in common. They also avoid uncertainty about whether their prospective partner is interested in meeting someone. And yet while marriages do sometimes result from commercial dating services, the consensus appears to be that they are a bad investment. The apparent reason is that, without meaning to, they act as a screening device that identifies people who have trouble initiating their own relationships. To be sure, sometimes a participant's trouble is merely that he or she is too busy. But often it is the result of personality problems or other, more worrisome difficulties. People who participate in dating services are indeed easier to meet, just as the advertisements say. But signaling theory says that, on the average, they are less worth meeting.

CONSPICUOUS CONSUMPTION AS ABILITY SIGNALING

Suppose that you have been unjustly accused of a serious crime and are look-ing for an attorney to represent you. And suppose your choice is between two lawyers who, so far as you know, are identical in all respects, except for their standard of consumption. One wears a threadbare polyester suit off the rack and arrives at the courthouse in a 15-year-old, rust-eaten Chevy Citation. The other wears an impeccably tailored sharkskin suit and drives a new BMW 740i. Which one would you hire?

Our simple signaling principles suggest that the latter attorney is probably a better bet. The reason is that a lawyer's ability level in a competitive market is likely to be mirrored closely by his income, which in turn will be positively cor-related with his consumption. There is obviously no guarantee that the lawyer who spends more on consumption will have higher ability. But as in other situ-ations involving risk, here too people must be guided by the laws of probabil-ity. And these laws say unequivocally to choose the better-dressed lawyer.

Where important decisions involving people we do not know well are involved, even weak signals of ability are often decisive. Close employment deci-sions are an obvious example. First impressions count for a lot during job inter-views, and as apparel manufacturers are fond of reminding us, we never get a second chance to make a first impression. Placement counselors have always stressed the importance of quality attire and a good address in the job search process. Even when the employer *knows* how good an applicant is, she may still care a great deal about how that person will come across to others. This will be especially true in jobs that involve extensive contact with outsiders who do *not* know how good the employee is.

Judging from their spending behavior, many single people seem to believe that their marriage prospects hinge critically on what clothes they wear and what cars they drive. At first glance, this seems curious because by the time most people marry, they presumably know one another well enough for such things not to count for much. Even so, many potential mates have been rejected at the outset for seeming "unsuitable." The trappings of success do not guar-antee that a person will marry well, but they do strengthen the chances of draw-ing a second glance.

The importance of consumption goods as signals of ability will be different for different occupations. Earnings and the abilities that count most among research professors are not strongly correlated, and most professors think noth-ing of continuing to drive a 15-year-old automobile if it still serves them reliably. But it would be a big mistake for an aspiring investment banker to drive such a car in the presence of his potential clients.

This example makes it clear that a person's incentive to spend additional money on conspicuous consumption goods will be inversely related to the amount and reliability of independent information that other people have about his abilities. The more people know about someone, the less he can influence their assessments of him by rearranging his consumption patterns in favor of observable goods. This may help explain why consumption patterns in small towns, which have highly stable social networks, are so different from those in big cities. The wardrobe a professional person "needs" in Iowa City, for example, costs less than half as much as the one that same person would need in Manhattan or Los Angeles. Similarly, because the reliability of information about a person increases with age, the share of income devoted to conspicuous consumption should decline over time. The more mature spending patterns of older people may say as much about the declining payoffs to ability signaling as about the increasing wisdom of age.

Note that conspicuous consumption as an ability signal confronts us with a dilemma. The concept of a tasteful wardrobe, like the notion of a fast car, is inescapably relative. To make a good first impression, it is not sufficient to wear clothes that are clean and mended. We must wear something that looks better than what most others wear. This creates an incentive for everyone to save less and spend more on clothing. But when *everyone* spends more on clothing, relative appearance remains unchanged. Conspicuous consumption is thus essentially a positional good (see Chapter 5). In the familiar stadium metaphor, all spectators leap to their feet to get a better view of an exciting play, only to find the view no better than if all had remained seated. Here, too, the aggregate outcome of individually rational behavior is markedly different from what people hoped.

As a group, it might pay to spend much less on conspicuous consumption and to save much more for retirement. But if conspicuous consumption strongly influences estimates of ability, it will not pay any individual, acting alone, to take this step.

ADVERSE SELECTION

When a trading opportunity is presented to a heterogeneous group of potential traders, those who accept it will be different—and in some specific sense, worse—on the average, than those who do not. For example, the used cars that are for sale are of lower quality than the used cars that are not for sale; and the participants in dating services are generally less worth meeting than others. Both illustrate the lemons principle, and are also sometimes referred to as examples of *adverse selection*. Adverse selection is the process by which "undesirable" members of a population of buyers or sellers are more likely to participate in a voluntary exchange.

Adverse selection Process by which the less desirable potential trading partners volunteer to exchange.

Adverse selection is especially important in insurance markets, where it often eliminates exchange possibilities that would be beneficial to both consumers and insurance companies alike. To remain in business, an insurance company must have revenues from premiums that cover the claims it pays out plus its administrative expenses. Its premiums therefore must closely reflect the likelihood of claims being filed. Not all potential consumers, however, are equally likely to file claims. In the automobile collision insurance case, for example, some drivers are several times more likely to have accidents than others.

If insurance companies could identify the most risky drivers, they could adjust their premiums accordingly. To some extent, of course, they attempt to do precisely that, charging higher rates for drivers with a history of accidents or serious traffic violations or even for those having no prior insurance history. (More below on how they also set different rates for people with identical records who belong to different groups.) But these adjustments are at best imperfect. Some people who have had neither an accident nor a traffic ticket are nonetheless much more at risk than many drivers with blemished records. Within any broad category of policy, there will inevitably be wide variation in the riskiness of potential policyholders.

Competitive pressure in the insurance market will in general force premiums to reflect the average level of risk for policies in a given category. This means that drivers who know they are much riskier than average face an attractive price on insurance. The other side of this coin, however, is that the same premium is unattractive to drivers who know they are much less risky than average. The result is that many of the least risky drivers will be induced to self-insure. And when that happens, the average riskiness of the drivers who do buy insurance goes up, which necessitates a rise in premiums. This increase, in turn, makes the insurance even less attractive to less risky drivers, inducing still more of them to self-insure. In the end, all but the worst drivers may be excluded from participation in the insurance market. This is an unfortunate outcome for many careful drivers, who would gladly pay an insurance premium that was anywhere close to the expected value of their losses.

STATISTICAL DISCRIMINATION

As noted earlier, automobile insurance companies often try to tailor their rates to the driving records of individual policyholders. In addition, most companies charge different rates to people with identical driving records if they happen to belong to groups with significantly different average risk. Perhaps the most conspicuous example is the extremely high rate for single male drivers under 25 years of age. The average accident rate for drivers in this group is much higher than for any other demographic category. Even so, plenty of males under 25 are exceptionally good drivers. My second son (the one who always eats his favorite foods last) is a clear example, and there are surely several others in your class. The difficulty is that insurance companies cannot identify these drivers at reasonable cost.

In California, many auto insurance companies charge different rates depending on what part of a city you live in. Their rationale is that traffic congestion, theft, vandalism, uninsured drivers, and other factors that influence claims differ greatly from neighborhood to neighborhood.[5] The awkward result,

---

[5]See Eric Smith and Randall Wright,"Why Is Automobile Insurance in Philadelphia So Damned Expensive?," *American Economic Review*, 82, 1992: 756−772.

however, is that people who live just 50 yards from one another in adjacent zip codes sometimes end up paying substantially different insurance rates.

Many have complained that such rate differentials are inherently unfair. But before judging the insurance companies, it is important to understand what would happen to one that abandoned these differentials. Suppose, for example, that a company decided to sell insurance at the same price to all drivers with clean records. If it retained its current list of policyholders, this would mean lowering its current rates for people in unsafe neighborhoods, teenage males, and other high-risk groups, and raising them for everyone else. But why should older drivers from safe neighborhoods then remain with the company? They could save by switching to a company that had stuck with the old rate structure, and many of them would surely do so. By the same token, members of high-risk groups who now hold policies with other companies would have a strong incentive to switch to the one with the new rate structure. In the end, the company would be left with only policyholders from high-risk groups. The company could stick with its new program of charging the same rate for everyone, but that rate would have to be high enough to cover the claims generated by the highest risk group of all.

Recognizing this problem, some states are considering laws to outlaw group insurance rating. The argument is that if *all* companies are forced to offer a single rate, members of low-risk groups cannot escape rate increases by switching to other companies. The difficulty with this approach, however, is that the government cannot force private insurance companies to provide insurance against their will. As a result, many companies will pull out of those areas that are costliest to serve, leaving their former customers to fend for themselves.

Choice Under Uncertainty

No matter how much time and energy we spend gathering information, most choices must be made without complete knowledge about the relevant alternatives. The choice between, say, taking a ski trip or buying a new CD player can be made more intelligently if we consult sources like the National Weather Service and *Consumer Reports*. And yet, in the end, we simply cannot rule out possibilities like bad weather or defective computer chips. Such risks are a prominent feature of many of our most important decisions. Our task in the remainder of this chapter is to enlarge the basic consumer choice model in Chapter 3 to accommodate them.

PROBABILITY AND EXPECTED VALUE

Choosing a university to attend, a person to marry, an occupation to pursue, even a movie to see—in each case there are likely to be important characteristics of the alternatives that you are uncertain about at the moment of choice. Sometimes your choice is between two alternatives that are equally risky (the choice, for example, between two blind dates); other times it will be between a little-known alternative and a relatively familiar one (for instance, the decision of whether to transfer to another university or to stay where you are).

Economic decisions made under uncertainty are essentially gambles. We have a variety of intuitions about what makes for an attractive gamble, and many of these intuitions carry over into the realm of economic choices. To illustrate, consider the following series of gambles involving the toss of a fair coin.

Gamble 1.   If the coin comes up heads, you win $100; if tails, you lose $0.50.

This is a gamble you are unlikely ever to be offered in a profit-making casino. The winning outcome is 200 times larger than the losing outcome and the two outcomes are equally likely. Only people whose religious faith proscribes gambling would consider turning this gamble down, and even for them, the choice might be difficult. (They might, for example, think it best to take the gamble and donate their winnings to charity.)

Gamble 2.   If heads, you win $200; if tails, you lose $100.

With a winning outcome only twice as large as the losing outcome, this bet is obviously less attractive than the first, but it too would be accepted by many people.

Finally, consider a third gamble. It is the same as the second except the payoffs are multiplied by 100.

Gamble 3.   If heads, you win $20,000; if tails, you lose $10,000; losers are allowed to pay off their loss in small monthly payments spread out over 30 years.

If put to the test, most people would refuse this bet, even though its payoffs are in exactly the same proportion as those in gamble 2. It is the task of a theory of choice under uncertainty to explain this pattern of behavior.

One important property of a gamble is its *expected value,* a weighted average of all its possible outcomes, where the weights are the respective probabilities. The probability that a fair coin comes up heads when tossed is 1/2. One way of interpreting this statement is to say that it means that if a fair coin were tossed a very large number of times, it would come up heads half the time, tails the other half of the time. Thus, the three bets described above have expected values of

Expected value
The sum of all possible outcomes, weighted by its respective probability of occurrence.

$$EV_1 = (1/2)\$100 + (1/2)(-\$0.50) = \$49.75; \tag{6.1}$$
$$EV_2 = (1/2)\$200 + (1/2)(-\$100) = \$50; \tag{6.2}$$

and

$$EV_3 = (1/2)\$20,000 + (1/2)(-\$10,000) = \$5000, \tag{6.3}$$

where the notation EV_i denotes the expected value of gamble i, where $i = 1, 2, 3$.

A gamble is clearly more attractive if it has a positive expected value rather than a negative one. But from the way most people respond to these three hypothetical gambles, it is clear that having a positive expected value is by no means sufficient to make a gamble attractive. On the contrary, gamble 3 has the highest expected value of the three, yet is the one least likely to be accepted. By contrast, gamble 1, which has the lowest expected value, is the one most likely to be chosen.

Now, the lesson is obviously not that having a higher expected value is a bad thing in itself. Rather, it is that in addition to the expected value of a gamble, most people also consider how they feel about each of its possible outcomes. The feature that makes gamble 3 so unattractive to most people is that there is a 50-50 chance of the extremely unpleasant outcome of losing $10,000. Gamble 2 also contains an unpleasant possibility, namely, a 50-50 chance of losing $100. But this is an outcome many people feel they could live with. Gamble 1 is by far the easiest choice for most people because its positive outcome is large enough to make a difference, while its negative outcome is too small to really matter.

THE VON NEUMANN–MORGENSTERN EXPECTED UTILITY MODEL

Expected utility
The expected utility of a gamble is the expected value of utility over all possible outcomes.

The formal economic theory of choice between uncertain alternatives was advanced by John von Neumann, a distinguished mathematician at the Institute for Advanced Study, and Oskar Morgenstern, a Princeton economist. Its central premise is that people choose the alternative that has not the highest expected value but the highest *expected utility*. Their theory of expected utility maximization assumes a utility function U that assigns a numerical measure to the satisfaction associated with different outcomes. *The expected utility of a gamble is the expected value of utility over all possible outcomes.*

For the sake of simplicity, we will consider the outcome of a gamble to be defined uniquely by the amount of total wealth to which it corresponds. For example, if a consumer with an initial wealth level of 1000 accepted gamble 1 above and won, the outcome would be a total wealth of $1000 + 100 = 1100$, and the consumer's utility would be $U(1100)$. If he lost, his wealth would be $1000 - 0.50 = 999.50$, his utility $U(999.50)$. More generally, if M_0 is the consumer's initial wealth level, the expected utility of accepting the first gamble would be

$$\text{EU}_1 = (1/2)\, U(M_0 + 100) + (1/2)\, U(M_0 - 0.50). \qquad (6.4)$$

If your choice is between accepting gamble 1 or refusing it, and you refuse it, your expected utility will simply be the utility of the wealth level M_0, namely, $U(M_0)$. Faced with this choice, the von Neumann–Morgenstern expected utility criterion tells you to accept the gamble if and only if EU_1 is larger than $U(M_0)$.

EXAMPLE 6-1 *Suppose Smith's utility function is given by $U(M) = \sqrt{M}$. If Smith has an initial wealth of 10,000, which of the above gambles has the highest expected utility?*

The three expected utilities are given by

$$EU_1 = (1/2)\sqrt{10{,}100} + (1/2)\sqrt{9999.50} = 100.248,$$
$$EU_2 = (1/2)\sqrt{10{,}200} + (1/2)\sqrt{9900} = 100.247,$$

and

$$EU_3 = (1/2)\sqrt{30{,}000} + (1/2)\sqrt{0} = 86.603,$$

so gamble 1 is the most attractive of the three for Smith.

The key insight of the theory is that the expected values of the outcomes of a set of alternatives need not have the same ranking as the expected utilities of the alternatives. Differences in these orderings arise because utility is often a nonlinear function of final wealth. In the empirically most common case, utility is assumed to be a *concave* function of total wealth, which means that the utility function has the characteristic profile shown in Figure 6-2. More formally, a function $U(M)$ is said to be concave if for any pair of values M_1 and M_2, the function lies above the chord joining the points $[M_1, U(M_1)]$ and $[M_2, U(M_2)]$. The utility function $U = \sqrt{M}$ is a concave function of M. A utility function that is concave in M is also said to exhibit **diminishing marginal utility** of wealth. Marginal utility is simply the slope of the utility function,[6] and a utility function with diminishing marginal utility is one whose slope declines as M increases. Intuitively, the meaning of diminishing marginal utility of wealth is that the more wealth a consumer has, the smaller will be the increase in his utility caused by a 1-unit increase in wealth.

Persons whose utility functions are concave in total wealth are said to be **risk averse**, which means that they would always refuse a gamble whose expected value is zero. Gambles with an expected value of zero are called *fair gambles*.

Consider, for example, a gamble G in which you win \$30 if the coin comes up heads, but lose \$30 if tails. The expected value of this gamble is $(1/2)30 + (1/2)(-30) = 0$, so it is a fair gamble. For a person with an initial wealth level of 40, and utility function given by $U = U(M)$, the expected utility of this gamble is

$$EU_G = 0.5U(40 - 30) + 0.5U(40 + 30) = 0.5U(10) + 0.5U(70). \tag{6.5}$$

For any fair gamble, the expected value of your wealth if you accept the gamble is the same as the certain value of your wealth if you refuse the gamble. Here, the expected value of wealth when you take the gamble is equal to 40. If you refuse the gamble, you will have a certain wealth level of 40, which yields utility

Diminishing marginal utility For a utility function defined by wealth, one in which the marginal utility declines as wealth rises.

Risk averse Preferences described by a utility function with diminishing marginal utility of wealth.

Fair gamble A gamble whose expected value is zero.

---

[6]See the appendix to Chapter 3, which can be found in the "For the Instructor" section at our Web site www.mhhe.com/economics/frank4, for a more extended discussion of marginal utility.

FIGURE 6-2
Any arc of a con-
cave utility function
lies above the corre-
sponding chord.

A CONCAVE UTILITY FUNCTION

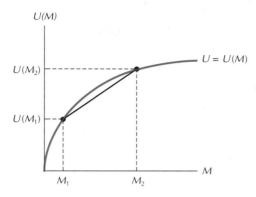

equal to $U(40)$. Expected utility theory says that if $EU_G > U(40)$, you should
accept the gamble; otherwise you should refuse it.

The expected utility of a gamble has a straightforward geometric interpretation. We first construct the chord that joins the points on the utility function that
correspond to losing and winning the gamble, respectively (that is, the points A
and C in Figure 6-3). For the utility function shown in Figure 6-3, the expected
utility of the gamble is equal to $0.5(18) + 0.5(38) = 28$. Note that this value corresponds to the point on the chord between A and C that lies directly above the
expected value of wealth under the gamble (40). Note that the expected utility
of refusing the gamble is simply $U(40) = 32$, which is clearly larger than the
expected utility of the gamble itself.

FIGURE 6-3
The expected utility
of a gamble lies on
the chord joining
points A and C. If
the probability of
winning is 1/2, the
expected utility lies
halfway between A
and C. Since a point
on the arc of a con-
cave function al-
ways lies above the
corresponding point
on the chord, the
expected utility of a
fair gamble will al-
ways be less than
the utility of refusing
the gamble.

A RISK-AVERSE PERSON WILL ALWAYS REFUSE A FAIR GAMBLE

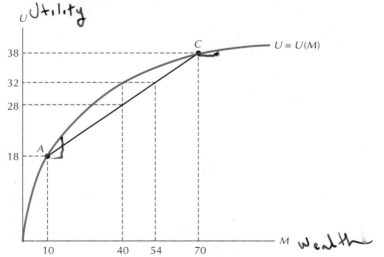

Indeed, it is clear from Figure 6-3 that a risk-averse person will refuse not only fair gambles but even some that have positive expected value. For the particular utility function shown, all gambles that result in an expected value of final wealth less than 54 yield a lower expected utility than that of standing pat with the initial wealth level 40.

The gambles we have considered so far have been ones decided by the toss of a coin. With probability 1/2, a good outcome occurred; with probability 1/2, a bad outcome. In general, however, the probability of winning a gamble can be any number between 0 and 1. But as the following example and exercise illustrate, the expected utility of a gamble may still be interpreted as a point on the chord joining the winning and losing endpoints, even when the probability of winning is something other than 1/2.

EXAMPLE 6-2 *Your utility function is $U = \sqrt{M}$ and your initial wealth is 36. Will you accept a gamble in which you win 13 with probability 2/3 and lose 11 with probability 1/3?*

The expected utility of the gamble is given by

$$EU_G = (2/3)\sqrt{36 + 13} + (1/3)\sqrt{36 - 11} = 14/3 + 5/3 = 19/3.$$

If you refuse the gamble, your utility will be $\sqrt{36} = 6$, which is smaller than 19/3, so you should accept the gamble.

EXERCISE 6-1

Graph the utility function in Example 6-2 for $0 < M < 50$. Locate the points on the utility function that correspond to the winning and losing outcomes of the gamble in Example 6-2. Draw the chord between these two points, labeling the winning endpoint C, the losing endpoint A. What fraction of AC must you move from C before reaching the expected utility of the gamble?

The general rule illustrated by Exercise 6-1 is that if the probability of winning is p and the probability of losing is $1 - p$, then the expected utility lies a fraction of $1 - p$ to the left of point C, the winning endpoint of the chord joining the winning and losing points on the utility function.

One intuitive rationale for the assumption that most people are risk averse is that increments to total wealth yield diminishing marginal utility—which, again, means that the more wealth a consumer has, the smaller will be the increase in his utility caused by a 1-unit increase in wealth. Most of us are comfortable with the idea that an extra $100 means more to a person if his total wealth is $4000 than it would if his total wealth were $1 million. Note that this intuition is equivalent to saying that the utility function is concave in total wealth—which in turn implies that a given gain in wealth produces a smaller gain in utility than the loss that would be caused by a comparable loss in wealth.

Whether people are risk averse is of course an empirical question. We do know that at least some people are not risk averse some of the time (such as those who climb sheer rock cliffs, or go hang-gliding in gusty winds). And we also know that most of us are not risk averse at least some of the time (as, for example, when we play roulette in Atlantic City, or any other game of chance with negative expected value).

Risk seeking
Preferences described by a utility function with increasing marginal utility of wealth.

Consider a person with an initial wealth of M_0 who is confronted with a gamble that pays B with probability $1/2$ and $-B$ with probability of $1/2$. If this person is a ***risk seeker***, her utility function will look like the one pictured in Figure 6-4. It is *convex* in total wealth, which implies that the expected utility of accepting a fair gamble, EU_G, will be larger than the utility of refusing it, $U(M_0)$. Geometrically, a convex utility function is one whose slope increases with total wealth.

EXERCISE 6-2

> Consider a person with an initial wealth level of 100 who faces a chance to win 20 with probability $1/2$ and to lose 20 with probability $1/2$. If this person's utility function is given by $U(M) = M^2$, will she accept this gamble?

FIGURE 6-4
Any arc of a convex function lies below the corresponding chord. For a risk seeker, the expected utility of a fair gamble, EU_G, will always exceed the utility of refusing the gamble, $U(M_0)$.

THE UTILITY FUNCTION OF A RISK-SEEKING PERSON IS CONVEX IN TOTAL WEALTH

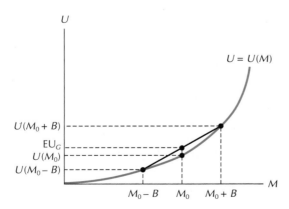

Risk neutral
Preferences described by a utility function with constant marginal utility of wealth.

   A person is said to be *risk neutral*, finally, if he is generally indifferent between accepting or refusing a fair gamble. The utility function of a risk-neutral person will be linear, like the one shown in Figure 6-5.

EXERCISE 6-3

Consider a person with an initial wealth level of 100 who faces a chance to win 20 with probability 1/2 and to lose 20 with probability 1/2. If this person's utility function is given by $U(M) = M$, will she accept this gamble?

EXAMPLE 6-3

Suppose it is known that some fraction z of all personal computers are defective. The defective ones, however, cannot be identified except by those who own them. Consumers are risk neutral and value nondefective computers at $2000 each. Computers do not depreciate physically with use. New computers sell for $1000, used ones for $500. What is z?

Because of the lemons principle, we know that all used computers that are for sale must be defective. (The owners of nondefective computers could not sell them for what they are worth in the used market, so they hold on to them.) Accordingly, the price of a used computer is the same as the value of a new defective one. (Recall that being used, by itself, doesn't cause the machines to depreciate.) Because consumers are risk neutral, the price of a new computer—$1000—is simply a weighted average of the values of nondefective and defective computers, where the weights are the respective probabilities. Thus we have

$$\$1000 = \$500z + \$2000 \,(1 - z), \tag{6.6}$$

which solves for $z = 2/3$.

EXERCISE 6-4

Suppose one in every four new personal computers is defective. The defective ones, however, cannot be identified except by those who own them. Consumers are risk neutral and value nondefective computers at $2000 each. Computers do not depreciate physically with use. If used computers sell for $600, how much do new ones sell for?

FIGURE 6-5
A risk-neutral consumer is indifferent between accepting or refusing a fair gamble, because the expected utility of accepting, EU_G, is the same as the certain utility of refusing, $U(M_0)$.

RISK NEUTRALITY

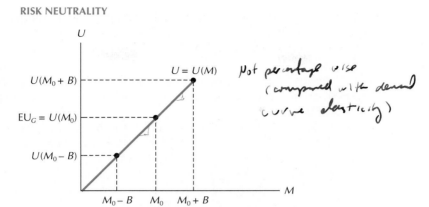

Not percentage wise (compared with demand curve elasticity)

The gambles we have considered thus far have had only two outcomes. In general, however, a gamble can have any number of possible outcomes. The expected value of a gamble with more than two outcomes is, as before, a weighted sum of the possible outcomes, where the weights are again the respective probabilities. For example, a gamble with three possible outcomes, B_1, B_2, and B_3, which occur with probabilities p_1, p_2, and p_3, respectively, has an expected value of $p_1B_1 + p_2B_2 + p_3B_3$. Because the probabilities must add up to 1, we know that $p_3 = (1 - p_1 - p_2)$. The expected utility of this gamble is therefore $p_1U(B_1) + p_2U(B_2) + (1 - p_1 - p_2)U(B_3)$.

To gain added facility with the concepts of the expected utility model, it is helpful to work through some simple numerical examples. In the next example we use a payoff tree to illustrate the outcomes and probabilities for a decision under uncertainty.

*E*XAMPLE *6-4* *Sarah has a von Neumann–Morgenstern utility function given by $U = 1 - 1/M$, where M is the present value of her lifetime income. If Sarah becomes a teacher, she will make $M = 5$ with probability 1. If she becomes an actress, she will make $M = 400$ if she becomes a star, but only $M = 2$ if she fails to become a star. The probability of her becoming a star is 0.01. Smith is an infallible judge of acting talent. After a brief interview, he can state with certainty whether Sarah will become a star. What is the most she would be willing to pay for this information?*

> To answer this question, we must first calculate Sarah's expected utility if she lacks access to Smith's information. If she were to become a teacher, she will have a lifetime income of 5 with probability 1, so her expected utility would be simply
>
> $$U_T = 1 - 1/5 = 0.8.$$

If instead she pursued an acting career, her expected utility would be

$$EU_A = 0.01(1 - 1/400) + 0.99(1 - 1/2) = 0.505.$$

Because her expected utility is higher by becoming a teacher rather than an actress, she will become a teacher and have an expected utility of 0.8.

Now suppose that she has access to an interview with Smith that will reveal with certainty whether she would become a star if she pursued an acting career. And suppose that the charge for this interview is P, where P is measured in the same units as M (see Figure 6-6).

The clear advantage of having the information Smith provided is that if he says she would succeed as an actress, she can then avail herself of that lucrative, but otherwise too risky, career path. If Smith says she would not succeed, however, she can choose teaching with no regrets. Her expected utility if she pays P for the interview is given by

$$EU_I = 0.01[1 - 1/(400 - P)] + 0.99[1 - 1/(5 - P)]. \tag{6.7}$$

To find the maximum amount that Smith can charge for an interview, we set EU_I equal to Sarah's expected utility if she lacks information and solve for P (recall that if she lacks information, she becomes a teacher and gets $U_T = 0.8$):

$$EU_I = 0.01[1 - 1/(400 - P)] + 0.99[1 - 1/(5 - P)] = U_T = 0.8. \tag{6.8}$$

As an exercise, you can verify that a value of P of approximately 0.0494 solves this equation. For any price less than that, Sarah should pay Smith for his evaluation. But if Smith charges more than 0.0494, Sarah should skip the interview and become a teacher.

FIGURE 6-6
Under the assumed payoffs, the expected utility of becoming an actress is less than the expected utility of becoming a teacher. But because a successful actress earns so much more than a teacher, information about whether an acting career would be successful has obvious economic value.

THE VALUE OF REDUCING UNCERTAINTY

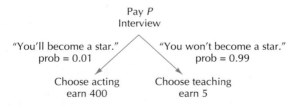

As the preceding example clearly illustrates, information that helps reduce uncertainty has economic value. And this is reflected in the fact that we employ vocational testing services, guidance counselors, and a variety of other professionals to generate just this type of information.

E_{XAMPLE} 6-5 *Suppose you have been accepted by two colleges, A and B. A is a much more demanding and also a more prestigious institution than B. In all respects other than the possible influence each school will have on your career prospects, you are indifferent between the two. B is a safe option in the sense that you know you will do reasonably well academically there, and that after graduation you will land an "adequate" job. If you manage to survive academically at A, you will land a "great" job; but it is also possible that you will do poorly there, in which case you will end up in a "bad" job. Figure 6-7 shows the lifetime wealth levels for each type of job and the corresponding probabilities of getting each type for the two schools. If your utility function of lifetime wealth is U(M) = $\sqrt{M}$, which college should you attend?*

Your expected utilities of attending the two colleges are given by

$$EU_A = 0.6\sqrt{1,000,000} + 0.4\sqrt{250,000} = 800 \qquad (6.9)$$

and

$$EU_B = \sqrt{690,000} = 830.7, \qquad (6.10)$$

and since EU_B is greater than EU_A, you should attend B. Notice, however, that your expected lifetime wealth after attending A [namely, $0.6(1,000,000) + 0.4(250,000) = 700,000$] would be higher than after attending B (690,000). That B is nonetheless more attractive to you is a consequence of the fact that your utility function, $U = \sqrt{M}$, is concave. The slightly higher expected wealth from attending A is not sufficient to compensate for the risk associated with that choice (see Figure 6-8).

$E_{XERCISE}$ 6-5

Certainty equivalent value The certainty equivalent value of a gamble is the sum of money for which an individual would be indifferent between receiving that sum and taking the gamble.

In Example 6-5, how low would the lifetime wealth of the acceptable job have had to be before college A would have been more attractive?

The answer to the question asked in Exercise 6-5 is called the ***certainty equivalent value*** of the gamble associated with attending college A. The certainty equivalent value of a gamble is the sum of money for which an individual would be indifferent between receiving that sum and taking the gamble.

Exposure to risk is an undesirable thing for risk-averse consumers, enough so

FIGURE 6-7
If you go to college *B*, you get an adequate job with certainty. If you go to the more prestigious college *A*, you get a great job with probability 0.6. But with probability 0.4 you will flunk out of *A*, in which case you will get a bad job.

CAREER PROSPECTS AFTER ATTENDING COLLEGES *A* AND *B*

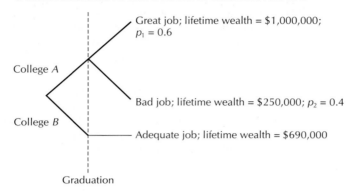

College *A*

Great job; lifetime wealth = $1,000,000; $p_1 = 0.6$

Bad job; lifetime wealth = $250,000; $p_2 = 0.4$

College *B*

Adequate job; lifetime wealth = $690,000

Graduation

that they are often willing to sacrifice substantial resources in order to reduce it. Thus, the certainty equivalent value of a gamble is less than the expected value of a gamble for risk-averse consumers. As you showed in Exercise 6-5, the consumer in Example 6-5 would have been willing to accept an outcome with $60,000 smaller expected lifetime wealth in order to avoid the possibility of landing in a bad job.

INSURING AGAINST BAD OUTCOMES

When the risks that different consumers confront are *independent* of one another (that is, when the likelihood of a bad outcome happening to one consumer is independent of the likelihood of one happening to another), it will often be possible for consumers to act collectively to achieve a result they all prefer.

Suppose, for example, that 1000 people like the one in Example 6-5 made an

FIGURE 6-8
The expected value of lifetime wealth is higher when you go to *A* ($700,000) than when you go to *B* ($690,000). But a risk-averse person will nonetheless choose *B*, because it has higher expected utility (830.6) than *A* (800).

THE EXPECTED UTILITIES OF ALTERNATIVE COLLEGE CHOICES

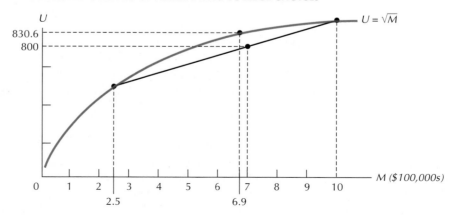

$U = \sqrt{M}$

agreement to attend college *A* and then pool their incomes afterward. If the individual probabilities of finding good jobs are independent, the proportion of people in a large group finding good jobs will be almost exactly 60 percent. (More on this point below.) And with 60 percent of the people getting good jobs and the remaining 40 percent getting bad ones, each person's share in the total wealth in the pool would be $700,000.

By agreeing to pool their incomes, then, people could eliminate virtually all the uncertainty associated with attending college *A*. If the alternative were to attend college *B* and earn $690,000, people would be willing to pay up to $10,000 each for the privilege of joining an income pool. As long as the costs of organizing the pool are less than $10,000/person, everyone can benefit by such a *risk-sharing* arrangement.

Law of large numbers A statistical law that says that if an event happens independently with probability *p* in each of *N* instances, the proportion of cases in which the event occurs approaches *p* as *N* grows larger.

Risk sharing, or *risk pooling,* works because of a statistical property called the *law of large numbers*. This law says that if an event happens independently with probability *p* for each of a large number of individuals, then the *proportion* to whom it happens in a given year will almost never deviate significantly from *p*. Suppose the event is that of a fire destroying a private home, and that it happens with probability 0.001 for each home in a given year. For a small collection of individual homes, the proportion destroyed by fire can vary sharply from year to year. But in a sample of, say, 1,000,000 homes, we can be reasonably sure that the number destroyed by fire in a given year will be very close to 1000 (so that the proportion destroyed—1000/1,000,000—would be 0.001).

The law of large numbers also shows up clearly in the proportion of heads observed in *N* flips of a fair coin. The probability of getting heads on a single toss of a fair coin is 1/2, and it is not at all unlikely to get heads 2/3 of the time or more when you toss a coin only, say, 6 times. (You get at least 4 heads in 6 tosses 34.4 percent of the time!) But toss a fair coin 10,000 times and the percentage of heads will lie between 49 and 51 percent more than 95 percent of the time.

For individuals, or even small groups of individuals, accidental losses pose a problem of inherent uncertainty. But for a large group of individuals, the proportion of people who will have accidents is extremely stable and predictable. And this property of the law of large numbers makes it possible for people to reduce their risk exposure through pooling arrangements.

Another method of risk sharing is the practice of joint ownership of business enterprises. When a new business starts, two things can happen. The business can succeed, in which case its owners earn a lot of money. Alternatively—and much more likely—it can fail, in which case they lose all or part of their initial investments. Starting a business is thus a gamble, much like any other. Consider a business venture that requires an initial investment of $10,000. Suppose that with probability 1/2 you lose this initial investment, and with probability 1/2 you not only get it back but also earn a dividend of $20,000. This venture is thus essentially the same as gamble 3 considered earlier. It is clear that while the expected value of this enterprise is positive (namely, $5000), many people would find it unacceptably risky. But if 100 people pooled their resources and shared the investment, the venture would suddenly look exactly like gamble 2—each person would stand to lose $100 with probability 1/2 or gain $200 with probability 1/2. Without changing the business venture itself at all, it has suddenly become attractive to a great many more people.

Partnerships, joint stock companies, racehorse syndicates, and a host of other similar institutional arrangements enable people to translate unacceptably large risks into much more palatable small ones. Someone with a lot of wealth to invest can keep her risk to a minimum by investing it in numerous independent projects. There is a good chance that *some* of these projects will fail, but very little chance that a substantial portion of them will.

Another example of collective action to reduce uncertainty is the operation of insurance markets. Consider the case of automobile liability insurance. An accident that causes death or serious injury can easily result in a court judgment of several million dollars against the driver. The likelihood of such a bad outcome is remote, but the consequences are so dire that few families could bear them. Private insurance companies offer a means for consumers to share this risk. By contributing an annual premium of several hundred dollars each, the policyholders create a pool of revenues that is large enough to settle the small handful of judgments awarded each year. Because of the law of large numbers, insurance companies can predict very accurately how much revenue they will need to cover their benefit claims. In effect, each party accepts a sure small loss (its insurance premium) in return for a guarantee of not having to bear a much larger one.

For the average consumer, insurance for sale in a private marketplace will always be an unfair gamble, in the specific sense defined earlier. To see why, note first that if an insurance company paid out exactly the same amount in benefits as it collected in premiums, then buying insurance would be a fair gamble—the amount a policyholder got back in benefits would be equal, on the average, to the amount she paid in premiums. But a private insurance company must collect more in premiums than it pays out in benefits, because it must also cover its administrative costs. Sales agents, bookkeepers, claims investigators, and the rent on the company's offices must all be paid for out of premiums. So, on the average, consumers get back less in benefits than they pay in premiums. That most people prefer a small unfair gamble (buying insurance) to a much larger fair one (taking their chances without insurance) is often cited as evidence that most people are risk averse.

THE RESERVATION PRICE FOR INSURANCE

What is the most a consumer would pay for insurance against a loss? Suppose a risk-averse consumer with an initial wealth of 700 has the utility function $U(M)$, as shown in Figure 6-9. If he faces the prospect of a loss of 600 with probability 1/3, his expected utility is $(1/3)U(100) + (2/3)U(700) = (1/3)(18) = (2/3)(36) = 30$. (See Figure 6-9, and note that his expected utility lies on the chord joining A and C at the point directly above $M = 500$, his expected wealth without insurance.) Now suppose this consumer could buy an insurance policy that completely covered the loss. What is the most he would be willing to pay for such a policy?

THE RESERVATION PRICE FOR INSURANCE

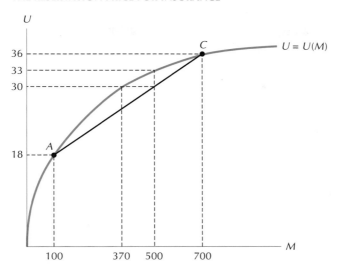

From Figure 6-9, we see that if he paid 330 for it, his utility would be $U(700 − 330) = U(370) = 30$, whether or not a loss occurred. Since this is exactly the same as his expected utility if he did not buy the policy, he would be indifferent between buying and not buying it. 330 is thus his *reservation price* for the policy, the most he would be willing to pay for it. Note that $700 − 330 = 370$ is the *certainty equivalent value* of the gamble of getting $700 − 600$ with probability 1/3 and 700 with probability 2/3. If I is the actual price of the insurance, and is less than 330, then the consumer will buy the policy and get consumer surplus from it of $330 − I$.

More generally, suppose a risk-averse consumer with an initial wealth of M_0 has the utility function $U(M)$ shown in Figure 6-10. If she faces the prospect of a loss L with probability p, her expected utility is $pU(M_0 − L) + (1 − p)U(M_0)$. From Figure 6-10, we see that if she paid R for an insurance policy against this loss, her utility would be $U(M_0 − R)$, whether or not a loss occurred. Since this is exactly the same as her expected utility if she did not buy the policy, she would be indifferent between buying and not buying it. In this more general case, R is her reservation price. $M_0 − R$ is the certainty equivalent value of the gamble of getting $M_0 − L$ with probability p and M_0 with probability $1 − p$. Finally, if I is the actual price of the insurance, and is less than R, then the consumer will buy the policy and get consumer surplus of $R − I$.

APPLICATION: ALWAYS SELF-INSURE AGAINST SMALL LOSSES

As noted earlier, insurance provided in private markets will have negative expected value because of the resources used by the company to administer its policies. The phenomenon of adverse selection provides another reason to

FIGURE 6-10
If this consumer paid R for an insurance policy against a loss of L that occurred with probability p, her utility, $U(M_0 - R)$, would be the same as her expected utility without the insurance, $pU(M_0 - L) + (1 - p)U(M_0)$.

THE RESERVATION PRICE FOR INSURANCE AGAINST A LOSS L OCCURRING WITH PROBABILITY p

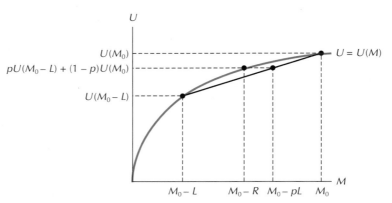

Moral hazard
The tendency whereby people expend less effort protecting those goods that are insured against theft or damage.

self-insure when the size of the potential loss is manageable. It says that insurance premiums must be large enough to cover the cost of serving the typical policyholder, who will have a greater risk of losses than the average person.

Still another reason that insurance premiums exceed the expected value of the average person's losses is the problem of **moral hazard**. Many people whose cars are insured, for example, will not take great care to prevent them from being damaged or stolen. Precautions are costly, after all, and if potential losses are fully covered, there is less reason to incur these costs.

Despite the fact that insurance premiums must cover administrative expenses, adverse selection, and the costs of moral hazard, most of us still find it prudent to insure against major losses, like damage to our homes by fire. But many people also insure against a host of much smaller losses.

Buying insurance against minor losses violates the strategy of always picking the alternative with the highest expected outcome when only small outcomes are at stake. Automobile collision insurance policies typically offer a choice of the amount of each claim to leave uncovered—the "deductible provision," as it is called. If you choose the $200 deductible provision, for example, your insurance policy will cover all but the first $200 of any damage claim. Policies with this provision are cheaper than those without, because the company not only does not have to pay the first $200 in damages, but it also avoids the trouble and expense of processing numerous small damage claims. Because of this additional cost reduction, the amount you expect to save in premiums is larger than the extra amount you expect to spend on repairs. And the higher deductible provision you choose, the greater the expected savings will be. Rather than insure fully against collision damage, it thus makes much more sense to choose a large deductible provision and deposit the savings in an interest-bearing account.

How large a deductible provision? The larger the better, subject to the proviso that you have enough resources on hand to take care of the uncovered portion of any damage claim. Indeed, for many middle- and upper-income consumers, and for those with older cars that are not worth very much, the most sensible strategy is not to buy automobile collision insurance at all.

But what if you follow this strategy and then someone smashes your new $20,000 automobile beyond repair? Naturally, you will feel bad. But be careful not to fall victim to the bad-outcome-implies-bad-decision fallacy. After all, the odds of such an accident were very low to begin with, and even having had one, your premium savings over the course of a lifetime will be more than enough to cover the damages. Relative to the alternative of buying collision insurance, going without collision insurance is a better-than-fair gamble, and if you are wealthy enough to withstand the worst outcome, you should take it.

Caution: Always Insure Against Major Losses.   Lest there be any misunderstanding, the advice of the last section does not apply to major losses. If a major loss is defined as one that will deprive you of a significant fraction of your lifetime wealth, you should always insure against such losses. You should carry major medical insurance, with deep coverage against both catastrophic illness and loss of income from disability; you should carry an umbrella liability insurance policy against the possibility of a ruinous court judgment; if you live on a flood plain, you should carry flood insurance; and so on.

Ironically, however, many people leave these life-shattering risks uncovered, while at the same time insuring themselves fully against the possible theft of their television sets. The savvy expected utility maximizer will know to avoid this ill-advised pattern of behavior.

Summary

Potential parties to an economic exchange often share many common goals, but in an important respect they must be viewed as adversaries. In both product and labor markets, both buyers and sellers face powerful incentives to misrepresent their offerings.

For messages between potential adversaries to be credible, they must be costly to fake. A firm with extensive sunk costs, for example, can communicate credibly that it offers a reliable product because if it fails to satisfy its customers, the firm stands to lose a lot of money. By contrast, a street vendor, for whom the costs of going out of business are very low, has a much more difficult time persuading buyers he offers high quality.

Messages between potential adversaries must also satisfy the full-disclosure principle, which means that if one party is able to disclose favorable information about itself, others will feel pressure to disclose parallel information, even if considerably less favorable. The producer of a low-quality product does not *want* to signal his product's inferior status by offering only limited warranty coverage. But unless he does so, many buyers will make an even less favorable assessment.

When a trading opportunity confronts a mixed group of potential traders, the ones who accept it will be different—and in some way, worse—on the average, than those who reject it. Cars that are offered for sale in the secondhand market are of lower quality than those that are not for sale; participants in dating services are generally less worth meeting than others; and so on. These are illustrations of the lemons principle, and are also sometimes referred to as examples of adverse selection.

Because of the problem of adverse selection, firms are under heavy competitive pressure to find out all the information they possibly can about potential buyers and employees. These pressures often translate into the phenomenon of statistical discrimination. In insurance markets, people from groups with different accident rates will often pay different premiums, even though their individual driving records are identical. This pricing pattern creates an understandable sense of injustice on the part of individuals adversely affected by it. In competitive markets, however, any firm that abandoned this policy could not expect to survive for long.

The analytical tool for dealing with choice under uncertainty is the von Neumann–Morgenstern expected utility model. This model begins with a utility function that assigns a numerical measure of satisfaction to each outcome, where outcomes are defined in terms of the final wealth to which they correspond. The model says that a rational consumer will choose between uncertain alternatives so as to maximize his expected utility, a weighted sum of the utilities of the outcomes, where the weights are their respective probabilities of occurrence.

The central insight of the expected utility model is that the ordering of the expected values of a collection of gambles will often be different from the ordering of the expected utilities of those gambles. The differences in these rankings arise because of nonlinearities in the utility function, which in turn summarize the consumer's attitude toward risk. The concave utility function, any arc of which always lies above the corresponding chord, leads to risk-averse behavior. Someone with such a utility function will always refuse a fair gamble, which is defined as one with an expected value of zero. A person with a convex utility function, any arc of which lies below the corresponding chord, is said to be a risk seeker. Such a person will always accept a fair gamble. A person with a linear utility function is said to be risk neutral, and is always indifferent between accepting and refusing a fair gamble.

Insurance purchased in private markets is generally an unfair gamble, not only because of the administrative costs included in insurance premiums, but also because of adverse selection and moral hazard. The fact that most people nonetheless buy substantial amounts of insurance is taken as evidence that risk aversion is the most empirically relevant case. This observation is further supported by the pervasiveness of risk-sharing arrangements like joint stock ownership.

An appendix to this chapter (see the "For the Instructor" section at our Web site www.mhhe.com/economics/frank4) discusses search theory and the winner's curse.

Questions for Review

1. Why must a signal between potential adversaries be costly to fake?

2. Explain why, despite the potential adversary relationship between sellers and buyers, commercial advertising nonetheless transmits information about product quality.

3. What practical difficulty confronts laws that try to regulate what questions can be asked of job applicants during employment interviews?

4. How does statistical discrimination affect the distribution of insurance premiums within a group?

5. How does statistical discrimination affect the average insurance premium paid by members of different groups?

6. Why is it intuitively plausible to assume that most people are risk averse?

7. Give some examples of behavior that seem inconsistent with the assumption of risk aversion.

8. Explain, in your own words, why it makes sense to self-insure against minor losses.

9. Give some examples in which people do not self-insure against minor losses.

Problems

1. Suppose the messiness of apartments is measured on a scale from 0 to 100, with 0 the cleanest and 100 the messiest. Suppose also that the distribution of apartments by messiness is as shown in the diagram. That is, suppose 10 percent of the apartments lie between 0 and 20, 20 percent between 20 and 40, and so on.

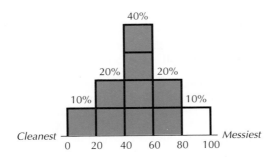

Suppose, finally, that all parents tried to teach their children never to let anyone in to see their apartments if they were over 80 on the messiness scale. If such a rule of thumb were widely observed, what would be your best estimate of the messiness index of someone who said, "You can't come in now, my place is a pit"? In a world in which everyone makes use of all available information, would you expect this rule of thumb to be stable? What do you conclude from the fact that people really do sometimes refuse admission on the grounds that their apartments are too messy?

2. Explain in detail what will happen to an insurance company that charges teenage males the same rates for automobile insurance as it charges its other customers.

3. It is known that some fraction d of all new cars is defective. Defective cars cannot be identified as such except by the people who own them. Each consumer is risk neutral and values a nondefective car at $6000. New cars sell for $4000 each, used ones for $1000. If cars do not depreciate physically with use, what is d?

4. A new motorcycle sells for $9000, while a used motorcycle sells for $1000. If there is no depreciation and risk-neutral consumers know that 20 percent of all new motorcycles are defective, how much do consumers value a nondefective motorcycle?

5. The exhaust system on your 1986 Escort needs to be replaced, and you suspect that the price of a new exhaust system is the same as what you would get if you tried to sell the car. If you know that the car is otherwise okay, what relevance does Akerlof's model of lemons have to your decision about whether to purchase a new exhaust system?

6. What grounds are there for assuming that a randomly chosen social worker is less likely to cheat you in cards than a randomly chosen person?

7. At the turn of this century, most banks required tellers to have a high school diploma. Even though the tasks currently performed by tellers in most banks can still be performed by persons who have mastered the high school curriculum, many banks now require that their tellers have college diplomas. Assuming that the real costs of college education are lower now than at the turn of the century and that these costs are lower for persons of higher ability, construct an explanation for why banks might have raised their hiring standards.

8. What is the expected value of a random toss of a die? (Fair and six-sided.)

9. A fair coin is flipped twice and the following payoffs are assigned to each of the four possible outcomes:

    H-H: win 20; H-T: win 9; T-H: lose 7; T-T: lose 16.

What is the expected value of this gamble?

10. Suppose your utility function is given by $U = \sqrt{M}$, where M is your total wealth. If M has an initial value of 16, will you accept the gamble in the preceding problem?

11. Suppose you have $10,000 to invest. A broker phones you with some information you requested on certain junk bonds. If the company issuing the bonds posts a profit this year, it will pay you a 40 percent interest rate on the bond. If the company files for bankruptcy, you will lose all you invested. If the company breaks even, you will earn a 10 percent interest rate. Your broker tells you there is a 50 percent chance that they will break even and a 20 percent chance that the company will file for bankruptcy. Your other option is to invest in a risk-free government bond that will guarantee 8 percent interest for 1 year.

    a. What is the expected interest rate for the junk bond investment?
    b. Which investment will you choose if your utility function is given by $U = M^2$?
    c. Which investment will you choose if your utility function is given by $U = \sqrt{M}$?

12. Suppose your current wealth, M, is 100 and your utility function is $U = M^2$. You have a lottery ticket that pays $10 with a probability of 0.25 and $0 with a probability of 0.75. What is the minimum amount for which you would be willing to sell this ticket?

13. Your utility function is $\sqrt{M}$. Your current wealth is \$400,000. There is a 0.00001 probability that your legal liability in an automobile accident will reduce your wealth to \$0. What is the most you would pay for insurance to cover this risk?

14. A farmer's hens lay 1000 eggs/day, which he sells for 10 cents each, his sole source of income. His utility function is $U = \sqrt{M}$, where M is his daily income. Each time a farmer carries eggs in from the hen house, there is a 50 percent chance he will fall and break all the eggs. Assuming he assigns no value to his time, is he better off by carrying all the eggs in one trip or by carrying 500 in each of two trips? (*Hint:* There are three possibilities when he takes two trips: 1000 broken eggs, 500 broken eggs, and no broken eggs. What is the probability of each of these outcomes?)

15. Your current wealth level is $M = 49$ and you are forced to make the following wager: if a fair coin comes up heads, you get 15; you lose 13 if it comes up tails. Your utility function is $U = \sqrt{M}$.

   a. What is the expected value of this gamble?
   b. What is its expected utility?
   c. How would your answers change if the payoff for tails fell to a loss of 15?
   d. What is the most you would pay to get out of the gamble described in (c)?

16. Smith has an investment opportunity that pays 33 with probability 1/2 and loses 30 with probability 1/2.

   a. If his current wealth is $M = 111$, and his utility function is $U = \sqrt{M}$, will he make this investment?
   b. Will he make it if he has two equal partners? (Be sure to calculate the relevant expected utilities to at least two decimal places.)

17. John has a von Neumann–Morgenstern utility function given by $U = \sqrt{M}$, where M is his income. If he becomes an economics professor, he will make $M = 81/\text{yr}$ with probability 1. If he becomes an attorney, he will make $M = 900/\text{yr}$ if he becomes a partner in a Wall Street firm, but only $M = 25/\text{yr}$ if he fails to make partner. The probability of him becoming a partner is 0.2. Smith is an infallible judge of legal talent. After a brief interview, he can state with certainty whether John will become a partner. What is the most John would be willing to pay for this information? (Set up the relevant equation. You don't need to solve it.)

*18. In the preceding question, assuming that the interview is costless for Smith to conduct, is he getting the highest possible expected income for himself by charging John the same fee regardless of the outcome of the interview?

*19. There are two groups of equal size, each with a utility function given by $U(M) = \sqrt{M}$, where $M = 100$ is the initial wealth level for every individual. Each member of group 1 faces a loss of 36 with probability 0.5. Each member of group 2 faces the same loss with probability 0.1.

   a. What is the most a member of each group would be willing to pay to insure against this loss?

---

*Problems marked with an asterisk (*) are more difficult.

b. In part (a), if it is impossible for outsiders to discover which individuals belong to which group, will it be practical for members of group 2 to insure against this loss in a competitive insurance market? (For simplicity, you may assume that insurance companies charge only enough in premiums to cover their expected benefit payments.) Explain.

c. Now suppose that the insurance companies in part (b) have an imperfect test for identifying which persons belong to which group. If the test says that a person belongs to a particular group, the probability that he really does belong to that group is $x < 1.0$. How large must x be in order to alter your answer to part (b)?

*20. There are two groups, each with a utility function given by $U(M) = \sqrt{M}$, where $M = 144$ is the initial wealth level for every individual. Each member of group 1 faces a loss of 44 with probability 0.5. Each member of group 2 faces the same loss with probability 0.1.

a. What is the most a member of each group would be willing to pay to insure against this loss?

b. If it is impossible for outsiders to discover which individuals belong to which group, how large a share of the potential client pool can the members of group 1 be before it becomes impossible for a private company with a zero-profit constraint to provide insurance for the members of group 2? (For simplicity, you may assume that insurance companies charge only enough in premiums to cover their expected benefit payments and that people will always buy insurance when its price is equal to or below their reservation price.) Explain.

*21. Given a choice between A (a sure win of 100) and B (an 80 percent chance to win 150 and a 20 percent chance to win 0), Smith picks A. But when he is given a choice between C (a 50 percent chance to win 100 and a 50 percent chance to win 0) and D (a 40 percent chance to win 150 and a 60 percent chance to win 0), he picks D. Show that Smith's choices are inconsistent with expected utility maximization.

Answers to In-Chapter Exercises

6-1. The expected utility of the gamble corresponds to point D, which lies one-third of the way from C to A.

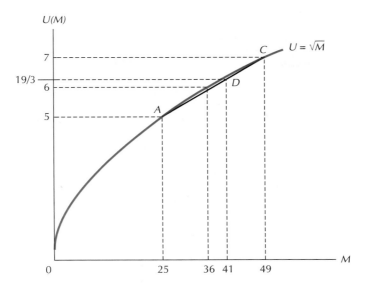

6-2. If she accepts the gamble, her expected utility is given by $EU_G = (1/2)(120^2) + (1/2)(80^2) = 10{,}400$. Her utility if she refuses the gamble is only $100^2 = 10{,}000$, and so she should accept the gamble.

6-3. If she accepts the gamble, her expected utility is given by $EU_G = (1/2)(120) + (1/2)(80) = 100$. Her utility if she refuses the gamble is also 100, and so she is indifferent between accepting and refusing the gamble.

6-4. As in Example 6-3, the key step here is to see that the only used computers for sale will be defective. Because of the lemons principle, the owner of a good computer could not sell it for what it is worth to him in the secondhand market. So if the value of a defective computer is $600, then the value of a new computer to a risk-neutral buyer must be $(1/4)(\$600) + (3/4)(\$2000) = \$1650$.

6-5. Equate the expected utility of attending A to the utility of a job with a salary level of M', and solve for M':

$$EU_A = 800 = \sqrt{M'},$$

which yields $M' = \$640{,}000$.

CHAPTER

7

Explaining Tastes: The Importance of Altruism and Other Nonegoistic Behavior

The central assumption of microeconomic analysis is that people are rational. There is far from universal agreement, however, on just what this means. Two important definitions of rationality are the so-called *present-aim* and *self-interest* standards.[1] Recalling our discussion in Chapter 1, a person is rational under the present-aim standard if she is efficient in the pursuit of whatever aims she happens to hold at the moment of action. No attempt is made, under this standard, to assess whether her aims themselves make any sense. If someone has a preference for self-destructive behavior, for example, the only requirement for rationality under the present-aim standard is that she pursue that behavior in the most efficient available way. Under the self-interest standard, by contrast, it is assumed at the outset that people's motives are congruent with their material interests. Motives such as altruism, fidelity to principle, a desire for justice, and the like are simply not considered under the self-interest standard.

In textbook accounts of rational choice, economists often embrace the present-aim standard. Tastes are given exogenously, we say, and there is no logical basis for questioning them. In the words of the nineteenth-century economist Jeremy Bentham, a taste for pushpins is no less valid than a taste for poetry.

The difficulty with the present-aim standard is what the late University of Chicago economist George Stigler might have called the "crankcase oil" problem.

---

[1] See Derek Parfit, *Reasons and Persons*, Oxford: Clarendon, 1984.

If we see a person drink the used crankcase oil from his car, and he then writhes in agony and dies, we can assert that he must have *really* liked crankcase oil. (Why else would he have drunk it?) Virtually any behavior, no matter how bizarre, can be "explained" after the fact by simply assuming a taste for it. Thus the chief attraction of the present-aim model turns out also to be its biggest liability. Because it allows us to explain everything, we end up explaining nothing.

With this difficulty in mind, most economists assume some version of the self-interest standard of rationality in their actual research. This is the approach we took in previous chapters, and as we have seen, it generates many powerful insights into human behavior. It helps explain, for example, why car pools form in the wake of increases in gasoline prices; why the members of "service" organizations, such as the Rotary and Kiwanis clubs, are more likely to be real estate salespersons, dentists, insurance agents, and others with something to sell than to be postal employees or airline pilots; and so on. Without question, self-interest is an important human motive.

Yet narrow self-interest is surely not the only human motive. Travelers on interstate highways leave tips for waitresses they will never see again. Participants in bloody family feuds seek revenge even at ruinous cost to themselves. People walk away from profitable transactions whose terms they believe to be "unfair." The British spend vast sums to defend the desolate Falklands, even though they have little empire left against which to deter future aggression. (The Argentine writer Jorge Luis Borges likened the war to two bald men fighting over a comb.) In these and countless other ways, people do not seem to be maximizing utility functions of the egoistic sort.

Chapter Preview

The self-interest model ignores the fact that most of us pursue a variety of goals that seem to conflict with narrow self-interest. We begin this chapter with an example of how unselfish motivations can be incorporated into the rational choice model—in this case, a straightforward application of the present-aim standard. But our real challenge is to explore how such motivations might have come to be held in the first place. We are all comfortable with the notion that someone who deliberately strives to be more spontaneous is doomed to fail. So, too, we will see that persons whose only goal is to promote their own interests face a difficulty of a similar sort. There are important problems that selfish persons simply are not able to solve very well.

In the descriptive realm, we will see that it is possible to do a much better job of predicting people's behavior when we take certain nonegoistic sources of motivation into account.

An Application of the Present-Aim Standard: Altruistic Preferences

Because we know from experience that not everyone has the narrowly selfish preferences assumed by the self-interest model, it is tempting to broaden the analysis by simply adding additional tastes—by assuming, for example, that people derive satisfaction from a variety of behaviors that conflict with narrowly defined self-interest, such as donating money to charity, voting, disposing of litter properly, and so on. Let us explore how the notion that some people have altruistic preferences can be incorporated formally into our model of rational choice.

Consider, for example, the case of Franny, who cares not only about her own income level but also about Zooey's. Such preferences can be represented in the form of an indifference map defined over their respective income levels, and might look something like the one shown in Figure 7-1. Note that Franny's indifference curves are negatively sloped, which means that she is willing to tolerate a reduction in her own income in return for a sufficiently large increase in Zooey's. Note also that her indifference curves exhibit diminishing MRS, which

FIGURE 7-1
Franny would be willing to have less income in order for Zooey to have more.

THE INDIFFERENCE MAP FOR FRANNY, AN ALTRUISTIC PERSON

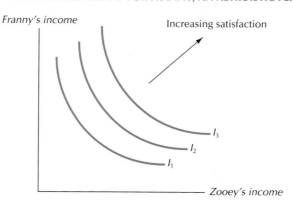

FIGURE 7-2
At point *C*, Franny's MRS between her income and Zooey's is exactly equal to the absolute value of the slope of her budget constraint. Given her preferences, the best she can do is give $19,000 of her original $50,000 income to Zooey, keeping $31,000 for herself.

THE OPTIMAL INCOME TRANSFER FROM AN ALTRUISTIC PERSON

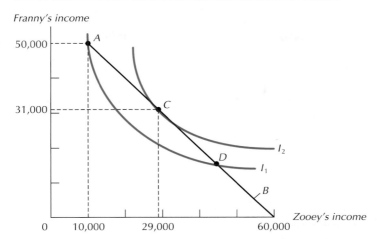

means that the more income Franny has, the more she is willing to give up in order to see Zooey have more.

The question that Franny confronts is whether she would be better off if she gave some of her income to Zooey. In order to answer this question, we first need to display the relevant budget constraint confronting Franny. Suppose her initial income level is $50,000/yr and that Zooey's is $10,000, as denoted by the point labeled *A* in Figure 7-2. What are Franny's options? She can retain all her income, in which case she stays at *A*. Or she can give some of it to Zooey, in which case she will have $1 less than $50,000 for every $1 she gives him. Her budget constraint here is thus the locus labeled *B* in Figure 7-2, which has a slope of −1.

If Franny keeps all her income, she ends up on the indifference curve labeled I_1 in Figure 7-2. But because her MRS exceeds the slope of her budget constraint at *A*, it is clear that she can do better. The fact that MRS > 1 at *A* tells us that she is willing to give up more than a dollar of her own income to see Zooey have an extra dollar. But the slope of her budget constraint tells us that it costs her only a dollar to give Zooey an extra dollar. She is therefore better off if she gives some of her income to Zooey. The optimal transfer is represented by the tangency point labeled *C* in Figure 7-2. The best she can do is to give $19,000 of her income to Zooey.

Note, however, that the conclusion would have been much different if Franny had started not at *A* but at *D* in Figure 7-2. Then her budget constraint would have been only that portion of the locus *B* that lies below *D*. (She does not have the option of making negative gifts to Zooey!) And since her MRS at *D* is less than 1, she will do best to give no money to Zooey at all. (Recall from Chapter 3 that such outcomes are called corner solutions.)

*E*XAMPLE *7-1* *Smith's utility function is given by $U_S = M_S M_J$, where M_S is Smith's wealth level and M_J is Jones's. Initially, Smith has 90 units of wealth and Jones has 10. If Smith is a utility maximizer, should he transfer some of his wealth to Jones, and if so, how much? Draw Smith's initial indifference curve and the indifference curve when each has 50 units of wealth. Also draw Smith's budget constraint in the $M_S M_J$ plane.*

Together, Smith and Jones have a total of 100 units of wealth. This means that if Smith's wealth is M_S, then Jones's is $100 - M_S$. Smith's utility function may thus be written as $U_S = M_S(100 - M_S)$, which is plotted in the top panel of Figure 7-3. Note that Smith's utility attains a maximum of 2500 when $M_S = 50$. At the initial allocation of wealth, Smith's utility is only 900. So if Smith is a utility maximizer, he should transfer 40 units of his wealth to Jones. The heavy line in the bottom panel is Smith's budget constraint in the $M_S M_J$ plane. Note that the $U_S = 2500$ indifference curve is tangent to this budget constraint when $M_S = M_J = 50$.

The Strategic Role of Preferences

The attractive feature of the present-aim standard of rationality is that it lets us broaden our analysis to embrace nonegoistic motives whose existence is empirically well documented. Yet as noted, the lingering methodological difficulty is that unless we impose some constraints on ourselves, the present-aim standard allows us to explain virtually any bizarre behavior by simply positing a taste for it. Our dilemma is how to expand our view of human motives without at the same time becoming vulnerable to Stigler's crankcase oil objection.

Biologists have discovered a way out of this dilemma, one that rests on an analysis that is quintessentially microeconomic in character. In biology, an organism's tastes are not arbitrarily given, as they are in economic models. Rather, biologists assume that tastes are forged by the pressures of natural selection to help organisms solve important problems in their environments. Consider the example of the common human taste for sweets. How would biologists explain such a taste? Their argument is straightforward. It begins with the observation that certain kinds of sugars—in particular, those commonly found in ripened fruit—were more easily digested than other sugars by our primate ancestors. The next step is to assume an initial degree of variability of tastes across individuals—that is, to assume that some individuals were more predisposed than others to "like" the kinds of sugars found in ripened fruit. Motivated by this taste, these primates were more likely than others to eat ripened fruit. Because the sugars in ripened fruit are more easily digested, individuals who liked these sugars were more likely than others to survive and leave offspring. And because of this advantage, the genes for liking the kinds of sugars found in ripened fruit eventually spread throughout the population.

FIGURE 7-3
The top panel shows
that Smith's utility is
maximized by keep-
ing only 50 units of
wealth for himself.
The heavy line in the
bottom panel is
Smith's budget con-
straint in the $M_S M_J$
plane. Note that the
$U_S = 2500$ indiffer-
ence curve is tangent
to that budget con-
straint at $M_S = 50$.

A UTILITY-MAXIMIZING ALTRUIST

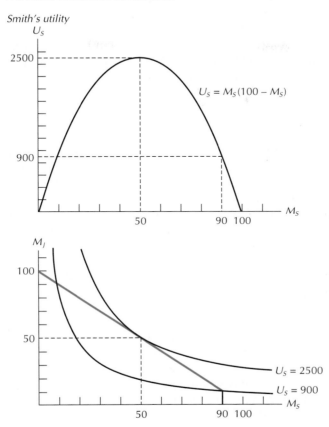

Thus, in the biologist's account, our taste for sweets is a characteristic we inher-
ited from our ancestors, in whom it evolved for functional reasons.

There is evidence that this particular taste is no longer functional in our
current environment. In earlier times, the sugars found in ripened fruits were
sufficiently scarce that there was no practical danger of overconsuming them.
Now, with sweets so plentiful, our taste for them sometimes leads us to
overindulge, with various adverse consequences. If these consequences were sufficiently severe, evolutionary pressures would eventually diminish our taste for
sweets. But since changes of this sort often require thousands of generations, it
is almost certainly a taste we are stuck with for now.

The taste for sweets is a simple preference, in the sense that it would have
been useful to an individual irrespective of whether others in the population
shared that taste. Other tastes, however, are more complex, in the sense that the
usefulness of having them depends on the fraction of other individuals in the

population who share them. This second type we will call a *strategic preference,* one that helps the individual solve important problems of social interaction. An early example of a strategic preference in the biological literature focused on the taste for aggressive behavior. A careful examination of the biologist's model of the evolution of this taste helps fix ideas for our subsequent analysis of a variety of other important strategic preferences.

A PARABLE OF HAWKS AND DOVES

To begin, consider a population that consists of individuals who are the same except with respect to their taste for aggressive behavior. One type of individual, called a "hawk," has a strong preference for such behavior.[2] The other type, called a "dove," strictly prefers to avoid aggressive behavior. Which of these two types an individual happens to be matters only when it comes into conflict with another individual over an important resource—food, a mate, whatever. The hawk's strategy is always to fight for the resource. The dove's strategy is never to fight.

If these two types compete for the scarce resources required for survival, which type will win out? At first glance, it might seem as if the hawks would, since they would always prevail in their conflicts with doves. But this view overlooks what happens when two hawks confront one another. Since both individuals are now predisposed to be aggressive, a bitter fight may ensue. Depending on the consequences of such a fight, it may thus be a risky proposition indeed to be a hawk.

The potential disadvantage of being a hawk becomes even clearer when we examine what happens when two doves confront one another over an important resource. In these encounters, the costs of a bloody battle are avoided, and the doves share the resource.

In our hypothetical population, pairs of individuals interact with one another at random and there are three possible pairings: (1) two doves, (2) two hawks, and (3) a hawk and a dove. To see how this population will evolve, we need to know the payoffs for each of these three types of interaction. To make our analysis manageable, let us assume that a biologist has gathered data that enable us to express these payoffs in units of some common measure—say, calories. Suppose the conflict involves food that contains 12 calories. When two doves interact, they share the food so that each receives a payoff of 6 calories. When a hawk and a dove interact, the dove defers to the hawk, so the hawk gets 12 calories, the dove none. Finally, when two hawks interact, the winner of the ensuing fight gets the 12 calories, the loser none. The fight itself, however, consumes 10 calories for each hawk, which means that the net payoff is $12 - 10 = 2$ calories for the winning hawk, and -10 calories for the losing hawk. Over the course of many encounters between hawks, any given hawk

---

[2]The names "hawk" and "dove" are used metaphorically here to describe members of the same species who have different tastes for aggressive behavior.

Two individuals are in conflict over food worth 12 calories. When two hawks meet, a fight ensues that consumes 10 calories each, leaving an average net payoff of −4 calories per hawk. When doves and hawks meet, doves defer, so hawks get 12 calories, doves 0. When two doves meet, they share the food, so each gets 6 calories.

TABLE 7-1 THE HAWK-DOVE PAYOFF MATRIX

		Individual Y	
		Hawk	**Dove**
Individual X	**Hawk**	−4 calories for each	12 calories for X 0 calories for Y
	Dove	0 calories for X 12 calories for Y	6 calories for each

can expect to win half the time and lose half the time. Thinking of hawks as a whole, then, the average payoff from hawk-hawk encounters is $(2 - 10)/2 = -4$ calories per individual.

If we let X and Y represent two individuals from the population, the average payoffs for the different combinations of interactions are summarized in Table 7-1.

As biologists view the matter, the question of whether it is better to be a hawk or to be a dove is answered by computing which type gets more calories on the average. To do this, we must first know the likelihood of each type of interaction. To illustrate, suppose that half the population initially consists of hawks, the other half of doves. Then, half of each individual's interactions would be with hawks, the other half with doves. For a hawk, then, the average payoff, denoted P_H, would be a weighted average of the two payoff values:

$$P_H = (\tfrac{1}{2})(-4) + (\tfrac{1}{2})(12) = 4. \tag{7.1}$$

The corresponding average payoff for a dove, denoted P_D, would be

$$P_D = (\tfrac{1}{2})(0) + (\tfrac{1}{2})6 = 3. \tag{7.2}$$

The implicit assumption in the biologist's view of the competition between hawks and doves is that whichever type garners a larger number of calories will tend to raise larger families and will thus make up an increasing share of the total population. We have just seen that in a population initially split 50-50 between the two types, the hawks will get more calories than the doves, and this means that the hawks' share of the total population will grow.

Suppose we use h to denote the fraction of the population that consists of hawks (so that, in the example just considered, we had $h = \tfrac{1}{2}$). Then, since the population shares of the two types must sum to 1, we know that $1 - h$ will be the fraction of the population that consists of doves. For such a population, the average payoff for hawks is again a weighted average of the two types of hawk payoffs, where now the weights are the respective population shares, h and $(1 - h)$:

$$P_H = (h)(-4) + (1 - h)(12) = 12 - 16h. \tag{7.3}$$

The corresponding general expression for the average payoff for doves is

$$P_D = (h)(0) + (1 - h)6 = 6 - 6h. \tag{7.4}$$

For example, if the share consisting of hawks were four-fifths, hawks would encounter other hawks in their interactions four-fifths of the time, doves the remaining one-fifth of the time, making the average payoff for hawks $P_H = (\frac{4}{5})(-4) + (\frac{1}{5})(12) = -0.8$. The corresponding average for doves would be $P_D = (\frac{4}{5})(0) + (\frac{1}{5})(6) = 1.2$. So when hawks make up four-fifths of the population, their average payoff will be smaller than the average payoff for doves, and this means that the hawks' share of the population will begin to fall.

To see whether the population shares will settle at some equilibrium, we plot the average payoff curves for the two types and look for a point at which they cross. As shown in Figure 7-4, this occurs when $h = 0.6$. This means that when 60 percent of the population consists of hawks, the remaining 40 percent of doves, each type will receive an average payoff of 2.4 calories per interaction. With equal average payoffs, the two types will tend to have equally many offspring, which implies that their respective shares of the population will remain unchanged.

Note that the equilibrium point identified in Figure 7-4 is stable: If the population share of hawks were ever to deviate from 0.6, there would immediately be forces pulling it back to 0.6. For example, if the share of hawks for some reason dipped to 0.5, the average payoff curves in Figure 7-4 show that the average payoff for hawks would exceed the average payoff for doves, and this would cause the hawks' population share to rise. Conversely, if the share of hawks somehow rose to 0.7, then the hawks' average payoff would be smaller than the doves', and this would cause the hawks' population share to fall.

FIGURE 7-4
The average payoffs for both hawks and doves are declining functions of the share of the population consisting of hawks. The mixture of the two types is in equilibrium when the average payoffs are the same for the two types.

AVERAGE PAYOFFS FOR HAWKS AND DOVES

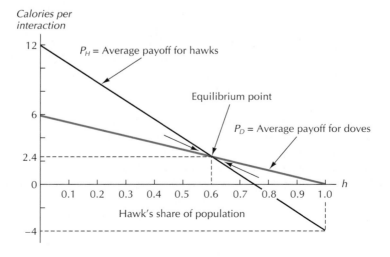

EXERCISE 7-1

In the example discussed above, suppose now that the payoffs are altered as follows: When two doves interact, each earns 3 units; when two hawks interact, each earns 1 unit; and when a dove and a hawk interact, the former gets a payoff of 2 units, the latter a payoff of 6 units. What will be the equilibrium population share of each type?

The hawks and doves example illustrates how the usefulness of a preference for a certain mode of behavior depends on the frequency with which others in the population also prefer that behavior. Being a hawk (preferring aggression) can be advantageous, but only up to a point. For once hawks become sufficiently numerous, it then becomes advantageous to be a dove. The population is in equilibrium only when the average payoffs for the two tastes are the same.

The hawks and doves example also illustrates an important property of evolution by natural selection, which is that traits are favored for their effects on *individual* payoffs, not for their effects on the payoffs of populations as a whole. Note in Figure 7-4 that the population as a whole would be better off if there were no hawks at all ($h = 0$). For in a population consisting only of doves, all individuals would receive 6 calories per interaction, a dramatic improvement over the equilibrium value of 2.4. But a population consisting only of doves would not be evolutionarily stable. A hawk could invade such a population and make rapid headway because of its success when interacting with doves.

The rational choice model introduced in Chapter 3 regards the consumer's tastes as given, a set of goals the consumer strives to fulfill. Ecological models like the hawks and doves example take a step back and ask where those tastes come from. These models view preferences not as ends in themselves but as a means by which individuals achieve important material objectives (in the hawks and doves case, the acquisition of calories needed to survive and reproduce).

With the workings of the hawks and doves model firmly in mind, we are now in a position to analyze how a variety of other tastes might have emerged. In particular, we focus on how certain unselfish motives often help people solve an important class of problems that arise in economic and social interaction.

The Commitment Problem

One of the most frequently discussed examples in which the pursuit of self-interest is self-defeating is the so-called *prisoner's dilemma*. The mathematician A. W. Tucker is credited with having discovered this simple game, whose name derives from the anecdote originally used to illustrate it. Two prisoners are held in separate cells for a serious crime that they did, in fact, commit. The prosecutor, however, has only enough hard evidence to convict them of a minor offense, for which the penalty is, say, a year in jail. Each prisoner is told that if one confesses while the other remains silent, the confessor will go scot free while the other will spend 20 years in prison. If both confess, they will get an intermediate sentence, say, 5 years. Table 7-2 summarizes these payoffs. The two prisoners are not allowed to communicate with one another.

The dominant strategy in the prisoner's dilemma is to confess. No matter what Y does, X gets a lighter sentence by speaking out—if Y too confesses, X gets 5 years instead of 20; and if Y remains silent, X goes free instead of spending a year in jail. The payoffs are perfectly symmetric, so Y also does better to confess, no matter what X does. The difficulty is that when each behaves in a self-interested way, both do worse than if each had shown restraint. Thus, when both confess, they get 5 years, instead of the 1 year they could have gotten by remaining silent.

Although the prisoners are not allowed to communicate with one another, it would be a mistake to assume that this is the real source of difficulty. Their problem is rather a lack of *trust*. A simple promise not to confess does not change the material payoffs of the game. (If each could promise not to confess, each would *still* do better if he broke his promise.)

The prisoner's dilemma is an example of a broader class of problems called *commitment problems*. The common feature of these problems is that people can do better if they can commit themselves to behave in a way that will later be inconsistent with their own material interests. In the prisoner's dilemma, for example, if the prisoners could commit themselves to remain silent, they would do better than if left free to pursue their narrow material interests.

University of Maryland economist Thomas Schelling[3] provided another vivid illustration of a commitment problem. Schelling described a kidnapper who suddenly gets cold feet. He wants to set his victim free but is afraid he will go to the police. In return for his freedom, the victim gladly promises not to do so. The problem, however, is that both realize it will no longer be in the victim's interest to keep this promise once he is free. And so the kidnapper reluctantly concludes that he must kill him. The kidnapper's belief that the victim will act in a rational, self-interested way spells apparent doom for the victim.

Schelling suggested the following way out of the dilemma: "If the victim has committed an act whose disclosure could lead to blackmail, he may confess it; if not, he might commit one in the presence of his captor, to create a bond that will ensure his silence."[4] (Perhaps the victim could allow the kidnapper to photograph him in the process of committing some unspeakably degrading act.) The blackmailable act serves here as a *commitment device*, something that provides the victim with an incentive to keep his promise.[5] Keeping it will still be unpleasant

---

[3]Thomas Schelling, *The Strategy of Conflict*, Cambridge, MA: Harvard University Press, 1960.

[4]Ibid., pp. 43–44.

[5]Note the analogy to the commitment devices we discussed in Chapter 6, whereby people forced themselves to save.

No matter what the other player does, each player always gets a shorter sentence by confessing. And if each player confesses, each gets 5 years. Yet if both players had remained silent, each would have gotten only 1 year in jail. Here the individual pursuit of self-interest produces a worse outcome for each player.

TABLE 7-2 THE PRISONER'S DILEMMA

		Prisoner **Y**	
		Confess	**Remain silent**
Individual X	**Confess**	5 years for each	0 years for X 20 years for Y
	Remain silent	20 years for X 0 years for Y	1 year for each

for him once he is freed, but clearly less so than not being able to make a credible promise in the first place.

In everyday economic and social interaction, we repeatedly encounter commitment problems like the prisoner's dilemma, or like the one confronting Schelling's kidnapper and victim. The solution Schelling suggested tries to eliminate the problem by altering the relevant material incentives. Unfortunately, however, this approach will not always be practical.

An alternative approach is to alter the psychological rewards that govern behavior—in economic terms, to have preferences that lead people to behave in ways contrary to narrow self-interest. Suppose, for example, the kidnap victim was known to be a person who would feel bad if he broke a promise. Such a feeling, if sufficiently strong, would deter him from going to the police even after it became in his material interests to do so. And this knowledge would enable the kidnapper to set him free.

Illustration: The Cheating Problem

The functional role of unselfish motives can be seen more clearly with the help of an example of a simple ecology in which egoists are pitted against nonegoists in a struggle to survive. The commitment problem they face arises in joint business ventures, each of which consists of a pair of individuals. In these ventures each person can behave in either of two ways: He can "cooperate," which means to deal honestly with his partner, or he can "defect," which means to cheat his partner. The payoffs to each of two representative partners, Smith and Jones, depend on the combination of behaviors chosen in the manner shown in Table 7-3. These payoffs confront the partners with a monetary version of the prisoner's dilemma. Note that Jones gets a higher payoff by defecting, no matter what Smith does, and that the same is true for Smith. If Jones believes Smith will behave in a self-interested way, he will predict that Smith will defect. And if only to protect himself, he may feel compelled to defect as well. When both defect, each gets only a 2-unit payoff. The frustration, as in all dilemmas of this sort, is that both could have done better. Had they cooperated, each would have gotten a 4-unit payoff.

Now suppose we have not just Smith and Jones but also a large population.

The payoffs in the table have the same structure as the payoffs in the prisoner's dilemma. Holding the other player's behavior fixed, each player does best by defecting. Yet when each defects, each gets only 2, whereas each gets 4 when both cooperate.

TABLE 7-3   MONETARY PAYOFFS IN A JOINT VENTURE

		Smith	
		Defect	**Cooperate**
Jones	**Defect**	2 for each	0 for Smith 6 for Jones
	Cooperate	6 for Smith 0 for Jones	4 for each

Pairs of people again form joint ventures and the relationship between behavior and payoffs for the members of each pair is again as given in Table 7-3. Suppose further that everyone in the population is of one of two types—cooperator or defector. A cooperator is someone who, possibly through intensive cultural conditioning, has developed a heritable capacity to experience a moral sentiment that predisposes him to cooperate. A defector is someone who either lacks this capacity or has failed to develop it.

In this scheme, cooperators are altruists in the sense that they refrain from cheating even when there is no possibility of being detected. Viewed in the narrow context of the choice at hand, this behavior is clearly contrary to their material interests. Defectors, by contrast, are pure opportunists. They always make whatever choice will maximize their personal payoffs. As in the hawks and doves example considered earlier, our task here is to determine what will happen when people from the two groups are thrown into a survival struggle against one another. As we will see, the answer depends critically on how easily the two types may be distinguished from one another. We consider several possibilities in turn.

POPULATION MOVEMENTS WHEN COOPERATORS AND DEFECTORS LOOK ALIKE

Suppose, for argument's sake, that cooperators and defectors look exactly alike, thus making it impossible to distinguish the two types. In this hypothetical ecology, this means that, as in the hawks and doves example, individuals will pair at random. Naturally, cooperators (and defectors, for that matter) would like nothing better than to pair with cooperators, but they have no choice in the matter. Because everyone looks the same, they must take their chances. The expected payoffs to both defectors and cooperators therefore depend on the likelihood of pairing with a cooperator, which in turn depends on the proportion of cooperators in the population.

Let c denote the fraction of the population that consists of cooperators. If a cooperator interacts with a randomly chosen person from the population, the probability of that person also being a cooperator will be c. The probability of that person being a defector is $1 - c$. Since a cooperator gets a payoff of 4 units when he interacts with another cooperator and a payoff of 0 when he interacts with a defector, the expected, or average, payoff for each cooperator in this case can be written as

$$P_C = c(4) + (1 - c)(0) = 4c. \tag{7.5}$$

Thus, when half of the population consists of cooperators ($c = \frac{1}{2}$), a cooperator has a 50-50 chance of interacting with another cooperator, in which case he will get 4 units, and a 50-50 chance of interacting with a defector, in which case he will get 0 units. His expected payoff here is a weighted average of these two outcomes, namely, 2 units.

EXERCISE 7-2

What is a cooperator's average payoff when $c = 0.9$?

The corresponding expression for the average payoff for defectors is given by

$$P_D = 6c + 2(1 - c) = 2 + 4c. \tag{7.6}$$

The average payoff relationships for the monetary values assumed in this illustration are shown in Figure 7-5 on the next page.

When cooperators and defectors look exactly the same, how will the population evolve over time? As in the hawks and doves example, the rule here is that each individual reproduces in proportion to its average payoff: Those with larger material payoffs have the resources necessary to raise larger numbers of offspring.[6] Recall that in the hawks and doves example the average payoff curves for the two types intersected, resulting in a stable population share for each type. In the current case, however, the average payoff curves do not intersect. Since defectors always receive a higher average payoff here, their share of the population will grow over time. Cooperators, even if they make up almost the entire population to begin with, are thus destined for extinction. When cooperators and defectors look alike, genuine cooperation cannot emerge. In a crude way, this case provides the underlying rationale for the self-interest model's assumption of egoistic behavior.

Note in Figure 7-5 that in a population consisting only of cooperators ($c = 1.0$), everyone's payoff would be 4 units, or twice as much as everyone gets in the equilibrium consisting only of defectors. As in the hawks and doves example, we see in this case too that tastes evolve according to their effect on individual, not group, payoffs.

---

[6]In very recent times, of course, there has been a *negative* relationship between income and family size. But if preferences were forged by natural selection, the relationship that matters is the one that existed during most of evolutionary history. And that relationship was undisputedly positive: Periods of famine were frequent and individuals with greater material resources saw many more of their children reach adulthood. Moreover, most early societies were polygynous—their wealthiest members usually claimed several wives, leaving many of the poor with none.

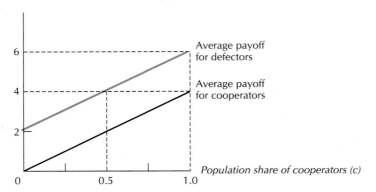

FIGURE 7-5
The expected pay-offs for both cooper-ators and defectors increase with the percentage of coop-erators in the popu-lation. But no matter what the initial pop-ulation share of co-operators is, cooperators earn a lower average pay-off than defectors. This means that co-operators are des-tined for extinction.

POPULATION MOVEMENTS WHEN COOPERATORS ARE EASILY IDENTIFIED

Now suppose everything is just as before except that cooperators and defectors are perfectly distinguishable from each other. For concreteness, suppose that sympathy is the emotion that motivates cooperation, and that there is an observ-able symptom present in people who experience this emotion (perhaps a "sym-pathetic manner"). Defectors lack this observable symptom; or, more generally, they may try to mimic it, but fail to get it exactly right.

If this symptom is observable at a glance, the tables are completely turned. Cooperators can now interact selectively with one another and be assured of a payoff of 4 units. No cooperator need ever interact with a defector. Defec-tors are left to interact with one another, for which they get a payoff of only 2 units.

Since all element of chance has been removed from the interaction process, payoffs no longer depend on the proportion of cooperators in the population (see Figure 7-6). Cooperators always get 4, defectors always get 2.

This time the cooperators' larger payoffs enable *them* to raise larger families, which means they will make up an ever growing share of the population. When cooperators can be easily identified, it is the defectors who face extinction.

MIMICRY WITHOUT COST OR DELAY

The defectors need not go quietly into the night, however. Suppose there arises a mutant strain of defectors, one that behaves exactly like other defectors but in which each individual has precisely the same symptoms of trustworthiness as cooperators. Since this particular strain of defectors looks exactly the same as cooperators, it is impossible for cooperators to discriminate against them. Each impostor is therefore just as likely to interact with a cooperator as a genuine cooperator is. This, in turn, means that the mutant defectors will have a higher expected payoff than the cooperators.

FIGURE 7-6
When cooperators can be identified at a glance, they can always interact with one another and get a payoff of 4 units. Defectors are left to interact with each other, and get a payoff of 2 units. In this case, it is the defectors who become extinct.

AVERAGE PAYOFFS WHEN COOPERATORS AND DEFECTORS ARE PERFECTLY DISTINGUISHABLE

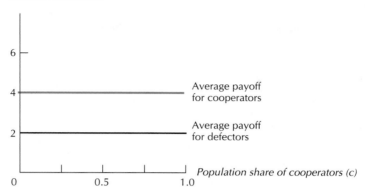

The nonmutant defectors—those who continue to look different from cooperators—will have a lower payoff than both of these groups and, as before, are destined for extinction. But unless the cooperators adapt in some way, they too face the same fate. When defectors can perfectly mimic the distinguishing feature of cooperators with neither cost nor delay, the feature loses all power to distinguish. Cooperators and the surviving defectors again look exactly alike, which again spells doom for the cooperators.

IMPERFECT MIMICRY AND THE COSTS OF VIGILANCE

Defectors, of course, have no monopoly on the power to adapt. If random mutations alter the cooperators' distinguishing characteristic, the defectors will be faced with a moving target. Imagine that symptoms by which cooperators originally managed to distinguish themselves can be imperfectly mimicked by defectors. If the two types could be distinguished at a glance, defectors would again be doomed. But suppose it requires effort to differentiate between a cooperator and a defector. For concreteness, suppose inspection costs 1 unit. Paying this cost is like buying a pair of invisible glasses that enable cooperators and defectors to be distinguished at a glance. For those who do not pay, the two types remain perfectly indistinguishable.

To see what happens this time, suppose the payoffs are again as given in Table 7-3, and consider the decision facing a cooperator who is trying to decide whether to pay the cost of vigilance. If he pays it, he can be assured of interacting with another cooperator and will thus get a payoff of $4 - 1 = 3$ units. If he does not, his payoff is uncertain. Cooperators and defectors will look exactly alike to him and he must take his chances. If he happens to interact with another cooperator, he will get 4 units. But if he interacts with a defector, he will get zero. Whether it makes sense to pay the 1-unit cost of vigilance thus depends on the likelihood of those two outcomes.

Suppose the population share of cooperators is 90 percent. By not paying the cost of vigilance, a cooperator will interact with another cooperator 90 percent of the time, with a defector only 10 percent. His payoff will thus have an average value of $(0.9)(4) + (0.1)(0) = 3.6$. Since this is higher than the 3-unit net payoff he would get if he paid the cost of vigilance, it is clearly better not to pay it.

Now suppose the population share of cooperators is not 90 percent but 50 percent. If our cooperator does not pay the cost of vigilance, he will now have only a 50-50 chance of interacting with a cooperator. His average payoff will thus be only 2 units, or 1 unit less than if he had paid the cost. On these odds, it would clearly be better to pay it.

The numbers in this example imply a "breakeven point" obtained by solving the following equation for c:

$$4c = 3, \tag{7.7}$$

which yields $c = 0.75$. Thus, when the population share of cooperators is 75 percent, a cooperator's expected payoff if he does not pay the cost of vigilance ($4c$) is exactly equal to his certain payoff if he does (3). A cooperator who does not pay the cost has a 75 percent chance at a payoff of 4 units, and a 25 percent chance of getting zero, which means an average payoff of 3 units, the same as if he had paid the cost. When the population share of cooperators is below 75 percent, it will always be better for him to pay the cost of vigilance. When the population share of cooperators is above 75 percent, it will never be better for him to pay the cost of vigilance.

EXERCISE 7-3

In a population with 60 percent cooperators and a cost of vigilance equal to 1.5, should a cooperator pay the cost of vigilance?

With the breakeven rule in mind, we can now say something about how the population will evolve over time. When the population share of cooperators is below 75 percent, cooperators will all pay the cost of vigilance and get a payoff of 3 units by cooperating with one another. It will not be in the interests of defectors to bear this cost, because the vigilant cooperators would not interact with them anyway. The defectors are left to interact with one another and get a payoff of only 2 units. Thus, if we start with a population share of cooperators less than 75 percent, the cooperators will get a higher average payoff, which means that their share of the population will grow.

In populations that consist of more than 75 percent cooperators, the tables are turned. Now it no longer makes sense to pay the cost of vigilance. Cooperators and defectors will thus interact at random, which means that defectors will have

FIGURE 7-7

When the share of cooperators exceeds 75 percent, it does not pay cooperators to bear the cost of vigilance. As a result, the expected payoff for defectors exceeds the expected payoff for co-operators, and the share of cooperators declines. When the share of cooperators is less than 75 per-cent, cooperators pay the cost of vigi-lance and thereby avoid interaction with defectors. In this region the coop-erators receive higher payoffs than defectors, and the share of cooperators increases as a result. From any starting point, the popula-tion eventually sta-bilizes at 75 percent cooperators.

AVERAGE PAYOFFS WITH COSTS OF VIGILANCE

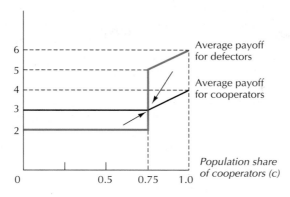

a higher average payoff. This difference in payoffs, in turn, will cause the pop-ulation share of cooperators to shrink.

For the values assumed in this example, the average payoff schedules for the two groups are plotted in Figure 7-7. As noted, the cooperators' schedule lies above the defectors' for shares smaller than 75 percent, but below it for larger shares. The sharp discontinuity in the defectors' schedule reflects the fact that, to the left of 75 percent, all cooperators pay for vigilance, while to the right of 75 percent, none of them does. Once the population share of cooperators passes 75 percent, defectors suddenly gain access to their victims. The evolutionary rule, once again, is that higher relative payoffs result in a growing population share. This rule makes it clear that the population in this example will stabilize at 75 percent cooperators.

Now, there is obviously nothing magic about this 75 percent figure. Had the cost of vigilance been lower than 1 unit, for example, the population share of cooperators would have been larger.

EXERCISE 7-4

> What will be the equilibrium population share of cooperators if the cost of vigilance is 0.5 unit?

An increase in the payoff when cooperators pair with one another would also increase the equilibrium population share of cooperators. The point of the exam-ple is that when there are costs of vigilance, there will be pressures that pull the population toward some stable mix of cooperators and defectors. As in the hawks and doves example considered earlier, once the population settles at this mix, members of both groups have the same average payoff and are therefore equally likely to survive. There is an ecological niche, in other words, for both groups. This result stands in stark contrast to the view that only opportunism can survive in a bitterly competitive material world.

The central assumption behind the claim that certain nonegoistic motives or preferences can help solve commitment problems is that the presence of these motives can somehow be discovered by others. Since the publication of Charles Darwin's 1872 book *The Expression of Emotions in Man and Animals,* much has been learned about the observable manifestations of motivational states. Psychologists, for example, have confirmed Darwin's claim that certain facial expressions are characteristic of specific emotions. These expressions, which are the result of complex combinations of facial muscle movements, are extremely difficult to produce on demand, yet appear spontaneously when the corresponding emotion is experienced.

Consider, for instance, the schematic expression in Figure 7-8. The distinct configuration of the eyebrows—elevated in the center of the brow, sloping downward toward the sides—is produced by a specific combination of the pyramidal muscles (located near the bridge of the nose) and the corrugator muscles (located near the center of the brow). Only 15 percent of experimental subjects are able to produce this expression on demand. By contrast, virtually all subjects exhibit it spontaneously when they experience grief, sadness, or concern.

Psychologists have also found that posture and other elements of body language, the pitch and timbre of the voice, the rate of respiration, and even the cadence of speech are systematically linked to underlying motivational states. Because the relevant linkages are beyond conscious control in most people, it is difficult to conceal from others the experience of certain emotions, and equally difficult to feign the characteristic expressions of these emotions on occasions when they are not actually experienced. For this reason, we are able to use such clues to form estimates of the emotional makeup of others, which in turn help us to form judgments about their preferences.[7] In addition to facial expressions and other physical symptoms of emotion, we rely on reputation and a variety of other clues to predict the behavior of potential partners.[8]

A Simple Thought Experiment

Perhaps the following simple thought experiment will help you decide whether you think you are able to make reliable character judgments about other people.

---

[7]The term "preferences" may not fully capture the essence of what we are trying to assess in potential partners. "Character" or "moral sentiments" may come closer.

[8]For a discussion of the role of reputation and other factors, see Chapter 4 of my *Passions Within Reason.*

FIGURE 7-8
Specific emotions summon characteristic facial expressions. Because these expressions are extremely difficult to display through conscious manipulation of the relevant facial muscles, the expressions serve as reliable indicators of the underlying motivational states.

THE EXPRESSION OF GRIEF, SADNESS, OR CONCERN

Imagine you have just gotten home from a crowded concert and discover you have lost $1000 in cash. The cash had been in your coat pocket in a plain envelope with your name written on it. Do you know anyone, not related to you by blood or marriage, who you feel certain would return it to you if he or she found it?

For the sake of discussion, I will assume that you are not in the unenviable position of having to answer no. Think for a moment about the person you are sure would return your cash; call her "Virtue." Try to explain *why* you feel so confident about her. Note that the situation was one where, if she had kept the cash, you could not have known it. On the basis of your other experiences with her, the most you could possibly know is that she did not cheat you in *every* such instance in the past. Even if, for example, she returned some lost money of yours in the past, that would not prove she didn't cheat you on some other occasion. (After all, if she *had* cheated you in a similar situation, you wouldn't know it.) In any event, you almost certainly have no logical basis in experience for inferring that Virtue would not cheat you now. If you are like most participants in this thought experiment, you simply believe you can fathom her inner motives: You are sure she would return your cash because you are sure she would feel terrible if she did not.

For preferences to serve as commitment devices, it is not necessary to be able to predict other people's preferences with certainty. Just as a weather forecast of 20 percent chance of rain can be invaluable to someone who must plan outdoor activities, so can probabilistic assessments of character traits be of use to people who must choose someone to trust. It would obviously be nice to be accurate in every instance. But it will often suffice to be right only a fraction of the time. And most people firmly believe they can make reasonably accurate character judgments about people they know well. If you share this belief, you are in a position to see clearly why the unbridled pursuit of self-interest will often be self-defeating.

Here are two more examples of commitment problems and how nonegoistic preferences can help solve them:

- **The deterrence problem.** Suppose Jones has a $200 leather briefcase that Smith covets. If Smith steals it, Jones must decide whether to press charges. If he does, he will have to go to court. He will get his briefcase back and Smith will spend 60 days in jail, but the day in court will cost him $300 in lost earnings. Since this is more than the briefcase is worth, it would clearly not be in his material interest to press charges. (To eliminate an obvious complication, suppose Jones is about to move to a distant city, so there is no point in his adopting a tough stance in order to deter future theft.) Thus, if Smith knows Jones is a purely rational, self-interested person, he is free to steal the briefcase with impunity. Jones may threaten to press charges, but his threat would be empty.

  But now suppose that Jones is *not* a pure egoist—that if Smith steals his briefcase, he will become outraged and think nothing of losing a day's earnings, or even a week's, in order to see justice done. If Smith knows this, he will let the briefcase be. If people expect us to respond irrationally to the theft of our property, we will seldom need to because it will not be in their interests to steal it. Being predisposed to respond irrationally serves much better here than being guided only by material self-interest.

- **The bargaining problem.** In this example, Smith and Jones again face the opportunity of a profitable joint venture. There is some task that they alone can do, which will net them $1000 total. Suppose Jones has no pressing need for extra money, but Smith has important bills to pay. It is a fundamental principle of bargaining theory that the party who needs the transaction least is in the strongest position. The difference in their circumstances thus gives Jones the advantage. Needing the gain less, he can threaten, credibly, to walk away from the transaction unless he gets the lion's share of the take, say, $900. Rather than see the transaction fall through, it will then be in Smith's interest to capitulate.

  But suppose Jones knows that Smith cares not only about how much money he receives in absolute terms but also about how the total is divided between them. More specifically, suppose Jones knows that Smith is committed to a norm of fairness that calls for the total to be divided evenly. If Smith's commitment to this norm is sufficiently strong, he will refuse Jones's one-sided offer, even though he would do better, in purely material terms, by accepting it. The irony is that if Jones knows this, he will not confront Smith with a one-sided offer in the first place.

*Tastes Not Only **Can** Differ, They **Must** Differ*

The examples we examined in this chapter suggest that economic forces may create a stable environmental niche not only for egoists but for altruists as well. We saw that a population consisting of only one of these types could always be invaded by the other. Our exercise thus tells us that people's tastes not only *can* differ, they *must* differ.

This message stands in stark contrast to the message of a celebrated article by University of Chicago economists George Stigler and Gary Becker, who at the time were strongly critical of explanations of behavior based on the assumption of differing tastes.[9] To say that people behave differently merely because they have different tastes, they argued, is an intellectual cop-out, an abandonment of the scholar's quest to get to the bottom of things. The best explanation of behavioral differences, in their view, is one that assumes people have the same tastes but face different prices and incomes.

Note that Stigler and Becker were stating the classical criticism of the present-aim version of rational choice theory—namely, that it serves up an instant explanation of any and all behavior. We may agree wholeheartedly with this criticism, yet this should not blind us to the fact that differences in tastes do exist—indeed must exist—and often imply important differences in behavior. The advantage of the commitment model is that its view of tastes as means rather than ends helps constrain the open-ended nature of the present-aim standard. The commitment model's functional view of preferences suggests that the repertoire of tastes be expanded beyond the simple egoistic tastes assumed in the self-interest model, but only upon showing that the holding of a specific taste is advantageous (or at least not fatally disadvantageous) in a material sense.

APPLICATION: VOTING IN PRESIDENTIAL ELECTIONS

As we saw in Example 1-11 in Chapter 1, the self-interest version of the rational choice model predicts that people will not vote in presidential elections. The reason, in a nutshell, is that while there are almost always costs involved in voting, there is virtually no chance that a single vote will tip the balance of the election.

But consider a person who has been taught that it is a citizen's duty to vote in presidential elections. If this message has sunk in at a deep level, its effect is to alter the person's preferences. For such a person, voting now becomes an end in itself, something that provides satisfaction.[10]

---

[9]George Stigler and Gary Becker, "De Gustibus Non Est Disputandum," *American Economic Review, 67,* September 1977. In fairness, I should add that Gary Becker has more recently embraced a much richer view about the admissible range of preferences.

[10]Here too, it might seem more descriptive to say that a person votes not because it gives her pleasure but because she thinks it is the right thing to do. Analytically, however, both descriptions may be represented by saying that the act of voting augments utility.

Her decision of whether to vote can now be analyzed in much the same way as we analyze other economic choices. To illustrate, consider a consumer whose utility is given by the following function:

$$U = 2M + 100V, \tag{7.8}$$

where M is the dollar value of her annual consumption of the composite good, and V takes the value 1 if she votes and 0 if she does not. Suppose further that this consumer finances her consumption by working at a job that pays \$50/hr for as many hours as she chooses to work. And suppose, finally, that in order to vote she must spend a total of 30 minutes traveling to and from the polling place, where she also must stand in line before casting her ballot. If she regards her transit time and waiting time as neither more nor less unpleasant than working an equivalent amount of time at her job, how long must the line at the polls be before she will decide not to vote?

Suppose we let t represent the length of the line at the polls, measured in hours. Then the total time required to vote, including travel time, is equal to $(t + 0.5)$ hr. Given that she can earn \$50/hr at her job, the opportunity cost of her voting is thus \$$(50t + 25)$. And since she gets 2 units of utility from each dollar of consumption of the composite good (see Equation 7.8), the opportunity cost of voting in utility terms is equal to $100t + 50$ units. On the benefit side, she stands to gain 100 units of utility by voting. The maximum acceptable length of the polling line is the value of t that equates the costs and benefits of voting in utility terms. This value of t is found by solving the equation

$$100t + 50 = 100, \tag{7.9}$$

which yields $t = \frac{1}{2}$, or 30 minutes. So the model predicts that if the line at the polling place is shorter than 30 minutes, she will vote; if longer, she will not vote; and if equal to 30 minutes, she will be indifferent between voting and not voting.

APPLICATION: CONCERNS ABOUT FAIRNESS

As an additional illustration of how predictions change when we take nonegoistic motives into account, consider the following example set forth by the German economist Werner Guth. Guth and his colleagues set out to discover how people would behave in a simple game designed to test for the presence of concerns about fairness.

The game is called the *ultimatum bargaining game* and involves two players, an *allocator* and a *receiver*. It begins by giving the allocator a fixed sum of money, say, \$20. The allocator must then make a proposal about how the money should be divided between him and the receiver—for example, he might propose \$10 for himself and \$10 for the receiver. The receiver's task is then either to accept or reject the proposal. If he accepts it, then they each receive the amounts proposed. If he rejects it, however, each player receives nothing. The \$20 simply reverts to the experimenters. The players in the game are strangers to one another and will play the game only once.

What does the self-interest model predict will happen here? To answer this question, we begin by assuming that each player cares only about his final wealth level, not about how much the other player gets. Now suppose the allocator proposes to keep $P_A = \$15$ for himself and to give the remaining $\$20 - P_A = \$5$ to the receiver, and that the receiver accepts this proposal. If M_A and M_R were their respective wealth levels before the experiment, their final wealth levels will then be $M_A + \$15$ and $M_R + \$5$.

If, on the other hand, the receiver rejects the allocator's proposal, then their final wealth levels will be M_A and M_R. Knowing this, the allocator can conclude that the receiver will get a higher wealth level by accepting the proposal than by rejecting it, provided only that P_A is less than $20. If the money cannot be divided into intervals any smaller than 1 cent, the self-interest model thus predicts unequivocally that the allocator will propose to keep $19.99 for himself and to give the remaining 1 cent to the receiver. The receiver may not be pleased about this one-sided offer, but the self-interest model says he will accept it nonetheless because $M_R + \$0.01 > M_R$. By the logic of the self-interest model, the receiver reasons that, whereas a gain of 1 cent is not much, it is better than nothing, which is what he would get if he refused the offer. Because the game is played only once, there is no point in refusing in the hope of encouraging a more favorable offer next time.

What prediction would we reach if we acknowledge that the receiver cares not just about his final wealth level but also about fairness? It is natural to say that the fairest split of the surplus in an ultimatum bargaining game is 50-50. Let S denote the total sum of money to be divided, and let $P/S = (20 - P_A)/S$ be the share of this surplus the receiver would get if he accepted the proposal. A convenient way to express the receiver's concern about fairness is by saying that his satisfaction declines as the ratio P/S deviates—in either direction—from the value 0.5. Thus, the receiver's indifference map defined over M_R and P/S might look roughly as shown in Figure 7-9 (next page). The indifference curves shown embody the additional assumption that a one-sided division is more objectionable if it favors the other person—which is another way of saying that the MRS rises more sharply when we move to the left from $P/S = 0.5$ than when we move to the right.[11]

Let us now evaluate the one-sided proposal predicted by the standard self-interest model, where $P_A = \$19.99$ and $P = \$0.01$. If the receiver accepts this proposal, he will end up at the point $(0.01/20, M_R + 0.01)$, labeled C in Figure 7-10. If, on the other hand, he rejects the proposal, he will have virtually the same wealth level, M_R. If rejecting may be considered to result in a P/S value of 0.5 (since neither party gains ground at the other's expense), the receiver will thus end up at point D in Figure 7-10. And because D lies on a higher indifference curve than C, he does best to reject the proposal. (If he accepted it, the trivial

---

[11]The point made in this example would be essentially the same if the receiver's indifference curves in Figure 7-9 were downward sloping throughout.

FIGURE 7-9
In many situations, the fairest division of a surplus is when each party receives an equal share. When people value fairness for its own sake, the indifference curves between final wealth and own share of the surplus are U-shaped, which means that people need to be compensated for accepting divisions that deviate from equality.

THE TRADEOFF BETWEEN ABSOLUTE WEALTH AND RELATIVE GAIN

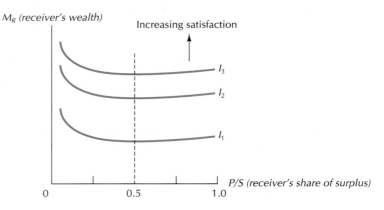

FIGURE 7-10
Accepting a one-sided offer places the receiver at point C. By refusing the offer, he ends up at D, where, even though his final wealth is slightly lower, he is on a higher indifference curve.

THE GAIN FROM REJECTING A ONE-SIDED OFFER

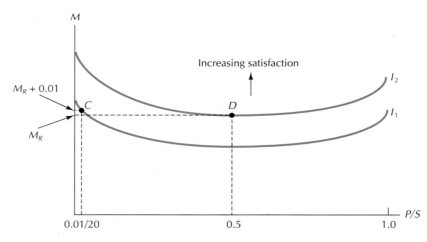

increase in his wealth would be insufficient to compensate for the disutility of the one-sided transaction.) More important, if the allocator knows that the receiver has such preferences, he will never make a one-sided offer in the first place.

In the foregoing example, it cost the receiver only a penny to punish the allocator for making a one-sided offer. Are people willing to turn down one-sided offers where substantially larger losses are involved? Werner Guth and his colleagues conducted these experiments with amounts as large as $50. They found that, even at this level, it is common to see the receiver reject if the allocator offers less than 20 percent of the total.

At some point, of course, concerns about fairness are likely to give way to concerns about the absolute gain itself. It would be surprising indeed if the receiver rejected a proposal that he get 10 percent of, say, $1 million. Here, most people would surely find the pair (0.1, M_R + $100,000) more attractive than (0.5, M_R).

*E*XAMPLE *7-2* *Hatfield's utility function is given by $U_H = M_H/\sqrt{M_M}$, where M_H is Hatfield's wealth level and M_M is McCoy's. McCoy's utility function takes a similar form: $U_M = M_M/\sqrt{M_H}$. Suppose $M_H = M_M = 4$ initially, and suppose there is a task, neither pleasant nor unpleasant, that Hatfield and McCoy can perform together and that will generate an additional 2 units of wealth for the two men to divide. Neither man can perform the task alone or with anyone else. What is the smallest payment Hatfield would accept in return for this task? (McCoy is paid the difference between 2 and the amount paid to Hatfield.) Is this task feasible?*

> The utility functions in this example are ones in which each person feels better when his own wealth increases but feels worse when the other person's wealth increases. The effect of the task is to increase the wealth of both people. The question is thus whether the positive effect of having more income from performing the task outweighs the negative effect of the other person also having more income. Hatfield's initial utility level is $4/\sqrt{4} = 2$. Suppose he does the task with McCoy and receives a payment of P, leaving $2 - P$ for McCoy. Hatfield's utility level would then be $U_H = (4 + P)/\sqrt{(4 + 2 - P)} = (4 + P)/\sqrt{(6 - P)}$. The lowest acceptable utility payment for Hatfield is the one that keeps his utility at the same level as if he did not participate: $(4 + P)/\sqrt{(6 - P)} = 2$. Rearranging terms, we have $P^2 + 12P - 8 = 0$, which solves for $P = 0.63$ (see footnote 12). Since the problem is symmetric, this is also the minimum payment that would be acceptable to McCoy. And since the total gain from doing the project (2) is more than enough for each person to get 0.63, they will do it. For example, if each takes a payment of 1, each will have a utility level of $(4 + 1)/\sqrt{(4 + 1)} = \sqrt{5}$, which is greater than the initial utility level of 2.

The Importance of Tastes

The self-interest model assumes certain tastes and constraints and then calculates what actions will best serve those tastes. This model is widely used by economists and other social scientists, game theorists, military strategists, philosophers, and others. Its results influence decisions that affect us all. In its standard form, it assumes purely egoistic tastes—namely, for present and future consumption goods of various sorts, leisure, and so on. Envy, guilt, rage, honor, sympathy, love, and the like typically play no role.

The examples in this chapter, by contrast, emphasize the role of these

---

[12]Recall that the solution to an equation of the form $ax^2 + bx + c = 0$ is given by $x = \dfrac{-b \pm \sqrt{b^2 - 4ac}}{2a}$.

emotions in behavior. The rationalists speak of tastes, not emotions, but for analytical purposes, the two play exactly parallel roles. Thus, a person who is motivated to avoid the emotion of guilt may be equivalently described as someone with a "taste" for honest behavior.

Tastes have important consequences for action. The inclusion of tastes that help solve commitment problems substantially alters the predictions of self-interest models. We saw that it may pay people to feel concerned about fairness for its own sake, because feeling that way makes them better bargainers. Without taking into account concerns about fairness, we cannot hope to predict what prices stores will charge, what wages workers will demand, how long business executives will resist a strike, what taxes governments will levy, how fast military budgets will grow, or whether a union leader will be reelected.

The presence of conscience also alters the predictions of self-interest models. These models predict clearly that when interactions between people are not repeated, people will cheat if they know they can get away with it. Yet evidence consistently shows that most people do not cheat under these circumstances. Self-interest models also suggest that the owner of a small business will not contribute to the lobbying efforts of trade associations. Like one man's vote, her own contribution will seem too small a part of the total to make any difference. Yet many small businesses do pay dues to trade associations, and many people do vote. Charitable institutions also exist on a far grander scale than would ever be predicted by self-interest models.

There is nothing mystical about the emotions that drive these behaviors. On the contrary, they are an obvious part of most people's psychological makeup. What we have seen is why it might be advantageous, even in purely material terms, to have concerns that motivate unselfish behavior.

IS MATERIAL GAIN AN "APPROPRIATE" MOTIVE FOR MORALITY?

Some may object that the prospect of material gain is somehow an improper motive for adopting moral values. But this objection misconstrues the fundamental message of this chapter, which is that nonegoistic motives confer material advantage only if the satisfaction people take from doing the right thing is *intrinsic* to the behavior itself. Otherwise, the person will lack the necessary motivation to make self-sacrificing choices when no one is looking, and once other people sense that aspect of his character, material advantages will not, in fact, follow. By the very nature of the commitment problem, moral sentiments cannot lead to material advantage unless they are heartfelt.

Summary

Prisoner's dilemmas and other forms of commitment problems abound in economic transactions. Being known not to have strictly self-interested preferences can be extremely useful for solving these problems.

In order for such preferences to be advantageous, others must be able to discern that one has them. If preferences could be observed without cost or uncertainty, there would be only cooperative people in the world. But because costs and uncertainty are an inherent part of the process, there will always be an ecological niche for at least some of the opportunistic people assumed in conventional self-interest models.

The two main points of this chapter are (1) the self-interest model, which assumes that everyone behaves opportunistically, is destined to make important errors in predicting actual behavior; and (2) people who are concerned about the interests of others need not suffer on that account, even in purely material terms. Because others can recognize the kind of people they are, opportunities will be open to them that would not be open to the opportunist.

Questions for Review

1. Summarize in your own words the major difficulties of the present-aim and self-interest standards of rationality.

2. Explain the role of rational analysis in the psychologist's model of human motivation.

3. Try to think of at least two commitment problems you personally encountered during the last year.

4. In the commitment model, what role is played by the observability of preferences?

5. Explain how the military arms race between the United States and the former Soviet Union had the same formal structure as a prisoner's dilemma.

Problems

1. A population consists of two types, "friendlies" and "aggressives." Each individual interacts with a randomly chosen member of the population. When two friendlies interact, each earns 3 units. When two aggressives interact, each earns 0 units. When a friendly and an aggressive interact, the former gets a payoff of 1 unit, the latter a payoff of 5 units. The growth rate of each type is proportional to its average payoff. What will be the equilibrium population shares of each type?

2. Consider a population with two types of people, C's and D's. Interactions among various combinations of the two types produce the following payoffs:

    C-C: 6 each
    C-D: 8 for D, 0 for C
    D-D: 4 each

Goggles are available at a cost of 1 unit that enable the wearer to identify each person's type with certainty. Without the goggles the two types are indistinguishable.

   a. What will be the equilibrium population shares of the two types?
   b. How would your answer differ if the payoff for D-D interactions was 5.5?

3. Alphonse's utility function is given by

$$U_A = M_A M_G,$$

where M_A and M_G are the wealth levels of Alphonse and Gaston, respectively. If Alphonse's initial wealth level is 100 while Gaston's is only 20, how much of his wealth will Alphonse give to Gaston?

4. Abdul's utility function is given by

$$U_A = \frac{M_A^2}{M_B^2},$$

where M_A is Abdul's wealth level and M_B is Benjamin's wealth level. Benjamin's utility function is given by

$$U_B = \frac{M_B^2}{M_A^2}.$$

Suppose $M_A = M_B = 10$ initially, and suppose there is a joint project that Abdul and Benjamin can undertake that will generate an additional 10 units of wealth to divide between them. The project is neither pleasant nor unpleasant. What is the minimum payment Abdul must be given to secure his agreement to perform the project? What is the minimum payment Benjamin must be given? Will they perform the project?

5. Now, suppose Benjamin's utility function is given by $U_B = M_B^2$ in Problem 4. And suppose Abdul signs a contract saying that he will donate 20 to a cause he opposes in the event that he receives less than 90 percent of any money he earns jointly with Benjamin. Will Benjamin accept a take-it-or-leave-it offer of 1 unit from Abdul?

6. Describe the advantages and disadvantages of electing a political leader who is known to favor harsh military reprisals against foreign aggression, even when such reprisals are highly injurious to our own national interests.

7. Harold's utility is given by $U = 3M + 60V$, where M is the dollar value of his annual consumption of the composite good and V takes the value 1 if he votes and 0 if he does not. Harold finances his consumption by working at a job that pays $30/hr for as many hours as he chooses to work. In order to vote he must spend a total of 20 minutes traveling to and from the polling place, where he must stand in line before casting his ballot. If he regards his transit time and waiting time as neither more nor less unpleasant than working an equivalent amount of time at his job, how long must the line at the polls be before Harold will decide not to vote?

Answers to In-Chapter Exercises

7-1. Let h denote the share of hawks in the population, so that $1 - h$ denotes the share of doves. Since the two types interact at random with other members of the population, the expected payoff for doves is given by

$$P_D = 3(1 - h) + 2(h) = 3 - h.$$

The corresponding expected payoff for hawks is

$$P_H = 6(1 - h) + 1(h) = 6 - 5h.$$

The population mix is in equilibrium when the expected payoffs of the two types are the same. If h^* denotes the equilibrium share of hawks, we have

$$3 - h^* = 6 - 5h^*,$$

which solves for $h^* = \frac{3}{4}$. The equilibrium share of doves is $1 - h^* = \frac{1}{4}$.

7-2. $P_C = 0.9(4) + 0.1(0) = 3.6.$

7-3. If all cooperators pay the cost of vigilance, each will get a payoff of $4 - 1.5 = 2.5$. If none pays the cost of vigilance, the expected payoff will be

$$P_C = 0.6(4) + 0.4(0) = 2.4,$$

which is less than 2.5. So they should pay the cost of vigilance.

7-4. The payoff net of the cost of vigilance is now $4 - 0.5 = 3.5$. If C's do not pay the cost of vigilance, their expected payoff is again given by $P_C = 4c$. To find the breakeven level of c, we solve $4c' = 3.5$, which yields $c' = \frac{7}{8}$.

For $c < \frac{7}{8}$, the C's have a higher expected payoff if they pay the cost. For $c > \frac{7}{8}$, they have a higher expected payoff if they simply take their chances. For $c < \frac{7}{8}$, the D's will be forced to interact with one another, which gives the D's a payoff of 2. Once $c > \frac{7}{8}$, however, the C's stop paying the cost and the expected payoff for the D's becomes

$$P_D = c6 + (1 - c)2 = 2 + 4c.$$

The expected payoff functions for the C's and D's are now as shown in the diagram:

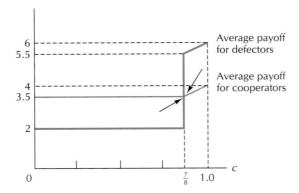

Note that the average payoff for C's is greater than for D's whenever $c < \frac{7}{8}$, while the expected payoff for D's exceeds that of C's whenever $c > \frac{7}{8}$. The result is that if we start with $c > \frac{7}{8}$, the population share of C's will shrink to $\frac{7}{8}$, because the growth rate of D's will be faster than that of C's. If we start with $c < \frac{7}{8}$, the population share of C's will grow to $\frac{7}{8}$.

CHAPTER

8

Cognitive Limitations and Consumer Behavior

ornell University has two sets of faculty tennis courts, one outdoor, one indoor. Membership in the outdoor facility is available for a fixed fee per season. There is no additional charge based on actual court use. The indoor facility, by contrast, has not only a seasonal fee but also a $15 per hour charge for court time. The higher charges of the indoor facility reflect the additional costs of heat, electricity, and building maintenance. The indoor facility opens in early October, a time when the Ithaca weather can be anything from bright sunshine and mild temperatures to blowing sleet and snow. The outdoor courts remain open, weather permitting, until early November. There is a similar 1-month overlap in the operation of the two facilities in the spring.

Demand on the indoor facility is intense, and people who want to play regularly must commit themselves to buy a specific hour each week. Having done so, they must pay for the hour whether or not they use it. During good weather, almost everyone prefers to play on the outdoor courts, which are nestled in one of Ithaca's scenic gorges.

Here is the problem: You are committed to an indoor court at 3 P.M. on Saturday, October 20, the only hour you are free to play that day. It is a warm, sunny autumn afternoon. Where should you play, indoors or out?

I find that surprisingly many of my noneconomist partners balk when I say that playing on the outdoor courts is the only sensible thing to do. "But we've already paid for the indoor court," they invariably complain. I ask, "If both courts cost the same, which would you choose?" They immediately respond, "Outdoors." I then explain that both courts *do* cost the same—because our fee for the hour is going to be $15 no matter which place we play—indeed, no matter whether we play at all. The $15 is a sunk cost and should have no effect on our decision. Yet, even at this point, many people seem to feel uncomfortable about wasting the indoor court we have paid for. The alternative, however, is to waste an opportunity to play outdoors, which we all agree is something even more valuable! True enough, it is bad to be wasteful, but *something* is going to be wasted, no matter which place we play.

Eventually, most people come around to the notion that it is more sensible to abandon the indoor court, even though paid for, and play outdoors on sunny fall days. The rational choice model says unequivocally that this is what we should do. But it does not seem to be the natural inclination of most people. On the contrary, in the absence of a prodding economist, most people who have paid for an indoor court end up using it, even on the most pleasant days.

Chapter Preview

In Chapter 7 we saw why motives other than self-interest might be important. These motives often lead people to behave in ways that are considered irrational under the self-interest model. But irrational or not, behaviors like tipping on the road or returning lost wallets to their owners are undertaken without regret. If a rationalist were to point out that there is no way a waiter in a distant city could retaliate for not having been left a tip, most of us would respond, "So what?" We would not suddenly regret having left tips all our lives.

Our focus in this chapter is on irrational behavior of an altogether different sort, behavior that is the result of failure to see clearly how best to achieve a desired result. Failure to ignore the sunk costs of the indoor tennis court is one example. Unlike the behaviors considered in the last chapter, people often *do* want to alter these behaviors once their consequences become clear to them.

In addition to failing to ignore sunk costs, we will see that people violate the prescriptions of rational choice models in a variety of other ways. The important point, for our purposes, is that these violations are often systematic. We will examine several behavioral models of choice that often do a much better job of predicting actual decisions than the rational choice model. It is important to remember, however, that these behavioral models claim no normative significance. They tell us, for instance, that we often *do* tend to ignore sunk costs, not that we *should* ignore them.

The rational choice model says we can make better decisions by ignoring sunk costs, and most people, on reflection, strongly agree. The value of behavioral models is that that they call our attention to situations in which we are likely to make mistakes. They are an important tool for helping us avoid common pitfalls in decision making.

Bounded Rationality

The Nobel laureate Herbert Simon was the first to impress upon economists that human beings are incapable of behaving like the rational beings portrayed in standard rational choice models. Simon is a pioneer in the field of artificial intelligence and stumbled upon this realization in the process of trying to instruct a computer to "reason" about a problem. He discovered that when we ourselves confront a puzzle, we rarely reach a solution in a neat, linear fashion. Rather, we search in a haphazard way for potentially relevant facts and information, and usually quit once our understanding reaches a certain threshold. Our conclusions are often inconsistent, even flatly incorrect. But much of the time, we come up with serviceable, if imperfect, solutions. In Simon's terms, we are "satisficers," not maximizers.

Subsequent economists have taken Simon's lead and developed a sophisticated literature on decision making under incomplete information. We now realize that when information is costly to gather, and cognitive processing ability is limited, it is not even rational to make fully informed choices of the sort portrayed in simple models. Paradoxically, it is irrational to be completely well informed! The literature on decision making under incomplete information, far from being a challenge to the rational choice model, has actually bolstered our confidence in it.

But there is another offshoot of Simon's work, one that is less friendly to the rational choice model. This research, strongly influenced by cognitive psychologists Daniel Kahneman and Amos Tversky, demonstrates that even with transparently simple problems, people often violate the most fundamental axioms of rational choice. Choosing whether to play tennis indoors or out is a case in point. The relevant facts in this problem could hardly be any simpler, and yet, as noted, people consistently choose irrationally.

Such examples are by no means isolated. One of the most cherished tenets of the rational choice model is that wealth is fungible. Fungibility implies, among other things, that our total wealth, not the amount we have in any particular account, determines what we buy. Kahneman and Tversky, however, provided a vivid experimental demonstration to the contrary.[1] They tell one group of people to imagine that, having earlier purchased tickets for $10, they arrive at the theater to discover they have lost them. Members of a second group are told to picture themselves arriving just before the performance to buy their tickets when they find each of them has lost $10 on the way to the theater. People in both groups are then asked whether they will continue with their plans to attend the performance. In the rational choice model, the forces governing this decision are the same for both groups. Losing a $10 ticket should have precisely the same effect as losing a $10 bill. (Recall from Chapter 3 the rule that if tastes and budget constraints are the same, decisions should also be the same.) And yet, in repeated trials, most people in the lost-ticket group say they would not attend the performance, while an overwhelming majority—88 percent—in the lost-bill group say they would.

---

[1]See Amos Tversky and Daniel Kahneman, "The Framing of Decisions and the Psychology of Choice," *Science, 211,* 1981: 453–458.

Kahneman and Tversky explained that people apparently organize their spending into separate "mental accounts" for food, housing, entertainment, general expenses, and so on. People who lose their tickets act as if they debit $10 from their mental entertainment accounts, while those who lose $10 debit their general expense account. For people in the former group, the loss makes the apparent cost of seeing the show rise from $10 to $20, whereas for those in the second it remains $10.

The rational choice model makes clear that the second group's assessment is the correct one. And on reflection, most people do, in fact, agree that losing a ticket is no better reason not to see the performance than losing a $10 bill.

The Asymmetric Value Function

The rational choice model says that people should evaluate events, or collections of events, in terms of their overall effect on total wealth. Suppose A is the event that you get an unexpected gift of $100 and B is the event that you return from vacation to find an $80 invoice from the city for the repair of a broken water line on your property. According to the rational choice model, you should regard the occurrence of these two events as a good thing, because their net effect is a $20 increase in your total wealth.

Kahneman and Tversky found, however, that people seem to weigh each event separately, and attach considerably less importance to the gain than to the loss—so much less that many people actually refuse to accept pairs of events that would increase their overall wealth!

In the rational choice model, this of course can never happen. Confronted with the two events A and B described above, a person with an initial wealth of M_0 knows exactly how to react. The combined effect of A (a $100 gain) and B (an $80 loss) is to increase his wealth to $M_0 + 20$. And since utility is an increasing function of total wealth, the two events taken together cause utility to increase from U_0 to U_1, as shown in Figure 8-1.

FIGURE 8-1
Under the rational choice model, any combination of events that increases total wealth will also increase total utility.

UTILITY OF A PAIR OF EVENTS THAT INCREASES TOTAL WEALTH

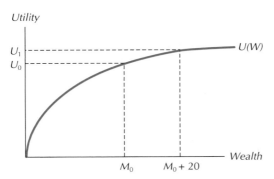

Kahneman and Tversky proposed that people evaluate alternatives not with the conventional utility function, but instead with a *value function* that is defined over *changes* in wealth. One important property of this value function is that it is much steeper in losses than in gains. In Figure 8-2, for example, note how it assigns a much larger value, in absolute terms, to a loss of $80 than to a gain of $100. Note also that the value function is concave in gains and convex in losses. This property is the analog of diminishing marginal utility in the traditional model. It says that the impact of incremental gains or losses diminishes as the gains or losses become larger.

Kahneman and Tversky emphasized that their value function is a purely descriptive device. They are trying to summarize regularities in the ways people actually seem to make choices. They make no claim that people *should* choose in the ways predicted by their value function.

According to Kahneman and Tversky, it is very common for people to evaluate each item of a collection of events separately and then make decisions on the basis of the sum of the separate values. In this example, $V(100)$ is much smaller, in absolute terms, than $V(-80)$. Because the algebraic sum of the two is less than zero, anyone who employs this decision mechanism will refuse the pair of opportunities A and B, even though their net effect is to increase total wealth by $20.

There are really two important features of the Kahneman and Tversky value function. One is that people treat gains and losses asymmetrically, giving the latter much heavier weight in their decisions than the former. The second is that people evaluate events first and then add the separate values together. The first of these features does not necessarily imply irrational behavior. There is nothing inconsistent, after all, about feeling that a loss causes more pain than the happiness caused by a gain of the same magnitude. What *does* often appear irrational is the second step—treating each event separately, rather than considering their combined effect.

FIGURE 8-2
Unlike the traditional utility function, the value function is defined over *changes* in total wealth. It is steeper in losses than in gains, concave in gains, and convex in losses.

THE KAHNEMAN-TVERSKY VALUE FUNCTION

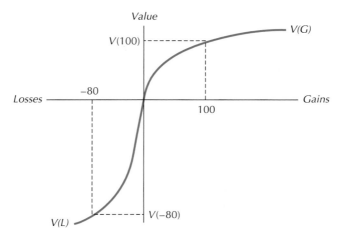

This is essentially a question about how to frame events. If someone pointed out to a person that the net effect of two events A and B was to increase her wealth by $20, she would probably quickly agree to allow the events to happen. Framed as an entity, they are obviously an improvement over the status quo. The problem is that, in actual decisions, it may seem more natural to frame the events separately.

Another example helps illustrate this point. Recently, a corporation made available to its employees a new medical insurance plan. The old plan paid 100 percent of all covered medical expenses, and the premium was approximately $500/yr per family. The new plan has a $200 deductible feature—people must pay the first $200 in medical expenses each year, but once that threshold is reached, the insurance again pays 100 percent. The premium for the new plan is $250/yr, half that of the old plan. Employees have the option of staying with the old plan or switching to the new.

Seen through the lens of the rational choice model, the new plan dominates the old. The $250 savings in premiums is more than enough to compensate for the $200 deductible feature. Families that incur less than $200/yr in medical expenses do even better under the new plan. Nonetheless, many employees are adamant in their wish to remain on the old plan. If some people code the $250 premium savings and the $200 extra in medical bills as separate events, the asymmetric value function predicts just such behavior. As indicated in Figure 8-3, the $200 loss weighs in more heavily than the $250 gain.

Sunk Costs

Another basic tenet of the rational choice model is that sunk costs should be ignored in decisions. In the tennis example at the beginning of this chapter, we saw that it

FIGURE 8-3
Because the savings in premiums ($250) is larger than the largest possible increase in uncovered expenses ($200), the new plan is necessarily better than the old. But if people code gains and losses separately, they may nonetheless refuse to switch to the new policy.

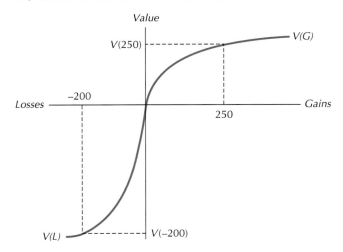

REJECTION OF A DOMINANT INSURANCE PLAN

is this principle, not sunk cost, that is sometimes ignored. Economist Richard Thaler argued that such examples are not isolated, that people in fact show a general tendency not to ignore sunk costs. Thaler is the author of the all-you-can-eat pizza experiment we discussed in Chapter 1. Recall that in the experiment the diners whose admission charges were refunded ate substantially fewer slices of pizza than the others. Thaler offered several other vivid illustrations of the pattern.

One is a thought experiment in which you are asked first to imagine that you have bought a pair of very fashionable shoes for $200, only to discover that they are painfully tight. They improve slightly after being broken in, but still cause considerable discomfort. What do you do with these shoes, continue wearing them or give them away? Would your response be any different if you had not bought the shoes but instead had received them as a gift?

Under the rational choice model, it should not matter whether you bought the shoes or were given them. Either way, you own them now, and the only question is whether the discomfort they cause is serious enough to discontinue wearing them. People in both categories should be equally likely to discontinue wearing the shoes. Contrary to this prediction, however, people are much more likely to say they would abandon the shoes if they received them as a gift. Having shelled out $200 apparently makes many people determined to endure them.

One final sunk cost example: Suppose you have just paid $40 for tickets to a basketball game to be played tonight in an arena 60 miles north of your home. Suddenly it starts snowing heavily and the roads north, while passable, are difficult. Do you still go to the game? Would your answer have been different if, instead of having bought the tickets, you had received them for free? Thaler finds that most people who bought the tickets would go, whereas most of those who were given them say they would stay home. According to the rational choice model, of course, the decision should be the same in either case. If your expected pleasure of seeing the game exceeds the expected hassle of the drive, you should go; otherwise stay home. Neither element in this cost-benefit calculation should depend on how you obtained the tickets.

Out-of-Pocket Costs Versus Opportunity Costs

Thaler suggested that our tendency not to ignore sunk costs may be given a simple interpretation in terms of the Kahneman and Tversky value function. In terms of the tennis example, failure to play on the outdoor courts on a nice day is coded mentally as a forgone gain, whereas not playing on the $15 indoor court you have already paid for is coded as a loss. Even though the gain is larger than the loss here, the greater steepness of the value function in the loss domain creates a bias in favor of the indoor court.

Much the same interpretation is supported by a number of other plausible examples.[2] Consider a person who in 1955 bought a case of wine for $5/bottle. Today the same wine sells for $100/bottle. His wine merchant offers him $60/bottle for it and he refuses, even though the most he would pay for the same wine today is $35/bottle. The rational choice model rules out such behavior. But if out-of-pocket expenses (for example, for the purchase of additional wine) are coded as losses, while opportunity costs (for example, of not selling the wine to the merchant) are coded as forgone gains, then the asymmetric value function allows for just such a response.

An even more common example is the case of tickets to premium entertainment events. Tickets to the 1995 Super Bowl sold for $250 through official channels, but in the open market went for prices as high as $2500. Thousands of fans used their $250 tickets to attend the game, thus passing up the opportunity to sell them for $2500. Very few of these fans, however, would have spent $2500 to buy a ticket for the game.

Thaler offered the parallel example of the man who would refuse to mow his neighbor's lawn for $20 yet mows his own identical lawn, even though his neighbor's son would be willing to mow it for him for only $8. This behavior, as well as the behavior of the Super Bowl fans, is also consistent with the notion that out-of-pocket expenses are coded as losses, opportunity costs as forgone gains.

Hedonic Framing

Kahneman and Tversky's value function suggested specific ways that sellers, gift givers, and others might frame their offerings to enhance their appeal.[3] Thaler mentioned these four specific strategies:

- **Segregate gains.** Because the value function is concave in gains, a higher total value results when we decompose a large gain into two (or more) smaller ones. Thus, Figure 8-4 shows that a gain of 100 creates more total value if decomposed into two separate gains of 60 and 40. The moral here, as Thaler said, is "Don't wrap all the Christmas presents in a single box."

    Thaler tested the empirical validity of this recommendation by asking people which of the following two persons they thought would be happier: *A*, who is given two lottery tickets, one of which wins $50, the other $25; or *B*, who is given one lottery ticket, which wins $75. Of the people he asked, 64 percent responded that *A* would be happier, 18 percent said *B*, and 17 percent thought the two would be equally happy. The rational choice model, of course, says that both would be equally happy.

---

[2]See R. Thaler, "Toward a Positive Theory of Consumer Choice," *Journal of Economic Behavior and Organization*, 1980.

[3]The material in this section draws extensively on the arguments and evidence presented in R. Thaler, "Mental Accounting and Consumer Choice," *Marketing Science*, 4, 1985.

FIGURE 8-4
Because the value
function is concave
in gains, the total
value of two small
gains taken
separately
[$V(60) + V(40)$] is
larger than the value
of their sum
[$V(100)$].

THE BENEFIT OF SEGREGATING GAINS

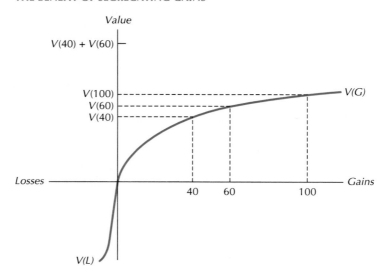

• **Combine losses.** The convexity of the value function in the loss domain implies that two separate losses will appear less painful if they are combined into a single, larger loss. As shown in Figure 8-5, for example, separate losses of 20 and 30 have a combined value that is larger, in absolute terms, than the value of a loss of 50.

FIGURE 8-5
Because the value
function is convex
in losses, the effect
of two losses taken
separately
[$V(-20) + V(-30)$]
is more painful than
the effect of their
sum [$V(-50)$].

THE BENEFIT OF COMBINING LOSSES

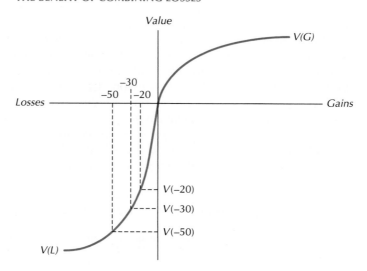

FIGURE 8-6
Because the value function is steeper in losses than in gains, the pain of a loss [$V(-200)$] will often exceed the pleasure of a slightly larger gain [$V(250)$]. The pain of such a loss can be avoided when it is possible to combine it with the larger gain to produce a positive net effect [$V(50)$].

THE BENEFIT OF OFFSETTING A LOSS WITH A LARGER GAIN

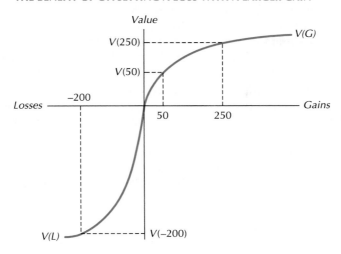

To test this prediction about the efficacy of combining losses, a sample of subjects was asked who would feel worse: *A*, who gets one letter from the Internal Revenue Service saying he owes $150; or *B*, who gets two letters, one from the IRS saying he owes $100, another from the state tax authorities saying he owes $50. (The subjects were also told that there would be no repercussions other than the additional tax payments themselves.) Here are their responses: 76 percent said that *B* would feel worse, 16 percent said *A*, and 8 percent said there would be no difference. The rational choice model, again, says that the two should feel the same.

Marketers seem to have discovered the principle that losses are less painful when combined than when taken separately. A $2000 Jacuzzi, for example, seems much cheaper when its price is added together with that of a $150,000 house than it does when it is evaluated in isolation. The $150,000 expense of the house already has the buyer so far out on the flattened part of the value function that an extra $2000 seems to cause very little additional injury.

- **Offset a small loss with a larger gain.** The greater steepness of the value function in the loss domain can be avoided whenever a loss can be combined with a larger gain. Thus, the effect of a gain of 250 and a loss of 200, evaluated separately, is to produce a net value that is negative. As shown in Figure 8-6, however, the effect of lumping the two together is clearly positive.

To test your intuition about the advantage of offsetting a loss with a larger gain, ask yourself which person you think would be happier: *A*, who wins $100 in the state lottery but the same day drops a bottle of ink and does $80 worth of damage to his living room rug; or *B*, who wins $20 in the lottery? Of a large sample of subjects who were asked this question, 70 percent responded *B*, 25 percent said *A*, and 5 percent thought the two would be equally happy.[4] The rational choice model, which predicts the latter outcome, is again in conflict with the majority view.

Recall our earlier discussion of the company whose employees were reluctant to adopt the new medical insurance plan. This company might have won much stronger acceptance for the plan had it framed the decision in terms of the net effect, rather than as a separate loss and gain.

- **Segregate small gains from large losses.** A sample of subjects was asked which of these persons is more upset: *A*, whose car sustains $200 damage in the parking lot the same day he wins $25 in the office football pool; or *B*, whose car sustains $175 damage in the parking lot? Of those responding, 72 percent said *B* would be more upset, 22 percent picked *A*, and 6 percent said they would be equally upset. The rational choice model predicts they would be equally upset, because they suffer exactly the same reduction in their wealth. The Kahneman and Tversky value function, by contrast, predicts that *B* would be more upset, which accords with most people's responses.

Thaler called the segregation of a small gain from a big loss the "silver-lining effect" and argued that it may help explain why so many merchants offer cash rebates on their products. ("Buy a new Dodge before October 1st and get $1200 cash back!") Viewed in the context of the rational choice model, this practice seems to be dominated by the simple alternative of reducing the price of the product. The reason is that the buyer must pay sales tax on the whole price of the item, including any amount he gets back as a rebate. In New York City, which has an $8\frac{1}{4}$ percent sales tax, this means paying $99 more for a car with a $1200 rebate than for the identical car with a $1200 price reduction. And yet the practice persists. If it leads people to code the price of the product as a loss and the rebate as a gain (see Figure 8-7), the value function approach makes clear why it might be so effective.

Choice Under Uncertainty

The standard model of rational choice under uncertainty is the von Neumann–Morgenstern expected utility model discussed in Chapter 6. This model provides valuable *guidance* about how best to choose between uncertain alternatives. But Kahneman and Tversky showed that it does not always provide a good *description* of the way people actually decide.[5] To illustrate, they presented a series of choices to a group of volunteer subjects. They began with the following problem, which elicited responses that were perfectly consistent with the expected utility model:

---

[4]R. Thaler, op. cit., 1985.

[5]See Amos Tversky and Daniel Kahneman, "Judgment Under Uncertainty: Heuristics and Biases," *Science, 185,* 1974: 1124–1131.

FIGURE 8-7
If a cash rebate is coded as a separate gain [$V(1200)$], and the price of the product as a loss [$V(-11,200)$], then the total effect [$V(1200)$] + [$V(-11,200)$] is less painful than when the product is offered at a lower price [$V(-10,000)$].

THE SILVER-LINING EFFECT AND CASH REBATES

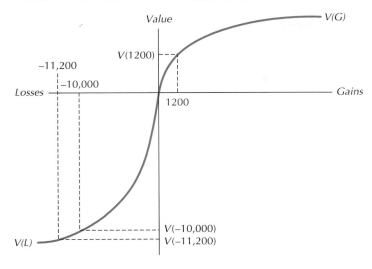

Problem 1. Choose between

    A: A sure gain of $240   (84%)

and

    B: A 25% chance of getting $1000 and a 75% chance of getting $0.   (16%)

The numbers in parentheses indicate the percentage of subjects who picked each alternative. Here, most people chose the sure gain of $240, even though the expected value of the lottery, at $250, was $10 higher. To verify that this pattern is consistent with the expected utility model, let U denote a subject's utility function, defined on total wealth, and let M denote her initial wealth in dollars. Then the expected utility of choice A is $U(M + 240)$, whereas the expected utility of choice B is $0.25U(M + 1000) + 0.75U(M)$. If utility is a concave function of total wealth (that is, if people are risk averse), we see in Figure 8-8 why A might easily have been more attractive than B.

Subjects were then asked to consider an apparently very similar problem:

Problem 2. Choose between

    C: A sure loss of $750   (13%)

and

    D: A 75% chance of losing $1000 and a 25% chance of losing $0.   (87%)

FIGURE 8-8
If the utility function is sufficiently concave, $U(M + 240)$ will exceed the expected utility of a gamble with positive expected value, $0.25\ U(M + 1000) + 0.75\ U(M)$.

A RISK-AVERSE PERSON WILL USUALLY PREFER A SURE GAIN TO A LOTTERY WITH SLIGHTLY HIGHER EXPECTED VALUE

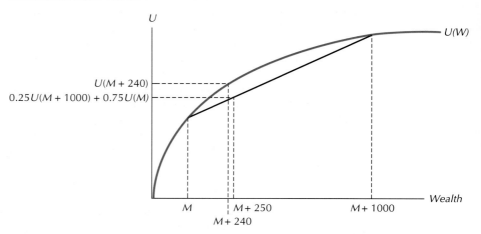

This time the lottery has the same expected value as the sure option. Under the expected utility model, risk-averse subjects therefore ought to choose the sure alternative once again. But this time we see a dramatic reversal. More than 6 times as many people chose the lottery as chose the sure loss of $750.

Finally, the subjects were asked to consider the following problem:

Problem 3. Choose between

> *E:* A 25% chance of getting $240 and a 75% chance of losing $760 (0%)

and

> *F:* A 25% chance of getting $250 and a 75% chance of losing $750. (100%)

Viewed in isolation, the responses to Problem 3 are completely unsurprising. The lottery in *E* is simply worse in every way than the one in *F*, and only someone who wasn't paying attention would have chosen *E*. But note that lottery *E* is what we get when we combine choices *A* and *D* from Problems 1 and 2; and that, similarly, lottery *F* is the result of combining choices *B* and *C* from the two earlier problems. In the first two problems, the combination of *B* and *C* was chosen by fewer subjects (3 percent) than any other, whereas the combination *A* and *D* was by far the most popular (chosen by 73 percent of all subjects)—even though the combination of *A* and *D* is strictly dominated by the combination of *B* and *C*. Such findings, needless to say, pose a sharp challenge to the expected utility model.

Kahneman and Tversky argued that the observed pattern is exactly what would have been predicted using their asymmetric value function. In Problem

1, for example, note that the choice is between a certain gain and a lottery whose possible outcomes are nonnegative. Since the value function is concave in gains, and since the expected value of the lottery is only slightly larger than the sure alternative, it predicts the choice of the latter.

In Problem 2, by contrast, the choice is between a certain loss, on the one hand, and a lottery, each of whose outcomes is a loss, on the other. Since the value function is convex in losses, it predicts risk-seeking behavior with respect to such a choice, and this, of course, is just what we saw. Because Problem 3 forced people to amalgamate the relevant gains and losses, subjects were easily able to see that one pair of alternatives dominated the other, and chose accordingly.

It is tempting to suppose that violations of the expected utility model occur only when the problem is sufficiently complicated that people have difficulty computing what the model prescribes. But Kahneman and Tversky showed that the outcomes of even the simplest of decisions can be manipulated by framing the alternatives slightly differently.

For example, they asked a group of subjects to choose between various policy responses to a rare disease that would claim 600 lives if we did nothing. One group was asked to choose either program *A*, which would save exactly 200 lives with certainty, or program *B*, which would save 600 lives with probability 1/3 and zero lives with probability 2/3. Here, 72 percent of all subjects chose program *A*. A second group was asked to choose either program *C*, under which exactly 400 people would die, or program *D*, under which there is a 1/3 chance no one will die and 2/3 chance that all 600 will die. This time, 78 percent of all subjects chose program *D*.

A moment's reflection reveals that programs *A* and *C* are exactly the same, as are programs *B* and *D*. And yet subjects from the two groups chose dramatically differently. Kahneman and Tversky explained that the first group coded "lives saved" as gains, and were therefore risk averse in choosing between *A* and *B*. Similarly, the second group coded deaths as losses, which led them to be risk seeking in the choice between *C* and *D*.

It is also tempting to suppose that behavior inconsistent with the prescriptions of the expected utility model is largely confined to situations involving novice decision makers, or situations where little of importance is at stake. Kahneman and Tversky found, however, that even experienced physicians make similarly inconsistent recommendations about treatment regimens when the problems are framed in slightly different ways. The moral is that we are all well advised to be cautious when making decisions under uncertainty. Try framing the relevant alternatives in different ways and see if it makes any difference. And if it does, try to reflect on which of the formulations best captures your underlying concerns.

Judgmental Heuristics and Biases

Many of the examples considered so far make it clear that even when people have precisely the relevant facts at their fingertips, they often fail to make rational decisions. There is yet another difficulty confronting the rational choice model, namely, that we often draw erroneous inferences about what the relevant facts are. More important, many of the errors we make are systematic, not random. Kahneman and Tversky identified three particularly simple heuristics, or rules of thumb, that people use to make judgments and inferences about the environment.[6] These heuristics are efficient in the sense that they help us economize on cognitive effort and give roughly correct answers much of the time. But they also give rise to large, predictable errors in many cases. Let us consider each of the three heuristics in turn.

AVAILABILITY

We often estimate the frequency of an event, or class of events, by the ease with which we can summon examples from memory. Much of the time, there is a close positive correlation between the ease with which we can do so and the true frequency of occurrence. It is easier, after all, to recall examples of things that happen often.

But frequency of occurrence is not the only factor that determines ease of recall. If people are asked, for example, whether there are more murders than suicides in New York State each year, almost everyone confidently answers yes. And yet there are always more suicides! Kahneman and Tversky explained that we think there are more murders because murders are more "available" in memory. Memory research demonstrates that it is much easier to recall an event the more vivid or sensational it is. Even if we had heard about equally many suicides as murders, it is on this account likely that we will be able to remember a much larger proportion of the murders.

Other elements in the mechanics of memory can also affect the availability of different events. Ask yourself, for example, whether more words in the English language start with the letter r than words that have r as their third letter. Most people answer confidently that many more words start with r, but in fact many more words have r as their third letter. We store words in memory much as they are stored in a dictionary—alphabetically, beginning with the first letter. We know plenty of words with r as their third letter, but it is no easier to remember them than it is to find them in a dictionary.

Events also tend to be more available in memory if they have happened more recently. A large body of research indicates that people tend to assign too much weight to recent information when making assessments about relative performance. In baseball, for example, a player's lifetime batting average against a certain pitcher is the best available predictor of how he will do against that pitcher in his next time at bat. It is apparently not uncommon, however, for a manager to bench a hitter against a pitcher he has performed poorly against the last couple

---

[6]See Tversky and Kahneman, ibid.

of times out, even though he hit that same pitcher very well during a span of many years. The problem is that the manager estimates the player's performance by examples of it that spring easily to mind. And the most recent examples are the easiest ones to think of.

Economically, the availability bias is important because we often have to estimate the relative performance of alternative economic options. Managers of companies, for example, must weigh the merits of different employees for promotion. The most effective managers will be those who guard against the natural tendency to put too much weight on recent performance.

REPRESENTATIVENESS

Kahneman and Tversky also discovered an interesting bias in the way we attempt to answer questions of the forms, "What is the likelihood that object *A* belongs to class B?" For example, suppose Steve is a shy person and we want to estimate the likelihood that he is a librarian rather than a salesperson. Most people are eager to respond that Steve is much more likely to be a librarian, because shyness is thought to be a representative trait for librarians, but rather an unusual one for salespersons. Such responses are often biased, however, because the likelihood of belonging to the category in question is influenced by many other important factors besides representativeness. Here, it is heavily influenced by the relative frequencies of salespersons and librarians in the overall population.

A simple example conveys the essence of the problem. Suppose that 80 percent of all librarians are shy, but only 20 percent of all salespeople. Suppose further that there are nine salespeople in the population for every librarian. Under these reasonable assumptions, if we know that Steve is shy and that he is either a librarian or a salesman, what is the probability that he is a librarian? The relevant numbers for answering this question are displayed in Figure 8-9. There, we

FIGURE 8-9
Even though shyness is more representative of librarians than of salespersons, a shy person is much more likely to be a salesperson than a librarian. The reason is that there are many more salespersons than librarians.

DISTRIBUTION BY TYPE OF LIBRARIANS AND SALESPERSONS

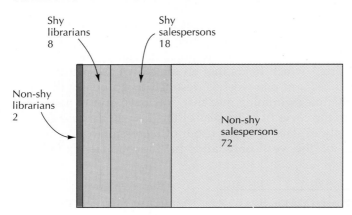

Shy librarians 8

Shy salespersons 18

Non-shy librarians 2

Non-shy salespersons 72

see that even though a much larger proportion of librarians are shy, there are more than twice as many shy salespersons as there are shy librarians. The reason, of course, is that there are so many more salespeople than librarians. Out of every 100 people here, 26 of them are shy—18 salespersons and 8 librarians. This means that the odds of a shy person being a librarian are only 8/26, or just under one-third. Yet most people who confront this example are reluctant to say that Steve is a salesperson, because shyness is so unrepresentative of salespersons.

EXERCISE 8-1

Suppose 90 percent of all librarians are shy but only 20 percent of all salespersons are, and that there are 4 times as many salespersons as librarians. What is the likelihood that a randomly chosen shy person is a librarian, given that he is either a salesperson or a librarian?

Another example of the representativeness bias is the statistical phenomenon known as the *regression effect,* or *regression to the mean.* Suppose a standard IQ test is administered to 100 people and that the 20 who score highest have an average score of 122, or 22 points above the average for the population. If these same 20 people are then tested a second time, their average score will almost always be substantially smaller than 122. The reason is that there is a certain amount of randomness in performance on IQ tests, and the people who did best on the first test are likely to include disproportionately many whose performances happened to be better than usual on that particular test.

We have substantial firsthand experience with regression effects in our daily lives (for example, the sons of unusually tall fathers tend to be shorter than their fathers). Kahneman and Tversky noted, however, that we often fail to make adequate allowance for it in our judgments because, they conjectured, we feel intuitively that an output (for example, an offspring) should be representative of the input (for example, the parent) that produced it.

It has long been observed that the rookie of the year in major league baseball (and in other sports as well) often has a mediocre second season. This has been attributed to the "sophomore jinx." A related phenomenon is the *"Sports Illustrated* jinx," which holds that an athlete whose picture appears on the cover of *Sports Illustrated* one week is destined to do poorly the next. Shirley Babashoff, the Olympic swimming medalist, was once said to have refused to have her picture on the cover of *SI* for fear of the jinx.[7] Both these supposed jinxes, however, are easily explained as the result of regression to the mean. Someone gets to be rookie of the year only after having had an extraordinarily good season.

---

[7]See Thomas Gilovich, *How We Know What Isn't So,* New York: The Free Press, 1991.

Similarly, athletes appear on the cover of *SI* only after an unusually strong performance. Their subsequent performance, even if still well above average, will almost inevitably fall below the standard that earned them their accolades.

An especially pernicious consequence of our failure to take into account regression to the mean is the effect it has on our estimates of the relative efficacy of praise and blame. Psychologists have long demonstrated that praise and other forms of positive reinforcement are much more effective than punishment or blame for teaching desired skills. But people would be unlikely to draw this inference from experience if they were unmindful of the importance of regression to the mean.

The reason is that, quite independently of whether a person is praised or blamed, a good performance is likely to be followed by a lesser one and a bad performance by a better one. Someone who praises good performances is therefore likely to conclude, erroneously, that praise perversely *causes* worse performance. Conversely, someone who denigrates poor performance is likely to spuriously attribute to his action the improvement that in fact results from regression effects. The co-movements of praise, blame, and performance would convince all but the most sophisticated analyst that blame works and praise doesn't. Managers who are trying to elicit the most effective performances from their employees can ill afford to make this mistake.

ANCHORING AND ADJUSTMENT

In one common strategy of estimation, known as "anchoring and adjustment," people first choose a preliminary estimate—an anchor—and then adjust it in accordance with whatever additional information they have that appears relevant. Kahneman and Tversky have discovered that this procedure often leads to biased estimates, for two reasons. First, the initial anchor may be completely unrelated to the value to be estimated. And second, even when it is related, people tend to adjust too little from it.

To demonstrate the anchoring and adjustment bias, Kahneman and Tversky asked a sample of students to estimate the percentage of African countries that are members of the United Nations. Each person was first asked to spin a wheel that generated a number between 1 and 100. The student was then asked whether his estimate was higher or lower than that number. And finally, the student was asked for his numerical estimate of the percentage. The results were nothing short of astonishing. Students who got a 10 or below on the spin of the wheel had a median estimate of 25 percent, whereas the corresponding figure for those who got a 65 or above was 45 percent.

Each student surely *knew* that the initial random number had no possible relevance for estimating the percentage of African nations that belong to the U.N. Nonetheless, the numbers had a dramatic effect on the estimates they reported. In similar problems, any number close at hand seems to provide a convenient starting point. Kahneman and Tversky reported that giving the students monetary payoffs for accuracy did not alter the size of the bias.

In another illustration, two groups of high school students were asked to estimate the product of 8 numbers within 5 seconds. The first group was given this expression:

$$8 \times 7 \times 6 \times 5 \times 4 \times 3 \times 2 \times 1,$$

while the second group was given exactly the same numbers in reverse order:

$$1 \times 2 \times 3 \times 4 \times 5 \times 6 \times 7 \times 8.$$

The time limit prevents most students from performing the entire calculation (which would lead to the correct answer of 40,320). What many of them apparently do is to perform the first few multiplications (their anchor), and then project an estimate of the final result. For both groups of students, these anchors turn out not to be very appropriate and the projections turn out to be grossly insufficient. The resulting bias displays exactly the predicted pattern: The median estimate for the first group was 2250; for the second group, only 512.

An important economic application of the anchoring and adjustment bias is in estimating the failure rates of complex projects. Consider, for example, starting a new business. To succeed, it is necessary that each of a large number of events happens. Satisfactory financing must be obtained, a workable location found, a low-cost production process designed, sufficiently skilled labor hired, an effective marketing campaign implemented, and so on. The enterprise will fail if any one of these steps fails. When many steps are involved, the failure rate is invariably high, even when each step has a high probability of success. For example, a program involving 10 steps, each with a success rate of 90 percent, will fail 65 percent of the time. When estimating failure rates for such processes, people tend to anchor on the low failure rate for the typical step, from which they make grossly insufficient adjustments. The anchoring and adjustment bias may thus help explain why the overwhelming majority of new businesses fail.

The Psychophysics of Perception

Weber-Fechner law The property of perception whereby the just noticeable difference in a stimulus tends to be proportioned to the value of the stimulus.

There is yet another pattern to the way we perceive and process information that has importance in economic applications. It derives from the so-called *Weber-Fechner law* of psychophysics. Weber and Fechner set out to discover how large the change in a stimulus had to be before we could perceive the difference in intensity. Most people, for example, are unable to distinguish a 100-watt light bulb from a 100.5-watt light bulb. But how large does the difference in brightness have to be before people can reliably identify it? Weber and Fechner found that the minimally perceptible difference is roughly proportional to the original intensity of the stimulus. Thus the more intense the stimulus is, the larger the difference has to be, in absolute terms, before we can tell the difference.

Thaler suggested that the Weber-Fechner law seems to be at work when people decide whether price differences are worth worrying about. Suppose, for example, you are about to buy a clock radio in a store for $25 when a friend informs you that the same radio is selling for only $20 in another store only 10 minutes away. Do you go to the other store? Would your answer have been different if you had been about to buy a television for $500 and your friend told you the same set was available at the other store for only $495? Thaler found that most people answer yes to the first question and no to the second.

In the rational choice model, it is inconsistent to answer differently for the two cases. A rational person will travel to the other store if and only if the benefits of doing so exceed the costs. The benefit is $5 in both cases. The cost is also the same for each trip, whether it is to buy a radio or a television. If it makes sense to go in one case, it also makes sense in the other.

The Difficulty of Actually Deciding

In the rational choice model, there should be no difficult decisions. If the choice between two alternatives is a close call—that is, if the two alternatives are predicted to yield approximately the same utility—then it should not make much difference which is chosen. Alternatively, if one of the options clearly has a higher expected utility, the choice should again be easy. Either way, the chooser has no obvious reasons to experience anxiety and indecision.

In reality, of course, we all know that difficult decisions are more the rule than the exception. There are many pairs of alternatives over which our utility functions just don't seem to assign clear, unambiguous preference rankings. The difficulty is most pronounced when the alternatives differ along dimensions that are hard to compare. If the three things we care about in a car are, say, comfort, fuel economy, and safety, it will be easy to decide between two cars if one is safer and more comfortable and has better gas mileage than the other. But what if one is much more comfortable and has much worse gas mileage? In principle, we are supposed to have indifference curves that tell us the rate at which we would be willing to trade one characteristic for the other. In practice, however, we often seem to find it difficult to summon the information implicit in these curves. And the very act of trying to do so often seems to provoke disquiet. For instance, it is not uncommon for people to dwell on the possibility that they will regret whichever choice they make. ("If I pick the more comfortable car, what will happen if I then get transferred to a job that requires a long daily commute?")

Such difficulties appear to cast doubt on a fundamental axiom of rational choice theory, namely, that choices should be independent of irrelevant alternatives. This axiom is often illustrated by a story like the following. A man comes into a delicatessen and asks what kind of sandwiches there are. The attendant answers that they have roast beef and chicken. The patron deliberates for a few moments and finally asks for a roast beef sandwich. The counterman says, "Oh, I forgot to mention, we also have tuna." To this the patron responds, "Well, in

FIGURE 8-10
By suitably manipu-
lating the monthly
rents and distances
from campus, it is
possible to get a
group of students to
split 50-50 in their
choices between *A*.
and *B*.

CHOOSING BETWEEN TWO APARTMENTS

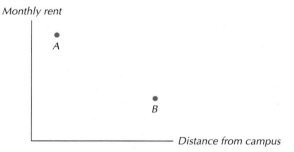

that case I guess I'll have chicken." According to the rational choice model, the availability of tuna should matter only if it is the alternative the patron most prefers. There is no intelligible basis for its availability to cause a switch from roast beef to chicken.

Tversky performed some intriguing experiments that suggest choice may not, in fact, always be independent of irrelevant alternatives. One of his examples is the choice between apartments that differ along two dimensions, monthly rent and distance from campus. From a student's point of view, an apartment is more attractive the closer it is to campus and the lower its monthly rent. A group of students was asked to choose between two apartments like the pair shown in Figure 8-10. Notice in the figure that neither apartment dominates the other. *A* is more expensive, but *B* is farther from campus. We expect that students who are relatively more concerned about rent will choose apartment *B*, while those who care primarily about commuting time will pick *A*. By manipulating the distance and rent, it is easy to get a group of students to divide roughly 50-50 between the two apartments.

So far, no surprises. But now Tversky adds a third apartment, *C*, to the list of choices, giving us the set depicted in Figure 8-11. Notice that *C* is dominated by *B*—that is, it is both farther from campus *and* more expensive than *B*. In terms of the rational choice model, it is a classic example of an irrelevant alternative.

FIGURE 8-11
Because *C* is domi-
nated by *B*, no one
should ever choose
it. But while no one
does choose *C*, its
availability makes
people much more
likely to choose *B*.

ADDING AN IRRELEVANT ALTERNATIVE

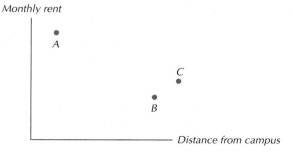

Faced with the choice *A, B,* and *C,* no rational consumer would ever choose *C.* And indeed, in actual experiments, hardly anyone ever does.

The surprise is that options like *C* turn out to affect people's choices between the remaining options. Tversky and his colleagues discovered that when an apartment like *C* is added to the pair *A* and *B,* the effect is to shift people's choices substantially in favor of *B.* Before *C* was available, students divided 50-50 between *A* and *B.* Once *C* was added, however, more than 70 percent of the students chose *B,* the option that dominates *C.*

Many people apparently find the original choice between *A* and *B* a difficult one to make. The appearance of *C* gives them a comparison they can make comfortably, namely, the one between *B* and *C.* Tversky hypothesized that this creates a "halo effect" for *B,* which makes it much more likely to be chosen over *A.* Perhaps a similar effect might cause the availability of tuna to cause someone to switch his decision from roast beef to chicken. Whatever the reason for such behavior, it is clear that it violates the axiom that choice is independent of irrelevant alternatives.

Summary

Numerous examples of behavior contradict the predictions of the standard rational choice model. People apparently often fail to ignore sunk costs. They play tennis indoors when, by their own account, they would prefer to play outside. They behave differently when they lose a ticket than when they lose an equivalent amount of cash. Psychologists argue that such behavior is the result of limitations in human cognitive capacity. People use mental accounting systems that reduce the complexity of their decisions, sometimes at the expense of consistency with the axioms of rational choice.

An important class of departures from rational choice appears to result from the asymmetric value function described by Kahneman and Tversky. In contrast to the rational choice model, which uses a utility function defined on total wealth, Kahneman's and Tversky's descriptive theory uses a value function defined over changes in wealth. Unlike the traditional model, it gives losses much heavier decision weight than gains. This feature makes decisions extremely sensitive to how the alternatives are framed. A pair of gains, for example, is more attractive if presented separately than if lumped together. Losses, by contrast, have less impact if amalgamated than if taken separately. Also, a loss combined with a slightly larger gain produces a positive effect, whereas taken separately their net effect is negative; and finally, a small gain segregated from a large loss produces less of a negative effect than the two lumped together. The rational choice model, by contrast, says that none of these framing effects should matter.

Decisions under uncertainty also often violate the prescriptions of the expected utility model. And again, the asymmetric value function provides a consistent description of several important patterns. People tend to be risk averse in the domain of gains but risk seeking in the domain of losses. The result is that subtle differences in the framing of the problem can shift the mental reference point used for reckoning gains and losses, which, in turn, can produce radically different patterns of choice.

Another important departure from rational choice occurs in the heuristics, or rules of thumb, people use to make estimates of important decision factors. The availability heuristic says that one way people estimate the frequency of a given class of events is by the ease with which they can recall relevant examples. This leads to predictable biases because actual frequency is not the only factor that governs how easy it is to recall examples. People tend to overestimate the frequency of vivid or salient events, and of other events that are especially easy to retrieve from memory.

Another important heuristic is representativeness. People estimate the likelihood that an item belongs to a given class by how representative it is of that class. We saw that this often leads to substantial bias because representativeness is only one of many factors that govern this likelihood. Shyness may indeed be a trait representative of librarians, but because there are so many more salespeople than librarians, it is much more likely that a randomly chosen shy person is a salesperson than a librarian.

Anchoring and adjustment is a third heuristic that often leads to biased estimates of important decision factors. This heuristic says that people often make numerical estimates by first picking a convenient (but sometimes irrelevant) anchor and then adjusting from it (usually insufficiently) on the basis of other potentially relevant information. This procedure often causes people to underestimate the failure rate of projects with many steps. Such a project fails if any one of its essential elements fails, which means that even if the failure rate of each element is extremely low, a project with many elements is nonetheless very likely to fail. Because people tend to anchor on the failure rate for the typical step, and adjust insufficiently from it, they often grossly overestimate the likelihood of success. This may help explain the naive optimism of people who start new businesses.

Another departure from rational choice traces to the psychophysics of perception. Psychologists have discovered that the barely perceptible change in any stimulus is proportional to its initial level. This seems to hold true as well when the stimulus in question is the price of a good or service. People think nothing of driving across town to save $5 on a $25 radio, but would never dream of doing so to save $5 on a $500 TV set.

Finally, departures from rational choice may occur because people simply have difficulty choosing between alternatives that are hard to compare. The rational choice model assumes that we have complete preference orderings, but in practice, it often seems to require a great deal of effort for us to decide how we feel about even very simple alternatives.

Behavioral models of choice often do a much better job of predicting actual decisions than the rational choice model. It is important to remember, however, that the behavioral models claim no normative significance. That is, the mere fact that they predict, for example, that people often *do* ignore sunk costs should not be taken to mean that people *should* ignore them. The rational choice model says we can make better decisions by ignoring sunk costs, and most people, on reflection, strongly agree. In this respect, behavioral models of choice are an important tool for helping us avoid common pitfalls in decision making.

Questions for Review

1. Suppose you were the owner of a small business and were asked the maximum you would be willing to pay in order to attend a course in the traditional theory of rational choice. In which case would your answer be larger: (1) if it were known that people always behave in strict accordance with the predictions of rational choice theory; or (2) if it were known that people's behavior often departs systematically from the predictions of rational choice theory?

2. Why is it rational to make decisions with less than complete information?

3. Distinguish between (1) the best decision and (2) the decision that leads to the best possible outcome.

4. Is there anything irrational about weighing gains less heavily than losses?

5. The policy of one school was to punish students for being late, while the corresponding policy in an otherwise identical school was to reward students for being on time. If effectiveness is measured by behavior on the day following punishment or reward, which policy would seem to be more effective? Is this standard of effectiveness a good one?

Problems

1. Suppose your happiness is given by a Kahneman-Tversky value function like the one shown in the diagram.

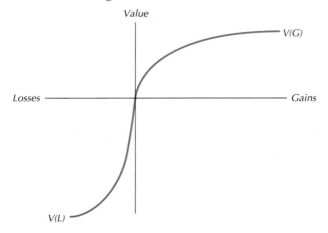

You have decided to apply the principles of hedonic framing to put the most favorable spin on the various combinations of events that occur in your life. How should you then view the following combinations of events?

    a. A gain of $500 and a loss of $50.
    b. A gain of $50 and a loss of $500.
    c. A gain of $500 and a gain of $600.
    d. A loss of $500 and a loss of $600.

2. Sears Roebuck has hired you as a consultant to give it marketing advice about how to sell its new all-terrain vehicle. On the basis of the material covered in this chapter, suggest two specific marketing strategies for Sears to consider.

3. Give two examples of how the framing of alternatives tends to produce systematic effects on people's choices.

4. Studies have shown that in the New York City subway crime rates fall in the years following increased police patrols. Does this pattern suggest that the increased patrols are the *cause* of the crime reductions?

5. Claiborne is a gourmet. He makes it a point never to visit a restaurant a second time unless he has been served a superb meal on his first visit. He is puzzled at how seldom the quality of his second meal is as high as the first. Should he be?

6. Dalgliesh the detective fancies himself a shrewd judge of human nature. In careful tests it has been discovered that he is right 80 percent of the time when he says that a suspect is lying. Dalgliesh says that Jones is lying. The polygraph expert, who is right 100 percent of the time, says that 40 percent of the subjects interviewed by Dalgliesh are telling the truth. What is the probability that Jones is lying?

7. A witness testifies that the taxicab that struck and injured Smith in a dark alley was green. On investigation, the attorney for Green Taxi Company discovers that the witness identifies the correct color of a taxi in a dark alley 80 percent of the time. There are two taxi companies in town, Green and Blue. Green operates 15 percent of all local taxis. The law says that the Green Taxi Company is liable for Smith's injuries if and only if the probability that it caused them is greater than 0.5. Is Green liable? Explain.

8. Last week your travel agent called to tell you that she had found a great fare, $667, for your trip to the United Kingdom later this month. This fare was almost $400 below the APEX (advance purchase excursion) fare. You told her to book it immediately and went around the department telling everyone about your great bargain. An hour later she called you back and told you that the reservation agent at British Airways had made a mistake and that the quoted fare did not exist. Your agent said she would hunt around and do the best she could for you. A few days later she found a ticket consolidator that could book you on the same British Airways flight for $708, a figure still well below what you originally had expected to pay. This time you didn't go around the department bragging about your bargain. How might the material in this chapter be used to shed light on your behavior?

9. In planning your next vacation, you have narrowed your choices down to two packages offered by your travel agent, a week in Hawaii for $1200 or a week in Cancun for $900. You are indifferent between these choices. You see an ad in the travel sec-

tion of the newspaper for a week in Hawaii, with accommodations identical to those offered by your agent, for $1300. According to the theory of rational choice, should the information in the newspaper ad influence your vacation plans? Explain.

10. Mary will drive across town to take advantage of a 40 percent–off sale on a $40 blouse but will not do so to take advantage of a 10 percent–off sale on a $1000 stereo. Assuming that her alternative is to pay list price for both products at the department store next to her home, is her behavior rational?

11. Hal is having difficulty choosing between two tennis rackets, A and B. As shown in the diagram, B has more power than A, but less control. According to the rational choice model, how will the availability of a third alternative—racket C—influence Hal's final decision? If Hal behaves like most ordinary decision makers in this situation, how will the addition of C to his choice set matter?

Power

Answer to In-Chapter Exercise

8-1. If there are 4 times as many salespersons as librarians, then there will be 80 salespersons for every 20 librarians. Of the 80 salespersons, 20 percent, or 16, will be shy. Of the 20 librarians, 90 percent, or 18, will be shy. Thus, the likelihood that a shy person is a librarian is $18/(18 + 16) = 0.53$.

PART THREE

The Theory of the Firm and Market Structure

The economic theory of the firm assumes that the firm's primary goal is to maximize profits. Profit maximization requires the firm to expand its output whenever the benefits of doing so exceed the costs. Our agenda in the first two chapters of Part Three is to develop the cost side of this calculation. Chapter 9 begins with the theory of production, which shows how labor, capital, and other inputs are combined to produce output. Making use of this theory, Chapter 10 then describes how the firm's costs vary with the amount of output it produces.

The next three chapters consider the benefit side of the firm's calculation under four different forms of market structure. Chapter 11 looks at the perfectly competitive firm, for which the benefit of selling an extra unit of output is exactly equal to its price. Chapter 12 examines the monopoly firm, or sole supplier of a good for which there are no close substitutes. For such a firm, the benefit of selling an extra unit of output is generally less than its price because it must cut its price on existing sales in order to expand its output. Chapter 13 looks at two intermediate forms of market structure, monopolistic competition and oligopoly. In making decisions about output levels, monopolistically competitive firms behave just like monopolists. By contrast, the oligopolist must take account of strategic responses of its rivals when it calculates the benefits of expanding output.

CHAPTER 9

Production

Many people think of production as a highly structured, often mechanical process whereby raw materials are transformed into finished goods. And without doubt, a great deal of production—like a mason's laying bricks for the walls of a house—is of roughly this sort. Economists emphasize, however, that production is also a much more general concept, encompassing many activities not ordinarily thought of as such. We define it as *any activity that creates present or future utility*.

Thus, the simple act of telling a joke constitutes production. In *Annie Hall*, Woody Allen (Figure 9-1) tells the story of the man who complains to his analyst that his brother thinks he's a chicken. "Why don't you tell him he's *not* a chicken?" asks the analyst, to which the man responds, "I can't, I need the eggs." Once a joke is told, it leaves no more tangible trace than a pleasant memory. But under the economic definition of production, Woody Allen is as much a production worker as the artisan whose chisel and lathe mold an ashwood log into a Louisville Slugger baseball bat. The person who delivers a singing telegram is also engaged in production; so is the doctor who gives my child a tetanus shot; the lawyer who draws up my will; the people who collect my garbage on Wednesday mornings; the postal worker who delivers my tax return to the IRS; and even the economists who write about production.

FIGURE 9-1   **A PRODUCTION WORKER**

Photograph by Phillippe Halsman
© Yvonne Halsman

Chapter Preview

In our discussions of consumer choice during the preceding chapters, an existing menu of goods and services was taken for granted. But where do these goods and services come from? In this chapter we will see that their production involves a decision process very similar to the one we examined in earlier chapters. Whereas our focus in earlier chapters was on the economic decisions that underlie the demand side of the market relationship, our focus in the next seven chapters is on the economic decisions that underlie the supply side.

In this chapter we describe the production possibilities available to us for a given state of technology and resource endowments. We want to know how output varies with the application of productive inputs in both the short run and the long run. Answers to these questions will set the stage for our efforts in the next chapter to describe how firms choose among technically feasible alternative methods of producing a given level of output.

The Input-Output Relationship, or Production Function

There are several ways to define production. One definition, mentioned above, is that it is any activity that creates present or future utility. Production may be equivalently described as a process that transforms inputs (factors of production) into outputs. (The two descriptions are equivalent because output is something that creates present or future utility.) Among the inputs into production, economists have traditionally included land, labor, capital, and the more elusive

FIGURE 9-2
The production function transforms inputs like land, labor, capital, and management into output. The box in the diagram embodies the existing state of technological knowledge. Because knowledge has been accumulating over time, we get more output from a given combination of inputs today than we would have gotten in the past.

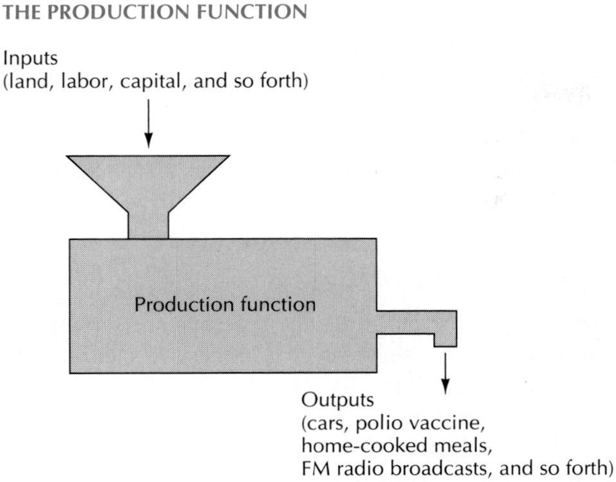

THE PRODUCTION FUNCTION

Inputs
(land, labor, capital, and so forth)

Production function

Outputs
(cars, polio vaccine,
home-cooked meals,
FM radio broadcasts, and so forth)

Production function The relationship that describes how inputs like capital and labor are transformed into output.

category called entrepreneurship.[1] To this list, it has become increasingly common to add such factors as knowledge or technology, organization, and energy.

A *production function* is the relationship by which inputs are combined to produce output. Schematically, it may be represented as the box in Figure 9-2. Inputs are fed into it, and output is discharged from it. The box implicitly embodies the existing state of technology, which has been improving steadily over time. Thus, a given combination of productive inputs will yield a larger number of cars with today's technology than with the technology of 1970.

A production function may also be thought of as a cooking recipe. It lists the ingredients and tells you, say, how many pancakes you will get if you manipulate the ingredients in a certain way.[2]

Yet another way of describing the production function is to cast it in the form of a mathematical equation. Consider a production process that employs two inputs, capital (K) and labor (L), to produce meals (Q). The relationship between K, L, and Q may be expressed as

$$Q = F(K, L), \tag{9.1}$$

where F is a mathematical function that summarizes the process depicted in Figure 9-2. It is no more than a simple rule that tells how much Q we get when we

---

[1]"Entrepreneurship" is defined as "the process of organizing, managing, and assuming responsibility for a business enterprise" (*Random House College Dictionary*). An entrepreneur is thus, by definition, a risk-taker.

[2]In some recipes, the ingredients must be mixed in fixed proportions. Other recipes allow substitution between ingredients, as in a pancake recipe that allows milk and oil to be substituted for eggs. Production functions can be of either of these two types.

employ specific quantities of K and L. By way of illustration, suppose the production function for meals is given by $F(K, L) = 2KL$, where K is measured in equipment-hours per week,[3] L is measured in person-hours per week, and output is measured in meals per week. For example, 2 equipment-hr/wk combined with 3 person-hr/wk would yield $2(2)(3) = 12$ meals/wk with this particular production function. The relationship between K, L, and weekly output of meals for the production function $Q = 2KL$ is summarized in Table 9-1.

INTERMEDIATE PRODUCTS AND VALUE ADDED

Intermediate products Products that are transformed by a production process into products of greater value.

Capital (as embodied, for example, in the form of stoves and frying pans) and labor (as embodied in the services of a chef) are clearly by themselves insufficient to produce meals. Raw foodstuffs are also necessary. The production process described by Equation 9.1 is one that transforms raw foodstuffs into the finished product we call meals. In this process, foodstuffs are *intermediate products*, ones that are transformed into something more valuable by the activity of production. Strictly speaking, the output of this process is not the meals themselves, but the *value added* to the raw foodstuffs. For example, if a chef and her equipment transformed $50 worth of raw foodstuffs into meals with a total value of $150, the resulting output would be measured as the $100 of value added.

For the sake of simplicity, we will ignore the complication of intermediate goods in the examples we discuss in this chapter. But this feature could be built into all these examples without changing any of our essential conclusions.

---

[3]Here, 1 frying pan-hr/wk is 1 frying pan used for 1 hour during the course of a week. Thus, a frying pan that is in use for 8 hr/day for each day of a 5-day workweek would constitute 40 frying pan-hr/wk of capital input.

The entries in the table represent output, measured in meals per week, and are calculated using the formula $Q = 2KL$.

TABLE 9-1   THE PRODUCTION FUNCTION $Q = 2KL$

		Labor (person-hours/wk)				
		1	2	3	4	5
	1	2	4	6	8	10
Capital	2	4	8	12	16	20
(equipment-hours/wk)	3	6	12	18	24	30
	4	8	16	24	32	40
	5	10	20	30	40	50

FIXED AND VARIABLE INPUTS

The production function tells us how output will vary if some or all of the inputs are varied. In practice, there are many production processes in which the quantities of at least some inputs cannot be altered quickly. The FM radio broadcast transmission of classical music is one such process. To carry it out, complex electronic equipment is needed, and also a music library and a large transmission tower. Records and compact discs can be purchased in a matter of hours. But it may take weeks to acquire the needed equipment to launch a new station, and months or even years to purchase a suitable location and construct a new transmission tower.

Long run The shortest period of time required to alter the amounts of all inputs used in a production process.

The *long run* for a particular production process is defined as the shortest period of time required to alter the amounts of *every* input. An input whose quantity may be freely altered is called a *variable input*. One whose quantity cannot be altered—except perhaps at prohibitive cost—within a given time period is called a *fixed input* with respect to that time period. In the long run, all inputs are variable inputs, by definition. The *short run,* by contrast, is defined as that period during which one or more inputs cannot be varied. In the classical music broadcast example, records and compact discs are variable inputs in the short run, but the broadcast tower is a fixed input. If sufficient time elapses, however, even it becomes a variable input. In some production activities, like those of a street-corner hot dog stand, even the long run does not involve an extended period of time.

Short run The longest period of time during which at least one of the inputs used in a production process cannot be varied.

Production in the Short Run

Consider again the production process described by $Q = F(K, L) = 2KL$, the simple two-input production function described in Table 9-1. And suppose we are concerned with production in the short run—here, a period of time in which the labor input is freely variable but the capital input is fixed, say, at the value $K = K_0 = 1$. With capital held constant, output becomes, in effect, a function of only the variable input, labor: $F(K, L) = 2K_0L = 2L$. This means we can plot the production function in a two-dimensional diagram, as in Figure 9-3a. For this particular $F(K, L)$, the short-run production function is a straight line through the origin whose slope is 2 times the fixed value of K: Thus, $\Delta Q/\Delta L = 2K_0$. In Figure 9-3b, note that the short-run production rotates upward to $F(K_1, L) = 6L$ when K rises to $K_1 = 3$.

EXERCISE 9-1

Graph the short-run production function for $F(K, L) = \sqrt{K}\sqrt{L}$ when K is fixed at $K_0 = 4$.

FIGURE 9-3
Panel *a* shows the
production function,
$Q = 2KL$, with K
fixed at $K_0 = 1$.
Panel *b* shows how
the short-run pro-
duction function
shifts when K is in-
creased to $K_1 = 3$.

A SPECIFIC SHORT-RUN PRODUCTION FUNCTION

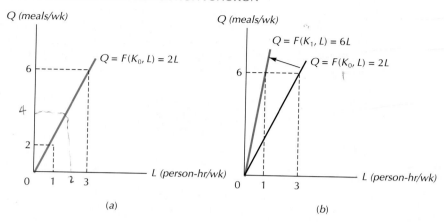

(a) (b)

As you saw in Exercise 9-1, the graphs of short-run production functions will not always be straight lines. The short-run production function shown in Figure 9-4 has several properties that are commonly found in production functions observed in practice. First, it passes through the origin, which is to say that we get no output if we use no variable input. Second, initially the addition of variable inputs augments output at an increasing rate: moving from 1 to 2 units of labor yields 10 extra units of output, while moving from 2 to 3 units of labor gives 13 additional units. Finally, the function shown in Figure 9-4 has the property that beyond some point ($L = 4$ in the diagram), additional units of the vari-

FIGURE 9-4
The curvilinear
shape shown here is
common to many
short-run production
functions. Output
initially grows at an
increasing rate as la-
bor increases. Be-
yond $L = 4$, output
grows at a diminish-
ing rate with in-
creases in labor.

ANOTHER SHORT-RUN PRODUCTION FUNCTION

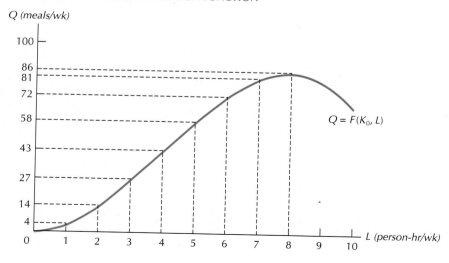

able input give rise to smaller and smaller increments in output. Thus, the move from 5 to 6 units of labor yields 14 extra units of output, while the move from 6 to 7 units of labor yields only 9. For some production functions, the level of output may eventually decline with additional units of the variable input beyond some point, as happens here for $L > 8$. With a limited amount of capital to work with, additional workers may eventually begin to get in one another's way.

The property that output initially grows at an increasing rate may stem from the benefits of division of tasks and specialization of labor. With one employee, all tasks must be done by the same person, while with two or more employees, tasks may be divided and employees may better perform their dedicated tasks. (Similar logic applies to specializing in one task within any period of time.)

The final property noted about the short-run production function in Figure 9-4—that beyond some point, output grows at a diminishing rate with increases in the variable input—is known as the *law of diminishing returns*. And although it too is not a universal property of short-run production functions, it is extremely common. The law of diminishing returns is a short-run phenomenon. Formally, it may be stated as follows:

Law of diminishing returns If other inputs are fixed, the increase in output from an increase in the variable input must eventually decline.

> *If equal amounts of a variable input are added and all other inputs are held fixed, the resulting increments to output will eventually diminish.*

Writing in the nineteenth century, the British economist Thomas Malthus argued that the law of diminishing returns implied eventual misery for the human race. The difficulty is that agricultural land is fixed, and beyond some point, the application of additional labor will yield ever smaller increases in food production. The inevitable result, as Malthus saw it, is that population growth will drive average food consumption down to the starvation level.

Whether Malthus's prediction will be borne out in the future remains to be seen. But he would never have imagined that food production per capita would be more than 20 times as great in 1985 as it was a century earlier. Note carefully, however, that the experience of the last 100 years does not contradict the law of diminishing returns. What Malthus did not foresee was the explosive growth in agricultural technology—not to mention large infusions of additional capital—that together have far outstripped the effect of a fixed supply of land. Still, the ruthless logic of Malthus's observation remains. No matter how advanced our technology, it would be clearly impossible to grow enough food in a single flowerpot to feed all the world's people. By extension, if population continues to grow, it is just a matter of time before even the richest nations confront food shortages.

Technological improvements in production are represented graphically by an upward shift in the production function. In Figure 9-5, for example, the curves labeled F_1 and F_2 are used to denote the agricultural production functions in 1797

FIGURE 9-5
F_1 represents the production function for food in the year 1797. F_2 represents the corresponding function for 1997. The effect of technological progress in food production is to cause F_2 to lie above F_1. Even though the law of diminishing returns applies to both F_1 and F_2, the growth in food production between 1797 and 1997 has more than kept pace with the growth in labor inputs over the same period.

THE EFFECT OF TECHNOLOGICAL PROGRESS IN FOOD PRODUCTION

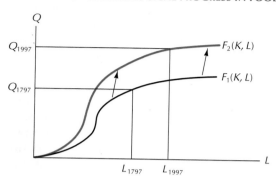

and 1997, respectively. The law of diminishing returns applies to each of these curves, and yet the growth in food production has kept pace with the increase in labor input during the period shown.

TOTAL, MARGINAL, AND AVERAGE PRODUCTS

Total product curve A curve showing the amount of output as a function of the amount of variable input.

Short-run production functions like the one shown in Figures 9-4 and 9-5 are often referred to as *total product curves*. They relate the total amount of output to the quantity of the variable input. Also of interest in many applications is the *marginal product* of a variable input. It is defined as *the change in the total product that occurs in response to a unit change in the variable input (all other inputs held fixed).* A business manager trying to decide whether to hire or fire another worker has an obvious interest in knowing what the *marginal product* of labor is.

More formally, if ΔL denotes a small change in the variable input, and ΔQ denotes the resulting change in output, then the marginal product of L, denoted MP_L, is defined as

Marginal product Change in total product due to a 1-unit change in the variable input.

$$MP_L = \frac{\Delta Q}{\Delta L}. \tag{9.2}$$

Geometrically, the marginal product at any point is simply the slope of the total product curve at that point, as shown in the top panel of Figure 9-6.[4] For example, the marginal product of labor when $L = 2$ is $MP_{L=2} = 12$. Likewise, $MP_{L=4} = 16$ and $MP_{L=7} = 6$ for the total product curve shown in Figure 9-6. Note, finally, that MP_L is negative for values of L greater than 8.

The marginal product curve itself is plotted in the bottom panel in Figure 9-6. Note that it rises at first, reaches a maximum at $L = 4$, and then declines, finally becoming negative for values of L greater than 8. Note in the diagram that the

---

[4]The formal definition of the marginal product of a variable input is given by $MP(L) = \partial F(K, L)/\partial L$.

FIGURE 9-6
At any point, the marginal product of labor, MP_L, is the slope of the total product curve at that point (top panel). For the production function shown in the top panel, the marginal product curve (bottom panel) initially increases as labor increases. Beyond $L = 4$, however, the marginal product of labor decreases as labor increases. For $L > 8$ the total product curve declines with L, which means that the marginal product of labor is negative in that region.

THE MARGINAL PRODUCT OF A VARIABLE INPUT

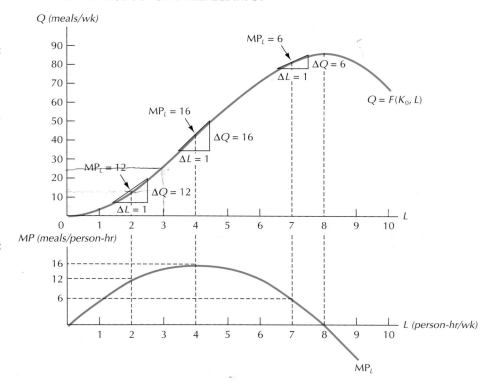

maximum point on the marginal product curve corresponds to the inflection point on the total product curve, the point where its curvature switches from convex (increasing at an increasing rate) to concave (increasing at a decreasing rate). Note also that the marginal product curve reaches zero at the value of L at which the total product curve reaches a maximum.

As we will see in greater detail in later chapters, the importance of the marginal product concept lies in the fact that decisions about running an enterprise most naturally arise in the form of decisions about *changes*. Should we hire another engineer or accountant? Should we reduce the size of the maintenance staff? Should we install another Xerox machine? Should we lease another delivery truck?

To answer such questions intelligently, we must compare the benefit of the change in question with its cost. And as we will see, the marginal product concept plays a pivotal role in the calculation of the benefits when we alter the level of a productive input. Looking at Figure 9-6, we may identify a range of values of the variable input that a rational manager would never employ. In particular, as long as labor commands a positive wage, such a manager would never want to employ the variable input in the region where its marginal product is negative ($L > 8$ in Figure 9-6). Equivalently, he would never employ a variable input past the point where the total product curve reaches its maximum value (where $MP_L = 0$).

EXERCISE 9-2

What is the marginal product of labor when $L = 3$ in the short-run production function shown in Figure 9-3a? When $L = 1$? Does this short-run production function exhibit diminishing returns to labor?

Average product
Total output divided by the quantity of the variable input.

The *average product* of a variable input is defined as the total product divided by the quantity of that input. Denoted AP_L, it is thus given by

$$AP_L = \frac{Q}{L}. \qquad (9.3)$$

Geometrically, the average product is the slope of the line joining the origin to the corresponding point on the total product curve. Three such lines, R_1, R_2, and R_3, are drawn to the total product curve shown in the top panel in Figure 9-7. The average product at $L = 2$ is the slope of R_1, which is $\frac{14}{2} = 7$. Note that R_2 intersects the total product curve in two places—first, directly above $L = 4$, and then directly above $L = 8$. Accordingly, the average products for these two values of L will be the same—namely, the slope of R_2, which is $\frac{43}{4} = \frac{86}{8} = 10.75$. R_3 intersects the total product curve at only one point, directly above $L = 6$. The average product for $L = 6$ is thus the slope of R_3, $\frac{72}{6} = 12$.

EXERCISE 9-3

For the short-run production function shown in Figure 9-3a, what is the average product of labor at $L = 3$? At $L = 1$? How does average product compare to marginal product at these points?

The Relationships Among Total, Marginal, and Average Product Curves

Because of the way the total, marginal, and average products are defined, systematic relationships exist among them. The top panel in Figure 9-7 shows a total product curve and three of the rays whose slopes define the average product of the variable input. The steepest of the three rays, R_3, is tangent to the total prod-

FIGURE 9-7
The average product at any point on the total product curve is the slope of the ray to that point. For the total product curve shown in the top panel, AP_L rises with $L = 6$, then declines. At $L = 6$, $MP_L = AP_L$. For any $L < 6$, $MP_L > AP_L$, and for any $L > 6$, $MP_L < AP_L$.

TOTAL, MARGINAL, AND AVERAGE PRODUCT CURVES

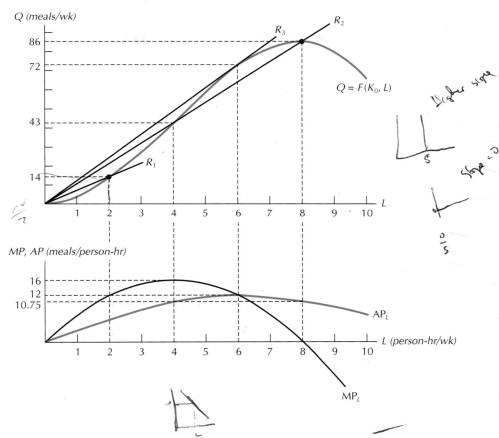

uct curve at $L = 6$. Its slope, $\frac{72}{6} = 12$, is the average product of labor at $L = 6$. The marginal product of labor at $L = 6$ is defined as the slope of the total product curve at $L = 6$, which happens to be exactly the slope of R_3, since R_3 is tangent to the total product curve. Thus $AP_{L=6} = MP_{L=6}$, as shown in the bottom panel by the fact that the AP_L curve intersects the MP_L curve for $L = 6$.

For values of L less than 6, note in the top panel in Figure 9-7 that the slope of the total product curve is larger than the slope of the ray to the corresponding point. Thus, for $L < 6$, $MP_L > AP_L$, as reflected in the bottom panel. Note also in the top panel that for values of L greater than 6, the slope of the total product curve is smaller than the slope of the ray to the corresponding point. This means that for $L > 6$, we have $AP_L > MP_L$, as shown in the bottom panel in Figure 9-7.

Note finally in Figure 9-7 that for extremely small values of L, the slope of the ray to the total product curve becomes indistinguishable from the slope of the total product curve itself. This tells us that for $L = 0$, average and marginal products are the same, which is reflected in the bottom panel in Figure 9-7 by the fact that both curves emanate from the same point.[5]

The relationship between the marginal and average product curves may be summarized as follows: *When the marginal product curve lies above the average product curve, the average product curve must be rising; and when the marginal product curve lies below the average product curve, the average product curve must be falling. The two curves intersect at the maximum value of the average product curve.* A moment's reflection on the definitions of the two curves makes the intuitive basis for this relationship clear. If the contribution to output of an additional unit of the variable input exceeds the average contribution of the variable inputs used thus far, the average contribution must rise. This effect is analogous to what happens when a student with a 3.8 grade point average joins a fraternity whose other members have an average GPA of 2.2: The new member's presence causes the group's GPA to rise. Conversely, adding a variable input whose marginal product is less than the average product of existing units is like adding a new fraternity member with a GPA of 1.7. Here, the effect is for the existing average to fall.[6]

EXERCISE 9-4

Consider a short-run production process for which $AP_{L=10} = 7$ and $MP_{L=10} = 12$. Will $AP_{L=10.1}$ be larger or smaller than $AP_{L=10}$ for this process?

The Practical Significance of the Average-Marginal Distinction

The distinction between average and marginal products is of central importance to anyone who must allocate a scarce resource between two or more productive activities. The specific question is, how should the resource be allocated in order to maximize total output? The following examples make clear the issues posed by this problem and the general rule required to solve it.

---

[5]For the production function shown, that point happens to be the origin, but in general it need not be.

[6]Mathematically, the result that MP intersects AP at the maximum value of AP can be shown by noting that the necessary condition for a maximum of AP is that its first partial derivative with respect to L be zero:

$$\partial(Q/L)/\partial L = [L(\partial Q/\partial L) - Q]/L^2 = 0,$$

from which it follows that $\partial Q/\partial L = Q/L$.

Read through the following scenario carefully and try to answer the question posed at the end:

Suppose you own a fishing fleet consisting of a given number of boats, and can send your boats in whatever numbers you wish to either of two ends of an extremely wide lake, east or west. Under your current allocation of boats, the ones fishing at the east end return daily with 100 pounds of fish each, while those in the west return daily with 120 pounds each. The fish populations at each end of the lake are completely independent, and your current yields can be sustained indefinitely. Should you alter your current allocation of boats?

Most people, especially those who have not had a good course in microeconomics, answer confidently that the current allocation should be altered. Specifically, they say that the fishing fleet owner should send more boats to the west side of the lake. Yet, as the following example illustrates, even a rudimentary understanding of the distinction between the average and marginal products of a productive resource makes clear that this response is not justified.

*E*XAMPLE 9-1   *In the fishing fleet scenario just described, suppose the relationship between the number of boats sent to each end and the number of pounds caught per boat is as summarized in Table 9-2. Suppose further that you have four boats in your fleet, and that two currently fish the east end while the other two fish the west end. (Note that all of these suppositions are completely consistent with the facts outlined in the scenario.) Should you move one of your boats from the east end to the west end?*

From the entries in Table 9-2, it follows that your total output under the current allocation is 440 pounds of fish per day (100 pounds from each of the two boats at the east end, 120 from each of the two at the west end). Now suppose you transfer one boat from the east end to the west end, which means you now have three boats in the west and only one in the east. From the figures in Table 9-2, we see that your total output will now be only 430 pounds per day, or 10 pounds per day less than under the current allocation. So, no, you should not move an extra boat to the west end. Neither, for that matter, should you send one of the west end boats to the east end. Loss of a boat from the west end would reduce the total daily catch at that end by 110 pounds (the difference between the 240 pounds caught by two boats and the 130 that would be caught by one), which is more than the extra 100 pounds you would get by having an extra boat at the east end. The current allocation of two boats to each end is optimal.

The average catch per boat is constant at 100 pounds per boat for boats sent to the east end of the lake. The average catch per boat is a declining function of the number of boats sent to the west end.

TABLE 9-2   **AVERAGE PRODUCT, TOTAL PRODUCT, AND MARGINAL PRODUCT (LB/DAY) FOR TWO FISHING AREAS**

Number of boats	East end			West end		
	AP	TP	MP	AP	TP	MP
0	0	0		0	0	
			100			130
1	100	100		130	130	
			100			110
2	100	200		120	240	
			100			90
3	100	300		110	330	
			100			70
4	100	400		100	400	

The general rule for allocating a resource efficiently across different production activities is to allocate each unit of the resource to the production activity where its marginal product is highest. This form of the rule applies to resources, such as boats, that are not perfectly divisible, and also to cases where the marginal product of a resource is always higher in one activity than in another.[7] For a resource that is perfectly divisible, and for activities for which the marginal product of the resource is not always higher in one than in the others, the rule is to *allocate the resource so that its marginal product is the same in every activity.*

Many people, however, "solve" these kinds of problems by allocating resources to the activity with the highest *average* product, or by trying to equalize *average* products across activities. The reason that this particular wrong answer often has appeal is that people often focus on only part of the relevant production process. By sending only two boats to the west end, the average catch at that end is 20 pounds per day greater than the average catch per boat at the east end. But note that if you send a third boat to the west end, that boat's contribution to the total amount of fish caught at the west end will be only 90 pounds per day (the difference between the 330 pounds caught by three boats and 240 pounds caught by two). What people often tend to overlook is that the third boat at the west end catches some of the fish that would otherwise have been caught by the first two.

As the figures in Table 9-2 illustrate, the opportunity cost of sending a third boat to the west end is the 100 pounds of fish that will no longer be caught at the east end. But since that third boat will add only 90 pounds to the daily catch at the west end, the best that can be done is to keep sending two boats to each end of the lake. The fact that either of the two boats currently fishing at the east

---

[7]See Example 9-2.

end could catch 10 pounds per day more by moving to the west end is no cause for concern to a fishing fleet owner who understands the distinction between average and marginal products.

EXERCISE 9-5

> Explain why we cannot necessarily conclude that the baseball pitcher should throw more fastballs in the following scenario: You are a baseball pitcher who throws two different kinds of pitches: fastball and curve. Your team statistician tells you that at the current rate at which you employ these pitches, batters hit .275 against your curve, only .200 against your fastball. Should you alter your current mix of pitches?

Example 9-1 produced what economists call an *interior solution*—one in which each of the production activities is actually employed. But not all problems of this sort have interior solutions. As the next example will make clear, there are cases where one activity simply dominates the other.

EXAMPLE 9-2

Same as Example 9-1, except now all entries in the west end total product column of Table 9-2 are equal to 120 lb/day.

> The difference between this example and Example 9-1 is that this time there is no drop-off in the rate at which fish are caught as more boats are sent to the west end of the lake. So this time the average product of boats sent to the west end is identical to their marginal product. And since the marginal product is always higher for boats sent to the west end, the optimal allocation is to send all four boats to that end.

Cases like the one illustrated in Example 9-2 are by no means unusual. But by far the more common, and more interesting, production decisions are the ones that involve interior solutions like the one we saw in Example 9-1, where some positive quantity of the productive input must be allocated to each activity.

EXAMPLE 9-3

Suppose that from the last minute you devoted to Problem 1 on your first economics exam you earned 4 extra points, while from the last minute devoted to Problem 2 you earned 6 extra points. The total number of points you earned on these two questions were 20 and 12, respectively, and the total time you spent on each was the same. How—if at all—should you have reallocated your time between them?

The rule for efficient allocation of time spent on exams is the same as the rule for efficient allocation of any resource: the marginal product of the resource should be the same in each activity. From the information given, the marginal product of your last minute spent on question 2 was 6 points, or 2 points more than the marginal product of the last minute spent on question 1. Even though the average product of your time spent on question 1 was higher than on question 2, you would have scored more points if you had spent less time on question 1 and more time on question 2.

Production in the Long Run

The examples discussed thus far have involved production in the short run, where at least one productive input cannot be varied. In the long run, by contrast, all factors of production are by definition variable. In the short run, with K held fixed in the production function $Q = F(K, L)$, we were able to describe the production function in a simple two-dimensional diagram. With both K and L variable, however, we now require three dimensions instead of two. And when there are more than two variable inputs, we require even more dimensions.

This creates a problem similar to the one we encountered in Chapter 3 when the consumer was faced with a choice between two or more products: We are not very adept at graphical representations involving three or more dimensions. For production with two variable inputs, the solution to this problem is similar to the one we adopted in Chapter 3.

To illustrate, consider again the production function we discussed earlier in this chapter:

$$Q = F(K, L) = 2KL, \tag{9.4}$$

and suppose we want to describe all possible combinations of K and L that give rise to a particular level of output—say, $Q = 16$. To do this, we solve $Q = 2KL = 16$ for K in terms of L, which yields

$$K = \frac{8}{L}. \tag{9.5}$$

Isoquant The set of all input combinations that yield a given level of output.

The (L, K) pairs that satisfy Equation 9.5 are shown by the curve labeled $Q = 16$ in Figure 9-8. The (L, K) pairs that yield 32 and 64 units of output are shown in Figure 9-8 as the curves labeled $Q = 32$ and $Q = 64$, respectively. Such curves are called **isoquants,** and are defined formally as *all combinations of variable inputs that yield a given level of output.*

FIGURE 9-8
An isoquant is the
set of all (L, K) pairs
that yield a given
level of output. For
example, each (L, K)
pair on the curve la-
beled $Q = 32$ yields
32 units of output.
The isoquant map
describes the prop-
erties of a produc-
tion process in
much the same way
as an indifference
map describes a
consumer's prefer-
ences.

PART OF AN ISOQUANT MAP FOR THE PRODUCTION FUNCTION $Q = 2KL$

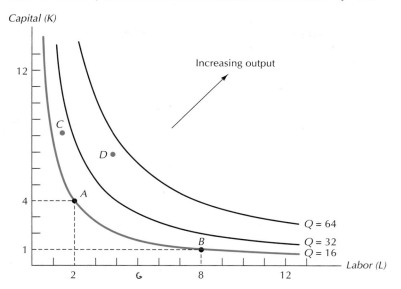

Note the clear analogy between the isoquant and the indifference curve of consumer theory. Just as an indifference map provides a concise representation of a consumer's preferences, an *isoquant map* provides a concise representation of a production process.

On an indifference map, movements to the northeast correspond to increasing levels of satisfaction. Similar movements on an isoquant map correspond to increasing levels of output. A point on an indifference curve is preferred to any point that lies below that indifference curve, and less preferred than any point that lies above it. Likewise, any input bundle on an isoquant yields more output than any input bundle that lies below that isoquant, and less output than any input bundle that lies above it. Thus, bundle C in Figure 9-8 yields more output than bundle A, but less output than bundle D.

The only substantive respect in which the analogy between isoquant maps and indifference maps is incomplete has to do with the significance of the labels attached to the two types of curves. From Chapter 3 recall that the actual numbers assigned to each indifference curve were used to indicate only the relative rankings of the bundles on different indifference curves. The number we assign to an isoquant, by contrast, corresponds to the actual level of output we get from an input bundle along that isoquant. With indifference maps, we are free to relabel the indifference curves in any way that preserves the original ranking of bundles. But with isoquant maps, the labels are determined uniquely by the production function.

THE MARGINAL RATE OF TECHNICAL SUBSTITUTION

Marginal rate of technical substitution (MRTS)
The rate at which one input can be exchanged for another without altering the total level of output.

Recall from our discussion of consumer theory in Chapter 3 that the marginal rate of substitution is the rate at which the consumer is willing to exchange one good for another along an indifference curve. The analogous concept in production theory is called the *marginal rate of technical substitution,* or *MRTS.* It is the rate at which one input can be exchanged for another without altering output. In Figure 9-9, for example, the MRTS at A is defined as the absolute value of the slope of the isoquant at A, $|\Delta K/\Delta L|$.

In consumer theory, we assumed that the marginal rate of substitution diminishes with downward movements along an indifference curve. For most production functions, the MRTS displays a similar property. Holding output constant, the less we have of one input, the more we must add of the other input to compensate for a one-unit reduction in the first input.

A simple but very important relationship exists between the MRTS at any point and the marginal products of the respective inputs at that point. In a small neighborhood of point A in Figure 9-9, suppose we reduce K by ΔK and augment L by an amount ΔL just sufficient to maintain the original level of output. If MP_{KA} denotes the marginal product of capital at A, then the reduction in output caused by the loss of ΔK is equal to $MP_{KA}\Delta K$. Using MP_{LA} to denote the marginal product of L at A, it follows similarly that the gain in output resulting from the extra ΔL is equal to $MP_{LA}\Delta L$. Finally, since the reduction in output from having less K is exactly offset by the gain in output from having more L, it follows that

$$MP_{KA}\ \Delta K = MP_{LA}\ \Delta L. \tag{9.6}$$

Cross-multiplying, we get

$$\frac{MP_{LA}}{MP_{KA}} = \frac{\Delta K}{\Delta L}, \tag{9.7}$$

which says that the MRTS at A is simply the ratio of the marginal product of L to the marginal product of K. This relationship will have an important application in the next chapter, where we will take up the question of how to produce a given level of output at the lowest possible cost.

EXERCISE 9-6

Given a firm's current level of capital and labor inputs, the marginal product of labor for its production process is equal to 3 units of output. If the marginal rate of technical substitution between K and L is 9, what is the marginal product of capital?

FIGURE 9-9
The MRTS is the rate at which one input can be exchanged for another without altering total output. The MRTS at any point is the absolute value of the slope of the isoquant that passes through that point. If ΔK units of capital are removed at point A, and ΔL units of L are added, output will remain the same at Q_0 units.

THE MARGINAL RATE OF TECHNICAL SUBSTITUTION

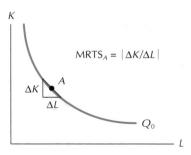

$$MRTS_A = |\Delta K/\Delta L|$$

In consumer theory, the shape of the indifference curve tells us how the consumer is willing to substitute one good for another. In production theory, an essentially similar story is told by the shape of the isoquant. Figure 9-10 illustrates the extreme cases of inputs that are perfect substitutes (*a*) and perfect complements (*b*). Figure 9-10*a* describes a production process in which cars and gasoline are combined to produce trips. The input of gasoline comes in two brands, Texaco and Amoco, which are perfect substitutes for one another. We can substitute 1 gallon of Amoco for 1 gallon of Texaco and still produce the same number of trips as before. The MRTS between Texaco and Amoco remains constant at 1 as we move downward along any isoquant.

Figure 9-10*b* describes a production process for typing letters using the two inputs of typewriters and typists. In this process, the two inputs are perfect complements. Here, inputs are most effectively combined in fixed proportions. Having more than one typewriter per typist doesn't augment production, nor does having more than one typist per typewriter.

FIGURE 9-10
In panel *a*, we get the same number of trips from a given total quantity of gasoline, no matter how we mix the two brands. Amoco and Texaco are perfect substitutes in the production of automobile trips. In panel *b*, typewriters and typists are perfect complements in the process of typing letters.

ISOQUANT MAPS FOR PERFECT SUBSTITUTES AND PERFECT COMPLEMENTS

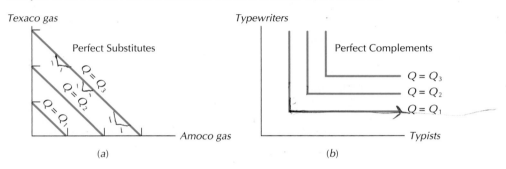

Returns to Scale

A question of central importance for the organization of industry is whether production takes place most efficiently at large scale rather than small scale (where "large" and "small" are defined relative to the scale of the relevant market). This question is important because the answer dictates whether an industry will end up being served by many small firms or only a few large ones.

The technical property of the production function used to describe the relationship between scale and efficiency is called *returns to scale*. The term tells us what happens to output when all inputs are increased by exactly the same proportion. Because returns to scale refer to a situation in which all inputs are variable, *the concept of returns to scale is an inherently long-run concept.*

Increasing returns to scale
The property of a production process whereby a proportional increase in every input yields a more than proportional increase in output.

A production function for which proportional changes in all inputs lead to a more than proportional change in output is said to exhibit **increasing returns to scale.** For example, if we double all inputs in a production function with increasing returns to scale, we get more than twice as much output as before. As we will see in Chapters 12 and 13, such production functions generally give rise to conditions in which a small number of firms supply most of the relevant market.

Increasing returns to scale often result from the greater possibilities for specialization in large organizations. Adam Smith illustrated this point by describing the division of labor in a pin factory:

> One man draws out the wire, another straightens it, a third cuts it, a fourth points it, a fifth grinds it at the top for receiving the head; to make the head requires two or three distinct operations. . . . I have seen a small manufactory . . . of this kind where only ten men were employed . . . [who] could, when they exerted themselves, make among them about twelve pounds of pins in a day. There are in a pound upwards of four thousand pins of middling size. Those ten persons, therefore, could make among them upwards of forty-eight thousand pins in a day. Each person, therefore, making a tenth part of forty-eight thousand pins might be considered as making four thousand eight hundred pins in a day. But if they had all wrought separately and independently . . . they could not each of them have made twenty, perhaps not one pin in a day. . . .[8]

The airline industry is often cited as a modern example of an industry with increasing returns to scale. Industry professionals have long stressed that having a large number of flights helps an airline fill each flight by feeding passengers from its incoming flights to its outgoing flights. Local airport activities also exhibit increasing returns to scale. Ticket-counter space, ticket agents, reservations equipment, baggage-handling equipment, ground crews, and passenger-boarding facilities are all resources that are utilized more efficiently at high activity levels than at low activity levels. (The ticket counters, gates, and agents of a carrier with only a few flights a day will stand idle much of the time.) As a consequence of the law

---

[8]Adam Smith, *The Wealth of Nations*, New York: Everyman's Library, 1910 (1776), Book 1, p. 5.

Constant returns to scale The property of a production process whereby a proportional increase in every input yields an equal proportional increase in output.

Decreasing returns to scale The property of a production process whereby a proportional increase in every input yields a less than proportional increase in output.

of large numbers,[9] moreover, it follows that maintenance operations, flight crew scheduling, and other inventory-related activities are all accomplished more efficiently on a large scale than on a small scale. Increasing returns to scale in commercial air transport constitute the underlying explanation for why the industry has been moving toward ever larger airlines in the last decade.

A production function for which a proportional change in all inputs causes output to change by the same proportion is said to exhibit *constant returns to scale.* In such cases, doubling all inputs results in a doubling of output. In industries in which production takes place under constant returns to scale, large size is neither an advantage nor a disadvantage.

Finally, a production function for which a proportional change in all inputs causes a less than proportional change in output is said to exhibit *decreasing returns to scale.* Here large size is a handicap, and we do not expect to see large firms in an industry in which production takes place with decreasing returns to scale. As we will see in Chapter 11, the constant and decreasing returns cases often enable many sellers to coexist within the same narrowly defined markets.

A production function need not exhibit the same degree of returns to scale over the entire range of output. On the contrary, a commonly observed pattern is for there to be increasing returns to scale at low levels of output, followed by constant returns to scale at intermediate levels of output, followed finally by decreasing returns to scale at high levels of output. The isoquant map for such a production function is discussed after the following application.

APPLICATION: PREFABRICATION VERSUS ON-SITE CONSTRUCTION

When construction crews build a wood-frame house, they usually construct framing for the walls at the construction site. By contrast, they often buy prefabricated framing for the roof. Why this difference?

There are two key differences between wall framing and roof framing: (1) cutting the lumber for roof framing involves many complicated angle cuts, whereas the right-angle cuts required for wall framing are much simpler (see Figure 9-11); and (2) sections of roof framing of a given size are all alike, whereas wall sections differ according to the placement of window and door openings. Both properties of roof framing lead to substantial economies of scale in production. First, the angle cuts they require can be made much more rapidly if a frame or "jig" can be built that guides the lumber past the saw-blade at just the proper angle. It is economical to set up such jigs in a factory where thousands of cuts are made each day, but it usually does not pay to use this method for the limited number of cuts required at any one construction site. Likewise, automated methods are easy to employ for roof framing by virtue of its uniformity. The idiosyncratic nature of wall framing, by contrast, militates against the use of automated methods.

---

[9]See Chapter 6.

FIGURE 9-11
The angular cuts and standard shapes characteristic of roof framing are more conducive to economies of scale than are the rectangular cuts and idiosyncratic layouts of wall framing. This difference helps explain why wall framing is generally built at the construction site while roof framing is more often prefabricated.

PREFABRICATED VERSUS ON-SITE CONSTRUCTION

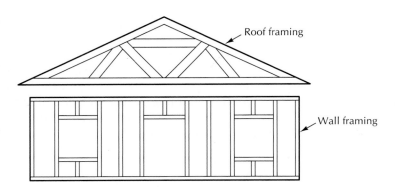

Roof framing

Wall framing

So the fact that there are much greater economies of scale in the construction of roof framing than wall framing helps account for why wall framing is usually built at the construction site while roof framing is more often prefabricated.

SHOWING RETURNS TO SCALE ON THE ISOQUANT MAP

A simple relationship exists between a production function's returns to scale and the spacing of its isoquants.[10] Consider the isoquant map in Figure 9-12. As we move outward into the isoquant map along the ray labeled R, each input grows by exactly the same proportion. The particular production function whose isoquant map is shown in the diagram exhibits increasing returns to scale in the region from A to C. Note, for example, that when we move from A to B, both inputs double while output goes up by a factor of 3; likewise, when we move from B to C, both inputs grow by 50 percent while output grows by 100 percent. In the region from C to F, this same production function exhibits constant returns to scale. Note, for example, that when we move from D to E, both inputs grow by 25 percent and output also grows by 25 percent. Finally, the production function whose isoquant map is shown in Figure 9-12 exhibits decreasing returns to scale in the region to the northeast of F. Thus, when we move from F to G, both inputs increase by 16.7 percent while output grows by only 11.1 percent.

THE DISTINCTION BETWEEN DIMINISHING RETURNS AND DECREASING RETURNS TO SCALE

It is important to bear in mind that decreasing returns to scale have nothing whatsoever to do with the law of diminishing returns. Decreasing returns to scale refer to what

---

[10]The discussion in this section applies to *homothetic* production functions, an important class of production functions defined by the property that the slopes of all isoquants are constant at points along any ray.

FIGURE 9-12
In the region from A to C, this production function has increasing returns to scale. Proportional increases in input yield more than proportional increases in output. In the region from C to F, there are constant returns to scale. Inputs and output grow by the same proportion in this region. In the region northeast of F, there are decreasing returns to scale. Proportional increases in both inputs yield less than proportional increases in output.

RETURNS TO SCALE SHOWN ON THE ISOQUANT MAP

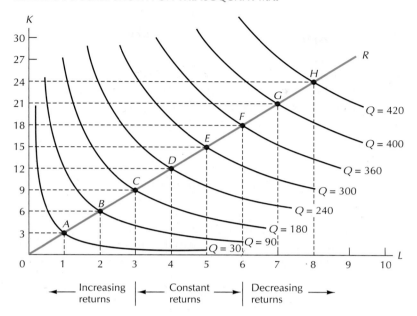

happens when *all* inputs are varied by some proportion. The law of diminishing returns, by contrast, refers to the case in which one input varies while all others are held fixed. As an empirical generalization, it applies with equal force to production functions having increasing, constant, or decreasing returns to scale.

THE LOGICAL PUZZLE OF DECREASING RETURNS TO SCALE

If the production function $Q = F(K, L)$ is a complete description of the corresponding production process, it is difficult to see how any production function could ever exhibit decreasing returns to scale in practice. The difficulty is that we ought to be able to duplicate the process used to produce any given level of output, and thereby achieve constant returns to scale. To illustrate, suppose first that $Q_0 = F(K_0, L_0)$. If we now want to produce $2Q_0$ units of output, we can always do so by again doing what we did the first time—namely, by again combining K_0 and L_0 to get Q_0 and adding that to the Q_0 we already have. Similarly, we can get $3Q_0$ by carrying out $F(K_0, L_0)$ three times in succession. Simply by carrying out the process again and again, we can get output to grow in the same proportion as inputs, which means constant returns to scale. And for reasons similar to the ones discussed above for the airline industry, it will often be possible to do even better than that.

In cases where it is not possible to at least double our output by doubling both K and L, we seem forced to conclude that there must be some important input besides K and L that we are failing to increase at the same time. This input is variously referred to as "organization" or "communication," the idea being that when a firm gets past a certain size, it somehow starts to get out of control. Others claim that it is the shortage of managerial or entrepreneurial resources that creates bottlenecks in production. If there is indeed some unmeasured input that is being held fixed as we expand K and L, then we are still in the short run by definition. And there is no reason to expect to be able to double our output by doubling only some of our inputs.

Summary

Production is any activity that creates current or future utility. A production function summarizes the relationship between inputs and outputs. The short run is defined as that period during which at least some inputs are fixed. In the two-input case, it is the period during which one input is fixed, the other freely variable.

The marginal product of a variable input is defined as the change in output brought forth by an additional unit of the variable input, all other inputs held fixed. The law of diminishing returns says that beyond some point the marginal product declines with additional units of the variable input.

The average product of a variable input is the ratio of total output to the quantity of the variable input. Whenever marginal product lies above average product, the average product will increase with increases in the variable input. Conversely, when marginal product lies below average product, average product will decline with increases in the variable input.

An important practical problem is that of how to allocate an input across two productive activities in such a way as to generate the maximum possible output. In general, two types of solutions are possible. A corner solution occurs when the marginal product of the input is always higher in one activity than in the other. In that case, the best thing to do is to concentrate all the input in the activity where it is most productive.

An interior solution occurs whenever the marginal product of the variable input, when all of it is placed in one activity, is lower than the marginal product of the first unit of the input in the other activity. In this case, the output-maximizing rule is to distribute the input across the two activities in such a way that its marginal product is the same in both. Even experienced decision makers often violate this simple rule. The pitfall to be on guard against is the tendency to equate not marginal but average products in the two activities.

The long run is defined as the period required for all inputs to be variable. The actual length of time that corresponds to the short and long runs will differ markedly in different cases. In the two-input case, all of the relevant information about production in the long run can be summarized graphically by the isoquant map. The marginal rate of technical substitution is defined as the rate at which one input can be substituted for another without altering the level of output. The MRTS at any point is simply the absolute value of the slope of the isoquant at that point. For most production functions, the MRTS will diminish as we move downward to the right along an isoquant.

A production function is said to exhibit constant returns to scale if a given proportional increase in all inputs produces the same proportional increase in output. A production function is said to exhibit decreasing returns to scale if a given proportional increase in all inputs results in a smaller proportional increase in output. And, finally, a production function is said to exhibit increasing returns to scale if a given proportional increase in all inputs causes a greater proportional increase in output. Production functions with increasing returns to scale are also said to exhibit economies of scale. Returns to scale constitute a critically important factor in determining the structure of industrial organization.

An appendix to this chapter (see the "For the Instructor" section at our Web site www.mhhe.com/economics/frank4) considers several mathematical extensions of production theory. Topics covered include applications of the average marginal distinction, specific mathematical forms of the production function, and a mathematical treatment of returns to scale in production.

Questions for Review

1. List three examples of production that a noneconomist might not ordinarily think of as production.

2. Give an example of production in which the short run lasts at least 1 year.

3. Why should a person in charge of hiring productive inputs care more about marginal products than about average products?

4. A wag once remarked that when a certain government official moved from New York to California, the average IQ level in both states went up. Interpret this remark in the context of the average-marginal relationships discussed in the chapter.

5. How is an isoquant map like an indifference map? In what important respect do the two constructs differ?

6. Distinguish between diminishing returns to a variable input and decreasing returns to scale.

7. *True or false:* If the marginal product is decreasing, then the average product must also be decreasing. Explain.

8. A factory adds a worker and subsequently discovers that the average product of its workers has risen. *True or false:* The marginal product of the new worker is less than the average product of the plant's workers before the new employee's arrival.

9. Currently, 2 units of labor and 1 unit of capital produce 1 unit of output. If you double both the inputs (4 units of labor and 2 units of capital), what can you conclude about the output produced under constant returns to scale? Decreasing returns to scale? Increasing returns to scale?

$$\frac{216}{4}$$
$$68^4$$

Problems

1. Graph the short-run total product curves for each of the following production functions if K is fixed at $K_0 = 4$.

    a. $Q = F(K, L) = 2K + 3L$.
    b. $Q = F(K, L) = K^2 L^2$. $= 4L^2 \quad 16L^2$

2. Do the two production functions in Problem 1 obey the law of diminishing returns?

3. Suppose the marginal product of labor is currently equal to its average product. If you were one of ten new workers the firm was about to hire, would you prefer to be paid the value of your average product or the value of your marginal product? Would it be in the interests of an employer to pay you the value of your average product?

4. The following table provides partial information on total product, average product, and marginal product for a production function. Using the relationships between these properties, fill in the missing cells.

Labor	Total product	Average product	Marginal product
0		0	
1	180		
			140
2			
3	420		
4		120	

5. The Philadelphia Police Department must decide how to allocate police officers between West Philadelphia and Center City. The average product, total product, and marginal product in each of these two areas are given in the table below. Currently the police department allocates 200 police officers to Center City and 300 to West Philadelphia. If police can be redeployed only in groups of 100, how, if at all, should the police department reallocate its officers to achieve the maximum number of arrests?

Number of police	West Phily			Center City		
	AP	TP	MP	AP	TP	MP
0	0	0		0	0	
			40			45
100	40	40		45	45	
			40			35
200	40	80		40	80	
			40			25
300	40	120		35	105	
			40			15
400	40	160		30	120	
			40			5
500	40	200		25	125	

6. Suppose a crime wave hits West Philadelphia, so that the marginal product and average product of police officers are now 60 arrests per hour for any number of police officers. What is the optimal allocation of 500 police officers between the two areas now?

7. A firm's short-run production function is given by

$$Q = \tfrac{1}{2} L^2 \qquad \text{for } 0 \le L \le 2$$

and

$$Q = 3L - \tfrac{1}{4}L^2 \qquad \text{for } 2 < L \le 7.$$

   a. Sketch the production function.
   b. Find the maximum attainable production. How much labor is used at that level?
   → c. Identify the ranges of L utilization over which the marginal product of labor is increasing and decreasing.
   → d. Identify the range over which the marginal product of labor is negative.

8. Suppose that from the last minute you devoted to Problem 10 on an exam you earned 2 extra points, while from the last minute devoted to Problem 8 you earned 4 extra points. The total number of points you earned on these two questions were 8 and 6, respectively, and the total time you spent on each was the same. How—if at all—should you have reallocated your time between them?

9. Suppose capital is fixed at 4 units in the production function $Q = KL$. Draw the total, marginal, and average product curves for the labor input.

10. Identify the regions of increasing, constant, and decreasing returns to scale on the isoquant map below.

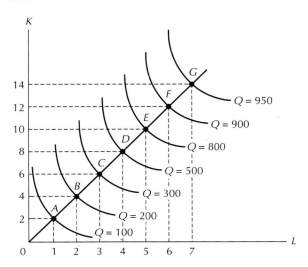

11. When Paul Samuelson switched from physics to economics, Robert Solow is said to have remarked that the average IQ in both disciplines went up. A bystander responded that Solow's claim must be wrong because it implies that the average IQ

for academia as a whole (which is a weighted average of the average IQ levels for each discipline) must also have gone up as a result of the switch, which is clearly impossible. Was the bystander right? Explain.

Answers to In-Chapter Exercises

9-1.   For $K = 4$, $Q \sqrt{4} \sqrt{L} = 2\sqrt{L}$.

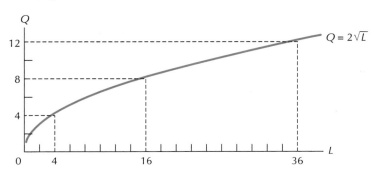

9-2.   The slope of the total product curve in Figure 9-3a is 2 for all values of L. So $MP_{L=3} = 2$.

9-3.   The slope of the ray to any point on the total product curve is 2, and so $AP_{L=3} = 2$. When the total product curve is a ray, as here, $AP_L = MP_L$ is constant for all values of L.

9-4.   Because $AP_{L=10} < MP_{L=10}$, AP will rise when L increases, and so $AP_{L=10.1} > AP_{L=10}$.

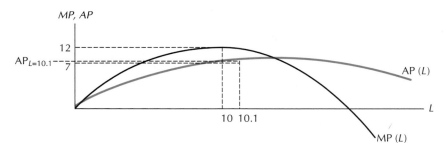

9-5.   We cannot say that the pitcher should throw more fastballs without first knowing how a change in the proportion of pitches thrown would alter the effectiveness of both types of pitches. In particular, throwing more fastballs is likely to decrease the effectiveness not only of the additional fastballs thrown, but of all other fastballs as well. And if this loss exceeds the gain from switching from curves to fastballs, more fastballs should not be thrown.

9-6.   From the relationship $MP_L/MP_K = MRTS$, we have $3/MP_K = 9$, which yields $MP_K = \frac{1}{3}$.

CHAPTER
10

Costs

More than 30 years ago, I was a high school math and science teacher in Sanischare, a small village in eastern Nepal. During my 2 years there, one of the country's few roads was in the process of being built through Sanischare. Once the right-of-way was cleared and the culverts and bridges laid in, the next step was to spread gravel over the roadbed. As at almost every other stage of the process, the methods employed at this step were a page torn from another century. The Nepalese workmen squatted by the side of the road in the blazing sun, tapping away at large rocks with their hammers. In a 12-hour day, each worker would produce a small mound of gravel, not enough to cover even one running foot of roadbed. But there were a lot of people working, and eventually the job was done.

In the United States, of course, we build roads very differently. We do not hire people to hammer rocks into gravel by hand. Instead, we have huge machines that pulverize several tons of rock each minute. The reason for this difference seemed obvious to me at the time: Nepal, being a very poor country, simply couldn't afford to buy the expensive equipment used in the industrialized nations. But this explanation, I now realize, is wrong. As we will see, it still would have made sense for Nepal to make gravel with manual labor even if it had had vast surplus revenues in its national treasury, because labor is very cheap relative to capital equipment there.

Chapter Preview

In this chapter we translate the theory of production developed in Chapter 9 into a coherent theory of costs. Our task in Chapter 9 was to establish the relationship between the quantities of inputs employed and the corresponding level of output, but here we forge the link between the quantity of output produced and the cost of producing it.

Our first step is to tackle the question of how costs vary with output in the short run. This question turns out to be more involved than it sounds, for there are seven different types of costs to keep track of, namely, total cost, variable cost, fixed cost, marginal cost, average total cost, average variable cost, and average fixed cost. This array sounds bewildering at first, but the links between the different cost concepts are actually very clear and simple. And each turns out to be important for the study of firm behavior, which is our principal concern in the chapters to follow.

Of even greater importance for the structure and conduct of industry is the question of how costs vary with output in the long run. Here, we begin with the question of how to produce a given level of output—say, a mile of road, either here or in some other country—at the lowest possible cost. A given quantity can be produced many ways: We need to find the cheapest way, the most appropriate method for existing factor prices. The answer to this question enables us to explore how costs are related to returns to scale in production.

Costs in the Short Run

To see how costs vary with output in the short run, it is convenient to begin with a simple production example of the sort we discussed in Chapter 9. Suppose Kelly's Cleaners washes bags of laundry using labor (L) and capital (K). Labor is purchased in the open market at a wage rate $w = \$10/\text{person-hr.}$[1] Capital is fixed in the short run. The relationship between the variable input and the total number of bags washed per hour is summarized in Table 10-1. Note that output initially grows at an increasing rate with additional units of the variable input (as L grows from 0 to 4 units), then grows at a diminishing rate (as L grows from 4 to 8 units).

The total cost of producing the various levels of output is simply the cost of all the factors of production employed. If Kelly owns his own capital, its rental value is an implicit cost, the money Kelly could have earned if he had sold his capital and invested the proceeds in, say, a government bond (see Chapter 1). Suppose Kelly's capital is fixed at 120 machine-hr/hr, the rental value of each of which is $r = \$0.25/\text{machine-hr,}$[2] for a total capital rental of $30/hr. This cost is

---

[1] A person-hour is one person working for 1 hour. In Chapter 14 we will consider how input prices are determined. For the present, we simply take them as given.

[2] A machine-hour is one machine working for 1 hour.

The entries in each row of the right column tell the quantity of output produced by the quantity of variable input in the corresponding row of the left column. This production function initially exhibits increasing, then diminishing, returns to the variable input.

TABLE 10-1   THE SHORT-RUN PRODUCTION FUNCTION FOR KELLY'S CLEANERS

Quantity of labor (person-hr/hr)	Quantity of output (bags/hr)
0	0
1	4
2	14
3	27
4	43
5	58
6	72
7	81
8	86

Fixed cost (FC) Cost that does not vary with the level of output in the short run.

fixed cost (FC), which means that it does not vary in the short run as the level of output varies. More generally, if K_0 denotes the amount of capital and r is its rental price per unit, we have

$$FC = rK_0. \tag{10.1}$$

Other examples of fixed cost might include property taxes, insurance payments, interest on loans, and other payments to which the firm is committed in the short run and which do not vary as the level of output varies. Business managers often refer to fixed costs as *overhead costs.*

Variable cost (VC) Cost that varies with the level of output in the short run.

Variable cost (VC) is defined as the total cost of the variable factor of production at each level of output.[3] To calculate VC for any given level of output in this example, we simply multiply the amount of labor needed to produce that level of output by the hourly wage rate. Thus, the variable cost of 27 bags/hr is ($10/person-hr) (3 person-hr/hr) = $30/hr. More generally, if L_1 is the quantity of labor required to produce an output level of Q_1 and w is the hourly wage rate, we have

$$VC_{Q1} = wL_1. \tag{10.2}$$

Note the explicit dependence of VC on output in the notation on the left-hand side of Equation 10.2, which is lacking in Equation 10.1. This is to emphasize that variable cost depends on the output level produced, whereas fixed cost does not.

---

[3]In production processes with more than one variable input, variable cost refers to the cost of *all* such inputs.

Total cost (TC)
All costs of production: the sum of variable cost and fixed cost.

Total cost (TC) is the sum of FC and VC. If Kelly wishes to wash 43 bags/hr, the total cost of doing so will be $30/hr + ($10/person-hr) (4 person-hr/hr) = $70/hr. More generally, the expression for total cost of producing an output level of Q_1 is written

$$TC_{Q1} = FC + VC_{Q1} = rK_0 + wL_1. \tag{10.3}$$

Table 10-2 shows fixed, variable, and total cost for corresponding output levels for the production function given in Table 10-1. The relationships among the various cost categories are most clearly seen by displaying the information graphically, not in tabular form. The short-run production function from Table 10-1 is plotted in Figure 10-1. Recall from Chapter 9 that the initial region of upward curvature ($0 \leq L \leq 4$) of the production function corresponds to increasing returns to the variable input. Beyond the point $L = 4$, the production function exhibits diminishing returns to the variable input.

GRAPHING THE TOTAL, VARIABLE, AND FIXED COST CURVES

Not surprisingly, the shape of the variable cost curve is systematically related to the shape of the short-run production function. The connection arises because the production function tells us how much labor we need to produce a given level of output, and this quantity of labor, when multiplied by the wage rate, gives us variable cost. Suppose, for example, we want to plot the variable cost of producing 58 units of output. We first note from the production function shown in Figure 10-1 that 58 units of output require 5 units of labor, which, at a wage rate of $10/person-hr, gives rise to a variable cost of (5)(10) = $50/hr. So in Figure 10-2 (page 314), the output level of 58 is plotted against a variable cost of $50/hr. Similarly, note from the production function that 43 units of output require 4 units of labor, which, at the $10 wage rate, gives rise in Figure 10-

The fixed cost of capital is $30/hr, and the cost per unit of the variable factor (L) is $10/hr. Total cost is calculated as the sum of fixed cost and variable cost.

TABLE 10-2 OUTPUTS AND COSTS

Q	FC	VC	TC
0	30	0	30
4	30	10	40
14	30	20	50
27	30	30	60
43	30	40	70
58	30	50	80
72	30	60	90
81	30	70	100
86	30	80	110

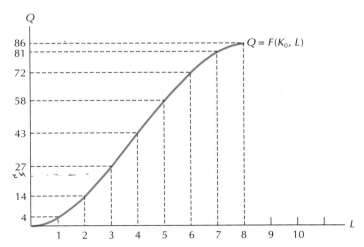

FIGURE 10-1
This production process shows increasing returns to the variable input up to the variable input up to $L = 4$, and diminishing returns thereafter.

OUTPUT AS A FUNCTION OF ONE VARIABLE INPUT

2 to a variable cost of \$40/hr. In like fashion, we can generate as many additional points on the variable cost curve as we choose.

Of particular interest is the relationship between the curvature of the production function and that of the variable cost curve. Note in Figure 10-1 that $L = 4$ is the point at which diminishing returns to the variable factor of production set in. For values of L less than 4, there are increasing returns to L, which means that increments in L produce successively larger increments in Q in that region. Put another way, in this region a given increase in output, Q, requires successively smaller increments in the variable input, L. As a result, variable cost grows at a diminishing rate for output levels less than 43. This is reflected in Figure 10-2 by the downward-curving shape of the variable cost curve for output levels between 0 and 43.

Once L exceeds 4 in Figure 10-1, we enter the region of diminishing returns. Here, successively larger increments in L are required to produce a given increment in Q. In consequence, variable cost grows at an increasing rate in this region. This is reflected in the upward-curving shape of the variable cost curve in Figure 10-2 for output levels in excess of 43.

Because fixed costs do not vary with the level of output, their graph is simply a horizontal line. Figure 10-2 shows the fixed, variable, and total cost curves (FC, VC, and TC) for a representative production function. Note in the figure that the variable cost curve passes through the origin, which means simply that variable cost is zero when we produce no output. The total cost of producing zero output is equal to fixed costs, FC. Note also in the figure that the vertical distance between the VC and TC curves is everywhere equal to FC. This means that the total cost curve is parallel to the variable cost curve and lies FC units above it.

FIGURE 10-2
These curves are for the production function for Kelly's cleaners, shown in Figure 10-1. The variable cost curve passes through the origin, which means that the variable cost of producing zero units of output is equal to zero. The TC curve, which is the sum of the FC and VC curves, is parallel to the VC curve and lies FC = 30 units above it.

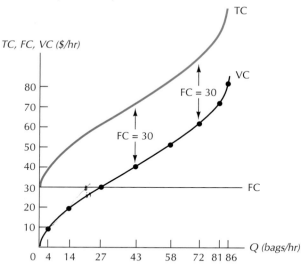

THE TOTAL, VARIABLE, AND FIXED COST CURVES

EXAMPLE 10-1 Suppose the production function is given by Q = 3KL, where K denotes capital and L denotes labor. The price of capital is $2/machine-hr, the price of labor is $24/person-hr, and capital is fixed at 4 machine-hr/hr in the short run. Graph the TC, VC, and FC curves for this production process.

Unlike the production process shown in Figure 10-1, the process in this example is one in which there are everywhere constant returns to the variable factor of production. As shown in Figure 10-3, output here is strictly proportional to the variable input.

To derive the total cost function from this production function, we must first discover how much capital and labor are required to produce a given level of output in the short run. Since K is fixed at 4 machine-hr/hr, the required amount of labor input is found by solving Q = 3KL = 3(4)L for L = Q/12. The total cost of producing Q units of output per hour is therefore given by

$$TC(Q) = (\$2/\text{machine-hr})(4 \text{ machine-hr}/\text{hr})$$
$$+ (\$24/\text{person-hr})\left(\frac{Q}{12} \text{ person-hr}/\text{hr}\right) = \$8/\text{hr} + \$2Q/\text{hr}. \quad (10.4)$$

The \$8/hr expenditure on capital constitutes fixed cost. Variable cost is total cost less fixed cost, or

$$VC_Q = 2Q. \tag{10.5}$$

The total, variable, and fixed cost curves are plotted in Figure 10-4.

FIGURE 10-3
This short-run production function exhibits constant returns to L over the entire range of L. There is neither a region of increasing returns nor a region of diminishing returns to L.

THE PRODUCTION FUNCTION $Q = 3KL$, WITH $K = 4$

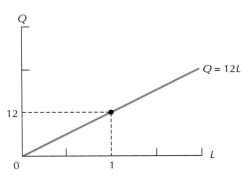

FIGURE 10-4
With K fixed at 4 machine-hr/hr in the short run and a price of K of $r = \$2$/machine-hr, fixed costs are \$8/hr. To produce Q units of output per hour requires $Q/12$ person-hr/hr of labor. With a price of labor of \$24/person-hr, variable cost is $2Q$/hr. Total cost is \$8/hr + \$2Q/hr.

THE TOTAL, VARIABLE, AND FIXED COST CURVES FOR THE PRODUCTION FUNCTION $Q = 3KL$

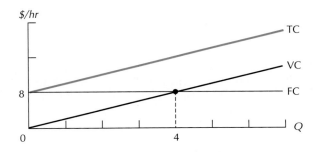

EXERCISE 10-1

Same as Example 10-1 except the price of capital $r = \$4$/machine-hr.

OTHER SHORT-RUN COSTS

Average fixed cost (AFC) Fixed cost divided by the quantity of output.

Average fixed cost (AFC) is fixed cost divided by the quantity of output. For example, the average fixed cost of washing 58 bags/hr is ($30/hr) ÷ (58 bags/hr) = $0.517/bag. More generally, the average fixed cost of producing an output level of Q_1 is written

$$\text{AFC}_{Q1} = \frac{\text{FC}}{Q_1} = \frac{rK_0}{Q_1}. \tag{10.6}$$

Note in Equation 10.6 that, unlike FC, AFC depends on the level of output produced.

Average variable cost (AVC) Variable cost divided by the quantity of output.

Average variable cost (AVC) is variable cost divided by the quantity of output. If Kelly washes 72 bags/hr, his AVC will be ($10/person-hr) (6 person-hr/hr) ÷ 72 bags/hr = $0.833/bag. The average variable cost of producing an output level Q_1 may be written as

$$\text{AVC}_{Q1} = \frac{\text{VC}_{Q1}}{Q_1} = \frac{wL_1}{Q_1}. \tag{10.7}$$

Average total cost (ATC) Total cost divided by the quantity of output.

Average total cost (ATC) is total cost divided by the quantity of output. And since total cost is the sum of total fixed cost and total variable cost, it follows that ATC is the sum of AFC and AVC. For example, the ATC of washing 58 bags/hr is ($30/hr) ÷ (58 bags/hr) + ($10/person-hr) (5 person-hr/hr) ÷ (58 bags/hr) = $0.517/bag + $0.862/bag = $1.379/bag. The average total cost of producing Q_1 units of output is given by

$$\text{ATC}_{Q1} = \text{AFC}_{Q1} + \text{AVC}_{Q1} = \frac{rK_0 + wL_1}{Q_1}. \tag{10.8}$$

Marginal cost (MC) Change in total cost that results from a 1-unit change in output.

Marginal cost (MC), finally, is the change in total cost that results from producing an additional unit of output.[4] In going from 58 to 72 bags/hr, for example, total costs go up by $10/hr, which is the cost of hiring the extra worker needed to achieve that increase in output. Since the extra worker washes an extra 14 bags/hr, the marginal cost of the additional output in per-bag terms is ($10/hr) ÷ (14 bags/hr) = $0.714/bag. More generally, if ΔQ denotes the change in output from an initial level of Q_1, and ΔTC_{Q1} denotes the corresponding change in total cost, marginal cost at Q_1 is given by

$$\text{MC}_{Q1} = \frac{\Delta \text{TC}_{Q1}}{\Delta Q}. \tag{10.9}$$

Because fixed cost does not vary with the level of output, the change in total cost

---

[4]In calculus terms, the definition of marginal cost is simply $\text{MC}_Q = d\text{TC}_Q/d\text{Q}$.

when we produce ΔQ additional units of output is the same as the change in variable cost. Thus an equivalent expression for marginal cost is

$$MC_{Q1} = \frac{\Delta VC_{Q1}}{\Delta Q}, \tag{10.10}$$

where ΔVC_{Q1} represents the change in variable cost when we produce ΔQ units of additional output.

GRAPHING THE SHORT-RUN AVERAGE AND MARGINAL COST CURVES

Since FC does not vary with output, average fixed cost declines steadily as output increases. Suppose McGraw-Hill's fixed costs in producing this textbook were approximately \$200,000. If only 1000 copies were produced, its average fixed cost would be \$200/book. But if the publisher produces 20,000 copies, AFC will fall to \$10/book. McGraw-Hill's best-selling economics principles text, by Campbell McConnell and Stanley Brue, is nearly twice as long as this book, and yet its average fixed cost comes to little more than \$1/book. The process whereby AFC falls with output is often referred to as "spreading overhead costs."

For the fixed cost curve FC shown in the top panel in Figure 10-5, the corresponding average fixed cost curve is shown in the bottom panel as the curve labeled AFC. Like all other AFC curves, it takes the form of a rectangular hyperbola. As output shrinks toward zero, AFC grows without bounds, and it falls ever closer to zero as output increases. Note that the units on the vertical axis of the AFC curve are dollars per unit (\$/unit) of output, and that the vertical axis of the FC curve, by contrast, is measured in dollars per hour (\$/hr).

Geometrically, average variable cost at any level of output Q, which is equal to VC/Q, may be interpreted as the slope of a ray to the variable cost curve at Q. Notice in the top panel in Figure 10-5 that the slope of a ray to the VC curve declines with output up to the output level Q_2; thereafter it begins to increase. The corresponding average variable cost curve, shown in the bottom panel in Figure 10-5, therefore reaches its minimum value at Q_2, the output level at which the ray R_2 is tangent to the variable cost curve. Beyond that point, the AVC curve increases with output.

The graph of the ATC curve is generated in an analogous fashion. For any level of output, ATC is the slope of the ray to the total cost curve at that output level. For the total cost curve in the top panel in Figure 10-5, the corresponding ATC curve is plotted in the bottom panel of the diagram. Note that the minimum point on ATC in the bottom panel occurs at Q_3, the output level for which the ray R_1 is tangent to the TC curve in the top panel.

Recall that because TC = FC + VC, it follows that ATC = AFC + AVC (simply divide both sides of the former equation by output). This means that the vertical distance between the ATC and AVC curves at any level of output will always be the corresponding level of AFC. Thus the vertical distance between

FIGURE 10-5
The MC curve intersects the ATC and AVC curves at their respective minimum points.

THE MARGINAL, AVERAGE TOTAL, AVERAGE VARIABLE, AND AVERAGE FIXED COST CURVES

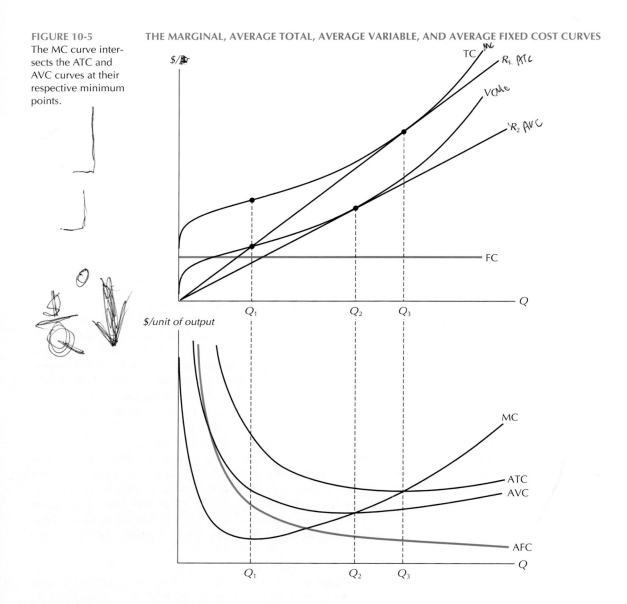

ATC and AVC approaches infinity as output declines toward zero, and shrinks toward zero as output grows toward infinity. Note also in Figure 10-5 that the minimum point on the AVC curve occurs for a smaller unit of output than does the minimum point on the ATC curve. Because AFC declines continuously, ATC continues falling even after AVC has begun to turn upward.

EXAMPLE 10-2 *Construct a table showing the average fixed costs, average variable cost, average total cost, and marginal cost using the information in Table 10-1 for Kelly's Cleaners. Then graph these average costs.*

We calculate the average fixed cost as fixed costs divided by quantity AFC = FC/Q, average variable cost as variable cost divided by quantity AVC = VC/Q, and average total cost as total cost divided by quantity ATC = TC/Q. We calculate marginal cost by a finding the difference in total cost divided by the difference in quantity MC = ΔTC/ΔQ to fill in the table below. The average cost curves are illustrated in Figure 10-6.

OUTPUTS AND COSTS

Q	AFC	AVC	ATC	MC*
0	∞	–	∞	
				2.50
4	7.50	2.50	10.00	
				1.0
14	2.14	1.43	3.57	
				0.77
27	1.11	1.11	2.22	
				0.63
43	0.70	0.93	1.63	
				0.67
58	0.52	0.86	1.38	
				0.71
72	0.42	0.83	1.25	
				1.11
81	0.37	0.86	1.23	
				2.0
86	0.35	0.93	1.28	

*The marginal cost entries are placed between the lines of the table to indicate that each entry represents the cost of moving from the preceding output level to the next.

FIGURE 10-6
ATC is the sum of
AVC and AFC. AFC
is declining for all
values of Q.

QUANTITY VS. AVERAGE COSTS

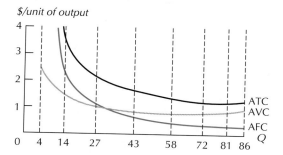

EXERCISE 10-2

If FC takes the value 20, what is the vertical distance between the ATC and AVC curves in Figure 10-5 when $Q = 10$?

In terms of its role in the firm's decision of how much output to produce, by far the most important of the seven cost curves is the *marginal cost curve*. The reason, as we will see in the coming chapters, is that the firm's typical operating decision involves the question of whether to expand or contract its current level of output. To make this decision intelligently, the firm must compare the relevant costs and benefits. The cost of expanding output (or the savings from contracting) is by definition equal to marginal cost.

Geometrically, marginal cost at any level of output may be interpreted as the slope of the total cost curve at that level of output. And since the total cost and variable cost curves are parallel, marginal cost is also equal to the slope of the variable cost curve. (Recall that the variable cost component is all that varies when total cost varies, which means that the change in total cost per unit of output must be the same as the change in variable cost per unit of output.)

Notice in the top panel in Figure 10-5 that the slope of the total cost curve decreases with output up to Q_1, and rises with output thereafter.[5] This tells us that the marginal cost curve, labeled MC in the bottom panel, will be downward sloping up to Q_1 and upward sloping thereafter. Q_1 is the point at which diminishing returns set in for this production function, and diminishing returns are what accounts for the upward slope of the short-run marginal cost curve.

At the output level Q_3, the slope of the total cost curve is exactly the same as the slope of the ray to the total cost curve (the ray labeled R_1 in the top panel in Figure 10-5). This tells us that marginal cost and average total cost will take

---

[5]A point at which the curvature changes is called an *inflection point*.

precisely the same value at Q_3. To the left of Q_3, the slope of the total cost curve is smaller than the slope of the corresponding ray, which means that marginal cost will be smaller than average total cost in that region. For output levels in excess of Q_3, the slope of the total cost curve is larger than the slope of the corresponding ray, so marginal cost will be larger than average total cost for output levels larger than Q_3. These relationships are reflected in the average total cost and marginal cost curves shown in the bottom panel in Figure 10-5. Notice that the relationship between the MC and AVC curves is qualitatively similar to the relationship between the MC and ATC curves. One common feature is that MC intersects each curve at its minimum point. Both average cost curves have the additional property that *when MC is less than average cost (either ATC or AVC), the average cost curve must be decreasing with output; and when MC is greater than average cost, average cost must be increasing with output.*

Note also that both of these relationships are very much like the ones among marginal and average product curves discussed in Chapter 9. They follow directly from the definition of marginal cost. Producing an additional unit whose cost exceeds the average (either total or variable) cost incurred thus far has the effect of pulling the average cost up. Conversely, an extra unit whose cost is less than the average will necessarily pull down the average.

Finally, note in the bottom panel in Figure 10-5 that the units on the vertical axis of the marginal cost curve diagram are again dollars per unit ($/unit) of output, the same as for the three short-run average cost curves. All four of these curves can thus be displayed in a single diagram. But you must never, *ever*, attempt to place any of these four curves on the same axes with the total cost, variable cost, or fixed cost curves. The units measured along the vertical axes are simply not compatible.[6]

*E*XAMPLE 10-3 *Suppose output is given by the production function $Q = 3KL$, where K denotes capital and L denotes labor. The price of capital is $2/machine-hr, the price of labor is $24/person-hr, and capital is fixed at 4 units in the short run (this is the same production function and input prices as in Example 10-1). Graph the ATC, AVC, AFC, and MC curves.*

> Recall from Example 10-1 that the total cost curve for this process is given by
>
> $$TC_Q = 8 + 2Q. \tag{10.11}$$
>
> Marginal cost is the slope of the total cost curve, which here is equal to $2/unit of output:

---

[6]A colleague tells of an occasion when he issued this warning forcefully to his class of intermediate microeconomics students. He was team-teaching the course that semester with a professor whose competence was very much in doubt. All doubt was resolved when, in the very next class meeting, his coteacher began his lecture by drawing the TC, ATC, and MC curves on a single set of axes.

$$MC_Q = \frac{\Delta TC_Q}{\Delta Q} = 2. \qquad (10.12)$$

Average variable cost is given by VC_Q/Q, which is also \$2/unit of output:

$$AVC_Q = \frac{2Q}{Q} = 2. \qquad (10.13)$$

When marginal cost is constant, as in this production process, it will always be equal to AVC.

Average fixed cost is given by

$$AFC_Q = \frac{8}{Q}, \qquad (10.14)$$

and average total cost is given by

$$ATC_Q = 2 + \frac{8}{Q}, \qquad (10.15)$$

in this example. The marginal and average cost curves are as shown in the bottom panel in Figure 10-7, where the top panel reproduces the corresponding total, variable, and fixed cost curves.

Allocating Production Between Two Processes

In Chapter 9, we saw that the problem of allocating a fixed resource between two production activities is solved by the allocation that equates the marginal product of the resource in each. There is a very closely related problem that can be solved with the cost concepts developed in this chapter. Here, the problem is to divide a given production quota between two production processes in such a way as to produce the quota at the lowest possible cost.

Let Q_T be the total amount to be produced, and let Q_1 and Q_2 be the amounts produced in the first and second processes, respectively. And suppose the marginal cost in either process at very low levels of output is lower than the marginal cost at Q_T units of output in the other (which ensures that both processes will be used).[7] *The values of Q_1 and Q_2 that solve this problem will then be the ones that result in equal marginal costs for the two processes.*

---

[7]Suppose the marginal cost at $Q = Q_T$ using production function A were less than the marginal cost at $Q = 0$ for production process B: $MC_{Q_T}^A < MC_0^B$. Then the cheapest way of producing Q_T would be to use only process A.

FIGURE 10-7
For production processes with constant marginal cost, average variable cost and marginal cost are identical. Marginal cost always lies below ATC for such processes.

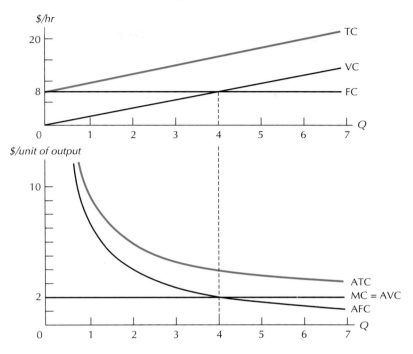

COST CURVES FOR A SPECIFIC PRODUCTION PROCESS

To see why, suppose the contrary—that is, suppose that the cost-minimizing allocation resulted in higher marginal costs in one process than in the other. We could then shift one unit of output from the process with the higher marginal cost to the one with the lower. Because the result would be the same total output as before at a lower total cost, the initial division could not have been the cost-minimizing one.

In Chapter 9 we saw that two production processes could have equal marginal products even though their average products differed substantially. Here, too, it is possible for two production processes to have equal marginal costs even though their average costs differ markedly. The cost-minimizing condition does not require average cost levels in the two processes to be the same, and indeed, in practice, they will often take substantially different values.

EXAMPLE 10-4 *Suppose production processes A and B give rise to the following marginal and average total cost curves:*

$$MC^A = 12Q^A, \qquad ATC^A = 16/Q^A + 6Q^A,$$
$$MC^B = 4Q^B, \qquad ATC^B = 240/Q^B + 2Q^B,$$

where the superscripts denote processes A and B, respectively. What is the least costly way to produce a total of 32 units of output?

The minimum-cost condition is that $MC^A_{Q^A}$, $MC^B_{Q^B}$, with $Q^A + Q^B = 32$. Equating marginal costs, we have

$$12Q^A = 4Q^B. \qquad (10.16)$$

Substituting $Q^B = 32 - Q^A$ into Equation 10.16, we have

$$12Q^A = 128 - 4Q^A, \qquad (10.17)$$

which solves for $Q^A = 8$. $Q^B = 32 - 8 = 24$ takes care of the remaining output, and at these output levels, marginal cost in both plants will be \$96/unit of output (see Figure 10-8). The line $MC^T = 3Q^T$ is the horizontal sum of MC^A and MC^B.[8] We can also see the output that equates marginal cost by summarizing the marginal cost information in a table as below.

Q	MC^A	MC^B	MC^T
0	0	0	0
8	96	32	24
16	192	64	48
24	288	96	72
32	384	128	96

The average total cost values that correspond to this allocation are $ATC^A = \$50$/unit of output and $ATC^B = \$58$/unit of output. From the average total cost curves we can deduce total cost curves in this example (just multiply ATC by Q).[9] They are given by $TC^A = 16 + 6(Q^A)^2$ and $TC^B = 240 + 2(Q^B)^2$. The cost-minimizing allocation results in $TC^A = \$400$ and $TC^B = \$1392$, illustrating that the cost-minimizing allocation does not require equality of total costs either.

EXERCISE 10-3

Same as Example 10-3 except the total output is 12.

---

[8]MC^T is found by solving $Q^T = Q^A + Q^B = MC/12 + MC/4 = MC/3$ for $MC^T = 3Q^T$.
[9]Note that $MC^A = dTC^A/dQ^A = d[16 + 6(Q^A)^2]/dQ^A = 12Q^A$ and $MC^B = dTC^B/dQ^B = d[240 + 2(Q^B)^2]/dQ^B = 4Q^B$.

FIGURE 10-8
To produce a given total output at minimum cost, it should be allocated across production activities so that the marginal cost of each activity is the same.

THE MINIMUM-COST PRODUCTION ALLOCATION

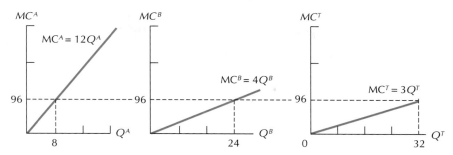

The Relationship Among MP, AP, MC, and AVC

In Chapter 9, we saw that the marginal product curve cuts the average product curve at the maximum value of the AP curve. And in this chapter, we saw that the marginal cost curve cuts the average variable cost curve at the minimum value of the AVC curve. There is a direct link between these relationships. To see the connection, note first that from the definition of marginal cost we have MC $= \Delta VC/\Delta Q$. When labor is the only variable factor, $\Delta VC = \Delta wL$ so that $\Delta VC/\Delta Q$ is equal to $\Delta wL/\Delta Q$. If wages are fixed, this is the same as $w\Delta L/\Delta Q$. And since $\Delta L/\Delta Q$ is equal to $1/MP$, it follows that

$$\mathrm{MC} = \frac{w}{\mathrm{MP}}. \tag{10.18}$$

In similar fashion, note from the definition of average variable cost that AVC $=$ VC$/Q = wL/Q$, and since L/Q is equal to $1/AP$, it follows that

$$\mathrm{AVC} = \frac{w}{\mathrm{AP}}. \tag{10.19}$$

From Equation 10.18, we see that the minimum value of marginal cost corresponds to the maximum value of MP. Likewise, it follows from Equation 10.19 that the minimum value of AVC corresponds to the maximum value of AP. The top panel in Figure 10-9 plots the AP and MP curves as functions of L. The bottom panel uses Equations 10.18 and 10.19 to plot the corresponding MC and AVC curves as functions of L. (Normally, the MC and AVC curves are plotted as functions of Q. The value of Q that corresponds to a given value of L in the bottom panel may be calculated by multiplying L times the corresponding value of AP_L.) Note that the MP curve in the top panel takes its maximum value at $L = L_1$, and that the minimum value of the MC curve in the bottom panel occurs at the output level (Q_1) that corresponds to $L = L_1$. Note also that the AP curve in the top panel takes its maximum value at $L = L_2$, and that the minimum value of the AVC curve in the bottom panel occurs at the output level (Q_2) that corresponds to $L = L_2$.

FIGURE 10-9
Normally, the MC and AVC curves are plotted with Q on the horizontal axis. In the bottom panel, they are shown as functions of L. The value of Q that corresponds to a given value of L is found by multiplying L times the corresponding value of AP_L. The maximum value of the MP curve, at $L = L_1$, top panel, corresponds to the minimum value of the MC curve, at $Q = Q_1$, bottom panel. Similarly, the maximum value of the AP curve, at $L = L_2$, top panel, corresponds to the minimum value of the AVC curve, at $Q = Q_2$, bottom panel.

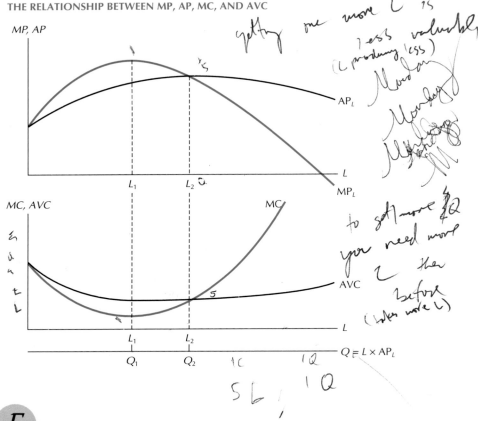

THE RELATIONSHIP BETWEEN MP, AP, MC, AND AVC

Exercise 10-4

For a production function at a given level of output in the short run, the marginal product of labor is greater than the average product of labor. How will marginal cost at that output level compare with average variable cost?

Costs in the Long Run

In the long run all inputs are, by definition, freely variable. If the manager of the firm wishes to produce a given level of output at the lowest possible cost and is free to choose any input combination she pleases, which one should she choose? As we will see in the next section, the answer to this question depends on the relative prices of capital and labor.

CHOOSING THE OPTIMAL INPUT COMBINATION

No matter what the structure of industry may be—monopolistic or atomistically competitive, capitalist or socialist, industrialized or less developed—the objective of most producers is to produce a given level and quality of output at the lowest possible cost. Equivalently, the producer wants to produce as much output as possible from any given expenditure on inputs.

Let us begin with the case of a firm that wants to maximize output from a given level of expenditure. Suppose it uses only two inputs, capital (K) and labor (L), whose prices, measured in dollars per unit of input per day, are $r = 2$ and $w = 4$, respectively. What different combinations of inputs can this firm purchase for a total expenditure of $C = \$200/day$? Notice that this question has the very same structure as the one we encountered in the theory of consumer behavior in Chapter 3 ("With an income of M, and facing prices of P_X and P_Y, what combinations of X and Y can the consumer buy?"). In the consumer's case, recall, the answer was easily summarized by the budget constraint. The parallel information in the case of the firm is summarized by the *isocost line*, shown in Figure 10-10 for the example given. Any of the input combinations on the locus labeled B can be purchased for a total expenditure of $\$200/day$. Analogously to the budget constraint case, the slope of the isocost line is the negative of the ratio of the input prices, $-w/r$.

EXERCISE 10-5

If $w = 3$ and $r = 6$, draw the isocost lines that correspond to total expenditure of $90 and $180 per unit of time.

FIGURE 10-10
For given input prices ($r = 2$ and $w = 4$ in the diagram), the isocost line is the locus of all possible input bundles that can be purchased for a given level of total expenditure C ($\$200$ in the diagram). The slope of the isocost line is the negative of the input price ratio, $-w/r$.

THE ISOCOST LINE

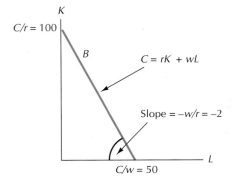

FIGURE 10-11
A firm that is trying
to produce the
largest possible out-
put for an expendi-
ture of *C* will select
the input combina-
tion at which the
isocost line for *C* is
tangent to an
isoquant.

THE MAXIMUM OUTPUT FOR A GIVEN EXPENDITURE

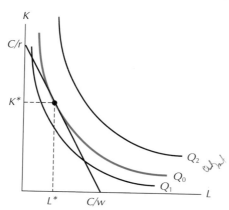

The analytic approach for finding the maximum output that can be produced for a given cost turns out to be very similar to the one for finding the optimal consumption bundle. Just as a given level of satisfaction can be achieved by any of a multitude of possible consumption bundles (all of which lie on the same indifference curve), so too can a given amount of output be produced by any of a host of different input combinations (all of which lie on the same isoquant). In the consumer case, we found the optimum bundle by superimposing the budget constraint onto the indifference map and locating the relevant point of tangency.[10] Here, we superimpose the isocost line onto the isoquant map. In Figure 10-11, the tangency point (L^*, K^*) is the input combination that yields the highest possible output (Q_0) for an expenditure of C.

As noted, the problem of producing the largest output for a given expenditure is solved in essentially the same way as the problem of producing a given level of output for the lowest possible cost. The only difference is that in the latter case we begin with a specific isoquant (the one that corresponds to the level of output we are trying to produce), then superimpose a map of isocost lines, each corresponding to a different cost level. In our first exercise, cost was fixed and output varied; this time, output is fixed and costs vary. As shown in Figure 10-12, the least-cost input bundle (L^*, K^*) corresponds to the point of tangency between an isocost line and the specified isoquant (Q_0).

Recall from Chapter 9 that the slope of the isoquant at any point is equal to $-MP_L/MP_K$, the negative of the ratio of the marginal product of L to the marginal product of K at that point. (Recall also from Chapter 9 that this ratio is called the marginal rate of technical substitution.) Combining this with the result that minimum cost occurs at a point of tangency with the isocost line (whose slope is $-w/r$), it follows that

---

[10]Except, of course, in the case of corner solutions.

THE MINIMUM COST FOR A GIVEN LEVEL OF OUTPUT

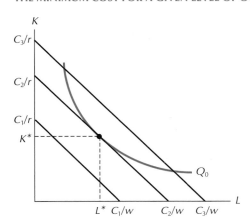

$$\frac{MP_{L^*}}{MP_{K^*}} = \frac{w}{r}, \tag{10.20}$$

where K^* and L^* again denote the minimum-cost values of K and L. Cross-multiplying, we have

$$\frac{MP_{L^*}}{w} = \frac{MP_{K^*}}{r}. \tag{10.21}$$

Equation 10.21 has a straightforward economic interpretation. Note first that
MP_L^* is simply the extra output obtained from an extra unit of L at the cost-minimizing point. w is the cost, in dollars, of an extra unit of L. The ratio MP_{L^*}/w
is thus the extra output we get from the last dollar spent on L. Similarly, MP_{K^*}/r
is the extra output we get from the last dollar spent on K. In words, Equation
10.21 tells us that when costs are at a minimum, the extra output we get from
the last dollar spent on an input must be the same for all inputs.

It is easy to show why, if that were not the case, costs would not be at a minimum. Suppose, for example, that the last units of both labor and capital
increased output by 4 units. That is, suppose $MP_L = MP_K = 4$. And again, suppose that $r = \$2$ and $w = \$4$. We would then have gotten only 1 unit of output
for the last dollar spent on L, but 2 units for the last dollar spent on K. We could
reduce spending on L by a dollar, increase spending on K by only 50 cents, and
get the same output level as before, saving 50 cents in the process. Whenever
the ratios of marginal products to input prices differ across inputs, it will always
be possible to make a similar cost-saving substitution in favor of the input with
the higher MP/P ratio.[11]

---

[11]Again, this statement is true except in the case of corner solutions.

More generally, we may consider a production process that employs not two but N inputs, $X_1, X_2, \ldots, X_N$. In this case, the condition for production of minimum cost as a straightforward generalization of Equation 10.21:

$$\frac{MP_{X_1}}{P_{X_1}} = \frac{MP_{X_2}}{P_{X_2}} = \cdots = \frac{MP_{X_N}}{P_{X_N}}. \tag{10.22}$$

EXAMPLE 10-5 *Why is gravel made by hand in Nepal but by machine in the United States?*

For simplicity, suppose that only two inputs—capital (K) and labor (L)—are involved in the transformation of rocks into gravel. (In the language of Chapter 9, rocks are an "intermediate product.") And suppose that any of the input combinations on the isoquant labeled $Q = 1$ ton in Figure 10-13 will yield 1 ton of gravel. Thus, the combination labeled ($L_{U.S.}^*$, $K_{U.S.}^*$) might correspond to the highly capital-intensive technique used in the United Nations (L_{Nepal}^*, K_{Nepal}^*) to the highly labor-intensive technique used in Nepal.

The reason the chosen techniques differ between countries is not that the United States is richer, as I had originally thought when I taught in Nepal; rather, it is that the relative prices of labor and capital differ so dramatically in the two countries. In Nepal, labor is cheaper than in almost any other nation. While I was living there, I paid 10 cents for a haircut and chiropractic neck adjustment (both administered by the same person). Wages in the United States, by contrast, are among the highest in the world. Construction equipment is traded in world markets and, aside from shipping costs, its price does not differ much from one country to another. If the price of capital, r, is roughly the same in the two countries and the price of labor, w, is much higher in the United States, it follows that the isocost line is much flatter in Nepal. And as shown in Figure 10-13, this fact alone is sufficient to account for the dramatic difference in production techniques.

EXERCISE 10-6

Suppose capital and labor are perfect complements in a one-to-one ratio. That is, suppose that $Q = min(L, K)$. Currently, the wage is $w = 5$ and the rental rate is $r = 10$. What is the minimum cost and method of producing $Q = 20$ units of output? Suppose the wage rises to $w' = 20$. If we keep total cost the same, what level of output can now be produced and what method of production (input mix) is used?

FIGURE 10-13
Countries where labor is cheap relative to capital will select labor-intensive techniques of production. Those where labor is more expensive will employ relatively more capital-intensive techniques.

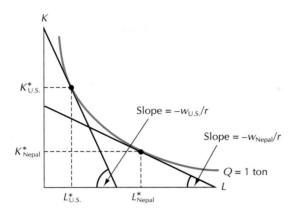

DIFFERENT WAYS OF PRODUCING 1 TON OF GRAVEL

EXERCISE 10-7

Repeat the previous exercise but now suppose capital and labor are perfect substitutes in a one-to-one ratio: $Q = K + L$.

APPLICATION: UNIONS AND MINIMUM WAGES

American labor unions have historically been among the most outspoken proponents of minimum wage legislation. They favor not only higher levels of the minimum wage, but also broader coverage. Yet almost all members of the Teamsters, AFL-CIO, or United Auto Workers unions already earn substantially more than the minimum wage, and so are not directly affected by changes in the legislation. Why, then, do these unions devote such great effort and expense to lobbying in favor of minimum wages?

One reason might be that their members are genuinely concerned about the economic well-being of workers less fortunate than themselves. No doubt many do feel such concern. But there are other disadvantaged groups—many of them even more deserving of help than low-wage workers—on whose behalf the unions might also have lobbied. Why doesn't the AFL-CIO work just as hard, for example, trying to get extra benefits for homeless children, or for the physically handicapped?

An understanding of the condition for production at minimum cost helps answer these questions. Note first that, on the average, union workers tend to be more skilled than nonunion workers. Unskilled labor and skilled labor are substitutes for one another in many production processes, giving rise to isoquants shaped something like the one shown in Figure 10-14. What mix of the

FIGURE 10-14
Unskilled labor and skilled labor are substitutes for one another in many production processes. When the price of unskilled labor rises, the slope of the isocost line rises, causing many firms to increase their employment of skilled (unionized) labor.

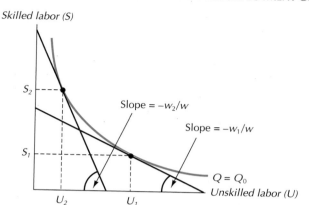

THE EFFECT OF A MINIMUM WAGE LAW ON EMPLOYMENT OF SKILLED LABOR

two skill categories the firm chooses to use will depend strongly on relative prices. Figure 10-14 shows the least costly mix for producing $Q = Q_0$ both before and after the enactment of the minimum wage statute. The wage rate for skilled labor is denoted by w. The prelegislation price of unskilled labor is w_1, which rises to w_2 after enactment of the law. The immediate effect is to increase the absolute value of the slope of the isocost line from w_1/w to w_2/w, causing the firm to increase its employment of skilled labor from S_1 to S_2, simultaneously reducing its employment of unskilled (nonunion) labor from U_1 to U_2.

Although most union workers are not affected directly by the minimum wage laws, these laws have the indirect consequence of increasing the demand for union labor.[12] Even if unions lacked their avowed concern for the well-being of unskilled, largely nonunion workers, there would thus be little mystery why unions devote so much of their resources in support of extensions of minimum wage legislation.

APPLICATION: RESTROOM MAINTENANCE

The substitution of capital for labor is sometimes motivated not by a change in factor prices, but by the introduction of new ideas. Consider, for example, the "offical toilet project" initiated several years ago by Jos van Bedaf, head manager of cleaning for the Schiphol airport in Amsterdam.[13] His problem was that the airport men's rooms, which were used by more than 100,000 patrons a year,

---

[12]Note that this example assumes that the firm will produce the same level of output after the minimum wage hike as before. As we will see in the next chapter, however, the firm will generally produce less output than before. If the output reduction is large enough, it could offset the firm's switch to skilled labor.

[13]This example is based on Stefan Verhagen, "Fly in the Pot," *Cornell Business*, April 21, 1992.

had a tendency to become messy and smelly despite frequent cleanings. Mr. van Bedaf's solution was not to intensify the efforts of maintenance crews but to make a minor change in the restroom equipment. Specifically, he requested that his sanitation equipment manufacturer supply the airport with urinals with the image of a housefly baked onto the center of each fixture's glazed ceramic surface. His theory was that the presence of this target would cause patrons to be much more accurate in their use of the facilities. The result? Dramatically cleaner facilities and a 20 percent reduction in cleaning costs. A national newspaper in the Netherlands rated the Schiphol facilities first on a list of clean restrooms.

THE RELATIONSHIP BETWEEN OPTIMAL INPUT CHOICE AND LONG-RUN COSTS

Given sufficient time to adjust, the firm can always buy the cost-minimizing input bundle that corresponds to any particular output level and relative input prices. To see how the firm's costs vary with output in the long run, we need only compare the costs of the respective optimal input bundles.

Output expansion path
The locus of tangencies (minimum-cost input combinations) traced out by an isocost line of given slope as it shifts outward into the isoquant map for a production process.

The curve labeled EE in Figure 10-15 shows the firm's *output expansion path.* It is the set of cost-minimizing input bundles when the input price ratio is fixed at w/r. Thus, when the price of K is r and the price of L is w, the cheapest way to produce Q_1 units of output is to use the input bundle S, which contains K_1^* units of K, L_1^* units of L, and costs TC_1. The bundle S is therefore one point on the output expansion path. In like fashion, the output level Q_2 is associated with bundle T, which has a total cost of TC_2; Q_3 is associated with U, which costs TC_3; and so on. In the theory of firm behavior, the long-run expansion path is the analog to the income-consumption curve in the theory of the consumer.

FIGURE 10-15
With fixed input prices r and w, bundles S, T, U, and others along the locus EE represent the least costly ways of producing the corresponding levels of output.

THE LONG-RUN EXPANSION PATH

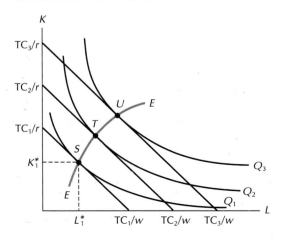

FIGURE 10-16
In the long run, the firm always has the option of ceasing operations and ridding itself of all its inputs. This means that the long-run total cost curve (top panel) will always pass through the origin. The long-run average and long-run marginal cost curves (bottom panel) are derived from the long-run total cost curves in a manner completely analogous to the short-run case.

THE LONG-RUN TOTAL, AVERAGE, AND MARGINAL COST CURVES

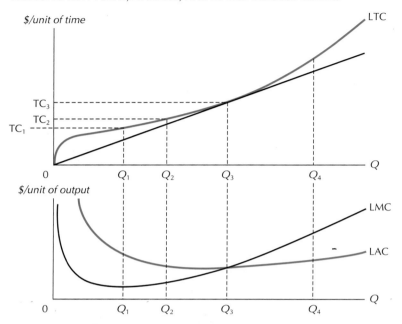

To go from the long-run expansion path to the long-run total cost curve, we simply plot the relevant quantity-cost pairs from Figure 10-15. Thus, the output level Q_1 corresponds to a long-run total cost of TC_1, Q_2 to TC_2, and so on. The result is the curve labeled LTC in the top panel in Figure 10-16. In the long run there is no need to distinguish among total, fixed, and variable costs, since all costs are variable.

The LTC curve will always pass through the origin because in the long run the firm can liquidate all of its inputs. If the firm elects to produce no output, it need not retain, or pay for, the services of any of its inputs. The shape of the LTC curve shown in the top panel looks very much like that of the short-run total cost curve shown in Figure 10-2. But this need not always be the case, as we will presently see. For the moment, though, let us take the shape of the LTC curve in the top panel in Figure 10-15 as given and ask what it implies for the long-run average and marginal cost curves.

Analogously to the short-run case, long-run marginal cost (LMC) is the slope of the long-run total cost curve:

$$LMC_Q = \frac{\Delta LTC_Q}{\Delta Q}. \tag{10.23}$$

In words, LMC is the cost to the firm, in the long run, of expanding its output by 1 unit.

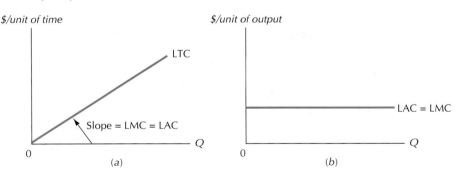

THE LTC, LMC, AND LAC CURVES WITH CONSTANT RETURNS TO SCALE

Long-run average cost (LAC) is the ratio of long-run total cost to output:

$$LAC_Q = \frac{LTC_Q}{Q} \tag{10.24}$$

Again, there is no need to discuss the distinctions among average total, fixed, and variable costs, since all long-run costs are variable.

The bottom panel in Figure 10-16 shows the LAC and LMC curves that correspond to the LTC curve shown in the top panel. The slope of the LTC curve is diminishing up to the output level Q_1 and increasing thereafter, which means that the LMC curve takes its minimum value at Q_1. The slope of LTC and the slope of the ray to LTC are the same at Q_3, which means that LAC and LMC intersect at that level of output. And again as before, the traditional average-marginal relationship holds: LAC is declining whenever LMC lies below it, and rising whenever LMC lies above it.

For a constant return to scale production function, doubling output exactly doubles costs.[14] Tripling all inputs triples output and triples costs, and so on. For the case of constant returns to scale, long-run total costs are thus exactly proportional to output. As shown in Figure 10-17a, the LTC curve for a production function with constant returns to scale is a straight line through the origin. Because the slope of LTC is constant, the associated LMC curve is a horizontal line, and is exactly the same as the LAC curve (Figure 10-17b).

When the production function has decreasing returns to scale, a given proportional increase in output requires a greater proportional increase in all inputs and hence a greater proportional increase in costs. The LTC, LMC, and LAC curves for a production function with decreasing returns to scale are shown in Figure 10-18. For the particular LTC curve shown in Figure 10-18a,

---

[14]Assuming, of course, that input prices remain the same as output varies.

FIGURE 10-18
Under decreasing returns, output grows less than in proportion to the growth in inputs, which means that total cost grows more than in proportion to growth in output.

THE LTC, LAC, AND LMC CURVES FOR A PRODUCTION PROCESS WITH DECREASING RETURNS TO SCALE

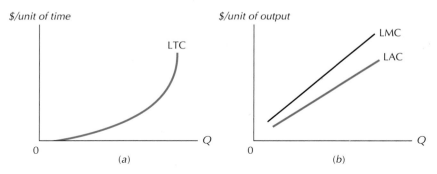

FIGURE 10-19
With increasing returns, the large-scale firm has lower average and marginal costs than the smaller-scale firm.

THE LTC, LAC, AND LMC CURVES FOR A PRODUCTION PROCESS WITH INCREASING RETURNS TO SCALE

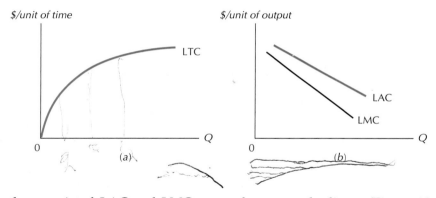

the associated LAC and LMC curves happen to be linear (Figure 10-18*b*), but this need not always happen. The general property of the decreasing returns case is that it gives rise to an upward-curving LTC curve, and upward-sloping LAC and LMC curves. Note yet another application of the average-marginal relationship: the fact that LMC exceeds LAC ensures that LAC must rise with output.

Consider, finally, the case of increasing returns to scale. Here, output grows more than in proportion to the increase in inputs. In consequence, long-run total cost rises less than in proportion to increases in output, as shown in Figure 10-17*a*. The accompanying LAC and LMC curves are shown in Figure 10-17*b*. The distinguishing feature of the LAC and LMC curves under increasing returns to scale is not the linear form shown in this particular example, but the fact that they are downward sloping.

The production processes whose long-run cost curves are pictured in Figure 10-17 to Figure 10-19 are "pure cases," exhibiting constant, decreasing, and increasing returns to scale, respectively, over their entire ranges of output. As

FIGURE 10-20
(a) LAC curves that slope downward throughout tend to be characteristic of natural monopolies. Unit costs are lowest when only one firm serves the entire market. (b) U-shaped LAC curves whose minimum points occur at a substantial share of total market output are characteristic of markets served by only a small handful of firms.

LAC CURVES CHARACTERISTIC OF HIGHLY CONCENTRATED INDUSTRIAL STRUCTURES

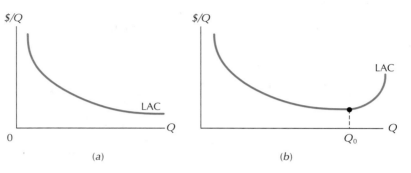

discussed in Chapter 9, however, the degree of returns to scale of a production function need not be the same over the whole range of output.

Long-Run Costs and the Structure of Industry

As noted in the preview to this chapter, long-run costs are important because of their effect on the structure of industry. A detailed elaboration of this role will be the subject of the coming chapters. Here, a brief overview of the key issues will help set the stage for that discussion.

When, as in Figure 10-20a, there are declining long-run average costs throughout, the tendency will be for a single firm to serve the market. If two firms attempted to serve such a market, with each producing only part of the total output sold, each would have higher average costs than if one of them alone served the market. The tendency in such a market will be for the firm that happens to grow larger to have a cost advantage that enables it to eliminate its rival. Markets characterized by declining long-run average cost curves are for this reason often referred to as **natural monopolies.**

Natural monopoly An industry whose market output is produced at the lowest cost when production is concentrated in the hands of a single firm.

Consider now the LAC curve shown in Figure 10-20b. The minimum point on this curve occurs at the output level Q_0. At that output level, the firm achieves its lowest possible unit cost of production. The output level Q_0 may be called the *minimum efficient scale:* the level of production required for LAC to reach its minimum level. If Q_0 constitutes a substantial share of industry output—more than, say, 20 percent—the industry will tend to be dominated by a small handful of firms. As in the natural monopoly case, a large number of small firms would be unlikely to survive in such a market, since each would have much higher average costs than larger firms. By contrast to the natural monopoly case, however, the upturn in the LAC beyond Q_0 will make it difficult for a single firm to serve the entire market. Markets served by firms with LACs like the one in Figure 10-20b are likely to be "highly concentrated," which means that a small number of firms will tend to account for the lion's share of all output sold.

FIGURE 10-21
The requirement for survival in any market is that a firm have the lowest possible unit costs. If the minimum point of a U-shaped LAC (Q_0 in panel *a*) occurs at a small fraction of market output, or if LAC is everywhere flat or rising (panels *b* and *c*, respectively), then small size and survival are compatible. Each firm will tend to produce only a small share of total market output.

LAC CURVES CHARACTERISTIC OF UNCONCENTRATED INDUSTRY STRUCTURES

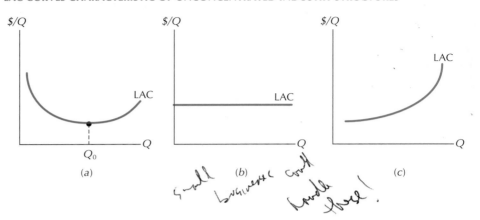

The long-run average cost curve associated with a market served by many firms is likely to take one of the three forms shown in Figure 10-21. If Q_0, the minimum point on the U-shaped average cost curve in panel *a*, constitutes only a small fraction of total industry output, we expect to see an industry populated by numerous firms, each of which produces only a small percentage of total industry output. Small size is also not a disadvantage when the production process is one that gives rise to a horizontal LAC curve like the one shown in panel *b*. For such processes, all firms—large or small—have the same unit costs of production. For the upward-sloping LAC curve shown in panel *c* in Figure 10-21, small size is not only compatible with survival in the marketplace but positively required, since large firms will always have higher average costs than smaller ones. As a practical matter, however, it is very unlikely that there could ever be an LAC curve that is upward sloping even at extremely small levels of output. (Imagine, for example, the unit costs of a firm that tried to produce $\frac{1}{100}$ of a pound of sugar.)

The relationship between market structure and the shape of the long-run average cost curve derives from the fact that, in the face of competition, market survival requires firms to have the lowest unit costs possible under existing production technology. Whether that happens at low or high levels of output depends entirely on the shape of the LAC curve.

The Relationship Between Long-Run and Short-Run Cost Curves

One way of thinking of the LAC curve is as an "envelope" of all the short-run average cost (SAC) curves. Suppose the SAC curves that correspond to 10,000 different levels of K were drawn in a diagram like Figure 10-22. If we then took a string and molded it to the outer contour of these SAC curves, it would trace out the shape of the LAC curve. In Figure 10-22, note that for the output level at which a given SAC is tangent to the LAC, the long-run marginal cost (LMC) of produc-

FIGURE 10-22
The LAC curve is the
"outer envelope" of
the SAC curves.
LMC = SMC at the
Q value for which
the SAC is tangent to
the LAC. At the min-
imum point on the
LAC, LMC = SMC
= SAC = LAC.

THE FAMILY OF COST CURVES ASSOCIATED WITH A U-SHAPED LAC

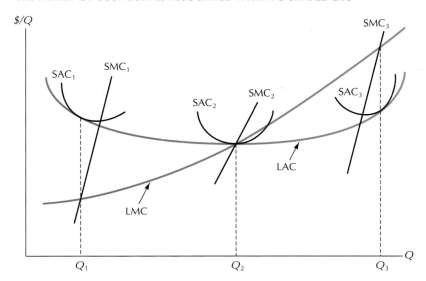

ing that level of output is the same as the short-run marginal cost (SMC). Thus, $LMC(Q_1) = SMC(Q_1)$, $LMC(Q_2) = SMC(Q_2)$, and $LMC(Q_3) = SMC(Q_3)$ (see foot-note 15). Note also that each point along a given SAC curve, except for the tangency point, lies above the corresponding point on the LAC curve. Note, finally, that at the minimum point on the LAC curve in Figure 10-22 ($Q = Q_2$), the long-run and short-run marginal and average costs all take exactly the same value.

Some intuition about the SAC-LAC relationship for a given SAC curve is afforded by noting that to the left of the SAC-LAC tangency, the firm has "too much" capital, with the result that its fixed costs are higher than necessary; and that to the right of the tangency, the firm has "too little" capital, so that dimin-ishing returns to labor drive its costs up. Only at the tangency point does the firm have the optimal quantities of both labor and capital for producing the cor-responding level of output.

Summary

Of all the topics covered in an intermediate microeconomics text, students usually find the material on cost curves by far the most difficult to digest. And for good reason, since the sheer volume of specific concepts can easily seem overwhelming

---

[15]These relationships are developed in greater detail in the appendix to this chapter in the "For the Instructor" section at our Web site www.mhhe.com/economics/frank4.

at first encounter. It is important to bear in mind, therefore, that all the various cost curves can be derived from the underlying production relationships in a very simple and straightforward manner.

Short-run cost curves, for example, all follow directly from the short-run production function. All short-run production functions we have discussed involved one fixed factor and one variable factor, but the theory would be exactly the same in the case of more than one fixed input. Short-run total costs are decomposed into fixed and variable costs, which correspond, respectively, to payments to the fixed and variable factors of production. Because of the law of diminishing returns, beyond some point we require ever larger increments of the variable input to produce an extra unit of output. The result is that short-run marginal cost, which is the slope of the short-run total cost curve, is increasing with output in the region of diminishing returns. Diminishing returns are also responsible for the fact that short-run average total and variable cost curves—which are, respectively, the slopes of the rays to the short-run total and variable cost curves—eventually rise with output. Average fixed costs always take the form of a rectangular hyperbola, approaching infinity as output shrinks toward zero, and falling toward zero as output grows increasingly large.

The problem of allocating a given production quota to two different production facilities is similar to the problem of allocating an available input across two different facilities. In the latter case, the goal is to maximize the amount of output that can be produced with a given amount of input. In the former, it is to produce a given level of output at the lowest total cost. The solution is to allocate the production quota so that the marginal cost is the same in each production process. This solution does not require that average costs be the same in each process, and in practice, they often differ substantially.

The optimal input bundle for producing a given output level in the long run will depend on the relative prices of the factors of production. These relative prices determine the slope of the isocost line, which is the locus of input bundles that can be purchased for a given total cost. The optimal input bundle will be the one that lies at the point of tangency between an isocost line and the desired isoquant. At the cost-minimizing point, the ratio of the marginal product of an input to its price will be the same for every input. Put another way, the extra output obtained from the last dollar spent on one input must be the same as the extra output obtained from the last dollar spent on any other input. Still another way of stating the minimum-cost condition is that the marginal rate of technical substitution at the optimizing bundle must be the same as the slope of the isocost line.

These properties of production at minimum cost help us understand why methods of production often differ sharply when relative factor prices differ sharply. We saw, for example, that it helps explain why developing countries often use labor-intensive techniques while their industrial counterparts choose much more capital-intensive ones, and why labor unions often lobby on behalf of increased minimum wages, even though virtually all of their members earn more than the minimum wage to begin with.

For a given level of output, long-run total costs can never be larger than short-run total costs for the simple reason that we have the opportunity to adjust all of our inputs in the long run, only some of them in the short run. The slope of the long-run average cost curve is a direct reflection of the degree of returns to scale in production. When there are increasing returns, LAC declines with output. With decreasing returns, by contrast, LAC rises with output. And finally, constant returns in production give rise to a horizontal LAC. A U-shaped LAC is one that corresponds to a production process that exhibits first increasing, then constant, and finally decreasing returns to scale. No matter what its shape, the LAC curve will always be an envelope of the corresponding family of SAC curves, each of which will be tangent to the LAC at one and only one point. At the output levels that correspond to these points of tangency, LMC and the corresponding SMC will be the same.

The relationship between market structure and long-run costs derives from the fact that survival in the marketplace requires firms to have the lowest costs possible with available production technologies. If the LAC curve is downward sloping, lowest costs occur when only one firm serves the market. If the LAC curve is U-shaped and its minimum point occurs at a quantity that corresponds to a substantial share of total market output, the lowest costs will occur when only a few firms serve the market. By contrast, if the minimum point on a U-shaped LAC curve corresponds to only a small fraction of total industry output, the market is likely to be served by many competing firms. The same will be true when the LAC curve is either horizontal or upward sloping.

An appendix to this chapter (see the "For the Instructor" section at our Web site www.mhhe.com/economics/frank4) considers the relationship between long-run and short-run costs in greater detail. It also develops the calculus approach to cost minimization.

Questions for Review

1. What is the relationship between the law of diminishing returns and the curvature of the variable cost curve?

2. What is the relationship between the law of diminishing returns and the slope of the short-run marginal cost curve?

3. In which production process is fixed cost likely to be a larger percentage of short-run total costs, book publishing or landscape gardening?

4. Why does the short-run MC curve cut both the ATC and AVC curves at their minimum points?

5. If the LAC curve is rising beyond some point, what can we say about the degree of returns to scale in production?

6. Why should the production of a fixed amount of output be allocated between two production activities so that the marginal cost is the same in each?

Problems

1. The Preservation Embalming Company's cost data have been partially entered in the table below. Following the sudden and unexpected death of the company's accountant, you are called on to fill in the missing entries.

Bodies embalmed	Total cost	Fixed cost	Variable cost	ATC	AVC	AFC	MC
0	24			–	–	–	
							16
1							
2			50				
3	108						
							52
4							
5					39.2		
6					47		

2. Sketch the short-run TC, VC, FC, ATC, AVC, AFC, and MC curves for the production function

$$Q = 3KL,$$

where K is fixed at 2 units in the short run, with $r = 3$ and $w = 2$.

3. When the average product of labor is the same as the marginal product of labor, how will marginal cost compare with average variable cost?

4. A firm has access to two production processes with the following marginal cost curves: $MC_1 = 0.4Q$ and $MC_2 = 2 + 0.2Q$.

   a. If it wants to produce 8 units of output, how much should it produce with each process?

   b. If it wants to produce 4 units of output?

5. A firm uses two inputs, K and L, in its production process and finds that no matter how much output it produces or how input prices vary, it always minimizes its costs by buying only one or the other of the two inputs. Draw this firm's isoquant map.

6. A firm finds that no matter how much output it produces and no matter how input prices vary, it always minimizes its costs by buying half as many units of capital as of labor. Draw this firm's isoquant map.

7. A firm purchases capital and labor in competitive markets at prices of $r = 6$ and $w = 4$, respectively. With the firm's current input mix, the marginal product of capital is 12 and the marginal product of labor is 18. Is this firm minimizing its costs? If so, explain how you know. If not, explain what the firm ought to do.

8. A firm has a production function $Q = F(K, L)$ with constant returns to scale. Input prices are $r = 2$ and $w = 1$. The output-expansion path for this production function at these input prices is a straight line through the origin. When it produces 5 units of output, it uses 2 units of K and 3 units of L. How much K and L will it use when its long-run total cost is equal to 70?

9. A firm with the production function $Q = F(K, L)$ is producing an output level Q^* at minimum cost in the long run. How will its short-run marginal cost when K is fixed compare with its short-run marginal cost when L is fixed?

10. A firm employs a production function $Q = F(K, L)$ for which only two values of K are possible, K_1 and K_2. Its SAC curve when $K = K_1$ is given by $SAC_1 = Q^2 - 4Q + 6$. The corresponding curve for $K = K_2$ is $SAC_2 = Q^2 - 8Q + 18$. What is this firm's LAC curve?

11. If a firm's LMC curve lies above its SMC curve at a given level of output, what will be the relationship between its SAC and LAC curves at that output level?

*12. A firm has a long-run total cost function:

$$LRTC(Q) = Q^3 - 20Q^2 + 220Q.$$

Derive expressions for long-run average cost and marginal cost, and sketch these curves.

*13. For the long-run total cost function

$$LRTC(Q) = Q^2 + 10,$$

sketch ATC, AVC, AFC, and MC.

*These problems are most easily solved using the calculus definition of marginal cost.

Answers to In-Chapter Exercises

10-1. The variable cost curve is the same as before; the FC and TC curves are shifted upward by 8 units. (See the following graph.)

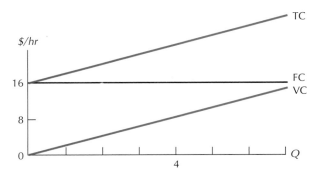

10-2. The vertical distance between the ATC and AVC curves is AFC. So we have $ATC_{10} - AVC_{10} = FC/10 = 20/10 = 2$.

10-3. Equating marginal costs, we have $12Q^A = 4Q^B$. Substituting $Q^B = 12 - Q^A$ yields $12Q^A = 48 - 4Q^A$, which solves for $Q^A = 3$. $Q^B = 12 - 3 = 9$ takes care of remaining output, and at these output levels, marginal cost in both plants will be \$36/unit of output.

10-4. When marginal product lies above average product, marginal cost lies below average variable cost. (See Figure 10-9.)

10-5.

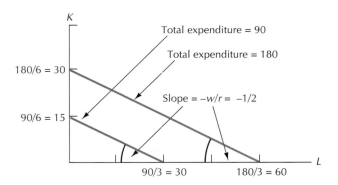

10-6. To produce 20 units of output, we will need $L = K = 20$. As $r = 10$ and $w = 5$, costs are

$$C = 10K + 5L = 200 + 100 = 300,$$

which may be rewritten as $K = 30 - \frac{1}{2}L$ in slope-intercept form. When the wage rises to $w = 20$, keeping costs at $C = 300$ requires that we find the point at which $K = L$ on the new isocost curve

$$C = 10K + 20L = 300,$$

which may be rewritten as $K = 30 - 2L$ in slope-intercept form. Setting $K = L$, we have

$$10K + 20L = 300 = 10L + 20L = 300 = 30L = 300 \rightarrow L = 10.$$

Thus, $L = K = 10$ and we produce $Q = 10$.

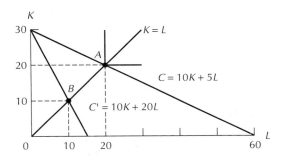

10-7. To produce 20 units of output, we will need $L = 20$ or $K = 20$. Since $r = 10$ and $w = 5$, costs are

$$C = \min \{10K, 5L\} = \min \{200, 100\} = 100.$$

When the wage rises to $w = 20$, keeping costs at $C = 100$ implies that

$$Q = \max\left\{\frac{100}{r}, \frac{100}{w}\right\} = \max\{10, 5\} = 10.$$

Thus, we use no labor ($L = 0$), all capital ($K = 10$), and produce $Q = 10$.

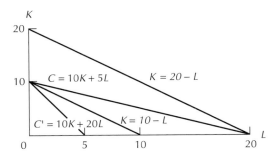

CHAPTER 11

Perfect Competition

Imagine yourself a member of the Colorado state legislature. You have been asked to vote for a bill whose purpose is to alleviate poverty among farmers in a rural county. Farmers in that county rent their farmland from landowners and are allowed to keep the proceeds from the sale of the crops they grow. Because of limited rainfall, their crops are usually meager, resulting in very low incomes for the average worker. The bill under consideration would authorize public funds to construct an irrigation system that would double the crop yields on the land in the county.

You strongly favor the objective of the bill and are about to vote in favor of it when you meet with your legislative aide, an intern who majored in economics in college. She urges you in the strongest possible terms not to vote for the bill. She concedes that the project would double crop yields, and she too is sympathetic to the goal of providing improved conditions for farmers. Even so, she insists that the bill would have little or no long-run effect on the earnings of farmers. Your aide has given you sound advice on similar matters in the past, and you decide to hear her out.

Chapter Preview

In this chapter we develop the analytical tools necessary for our hypothetical state legislator to assess his aide's advice, including a model of price and output determination in perfectly competitive markets. Our first step is to characterize the competitive firm's objective as that of earning the highest possible profits. This is clearly not the only goal a firm might pursue, but we will see several reasons why firms might often behave as if profits were all they cared about.

We then consider the four conditions that define a perfectly competitive market: (1) the existence of a standardized product, (2) price-taking behavior on the part of firms, (3) perfect long-run mobility of factors of production, and (4) perfect information on the part of consumers and firms. It turns out that none of these conditions is likely to be satisfied in practice for any industry. Nonetheless, we will see that the economic model of perfect competition often generates useful insights even when its structural preconditions are only approximately satisfied.

Next, using the cost curves discussed in Chapter 10, we derive the necessary condition for profit maximization in the short run. The rule calls for the firm to produce an output level at which its short-run marginal cost is equal to the price of the product. We will see that implementation of this rule fortunately does not require that firms have a detailed understanding of the economist's concept of marginal cost.

From the individual firm's supply decision, we move to the issue of industrywide supply. The technique for generating the industry supply schedule turns out to be closely analogous to the one for aggregating individual demand curves into a market demand curve: we simply add the individual firms' supply curves horizontally.

The industry short-run supply and demand curves interact to determine the short-run market price, which forms the basis for output decisions by individual firms. We will see that a firm's short-run profitability acts as a signal governing the movement of resources into and out of the industry—more specifically, that profits prompt resources to enter while losses prompt them to leave.

We will see that in the long run, if tastes and technology are unchanging, a competitive industry whose firms have U-shaped LAC curves will settle at an equilibrium price equal to the minimum value of the LAC curve. And we will also see that, under certain conditions, it will not be possible in such a market for anyone to enter into additional transactions that would benefit some people without at the same time harming some others.

The Goal of Profit Maximization

In studying not only perfect competition but also a variety of other market structures, economists traditionally assume that the firm's central objective is to maximize profit. Two things must be said about this assumption. The first is to clarify just what is meant by the term "profit," and the second is to explain why it often makes sense to assume that firms try to maximize it.

Profit—or, more precisely, *economic profit*—is defined as the difference between total revenue and total cost, where total cost includes all costs—both explicit and implicit—associated with resources used by the firm. This definition is significantly different from the one used by accountants and many other noneconomists, which does not subtract opportunity or implicit costs from total revenue. *Accounting profit* is simply total revenue less all explicit costs incurred.

To illustrate the distinction, suppose a firm produces 100 units of output per week by using 10 units of capital and 10 units of labor. Suppose the weekly price of each factor is $10/unit, and the firm owns its 10 units of capital. If output sells for $2.50/unit, the firm's total revenue will be $250/wk. To calculate the week's economic profit, we subtract from $250 the $100 spent on labor (an explicit cost) and the $100 opportunity cost of capital (an implicit cost), which leaves $50. (Under the assumption that the firm could have rented its capital to some other firm at the weekly rate of $10/unit, the $100 opportunity cost is simply the earnings forgone by using the capital in its own operation.) The week's accounting profit for this firm, by contrast, is $150, the difference between the $250 total revenue and the $100 out-of-pocket expenditure for labor.

Accounting profit may be thought of as the sum of two components: (1) *normal profit*, which is the opportunity cost of the resources owned by the firm (in this example, $100), and (2) economic profit, as defined above (here, $50). Economic profit is profit over and above the normal profit level.

The importance of the distinction between accounting and economic profits is driven home forcefully—if a bit fancifully—by the following example.

EXAMPLE 11-1 *Cullen Perot runs a miniature golf course in Valdosta, Georgia. He rents the course and equipment from a large recreational supply company and supplies his own labor. His monthly earnings, net of rental payments, are $800, and he considers working at the golf course just as attractive as his only other alternative, working as a grocery clerk for $800/mo.*

Now Cullen learns that his Uncle Ross has died and left him some land in New York City (the parcel bounded by the streets shown in Figure 11-1). The land has been cleared, and Cullen discovers that a construction company is willing to install and maintain a miniature golf course on it for a payment of $4000/mo. Cullen also commissions a market survey, which

FIGURE 11-1 POTENTIAL SITE FOR A MANHATTAN MINIATURE GOLF COURSE

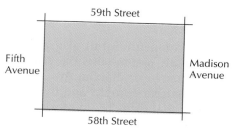

reveals that he would collect $16,000/mo in revenue by operating a miniature golf course there. (After all, there are many more potential golfers in Manhattan than in Valdosta.) After deducting the $4000/mo payment to the construction company, this would leave him with $12,000/mo free and clear. Given these figures, and assuming that the cost of living is the same in New York as in Valdosta, should Cullen, a profit maximizer, switch his operation to Manhattan?

Since he is a profit maximizer, he should switch to Manhattan only if his economic profit there will be higher than in Valdosta. Suppose, however, that Cullen is unfamiliar with the concept of economic profit and instead compares his accounting profits in the two locations. In Valdosta, his accounting profit is $800/mo, the amount he has left over after paying all his bills. In Manhattan, the corresponding figure will be $12,000/mo. On this comparison, he would quickly forsake Valdosta for New York.

If he compares economic profits, however, he will reach precisely the opposite conclusion. In Valdosta, his economic profit is zero once we account for the opportunity cost of his labor. (He could have earned $800/mo as a grocery clerk, exactly the amount of his accounting profit.) To calculate what his economic profits would be in New York, we must deduct from his $12,000/mo accounting profits not only the $800 monthly opportunity cost of his labor, but also the opportunity cost of his land. Few locations on earth command higher land prices than midtown Manhattan. Suppose we conservatively estimate that Cullen's land would sell for $100,000,000 in today's real estate market, and suppose that the interest rate is 1 percent/mo. The opportunity cost of devoting the land to a miniature golf course will then be $(0.01) \times (\$100,000,000) = \$1,000,000/mo$, which makes his monthly economic profit in Manhattan equal to $\$12,000 - \$800 - \$1,000,000 = -\$988,800$. Thus, if we assign any reasonable value to the opportunity cost of his land, it will obviously be better for Cullen to sell or rent it and remain in Valdosta. The reason Manhattan real estate is so expensive is that people can build skyscrapers on it and charge high rents to a multitude of tenants. To build a miniature golf course in midtown Manhattan would be like wearing diamonds on the soles of your shoes.

EXERCISE 11-1

In Example 11-1, how low would the monthly interest rate have to be before Cullen should relocate to Manhattan?

Let's turn now to the assumption of profit maximization. In order to predict what any entity—a firm, person, committee, or government—will do under specific conditions, some sort of assumption must be made about its goals. After all, if we know where people want to go, it's much easier to predict what they'll do to get there. Economists assume that the goal of firms is to maximize economic profits; then they try to discover what specific behaviors contribute to that objective.

Numerous challenges have been raised to the profit-maximization assumption. Some critics say the firm's goal is to maximize its chances of survival; others believe that it wants to maximize total sales or total revenues; and some even claim that firms don't try to maximize anything at all.

One reason for such skepticism is that examples abound in which the managers of firms appear incompetent and too poorly informed to take the kinds of actions required for maximizing profits. It is important to understand, however, that the assumption of profit maximization is not refuted by the existence of incompetent managers. On the contrary, a case can be made that, even in a world in which the actions of firms are initially random, there will be a long-run tendency for profit-maximizing behavior eventually to dominate.[1]

The argument is directly analogous to Charles Darwin's theory of evolution by natural selection, and it goes roughly as follows. First, in a world of random action, some firms will, purely by chance, come much closer than others to profit-maximizing behavior. The result will be that the former firms will have greater surplus revenues at their disposal, which will enable them to grow faster than their rivals. The other side of this coin is that firms whose behavior deviates most sharply from profit maximization are the ones most likely to go bankrupt. In the animal kingdom, food is an essential resource for survival, and profits play a parallel role in the competitive marketplace. Those firms with the highest profits are often considerably more likely to survive. The evolutionary argument concludes that, over long periods of time, behavior will tend toward profit maximization purely as a result of selection pressures in the competitive environment.

But the forces in support of profit maximization are not limited to the unintentional pressures of natural selection. They also include the actions of people who are very consciously pursuing their own interests. Bankers and other moneylenders, for example, are eager to keep their risks to a minimum, and for this reason, they prefer to do business with highly profitable firms. In addition to having more internal resources, such firms thus have easier access to external sources of capital to finance their growth. Another important force supporting profit-maximizing behavior is the threat of an outside takeover. The price of shares of stock in a firm is based on the firm's profitability (more on this point in Chapter 15), with the result that shares of stock of a non-profit-maximizing firm will often sell for much less than their potential value. This creates an opportunity for an outsider to buy the stock at a bargain price and then drive its price upward by altering the firm's behavior.

---

[1]See, for example, Armen Alchian, "Uncertainty, Evolution, and Economic Theory," *Journal of Political Economy*, 1950.

Another pressure in favor of profit maximization is that the owners of many firms compensate their managers in part by giving them a share of the firm's profits. This provides a clear financial incentive for managers to enhance profitability whenever and wherever opportunities arise for them to do so.

Let us note, finally, that the assumption of profit maximization does not imply that firms conduct their operations in the most efficient conceivable manner at all times. In the world we live in there are not only many intelligent, competent managers, but also a multitude who possess neither of these attributes. Needless to say, not every task can be assigned to the most competent person in the universe. In a sensible world, the most important tasks will be carried out by the best managers, the less important tasks by less competent ones. So the mere fact that we often observe firms doing silly things does not establish that they are not maximizing profits. To maximize profits means simply to do the best one can under the circumstances, and that will sometimes mean having to muddle along with uninspired managers.

Taken as a whole, the foregoing observations lend support to the assumption of profit maximization. We might even say that they place the burden of proof on those who insist that firms do not maximize profits. But they obviously do not establish conclusively that firms always pursue profits at the expense of all other goals. This remains an empirical question, and in the chapters to come we will see some evidence that firms sometimes fall short. Even so, the assumption of profit maximization is a good place to begin our analysis of firm behavior, and there is no question but that it provides useful insights into how firms respond to changes in input or product prices, taxes, and other important features of their operating environments.

The Four Conditions for Perfect Competition

To predict how much output a competitive firm will produce, economists have developed the *theory of perfect competition*. Four conditions define the existence of a perfectly competitive market. Let us consider each of them in turn.

1. Firms sell a standardized product. In a perfectly competitive market, the product sold by one firm is assumed to be a perfect substitute for the product sold by any other. Interpreted literally, this is a condition that is rarely if ever satisfied. Connoisseurs of fine wines, for example, insist that they can tell the difference between wines made from the same variety of grape grown on estates only a few miles apart. It is also difficult to speak of a market for even such a simple commodity as shirts, because shirts come in so many different styles and quality levels. If we define the market sufficiently narrowly, however, it is sometimes possible to achieve a reasonable degree of similarity among the products produced by competing firms. For instance, "Midwestern spring wheat" may not be exactly the same on different farms, but it is close enough that most buyers don't care very much where the wheat comes from.

2. Firms are price takers. This means that the individual firm treats the market price of the product as given. More specifically, it must believe that the market price will not be affected by how much output it produces. This condition is likely to be satisfied when the market is served by a large number of firms, each one of which produces an all but imperceptible fraction of total industry output. But a large number of firms are not always necessary for price-taking behavior. Even if there are only two firms in the market, for example, each may behave as a price taker if it believes that other firms stand ready to enter its market at a moment's notice.

3. Factors of production are perfectly mobile in the long run. One implication of this condition is that if a firm perceives a profitable business opportunity at a given time and location, it will be able to hire the factors of production it needs in order to take advantage of it. Similarly, if its current venture no longer appears attractive in relation to alternative business ventures, it is free to discharge its factors of production, which will then move to industries where opportunities are stronger. Of course, no one believes that resources are perfectly mobile. Labor, in particular, is not likely to satisfy this condition. People buy homes, make friends, enroll their children in schools, and establish a host of other commitments that make it difficult to move from one place to another. Nonetheless, the perfect mobility assumption is often reasonably well satisfied in practice, especially if we take into account that it is not always necessary for labor to move geographically in order for it to be mobile in an economic sense. Indeed, the firm can often move to the worker, as happened when New England shoe and textile factories relocated in the South in order to employ the less expensive labor available there.

4. Firms and consumers have perfect information. A firm has no reason to leave its current industry if it has no way of knowing about the existence of more profitable opportunities elsewhere. Similarly, a consumer has no motive to switch from a high-priced product to a lower-priced one of identical quality unless she has information about the existence of the latter. Here too the required condition is never satisfied in a literal sense. The world is sufficiently complex that there will inevitably be relevant features of it hidden from view. As a practical matter, the assumption of perfect information is usually interpreted to mean that people can acquire most of the information that is most relevant to their choices without great difficulty. Even this more limited condition will fail in many cases. As we saw in Chapter 8, people often have the relevant information right at their fingertips and yet fail to make sensible use of it. These observations notwithstanding, we will see that the state of knowledge is often sufficient to provide a reasonable approximation to the perfect information condition.

To help assess whether the assumptions underlying the model of perfect competition are hopelessly restrictive, it is useful to compare them to the assumptions that underlie the physicist's model of objects in motion. If you have taken a high school or college physics course, then you know (or once knew) that a force applied to an object on a frictionless surface causes that object to acceler-ate at a rate inversely proportional to its mass. Thus, a given force applied to a 10-kilogram object will cause that object to accelerate at twice the rate we observe when the same force is applied to a 20-kilogram object.

To illustrate this theory, physics teachers show us films of what happens when various forces are applied to a hockey puck atop a large surface of dry ice. These physicists understand perfectly well that there is an easily measured amount of friction between the puck and the dry ice. But they are also aware that the friction levels there are so low that the model still provides reasonably accurate predictions.

In the kinds of situations we are most likely to encounter in practice, friction is seldom as low as between a puck and a dry ice surface. This will be painfully apparent to you, for example, if you have just taken a spill on your Harley Sport-ster. But even here the physicist's laws of motion apply, and we can make adjust-ments for friction in order to estimate just how far a fallen rider will slide. And even where the model cannot be calibrated precisely, it tells us that the rider will slide farther the faster he was going when he fell, and that he will slide farther if the pavement is wet or covered with sand or gravel than if it is clean and dry.

With the economic model of perfect competition, the issues are very similar. In some markets, most notably for agricultural products, the four conditions come close to being satisfied. The predictions of the competitive model in these cases are in many ways as precise as those of the physicist's model applied to the puck on dry ice. In other markets, such as those for garbage trucks or earth-moving equipment, at least some of the conditions are not even approximately satisfied. But even in these cases, the competitive model can tell us something useful if we interpret it with sufficient care.

The Short-Run Condition for Profit Maximization

The first question we want our model of competitive firm behavior to be able to answer is, "How does a firm choose its output level in the short run?" Under the assumption that the firm's goal is to maximize economic profit, it will choose that level of output for which the difference between total revenue and total cost is largest.

Consider a firm with the short-run total cost curve labeled TC in the top panel in Figure 11-2. Like many of the firms we discussed in Chapter 10, this firm expe-riences first increasing, then decreasing, returns to its variable input, which pro-duces the familiar pattern of curvature in its total cost curve. Suppose this firm can sell its output at a price of $P_0 = \$18/\text{unit}$. Its total revenue per week will then be $18/unit of output times the number of units of output sold each week. For example, if the firm sells no output, it earns zero total revenue; if it sells 10 units of output per week, it earns $180/wk; if it sells 20 units/wk, it earns $360/wk; and so on. So for the perfectly competitive firm, which can sell as much or as little output as it chooses at a constant market price, total revenue is exactly

FIGURE 11-2
The total revenue curve is the ray labeled TR in the top panel. The difference between it and total cost (TC in the top panel) is economic profit (Π_Q in the bottom panel). At $Q = 0$, $\Pi_Q = -FC = -30$. Economic profit reaches a maximum ($\$12.60$/wk) for $Q = 7.4$.

REVENUE, COST, AND ECONOMIC PROFIT

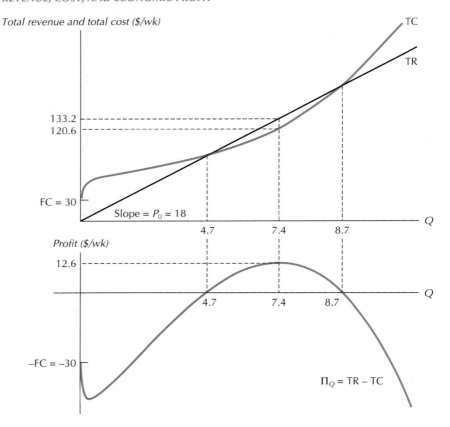

proportional to output. For the firm in this example, the total revenue curve is the line labeled TR in the top panel in Figure 11-2. It is a ray whose slope is equal to the product price, $P_0 = 18$.

The bottom panel in Figure 11-2 plots the difference between TR and TC, which is the curve labeled Π_Q, the notation traditionally used in economics to represent economic profit. Here, Π_Q is positive for output levels between $Q = 4.7$ and $Q = 8.7$, and reaches a maximum at $Q = 7.4$. For output levels less than 4.7 or greater than 8.7, the firm is earning economic losses, which is simply another way of saying that its economic profits are negative for those values of Q.

In the bottom panel in Figure 11-2, note also that the vertical intercept of the profit curve is equal to $-\$30$/wk, the negative of the firm's fixed cost. When the firm produces no output, it earns no revenue and incurs no variable cost but must still pay its fixed costs, so its profit when $Q = 0$ is simply $-FC$. If there were no positive output level for which the firm could earn higher profit than $-FC$, its best option would be to produce zero output in the short run.

Marginal revenue The change in total revenue that occurs as a result of a 1-unit change in sales.

The maximum profit point can also be characterized in terms of the relationship between output price and short-run marginal cost. Output price, which is equal to the slope of the total revenue curve, is also called *marginal revenue* (*MR*).[2] Marginal revenue is formally defined as *the change in revenue that occurs when the sale of output changes by 1 unit.* In the cost-benefit language of Chapter 1, MR is the benefit to the firm of selling an additional unit of output. If the firm wants to maximize its profits, it must weigh this benefit against the cost of selling an extra unit of output, which is its marginal cost.

The short-run marginal and average variable cost curves that correspond to the TC curve in Figure 11-2 are shown in Figure 11-3, where we again suppose that the firm can sell its output at a price of $P_0 = \$18/$unit. To maximize its economic profits, the firm should follow this rule: Provided P_0 is larger than the minimum value of AVC (more on the reason for this condition below), *the firm should produce a level of output for which marginal revenue, $P_0 = 18$, is equal to marginal cost on the rising portion of the MC curve.* For the particular cost curves shown in Figure 11-3, $P_0 = 18$ is indeed larger than the minimum value of AVC, and is equal to marginal cost at the quantity level $Q^* = 7.4$. The requirement that marginal revenue intersect marginal cost on the rising portion of marginal cost implies that marginal revenue intersects marginal cost from above. Thus marginal revenue lies below marginal cost past this point of intersection, and the firm has no incentive to expand output beyond this point (additional units would reduce profits).

As the following exercise demonstrates, the definitions of MR and MC tell us something about the relative values of the slopes of the TR and TC curves at the maximum-profit point in Figure 11-2.

FIGURE 11-3
A necessary condition for profit maximization is that price equal marginal cost on the rising portion of the marginal cost curve. Here, this happens at the output level $Q^* = 7.4$.

THE PROFIT-MAXIMIZING OUTPUT LEVEL IN THE SHORT RUN

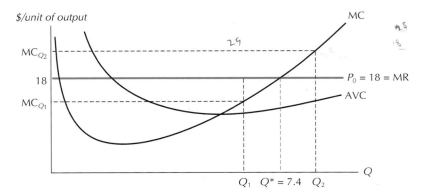

---

[2]As we will see in the next chapter, output price and marginal revenue are *not* the same for a monopolist.

EXERCISE 11-2

How do the slopes of the TC and TR curves compare at $Q = 7.4$ in Figure 11-2?

Why is "price = marginal cost" a necessary condition for profit maximization? Suppose we picked some other level of output, say, Q_1, that is less than Q^* = 7.4. The benefit to the firm of selling an additional unit of output will be P_0 = \$18 (its marginal revenue). The addition to total cost of producing an extra unit of output at Q_1 will be its marginal cost at the level of output, MC_{Q1}, which in Figure 11-3 is clearly less than \$18. It follows that for any level of output on the rising portion of the MC curve to the left of $Q^* = 7.4$, the benefit of expanding (as measured by marginal revenue) will be greater than the cost of expanding (as measured by marginal cost). This amounts to saying that profit will increase when we expand output from Q_1.

Now consider any level of output to the right of $Q^* = 7.4$, such as Q_2. At Q_2, the benefit of contracting output by 1 unit will be the resulting cost savings, which is marginal cost at that level of output, namely, MC_{Q2}. (Note here that we are using the term "benefit" to refer to the avoidance of a cost.) The cost to the firm of contracting output by 1 unit will be its marginal revenue, $P_0 = 18$, the loss in total revenue when it sells 1 unit less. (Here, not getting a benefit is a cost.) Since $MC_{Q2} > \$18$, the firm will save more than it loses when it contracts output by 1 unit. It follows that for any output level greater than $Q^* = 7.4$, the firm's profit will grow when it contracts output. The only output level at which the firm cannot earn higher profit by either expanding or contracting is $Q^* = 7.4$, the level for which the cost of any move is exactly equal to its benefit.[3]

---

[3]The firm's problem is to maximize $\Pi = PQ - TC_Q$, where TC_Q is the short-run total cost of producing Q units of output. The first-order condition for a maximum is given by

$$\frac{d\Pi}{dQ} = P - \frac{dTC_Q}{dQ} = P - MC_Q = 0,$$

which gives the condition $P = MC_Q$. The second-order condition for a maximum is given by

$$\frac{d^2\Pi}{dQ^2} = \frac{-dMC_Q}{dQ} < 0$$

or

$$\frac{dMC_Q}{dQ} > 0,$$

which tells us why we must be at a point on the rising portion of the marginal cost curve.

THE SHUTDOWN CONDITION

Shutdown condition If price falls below the minimum of average variable cost, the firm should shut down in the short run.

Recall that the rule for short-run profit maximization is to set price equal to marginal cost, provided price exceeds the minimum value of average variable cost. Why must price be greater than the minimum point of the AVC curve? The answer is that unless this condition is met, the firm will do better to shut down—that is, to produce no output—in the short run. To see why, note that the firm's *average revenue (AR)* per unit of output sold is simply the price at which it sells its product. (When price is constant for all levels of output, average revenue and marginal revenue are the same.)[4] If average revenue is less than average variable cost, the firm is taking a loss on each unit of output it sells. The firm's total revenue (average revenue times quantity) will be less than its total variable cost (AVC times quantity), and this means that it would do better by not producing any output at all.

As we saw in Figure 11-2, a firm that produces zero output will earn economic profit equal to the negative of its fixed costs. If the price of its product is less than the minimum value of its average variable costs, it would have even greater economic losses if it produced a positive level of output.

The two rules—(1) that price must equal marginal cost on a rising portion of the marginal cost curve and (2) that price must exceed the minimum value of the average variable cost curve—together define the short-run supply curve of the perfectly competitive firm. The firm's supply curve tells how much output the firm wants to produce at various prices. As shown by the heavy locus in Figure 11-4, it is the rising portion of the short-run marginal cost curve that lies above the minimum value of the average variable cost curve (which is $12/unit of output in this example). Below $P = 12$, the supply curve coincides with the vertical axis, indicating that the firm supplies zero output when price is less than min AVC. For prices above 12, the firm will supply the output level for which

---

[4]Note that $AR = TR/Q = PQ/Q = P$.

FIGURE 11-4
When price lies below the minimum value of average variable cost (here $12/unit of output), the firm will make losses at every level of output, and will keep its losses to a minimum by producing zero. For prices above min AVC, the firm will supply that level of output for which $P = MC$ on the rising portion of its MC curve.

THE SHORT-RUN SUPPLY CURVE OF A PERFECTLY COMPETITIVE FIRM

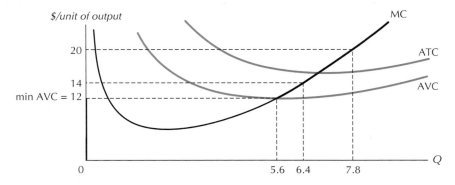

P = MC. Thus, prices of 14 and 20 will cause this firm to supply 6.4 and 7.8 units of output, respectively. The competitive firm acts here as both a price taker and a profit maximizer: taking the market price as given, it chooses the level of output that maximizes economic profit at that price.

Note in Figure 11-4 that the firm supplies positive output whenever price exceeds min AVC, and recall that average variable cost is less than average total cost, the difference being average fixed cost. It follows that no matter how small AFC is, there will be a range of prices that lie between the AVC and ATC curves. For any price in this range, the firm supplies the level of output for which P = MC, which means that it will lose money because P is less than ATC. For example, the firm whose cost curves are shown in Figure 11-4 cannot cover all its costs at a price of $14. Even so, its best option is to supply 6.4 units of output per week, because it would lose even more money if it were to shut down. Being able to cover variable costs does not assure the firm of a positive level of economic profit. But it is sufficient to induce the firm to supply output in the short run.

Note also in Figure 11-4 that the firm's short-run supply curve is upward sloping. This is because the relevant portion of the firm's short-run marginal cost curve is upward sloping, which, in turn, is a direct consequence of the law of diminishing returns.

The Short-Run Competitive Industry Supply

The short-run supply curve for a competitive industry is generated in a manner analogous to the one we used to generate the market demand curve in Chapter 5. In this case we simply announce a price and then add together the amounts each firm wishes to supply at that price. The resulting sum is industry supply at that price. Additional points on the industry supply curve are generated by pairing other prices with the sums of individual firm supplies at those prices.

Figure 11-5 illustrates the procedure for one of the simplest cases, an industry consisting of only two firms. At a price of $2/unit of output, only firm 1 (left panel) wishes to supply any output, and so its offering, Q_1 = 2 units of output per week, constitutes the entire industry supply at P = 2 (right panel). At P = 3, firm 2 enters the market (center panel) with an offering of Q_2 = 4. Added to firm 1's offering at P = 3—namely, Q_1 = 3—the resulting industry supply at P = 3 is Q = 7 (right panel). In like fashion, we see that industry supply at P = 7 is Q = 7 + 8 = 15. In Chapter 5, we saw that the market demand curve is the horizontal summation of the individual consumer demand curves. Here, we see that the market supply curve is the horizontal summation of the individual firm supply curves.

The horizontal summation of an individual firm's supplies into industry supply has a simple form when the firms in the industry are all identical. Suppose n firms each have supply curve $P = c + dQ_i$. To add up the quantities for the n firms into industry supply, we rearrange the firm supply curve $P = c + dQ_i$ to express quantity alone on one side $Q_i = (c/d) + (1/d)P$. Then industry supply is the sum of the quantities supplied Q_i by each of the n firms,

FIGURE 11-5
To get the industry supply curve (right panel), we simply add the individual firm supply curves (left and center panels) horizontally.

THE SHORT-RUN COMPETITIVE INDUSTRY SUPPLY CURVE

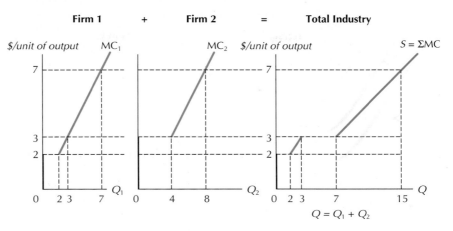

$$Q = nQ_i = n\left(-\frac{c}{d} + \frac{1}{d}P\right) = -\frac{nc}{d} + \frac{n}{d}P.$$

We can then rearrange industry supply $Q = -(nc/d) + (n/d)P$ to get it back in the form of price alone on one side: $P = c + (d/n)Q$. The intuition is that each one unit supplied by the industry is $1/n$ unit for each firm to supply. These calculations suggest a general rule for constructing the industry supply curve when firms are identical. If we have n individual firm supply curves $P = c + dQ_i$, then the industry supply curve is $P = c + (d/n)Q$.

*E*XAMPLE *11-2* *Suppose an industry has 200 firms, each with supply curve $P = 100 + 1000Q_i$. What is the industry supply curve?*

First, we need to rearrange the representative firm supply curve P 5 100 1 1000Qi to have quantity alone on one side:

$$Q_i = -\frac{1}{10} + \frac{1}{1000}P.$$

Then we multiply by the number of firms $n = 200$:

$$Q = nQ_i = 200Q_i = 200\left(-\frac{1}{10} + \frac{1}{1000}P\right) = -20 + \frac{1}{5}P.$$

Finally, we rearrange the industry supply curve $Q = -20 + (\frac{1}{5})P$ to have price alone on one side $P = 100 + 5Q$ to return to slope-intercept form.

EXERCISE 11-3

Suppose an industry has 30 firms, each with supply curve $P = 20 + 90Q_i$. What is the industry supply curve?

Short-Run Competitive Equilibrium

The individual competitive firm must choose the most profitable level of output to produce in response to a given price. But where does that price come from? As we saw in Chapter 2, it comes from the intersection of the supply and demand curves for the product. Recall that at the equilibrium price sellers are selling the quantity they wish to sell and buyers are buying the quantity they wish to buy.

In the left panel in Figure 11-6, the curve labeled D is the market demand curve for a product sold in a perfectly competitive industry. The curve labeled S is the corresponding short-run industry supply curve, the horizontal summation

FIGURE 11-6
The short-run supply and demand curves intersect to determine the short-run equilibrium price, $P^* = 20$ (left panel). The firm's demand curve is a horizontal line at $P^* = 20$ (right panel). Taking $P^* = 20$ as given, the firm maximizes economic profit by producing $Q_i^* = 80$ units/wk, for which it earns an economic profit of $\Pi_i = \$640$/wk (the shaded rectangle in the right panel).

SHORT-RUN PRICE AND OUTPUT DETERMINATION UNDER PURE COMPETITION

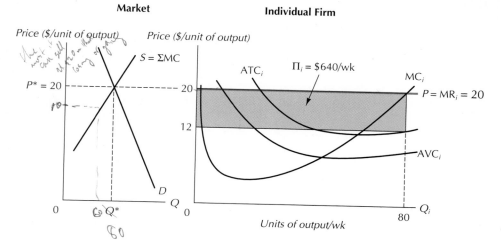

of the relevant portions of the individual short-run marginal cost curves.[5] These two curves intersect to establish the short-run competitive equilibrium price, here denoted $P^* = \$20/$unit of output. $P^* = 20$, in turn, is the price on which individual firms base their output decisions.

The conditions confronting a typical firm are shown in the right panel in Figure 11-6. The demand curve facing this firm is a horizontal line at $P^* = 20$. This means that it can sell as much or as little as it chooses at the market price of $20/unit. Put another way, any single firm can sell as much as it wants to without affecting the market price. If a firm charged more than the $20, it would sell no output at all because buyers would switch to a competing firm that sells for $20. A firm could charge less than $20, of course, but would have no motive to do so if its objective were to maximize economic profit, since it can already sell as much as it wants to at $20. The result is that even though the market demand curve is downward sloping, the demand curve facing the individual firm is perfectly elastic. (Recall from the definition of price elasticity in Chapter 5 that a horizontal demand curve has infinite price elasticity, which is the defining characteristic of the term "perfectly elastic.")

In the right panel in Figure 11-6, the representative firm maximizes its profit by equating $P^* = \$20/$unit to marginal cost at an output level of $Q_i^* = 80$ units/wk. At that output level its total revenue is $P^*Q_i^* = \$1600/$wk and its total costs are $ATC_{Q_i^*}Q_i^* = (\$12/$unit$)(80$ units/wk$) = \$960/$wk. Its economic profit is the difference between total revenue and total cost, $\$1600/$wk $- \$960/$wk $= \$640/$wk, and is represented by the shaded rectangle denoted Π_i. Equivalently, profits can be calculated as the difference between price ($20/unit) and average total cost ($12/unit) times the quantity sold (80 units/week).

Recall that the opportunity cost of resources owned by the firm constitutes part of the cost included in its average total cost curve. This is why we say that total revenues over and above total costs constitute economic profit. If the firm's revenue were exactly equal to its total cost, it would earn only a normal profit—which is to say, zero economic profit.

Facing a price equal to average total cost implies that total cost equals total revenue, and the firm earns zero economic profits. Thus price equal to the minimum of average total cost can be called the break even point—the lowest price at which the firm will not suffer negative profits in the short run.

The situation portrayed in Figure 11-6 and Table 11-1 is one in which the short-run equilibrium price enables the firm to make a positive economic profit. Another possibility is that the short-run supply and demand curves will intersect at an equilibrium price that is sufficiently high to induce firms to supply output, but not high enough to enable them to cover all their costs. This situation is shown in Figure 11-7 and Table 11-1. In the left panel, supply and demand intersect at a price $P^* = \$10/$unit of output, which lies above the minimum value

---

[5]Here, the "relevant portions" are those that lie above the respective values of min AVC.

At a price of 20, the firm earns economic profits, but at a price of 10, it suffers economic losses,

Table 11-1	ECONOMIC PROFITS VERSUS ECONOMIC LOSSES			
Q	ATC	MC	$\pi(P = 20)$	$\pi(P = 10)$
40	14	6	240	−160
60	12	10	480	−120
80	12	20	640	−160
100	15	31	500	−500

of the AVC curve of the firm shown in the right panel, but below that firm's ATC curve at the profit-maximizing level of output, $Q_i^* = 60$ units of output per week. The result is that the firm makes an economic loss of $P^*Q_i^* - \text{ATC}_{Q_i^*}Q_i^* = -\$120/\text{wk}$. This loss is shown in the right panel in Figure 11-7 by the shaded rectangle labeled Π_i. Note that this loss is less than $-\text{TFC}$, the value of economic profit when output is zero. Thus it makes sense to produce even when economic profit falls below zero in the short run.

EXERCISE 11-4

If the short-run marginal and average variable cost curves for a competitive firm are given by MC = $2Q$ and AVC = Q, how many units of output will the firm produce at a market price of $P = 12$? At what level of fixed cost will this firm earn zero economic profit?

FIGURE 11-7
The short-run supply and demand curves sometimes intersect to produce an equilibrium price $P^* = \$10$/unit of output (left panel) that lies below the minimum value of the ATC curve for the typical firm (right panel), but above the minimum point of its AVC curve. At the profit-maximizing level of output, $Q_i^* = 60$ units/wk, the firm earns an economic loss of $\Pi_i = -\$120$/wk.

A SHORT-RUN EQUILIBRIUM PRICE THAT RESULTS IN ECONOMIC LOSSES

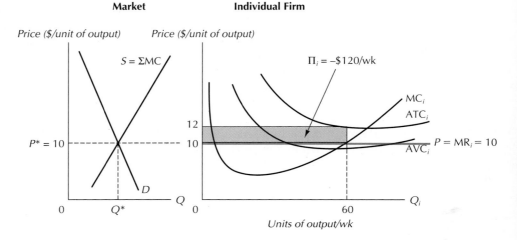

The Efficiency of Short-Run Competitive Equilibrium

Allocative efficiency A condition in which all possible gains from exchange are realized.

One of the most attractive features of competitive markets is the fact that they result in *allocative efficiency,* which means that they fully exploit the possibilities for mutual gains through exchange. To illustrate, let us consider the short-run equilibrium pictured in the left panel of Figure 11-8, and suppose that the cost curves pictured in the right panel are the same for each of 1000 firms in the industry.

In a competitive market in the short run, consumers give firms money, which firms use to buy variable inputs to produce the output that goes to consumers. To say that the competitive equilibrium leaves no room for further mutually beneficial exchange is the same thing as saying that there is no way for any producer and consumer to agree to a private transaction at any price other than $10. Of course, consumers would gladly pay less than $10 for an additional unit of output. But since $10 is equal to the value of the resources required to produce another unit (MC_i in the right panel of Figure 11-8), no firm would be willing to respond. Firms, for their part, would gladly produce an extra unit of output if the price were higher than $10. But with 100,000 units of output already in the market, there are no consumers left who are willing to pay more than $10 (left panel of Figure 11-8). At the short-run competitive equilibrium price and quantity, the value of the resources used to produce the last unit of output (as measured by short-run marginal cost) is exactly equal to the value of that unit of output to consumers (as measured by the price they are willing to pay for it). Firms may wish that prices were higher, and consumers may complain that prices are too high already. But two parties have no incentive to trade at any price other than the equilibrium price.

FIGURE 11-8
At the equilibrium price and quantity, the value of the additional resources required to make the last unit of output produced by each firm (MC in the right panel) is exactly equal to the value of the last unit of output to buyers (the demand price in the left panel). This means that further mutually beneficial trades do not exist.

SHORT-RUN COMPETITIVE EQUILIBRIUM IS EFFICIENT

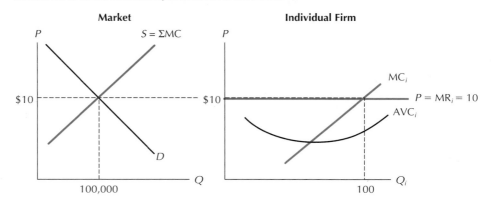

Producer Surplus

To say that a competitive market is efficient is to say that it maximizes the net benefits to its participants. In policy analysis, it is often useful to estimate the actual amount by which people and firms gain from their participation in specific markets. Suppose, for example, that a Third World government knows it can open up new markets for seafood by building a road from its coast to an interior region. If its goal is to use the country's resources as efficiently as possible, its decision about whether to build the road will depend on whether the benefits people and firms reap from these new markets exceed the cost of building the road.

In Chapter 4 we discussed the concept of consumer surplus as a measure of the benefit to the consumer of engaging in a market exchange. An analogous measure exists for producers. We call it *producer surplus,* and it measures how much better off the firm is as a result of having supplied its profit-maximizing level of output. It may seem tempting to say that the firm's producer surplus is simply its economic profit, but that will not generally be the case. To see why, first recall that in the short run if the firm produces nothing, it will sustain a loss equal to its fixed cost. If the price exceeds the minimum value of AVC, however, it can do better by supplying a positive level of output. How much better? The firm's gain compared with the alternative of producing nothing is the difference between total revenue and total variable cost at the output level where $P = MC$. Now recall that economic profit is the difference between total revenue and total cost and that total cost differs from variable cost by fixed cost; it follows that producer surplus is the sum of economic profit and fixed cost.[6] Diagrammatically, it is the area of the shaded rectangle shown in the left panel in Figure 11-9. In the short run, producer surplus is thus larger than economic profit, because the firm would lose more than its economic profit if it were prevented from participating in the market.

The right panel in Figure 11-9 shows an equivalent way of representing producer surplus. The alternative measure makes use of the fact that variable cost at any level of output is equal to the area under the marginal cost curve (below the shaded area in the right panel). To see why this is so, note that the variable cost of producing 1 unit of output is equal to marginal cost at 1 unit, MC_1; VC for 2 units is the sum of MC_1 and MC_2, and so on, so that $VC_Q = MC_1 + MC_2 + \cdots + MC_Q$, which is just the area under the MC curve. Hence the difference between the total revenue and total variable cost may also be expressed as the upper shaded area in the right panel in Figure 11-9.

Which of the two ways of measuring producer surplus is most useful will depend on the specific context at hand. If we are interested in the change in an existing producer surplus, the method shown in the right panel in Figure 11-9

Producer surplus
The dollar amount by which a firm benefits by producing a profit-maximizing level of output.

---

[6]If $\Pi = TR - TC$ and $TC = VC + FC$, then producer surplus $= TR - VC = TR - TC + FC = \Pi + FC$.

FIGURE 11-9
The difference between total revenue and total variable cost is a measure of producer surplus, the gain to the producer from producing Q_i^* units of output rather than zero. It can be measured as the difference between $P^*Q_i^*$ and $AVC_{Q_i^*}Q_i^*$ (shaded rectangle, left panel), or as the difference between $P^*Q_i^*$ and the area under the marginal cost curve (upper shaded area, right panel).

TWO EQUIVALENT MEASURES OF PRODUCER SURPLUS

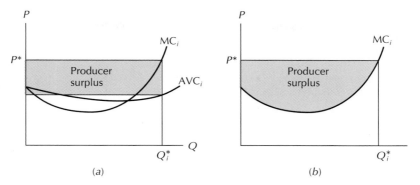

(a)   (b)

will usually be easiest to work with. But when we want to measure total producer surplus, it will often be easier to calculate the surplus by using the method shown in the left panel.

To measure aggregate producer surplus for a market, we simply add the producer surplus for each firm that participates. In cases where each firm's marginal cost curve is upward sloping for the bulk of its range, aggregate producer surplus will be well approximated by the area between the supply curve and the equilibrium price line, P^*, as shown in Figure 11-10.

Recall from Chapter 4 that a rough approximation of consumer surplus for the market as a whole is given by the area between the demand curve and the equilibrium price line, as indicated by the shaded upper triangle in Figure 11-11.[7] The total benefits from exchange in the marketplace may be measured by the sum of consumer and producer surpluses.

---

[7]Recall that this measure of consumer surplus is most accurate when income effects are small.

FIGURE 11-10
For any quantity, the supply curve measures the minimum price at which firms would be willing to supply it. The difference between the market price and the supply price is the marginal contribution to aggregate producer surplus at that output level. Adding these marginal contributions up to the equilibrium quantity Q^*, we get the shaded area, which is aggregate producer surplus.

AGGREGATE PRODUCER SURPLUS WHEN INDIVIDUAL MARGINAL COST CURVES ARE UPWARD SLOPING THROUGHOUT

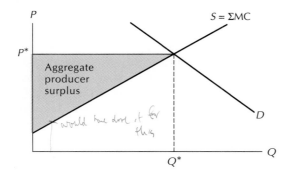

FIGURE 11-11
The sum of aggregate producer surplus (shaded lower triangle) and consumer surplus (shaded upper triangle) measures the total benefit from exchange.

THE TOTAL BENEFIT FROM EXCHANGE IN A MARKET

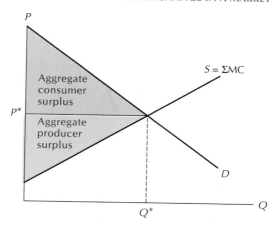

EXAMPLE 11-3 *Suppose there are two types of users of fireworks: careless and careful. Careful users never get hurt, but careless ones sometimes injure not only themselves, but also innocent bystanders. The short-run marginal cost curves of each of the 1000 firms in the fireworks industry are given by MC = 10 + Q, where Q is measured in pounds of cherry bombs per year and MC is measured in dollars per pound of cherry bombs. The demand curve for fireworks by careful users is given by P = 50 − 0.001Q (same units as for MC). Legislators would like to continue to permit careful users to enjoy fireworks. But since it is impractical to distinguish between the two types of users, they have decided to outlaw fireworks altogether. How much better off would consumers and producers be if legislators had the means to effect a partial ban?*

If the entire fireworks market is banned completely, the total of consumer and producer surplus will be zero. So to measure the benefits of a partial ban, we need to find the sum of consumer and producer surplus for a fireworks market restricted to careful users. To generate the supply curve for this market, we simply add the marginal cost curves of the individual firms horizontally, which results in the curve labeled S in Figure 11-12. The demand curve for careful users would intersect S at an equilibrium price of $30 and an equilibrium quantity of 20,000 lb/yr.

By outlawing the sale of fireworks altogether, legislators eliminate producer and consumer surplus values given by the areas of the two shaded triangles in Figure 11-12, which add to $400,000/yr. In the language of cost-benefit analysis, this is the cost imposed on producers and careful users. The benefit of the ban is whatever value the public assigns to the injuries prevented (net of the cost of denying careless users the right to continue). It is obviously no simple matter to

FIGURE 11-12
The upper shaded triangle is consumer surplus ($200,000/yr). The lower shaded triangle is producer surplus ($200,000/yr). The total benefit of keeping this market open is the sum of the two, or $400,000/yr.

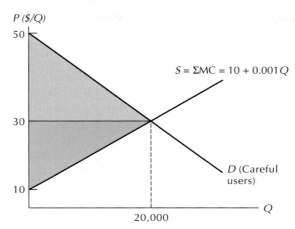

PRODUCER AND CONSUMER SURPLUS IN A MARKET CONSISTING OF CAREFUL FIREWORKS USERS

put a dollar value on the pain and suffering associated with fingers blown off by cherry bombs. In Chapter 14, we will discuss how at least rough estimates have been attempted in similar situations. But even in the absence of a formal quantitative measure of the value of injuries prevented, the public can ask itself whether the forgone surplus of $400,000/yr is a reasonable price to pay. Because virtually every state legislature has enacted a ban on the private sale and use of fireworks, the answer to this question seems to be an emphatic yes.

EXERCISE 11-5

What would the sum of consumer and producer surplus be in Example 11-2 if the demand curve for careful users were instead given by $P = 30 - 0.001Q$?

Adjustments in the Long Run

The firm's objective, in both the long run and the short run, is to earn the highest economic profit it can. In the preceding section we saw that a firm will sometimes find it in its interest to continue supplying output in the short run even though it is making economic losses. In the long run, however, a firm would prefer to go out of business if it could not earn at least a normal profit in its current industry.

Suppose that industry supply and demand intersect at the price level $P = 10$, as shown in the left panel in Figure 11-13. The cost curves for a representative firm are shown in the right panel in Figure 11-13. At $Q = 200$, the price of $10/unit of output exceeds SAC_2, with the result that the firm earns economic profit of $600 each time period. This profit is indicated by the shaded rectangle.

The situation depicted in Figure 11-13 is inherently unstable. The reason is that the existence of positive economic profits creates a powerful incentive for outsiders to enter the industry. Recall that the average cost curves already include the opportunity cost of the capital that a firm requires to do business. This means that an outsider can buy everything needed to duplicate the operations of one of the existing firms in the industry, and in the process earn an economic profit of $600 each time period.

As additional firms enter the industry, their short-run marginal cost curves are added to those of existing firms, which shifts the industry supply curve to the right. If only one firm entered the industry, there would be no significant effect on price. And with price virtually the same as before, each firm in the industry would continue to earn economic profits of $600 per time period. These profits will continue to act as a carrot to lure additional firms into the industry, and the accumulating rightward supply shift will gradually cause price to fall.

The left panel in Figure 11-14 portrays the rightward shift in industry supply that results from a significant amount of entry. The new supply schedule, S', intersects the demand schedule at $P = 8$, and this lower price level gives firms an incentive to readjust their capital stocks. In the right panel in Figure 11-14, note that the amount of capital that gives rise to the short-run cost curves SAC_3 and SMC_3 is optimal for the price level $P = 8$. Note also that the profit-maximizing level of output for $P = 8$ is $Q = 180$, and that this results in an economic profit of 540 per time period, as indicated by the shaded rectangle.

FIGURE 11-13
At the price level P = $10/unit, the firm has adjusted its plant size so that SMC_2 = LMC = 10. At the profit-maximizing level of output, Q = 200, the firm earns an economic profit equal to $600 each time period, indicated by the area of the shaded triangle.

A PRICE LEVEL THAT GENERATES ECONOMIC PROFIT

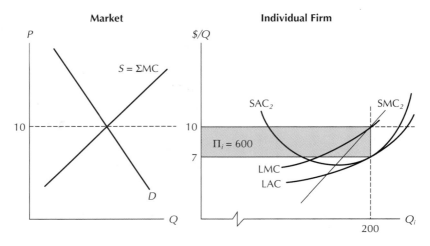

FIGURE 11-14
Entry of new firms causes supply to shift rightward, lowering price from 10 to 8. The lower price causes existing firms to adjust their capital stocks downward, giving rise to the new short-run cost curves SAC_3 and SMC_3. As long as price remains above short-run average cost (here, $SAC_3 = 5$), economic profits will be positive ($\Pi = \$540$ per time period), and incentives for new firms to enter will remain.

A STEP ALONG THE PATH TOWARD LONG-RUN EQUILIBRIUM

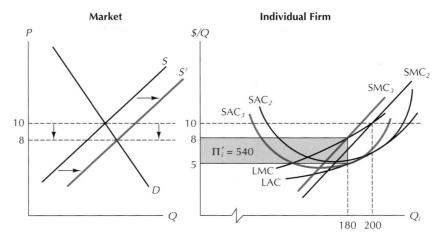

Note that the adjustment by existing firms to the lower price level shifts each of their short-run marginal cost curves to the left. In terms of its effect on the industry supply curve, this adjustment thus works in the opposite direction from the adjustment caused by the entry of new firms. But the *net* effect of the two adjustments must be to shift industry supply to the right. If it were not, price wouldn't have fallen in the first place, and there would have been no reason for existing firms to reduce their capital stocks.

Even after the adjustments described above take place, new and existing firms in the industry continue to earn positive economic profits. The new profit level is lower than before, but will still act as an incentive for additional entry into the industry. Further entry sets off yet another round of adjustment, as the continuing fall in price renders existing capital stocks too large. For industries whose firms have U-shaped long-run average cost curves, entry, falling prices, and capital stock adjustment will continue until these two conditions are met: (1) Price reaches the minimum point on the LAC curve (P^* in the right panel in Figure 11-15), and (2) all firms have moved to the capital stock size that gives rise to a short-run average cost curve that is tangent to the LAC curve at its minimum point (SAC^* in the right panel in Figure 11-15). Note in the right panel in Figure 11-15 that once all firms have reached this position, economic profit for each will be zero. The short-run marginal cost curve in the right panel is like the short-run marginal cost curve of all other firms in the industry, and when these curves are added horizontally, we get the industry supply curve shown in the left panel, which intersects the market demand curve at the long-run equilibrium price of P^*. This is the long-run competitive equilibrium position for the industry. Once it is reached, there will be no further incentive for new firms to enter the industry, because existing firms will all be earning an economic profit of zero.

In discussing the movement toward long-run competitive equilibrium, we began

FIGURE 11-15
If price starts above P^*, entry keeps occurring and capital stocks of existing firms keep adjusting until the rightward movement of the industry supply curve causes price to fall to P^*. At P^*, the profit-maximizing level of output for each firm is Q_i^*, the output level for which $P^* = SMC^* = LMC = SAC^* = LAC$. Economic profits of all firms are equal to zero.

THE LONG-RUN EQUILIBRIUM UNDER PERFECT COMPETITION

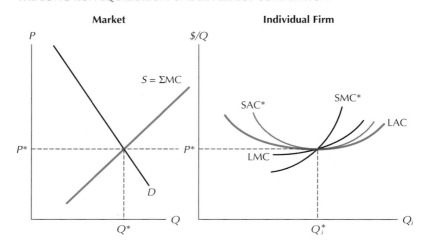

with an initial situation in which price was above the minimum value of long-run average cost and existing firms were all earning an economic profit. Suppose we had instead started with a situation in which price was below the minimum value of LAC. In that case, existing firms would be earning negative economic profits (that is, economic losses), which would be an incentive for some of them to leave the industry. The exodus would shift the supply curve leftward, causing an increase in price and movements by existing firms to adjust their capital stocks upward. This process would continue until all firms have once again settled into the long-run equilibrium position portrayed in the right panel in Figure 11-15.

The Invisible Hand

As Adam Smith saw clearly more than two centuries ago, it is the invisible hand of the self-interest motive—in particular, the carrot of economic profit, or the stick of economic losses—that drives competitive industries to their respective long-run equilibrium positions. But even though no firm consciously intends to promote the general social welfare, there are some remarkably attractive features of long-run competitive equilibrium. Price is equal to marginal cost, both long run and short run, which means that the equilibrium is efficient in the sense previously discussed: It exhausts all possibilities for mutually beneficial trades. The last unit of output consumed is worth exactly the same to the buyer as the resources required to produce it. Moreover, price is equal to the minimum point on the long-run average cost curve, which means that there is no less costly way of producing the product. Finally, all producers earn only a normal rate of profit, which is the opportunity cost of the resources they have invested in their firms. The public pays not a penny more than what it cost the firms to serve them.

Even more remarkable than these efficiency properties is the sheer volume of activity that is coordinated by the market mechanism. Throughout the dead of Ithaca winters, a food truck sits parked outside the Cornell dormitories all night, so that at 3 A.M. any student can take a few steps outside and purchase a fresh cup of coffee for 50 cents. No students had to instruct the operator of that truck to be there, or tell him where to buy paper cups or propane gas for his portable stove. The store near my house will sell me a new cartridge for my printer at a moment's notice, or a new carbide-tipped blade for the radial arm saw that sits in my garage. The butcher shop at my supermarket has fresh rabbit on Fridays and Saturdays, and a truck arrives each morning at dawn carrying fresh swordfish caught in the waters off the coast of Maine. On only a few hours' notice, several airlines stand ready to carry me to New York, Los Angeles, or Cedar Rapids, Iowa. All this activity, and much, much more, takes place without any central coordination at all, the result of a multitude of economic agents each acting in search of an economic profit.

In controlled economies, resources are allocated not by markets but by central planning committees. Because of natural limits on the amount of information such committees can process, they are unable to specify in exact detail the characteristics of the goods called for by their plans. Workers and managers in controlled economies are therefore often able to interpret their production orders in self-serving ways.

The famous Russian cartoon reprinted on this page, for example, shows the response of the manager of a roofing nail factory who was called on by the plan to deliver 10,000 pounds of roofing nails for the month of August. He alertly discovered that the easiest way to fulfill his quota was to produce a single 10,000-pound nail.

Whatever other faults it may have, the market system cannot be accused of producing products that people don't want to buy. In the market system, the consumer is sovereign, and firms that fail to provide what consumers want face economic extinction.[8]

— Кому нужен такой гвоздь?
— Это пустяки! Главное — мы сразу выполнили план по гвоздям...

"Who needs a nail as big as that?"

"Who cares? The important thing is we fulfilled the plan for nails in one fell swoop."

---

[8]Harvard economist John Kenneth Galbraith challenged this view. We will consider his arguments in Chapter 13.

The question of whether central plans are more efficient than market incentives was a hotly debated issue for most of the twentieth century. But no longer. Before their demise in the late 1980s, controlled economies all over the globe introduced marketlike incentives in a desperate attempt to revive their lagging production totals.

This is not to say that competitive markets lead to the best possible outcome in every instance. On the contrary, in later chapters we will see that market systems fall short in a variety of ways.

Moreover, the efficiency claims on behalf of competitive allocations are conditional on the initial distribution of resources among members of society. Markets are efficient at producing what people demand in the marketplace, and what gets produced depends on how much income specific people have. If you do not believe that the underlying distribution of resources is fair, there is no compelling reason for you to approve of the pattern of goods and services served up by competitive markets. But one need not take a naively optimistic view of the competitive process to appreciate its truly awesome power to draw order from complexity.

Application: The Cost of Extraordinary Inputs

THE IRRIGATION PROJECT

We are in a position now to return to the question with which we began this chapter, namely, whether a state-supported irrigation system that doubles crop yields will raise the incomes of poor farmers. Recall that the farmers in question live in an isolated county and rent their farm parcels from landowners.

First, let's consider the current situation in which no irrigation system exists. Farmers here may be viewed as the operators of small competitive firms. They rent land and supply their own labor, and keep the proceeds from selling their grain in a market so large that their own offerings have no appreciable effect on the price of grain, which is, say, $10/bushel. For the sake of simplicity, let us ignore the cost of seed, tools, and other minor inputs.

Suppose that an individual farmer can farm 40 acres and that without irrigation the land will yield 30 bushels of grain per acre per year. His total revenue from the sale of his grain will then be $12,000/yr, from which he must deduct the rent for his land. How will that rent be determined?

Suppose the alternative to working as a farmer is to work in a factory for $6000/yr, and that factory work is generally regarded as neither more nor less pleasant than farming. If the land rent were only, say, $5000/yr for a 40-acre parcel, then all the county's workers would prefer farming to working in the factories, because their net earnings would be $7000 instead of $6000. Assuming that there are many more factory workers than could farm the county's limited supply of farmland, there would be excess demand for farm parcels at a rental price of $5000/yr. Factory workers would bid against one another, and the bidding would continue until the rental price for a 40-acre parcel reached $6000/yr. At that price, a worker would have $6000 left over from the sale of his crops, which would leave him indifferent between the options of farming and factory work. The land rent could never exceed $6000 for very long under these conditions, for if it did, net farm incomes would fall below $6000/yr and everyone would want factory work instead of farming.

Now let's see what happens with the introduction of the irrigation project. With grain yields now 60 bushels/acre instead of 30, a 40-acre farm will produce $24,000 in annual total revenue instead of $12,000. If the land rent remained at its original $6000/yr level, a farmer would earn $18,000/yr instead of $6000. Indeed, it was the prospect of such a dramatic rise in farm incomes that has attracted so much support for the irrigation bill in the first place.

What the supporters of the bill have failed to recognize, however, is that land rents will not remain at $6000/yr after the introduction of the irrigation system. Needless to say, factory workers would bid vigorously for an opportunity to rent a farm parcel that would raise their income from $6000 to $18,000/yr. In the face of this bidding pressure, the rental price of farmland will continue to rise until it reaches a level of $18,000/yr. (If it were only $17,000, for example, a factory worker could switch to farming and raise his annual income from $6000 to $7000.) Once the annual rent for a 40-acre parcel reaches $18,000, the balance between farm and factory opportunities will be restored.

Recall that our hypothetical state legislator's aide recommended against the irrigation project on the grounds that it would not raise the incomes of farmers in the long run. She perceived correctly that the beneficiaries of the state-supported irrigation project would be not the impoverished farmers but the owners of the land. On the view that these owners already have high incomes, there is no social purpose served by spending tax dollars to increase their incomes further.[9]

This example illustrates the important idea that strong forces tend to equalize the average total costs of different firms in a competitive industry. Here, land prices adjusted to bring the average costs of the irrigated farms into balance with the average costs of growing crops elsewhere.

AN EFFICIENT MANAGER

Suppose one firm is like all others except that it employs an extraordinarily efficient manager. This manager is so efficient that the firm earns $500,000 of economic profit each year in an industry in which the economic profit of the other firms hovers very close to zero. If this manager received the same salary as all other managers, the firm that employed her would have much lower costs than all other firms in the industry. But then there would be a strong incentive for some other firm to bid this manager away by offering her a higher salary.

Suppose a new firm offered her $300,000 more than her current annual salary and she accepted. That new firm would then earn an economic profit of

---

[9]Of course, the irrigation project would still be attractive if its cost were less than the value of the extra grain that resulted.

$200,000/yr. That's not as good as an economic profit of $500,000/yr, but it is $200,000/yr better than the normal profit her original employer will earn without her.

Still other firms would have an incentive to offer even more for this manager. Theory tells us that the bidding should continue until the cost savings for which she is responsible are entirely incorporated into her salary—that is, until her salary is $500,000/yr higher than the salary of an ordinary manager. And once her salary is bid up to that level, the firm that hires her will no longer enjoy a cost advantage over the other firms in the industry. The existence of such competitive bidding for inputs makes it plausible to assume that all the firms in a competitive industry have roughly the same average total costs in equilibrium.

EXERCISE 11-6

Suppose all firms in an industry have "competent" managers and earn zero economic profit. The manager of one of the firms suddenly leaves and the firm finds that only incompetent applicants respond when the position is advertised at the original salary of $50,000/yr (which is the going rate for competent managers in this industry). Under an incompetent manager paid this salary, the firm will experience an economic loss of $20,000/yr. At what salary would it make sense for this firm to hire an incompetent manager?

The Long-Run Competitive Industry Supply Curve

We saw that the short-run supply curve for a perfectly competitive industry is the horizontal summation of the short-run marginal cost curves of its individual firms. But the corresponding long-run supply curve for a competitive industry is not the horizontal summation of the long-run marginal cost curves of individual firms. Our task in the next sections is to derive the long-run supply curve for competitive industries operating under a variety of different cost conditions.

LONG-RUN SUPPLY CURVE WITH U-SHAPED LAC CURVES

What does the long-run supply curve look like in an industry in which all firms have identical U-shaped long-run average cost (LAC) curves? Suppose, in particular, that these LAC curves are like the one labeled LAC_i in the right panel in Figure 11-16. Suppose the demand curve facing the industry is initially the one labeled D_1 in the left panel. Given this demand curve, the industry will be in long-run equilibrium when each firm installs the capital stock that gives rise to the short-run marginal cost curve labeled SMC_i in the right panel. The number

FIGURE 11-16
When firms are free
to enter or leave the
market, price cannot
depart from the min-
imum value of the
LAC curve in the
long run. If input
prices are unaffected
by changes in indus-
try output, the long-
run supply curve is
S_{LR}, a horizontal
line at the minimum
value of LAC.

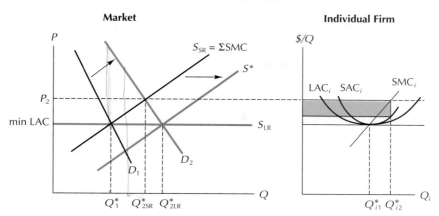

THE LONG-RUN COMPETITIVE INDUSTRY SUPPLY CURVE

of firms in the industry will adjust so that the short-run supply curve, denoted
S_{SR} in the left panel, intersects D_1 at a price equal to the minimum value of LAC_i.
(If there were more firms than that or fewer, each would be making either an
economic loss or a profit.)

Now suppose demand shifts rightward from D_1 to D_2, intersecting the short-
run industry supply curve at the price P_2. The short-run effect will be for each
firm to increase its output from Q_{i1}^* to Q_{i2}^*, which will lead to an economic profit
measured by the shaded rectangle in the right panel in Figure 11-16. With the
passage of time, these profits will lure additional firms into the industry until
the rightward supply shift (to S^* in the left panel) again results in a price of min
LAC. The long-run response to an increase in demand, then, is to increase industry output by increasing the number of firms in the industry. As long as the
expansion of industry output does not cause the prices of capital, labor, and other
inputs to rise, there will be no long-run increase in the price of the product.[10]

If demand had shifted to the left from D_1, a parallel story would have unfolded:
Price would have fallen in the short run, firms would have adjusted their offerings, and the resulting economic losses would have induced some firms to leave
the industry. The exodus would shift industry supply to the left until price had
again risen to min LAC. Here again the long-run response to a shift in demand is
accommodated by a change in the number of firms. With U-shaped LAC curves,
there is no tendency for a fall in demand to produce a long-run decline in price.

In summary, the long-run supply curve for a competitive industry with U-
shaped LAC curves and constant input prices is a horizontal line at the minimum value of the LAC curve. In the long run, all the adjustment to variations

---

[10]More follows on what happens when changes in industry output cause changes in input prices.

in demand occurs not through changing prices but through variations in the number of firms serving the market. Following possibly substantial deviations in the short run, price shows a persistent tendency to gravitate to the minimum value of long-run average cost.

INDUSTRY SUPPLY WHEN EACH LAC CURVE IS HORIZONTAL

As in the case of U-shaped LAC curves, the long-run industry supply curve when each firm's LAC curve is horizontal will again be a horizontal line (again assuming that input prices do not change with changes in industry output). But there is one salient difference between the two cases: When firms have identical U-shaped LAC curves, we can predict that each firm will produce the quantity that corresponds to the minimum point on its LAC. We thus get an industry composed of firms that all produce the same level of output.

In the case of horizontal LAC curves, by contrast, there is simply no unique minimum-cost point. LAC is the same at any level of output, which leads to an indeterminacy not present in the earlier case. We just cannot predict what the size distribution of firms will look like in the case of horizontal LAC curves. There may be a handful of large firms, many small ones, or a mixture of different sizes. All we can say with confidence is that price in the long run will gravitate toward the value of LAC.

THE EFFECT ON SUPPLY OF CHANGING INPUT PRICES

In our analysis of cost curves in Chapter 10, which forms the basis of our analysis of supply under perfect competition, an important assumption was that input prices do not vary with the amount of output produced. For a single firm whose input purchases constitute only a small fraction of the total input market, this assumption is plausible. In many cases, moreover, even the entire industry's demands for inputs constitute only a small share of the overall input market. For example, even if the insurance industry issues 20 percent more policies this year than last, it employs such a small percentage of the total available supplies of secretaries, computers, executives, and other inputs that the prices of these inputs should not be significantly affected. So here too we may reasonably assume that input prices do not depend on output.

But there are at least some industries in which the volume of inputs purchased constitutes an appreciable share of the entire input market. The market for commercial airliners, for example, consumes a significant share of the total amount of titanium sold each year. In such cases, a large increase in industry output will often be accompanied by significant increases in input prices.

Pecuniary diseconomy A rise in production cost that occurs when an expansion of industry output causes a rise in the prices of inputs.

When that happens, we have what is known as a ***pecuniary diseconomy***, a bidding up of input prices when industry output increases.[11] Even though the

---

[11]A *pecuniary diseconomy* thus implies that input prices will fall when industry output contracts.

FIGURE 11-17
When input prices rise with industry output, each firm's LAC curve will also rise with industry output (left panel). Thus the firm's LAC curve when industry output is Q_2 lies above its LAC curve when industry output is Q_1 (left panel). Firms will still gravitate to the minimum points on their LAC curves (Q_i^*, left panel), but because this minimum point depends on industry output, the long-run industry supply curve (S_{LR}, right panel) will now be upward sloping.

LONG-RUN SUPPLY CURVE FOR AN INCREASING COST INDUSTRY

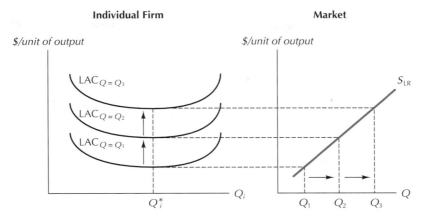

industry can expand output indefinitely without using more inputs per unit of output, the minimum point on each firm's LAC curve is nonetheless a rising function of industry output. For example, note in the left panel in Figure 11-17 that the firm's LAC curve for an industry output of Q_2 lies above its LAC curve for an industry output of $Q_1 < Q_2$, and that the LAC curve for an industry output of $Q_3 > Q_2$ lies higher still. To each industry output level there corresponds a different LAC curve, because input prices are different at every level of industry output. The long-run supply curve for such an industry will trace out the minimum points of these LAC curves. Thus, on the long-run industry supply curve (S_{LR}, right panel), Q_1 corresponds to the minimum point on the firm's LAC curve when industry output is Q_1 (left panel); Q_2 corresponds to the minimum point for the LAC curve for Q_2; and so on. With pecuniary diseconomies, the long-run supply curve will be upward sloping even though each individual firm's LAC curve is U-shaped. Pecuniary diseconomies also produce an upward-sloping industry supply curve when each firm's LAC curve is horizontal. Competitive industries in which rising input prices lead to upward-sloping supply curves are called *increasing cost industries.*

There are also cases in which the prices of inputs may fall significantly with expanding industry output. This will happen, for example, if inputs are manufactured using technologies in which there are substantial economies of scale. A dramatic increase in road building, for example, might facilitate greater exploitation of economies of scale in the production of earthmoving equipment, resulting in a lower price for that input. Such cases are called *pecuniary economies,* and give rise to a downward-sloping long-run industry supply curve, even where each firm's LAC curve is either horizontal or U-shaped. Competitive industries in which falling input prices lead to downward-sloping supply curves are called *constant cost industries.*

EXAMPLE 11-4 *Why do color photographs cost less than black-and-white photographs?*

When I was a boy, color photographs were a luxury, costing several times as much as black and white. Today, the photo-processing shop near my house charges $14.91 to develop and print a 36-exposure roll of black-and-white film, but only $6.99 for the same size roll of color film. This fall in the relative price of color photos has occurred despite the fact that the color process remains more complex than the one for black and white.

If color processing is more complex than black and white, why does it cost less? The answer is in part because of economies of scale in the production of the machinery used to make both types of prints. When color photography was in its infancy, film was expensive and the colors tended to fade rapidly, so most people used black and white. The high volume of black-and-white photo processing, in turn, made it possible to produce processing machines cheaply because of economies of scale. As the price of color film declined over time and its quality rose, more people began to use it and the demand for color-processing equipment gradually grew. And again because of economies of scale in the production of processing equipment, this led to a fall in the cost of an important input for color printmaking—a pecuniary economy. At the

FIGURE 11-18
Because of economies of scale in the production of equipment used to process film, the long-run supply curves of both color and black-and-white prints are downward sloping. In 1955, when the quality of color film was poor, most people demanded black and white, resulting in lower prices. In 1995, by contrast, demand for color is much greater than for black and white. The result is that color prints are now less expensive than black and white, even though color-processing equipment remains more complicated.

PECUNIARY ECONOMIES AND THE PRICE OF COLOR AND BLACK-AND-WHITE PHOTOS

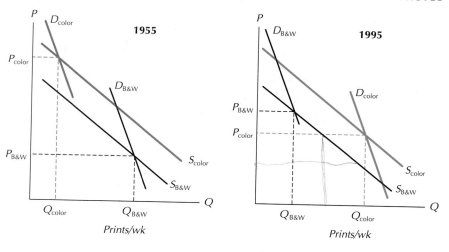

same time, the decline in production of black-and-white processing equipment led to an increase in its price—a pecuniary diseconomy.

The resulting changes in the equilibrium prices and quantities of the two types of prints are roughly as shown in Figure 11-18. Note that the relative positions of the two supply curves are the same for both years. This means that the printmaking industry would be willing to supply any given total quantity of black-and-white prints for a lower price than for the same quantity of color prints in both years. It is the change in demand patterns, together with downward-sloping supply curves in both markets, that explains the observed reversal in relative prices.

The Elasticity of Supply

Price elasticity of supply The percentage change in quantity supplied that occurs in response to a 1 percent change in product price.

In Chapter 5 we defined the price elasticity of demand as a measure of the responsiveness of the quantity demanded to variations in price. An analogous concept exists for measuring the responsiveness of the quantity supplied to variations in price. Naturally, it is called the *price elasticity of supply.* Suppose we are at a point (Q, P) on the industry supply curve shown in Figure 11-19, where a change in price of ΔP gives rise to a change of ΔQ in the quantity supplied. The price elasticity of supply, denoted ϵ^s, is then given by

$$\epsilon^s = \frac{\Delta Q}{\Delta P}\frac{P}{Q} \quad \text{(see footnote 12 below)}. \tag{11.1}$$

As in the case of elasticity of demand, supply elasticity has a simple interpretation in terms of the geometry of the industry supply curve. When ΔP is small, the ratio $\Delta P/Q$ is the slope of the supply curve, which means that the ratio $\Delta Q/\Delta P$ is the reciprocal of that slope. Thus the price elasticity of supply

---

[12]In calculus terms, supply elasticity is defined by

$$\epsilon^s = \frac{P}{Q}\frac{dQ}{dP}.$$

FIGURE 11-19
At point A, the elasticity of supply is given by $\epsilon^s =$ $(\Delta Q/\Delta P)(P/Q)$. Because the short-run supply curve is always upward sloping, the short-run elasticity of supply will always be positive. In the long run, elasticity of supply can be positive, zero, or negative.

THE ELASTICITY OF SUPPLY

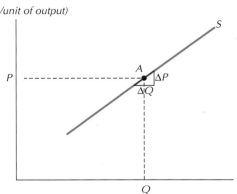

may be interpreted as the product of the ratio of price to quantity and the reciprocal of the slope of the supply curve:

$$\epsilon^s = \frac{P}{Q}\frac{1}{slope}.$$ (11.2)

EXAMPLE 11-5

Suppose the industry supply curve is P = −30 + 2Q. What is the price elasticity of supply when Q = 20?

At $Q = 20$, price is $P = -30 + 2Q = -30 + 2(20) = 10$ (see Figure 11-20). The slope of the linear supply curve is constant at

$$m = \frac{\text{rise}}{\text{run}} = \frac{\Delta P}{\Delta Q} = 2.$$

Thus the elasticity of supply at $(P = 10, Q = 20)$ is

$$\epsilon_s = \frac{1}{slope}\left(\frac{P}{Q}\right) = \frac{1}{2}\left(\frac{10}{20}\right) = \frac{1}{4}.$$

EXERCISE 11-7

What is the elasticity of supply at point A in Figure 11-19 if the price and quantity at A are given by 10 and 20, respectively, and the slope of the supply curve is 2?

FIGURE 11-20
The elasticity of supply at $Q = 20$ and $P = 10$

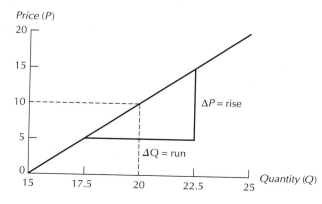

Because of the law of diminishing returns, the short-run competitive industry supply curve will always be upward sloping, which means that the short-run elasticity of supply will always be positive. For industries with a horizontal long-run supply curve, the long-run elasticity of supply is infinite. Output can be expanded indefinitely without a change in price. Because of pecuniary economies and diseconomies, long-run competitive industry supply curves may also be either downward or upward sloping in specific cases. The corresponding long-run elasticities of supply in these cases will be either negative or positive.

As noted earlier, most industries employ only a relatively small share of the total volume of inputs traded in the marketplace, which means that modest variations in industry output should have no significant effect on input prices in most industries. In practical applications of the competitive model, therefore, most economists adopt the working hypothesis that long-run supply curves are horizontal. Of course, this hypothesis can always be modified when there is evidence that pecuniary economies or diseconomies are important.

Applying the Competitive Model

As noted earlier in the chapter, economists recognize that no industries strictly satisfy the four requirements for perfect competition—a standardized product, firms as price takers, perfect factor mobility, and perfect information. For practical purposes, the important question is how far an industry can fall short of these conditions before general tendencies of the competitive model fail to apply. Unfortunately, there are no hard-and-fast rules for making this judgment. In industries where entry and exit are especially easy—such as the airline industry—a firm may behave as a price taker even in a market where it is the only competitor.[13] In industries where entry and exit are more difficult, even the existence of a relatively large number of established firms does not guarantee price-taking behavior. In the short run, especially, firms may be able to work out tacit agreements to restrain price competition even when there are extra-normal profits.

Despite this difficulty, experience has shown that many of the most important long-run properties of the competitive model apply in most industries, with the notable exception of those where the government erects legal barriers to entry (for example, by requiring a government license in order to participate in a market, as used to be the case in the airline industry).

By way of illustration, let's consider three brief applications that highlight some of the insights afforded by the perfectly competitive model.

---

[13]At a limited number of large airports, entry is difficult even in the airline industry. For these airports to accommodate carriers, new capacity will have to be built, which could take years or even decades.

PRICE SUPPORTS AS A DEVICE FOR SAVING FAMILY FARMS

At the beginning of this century, more than 20 percent of the U.S. labor force earned its living by farming. Today, the corresponding figure is less than 3 percent. This change is obviously not the result of a dramatic decline in food consumption. Rather, it is one of the many consequences of farming methods having become vastly more productive during this century.

As farm machinery has grown larger and more sophisticated, the size of land parcel at which long-run average cost curves cease declining has grown ever larger. Where family farms of fewer than 100 acres were once common in the American heartland, large corporate farms with several thousand acres have increasingly become the norm.

In terms of the competitive model developed in this chapter, the family farm may be thought of as a firm whose capital stock gives rise to the short-run cost curves denoted SAC_F and SMC_F in Figure 11-21. The corresponding cost curves for the corporate farm are denoted SAC_C and SMC_C. Competition has the effect of driving the long-run equilibrium price toward P^*, the minimum point on the LAC curve. At P^*, corporate farms earn a normal profit while family farms, with their higher costs, earn economic losses of Π_F, as measured by the shaded rectangle in Figure 11-21.

Despite the intense determination of many family farmers to remain on the land, large losses are simply not sustainable over a period of many years. Most farmers remain well past the time they are no longer able to earn a profit equal to the opportunity cost of their land. Many remain even long after they have ceased to earn the opportunity cost of their own labor. And a substantial number hang on by borrowing away most of the value of their only significant asset, their farmland. But credit cannot be extended without limit, and in the absence of government intervention, the long-run tendency has been for family farmers to leave the industry, selling whatever land they still own to the more efficient corporate farms.

Contrary to the stylized assumptions of the model of perfect competition, this process of resource mobility is far from perfect. Family farming is a way of life, one that people do not readily abandon when the terms of trade turn against

FIGURE 11-21
With the availability of modern farming methods, large farms have much lower unit costs than small ones. A price that covers cost for large corporate farms will produce large economic losses for family farms.

COST CURVES FOR FAMILY AND CORPORATE FARMS

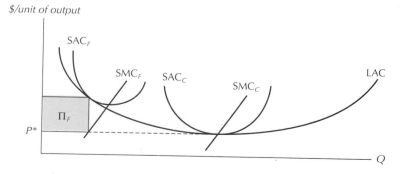

them. There is great sympathy among American voters for the plight of family farmers. We don't like to witness scenes on the nightly news of families huddled tearfully together as the auctioneer sells off the last of their possessions. We appreciate that these families have worked hard all their lives in an era when many others earn their living by selling crack or robbing convenience stores. Our sympathy for the family farmers has been translated by Congress into legislative programs designed to enable them to remain on their farms.

Price supports for agricultural products are among the most important of these programs. The details of the support programs are highly complex, but for the purpose of our analysis it will suffice to say that the government announces a price for a given product and then stands ready to buy whatever private buyers fail to purchase. One of the most important, if not always explicitly stated, goals of the price support programs is to keep prices high enough to prevent small family farms from going bankrupt.

Sad to say, these programs have failed miserably. Sadder still, even the most cursory understanding of competitive market dynamics would have made clear to Congress why this outcome was inevitable. To illustrate, suppose the price support is set at P_G in a market where the unsupported price would have been P^*. In Figure 11-22, we see that the short-run effect is to cause family farms to increase their output to Q_F, and to cause corporate farms to increase theirs to Q_C. At these output levels, family farms will earn an economic loss indicated by the color rectangle labeled Π_F in Figure 11-22, while corporate farms earn an economic profit indicated by the shaded rectangle Π_C.

In the short run, to the extent the new loss is smaller than the previous loss suffered by family farmers, the price support has had the intended effect of helping the family farmer. But the relief is destined to be transitory. To see why, note first that the same price support that reduces the short-run losses of family farms generates positive profits for corporate farms. We know, however, that positive profits are not sustainable in an industry in which there is freedom of entry. They will lure outsiders to bid for farmland so that they too may earn more than a normal rate of return. The effect of this bidding will be to cause land prices to

FIGURE 11-22
Price supports initially reduce the losses of family farms, while creating economic profits for corporate farms. In the long run, however, they serve only to bid up land prices.

THE SHORT-RUN EFFECT OF AGRICULTURAL PRICE SUPPORTS

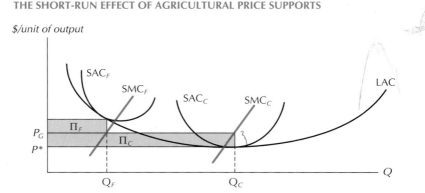

rise to the point where corporate farms no longer earn economic profits. But with land prices higher than before, the cost curves of all farms, corporate and family, shift upward. For owners, some of the sting of these economic losses is mitigated by the greater implicit value of their land. But for the many farm families who rent their land, there is no such compensation.

As technology continues to advance, and with it the scale of the most efficient farms, the stage is now set for another round of distress for family farms and the attendant pressure to increase the government price support level. A treadmill has been set in motion whereby the price support keeps escalating, only to set off another round of escalation in land prices. As a policy for protecting the long-term economic viability of family farms, the agricultural price support program could hardly have been more ill conceived.

Economists are not in a position to tell Congress whether trying to preserve the existence of the family farm is a worthwhile goal. That is a political question. But given that Congress has decided to pursue this objective, economists can give advice about what policies are most likely to be effective. The price supports failed because of the competitive bidding for land that was induced by them. Their long-run effect was to drive up the price of land, while doing little to ensure the survival of small family farms. A much more direct and efficient way to aid family farmers would be to reduce their income taxes; or, in the case of more extreme need, to give them outright cash grants.

THE ILLUSORY ATTRACTION OF TAXING BUSINESS

As noted in Chapter 2, political leaders often find it easier to propose new taxes on business than to collect additional taxes from individuals. Proposals to tax business usually include statements to the effect that "wealthy corporations can better afford to pay extra taxes than struggling workers can." But as we saw in Chapter 2, a tax placed on the product sold by an industry will in general be passed on, at least in part, to consumers.

Let us examine a perfectly competitive industry in which individual firms have identical U-shaped LAC curves like the one labeled LAC_i in the right panel in Figure 11-23. In the most common case, moderate variations in the industry's output will have no appreciable effect on its input prices, with the result that the long-run supply curve for this industry will be a horizontal line at the minimum point of LAC_i (the curve labeled S_{LR} in the left panel). If D is the market demand curve, then the equilibrium price will be Q_1^*.

Now suppose a tax of T dollars is collected on each unit of output sold in the market. The effect of this tax is to shift the LAC and SMC curves of each firm upward by T dollars (right panel in Figure 11-23). The new long-run industry supply curve is again a horizontal line at the minimum value of the LAC curve—this time the curve $S_{LR} + T$ in the left panel in Figure 11-23. The effect of the tax is to increase the price of the product by exactly T dollars. Industry output contracts from Q_1^* go Q_2^* (left panel), and this contraction is achieved by firms leaving the industry.

FIGURE 11-23
A tax of T dollars per unit of output raises the LAC and SMC curves by T dollars (right panel). The new long-run industry supply curve is again a horizontal line at the minimum value of LAC (left panel). Equilibrium price rises by T dollars (left panel), which means that 100 percent of the tax is passed on to consumers.

THE EFFECT OF A TAX ON THE OUTPUT OF A PERFECTLY COMPETITIVE INDUSTRY

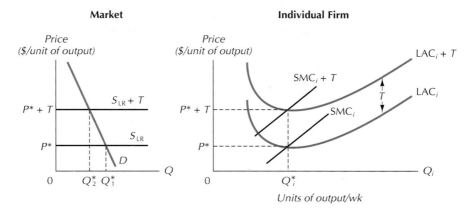

Thus we see that, for competitive industries whose firms have U-shaped LAC curves, and whose input prices are fixed (the most empirically relevant case), the burden of a tax on output falls entirely on consumers. As we will see in later chapters, there are a variety of legitimate reasons for taxing the output of specific industries. But the claim that corporations have more money than people do is simply not one of these reasons. Claims to the contrary are fraudulent, and an economically literate population would be unlikely to reelect politicians who defend taxing business on this ground.

If constant cost competitive industries are able to pass on 100 percent of taxes to buyers, why do industry lobbyists oppose taxes so strongly? Note in Figure 11-23 that one effect of a tax is to reduce total industry output. This reduction is achieved by some firms going out of business. Bankruptcy is never a pleasant experience for the owners of a firm, and on this account it is far from surprising that industry trade associations are so strongly opposed to new taxes.

THE ADOPTION OF COST-SAVING INNOVATIONS

The economist's emphasis on the competitive firm as a price taker sometimes creates the impression that competitive firms do little more than passively respond to impersonal price signals served up by the environment. This impression is deeply misleading. While it is true, for example, that an individual trucker can do little to affect trucking rates set in the open market, there is a great deal he can and must do to ensure his continued survival.

The short-run response to the dramatic fuel price increases of the 1970s automatically led to just the sorts of adjustments predicted by the competitive model: short-term losses, exit from the industry, gradually rising prices, and a gradual restoration of profitability for surviving firms. But the change in the environment also created opportunities that some firms actively exploited to their own advantage.

A case in point is one of the steps taken by truckers to reduce their consumption of fuel. Before 1970, the profile of the typical 18-wheel semi tractor-trailer truck was like the one shown in Figure 11-24a. The broad, flat expanse of the top of the trailer was directly exposed to the force of the oncoming wind, which at highway speeds was substantial. But diesel fuel cost only $0.30/gal in 1970, and so the penalty from having to run the engine a little harder was not large in those days.

With diesel prices over $1/gal by the early 1980s, however, that penalty became much more important—so much so that entrepreneurs devised ways of reducing it. One of the most successful innovations was the simple airfoil that now adorns the cab of virtually every large truck on the road. Shown in Figure 11-24b, its purpose is to deflect the wind to the top of the trailer. The profile of today's semi is still no aerodynamic masterpiece, but truckers estimate that the reduced wind resistance increases their mileage by 15 percent at highway speeds.

The truckers who were first to install the airfoils did so at a time when the industry price level was determined by the higher costs of running trucks that lacked them. As a result, these early adopters earned economic profits from their efforts. As time passed, however, more and more trucks began to sport the devices, and the industry price level gradually declined in response to the lower costs they made possible. At this point in history, it is rare to see an 18-wheeler that lacks an airfoil. By now it is safe to assume that the resultant cost savings have been fully reflected in lower trucking rates. The result is that the owner of a truck must now install an airfoil merely to be able to earn a normal rate of profit. Those who fail to install them pay the penalty of earning economic losses.

The lesson of this example is that the entrepreneur who earns economic profits is the one who adopts cost-saving innovations ahead of the competition. It is the search for such innovations that keeps even the price-taking firm from being merely a passive reactor to economic forces beyond its control.

FIGURE 11-24
With rising prices of diesel fuel, truckers began in the mid-1970s to install airfoils on the cabs of their trucks. Early adopters earned economic profits, while late adopters suffered economic losses.

THE CHANGING PROFILE OF THE 18-WHEELER

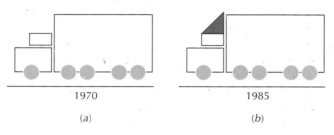

1970

1985

(a)

(b)

Summary

The assumed objective of the firm is to maximize its economic profits. Competitive pressures in the marketplace may render this a plausible assumption, even though it seems to impute an unrealistically high degree of purposefulness to the actions of many managers. Economic profit is the difference between total revenue and cost—both explicit and implicit—of all resources used in production. Economic profit is not to be confused with accounting profit, which is the difference between total revenue and the explicit cost of resources used.

The economic model of perfect competition assumes a standardized product, price-taking behavior on the part of the firms, perfect mobility of resources, and perfect information on the part of buyers and firms. In this sense, it is similar to the physicist's model of motion on frictionless surfaces. Both models describe idealized conditions that are rarely if ever met in practice, and yet each generates useful predictions and explanations of events we observe in the world.

The rule for profit maximization in the short run is to produce the level of output for which price is equal to short-run marginal cost on the rising portion of that curve. If price falls below the minimum value of average variable cost, the firm does best to produce no output in the short run. The individual firm's short-run supply curve is thus the rising portion of its short-run marginal cost curve that lies above the minimum point of its average variable cost curve.

The short-run industry supply curve is the horizontal summation of the individual firm's supply curves. It intersects the industry demand curve to determine the short-run equilibrium price. The individual competitive firm's demand curve is a horizontal line at the equilibrium price. If that price happens to lie above the minimum value of the long-run average cost curve, each firm will earn positive economic profits. If price is less than that value, each will suffer economic losses.

Long-run adjustments consist not only of alterations in the size of existing firms' capital stocks, but also of entry and exit of firms. Where firms have identical U-shaped LAC curves, the long-run equilibrium price will be the minimum value of that LAC curve, and each firm will produce the corresponding quantity.

Both long-run and short-run equilibrium positions are efficient in the sense that the value of the resources used in making the last unit of output is exactly equal to the value of that output to the buyer. This means that the equilibrium position exhausts all possibilities for mutually beneficial exchange. The long-run equilibrium has two additional attractive features: (1) Output is produced at the lowest possible unit cost, and (2) the seller is paid only the cost of producing the product. No economic profit is extracted from the buyer.

Under perfect competition with constant input prices, the long-run industry supply curve is a horizontal line, not only when LAC curves are horizontal, but also when they are U-shaped. When input prices are an increasing function of industry output, the industry supply curves in both cases will be upward sloping. When input prices decline with industry output, the competitive industry supply curve will be downward sloping.

The effect of competition for the purchase of unusually high quality inputs is to raise the price of those inputs until they no longer enable the firm that employs them to earn an economic profit. This is an extremely important part of the long-run adjustment process, and failure to account for it lies behind the failure of many well-intended economic policies.

Even price-taking firms must actively seek out means of reducing their costs of doing business. To the early adopters of cost-saving innovations goes a temporary stream of economic profit, while late adopters must suffer through periods of economic losses.

Questions for Review

1. What is the difference between economic profit and accounting profit, and how does this difference matter for actual business decisions?

2. Under what conditions will we expect firms to behave as price takers even though there are only a small number of other firms in the industry?

3. Would the market for dry cleaning be perfectly competitive in large cities such as San Francisco or New York City? Why or why not? How about in a small city such as Athens, Ohio, or Meredith, New Hampshire?

4. A firm's total revenue curve is given by $TR = aQ - 2Q^2$. Is this a perfectly competitive firm? Explain why or why not.

5. Does the fact that a business manager may not know the definition of marginal cost contradict the theory of perfect competition?

6. *True or false:* If marginal cost lies below average fixed cost, the firm should shut down in the short run. Explain.

7. What do economists mean when they say that the short-run competitive equilibrium is efficient?

8. *True or false:* In a constant cost industry, a tax of a constant, fixed amount on each unit of output sold will not affect the amount of output sold by a perfectly competitive firm in the long run. Explain.

9. Suppose all firms in a competitive industry are operating at output levels for which price is equal to long-run marginal cost. *True or false:* This industry is necessarily in long-run equilibrium.

10. *True or false:* Consumer surplus is the area between the demand curve and the price line. For a perfectly competitive firm the demand curve equals the price line. Thus, a perfectly competitive industry produces no consumer surplus.

11. Why are pecuniary economies and diseconomies said to be the exception rather than the rule?

12. Would you expect a firm that adopts cost-saving innovations faster than 80 percent of all firms in its industry to earn economic profits? If so, will there be any tendency for these profits to be bid away?

Problems

1. A competitive firm has the cost structure described in the following table. Graph the marginal cost, average variable cost, and average total cost curves. How many units of output will it produce at a market price of 32? Calculate its profits and show them in your graph.

Q	ATC	AVC	MC
1	44	4	8
2	28	8	16
4	26	16	32
6	31	24	48
8	37	32	64

2. If the short-run marginal and average variable cost curves for a competitive firm are given by SMC $= 2 + 4Q$ and AVC $= 2 + 2Q$, how many units of output will it produce at a market price of 10? At what level of fixed cost will this firm earn zero economic profit?

3. Each of 1000 identical firms in the competitive peanut butter industry has a short-run marginal cost curve given by

$$\text{SMC}_Q = 4 + Q.$$

If the demand curve for this industry is

$$P = 10 - \frac{2Q}{1000},$$

what will be the short-run loss in producer and consumer surplus if an outbreak of aflatoxin suddenly makes it impossible to produce any peanut butter?

4. Assuming the aflatoxin outbreak in Problem 3 persists, will the long-run loss in producer and consumer surplus be larger than, smaller than, or the same as the short-run loss?

5. A perfectly competitive firm faces a price of 10 and is currently producing a level of output where marginal cost is equal to 10 on a rising portion of its short-run marginal cost curve. Its long-run marginal cost is equal to 12. Its short-run average variable cost is equal to 8. The minimum point on its long-run average cost curve is equal to 10. Is this firm earning an economic profit in the short run? Should it alter its output in the short run? In the long run, what should this firm do?

6. All firms in a competitive industry have long-run total cost curves given by

$$\text{LTC}_Q = Q^3 - 10Q^2 + 36Q,$$

where Q is the firm's level of output. What will be the industry's long-run equilibrium? (*Hint:* Use either calculus or a graph to find the minimum value of the associated long-run average cost curve.) What will be the long-run equilibrium output level of the representative firm?

7. Same as Problem 6, except now

$$\text{LTC}_Q = Q^2 + 4Q.$$

Could any firm actually have this particular LTC curve? Why or why not?

8. The marginal and average cost curves of taxis in Metropolis are constant at $0.20/mile. The demand curve for taxi trips in Metropolis is given by $P = 1 - 0.00001Q$, where P is the fare, in dollars per mile, and Q is measured in miles per year. If the industry is perfectly competitive and each cab can provide exactly 10,000 miles/yr of service, how many cabs will there be in equilibrium and what will be the equilibrium fare?

9. Now suppose that the city council of Metropolis decides to curb congestion in the downtown area by limiting the number of taxis to 6. Applicants participate in a lottery, and the six winners get a medallion, which is a permanent license to operate a taxi in Metropolis. What will the equilibrium fare be now? How much economic profit will each medallion holder earn? If medallions can be traded in the marketplace and the rate of interest is 10 percent/yr, how much will the medallions sell for? (*Hint:* How much money would you have to deposit in a bank to earn annual interest equal to the profit made by a taxi medallion?) Will the person who buys a medallion at this price earn a positive economic profit?

10. Merlin is like all other managers in a perfectly competitive industry except in one respect: Because of his great sense of humor, people are willing to work for him for half the going wage rate. All other firms in the industry have short-run total cost curves given by

$$\text{STC}_Q = M + 10Q + wQ_2 \quad \text{(see footnote 14)},$$

where M is the salary paid to ordinary managers and w is the going wage rate for the industry. If all firms in the industry face an output price of 28, and if $w = 2$, how much more will Merlin be paid than the other managers in the industry?

11. You are the owner/manager of a small competitive firm that manufactures house paints. You and all your 1000 competitors have total cost curves given by

$$\text{TC} = 8 + 2Q + 2Q^2,$$

and the industry is in long-run equilibrium.

Now you are approached by an inventor who holds a patent on a process that will reduce your costs by half at each level of output.

   a. What is the most you would be willing to pay for the exclusive right to use this invention?
   b. Would the inventor be willing to sell at that price?

---

[14]The associated marginal cost curve is $d\text{STC}_Q/dQ = \text{MC}_Q = 10 + 2wQ$.

12. In the short run, a perfectly competitive firm produces output using capital services (a fixed input) and labor services (a variable input). At its profit-maximizing level of output, the marginal product of labor is equal to the average product of labor.

    a. What is the relationship between this firm's average variable cost and its marginal cost? Explain.

    b. If the firm has 10 units of capital and the rental price of each unit is \$4/day, what will be the firm's profit? Should it remain open in the short run?

13. A firm in a competitive industry has a total cost function of $TC = 0.2Q_2 - 5Q + 30$, whose corresponding marginal cost curve is $MC = 0.4Q - 5$. If the firm faces a price of 6, what quantity should it sell? What profit does the firm make at this price? Should the firm shut down?

14. The demand for gasoline is $P = 5 - 0.002Q$ and the supply is $P = 0.2 + 0.004Q$, where P is in dollars and Q is in gallons. If a tax of \$1/gal is placed on gasoline, what is the incidence of the tax? What is the lost consumer surplus? What is the lost producer surplus?

15. Suppose that bicycles are produced by a perfectly competitive, constant cost industry. Which of the following will have a larger effect on the long-run price of bicycles: (1) a government program to advertise the health benefits of bicycling, or (2) a government program that increases the demand for steel, an input in the manufacture of bicycles that is produced in an increasing cost industry?

16. Suppose a representative firm in a perfectly competitive, constant cost industry has a cost function $TC = 4Q^2 + 100Q + 100$. $4Q + 100 + \frac{1}{Q}100$ $P = 4$

    a. What is the long-run equilibrium price for this industry?

    b. If market demand is given by the function $Q = 1000 - P$, where P denotes price, how many firms will operate in this long-run equilibrium?

    c. Suppose the government grants a lump-sum subsidy to each firm that manufactures the product. If this lump-sum subsidy equals 36, what would be the new long-run equilibrium price for the industry?

17. The domestic supply and demand curves for Jolt coffee beans are given by $P = 10 + Q$ and $P = 100 - 2Q$, respectively, where P is the price in dollars per bushel, and Q is the quantity in millions of bushels per year. The U.S. produces and consumes only a trivial fraction of world Jolt bean output, and the current world price of \$30/bushel is unaffected by events in the U.S. market. Transportation costs are also negligible.

    a. How much will U.S. consumers pay for Jolt coffee beans, and how many bushels per year will they consume?

    b. How will your answers to part (a) change if Congress enacts a tariff of \$20/bushel?

    c. What total effect on domestic producer and consumer surplus will the tariff have? How much revenue will the tariff raise?

18. An Australian researcher has discovered a drug that weakens a sheep's wool fibers just above the sheep's skin. The drug sharply reduces the cost of shearing (cutting the wool off) sheep because the entire coat pulls off easily in one piece. The world wool market is reasonably close to the model of perfect competition in both the product and factor sides. Trace out all of the effects of the introduction of this new drug.

Answers to In-Chapter Exercises

11-1. Let r^* be the monthly interest rate for which Cullen's economic profit would be zero. Then r^* must satisfy $\$16,000 - \$4,000 - \$800 - r^*(\$100,000,000) = 0$, which yields $r^* = 0.000112$, or 0.0112 percent/mo. Cullen should relocate only if the interest rate is lower than r^*.

11-2. Marginal cost is the slope of the total cost curve, and marginal revenue is the slope of the total revenue curve. At the maximum profit point, $Q = 7.4$, the slopes of these two curves are exactly the same.

11-3. First, we need to rearrange the representative firm supply curve $P = 20 + 90Q_i$ to have quantity alone on one side.

$$Q_i = -\frac{2}{9} + \frac{1}{90}P.$$

Then we multiply by the number of firms $n = 30$.

$$Q = nQ_i = 30Q_i = 30\left(-\frac{2}{9} + \frac{1}{90}P\right) = -\frac{20}{3} + \frac{1}{3}P.$$

Finally, we rearrange the industry supply curve $Q = -\frac{20}{3} + \frac{1}{3}P$ to have price alone on one side, $P = 20 + 3Q$, to return to slope-intercept form.

11-4. Short-run profit maximization for a perfectly competitive firm occurs at the quantity where price equals marginal cost, $P = MC$, provided $P > \min AVC$ (otherwise, the firm shuts down). Since marginal cost is $MC = 2Q$, the market price $P = 12$ equals marginal cost $12 = 2Q$ at quantity $Q = 6$. Note that $\min AVC = 0$ here. We can express profits (with fixed costs separated out) as $\pi = (P - AVC)Q - FC$. Since average variable cost is $AVC = Q = 6$, the firm would earn profits of

$$\pi = (12 - 6)6 - FC = 36 - FC.$$

Thus, with fixed cost $FC = 36$, the firm would earn zero profits.

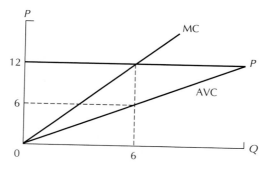

11-5. Total surplus is equal to the sum of the two shaded triangles shown below, which is $100,000/yr.

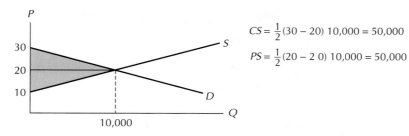

$$CS = \frac{1}{2}(30 - 20)\ 10{,}000 = 50{,}000$$

$$PS = \frac{1}{2}(20 - 2\ 0)\ 10{,}000 = 50{,}000$$

11-6. If the firm pays an incompetent manager only $30,000, it will continue to earn zero economic profit. It cannot pay any more than that without suffering an economic loss.

11-7. Using the formula $\epsilon^s = (P/Q)(1/slope)$, we have $\epsilon^s = \left(\frac{10}{20}\right)\left(\frac{1}{2}\right) = \frac{1}{4}$.

CHAPTER
12

Monopoly

Virtually every movie theater charges different admission prices to moviegoers who belong to different groups. Students pay one price, adults another, senior citizens still another. Some theaters sell "ten-packs" of movie tickets at a much lower unit price than the tickets they sell at the door. And people who attend showings at the dinner hour sometimes pay much less than those who attend evening showings. None of these practices would be expected under our model of perfect competition, which holds that all buyers pay a single price for a completely standardized product (the so-called *law of one price*).

The same theater operators who charge different ticket prices to different groups follow a very different practice when it comes to the sale of concession items. Here, the law of one price almost always prevails. Students, adults, senior citizens, major league baseball players, the clergy, service station attendants, and all other patrons pay exactly the same price for their popcorn. The same observation applies to the prices of soft drinks and candy. These prices, however, are usually much higher than we see for the same items sold in grocery stores and other retail establishments, certainly far greater than any reasonable measure of the marginal cost of providing them.

Both behaviors—charging differential admission prices on the one hand and uniformly high concession prices on the other—are, as we will see, perfectly consistent with what the economic model predicts about the single seller of a good or service.

Chapter Preview

In this chapter, our task is to examine the market structure that least resembles perfect competition—namely, *monopoly*, the case of a market served by a single seller of a product with no close substitutes. We will discuss four factors that lead to this market structure: (1) control over key inputs, (2) economies of scale, (3) patents, and (4) government licenses. We will then see that the monopolist's rule for maximizing profits in the short run is the same as the one used by perfectly competitive firms. The monopolist will expand output if the gain in revenue exceeds the increase in costs, and will contract output if the loss in revenue is smaller than the reduction in costs.

Next, we will examine the monopolist's behavior when confronted with the options of selling in several separate markets. Here again, the logic of cost-benefit analysis will provide a convenient framework for analyzing the firm's decision about whether to alter its current behavior.

Our next step is to examine the efficiency properties of the standard monopoly equilibrium. We will see that, unlike the perfectly competitive case, the monopoly equilibrium does not exhaust the potential gains from exchange. In general, the value to society of an additional unit of output will exceed the cost to the monopolist of the resources required to produce it. We will see that this finding has often been interpreted to mean that monopoly is less efficient than perfect competition. We will also see, however, that this interpretation is of only limited practical significance because the conditions that give rise to monopoly are rarely compatible with those required for perfect competition.

Our policy focus in the chapter is on the question of how the government should treat natural monopolies—markets characterized by downward-sloping long-run average cost curves. We will consider five policy alternatives: (1) state ownership, (2) private ownership with government price regulation, (3) competitive bidding by private firms for the right to be the sole provider of service, (4) vigorous enforcement of antitrust laws designed to prevent monopoly, and finally, (5) a complete *laissez-faire*, or hands-off, policy. Problems are inherent in each alternative, and we will see that the best policy generally will be different in different circumstances.

Defining Monopoly

A monopoly is a market structure in which a single seller of a product with no close substitutes serves the entire market. This definition could hardly appear any simpler, and yet it turns out to be exceedingly difficult to apply in practice. Consider the example of movie theaters with which the chapter began. Is a local movie house a monopoly under our definition? In smaller cities, at least, it is likely to be the only one showing a given film at a given time. Whether it is a monopoly obviously depends on what we mean by a close substitute. If, for example, the theater is currently showing *Halloween Part 8*, there are likely to be a rich variety of close substitutes for its product. Indeed, literally hundreds of low-grade blood-and-gore films are released each year, and the potential patrons of such films generally do not have to look far if they are dissatisfied with the terms available at any particular theater.

But what about a theater that is in the midst of an exclusive 6-month, first-run engagement of *Toy Story*? The first wholly computer-generated, full-length animated film, there was really no other movie quite like it at the time of its release. Anyone who wanted to see it while the excitement level was still high had only one seller to deal with.

The key feature that differentiates the monopoly from the competitive firm is the price elasticity of demand facing the firm. In the case of the perfectly competitive firm, recall, price elasticity is infinite. If a competitive firm raises its price only slightly, it will lose all its sales. A monopoly, by contrast, has significant control over the price it charges.

Empirically, one practical measure for deciding whether a firm enjoys significant monopoly power is to examine the cross-price elasticity of demand for its closest substitutes. In one famous antitrust case, the DuPont Corporation was charged with having an effective monopoly on the sale of cellophane. Even though the company sold more than 80 percent of all cellophane traded, it was able to defend itself against this charge by arguing that the cross-price elasticities between cellophane and its close substitutes—at the time, mainly waxed paper and aluminum foil—were sufficiently high to justify lumping all of these flexible-wrap products into a single market. DuPont sold less than 20 percent of total industry output under this broader market definition. In a controversial decision, the court deemed that small enough to sustain effective competition.

This is not to say, however, that cross-price elasticity provides a clear, unambiguous measure that distinguishes a product with close substitutes from one without. While there may not have been any other movie quite like *Toy Story*, there have always been lots of alternative ways to entertain oneself for 2 hours. For the person whose heart is set on seeing *Toy Story*, the theater operator is a monopolist, but for the person merely out in search of a good movie, the same theater operator faces stiff competition. The difference between perfect competition and monopoly often boils down to the question of which of these two types of buyers is more numerous. As in so many other cases in economics, the task of distinguishing between competition and monopoly remains as much an art as a science.

Note carefully that the distinction between monopoly and competition does not lie in any difference between the respective price elasticities of the *market* demand curves for the two cases. On the contrary, the market price elasticity of demand for products supplied by competitive firms is often much smaller than the price elasticity of demand facing a monopolist. The price elasticity of demand is smaller for wheat than for Polaroid cameras, even though wheat is produced under nearly perfectly competitive conditions while Polaroid's patents make it the only legal seller in most of its markets. The important distinction between monopoly and competition is that the demand curve facing the individual competitive firm is horizontal (irrespective of the price elasticity of the corresponding market demand curve), while the monopolist's demand curve is simply the downward-sloping demand curve for the entire market.

Four Sources of Monopoly

How does a firm come to be the only one that serves its market? Economists discuss four factors, any one or combination of which can enable a firm to become a monopoly. Let's consider these factors in turn.

1. Exclusive control over important inputs. The Perrier Corporation of France sells bottled mineral water. It spends millions of dollars each year advertising the unique properties of this water, which are the result, it says, of a once-in-eternity confluence of geological factors that created their mineral spring. In New York State, the Adirondack Soft Drink Company offers a product that is essentially tap water saturated with carbon dioxide gas. I am unable to tell the difference between Adirondack Seltzer and Perrier. But others feel differently, and for many of them there is simply no satisfactory substitute for Perrier. Perrier's monopoly position with respect to these buyers is the result of its exclusive control over an input that cannot easily be duplicated.

A similar monopoly position has resulted from the deBeers Diamond Mines' exclusive control over most of the world's supply of raw diamonds. Synthetic diamonds have now risen in quality to the point where they can occasionally fool even an experienced jeweler. But for many buyers, the preference for a stone that was mined from the earth is not a simple matter of greater hardness and refractive brilliance. They want *real* diamonds, and deBeers is the company that has them.

Exclusive control of key inputs is not a guarantee of permanent monopoly power. The preference for having a real diamond, for example, is based largely on the fact that mined diamonds have historically been genuinely superior to synthetic ones. But assuming that synthetic diamonds eventually do become completely indistinguishable from real ones, there will no longer be any basis for this preference. And as a result, the deBeers' control over the supply of mined diamonds will cease to confer monopoly power. New ways are constantly being devised of producing existing products, and the exclusive input that generates today's monopoly is likely to become obsolete tomorrow.

2. Economies of scale. When the long-run average cost curve (given fixed input prices) is downward sloping, the least costly way to serve the market is to concentrate production in the hands of a single firm. In Figure 12-1, for example, note that a single firm can produce an industry output of Q^* at an average cost of LAC_{Q^*}, while with two firms sharing the same market, average cost rises to $LAC_{Q^*/2}$. A market that is most cheaply served by a single firm is called a

FIGURE 12-1
When the LAC
curve is declining
throughout, it is al-
ways cheaper for a
single firm to serve
the entire industry.

NATURAL MONOPOLY

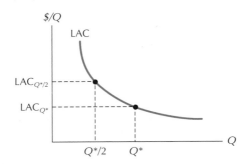

natural monopoly. A frequently cited example is the provision of local telephone service.

Recall from Chapter 11 that it is possible for the LAC curve to be downward sloping even in the absence of economies of scale. This can happen, for example, if the price of an important input falls significantly when industry output expands (a *pecuniary economy*, in the language of Chapter 11). Note carefully, however, that this case is *not* one that gives rise to natural monopoly. Input prices here depend on the level of industry output, not on the output of any one firm. Pecuniary economies will apply with equal force whether one or many firms serve the market.

Strictly speaking, then, it is the degree of returns to scale, not the slope of the LAC curve, that determines whether we have a natural monopoly. With fixed input prices, of course, there is always a one-to-one relationship between returns to scale and the slope of the LAC curve (see Chapter 10).

3. Patents. Most countries of the world protect inventions through some sort of patent system. A patent typically confers the right to exclusive benefit from all exchanges involving the invention to which it applies. There are costs as well as benefits to patents. On the cost side, the monopoly it creates usually leads, as we will see, to higher prices for consumers. On the benefit side, the patent makes possible a great many inventions that would not otherwise occur. Although some inventions are serendipitous, most are the result of long effort and expense in sophisticated research laboratories. If a firm were unable to sell its product for a sufficiently high price to recoup these outlays, it would have no economic reason to undertake research and development. Without a patent, competition would force price down to marginal cost, and the pace of innovation would be slowed dramatically. The protection from competition afforded by a patent is what makes it possible for the firm to recover its costs of innovation. In the United States, the life of a patent is 17 years, a compromise figure that is too long for many inventions, too short for many others. In particular, there is a persuasive argument that the patent life should be extended in the prescription drug industry, where the testing and approval process consumes all but a few years of the current patent period.[1]

4. Government licenses or franchises. In many markets, the law prevents anyone but a government-licensed firm from doing business. At rest areas on the Massachusetts Turnpike, for example, not just any fast-food restaurant is free to set up operations. The Turnpike Authority negotiates with several companies, chooses one, and then grants it an exclusive license to serve a particular area. As someone who likes Whoppers better than Big Macs, I am happy that the MassPike chose Burger King over McDonald's. But their choice is bound to disappoint many other buyers. The turnpike's purpose in restricting access in the first place is that there is simply not room for more than one establishment in these locations. In such cases, the government license as a source of monopoly is really a scale economy acting in another form. But government licenses are also required in a variety of other markets, such as the one for taxis, where scale economies do not seem to be an important factor. To raise revenues, many college campuses (such as Ohio State) sell exclusive rights to vending machine sales (such as only Coke or only Pepsi).

Government licenses are sometimes accompanied by strict regulations that spell out what the licensee can and cannot do. Where the government gives a chain restaurant an exclusive license, for example, the restaurant will often be required to charge prices no more than, say, 10 percent higher than it charges in its unregulated outlets. In other cases, the government simply charges an extremely high fee for the license, virtually forcing the licensee to charge premium prices. This is the practice of some airport authorities, who essentially auction their terminal counter space to the highest bidders. Your annoyance at having to pay $4 for a hot dog in LaGuardia Airport is thus more properly focused on the Port Authority of New York than on the vendor.

By far the most important of the four factors for explaining monopolies that endure in the long run is economies of scale. Production processes are likely to change over time, which makes exclusive control over important inputs only a transitory source of monopoly. Patents too are inherently transitory. Government licenses can of course persist for extended periods, but many of these licenses are merely an implicit recognition of scale economies that would lead to monopoly in any event.

With this brief overview of the causes of monopoly in mind, let us turn now to the question of what the consequences of monopoly are. In order to do this, we will proceed in much the same fashion as we did in our study of the competitive firm. That is, we will examine the firm's output decision and ask whether it leads to a situation in which all possible gains from exchange are exhausted. It will turn out that the answer to the latter question is generally no. But in formulating a government policy to improve on the results of

---

[1]Henry Grabowski, *Drug Regulation and Innovation*, Washington, DC: American Enterprise Institute, 1976.

unregulated monopoly, we will see that it is critical to understand the original source of monopoly.

The Profit-Maximizing Monopolist

As in the competitive case, we assume that the monopolist's goal is to maximize economic profit. And again as before, in the short run this means to choose the level of output for which the difference between total revenue and short-run total cost is greatest. The case for this motive is less compelling than in the case of perfect competition. After all, the monopolist's survival is less under siege than the competitor's, and so the evolutionary argument for profit maximization applies with less force in the monopoly case. Nonetheless, we will explore just what behaviors follow from the monopolist's goal of profit maximization.

THE MONOPOLIST'S TOTAL REVENUE CURVE

The key difference between the monopolist and the perfect competitor is the way in which total, and hence marginal, revenue varies with output. Recall from Chapter 11 that the demand curve facing the perfect competitor is simply a horizontal line at the short-run equilibrium market price—call it P^*. The competitive firm is a price taker, often because its own output is too small to have any discernible influence on the market price. Under these circumstances, the perfectly competitive firm's total revenue curve is a ray with slope P^*, as shown in Figure 12-2.

Now consider a monopolist with the downward-sloping demand curve $P = 80 - (\frac{1}{5})Q$ pictured in the top panel in Figure 12-3. For this firm too, total revenue is the product of price and quantity. At point A on its demand curve, for example, it sells 100 units of output per week at a price of $60/unit, giving a total revenue of $6000/wk. At B, it sells 200 units at a price of $40, so its total revenue at B will be $8000/wk, and so on. The difference between the monopolist and the competitor is that for the monopolist to sell a larger amount of

FIGURE 12-2
Price for the perfect competitor remains at the short-run equilibrium level P^* irrespective of the firm's output. Its total revenue is thus the product of P^* and the quantity it sells: TR = P^*Q.

THE TOTAL REVENUE CURVE FOR A PERFECT COMPETITOR

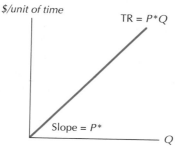

$/unit of time

TR = P^*Q

Slope = P^*

Q

FIGURE 12-3
For the monopolist to increase sales, it is necessary to cut price (top panel). Total revenue rises with quantity, reaches a maximum value, and then declines (middle panel). The quantity level for which the price elasticity of demand is unity corresponds to the midpoint of the demand curve, and at that value total revenue is maximized.

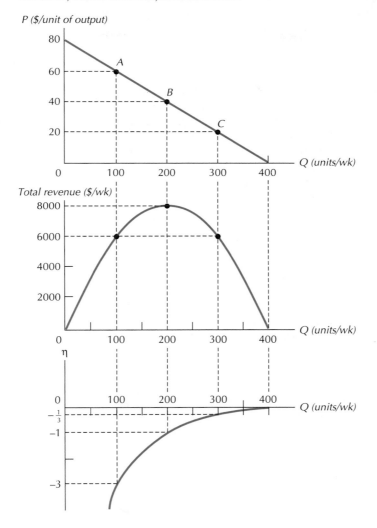

DEMAND, TOTAL REVENUE, AND ELASTICITY

output, he must cut his price—not only for the marginal unit but for all preceding units as well. As we saw in Chapter 5, the effect of a downward-sloping demand curve is that total revenue is no longer proportional to output sold. As in the competitive case, the monopolist's total revenue curve (middle panel in Figure 12-3) passes through the origin, because in each case selling no output generates no revenue. But as price falls, total revenue for the monopolist does not rise linearly with output. Instead, it reaches a maximum value at the quantity corresponding to the midpoint of the demand curve (*B* in the top panel), after which it again begins to fall. The corresponding values of the price elasticity of demand are shown in the bottom panel in Figure 12-3. Note that total revenue reaches its maximum value when the price elasticity of demand is unity.

EXERCISE 12-1

Sketch the total revenue curve for a monopolist whose demand curve is given by $P = 100 - 2Q$.

The top panel in Figure 12-4 portrays the short-run total cost curve and total revenue curve for a monopolist facing the demand curve shown in Figure 12-3. Economic profit, plotted in the bottom panel, is positive in the interval from $Q = 45$ to $Q = 305$, and is negative elsewhere. The maximum profit point occurs at $Q^* = 175$ units/wk, which lies to the left of the output level for which total revenue is a maximum ($Q = 200$).

FIGURE 12-4
Economic profit [$\Pi(Q)$ in the bottom panel] is the vertical distance between total revenue and total cost (TR and TC in the top panel). Note that the maximum-profit point, $Q^* = 175$, lies to the left of the output level at which TR is a maximum ($Q = 200$).

TOTAL COST, REVENUE, AND PROFIT CURVES FOR A MONOPOLIST

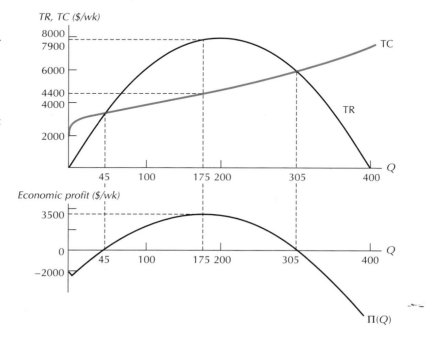

Notice in Figure 12-4 that the vertical distance between the short-run total cost and total revenue curves is greatest when the two curves are parallel (when $Q = 175$). Suppose this were not the case. For example, suppose that at the maximum-profit point the total cost curve were steeper than the total revenue curve. It would then be possible to earn higher profits by producing less output, because costs would go down by more than the corresponding reduction in total revenue. Conversely, if the total cost curve were less steep than the total revenue curve, the monopolist could earn higher profits by expanding output, because total revenue would go up by more than total cost.

MARGINAL REVENUE

Optimality condition for a monopolist A monopolist maximizes profit by choosing the level of output where marginal revenue equals marginal cost.

The slope of the total cost curve at any level of output is by definition equal to marginal cost at that output level. By the same token, the slope of the total revenue curve is the definition of *marginal revenue*.[2] As in the case of the perfectly competitive firm, we can think of marginal revenue as the change in total revenue when the sale of output changes by 1 unit. More precisely, suppose ΔTR_Q is the change in total revenue that occurs in response to a small change in output, ΔQ. Marginal revenue, denoted MR_Q, is then given by

$$MR_Q = \frac{\Delta TR_Q}{\Delta Q}. \tag{12.1}$$

Using this definition, a profit-maximizing monopolist in the short run will choose that level of output Q^* for which

$$MC_{Q^*} = MR_{Q^*} \qquad \text{(see footnote 3),} \tag{12.2}$$

provided marginal revenue intersects marginal cost from above. The monopolist wants to sell all units for which marginal revenue exceeds marginal cost, so marginal revenue should lie above marginal cost prior to the intersection (for some cost structures, marginal cost may decline initially and then increase, leading to two intersections of marginal cost and marginal revenue).

Recall that the analogous condition for the perfectly competitive firm is to choose the output level for which price and marginal cost are equal. Recalling that marginal revenue and price (P) are exactly the same for the competitive firm

---

[2] In calculus terms, marginal revenue is defined as the derivative dTR/dQ.

[3] This condition can also be justified by noting that the first-order condition for maximum profit is given by

$$\frac{d\Pi}{dQ} = \frac{d(TR - TC)}{dQ} = MR - MC = 0.$$

FIGURE 12-5
The area of rectangle *A* ($1000/wk) is the loss in revenue from selling the previous output level at a lower price. The area of rectangle *B* ($2500/wk) is the gain in revenue from selling the additional output at the new, lower price. Marginal revenue is the difference of these two areas ($2500 − $1000 = $1500/wk) divided by the change in output (50 units/wk). Here MR equals $30/unit, which is less than the new price of $50/unit.

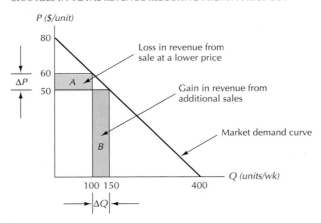

CHANGES IN TOTAL REVENUE RESULTING FROM A PRICE CUT

(when such a firm expands output by 1 unit, its total revenue goes up by *P*), we see that the profit-maximizing condition for the perfectly competitive firm is simply a special case of Equation 12.2.

In the case of the monopoly firm, marginal revenue will always be less than price.[4] To see why, consider the demand curve pictured in Figure 12-5, and suppose that the monopolist wishes to increase output from $Q_0 = 100$ to $Q_0 + \Delta Q = 150$ units/wk. His total revenue from selling 100 units/wk is ($60/unit) (100 units/wk) = $6000/wk. To sell an additional $\Delta Q = 50$ units/wk, he must cut his price to $60 − \Delta P = $50/unit, which means his new total revenue will be ($50/unit)(150 units/wk), which is equal to $7500/wk. To calculate marginal revenue, we simply subtract the original total revenue, $6000/wk, from the new total revenue, and divide by the change in output, $\Delta Q = 50$ units/wk. This yields $MR_{Q_0=100} = (\$7500/wk − \$6000/wk)/(50 \text{ units/wk}) = \$30/unit$, which is clearly less than the original price of $60/unit.

Another useful way of thinking about marginal revenue is to view it as the sum of the gain in revenue from new sales and the loss in revenue from selling the previous output level at the new, lower price. In Figure 12-5, the area of rectangle *B* ($2500/wk) represents the gain in revenue from the additional sales at the lower price. The area of rectangle *A* ($1000/wk) represents the loss in revenue from selling the original 100 units/wk at $50/unit instead of $60. Marginal revenue is the difference between the gain in revenue from additional sales and the loss in revenue from sales at a lower price, divided by the change in quantity. This yields ($2500/wk − $1000/wk)/(50 units/wk), which is again equal to $30/unit.

To explore how marginal revenue varies as we move along a straight-line demand curve, consider the demand curve pictured in Figure 12-6, and suppose

---

[4]There is actually one exception to this claim, namely, the case of the perfectly discriminating monopolist, discussed below.

FIGURE 12-6
When Q is to the left of the midpoint (M) of a straight-line demand curve (for example, $Q = Q_0$), the gain from added sales (area B) out-weighs the loss from a lower price for existing sales (area A). When Q is to the right of the midpoint (for example, $Q = Q_1$), the gain from added sales (area D) is smaller than the loss from a lower price for existing sales (area C). At the midpoint of the demand curve, the gain and the loss are equal, which means marginal revenue is zero.

MARGINAL REVENUE AND POSITION ON THE DEMAND CURVE

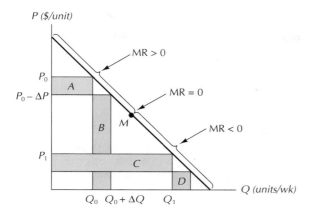

that the monopolist wishes to increase output from Q_0 to $Q_0 + \Delta Q$ units. His total revenue from selling Q_0 units is $P_0 Q_0$. To sell an additional ΔQ units, he must cut his price to $P_0 - \Delta P$, which means his new total revenue will be $(P_0 - \Delta P)(Q_0 + \Delta Q)$, which is equal to $P_0 Q_0 + P_0 \Delta Q - \Delta P Q_0 - \Delta P \Delta Q$. To calculate marginal revenue, simply subtract the original total revenue, $P_0 Q_0$, from the new total revenue, and divide by the change in output, ΔQ. This leaves $\text{MR}_{Q_0} = P_0 - (\Delta P / \Delta Q) Q_0 - \Delta P$, which is clearly less than P_0. As ΔP approaches zero, the expression for marginal revenue thus approaches[5]

$$\text{MR}_{Q_0} = P_0 - \frac{\Delta P}{\Delta Q} Q_0. \tag{12.3}$$

Equation 12.3 makes intuitive sense if we think of ΔQ as being a 1-unit change in output; P_0 would then be the gain in revenue from the sale of that extra unit, and $(\Delta P / \Delta Q) Q_0 = \Delta P Q_0$ would be the loss in revenue from the sale of the existing units at the lower price. We see again in Equation 12.3 that marginal revenue is less than price for all positive levels of output.

The fact that area B is larger than area A in Figure 12-6 means that marginal revenue is positive at Q_0. Once output moves past the midpoint (M in Figure 12-6) on a straight-line demand curve, however, the marginal revenue of a further expansion will be negative. Thus, the area of rectangle C is larger than the area of rectangle D in Figure 12-6, which means that marginal revenue at the output level Q_1 is less than zero.

---

[5]Note that when ΔP shrinks toward zero, the corresponding ΔQ does so as well. Because ΔP and ΔQ are both positive here, the ratio $\Delta P / \Delta Q$ is simply the negative of the slope of the demand curve.

MARGINAL REVENUE AND ELASTICITY

Yet another useful relationship links marginal revenue to the price elasticity of demand at the corresponding point on the demand curve. Recall from Chapter 5 that the price elasticity of demand at a point (Q, P) is given by

$$\eta = \frac{\Delta Q}{\Delta P} \frac{P}{Q}. \tag{12.4}$$

In Equation 12.4, the terms ΔQ and ΔP have opposite signs, because the demand curve is downward sloping. By contrast, recall that the ΔQ and ΔP terms in Equation 12.3, which also represent changes in P and Q as we move along the demand curve, are both positive. Suppose we redefine ΔQ and ΔP from Equation 12.4 so that both of these terms are positive. That equation then becomes

$$|\eta| = \frac{\Delta Q}{\Delta P} \frac{P}{Q}. \tag{12.5}$$

The purpose of making both ΔQ and ΔP positive is to be able to relate Equation 12.5 back to Equation 12.3. If we now solve Equation 12.5 for $\Delta P/\Delta Q = P/(Q|\eta|)$ and substitute into Equation 12.3, we get

$$MR_Q = P\left(1 - \frac{1}{|\eta|}\right). \tag{12.6}$$

Equation 12.6 tells us that the less elastic demand is with respect to price, the more price will exceed marginal revenue.[6] It also tells us that in the limiting case of infinite price elasticity, marginal revenue and price are exactly the same. (Recall from Chapter 11 that price and marginal revenue are the same for the competitive firm, which faces a horizontal, or infinitely elastic, demand curve.)

GRAPHING MARGINAL REVENUE

Equation 12.6 also provides a convenient way to plot the marginal revenue values that correspond to different points along a demand curve. To illustrate, consider the straight-line demand curve in Figure 12-7, which intersects the vertical

------

[6]Equation 12.6 can be derived using calculus as follows:

$$MR = \frac{d\text{TR}}{dQ} = \frac{d(PQ)}{dQ} = P + Q\frac{dP}{dQ} = P\left(1 + \frac{Q}{P}\frac{dP}{dQ}\right) = P\left(1 + \frac{1}{\eta}\right) = P\left(1 - \frac{1}{|\eta|}\right).$$

FIGURE 12-7
For the case of a
straight-line demand
curve, the corre-
sponding marginal
revenue curve is
also a straight line. It
has the same vertical
intercept as the de-
mand curve, and its
horizontal intercept
is half that of the de-
mand curve.

THE DEMAND CURVE AND CORRESPONDING MARGINAL REVENUE CURVE

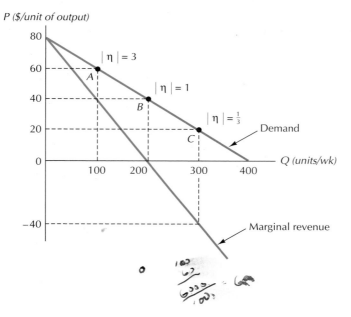

axis at a price value of $P = 80$. The elasticity of demand is infinite at that point, which means that $MR_0 = 80(1 - 1/|\eta|) = 80$. Although marginal revenue will generally be less than price for a monopolist, the two are exactly the same when quantity is zero. The reason is that at zero output there are no existing sales for a price cut to affect.

Now suppose we move, say, one-quarter of the way down the demand curve to point A, (100, 60). At that point, $|\eta| = 3$ (recall from Chapter 5 that the elasticity of demand at any point on a straight-line demand curve is simply the ratio of the bottom segment to the top segment of the demand curve at that point). Thus we have $MR_{100} = (60)(1 - \frac{1}{3}) = 40$.

Halfway down the demand curve, at point B, (200, 40), $|\eta| = 1$, which gives us $MR_{200} = (40)(1 - \frac{1}{1}) = 0$. This confirms our earlier finding (Chapter 5) that total revenue is at a maximum at the midpoint of a straight-line demand curve, where elasticity is unity.

Finally, consider point C, (300, 20), which is three-fourths of the way down the demand curve. Here $|\eta| = \frac{1}{3}$, so we have $MR_{300} = (20)[1-(1/\frac{1}{3})] = (20)(-2) = -40$. Thus, at $Q = 300$, the effect of selling an extra unit of output is to reduce total revenue by \$40/wk.

Filling in additional points in the same fashion, we quickly see that the marginal revenue curve associated with a straight-line demand curve is itself a straight line, one whose slope is twice that of the demand curve. The marginal revenue curve cuts the horizontal axis just below the midpoint of the demand

FIGURE 12-8
The marginal revenue curve has the same vertical intercept and twice the slope of the corresponding linear demand curve.

A SPECIFIC LINEAR DEMAND CURVE AND THE CORRESPONDING MARGINAL REVENUE CURVE

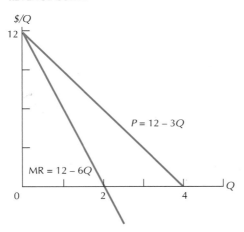

curve, and for all quantities larger than that marginal revenue is negative. Note that all points to the right of the midpoint of the demand curve have price elasticity values less than 1 in absolute value. The fact that marginal revenue is negative in this region thus fits our observation from Chapter 5 that a cut in price will reduce total revenue whenever demand is inelastic with respect to price.

*E*XAMPLE *12-1* *Find the marginal revenue curve that corresponds to the demand curve P = 12 − 3Q.*

The marginal revenue curve will have the same intercept as and twice the slope of the demand curve, which gives us MR = 12 − 6Q, as plotted in Figure 12-8.

The general formula for a linear demand curve is $P = a - bQ$, where a and b are positive numbers. The corresponding marginal revenue curve will be MR = $a - 2bQ$ (see footnote 7).

---

[7]Note that total revenue for the demand curve $P = a - bQ$ is given by TR = $aQ - bQ^2$. The corresponding marginal revenue curve is

$$\text{MR} = \frac{d\text{TR}}{dQ} = a - 2bQ.$$

FIGURE 12-9
Maximum profit oc-
curs at the output
level Q*, where the
gain in revenue from
expanding output
(or loss in revenue
from contracting
output), MR, is ex-
actly equal to the
cost of expanding
output (or the sav-
ings from contract-
ing output), SMC. At
Q*, the firm charges
P* and earns an
economic profit of Π.

THE PROFIT-MAXIMIZING PRICE AND QUANTITY FOR A MONOPOLIST

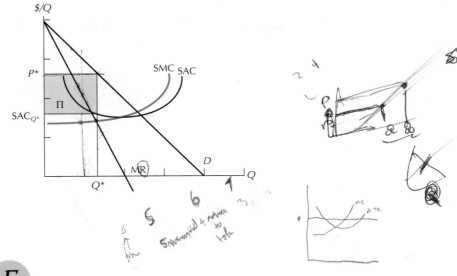

EXERCISE 12-2

> Sketch demand and marginal revenue curves for a monopolist whose
> market demand curve is given by $P = 100 - 2Q$.

GRAPHICAL INTERPRETATION OF THE SHORT-RUN PROFIT MAXIMIZATION CONDITION

Recall from Chapter 11 the graphical representation of the maximum-profit point
for the competitive firm in the short run. An analogous graphical representation
exists for the monopolist. Consider a monopolist with the demand, marginal revenue, and short-run cost curves pictured in Figure 12-9. The profit-maximizing
level of output for this firm is Q*, the one for which the marginal revenue and
marginal cost curves intersect. At that quantity level, the monopolist can charge
a price of P*, and by so doing will earn an economic profit equal to the shaded
rectangle labeled Π.

EXAMPLE 12-2

A monopolist faces a demand curve of $P = 100 - 2Q$ and a short-run total cost curve of
$TC = 640 + 20Q$. The associated marginal cost curve is $MC = 20$. What is the profit-maximizing price? How much will the monopolist sell, and how much economic profit will it
earn at that price?

The marginal revenue curve for this demand curve is MR = 100 − 4Q. Marginal cost is the slope of the total cost curve, which is constant at 20 in this example. Setting MR = MC, we have 100 − 4Q = 20, which yields the profit-maximizing quantity, $Q^* = 20$. Plugging $Q^* = 20$ back into the demand curve, we get the profit-maximizing price, $P^* = 60$. This solution is shown graphically in Figure 12-10, which also displays the average total cost curve for the monopolist. Note that at Q^* the ATC is 52, which means the monopolist earns an economic profit of 60 − 52 = 8 on each unit sold. With $Q^* = 20$, that makes for a total economic profit of 160.

Note in Figure 12-10 that the monopolist's fixed cost was irrelevant to the determination of the profit-maximizing output level and price. This makes sense intuitively, because fixed cost has no bearing on the gains and losses that occur when output changes.

EXERCISE 12-3

How would the profit-maximizing price and quantity change in Example 12-2 if the monopolist's total cost curve were instead given by TC = 640 + 40Q? The associated marginal cost curve is MC = 40.

FIGURE 12-10   **THE PROFIT-MAXIMIZING PRICE AND QUANTITY FOR SPECIFIC COST AND DEMAND FUNCTIONS**

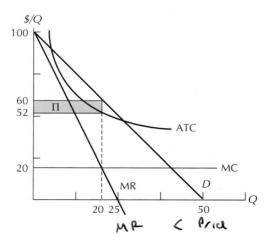

MR < Price

A PROFIT-MAXIMIZING MONOPOLIST WILL NEVER PRODUCE ON THE INELASTIC PORTION OF THE DEMAND CURVE

If a monopolist's goal is to maximize profits, it follows directly that she will never produce an output level on the inelastic portion of her demand curve. If she were to increase her price at such an output level, the effect would be to increase total revenue. The price increase would also reduce the quantity demanded, which, in turn, would reduce the monopolist's total cost. Since economic profit is the difference between total revenue and total cost, profit would necessarily increase in response to a price increase from an initial position on the inelastic portion of the demand curve. The profit-maximizing level of output must therefore lie on the elastic portion of the demand curve, where further price increases would cause both revenue and costs to go down.

THE PROFIT-MAXIMIZING MARKUP

The profit-maximization condition MR = MC can be combined with Equation 12.6, which says MR = $P[1 - (1/|\eta|)]$, to derive the profit-maximizing markup for the monopolist:

$$\frac{P - \text{MC}}{P} = \frac{1}{|\eta|} , \qquad (12.7)$$

which is the difference between price and marginal cost, expressed as a fraction of the profit-maximizing price. For example, if the price elasticity of demand facing a monopolist were equal to -2, the profit-maximizing markup would be $\frac{1}{2}$, which implies that the profit-maximizing price is twice marginal cost. Equation 12.7 tells us that the profit-maximizing markup grows smaller as demand grows more elastic. In the limiting case of infinitely elastic demand, the profit-maximizing markup is zero (which implies $P = $ MC), the same as in the perfectly competitive case.

THE MONOPOLIST'S SHUTDOWN CONDITION

In the case of the perfectly competitive firm, we saw that it paid to shut down in the short run whenever the price fell below the minimum value of average variable cost (AVC). The analogous condition for the monopolist is that there exists no quantity for which the demand curve lies above the average variable cost curve. The monopolist whose demand, marginal revenue, SMC, and AVC curves are shown in Figure 12-11, for example, has no positive level of output for which price exceeds AVC, and so the monopolist does best by ceasing production in the short run. He will then sustain a short-run economic loss equal to his fixed costs, but he would do even worse at any positive level of output.

FIGURE 12-11
Whenever average
revenue (the price
value on the de-
mand curve) is
lower than average
variable cost for
every level of out-
put, the monopolist
does best to cease
production in the
short run.

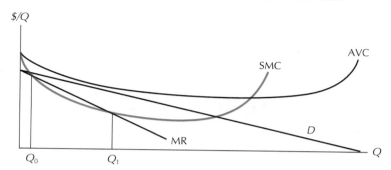

A MONOPOLIST WHO SHOULD SHUT DOWN IN THE SHORT RUN

Another way of stating the shutdown condition for a monopolist is to say that he should cease production whenever average revenue is less than average variable cost at every level of output. Average revenue is simply another name for price—the value of P along the monopolist's demand curve.[8]

Figure 12-11 also illustrates the important point that MR = MC is a necessary, but not sufficient, condition for maximum profit. Note in the figure that marginal revenue is equal to marginal cost at the output level Q_0. Why isn't this the maximum-profit point? Recall that in the case of the perfectly competitive firm, the maximum-profit condition called for price to equal marginal cost on a rising portion of the marginal cost curve, above the minimum point on the AVC curve. A somewhat different condition applies in the case of the monopolist. In Figure 12-11, note that at Q_0 the MR curve intersects the MC curve from below.[9] This means not only that Q_0 is not the maximum-profit point, but that it actually corresponds to a *lower* profit level than any of the other output levels nearby. For example, consider an output level just less than Q_0. At any such output level the gains from contracting output (MC) will exceed the losses (MR), so the firm does better to contract from Q_0. Now consider an output level just slightly larger than Q_0. For such an output level, the gains from expanding (MR) exceed the costs (MC), so the firm does better to expand. Thus, when the firm is at Q_0, it can earn higher profits by either contracting *or* expanding. Q_0 is called a *local minimum* profit point.[10]

---

[8]More formally, note that average revenue = TR/Q = PQ/Q = P.

[9]To "intersect from below at Q_0" means that as Q approaches Q_0 from the left, MR lies below MC and then crosses MC when Q = Q_0.

[10]The second-order condition for maximum profit is given by

$$\frac{d(\text{MR} - \text{MC})}{dQ} = \frac{d\text{MR}}{dQ} - \frac{d\text{MC}}{dQ} < 0,$$

which says simply that the slope of the marginal revenue curve must be less than the slope of the marginal cost curve.

Note also in Figure 12-11 that the MR curve intersects the MC curve a second time at the output level Q_1. This time the intersection occurs from above, and you can easily show as an exercise that Q_1 yields higher profits than any of the other output levels close by. (The argument runs exactly parallel to the one in the preceding paragraph.) We refer to points like Q_1 as *local maximum* profit points. But although Q_1 yields more profit than any nearby output level, the firm fails to cover its average variable cost at the level of output, and so does better simply to produce nothing at all. The point Q^* we saw earlier in Figure 12-9 is both a local maximum profit point and a *global maximum* profit point, the latter designation indicating that no other output level, including zero, yields higher profit. For a monopolist, a global maximum profit point might occur either on the rising or on the falling portion of the MC curve. But it must be at a point where the MR curve intersects the MC curve from above.

EXERCISE 12-4

Find the optimal price and quantity for the monopolist described by the information on the following table.

Q	P	MR	SMC	AVC
0	100	100	150	150
15	86	71	71	107
25	75	50	41	84
34	66	33	33	72
50	50	0	63	63

To recapitulate briefly, we have seen that the monopolist behaves like a perfectly competitive firm in the sense that each chooses an output level by weighing the benefits of expanding (or contracting) output against the corresponding costs. For both the perfect competitor and the monopolist, marginal cost is the relevant measure of the cost of expanding output. Fixed costs are irrelevant for short-run output decisions in both cases. For both the monopolist and perfect competitor, the benefits of expanding output are measured by their respective values of marginal revenue. For the competitor, marginal revenue and price are one and the same. For the monopolist, by contrast, marginal revenue is less than price. The competitor maximizes profit by expanding output until marginal cost equals price. The monopolist maximizes profit by expanding output until marginal cost equals marginal revenue, and

thus chooses a lower output level than if he had used the competitor's criterion. Both the monopolist and the perfect competitor do best to shut down in
the short run if price is less than average variable cost for all possible levels
of output.

A Monopolist Has No Supply Curve

As we saw in Chapter 11, the competitive firm has a well-defined supply curve.
It takes market price as given and responds by choosing the output level for
which marginal cost and price are equal. At the industry level, a shifting demand
curve will trace out a well-defined industry supply curve, which is the horizontal summation of the individual firm supply curves.

There is no similar supply curve for the monopolist. The reason is that the
monopolist is not a price taker, which means that there is no unique correspondence between price and marginal revenue when the market demand curve
shifts. Thus, a given marginal revenue value for one demand curve can correspond to one price, while the same value of marginal revenue for a second
demand curve corresponds to a different price. As a result, it is possible to
observe the monopolist producing Q^*_1 and selling at P^* in one period, and then
selling Q^*_2 at P^* in another period.

To illustrate, consider a monopolist with a demand curve of $P = 100 - Q$ and
with the same cost curves as in Example 12-2, in particular with MC = 20. The
marginal revenue curve for this monopolist is given by MR = $100 - 2Q$, and
equating MR to MC yields a profit-maximizing output level of $Q^* = 40$. The corresponding profit-maximizing price is $P^* = 60$. Note that this is the same as the
profit-maximizing price we saw for the monopolist in Example 12-2, even though
the demand curve here lies to the right of the earlier one.

When the monopolist's demand curve shifts, the price elasticity of demand at
a given price generally will also shift. But these shifts need not occur in the same
direction. When demand shifts rightward, for example, elasticity at a given price
may either increase or decrease, and the same is true when demand shifts leftward. The result is that there can be no unique correspondence between the price
a monopolist charges and the amount she chooses to produce. And hence we
say that the monopolist has no supply curve. Rather, she has a *supply rule*, which
is to equate marginal revenue and marginal cost.

Adjustments in the Long Run

In the long run, the monopolist is of course free to adjust all inputs, just as
the competitive firm is. What is the optimal quantity in the long run for a
monopolist with a given technology? The best the monopolist can do is to produce the quantity for which long-run marginal cost is equal to marginal rev-

enue. In Figure 12-12, that will mean choosing a capital stock that gives rise to the short-run average and marginal cost curves labeled SAC* and SMC*. For that level of capital stock, the short-run marginal cost curve passes through the intersection of the long-run marginal cost and marginal revenue curves. *Q** will be the profit-maximizing quantity in the long run, and it will sell at a price of *P**. For the conditions pictured in Figure 12-12, the long-run economic profit level, Π, will be positive, and is indicated by the area of the shaded rectangle.

As we saw in Chapter 11, economic profits tend to vanish in the long run in perfectly competitive industries. This tendency will sometimes be present for monopoly. To the extent that the factors that gave rise to the firm's monopoly position come under attack in the long run, there will be downward pressure on its profits. For example, competing firms may develop substitutes for important inputs that were previously under the control of the monopolist. Or in the case of patented products, competitors may develop close substitutes that do not infringe on existing patents, which are in any event only temporary.

But in other cases there may be a tendency for monopoly profits to persist even in the long run. The firm shown in Figure 12-12, for example, has a declining long-run average cost curve, which means that it may enjoy a persistent cost advantage over potential rivals. In such natural monopolies, economic profits may be highly stable over time. And the same, of course, may be true for a firm whose monopoly comes from having a government license. Persistent economic profits are indeed one of the major policy concerns about monopoly, as we discuss further later in the chapter.

FIGURE 12-12
The profit-maximizing quantity in the long run is *Q**, the output level for which LMC = MR. The profit-maximizing price in the long run is *P**. The optimal capital stock in the long run gives rise to the short-run marginal cost curve SMC*, which passes through the intersection of LMC and MR.

LONG-RUN EQUILIBRIUM FOR A PROFIT-MAXIMIZING MONOPOLIST

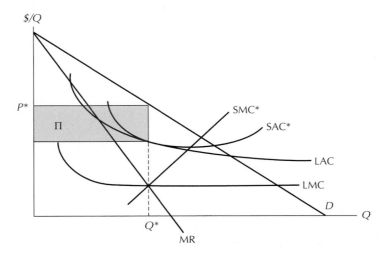

Price Discrimination

Our discussion thus far has assumed that the monopolist sells all its output at a single price. In reality, however, monopolists often charge different prices to different buyers, a practice that is known as *price discrimination*. The movie theater discount tickets discussed at the beginning of this chapter constitute one example. In the following sections, we analyze how the profit-maximizing monopolist behaves when it is possible to charge different prices to different buyers. When price discrimination is possible, a monopolist can transfer some of the gains from consumers into its own profits. However, we will see that not all the higher profits under price discrimination come at the expense of consumers. Efficiency is enhanced as the monopolist expands output toward the level at which demand intersects marginal cost.

SALE IN DIFFERENT MARKETS

Suppose the monopolist has two completely distinct markets in which she can sell her output. Perhaps she is the only supplier in the domestic market for her product, and the only one in a foreign market as well. If she is a profit maximizer, what prices should she charge and what quantities should she sell in each market?

Suppose the demand and marginal revenue curves for the two markets are as given in the left and middle panels in Figure 12-13. First note that if the monopolist is maximizing profit, her marginal revenue should be the same in each market. (If it weren't, she could sell 1 unit less in the market with lower MR and 1 unit more in the market with higher MR, and in the process increase her profit.) Given that MR in the two markets must be the same, the profit-max-

FIGURE 12-13
The marginal revenue curve for a monopolist who sells in two markets is the horizontal sum of the respective marginal revenue curves. The profit-maximizing output level is where the ΣMR curve intersects the MC curve, here, $Q^* = 10$. Marginal revenue in each market will be the same when $Q_1^* = 4$ and $Q_2^* = 6$ are sold in markets 1 and 2, respectively.

THE PROFIT-MAXIMIZING MONOPOLIST WHO SELLS IN TWO MARKETS

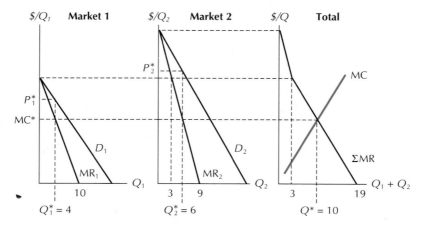

imizing total quantity will be the one for which this common value is the same as marginal cost. Graphically, the solution is to add the marginal revenue curves horizontally across the two markets, and produce the level of output for which the resulting curve intersects the marginal cost curve. In the right panel in Figure 12-13, the optimal total output is indicated by $Q^* = 10$ units. $Q_1^* = 4$ of it is sold in market 1 at a price of P_1^*, and the remaining $Q_2^* = 6$ in market 2 at a price of P_2^*.

EXAMPLE 12-3 A monopolist has marginal costs MC $=$ Q and home market demand P $=$ 30 $-$ Q. The monopolist can also sell to a foreign market at a constant price P_F $=$ 12. Find and graph the quantity produced, quantity sold in the home market, quantity sold in the foreign market, and price charged in the home market. Explain why the monopolist's profits would fall if it were to produce the same quantity but sell more in the home market.

The linear demand curve $P = 30 - Q$ has associated marginal revenue MR $= 30 - 2Q$. The profit-maximizing level of output for a monopolist selling to segmented markets occurs where ΣMR $=$ MC. The horizontal sum of the marginal revenues across markets is the home marginal revenue function MR_H up to home output where $MR_F = MR_H$, and then the foreign marginal revenue function $MR_F = 12$ for any further units (see Figure 12-14). Total marginal revenue equals marginal cost at $MR_F =$ MC, which solves for $Q = 12$. Marginal cost for this level of output equals home marginal revenue at $30 - 2Q_H = 12$, so $Q_H = 9$ with the remaining units sold abroad:

$$Q_F = Q - Q_H = 12 - 9 = 3.$$

In the home market, the monopolist charges

$$P_H = 30 - Q_H = 30 - 9 = 21.$$

Any further units sold at home would yield marginal revenue less than 12. Since sales to the foreign market yield a constant marginal revenue of 12, shifting sales to the home market would decrease profits due to the lost marginal revenue for each unit shifted.

FIGURE 12-14
The marginal revenue curve ΣMR follows MR^H as long as $MR^H \geq MR^F$, and then follows MR^F. The profit-maximizing output level is where the ΣMR curve intersects the MC curve, here $Q^* = 12$.

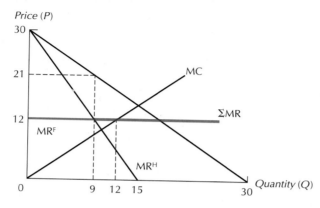

A MONOPOLIST WITH A PERFECTLY ELASTIC FOREIGN MARKET

EXERCISE 12-5

Suppose a monopolist sells in two separate markets, with demand curves given by $P_1 = 10 - Q_1$ and $P_2 = 20 - Q_2$, respectively. If her total cost curve is given by TC = 5 + 2Q (for which the associated marginal cost curve is given by MC = 2), what quantities should she sell and what prices should she charge in the two markets?

Note in Exercise 12-5 that the monopolist who sells in two markets charges a higher price in the market where demand is less elastic with respect to price.[11] Charging different prices to buyers in completely separate markets is often referred to as *third-degree price discrimination*. There is no special significance to the term "third-degree" beyond the fact that this type of price discrimination happened to have been the third one that appeared in an early taxonomy.

Examples of third-degree price discrimination abound. This textbook, for instance, is also offered in an international student edition that sells for about one-third the price of the domestic edition. Because the incomes of students are generally much lower in foreign markets than in the United States, the price elasticity of demand tends to be much higher in foreign than in U.S. markets. The price that maximizes profits in the U.S. market would discourage most Third World students from buying.

---

[11]This result follows from Equation 12.6, which says that MR = $P(1 - 1/|\eta|)$. Setting $MR_1 = MR_2$ yields $P_1/P_2 = (1 - 1/|\eta_2|)(1 - 1/|\eta_1|)$. Hence the higher price will be charged to customers with the lower price elasticity of demand.

Charging different patrons different admission prices for the same movie is another example. The higher price elasticities of senior citizens and students make it a good strategy for theater operators to set lower prices for these groups. Businesses that offer discount prices to students, senior citizens, and others sometimes portray their behavior as having been motivated by concern for the economic hardships confronting these groups. This concern is no doubt often heartfelt. But notice that the same pattern of behavior would be seen on the part of monopolists interested only in the bottom line.

Notice also that price discrimination is feasible only when it is impossible, or at least impractical, for buyers to trade among themselves. If students in other lands could trade with those in the United States, for example, it would not be possible to sell essentially the same book for $12 in Calcutta and $50 in New York. Entrepreneurial students would buy $12 books abroad and sell them to U.S. students for, say, $49; others, hoping to get in on the action, would cut price even further, and eventually the price differential would vanish. Buying at a low price from one source and reselling at a higher price is often called ***arbitrage***. Where arbitrage is practical, large price differentials for a single product cannot persist. Arbitrage ensures, for example, that the price of gold in London can never differ significantly from the price of gold in New York.

Arbitrage The purchase of something for costless risk-free resale at a higher price.

But arbitrage is not always practical. Student discounts enable theater operators to segment their markets because it is not possible for one person to see a movie at a low price and then sell the experience to someone else at a higher price. By the same token, it is practical for lawyers and doctors to charge different people different prices on the basis of differences in price elasticity of demand. But such market segmentation is more difficult for products like popcorn. If theater operators attempted to sell popcorn for $1 to students and for $3 to adults, some enterprising student would seize the arbitrage opportunity, selling popcorn to disgruntled adults for only $2. And under the pressure of competition from other arbitrageurs, the price differential would fall until the price differential was barely sufficient to make it worth the students' while to engage in the transaction.

THE PERFECTLY DISCRIMINATING MONOPOLIST

First-degree price discrimination is the term used to describe the largest possible extent of market segmentation. To illustrate, suppose a monopolist has N potential customers, each one of whom has a downward-sloping demand curve like the one labeled D_i in Figure 12-15. What is the most revenue the monopolist could extract from the sale of Q' units of output to such a customer? If the monopolist had to sell all units at the same price, the best he could do would be to charge P', which would yield a total revenue of $P'Q'$. But if he can charge different prices for different units of output, he can do much better. For example, he can sell the first Q_1 units at a price of P_1, the next $Q_2 - Q_1$ units at a price of P_2, and so on. If the intervals into which the monopolist can partition the product are arbitrarily small, this form of pricing will augment total revenue by the area of the shaded triangle in Figure 12-15.

PERFECT PRICE DISCRIMINATION

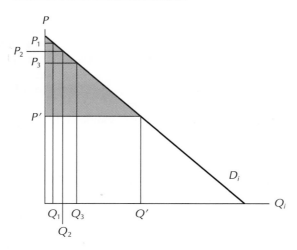

Had the monopolist been forced to charge a single price for all units, that shaded triangle would have been consumer surplus. When he is able to charge different prices for each unit, however, the monopolist captures all the consumer surplus. The consumer pays the maximum he would have been willing to pay for each unit, and as a result receives no surplus.

How much output will a profit-maximizing, perfectly discriminating monopolist produce? As always, the rule is to equate marginal revenue to marginal cost. Figure 12-16 portrays the demand, short-run marginal, and average total cost curves for a perfectly discriminating monopolist. But what is the marginal revenue curve for this monopolist? *It is exactly the same as his demand curve.* Because he can discriminate perfectly, he can lower his price to sell additional output without having to cut price on the output originally sold. Price and marginal revenue are one and the same, just as in the case of perfect competition. The best this firm can do is to produce Q^* units of output, each of which it sells at the highest price each of its buyers is willing to pay.

There are two salient points of comparison between the perfectly discriminating monopolist and the monopolist who cannot discriminate at all. The first is that the perfect discriminator produces a higher level of output because he need not be concerned with the effect of a price cut on the revenue from output produced thus far. He can cut price to the people who would not otherwise buy, and maintain higher prices to those who are willing to pay them.

A second important difference is that there generally is positive consumer surplus under the nondiscriminating monopolist, but none under the perfect discriminator. Because the nondiscriminator must charge the same price to all buyers, there is pressure on him not to set his price too high. If he sets it at the level the least elastic demanders are willing to pay, he will lose the patronage of

FIGURE 12-16
The marginal revenue curve for the monopolist who can discriminate perfectly is exactly the same as his demand curve. The profit-maximizing output is Q^*, the one for which the SMC and demand curves intersect. Economic profit (Π) is given by the shaded area.

THE PERFECTLY DISCRIMINATING MONOPOLIST

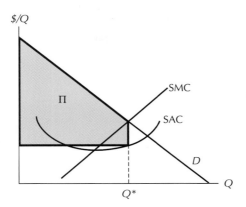

all others. As a result, the monopolist will not do this, and the least elastic demanders end up paying a price well below their respective reservation prices—hence the consumer surplus.

Perfect price discrimination is a never-attained theoretical limit. If a customer's demand curve were tattooed on his forehead, it might be possible for a seller to tailor each price to extract the maximum possible amount from every buyer. But in general, the details of individual demand are only imperfectly known to the seller. Merchants often estimate individual elasticity on the basis of information known about groups to which the individual belongs. A catalog merchant, for example, may print special editions with higher prices for mailing into high-income zip codes like 90213 (Beverly Hills, California).

Perhaps the closest thing we see to an in-depth assessment of individual elasticities is in the behavior of merchants in bazaars in the Middle East. The shrewd camel trader has had many years of experience in trying to assess how much a buyer with a given demographic and psychological profile is willing to pay. His stock in trade is to interpret the incongruous gesture, the furtive eye movement. But even here, the wily buyer may know how to conceal his eagerness to own the camel.

SECOND-DEGREE PRICE DISCRIMINATION

Yet another form of price discrimination is the practice by which many sellers post not a single price, but a schedule along which price declines with the quantity you buy. Thus, many electric utilities employ what are called *declining tail-block rate structures* by which the first, say, 300 kilowatt-hours per month are billed at 10 cents each, the next 700 at 8 cents, and all quantities over 1000 kilowatt-hours/mo at 5 cents each. Such rate structures are a form of *second-degree price discrimination*.

Figure 12-17 illustrates the effect of such a rate structure for a consumer with

FIGURE 12-17
The seller offers the first block of consumption (0 to Q_1) at a high price (P_1), the second block (Q_1 to Q_2) at a lower price (P_2), the third block (Q_2 to Q_3) at a still lower price (P_3), and so on. Even though second-degree price discrimination makes no attempt to tailor rates to the characteristics of individuals or specific groups, it often enables the monopolist to capture a substantial share of consumer surplus (the shaded area).

SECOND-DEGREE PRICE DISCRIMINATION

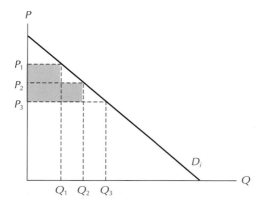

the demand curve labeled D_i. In comparison with the alternative of charging a price of P_3 for every unit, the quantity discount scheme increases the consumer's total payment by an amount equal to the shaded area.

Second-degree price discrimination is like first-degree in that it tries to extract consumer surplus from each buyer. The two principal differences are these: (1) The same rate structure is available to every consumer under second-degree schemes, which means that they make no attempt to tailor charges to elasticity differences among buyers; and (2) the limited number of rate categories tends to limit the amount of consumer surplus that can be captured under second-degree schemes. First-degree schemes get the whole triangle, whereas Figure 12-17 shows that second-degree schemes capture only part of it.

THE HURDLE MODEL OF PRICE DISCRIMINATION

Every seller would like to practice perfect price discrimination. The difficulty, as noted earlier, is that sellers lack the information on individual demand curves necessary to do so. Yet another important form of price discrimination consists of a technique whereby the firm induces the most elastic buyers to identify themselves. This is the *hurdle model of price discrimination*. The basic idea is that the seller sets up a hurdle of some sort and makes a discount price available to those buyers who elect to jump over it. The logic is that those buyers who are most sensitive to price will be much more likely than others to jump the hurdle.

One example of a hurdle is a rebate form included in the product package. To jump over the hurdle here means to go to the trouble of filling in the form, finding a stamp and an envelope, and then getting to the post office to mail it in. The firm's hope is that people who don't care much about price will be less likely than others to bother going through this process. If so, then people whose demands are less elastic end up paying the "regular" price, while those with more elastic demands pay the lower discount price.

It is a rare product whose seller does not use the hurdle model of differential pricing. Booksellers offer only high-priced hardback editions in the first year of publication. Buyers who don't care strongly about price buy these editions when they first come out. Others wait a year or two and then buy the much less expensive softcover edition. Here, the hurdle is having to endure the wait. Appliance sellers offer regular "scratch-'n-dent" sales at which machines with trivial cosmetic imperfections are sold for less than half their regular price. Here, there are two hurdles: having to find out when and where the sale takes place and having to put up with a scratch or dent (which most of the time will be out of sight). Airlines offer "super-saver" discounts of up to half off the regular coach fare. Here also there are two hurdles: having to make reservations a week or more in advance and having to stay over a Saturday night. Many retailers include discount coupons in their newspaper ads. Here, the hurdles are having to read the ads, clip the coupons, and get to the store before they expire. Some sellers post signs behind the counter saying "Ask about our special low price." Here, the hurdle is merely having to do the asking. But even this trivial hurdle can be remarkably effective, because many well-heeled buyers would find asking about a special price too unseemly even to contemplate.

None of these schemes perfectly segregates high-elasticity from low-elasticity buyers. For instance, there are some people who wait for the January white sales to buy their towels even though they would buy just as many if the sales weren't offered. But on the whole, the hurdles seem to function much as intended. A perfect hurdle would be one that imposes only a negligible cost on the buyers who jump it, yet perfectly separates buyers according to their elasticity of demand. Analytically, the effect of such a hurdle is portrayed in Figure 12-18, where P_H represents the "regular" price and P_L represents the discount price. With a perfect hurdle, none of the people who pay the discount price has a reservation price greater than or equal to the regular price, which means that all of them would have been excluded from the market had only the regular price been available.

The hurdle model need not be limited to the two-price version depicted in Figure 12-18. On the contrary, many sellers have developed it into a highly

FIGURE 12-18
When a hurdle is perfect, the only buyers who become eligible for the discount price (P_L) by jumping it are those who would not have been willing to pay the regular price (P_H). A perfect hurdle also imposes no significant costs on those who jump it.

A PERFECT HURDLE

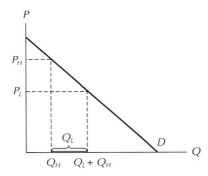

complex art form involving literally dozens of price-hurdle combinations. On its Los Angeles–Honolulu route alone, for example, United Airlines offers 37 different fares, each with its own set of restrictions. But no matter how simple or complex the scheme may be, its goal is the same—to give discounts to customers who would not otherwise buy the product.

The hurdle model is like first-degree price discrimination in that it tries to tailor prices to the elasticities of individual buyers. The principal difference is that even in its most sophisticated form, the hurdle model cannot hope to capture all the consumer surplus.

The Efficiency Loss from Monopoly

Recall from Chapter 11 the claim that perfect competition led to an efficient allocation of resources. This claim was based on the observation that in long-run competitive equilibrium, there are no possibilities for additional gains from exchange. The value to buyers of the last unit of output is exactly the same as the market value of the resources required to produce it.

How does the long-run equilibrium under monopoly measure up by the same criteria? Not very well, it turns out. To illustrate, consider a monopolist with constant long-run average and marginal costs and the demand structure shown in Figure 12-19. The profit-maximizing quantity for this monopolist is Q^*, which he will sell at a price of P^*. Note that at Q^*, the value of an additional unit of output to buyers is P^*, which is greater than the cost of producing an additional unit, LMC. This means that the single-price monopolist does not exhaust all possible gains from exchange. As we saw earlier, if it were possible for the monopolist to charge different prices to every buyer, output would expand to Q_C, which is the same amount we would see in a perfectly competitive industry under the same demand and cost conditions. If output did expand from Q^* to Q_C because of perfect price discrimination, the gain in producer surplus would be equal to the combined areas of the triangles labeled S_1 and S_2. Under perfect competition, the triangle S_1 would be part of consumer surplus. The cost to society of having such an industry served by a single-price monopolist, rather than by perfectly competitive sellers, will be the loss of that consumer surplus.

Thus, in pure efficiency terms, the perfectly discriminating monopolist and the perfectly competitive industry lead to the same result. The difference is that in the former case all the benefit comes in the form of producer surplus, in the latter case all in the form of consumer surplus. The efficiency loss from monopoly is the result of failure to price discriminate perfectly. This loss (the area of triangle S_1 in Figure 12-19) is called the *deadweight loss from monopoly*.

In the preceding analysis, it made sense to speak of the welfare loss from having monopoly rather than competition because the cost structure was one that is compatible with the existence of perfect competition. But with that kind of cost structure, only legal barriers could prevent the emergence of competition. The

FIGURE 12-19
A monopolist who charges a single price to all buyers will produce Q^* and sell at P^*. A competitive industry operating under the same cost conditions would produce Q_c and sell at P_c. In comparison with the perfectly competitive outcome, single-price monopoly results in a loss of consumer surplus equal to the area of $\Pi + S_1$. Since the monopolist earns Π, the cost to society is S_1—called the deadweight loss from monopoly.

THE WELFARE LOSS FROM A SINGLE-PRICE MONOPOLY

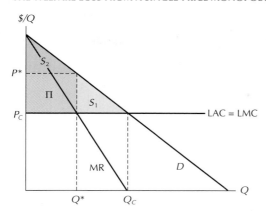

existence of economic profits (Π in Figure 12-19) would lure competitors into the industry until price and quantity were driven to P_c and Q_c, respectively.

Suppose the reason for having a monopoly with a flat LAC curve is that the firm enjoys patent protection for its product. Can we now say that the welfare loss from having a single-price monopoly is equal to the lost consumer surplus measured in Figure 12-19? Before answering, we must first ask, "What is the alternative to the current situation?" If it is a society without patent protection, we may well have never gotten the product in the first place, so it hardly makes sense to complain that, compared with pure competition, monopoly produces a welfare loss. True enough, the patent-protected single-price monopoly does not exhaust all possible gains from trade. But with the patent-protected monopoly, we do get a consumer surplus plus producer surplus of $S_2 + \Pi$, whereas we might have gotten nothing at all without the patent protection.

Public Policy Toward Natural Monopoly

These observations make clear that the relevant question is not whether monopoly is efficient in comparison with some unattainable theoretical ideal, but how it compares with the alternatives we actually confront. This question is nowhere more important than in the case of natural monopoly.

To keep the analysis simple, consider a technology in which total cost is given by

$$TC = F + MQ, \tag{12.8}$$

where Q is the level of output. And suppose the demand and marginal revenue curves for a single-price monopolist producing with this technology are as

FIGURE 12-20
The two main objections to single-price natural monopoly are that it earns economic profit (Π) and that it results in the loss of consumer surplus (S).

A NATURAL MONOPOLY

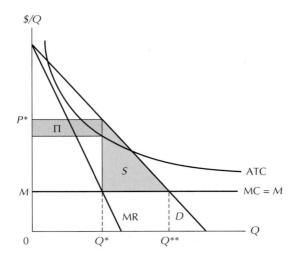

shown in Figure 12-20. The theoretical ideal allocation for this market would be to produce a quantity of Q^{**} and sell it at marginal cost, which here is equal to M. By contrast, the single-price monopoly produces only Q^* and sells it for P^*.

There are basically two objections to the equilibrium price-quantity pair of the single-price natural monopoly: (1) the *fairness objection*, which is that the producer earns an economic profit (Π); and (2) the *efficiency objection*, which is that price is above marginal cost, resulting in lost consumer surplus (S).

Policymakers may respond in a variety of ways to the fairness and efficiency objections. The five options considered below account for the most important alternatives.

1. STATE OWNERSHIP AND MANAGEMENT

Efficiency requires that price be equal to marginal cost. The difficulty this creates is that, for natural monopoly, marginal cost is below average total cost. Because private firms are not able to charge prices less than average cost and remain in business in the long run, the single-price firm has no alternative but to charge more than marginal cost. An option for getting around this particular difficulty is to have the state take over the industry. The attractive feature of this option is that the government is not bound, the way a private firm is, to earn at least a normal profit. It would thus be able to set a price equal to marginal cost, and absorb the resulting economic losses out of general tax revenues.

But there are also unattractive features of state ownership. Foremost among them is the fact that it often seems to weaken incentives for cost-conscious, efficient management. As Harvard University economist Harvey Leibenstein has

Drawing by Schrier. Copyright © 1981 Saturday Review, Inc.

"And then, after many years of business failures, Bertram finally made his fortune selling signs to the postal system saying 'Sorry, this window closed.'"

emphasized, an organization's costs depend not just on its technology, but also on the vigor with which it pursues efficiency. In Leibenstein's phrase, an organization that does not act energetically to curb costs is said to exhibit *X-inefficiency*.[12]

X-inefficiency is by no means the exclusive province of government. In widely varying degrees, it is found in private firms as well. Leibenstein argued that the extent to which X-inefficiency is a problem will depend on economic incentives, which suggests a theoretical reason for believing that it is likely to be more widespread in government. When a private firm cuts a dollar from its costs, its profit goes up by a dollar. By contrast, when the person in charge of a government agency cuts a dollar from her agency's budget, the effect is merely to shrink her fiefdom.

Several noted scholars have argued that the goal of most bureaucrats is to

X-inefficiency A condition in which a firm fails to obtain maximum output from a given combination of inputs.

---

[12]Harvey Leibenstein, "Allocative Efficiency vs. X-Efficiency," *American Economic Review*, June 1966: 392–415.

maximize their operating budgets.[13] This is not to deny that bureaucrats are for the most part sincere, dedicated public servants. But it is perhaps only human nature for a bureaucrat to think that her particular agency has the most important mission in government, and to lobby accordingly on its behalf.

Below we will consider some quantitative evidence that bears on the relative efficiency of state-managed and private firms. Even common experience, however, provides some relevant natural experiments. Each spring in northern U.S. cities, for example, municipal road crews repair the potholes left by winter while, at the same time, the parking lots of supermarkets, shopping centers, and other nongovernment road surfaces are under repair by private paving companies. The contrast between the two groups is often striking. It is common to see seven members of an eight-man municipal road crew leaning on their shovels smoking cigarettes, giving occasional advice to the newcomer among them as he lazily tamps asphalt into the holes. The private crews who work the parking lots, though often only half as large, usually fill many more potholes per day.

Another illuminating case study in the effects of state management is the Department of Motor Vehicles. Try to remember the last time you visited the DMV in person. Would you ever go there again if you didn't have to? If you are like most people, you came away with the impression that a manager of even very modest talents could have devised some way of performing that service more expeditiously. We may safely speculate that few people would elect to live in a society in which the DMV was in charge of a substantial share of productive activity.

Despite the X-inefficiency problem, state-operated natural monopoly may be the best solution in some cases. But there are other policy alternatives that offer many of the same benefits with fewer apparent costs.

2. STATE REGULATION OF PRIVATE MONOPOLIES

One such alternative is to leave ownership in private hands, while providing guidelines or regulations that limit pricing discretion. The stereotypical example of this approach is public regulation of private companies that provide electricity, water, and telephone service.

The main form of government price regulation employed in the United States is known as *rate-of-return regulation*, in which prices are set to allow the firm to earn a predetermined rate of return on its invested capital. Ideally, this rate of return would allow the firm to recover exactly the opportunity cost of its capital, which is to say, it would ideally be the same as the competitive rate of return on investment.

---

[13]See, for example, William Niskanen, *Bureaucracy and Representative Government*, Chicago: Aldine-Atherton, 1971; and Gordon Tullock, *The Politics of Bureaucracy*, Washington, DC: Public Affairs Press, 1965. But for a contrasting view, see Albert Breton and Ronald Wintrobe, *The Logic of Bureaucratic Conduct*, Cambridge: Cambridge University Press, 1982.

In practice, however, regulatory commissions can never be certain what the competitive rate of return will be in any period. If the rate they set lies below the competitive return, the firm will have an incentive to reduce the quality of its service, and eventually to go out of business. By contrast, if regulators set too high a rate of return, prices will be higher than necessary and the firm will earn an extra-normal profit. Neither of these outcomes is attractive, but regulatory commissions have traditionally decided that the problems caused by an insufficient rate of return are far more serious than those caused by an excessive one.

Harvey Averch and Leland Johnson were the first to explore in detail the consequences of a regulatory rate of return set higher than the cost of capital.[14] Their conclusion, in a nutshell, is that this practice gives the firm an incentive to substitute capital for other inputs in a way that inflates the cost of doing business. If the regulated utility's goal is to maximize profit, the behavioral path it will follow will be to make its "rate base"—the invested capital on which it earns the allowed rate of return—as large as possible. If the regulated monopolist can borrow capital at 8 percent/yr and is allowed to earn 10 percent/yr on each dollar invested, it can clear $20,000 of extra profit for every extra $1,000,000 of borrowed funds it invests.

At least two important distortions follow from the discrepancy between the allowed rate of return and the actual cost of capital. The first we may call the *gold-plated water cooler effect*. It refers to the fact that the regulated monopolist has an incentive to purchase more capital equipment than is actually necessary to produce any given level of output. Faced with a choice between buying a regular water cooler, for example, and a more expensive gold-plated one, the regulated monopolist has an incentive to opt for the latter. Regulatory commissions try to prevent the purchase of unnecessary equipment, but the complexities of day-to-day operations are too great to allow every decision to be monitored carefully.

A second distortion induced by rate-of-return regulation is peculiar to the monopolist who serves more than one separate market, and we may call it the *cross-subsidy effect*. Because the allowed rate of return exceeds the cost of capital, such a monopolist has an incentive to sell below cost in the more elastic market, and cross-subsidize the resulting losses by selling above cost in the less elastic market. The idea is that the below-cost price in the elastic market boosts sales by more than the above-cost price in the less elastic market curtails them. The resulting increase in output increases the requirements for capital to produce it, and hence increases the profits allowed by regulation.

---

[14]Harvey Averch and Leland Johnson, "Behavior of the Firm under Regulatory Constraint," *American Economic Review*, December 1962: 1052–1069. See also R. M. Spann, "Rate of Return Regulation and Efficiency in Production: An Empirical Test of the Averch-Johnson Thesis," *Bell Journal of Economics*, Spring 1974: 38–52.

FIGURE 12-21
A regulated monopolist is generally allowed to earn a rate of return that exceeds the actual cost of capital, which provides an incentive to acquire as much capital as possible. To increase output (thereby to increase the required capital stock), the monopolist can sell above cost in his less elastic market (market 1 in panel *a*) and use the resultant profits ($\Pi_1 > 0$) to subsidize the losses ($\Pi_2 < 0$) sustained by selling below cost in his more elastic market.

CROSS-SUBSIDIZATION TO BOOST TOTAL OUTPUT

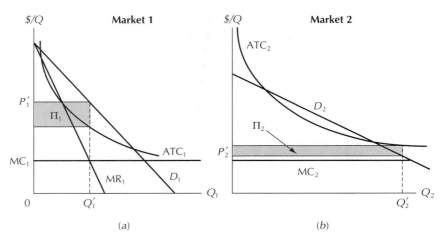

To illustrate, consider the regulated monopolist whose demand and cost curves for two markets are shown in Figure 12-21. The ATC curves are constructed to include the allowed rate of profit, which exceeds the cost of capital. Thus, when the monopolist is earning a zero profit in terms of the cost curves shown in Figure 12-21, he is really earning

$$\Pi = (r^a - r^c) K, \tag{12.9}$$

where r^a is the allowed rate of return, r^c the actual cost of capital, and K the size of the total capital stock. To maximize profit, the monopolist thus wants to make K as big as possible, which in turn means making the sum of the outputs sold in the two markets as large as possible. To do that, he will set MR = MC in the market with the less elastic demand (market 1 in panel *a*) and use the profits earned in that market (Π_1) to subsidize a price below average cost in the market with more elastic demand (market 2 in panel *b*). The aim, again, is to boost sales in the latter market by more than they are curtailed in the former. By selling the largest possible output, the monopolist is able to employ the largest possible capital stock, and thereby is able to earn the largest possible profit.

Regulatory pitfalls have not prevented governments in virtually every part of the world from continuing to intervene in the price and output decisions of important natural monopolies like electric utilities and local telephone service. Whether these interventions do more good than harm, in purely economic terms, remains an unsettled question. But they clearly seem to serve an important psychological function on behalf of a public that feels understandably uncomfortable about not having a buffer between itself and the sole supplier of a critical good or service.

3. EXCLUSIVE CONTRACTING FOR NATURAL MONOPOLY

In the title of a widely quoted article, UCLA economist Harold Demsetz asked the disarmingly simple question, "Why Regulate Monopoly?"[15] His point was that even though cost conditions may dictate that a market be served by a single supplier, there can still be vigorous competition to see who gets to *be* that supplier. In Demsetz's proposal, the government would specify in detail the service it wanted provided—fire protection, garbage collection, postal delivery, whatever—and then call for private companies to submit bids to supply the service. And to the low bidder would then go the contract.

This scheme has been tried with success in a number of different municipalities. The city of Scottsdale, Arizona, for example, has its fire protection services provided by a private contractor selected in this fashion. And the residents of Oakland, California, have their garbage collected each week not by municipal garbage workers but by the Oakland Scavenger Company, a private, profit-seeking firm. In both instances, the costs incurred in providing service are approximately half the cost of comparable services provided directly by municipal governments. In the fire protection case, moreover, there is hard evidence that the cost reductions are not achieved through reductions in the quality of service. Profit-seeking fire insurance companies, whose survival depends on their ability to assess risks accurately, charge no more for fire insurance in Scottsdale than they do in communities with municipal fire departments.[16] The advantage of private contracting for the provision of natural monopoly services is that it takes production out of the hands of bureaucrats, who are often not very good at keeping costs down.

Despite this advantage, however, it should be clear that private contracting is not necessarily a superior solution in every instance. Because the contract must specify the details of the service to be provided, it must go into extraordinary detail in the case of a complex service, such as telecommunications. Moreover, it must make provisions for how new contractors are to be selected. In the case of electric utilities, changing contractors necessarily involves the transfer of a vast, complex array of generation and distribution equipment. At what price should this equipment be sold? By the time all the *i*'s are dotted and the *t*'s crossed, the exclusive contracts for providing monopoly service may be so detailed as to be indistinguishable from direct economic regulation.

4. VIGOROUS ENFORCEMENT OF ANTITRUST LAWS

A major element in the policy arsenal for dealing with monopoly is the nation's antitrust laws. The most important of these are the Sherman Act (1890), which makes it illegal "to monopolize, or attempt to monopolize . . . any part of the

---

[15]Harold Demsetz, "Why Regulate Monopoly?" *Journal of Law and Economics*, April 1968: 55–65.

[16]For an extended survey of studies comparing private costs and public costs, see E. S. Savas, *Privatizing the Public Sector*, Chatham, NJ: Chatham House Publishers, 1982.

trade or commerce among the several States . . . ," and the Clayton Act (1914), one of whose provisions prevents corporations from acquiring shares in a competitor where the effect would be to "substantially lessen competition or create a monopoly."

In interpreting the antitrust laws, the U.S. Justice Department has developed guidelines that prohibit mergers between competing companies whose combined market share would exceed some predetermined fraction of total industry output. These guidelines are applied with highly varying degrees of zeal under different political administrations. As a general rule, Democrats have been far less tolerant of mergers than Republicans have.

In the case of industries with declining long-run average cost curves, the cost of production will be much higher if we are served by many firms than by only a few. The most vigorous supporters of the antitrust laws insist that the laws will not impede the formation of natural monopolies. But as we will see in Chapter 13, they may substantially postpone the time when economies of scale are fully realized.

One response to this difficulty would be to apply the antitrust laws to prevent only those mergers where significant cost savings would not be realized. The government is not in a good position, however, to distinguish one type of case from another. Congress was well aware of this, and explicitly ruled out consideration of cost savings as a rationale for allowing mergers. The result is that antitrust policy impedes all consolidations, even those that would lead to substantial reductions in cost.

5. A LAISSEZ-FAIRE POLICY TOWARD NATURAL MONOPOLY

As a fifth and final alternative for dealing with natural monopoly, let us consider the possibility of laissez faire, or doing nothing—just letting the monopolist produce whatever quantity she chooses and sell it at whatever price the market will bear. The obvious objections to this policy are the two we began with, namely,

FIGURE 12-22
By being able to offer a discount price to the most elastic portion of the demand curve, the two-price monopolist (panel *b*) expands the market, thereby causing a much smaller efficiency loss (area *Z*, panel *b*) than in the case of the single-price monopolist (area *W*, panel *a*).

THE EFFICIENCY LOSSES FROM SINGLE-PRICE AND TWO-PRICE MONOPOLY

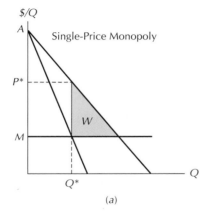

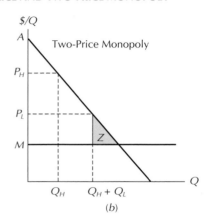

the fairness and efficiency problems. In this section, however, we will see that there may be at least some circumstances in which these problems are of only minimal importance.

Consider, in particular, a natural monopolist who uses the hurdle model of differential pricing. To keep the discussion simple, let's suppose she charges a regular price and also a discount price, the latter available to customers who clear some hurdle, such as mailing in a rebate form. How does the presence of this differential pricing device affect the fairness and efficiency objections to natural monopoly?

Consider first the efficiency objection. Recall that the problem is that the single-price monopolist charges a price above marginal cost, which excludes many potential buyers from the market, ones who value the product more highly than the value of the resources required to produce it.

For illustrative purposes, let's examine a natural monopolist with a total cost curve given by $F + MQ$ and a linear demand curve given by $P = A - BQ$. Figure 12-22a shows the demand and marginal cost curves for such a monopolist. If she is a single-price profit maximizer, she will produce Q^* and sell for P^*. But if she is able to charge one price to the buyers along the upper part of the demand curve and a lower price to all other buyers (Figure 12-22b), her profit-maximizing strategy will be to sell Q_H at the price P_H and $Q_H + Q_L$ at the price P_L.[17]

---

[17]For the single-price monopolist the profit function is given by

$$\Pi_1 = (A - BQ)\, Q - F - MQ.$$

The first-order condition for a maximum is given by

$$\frac{d\Pi_1}{dQ} = A - 2BQ - M = 0,$$

which yields a profit-maximizing quantity of $Q' = (A - M)/2B$, and a corresponding price of $P' = (A + M)/2$.

The profit function for the two-price monopolist, by contrast, is given by

$$\Pi_2 = (A - BQ_H)\, Q_H + (A - BQ_H - BQ_L)\, Q_L - F - M(Q_H + Q_L).$$

The first-order conditions for a maximum are given by

$$\frac{\partial \Pi_2}{\partial Q_H} = A - 2BQ_H - BQ_L - M = 0$$

and

$$\frac{\partial \Pi_2}{\partial Q_L} = A - BQ_H - 2BQ_L - M = 0,$$

which can be solved for

$$Q_H = \frac{A - M}{3B} = Q_L \quad \text{and} \quad P_L = \frac{A + 2M}{3} \quad \text{and} \quad P_H = \frac{2A + M}{3}.$$

Note that the efficiency loss associated with the two-price monopolist (lost consumer surplus, which is the area of triangle Z in panel b) is much smaller than the corresponding loss for the single-price monopolist (the area of triangle W in panel a).

In general, the more finely the monopolist can partition her market under the hurdle model, the smaller the efficiency loss will be. As noted earlier, it is common in most firms to see not one but a whole menu of different discount prices, each with a different set of restrictions (the deeper the discount, the more stringent the restriction). Given the wide latitude many firms have to expand their markets through hurdle pricing, the efficiency problem of natural monopoly will often be of only secondary importance.

What about the fairness problem? First, what *is* this problem? The popular perception of it is that the monopolist transfers resources from people who desperately need them (namely, poor consumers) to others who have more than they need to begin with (namely, wealthy shareholders). We will see below that, defined in this particular way, the problem is sometimes less serious than it appears.

The more general question of what constitutes a fair distribution of society's resources is a deep philosophical one, well beyond the scope of our discussion here. At the very least, however, we can say that no firm is entitled to acquire, through force or coercion, the power to extract excessive resources from other persons. But suppose the monopolist has become the lone seller in her market through completely benevolent means. This is not implausible. As a natural monopolist, her costs are by definition lower than if other firms also served the same market. And perhaps her cheerful and courteous service has also helped entrench her position. Does she then create an injustice by charging prices in excess of marginal cost?

Certainly consumers would be happier to pay only the marginal cost of production. But marginal cost is less than average cost in a natural monopoly, and so it is not possible for *everyone* to pay marginal cost and have the supplier remain in business. At best, *some* consumers can pay prices close to marginal cost, but others will have to pay substantially more. Even so, if the monopolist is earning an economic profit, we know that buyers are paying more, on the average, than the cost of the resources required to serve them. How can this be defended in the name of fairness?

Earlier we saw that hurdle pricing makes the monopoly allocation more efficient. It would be an exaggeration to say that the same hurdle model makes the existence of monopoly profits seem completely fair. But it does help mitigate some of the most serious objections to them.

Consider first the source of a given dollar of monopoly profit. From which buyers does this dollar come? It is straightforward to show that it cannot have come from the discount price buyer. Typical discount prices range from 15 to 50 percent off the so-called regular price, and seldom do more than half of all buyers pay the discount price. Taking an illustrative case in which the discount is 30 percent and half of all buyers receive it, we see that the monopolist's revenue would fall by 15 percent if everyone paid the discount price. Very few firms would remain profitable in the face of a 15 percent decline in total revenue.

It follows that if the monopolist is earning economic profit, the source of that profit is the buyer who pays the regular price. The fact that this buyer could have paid a discount price if he had been willing to jump the requisite hurdle tells us that the burden imposed on him is no greater than the trouble of jumping the hurdle. This is obviously not the same as saying that the regular-price buyer makes a voluntary charitable contribution to the monopolist. But it does take at least some of the sting out of the notion that the monopolist's customers are being cruelly victimized.

So much for the source of monopoly profit. What about its disposition? Who gets it? If we assume a corporate income tax rate of 40 percent, 40 cents of each dollar of monopoly profits goes to the U.S. Treasury. The remainder is paid out to shareholders, either directly through dividends or indirectly by reinvesting it into the company. Granted, the average income of shareholders is greater than that of citizens as a whole. But there are many low-income shareholders in the United States. Most employee pension funds, for example, are invested in the stock market, as are the private insurance holdings of many low-income individuals. So a considerable fraction of any dollar of monopoly profit will wind up in the hands of low-income shareholders.

But to take the worst possible case from a distributional point of view, let us suppose that what is left of the dollar of monopoly profit goes entirely to the wealthiest resident of Manhattan. Assume that she pays federal income tax at the rate of 40 percent on the 60 cents that the federal government hasn't already taken, leaving 36 cents. State and local income and sales taxes will claim an additional 9 cents, leaving only 27 cents in the hands of our wealthy shareholder.

To summarize then, the source of a dollar in monopoly profit is the regular-price buyer, someone who could have paid a discount price had he but taken a little extra trouble. Of that dollar, 64 cents goes to the federal treasury and another 9 cents to state and local governments. The disposition of more than 70 percent of the dollar is thus subject to governmental control. The remainder becomes income in the hands of shareholders, at least some of whom have low incomes to begin with. So it is by no means clear that the economic profit associated with natural monopoly creates distributional inequities of the sort commonly perceived.

Hurdles, of course, are seldom perfect. Inevitably they screen out some buyers who will not buy at the regular price. And much of the time, real resources must be expended in order to jump over these hurdles. Mailing in a rebate coupon may not take a lot of time, but the time it takes could certainly be better spent. And in at least some cases, tax avoidance will keep the government from collecting as much as the tax tables specify.

So what are we to conclude from this brief analysis of the five policy options for dealing with natural monopoly? The short answer is that each has problems. None completely eliminates the difficulties that arise when a single seller serves the market. Sometimes the least costly solution will be competitive contracting, other times direct state ownership. Regulation will continue to play a role in specific industries, particularly the traditional public utilities. And despite their many shortcomings, antitrust laws serve the public well by discouraging price-fixing and other anticompetitive practices. But in some cases, particularly those in which the monopolist has devised means of richly segmenting the market, the best option may be simply not to intervene at all.

DOES MONOPOLY SUPPRESS INNOVATION?

One of the most enduring topics of conversation among economic conspiracy buffs is the notion that monopolists deprive consumers of a spectrum of enormously valuable technological innovations. Who has not heard, for example, of how the lightbulb manufacturers have conspired to prevent revolutionary new designs for long-lasting lightbulbs from reaching the market?

Is the suppression of innovation yet another cost of monopoly that we ought to have considered in our analysis of public policy options? As the following example will make clear, the logic of profit maximization suggests that monopolists may not always be so eager to suppress innovation.

Example 12-4 *Suppose the current lightbulb design lasts 1000 hours. Now the lightbulb monopolist discovers how to make a bulb that lasts 10,000 hours for the same per-bulb cost of production. Will the monopolist introduce the new bulb?*

> Suppose we measure the quantity produced by the monopolist not as lightbulbs per se, but as the number of bulb-hours of lighting services. Thus, if the cost of producing the current design is, say, $1.00/bulb-hr, then the cost of the new design is only $0.10/bulb-hr. In Figure 12-23, D represents the market demand curve for lighting and MR the associated marginal revenue curve.

FIGURE 12-23
The cost of producing the new, efficient lightbulb, at $0.10/bulb-hr, is only one-tenth the cost of producing the current design, $1/bulb-hr. Because the monopolist's profits with the efficient design (area of *FGHK*) exceed its profits with the current design (area of *ABCE*), it will offer the new design.

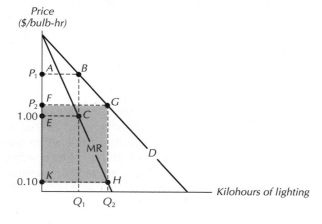

DOES MONOPOLY SUPPRESS INNOVATION?

Note that the profit-maximizing price and quantity for the current design, whose marginal cost is $1/bulb-hr, are P_1 and Q_1, respectively. For the new design, whose marginal cost is $0.10/bulb-hr, the profit-maximizing price and quantity are P_2 and Q_2. The monopolist's profit under the current design is the area of the rectangle $ABCE$. For the new design, the corresponding profit value is the area of the rectangle $FGHK$. And because the monopolist's profit is higher under the new design, it has every incentive to make that design available. Indeed, as some of you may recall, the availability of just such an efficient new lightbulb was announced several years ago.

This example does not imply that the monopolist's incentives to introduce innovations will always and everywhere be the same as a competitive firm's. But it should caution us against uncritical acceptance of claims that monopolists always deprive consumers of the benefits of the latest available technology.

Summary

Monopoly is the name given to the market structure in which a single firm serves the entire market. Four factors, acting alone or in combination, give rise to monopoly: (1) control over key inputs, (2) economies of scale, (3) patents, and (4) government licenses. In the long run, by far the most important of these is economies of scale.

Because the monopolist is the only seller in the market, his demand curve is the downward-sloping market demand curve. Unlike the perfect competitor, who can sell as much as he chooses at the market price, the monopolist must cut price in order to expand his output. The monopolist's rule for maximizing profits is the same as the one used by perfectly competitive firms. It is to expand output if the gain in revenue (marginal revenue) exceeds the increase in costs (marginal cost), and to contract if the loss in revenue is smaller than the reduction in costs. The pivotal difference is that marginal revenue is less than price for the monopolist, but equal to price for the perfect competitor.

When the monopolist can sell in several separate markets, he distributes output among them so that marginal revenue is the same in each. Here again, the familiar logic of cost-benefit analysis provides a convenient framework for analyzing the firm's decision about whether to alter its current behavior.

Unlike the perfectly competitive case, the monopoly equilibrium generally does not exhaust the potential gains from exchange. In general, the value to society of an additional unit of output will exceed the cost to the monopolist of the resources required to produce it. This finding has often been interpreted to mean that monopoly is less efficient than perfect competition. But this interpretation is of only limited practical significance, because the conditions that give rise to monopoly—in particular, economies of scale in production—are rarely compatible with those required for perfect competition.

Our policy focus in the chapter was on the question of how the government should treat natural monopolies—markets characterized by downward-sloping long-run average cost curves. We considered five policy alternatives: (1) state ownership, (2) private ownership with government price regulation, (3) competitive bidding by private firms for the right to be the sole provider of service, (4) vigorous enforcement of antitrust laws designed to prevent monopoly, and finally (5) a complete laissez-faire, or hands-off, policy. Problems arise with each of these alternatives, and the best policy will in general be different in different circumstances. The laissez-faire stance is most attractive in markets where the monopolist is able to employ the hurdle model of differential pricing. Allowing buyers to decide for themselves whether to become eligible for a discount price softens both the efficiency and fairness objections to natural monopoly.

Questions for Review

1. What four factors give rise to monopoly? In the long run, why is economies of scale the most important factor?

2. If the United States has thousands of cement producers but a small town has only one, is this cement producer a monopolist? Explain.

3. When is marginal revenue less than price for a monopolist? Explain.

4. Why does a profit-maximizing monopolist never produce on an inelastic portion of the demand curve? Would a revenue-maximizing monopolist ever produce on the inelastic portion of the demand curve?

5. Why is an output level at which MR intersects MC from below never the profit-maximizing level of output?

6. What effect will the imposition of a 50 percent tax on economic profit have on a monopolist's price and output decisions? (*Hint:* Recall that the assumed objective is to choose the level of output that maximizes economic profit.)

7. Suppose the elasticity of demand is $\eta = -3$. By how much does price exceed marginal cost? How does this markup of price over marginal cost compare with perfect competition?

8. *True or false:* A lump-sum tax on a monopolist will always increase the price charged by the monopolist and lower the quantity of output sold.

9. *True or false:* If a monopolist faces a perfectly horizontal demand curve, then the deadweight loss to the economy is zero.

10. What forces work against X-inefficiency in privately owned monopolies?

11. How does the hurdle method of price discrimination mitigate both the efficiency and fairness problems associated with monopoly?

Problems

1. You are a self-employed profit-maximization consultant specializing in monopolies. Five firms are currently seeking your advice, and although the information they have supplied to you is incomplete, your expert knowledge allows you to go back and make a definite recommendation in each case. Select one of the following recommendations for each firm in the short run:

    a. Remain at the current output level.
    b. Increase output.
    c. Reduce output.
    d. Shut down.
    e. Go back and recalculate your figures because the ones supplied can't possibly be right.

Firm	P	MR	TR	Q	TC	MC	ATC	AVC	Your recommendation
A	3.90	3.00		2000	7400	2.90		3.24	
B	5.90			10000		5.90	4.74	4.24	
C		9.00	44000	4000		9.00	11.90	10.74	
D	35.90	37.90		5000		37.90	35.90		
E	35.00		3990	1000	3300		at min value	23.94	

($P = AR$ noted above the P column)

2. A monopolist has a demand curve given by $P = 100 - Q$ and a total cost curve given by $TC = 16 + Q^2$. The associated marginal cost curve is $MC = 2Q$. Find the monopolist's profit-maximizing quantity and price. How much economic profit will the monopolist earn?

3. Now suppose the monopolist in Problem 2 has a total cost curve given by $TC = 32 + Q^2$. The corresponding marginal cost curve is still $MC = 2Q$, but fixed costs have doubled. Find the monopolist's profit maximizing quantity and price. How much economic profit does the monopolist earn?

4. Now suppose the monopolist in Problem 2 has a total cost curve given by $TC = 16 + 4Q^2$. The corresponding marginal cost curve is now $MC = 8Q$, and fixed costs are back to the original level. Find the monopolist's profit-maximizing quantity and price. How much economic profit does the monopolist earn?

5. Now suppose the monopolist in Problem 2 also has access to a foreign market in which he can sell whatever quantity he chooses at a constant price of 60. How much will he sell in the foreign market? What will his new quantity and price be in the original market?

6. Now suppose the monopolist in Problem 2 has a long-run marginal cost curve of MC = 20. Find the monopolist's profit-maximizing quantity and price. Find the efficiency loss from this monopoly.

7. Suppose a perfectly discriminating monopolist faces market demand $P = 100 - 10Q$ and has constant marginal cost MC = 20 (with no fixed costs). How much does the monopolist sell? How much profit does the monopolist earn? What is the maximum per-period license fee the government could charge the firm and have the firm still stay in business?

8. The demand by senior citizens for showings at a local movie house has a constant price elasticity equal to -4. The demand curve for all other patrons has a constant price elasticity equal to -2. If the marginal cost per patron is $1 per showing, how much should the theater charge members of each group?

9. During the Iran–Iraq war, the same arms merchant often sold weapons to both sides of the conflict. In this situation, a different price could be offered to each side because there was little danger that the country offered the lower price would sell arms to its rival to profit on the difference in prices. Suppose a French arms merchant has a monopoly of Exocet air-to-sea missiles and is willing to sell them to both sides. Iraq's demand for Exocets is $P = 400 - 0.5Q$ and Iran's is $P = 300 - Q$, where P is in millions of dollars. The marginal cost of Exocets is MC = Q. What price will be charged to each country?

10. If you have ever gone grocery shopping on a weekday afternoon, you have probably noticed some elderly shoppers going slowly down the aisles checking their coupon book for a coupon that matches each of their purchases. How is this behavior explained by the hurdle model of price discrimination?

11. A monopolist's price is $10. At this price the absolute value of the elasticity of demand is 2. What is the monopolist's marginal cost?

12. Suppose the government imposed a price ceiling on a monopolist (an upper bound on the price the monopolist can charge). Let $\overline{P}$ denote the price ceiling, and suppose the monopolist incurs no costs in producing output. *True or false:* If the demand curve faced by the monopolist is inelastic at the price $\overline{P}$, then the monopolist would be no better off if the government removed the price ceiling.

13. *The New York Times*, a profit-maximizing newspaper, faces a downward-sloping demand schedule for advertisements. When advertising for itself in its own pages (for example, an ad saying "Read Russell Baker in the Sunday *Times*"), is the opportunity cost of a given-size ad simply the price it charges its outside advertisers? Explain.

*14. Crazy Harry, a monopolist, has a total cost curve given by TC = $5Q + 15$. He sets two prices for his product, a regular price, P_H, and a discount price, P_L. Everyone is eligible to purchase the product at P_H. To be eligible to buy at P_L, it is necessary to present a copy of the latest Crazy Harry newspaper ad to the salesclerk. Suppose the only buyers who present the ad are those who would not have been willing to buy the product at P_H.

---

*This problem is most easily solved using the calculus method described in footnote 17.

a. If Crazy Harry's demand curve is given by $P = 20 - 5Q$, what are the profit-maximizing values of P_H and P_L?

b. How much economic profit does Harry make?

c. How much profit would he have made if he had been forced to charge the same price to all buyers?

d. Are buyers better or worse off as a result of Harry's being able to charge two prices?

15. An author has signed a contract in which the publisher promises to pay her $10,000 plus 20 percent of gross receipts from the sale of her book. *True or false*: If both the publisher and the author care only about their own financial return from the project, then the author will prefer a higher book price than the publisher.

16. A film director has signed a contract in which the production studio promises to pay her $1,000,000 plus 5 percent of the studio's rental revenues from the film, all of whose costs of production and distribution are fixed. *True or false*: If both the director and the studio care only about their own financial return from the project, then the director will prefer a lower film rental price than the studio.

Answers to In-Chapter Exercises

12-1. *TR ($/unit of time)*

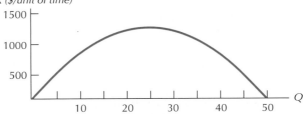

12-2. *$/unit of output*

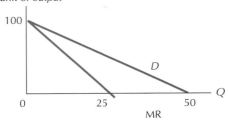

12-3. $MC = 40 = 100 - 4Q$, which solves for $Q^* = 15$, $P^* = 100 - 2Q^* = 70$.

12-4. The profit-maximizing level of output for a single-price monopolist occurs where $MR = MC$. Marginal revenue equals marginal cost at both $Q = 15$ and $Q = 34$, but $Q = 34$ has marginal revenue intersect from above and thus is the maximal one. However, even at $Q = 34$, price does not cover average variable cost ($66 = P$

$< \text{AVC} = 72$). The average variable cost curve lies everywhere above the demand curve (see figure), so the firm can do no better than earn profits equal to negative of the fixed costs. Thus, the optimal quantity is $Q = 0$: the firm should shut down!

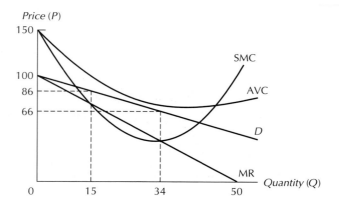

12-5. $MR_1 = 10 - 2Q_1$ (left panel), and $MR_2 = 20 - 2Q_2$ (center panel), so the horizontal summation of the MR curves is given by ΣMR (right panel). The profit-maximizing quantity is 13, 4 of which should be sold in market 1, the remaining 9 in market 2. The profit-maximizing prices are $P^*_1 = 6$ and $P^*_2 = 11$.

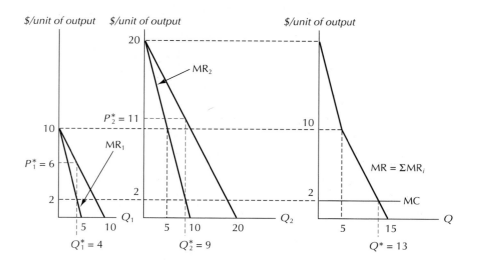

CHAPTER
13

Oligopoly and Monopolistic Competition

The military strategies of both the United States and the former Soviet Union were based on the doctrine of mutually assured destruction (MAD). The idea behind MAD was very simple: Both sides maintained sufficiently large and well-defended nuclear arsenals to ensure that each would be able to retaliate if the other launched a first strike. The prospect of a devastating counterstrike, according to the MAD theory, is what prevented each side from even considering a first strike.

The fact that neither side ever launched a first strike is interpreted by some people as evidence that the MAD strategy must have worked. And yet there is an apparent logical flaw in the strategy, one that suggests the real source of restraint must lie elsewhere. To appreciate the problem, put yourself in the shoes of a U.S. president who has just learned that the Russians have launched a first strike. At that moment, you know that the MAD strategy has already failed. For whatever reason, the threat of a counterstrike did not in fact deter the Russian first strike. Do you now order a counterstrike anyway? You realize that to do so will only increase the likelihood of total world destruction. True enough, American interests have been grievously damaged by the attack. But at that point, a counterstrike will only damage them further.

The logical difficulty with MAD is thus that each side knows perfectly well that once a first strike has already been launched, it will not be in the other side's interest to retaliate. And since each party knows this, the threat of a counterstrike loses all power to deter.

Or at least so it seems in theory. Perhaps the threat deters because each side fears the other might not respond rationally once it is the victim of a first strike. (A casual review of the American and Soviet leaders of the post–World War II period lends at least some credence to this interpretation.) But whether or not MAD is an effective defense strategy, its apparent flaw is troubling. The same logic that exposed this flaw suggests a simple way to repair it. It is to install a so-called doomsday machine—a tamper-proof device that will *automatically* retaliate once a first strike has been launched. Once each side became aware the other had such a device in place, the MAD strategy would be complete and a first strike truly would become unthinkable.

Chapter Preview

The nuclear deterrence issue confronts us with a *commitment problem* of the sort we saw in Chapter 7. To solve it, we must commit ourselves to a course of action that, if triggered, may prove disadvantageous. Similar kinds of *strategic interactions* between firms were ruled out in the market structures we studied in the last two chapters. In the perfect competition model, firms were assumed to ignore the actions of their adversaries. And in monopoly, the firm simply had no rivals to worry about. Both perfect competition and monopoly represent idealized forms. They are extraordinarily useful for generating insights about general tendencies but are rarely, if ever, encountered in practice. Our task in this chapter is to describe and explore the hybrid forms of industrial organization we deal with on a daily basis—namely, oligopoly and monopolistic competition.

Oligopoly refers to an industry in which there are only a few important sellers. These firms produce all, or most, of their industry's output. The logic of strategic interaction among oligopolistic rivals often has much the same flavor as the nuclear deterrence example. Among oligopolists, strategic interaction is not only present but occupies center stage.

We begin by comparing several simple models of interdependence in which firms make alternative assumptions about the behavior of their rivals. We will then see how collusive behavior and other forms of strategic interactions are illuminated by the mathematical theory of games; and we will see how even the threat of entry may have significant effects on the behavior of existing firms.

Monopolistic competition is defined by two seemingly simple conditions: (1) the existence of numerous firms each producing a product that is a close, but imperfect, substitute for the products of other firms; and (2) free entry and exit of firms. Our focus is on a simple spatial model of monopolistic competition. In this model, customers have particular locations or product characteristics that they most prefer. The result, we will see, is that firms tend to compete most intensively for the buyers of products that are most similar to their own.[1]

---

[1]Other traditional models of monopolistic competition are discussed in the appendix to this chapter, which can be found in the "For the Instructor" section at our Web site www.mhhe.com/economics/frank4.

Oligopoly

THE COURNOT MODEL

If a firm is considering a change in its output level or selling price, there are many possible assumptions it could make about the reactions of its rivals. It could assume, for example, that its rivals will continue producing at their current levels of output. Alternatively, it could assume that they would continue to charge their current prices. Or it could assume that they would react in various specific ways to its own price and output changes. In the sections that follow, we explore the implications of each alternative assumption.

We begin with the simplest case, the so-called *Cournot model*, in which each firm assumes that its rivals will continue producing at their current levels of output. Named for the French economist Auguste Cournot, who introduced it in 1838, this model describes the behavior of two firms that sell bottled water from mineral springs. A two-firm oligopoly is called a *duopoly*, and the Cournot model is sometimes referred to as the *Cournot duopoly model*, although its conclusions can easily be generalized to more than two firms.

The central assumption of the Cournot model is that each duopolist treats the other's quantity as a fixed number, one that will not respond to its own production decisions. This is a very weak form of interdependence, indeed, but we will see that even it leads to an outcome in which the behavior of each firm substantially affects its rival.

Suppose the total market demand curve for mineral water is given by

$$P = a - b\,(Q_1 + Q_2), \tag{13.1}$$

where a and b are positive numbers and Q_1 and Q_2 are the outputs of firms 1 and 2, respectively. Cournot assumed that the water could be produced at zero marginal cost, but this assumption is merely for convenience. Essentially similar conclusions would emerge if each firm had a constant positive marginal cost.

Let us look first at the profit-maximization problem facing firm 1. Given its assumption that firm 2's output is fixed at Q_2, the demand curve for firm 1's water is given by

$$P_1 = (a - bQ_2) - bQ_1, \tag{13.2}$$

which is rewritten to emphasize the fact that firm 1 treats Q_2 as given.

As Equation 13.2 shows, we get the demand curve for firm 1 by subtracting bQ_2 from the vertical intercept of the market demand curve. The idea is that firm 2 has skimmed off the first Q_2 units of the market demand curve, leaving firm 1 the remainder to work with.

If Q_2 were equal to zero, firm 1 would have the entire market demand curve to itself, as is indicated by D in Figure 13-1. If Q_2 is positive, we get firm 1's demand curve by shifting the vertical axis of the demand diagram rightward by

FIGURE 13-1
The Cournot duopo-
list's demand curve
is obtained by shift-
ing the vertical axis
rightward by the
amount produced
by the other duopo-
list (Q_2 in the dia-
gram). The portion
of the original mar-
ket demand curve
that lies to the right
of this new vertical
axis is the demand
curve facing firm 1.
Firm 1 then maxi-
mizes profit by
equating marginal
revenue and mar-
ginal cost, the latter
of which is zero.

THE PROFIT-MAXIMIZING COURNOT DUOPOLIST

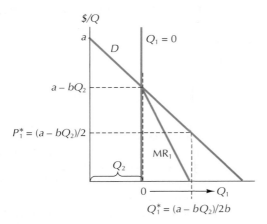

Q_2 units. Firm 1's demand curve is that portion of the original demand curve that lies to the right of this new vertical axis, and for this reason it is sometimes called a *residual demand curve.* The associated marginal revenue curve is labeled MR_1. Firm 1's rule for profit maximization is the same as for any other firm that faces a downward-sloping demand curve, namely, to equate marginal revenue and marginal cost. Marginal cost in this example is assumed to be zero, so the profit-maximizing level of output for firm 1 is that level for which its marginal revenue curve takes the value of zero.

The equilibrium outputs for a Cournot duopoly can be deduced from the residual demand diagram. Given that firm 2 is producing Q_2, firm 1 maximizes its profits by producing where marginal revenue equals marginal cost. Marginal revenue for firm 1 is given by $MR_1 = (a - bQ_2) - 2bQ_1$. Marginal revenue has twice the slope as demand, so marginal revenue intersects zero marginal cost at half the distance from the $Q_1 = 0$ axis to the horizontal intercept of the demand curve. By symmetry (the two firms are identical so they must behave the same), $Q_2 = Q_1$, which means that each of the three segments shown on the horizontal axis in Figure 13-1 has the same length. And this implies that each firm produces output equal to one-third of the distance from the origin to the horizontal intercept of the demand curve. The demand curve $P = a - bQ$ has a horizontal intercept of $Q = a/b$; hence, $Q_1 = Q_2 = a/(3b)$. A more general approach is to set marginal revenue equal to marginal cost and solve for the output of firm 1 in terms of the output of firm 2.[2]

$$Q_1^* = \frac{a - bQ_2}{2b}. \tag{13.3}$$

---

[2]For example, this more general approach is needed if firms are asymmetric (not identical) and thus would not produce the same level of output.

Reaction function A curve that tells the profit-maximizing level of output for one oligopolist for each amount supplied by another.

Economists often call Equation 13.3 firm 1's **reaction function**, and denote it by $Q_1^* = R_1(Q_2)$. This notation is suggestive because the reaction function tells how firm 1's quantity will react to the quantity level offered by firm 2.

Because the Cournot duopoly problem is completely symmetric, firm 2's reaction function has precisely the same structure:

$$Q_2^* = R_2(Q_1) = \frac{a - bQ_1}{2b}.$$ (13.4)

The two reaction functions are plotted in Figure 13-2. To illustrate the workings of the reaction function concept, suppose firm 1 initially produced a quantity of Q_1^0. Firm 2 would then produce the level of output that corresponds to Q_1^0 on its reaction function. Firm 1 would respond to that output level by picking the corresponding point on its own reaction function. Firm 2 would then respond by picking the corresponding point on its reaction function, and so on. The end result of this process is a stable equilibrium at the intersection of the two reaction functions. When both firms are producing $a/3b$ units of output, neither wants to change.[3]

How profitable are the Cournot duopolists? Since their combined output is $2a/3b$, the market price will be $P = a - b(2a/3b) = a/3$. At this price, each will

FIGURE 13-2
The reaction function for each duopolist gives its profit-maximizing output level as a function of the other firm's output level. The duopolists are in a stable equilibrium at the point of intersection of their reaction functions.

REACTION FUNCTIONS FOR THE COURNOT DUOPOLISTS

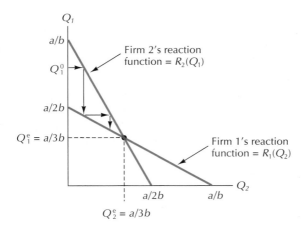

---

[3]To solve algebraically for firm 1's equilibrium level of output, we substitute $Q_1^* = Q_2^*$ into its reaction function and solve:

$$R_1(Q_2^*) = \frac{a - bQ_2^*}{2b} = \frac{a - bQ_1^*}{2b} = Q_1^*,$$

which yields $Q_1^* = a/3b$.

have total revenue equal to $(a/3)(a/3b) = a^2/9b$. And since neither firm has any production costs, total revenues and economic profits here are one and the same.

EXAMPLE 13-1 *Cournot duopolists face a market demand curve given by $P = 56 - 2Q$, where Q is total market demand. Each can produce output at a constant marginal cost of 20/unit. Graph their reaction functions and find the equilibrium price and quantity.*

> Figure 13-3a shows the residual demand curve facing firm 1 when firm 2 produces Q_2 units. Firm 1's marginal revenue curve has the same vertical intercept as its demand curve and is twice as steep. Thus the equation for firm 1's marginal revenue curve is $MR_1 = 56 - 2Q_2 - 4Q_1$. Equating MR_1 to marginal cost (20), we solve for firm 1's reaction function, $Q_1^* = R_1 = 9 - (Q_2/2)$. By symmetry, firm 2's reaction function is $R_2 = 9 - (Q_1/2)$. The two reaction functions are shown in Figure 13-3b, where they intersect at $Q_1 = Q_2 = 6$. Total market output will be $Q_1 + Q_2 = 12$. Consulting the market demand curve, we see that the market price will be $P = 56 - 2(12) = 32$.

EXERCISE 13-1

> Repeat Example 13-1 with the two firms facing a market demand curve of $P = 44 - Q$.

You may be wondering why the Cournot duopolists assume that their own production decisions will be ignored by their rivals. If so, you have asked a penetrating question, the same one posed by Cournot's critic, the French economist Joseph Bertrand. Let's now consider his alternative solution to the duopoly problem.

THE BERTRAND MODEL

Bertrand's insight was that from the buyer's perspective, what really counts is how the prices charged by the two firms compare. Since the duopolists are selling identical mineral water, every buyer will naturally want to buy from the seller with the lower price. Bertrand proposed that each firm chooses its price on the assumption that its rival's price would remain fixed. On its face, this assumption seems no more plausible than Cournot's, and since prices and quantities correspond uniquely along market demand curves, it may seem natural to wonder whether Bertrand's assumption even leads to a different outcome. On investigation, however, the outcomes turn out to be very different indeed.

FIGURE 13-3
Panel *a* shows the profit-maximizing output level for firm 1 (Q_1^*) when firm 2 produces Q_2. That and the parallel expression for firm 2 constitute the reaction functions plotted in panel *b*.

DERIVING THE REACTION FUNCTIONS FOR SPECIFIC DUOPOLISTS

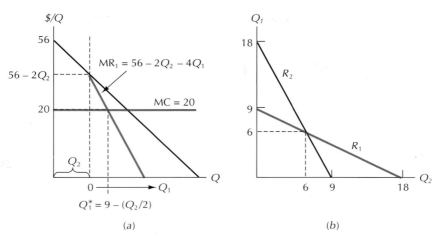

(a)

(b)

To illustrate, suppose the market demand and cost conditions are the same as in the Cournot example. And suppose firm 1 charges an initial price of P_0^1. Firm 2 then faces essentially three choices: (1) it can charge more than firm 1, in which case it will sell nothing; (2) it can charge the same as firm 1, in which case the two firms will split the market demand at that price; or (3) it can sell at a marginally lower price than firm 1, in which case it will capture the entire market demand at that price. The third of these options will always be by far the most profitable.[4]

As in the Cournot model, the situations of the duopolists are completely symmetric in the Bertrand model, which means that the option of selling at a marginally lower price than the competition will be the strategy of choice for both firms. Needless to say, there can be no stable equilibrium in which each firm undersells the other. The back-and-forth process of price-cutting will continue until it reaches its natural economic limit—namely, marginal cost, which in the mineral spring example is zero. (If instead we had considered an example in which both firms have the same positive marginal cost, price would have fallen to that value.) Once each firm has cut its price to marginal cost, it will have no incentive to cut further. With each firm selling at marginal cost, the duopolists will share the market equally.

EXAMPLE **13-2** *Bertrand duopolists face a market demand curve given by $P = 56 - 2Q$. Each can produce output at a constant marginal cost of 20/unit. Find the equilibrium price and quantity.*

---

[4]In the case of a price only infinitesimally smaller than firm 1's price, firm 2's profit will be virtually twice as large under option 3 as under option 2.

> The solution is both firms price at marginal cost $P = MC = 20$. Industry output is determined by market demand: $20 = 56 - 2Q$ implies $Q = 18$. The firms split the market equally, so each firm produces half of industry output $Q_1 = Q_2 = Q/2 = 9$.

EXERCISE 13-2

> If the market demand curve facing Bertrand duopolists is given by $P = 10 - Q$ and each has a constant marginal cost of 2, what will be the equilibrium price and quantity for each firm?

So we see that a seemingly minor change in the initial assumptions about firm behavior—that each duopolist takes its rival's price, not quantity, as given—leads to a sharply different equilibrium. Now we consider how another small change in the initial assumptions about firm behavior can lead to yet another equilibrium.

THE STACKELBERG MODEL

In 1934, the German economist Heinrich von Stackelberg asked the simple but provocative question, "What would a firm do if it knew its only rival were a naive Cournot duopolist?" The answer is that it would want to choose its own output level by taking into account the effect that choice would have on the output level of its rival.

Returning to the Cournot model, suppose firm 1 knows that firm 2 will treat firm 1's output level as given. How can it make strategic use of that knowledge? To answer this question, recall that firm 2's reaction function is given by $Q_2^* = R_2(Q_1) = (a - bQ_1)/2b$. Knowing that firm 2's output will depend on Q_1 in this fashion, firm 1 can then substitute $R_2(Q_1)$ for Q_2 in the equation for the market demand curve, which yields the following expression for its own demand curve:

$$P = a - b[Q_1 + R_2(Q_1)] = a - b\left(Q_1 + \frac{a - bQ_1}{2b}\right) = \frac{a - bQ_1}{2}. \qquad (13.5)$$

This demand curve and the associated marginal revenue curve are shown as D_1 and MR_1 in Figure 13-4. Since marginal cost is assumed to be zero in the mineral spring example, from 1's profit-maximizing output level will be the one for which MR_1 is zero, namely, $Q_1^* = a/2b$. The market price will be $a/4$.

FIGURE 13-4
When firm 1 knows firm 2 is a Cournot duopolist, it can take account of the effect of its own behavior on firm 2's quantity choice. The result is that it knows exactly what its demand curve will be.

THE STACKELBERG LEADER'S DEMAND AND MARGINAL REVENUE CURVES

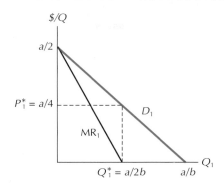

EXAMPLE 13-3 A Stackelberg leader and follower face a market demand curve given by $P = 56 - 2Q$. Each can produce output at a constant marginal cost of 20/unit. Find the equalibrium price and quantity.

The solution is found by substituting firm 2's reaction function $Q_2 = 9 - Q_1/2$ into the demand facing firm 1 $P = (56 - 2Q_2) - 2Q_1$ to find $P = 38 - Q_1$ with corresponding marginal revenue $MR_1 = 38 - 2Q_1$. Setting marginal revenue equal to marginal cost yields firm 1's output $Q_1 = 9$. Inserting firm 1's output into firm 2's reaction function yields firm 2's output $Q_2 = \frac{9}{2}$. Total industry output is $Q = Q_1 + Q_2 = \frac{27}{2}$, with price $P = 56 - 2Q = 56 - 27 = 29$.

EXERCISE 13-3

The market demand curve for a Stackelberg leader and follower is given by $P = 10 - Q$. If each has a marginal cost of 2, what will be the equilibrium price and quantity for each?

For obvious reasons, firm 1 is referred to as a *Stackelberg leader*. *Stackelberg follower* is the term used to describe firm 2. To help place the Stackelberg leader's behavior in clearer perspective, let's again consider the graph of the two firms' Cournot reaction functions, reproduced here as Figure 13-5. As we saw in Figure 13-4, $a/2b$ is the best output for firm 1 to produce once it takes into account that firm 2 will respond to its choice according to the reaction function $R_2(Q_1)$. Once firm 1 produces $a/2b$, firm 2 will consult R_2 and respond by producing

FIGURE 13-5
In the Stackelberg
model, firm 1 ig-
nores its own reac-
tion function from
the Cournot model.
It chooses its own
quantity to maxi-
mize profit, taking
into account the ef-
fect that its own
quantity will have
on the quantity of-
fered by firm 2.

THE STACKELBERG EQUILIBRIUM

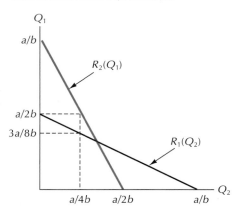

$a/4b$. Now here is the crucial step. If firm 1 thought that firm 2 would stay at $a/4b$ no matter what, its best bet would be to consult its own reaction function and produce the corresponding quantity, namely, $3a/8b$. By doing so, it would earn more than by producing $a/2b$. The problem is that firm 1 realizes that if it cuts back to $3a/8b$, this will elicit a further reaction from firm 2, culminating in a downward spiral to the intersection point of the two reaction functions. Firm 1 would do better to move to $3a/8b$ if it could somehow induce firm 2 to remain at $a/4b$. But it cannot. The best option open to firm 1 is therefore to grit its teeth and stay put at $a/2b$.

COMPARISON OF OUTCOMES

Now that we have considered three different types of behavior for duopolists, let's compare the outcomes of the different models. A monopoly confronting the same demand and cost conditions as Cournot duopolists would have produced $a/2b$ units of output at a price of $a/2$, earning an economic profit of $a^2/4b$ (see Figure 13-6). The interdependence between the Cournot duopolists thus causes price to be one-third lower and total quantity to be one-third higher than the corresponding values in the monopoly case.[5] Whereas the equilibrium price and quantity in the Cournot model differed by only a factor of one-third from those in the monopoly case, in the Bertrand model they are precisely the same as in the competitive case.[6]

---

[5]As a fraction of the output for a perfectly competitive industry, industry output under a Cournot duopoly is $N/(N + 1)$ with N firms. As the number of firms N becomes large, the Cournot industry output (and therefore price and profit) approaches that of a perfectly competitive industry. In this sense, Cournot duopoly is truly between monopoly and perfect competition.

[6]If firms choose capacity and then price, the outcome matches the Cournot equilibrium. See David Kreps and Jose Scheinkman "Quantity Precommitment and Bertrand Competition Yield Cournot Outcomes," *Bell Journal of Economics, 14*, 1983: 326–337.

FIGURE 13-6
The monopolist would maximize profit where marginal revenue equals zero, since there are no marginal production costs. The equilibrium price will be higher, and the equilibrium quantity lower, than in the Cournot case.

COMPARING EQUILIBRIUM PRICE AND QUANTITY

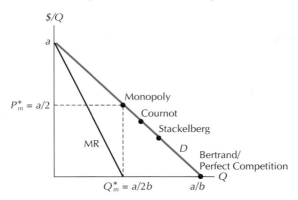

How well should the Stackelberg duopolists do? Naturally, the leader fares better since it is the one strategically manipulating the behavior of the follower. Referring to Figure 13-4 we see that firm 1's profit is $a^2/8b$, which is twice that of firm 2. As it happens, this is exactly what firm 1 would have earned had it and firm 2 colluded to charge the monopoly price, $a/2$, and split the market evenly (see Figure 13-6). The combined output of the two firms in the Stackelberg case is $3a/4b$, which is slightly higher than in the Cournot case, with the result that the market price, $a/4$, is slightly lower than in the Cournot case ($a/3$). The results of the four possibilities considered thus far are summarized in Table 13-1.

The Stackelberg model represents a clear improvement over the Cournot and Bertrand models in that it allows at least one of the firms to behave strategically. But why should only one firm behave in this fashion? If firm 1 can make strategic use of its rival's reaction function, why can't firm 2 do likewise? Suppose, in fact, that both firms try to be Stackelberg leaders. Each will then ignore its own reaction function and produce $a/2b$, with the result that total industry output and price will be a/b and 0, respectively, the same as in the Bertrand model. From the standpoint of consumers, this is a very desirable outcome, of course. But for the owners of the firms, universal strategic behavior leads to the worst possible outcome.

All four models assume a market demand curve of $P = a - bQ$ and marginal cost equal to zero. (Of course, if marginal cost is not zero, the entries will be all different from the ones shown.)

TABLE 13-1 **COMPARISON OF OLIGOPOLY MODELS**

Model	Industry output Q	Market price P	Industry profit Π
Shared monopoly	$Q_m = a/(2b)$	$P_m = a/2$	$\Pi_m = a^2/(4b)$
Cournot	$(4/3)Q_m$	$(2/3)P_m$	$(8/9)\Pi_m$
Stackelberg	$(3/2)Q_m$	$(1/2)P_m$	$(3/4)\Pi_m$
Bertrand	$2Q_m$	0	0
Perfect competition	$2Q_m$	0	0

COLLUSION AND THE THEORY OF GAMES

If two firms were savvy enough to operate as Stackelberg leaders, they should also be able to discover that a collusive agreement is the only way for them to achieve maximum profits. Since there are plenty of smart managers in the world, must we conclude that collusion is the rule, rather than the exception, in industries served by only a small number of firms?

As attractive as the collusive outcome is from the perspective of the firms involved, it turns out to be surprisingly difficult to sustain. Indeed, a recurring theme in the economics of oligopoly is that what it pays each firm to do individually often turns out to be very harmful to the interests of firms taken as a whole.

The basic problem confronting colluding oligopolists often has the same structure as the prisoner's dilemma game we saw in Chapter 7. Recall that in the original story used to illustrate the prisoner's dilemma, two prisoners are held in separate cells for a serious crime that they did in fact commit. The prosecutor, however, has only enough hard evidence to convict them of a minor offense, for which the penalty is, say, a year in jail. Each prisoner is told that if one confesses while the other remains silent, the confessor will go scot-free while the other spends 20 years in prison. If both confess, they will get an intermediate sentence, say, 5 years. These payoffs are summarized in Table 13-2. The two prisoners are not allowed to communicate with one another.

Situations like the prisoner's dilemma may be analyzed using the mathematical theory of games developed by John von Neumann and Oskar Morgenstern during the 1940s.[7] This theory begins by describing the three elements common to all games: (1) the players, (2) the list of possible strategies, and (3) the payoffs that correspond to each combination of strategies. In Table 13-2, the two players in the game are prisoner X and prisoner Y. Each player has two strategies: confess and remain silent. The payoffs to each combination of strategies: are the sentences they receive, which are summarized in the *payoff matrix* shown in Table 13-2.

Dominant strategy The strategy in a game that produces the best results irrespective of the strategy chosen by one's opponent.

Some games, like the prisoner's dilemma, have a ***dominant strategy***, which means a strategy that produces better results no matter what strategy the opposing player follows. The dominant strategy in the prisoner's dilemma is to confess. No matter what Y does, X gets a lighter sentence by speaking out: if Y too confesses, X gets 5 years instead of 20; and if Y remains silent, X goes free instead of spending a year in jail. The payoffs are perfectly symmetric, so Y also does better to confess, no matter what X does. The difficulty is that when each behaves in a self-interested way, both do worse than if each had shown restraint. Thus, when both confess, they get 5 years, instead of the 1 year they could have gotten by remaining silent.

To illustrate the analogy between the prisoner's dilemma and the problem confronting oligopolists who are trying to collude, let us consider two firms with

---

[7]See John von Neumann and Oskar Morgenstern, *Theory of Games and Economic Behavior*, 3d ed., Princeton, NJ: Princeton University Press, 1953.

Each player believes he will always get a shorter sentence by confessing, no matter what the other player does. And if each player confesses, each gets 5 years. Yet if both players had remained silent, each would have gotten only 1 year in jail. Here, the individual pursuit of self-interest produces a worse outcome for each player.

TABLE 13-2   THE PRISONER'S DILEMMA

		Prisoner Y	
		Confess	**Remain silent**
Prisoner X	**Confess**	5 years for each	0 years for X 20 years for Y
	Remain silent	20 years for X 0 years for Y	1 year for each

the same demand and cost conditions as in the mineral spring example. For the sake of concreteness, suppose that the market demand curve takes the specific form $P = 20 - Q$. Suppose the two firms are considering a collusive agreement under which each produces half the monopoly output and offers it for sale at the monopoly price. For the specific demand curve assumed, the monopoly price is 10, and the monopoly quantity is also 10. If the firms enter into, and abide by, this agreement, each will sell 5 units at a price of 10, thus making an economic profit of 50. On a strict profit criterion, there is no possibility for each firm to do better than that.

Yet this does not assure that each firm will abide by the agreement. Note that the payoffs to each firm depend on the combination of behaviors they choose. Each firm has two options—namely, to abide by the agreement or to defect. Again for the sake of concreteness, suppose that to defect means to cut price by 1 unit, from 10 to 9. If one firm abides by the agreement while the other defects, what will happen? Since the two firms are selling identical products, the defecting firm will capture the entire market because of its lower price. Selling 11 units at a price of 9, it will earn a profit of 99; the trusting cooperator sells no output and thus earns zero profit.

If both firms defect, they will end up splitting the 11 units of output sold at a price of 9, and each will make an economic profit of 49.50. Since each firm has two options—(1) cooperate, or abide by the agreement to charge 10; and (2) defect, or charge 9—there are four possible combinations of behavior. These combinations, and the profits that result from each, are summarized in Table 13-3.

Note in the table that it is a dominant strategy for each firm to defect. That is, each firm gets a higher payoff by defecting, no matter which option the other firm chooses. To illustrate, consider the choice facing firm 2. It says to itself, "Suppose firm 1 cooperates; which choice is best for me?" By cooperating when firm 1 cooperates, the firms end up in the upper left cell of the profit matrix in Table 13-3, which means each earns 50. But if firm 2 defects, the result will be the lower left cell, where it would end up earning 99. Now firm 2 says, "Suppose firm 1 defects. Which choice is best for me this time?" If firm 2 cooperates, we get the upper right

TABLE 13-3   PROFITS TO COOPERATION AND DEFECTION

		Firm 1	
		Cooperate $(P = 10)$	Defect $(P = 9)$
Firm 2	**Cooperate** $(P = 10)$	$\Pi_1 = 50$ $\Pi_2 = 50$	$\Pi_1 = 99$ $\Pi_2 = 0$
	Defect $(P = 9)$	$\Pi_1 = 0$ $\Pi_2 = 99$	$\Pi_1 = 49.50$ $\Pi_2 = 49.50$

cell of the profit matrix, where it earns 0. But if firm 2 defects, it earns 49.50. Thus, no matter which choice firm 1 makes, firm 2 earns higher profit by defecting.

By exactly parallel reasoning, defection is also a dominant strategy for firm 1. Note, however, that when each firm defects, each does worse than if each had cooperated. In this situation, behavior that is in the interest of each individual firm adds up to a result that is not in the interest of firms generally.

As this example is set up, the firms don't do much worse when each defects than when each cooperates. But firms that find it in their interest to defect once are likely to find it in their interest to do so again. If one now charges 8 while the other remains at 9, for example, the former will earn a profit of 96, while the latter earns 0. A firm need not feel a compelling desire to outdo its rival in order for defection to be an attractive option. On the contrary, its motive may be purely self-protective, the very rational fear that its rival will defect. As we saw in the Bertrand model, the resulting process of competitive price-cutting will terminate only when price has plummeted all the way down to marginal cost. At that point, recall, neither firm earns any profit at all. So the cost of failing to abide by a cooperative agreement can be very high indeed.

Application: The Advertising Arms Race in the Cigarette Industry. Oligopolists compete when not only along the price dimension, but through the use of advertising as well. And here too we see that what is in the interests of an individual firm is often not in the interests of firms taken as a whole.

When a firm in any given industry advertises its product, its demand increases for two reasons. First, people who never used that type of product before learn about it, and some will buy it. Second, other people who already consume a different brand of the same product may switch brands because of advertising. The first effect boosts sales for the industry as a whole. The second merely redistributes existing sales within the industry.

The American cigarette industry is an example of one in which the most important effect of advertising is believed to be brand-switching. In such industries, the decision of whether to advertise often confronts individual firms with a prisoner's dilemma. Table 13-4 shows the profits to a hypothetical pair of cigarette producers under the four possible combinations of their advertise/don't advertise decisions. If both firms advertise (lower right cell), each earns a profit of only 250, as compared with a profit of 500 each if neither advertises (upper left cell). So it is clearly better for neither firm to advertise than for both to advertise.

Yet note the incentives confronting the individual firm. Firm 1 sees that if firm 2 doesn't advertise, firm 1 can earn higher profits by advertising (750) than by not advertising (500). Firm 1 also sees that if firm 2 does advertise, firm 1 will again earn more by advertising (250) than by not advertising (0). It is thus a dominant strategy for firm 1 to advertise. And because the payoffs are symmetric, it is also a dominant strategy for firm 2 to advertise. So here too when each firm does what is rational from its own point of view, firms as a group do worse than if they had acted in concert.

Congress passed a law forbidding the advertising of cigarettes on television as of January 1, 1971. Its stated purpose was to protect people from messages that might persuade them to consume a product that has been proved hazardous to human health. The law seems to have achieved this purpose, at least in part, as evidenced by the steadily declining proportion of Americans who smoke. But the law has also had an unintended effect, which was to solve the prisoner's dilemma for American cigarette manufacturers. In the year before the law's enactment, cigarette manufacturers spent more than $300 million advertising their products. The corresponding figure for the following year was more than $60 million smaller, and much of that difference translated into higher profits for the industry. The advertising ban thus accomplished for the cigarette manufacturers what the imperatives of individual profit seeking could not—an effective way of limiting the advertising arms race.

The Nash Equilibrium Concept. When, as in the prisoner's dilemma, both parties have a dominant strategy in a game, the equilibrium for the game occurs when each plays the dominant strategy. But there are many games in which not every player has a dominant strategy. Consider, for example, the variation on the

In many industries the primary effect of advertising is to cause consumers to switch brands. In such industries, the dominant strategy is to advertise heavily (lower right cell), even though firms taken as a whole would do better by not advertising (upper left cell).

TABLE 13-4 THE ADVERTISING DECISION AS A PRISONER'S DILEMMA

		Firm 1	
		Don't advertise	**Advertise**
	Don't advertise	$\Pi_1 = 500$	$\Pi_1 = 750$
		$\Pi_2 = 500$	$\Pi_2 = 0$
Firm 2			
	Advertise	$\Pi_1 = 0$	$\Pi_1 = 250$
		$\Pi_2 = 750$	$\Pi_2 = 250$

advertising game shown in Table 13-5. No matter what firm 2 does, firm 1 does better to advertise; so advertise is the dominant strategy for firm 1. But now the same cannot be said of firm 2. If firm 1 advertises, firm 2 does best also to advertise. But if firm 1 does not advertise, firm 2 does best not to advertise. In contrast to the prisoner's dilemma, here the best strategy for firm 2 depends on the particular strategy chosen by firm 1.

Even though firm 2 does not have a dominant strategy in this game, we can say something about what is likely to happen. In particular, firm 2 is able to predict that firm 1 will advertise because that is a dominant strategy for firm 1. And since firm 2 knows this, it knows that its own best strategy is also to advertise. In this game, the lower right cell is called a *Nash equilibrium*,[8] which is defined as a combination of strategies such that each player's strategy is the best he can choose given the strategy chosen by the other player. Thus, at a Nash equilibrium, neither player has any incentive to deviate from its current strategy. Note that when each player follows his dominant strategy in a prisoner's dilemma, the result is a Nash equilibrium. But as we have seen, a Nash equilibrium does not require both players to have a dominant strategy.

Nash equilibrium
The combination of strategies in a game such that neither player has any incentive to change strategies given the strategy of his opponent.

Firm 1 earns higher profits by advertising, no matter what firm 2 does. Its dominant strategy is to advertise. But firm 2 has no dominant strategy. If firm 1 advertises, firm 2 does best also to advertise, but if firm 1 does not advertise, firm 2 does best not to advertise.

TABLE 13-5   A GAME IN WHICH FIRM 2 HAS NO DOMINANT STRATEGY

		Firm 1	
		Don't advertise	Advertise
	Don't advertise	$\Pi_1 = 500$ $\Pi_2 = 400$	$\Pi_1 = 750$ $\Pi_2 = 0$
Firm 2			
	Advertise	$\Pi_1 = 0$ $\Pi_2 = 300$	$\Pi_1 = 300$ $\Pi_2 = 200$

EXERCISE 13-4

Does either firm have a dominant strategy in the game below? Does the game have a Nash equilibrium?

---

[8]After John F. Nash, the American mathematician who introduced the concept in 1951.

		Firm 1	
		High research budget	Low research budget
Firm 2	**High research budget**	$\Pi_1 = 200$ $\Pi_2 = 40$	$\Pi_1 = 60$ $\Pi_2 = 100$
	Low research budget	$\Pi_1 = 0$ $\Pi_2 = 30$	$\Pi_1 = 40$ $\Pi_2 = 80$

Strategies for Repeated Play in Prisoner's Dilemmas. To say that the costs of failing to cooperate are high is simply another way of saying that there are powerful financial incentives to find some way to hold collusive agreements together. What the potential participants to a collusive agreement need is some way to penalize those who defect, thereby making it in their material interests not to do so. When a prisoner's dilemma confronts parties who will interact only once, this turns out to be very difficult to achieve. But when the participants expect to interact repeatedly in the future, new possibilities emerge.

Experimental research in the 1960s identified a very simple strategy that proves remarkably effective at keeping potential defectors in check.[9] The strategy is called *tit-for-tat,* and it works as follows: The first time you interact with someone, you cooperate. In each subsequent interaction you simply do what that person did in the previous interaction. Thus, if your partner defected on your first interaction, you would then defect on your next interaction with her. If she then cooperates, your move next time will be to cooperate as well.

Tit-for-tat is described as a "nice" strategy because of the propensity of players to cooperate on the first interaction. If two tit-for-tat players interact together over a long period of time, the result will be cooperation in each and every interaction. Tit-for-tat is also a "tough" strategy, however, because those who follow it always stand ready to punish defectors in the next interaction. Finally, it is a "forgiving" strategy, in the sense that a player is willing to cooperate with a former defector once she shows evidence of willingness to cooperate.

University of Michigan political scientist Robert Axelrod conducted an extensive analysis of how well the tit-for-tat strategy performs against other strategies for playing the repeated prisoner's dilemma game.[10] In an early round of Axelrod's computer simulations, tit-for-tat was the most successful strategy, in the sense that people who followed it earned more, on the average, than those using any of the other strategies tested. Axelrod then published this finding and invited experts from all over the world to try to design a better strategy. His challenge produced a host of ingenious counterstrategies. Axelrod found, however, that

---

[9]See Anatol Rapoport and A. Chammah, *Prisoner's Dilemma,* Ann Arbor: University of Michigan Press, 1965.

[10]Robert Axelrod, *The Evolution of Cooperation,* New York: Basic Books, 1984.

even these strategies, many of which had been put together for the specific purpose of defeating tit-for-tat, did not survive against it.

The success of tit-for-tat requires a reasonably stable set of players, each of whom can remember what other players have done in previous interactions. It also requires that players have a significant stake in what happens in the future, for it is only the fear of retaliation that keeps people from defecting. When these conditions are met, cooperators can identify one another and discriminate against defectors.

The conditions called for by the tit-for-tat strategy are often met in human populations. Many people do interact repeatedly, and most keep track of how others treat them. Axelrod has assembled persuasive evidence that these forces help explain how people actually behave. Perhaps the most impressive of all this evidence comes from accounts of the "live-and-let-live" system that developed in the trench warfare in Europe during World War I. In many areas of the war, the same enemy units lay encamped opposite one another in the trenches over a period of several years. Units were often closely matched, with the result that neither side had much hope of quickly defeating the other. Their choices were to fight intensively, with both sides sustaining heavy casualties, or to exercise restraint.

The conditions of interaction described by historian Tony Ashworth in his account of the trench fighting closely resemble those required for the success of tit-for-tat.[11] The identities of the players were more or less stable. Interactions between them were repeated, often several times daily, for extended periods. Each side could easily tell when the other side defected from the strategy. And each side had a clear stake in keeping its future losses to a minimum.

There is little doubt that tit-for-tat often did emerge as the strategy of choice for both Allied and German fighting units in World War I. Although strongly discouraged as a matter of official policy, restraint was sometimes conspicuously apparent. Referring to night patrol squads operating out of the trenches, Ashworth writes:

> . . . both British and Germans on quiet sectors assumed that should a chance face-to-face encounter occur, neither patrol would initiate aggression, but each would move to avoid the other. Each patrol gave peace to the other where aggression was not only possible, but prescribed, provided, of course, the gesture was reciprocated, for if one patrol fired so would the other.[12]

In the words of one of the participants in the conflict:

> We suddenly confronted, round some mound or excavation, a German patrol. . . . We were perhaps twenty yards from one another, fully visible. I waved a weary hand, as

---

[11]Tony Ashworth, *Trench Warfare: The Live and Let Live System*, New York: Holmes and Meier, 1980.
[12]Ibid., p. 103.

if to say, what is the use of killing each other? The German officer seemed to understand, and both parties turned and made their way back to their own trenches.[13]

Often, bombardments would occur only at specified times of day and would be directed away from the most vulnerable positions. Mealtimes and hospital tents, for example, were usually tacitly off limits.

The conditions discussed by Axelrod help to explain not only when people will cooperate, but also when they are most likely to *refrain* from cooperation. For example, he notes that mutual restraint in trench warfare began to break down once the end of the war was clearly in sight.

As in warfare, so, too, in the world of business. Companies pay their bills on time, Axelrod suggests, not because it is the right thing to do but because they require future shipments from the same suppliers. When future interactions appear unlikely, this tendency to cooperate often breaks down: "[An] example is the case where a business is on the edge of bankruptcy and sells its accounts receivable to an outsider called a 'factor.' This sale is made at a very substantial discount because

> once a manufacturer begins to go under, even his best customers begin refusing payment for merchandise, claiming defects in quality, failure to meet specifications, tardy delivery, or what-have-you. The great enforcer of morality in commerce is the continuing relationship, the belief that one will have to do business again with this customer, or this supplier, and when a failing company loses this automatic enforcer, not even a strong-arm factor is likely to find a substitute.[14]

One additional requirement for the success of tit-for-tat is that there not be a known, fixed number of future interactions. Indeed, if players know exactly how many times they will interact, then mutual cooperation on every move cannot be a Nash equilibrium. To see why, suppose each firm knew it was going to interact with its rival for, say, exactly 1000 more times. Each would then know that the other would defect on the last interaction, because there would be no possibility of being punished for doing so. But since each firm realizes that, it will also have no reason not to defect on the 999th interaction. After all, a defection will occur on the 1000th interaction no matter what it does on the round before. The same argument can be applied step-by-step back to the first interaction, with the result that the tit-for-tat strategy completely unravels.

The unraveling problem does not arise if there is not a known, fixed number of interactions.[15] If we suppose, for example, that there is always some positive

---

[13]Herbert Read, quoted in ibid., p. 104.

[14]Mayer, quoted in Axelrod, op. cit., pp. 59, 60.

[15]Another way the unraveling problem is avoided is if there is some positive probability that others will follow the tit-for-tat strategy even though, strictly speaking, it is not rational for them to do so. See David Kreps, Paul Milgrom, John Roberts, and Robert Wilson, "Rational Cooperation in Finitely Repeated Prisoner's Dilemmas," *Journal of Economic Theory*, 27, 1982: 245–252.

probability that a further interaction will ensue, then no interaction can ever be identified as being the last one, which means the threat of future punishment will always have at least some force. In the situations in which most firms find themselves (an exception being the bankruptcy case cited earlier), it seems plausible to assume that there will always be some probability of interaction in the future.

Is it inevitable, then, that the tit-for-tat strategy will produce widespread collusion among firms? By no means. One difficulty is that tit-for-tat's effectiveness depends on there being only two players in the game. In competitive and monopolistically competitive industries there are generally many firms, and even in oligopolies there are often several. When there are more than two firms, and one defects this period, how do the cooperators selectively punish the defector next period? By cutting price? That will penalize everyone, not just the defector. Even if there are only two firms in an industry, the problem remains that some other firm may enter the industry. So the would-be cooperators have to worry not only about each other, but also about the entire list of firms that might decide to compete with them. Each firm may see this as a hopeless task and decide to defect now, hoping to reap at least some extra-normal profit in the short run.

We will consider the threat of potential entry in greater detail in the sections to follow. For the moment, we may note that, as a purely empirical matter, cartel agreements and other forms of collusion have occurred frequently in the past but have tended to be highly unstable. Apparently the practical problems involved in implementing tit-for-tat in the environments confronting firms make it very difficult to hold collusive agreements together for long.

Sequential Games. The games we have considered so far have been ones in which both players must pick their strategies simultaneously. Each player had to choose his strategy knowing only the incentives facing his opponent, not the opponent's actual choice of strategy. But in many games, one player moves first, and the other is then able to choose his strategy with full knowledge of the first player's choice. The nuclear deterrence episode described at the beginning of this chapter is an example of such a game.

For the sake of illustration, suppose that the adversaries are the United States and the former USSR and that the USSR is considering whether to launch a nuclear strike against the United States. This decision may be portrayed in a "game tree" diagram like the one shown in Figure 13-7. If the first move is the USSR's, the game starts at point A. The first two branches of the game tree represent the USSR's alternatives of attacking and not attacking. If it attacks, then the United States finds itself at point B on the top branch of the game tree, where it must decide whether or not to strike back. If the United States retaliates, we end up at point D, where the payoffs are -100 for each country. If the United States does not retaliate, we end up at point E, where the payoffs are 100 for the USSR and -50 for the United States. (The units of these payoffs are purely arbitrary. The values chosen are intended to reflect each country's hypothetical relative valuation of the different outcomes.) The bottom half of the game tree represents the alternative in which the USSR does not attack. If the USSR chooses this alternative,

FIGURE 13-7
If the USSR attacks, the best option for the United States is not to retaliate (point *E*). If the USSR doesn't attack, the best option for the United States is also not to attack (point *G*). Since the USSR gets a higher payoff at *E* than at *G*, it will attack. If the United States is believed to be a payoff maximizer, its threat to retaliate against a first strike will not be credible.

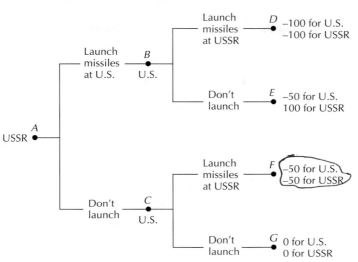

NUCLEAR DETERRENCE AS A SEQUENTIAL GAME

the United States finds itself at point *C*, where it again faces a decision about whether or not to launch missiles at the USSR. For argument's sake, suppose that the payoffs to the two countries under each alternative are shown on the bottom two branches of the game tree at points *F* and *G*, respectively. Given the assumed payoffs for each of the four possible outcomes of the game tree, the USSR can analyze what the United States will do under each alternative. If the USSR attacks (point *B*), the best option open to the United States is not to retaliate (point *E*). If the USSR does not attack (point *C*), the best option for the United States is also not to attack (point *G*). The USSR thus knows that if the United States is a payoff maximizer, the game will end at point *E* if the USSR attacks at point *G* if it does not attack. And since the USSR has a higher payoff at point *E*, it does best to attack. The United States may threaten to retaliate, but as long as its adversaries believe it is a payoff maximizer, such threats will lack credibility.

Now suppose that the United States could install a "doomsday machine"—a device that would automatically retaliate in the event of an attack by the USSR. The effect would be to eliminate the bottom half of the top branch of the game tree in Figure 13-7. The USSR would then know that if it attacked, the game would end at point *D*, where the USSR gets a payoff of −100. And since this is worse than the outcome if the USSR does not attack (point *G*), the best option open to the USSR would then be to leave its missiles in their silos.

Application: Strategic Entry Deterrence. The Sears Tower in Chicago is currently the tallest building in the United States. This status endows the building with a special form of prestige, enabling its owners to command higher rents than in otherwise similar office buildings. Now, suppose that company *X* is considering whether to build an even taller building. Suppose it knows that any firm that has permanent ownership of the tallest building will earn a large economic profit. Its concern, naturally, is that Sears (or some other firm) may build a still taller building, which would substantially diminish company X's payoff.

Both Sears and company X realize that they are participants in a sequential game of the type pictured in Figure 13-8. The game starts at point A, where X must decide whether to enter with a taller building. If it does not, Sears will receive a payoff of 100, X a payoff of 0. If X enters, however, the game moves to point B, where Sears must decide whether to build higher or stand pat. Suppose that if Sears builds higher, its payoff will be 30, while X will earn a payoff of -50; and that if Sears does not build higher, its payoff will be 40, while X will get a payoff of 60. Sears naturally wants X not to enter. It may even announce its intention to build a taller building in the event that X enters. But as long as X knows the payoffs facing Sears, it can conclude that the best option open to Sears once X enters is to stand pat. The Nash equilibrium of this sequential game is point E, where X enters and Sears stands pat.

Now suppose that before Sears had originally built its tower, it had the option of building a platform atop the building on which it could build an addition that would make the building taller. Building this platform costs 10 units, but reduces the cost of building a taller building by 20 units. If Sears had installed this platform, the sequential game between it and company X would then be as portrayed by the game tree in Figure 13-9. Sears's payoff at point D is now 40 (it saves 20 on building costs less the 10-unit cost of the platform). Its payoffs at C and E are each 10 units less than in Figure 13-8 (reflecting the cost of the platform). Despite the small magnitude of these changes in payoffs, the presence of the platform dramatically alters the outcome of the game. This time X can predict that if it enters with the tallest building, it will be in Sears's interest to add to its existing building, which means that X will receive a payoff of -50. As a result, X will not find it worthwhile to enter this market, and so the

FIGURE 13-8
If company X builds a skyscraper taller than the Sears Tower, Sears must decide whether to build higher (point D) or yield its status as the tallest building (point E). Because Sears earns a higher payoff at E than at D, it will not build higher. And since X knows that, it will enter the market despite Sears's threat to build a taller building.

THE DECISION TO BUILD THE TALLEST BUILDING

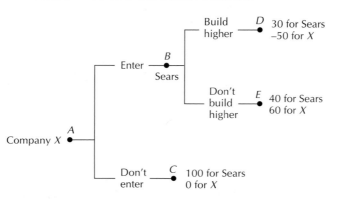

STRATEGIC ENTRY DETERRENCE

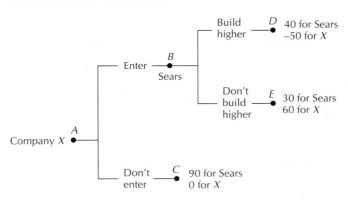

game will end at point C. The payoff to Sears at C is 90 (the original 100 minus the 10-unit cost of building the platform). Its 10-unit investment in the platform thus increases its net payoff by 50 (the difference between the 90-unit payoff it receives with the platform and the 40-unit payoff it would have received without it).[16]

CONTESTABLE MARKETS

In a widely discussed book, economists William Baumol, John Panzer, and Robert Willig suggested that oligopolies and even monopolies will sometimes behave much like perfectly competitive firms.[17] The specific condition under which this will happen, according to their theory, is that entry and exit be perfectly free. With costless entry, a new firm will quickly enter if an incumbent firm dares to charge a price above average cost. The name "contestable markets" refers to the fact that when entry is costless, we often see a contest between potential competitors to see which firms will serve the market.

Costless entry does not mean that it costs no money to obtain a production facility to serve a market. It means that there are no *sunk* costs associated with entry and exit. The most important piece of equipment required to provide air service in the New York–London market, for example, is a wide-bodied aircraft, which carries a price tag of almost $100 million. This is a hefty investment, to be sure, but it is not a sunk cost. If a firm wants to leave the market, it can sell

[16]Microsoft Explorer versus Netscape and Barnes & Noble versus Borders are more recent examples of strategic entry deterrence games.

[17]William Baumol, John Panzer, and Robert Willig, *Contestable Markets and the Theory of Industry Structure,* San Diego, CA: Harcourt Brace Jovanovich, 1982. For an accessible summary, see Baumol, "Contestable Markets: An Uprising in the Theory of Industry Structure," *American Economic Review,* 72, March 1982: 1–15.

or lease the aircraft to another firm, or make use of it in some other market. Contrast this case with that of a cement producer, which must spend a similar sum to build a manufacturing facility. Once built, the cement plant has essentially no alternative use. The resources that go into it are sunk costs, beyond recovery if the firm suddenly decides it no longer wants to participate in that market.

Why are sunk costs so important? Consider again the contrast between the air service market and the cement market. In each case we have a local monopoly. Because of economies of scale, there is room for only one cement factory in a given area and only one flight at a given time of day. Suppose in each case that incumbent firms are charging prices well in excess of average costs, and that in each case a new firm enters and captures some of the excess profit. And suppose, finally, that the incumbents react by lowering their prices, with the result that all the firms, entrants and incumbents alike, are losing money. In the cement market case, the entrant will then be stuck with a huge capital facility that will not cover its costs. The airline case, by contrast, carries no similar risk. If the market becomes unprofitable, the entrant can quickly pull out and deploy its asset elsewhere.

The contestable market theory is like other theories of market structure in saying that cost conditions determine how many firms will end up serving a given market. Where there are economies of scale, we expect to see only a single firm. Where there are U-shaped LAC curves whose minimum points occur at a substantial fraction of industry output, we expect only a few firms. With constant costs, there may be many firms. Where the contestable market theory differs from others is in saying that there is no clear relationship between the *actual* number of competitors in a market and the extent to which price and quantity resemble what we would see under perfect competition. Where the threat of entry is credible, incumbent firms are simply not free to charge prices that are significantly above cost.

Critics of the contestable market theory counter that there are important sunk costs involved in participation in *every* market.[18] Granted, in the airline case it is possible to lease an aircraft on a short-term basis; but that alone is not sufficient to start a viable operation. Counter space must be obtained at the airport terminal; potential passengers must be alerted to the existence of the new service, usually with an expensive advertising campaign. Reservations, baggage handling, and check-in facilities must be arranged. Ground service contracts for the aircraft must be signed, and so on. Each step involves irretrievable commitments of resources, and they add up to enough to make a brief stay in the market very costly indeed. The fiercest critics contend that so long as there are any sunk costs involved in entry and exit, the contestable market theory breaks down.

All the returns are not in yet on the contestable market theory. The critics have raised some formidable objections, but there do appear to be at least some settings where the insights hold up. In the intercity bus market, for example, either

---

[18]W. G. Shepherd, "Contestability vs. Competition," *American Economic Review, 74,* September 1984: 572–587.

Greyhound or Trailways is likely to be the only firm providing service in any given city-pair market. Traditional theories of market structure suggest that prices would be likely to rise steeply during holiday weekends, when substantially larger numbers of people travel. What we see in many markets, however, is that small charter bus companies offer special holiday service at fares no higher than normal. These companies often do little more than post a few leaflets on college campuses, stating their prices and schedules and giving a telephone number to call for reservations. The circumstances of the intercity bus industry come very close to the free entry ideal contemplated by the contestable market theory, and the results are much as it predicts. Much more remains to be said about just when the threat of entry will be a significant disciplining force, a subject we consider in more detail in the appendix to this chapter (www.mhhe.com/economics/frank4).

Another market structure close to perfect competition occurs if there is free entry but one firm's products are not perfect substitutes for the products of other firms. The degree of substitutability between products then determines how close to perfect competition the outcome achieves. One concrete way of thinking about lack of complete substitutability is distance. Gas across town is not a perfect substitute for gas at the nearest corner, especially not when your tank is reading below empty.[19]

Monopolistic Competition—A Spatial Interpretation

Imagine yourself a resident of a small island nation with a large lake in the middle of it. Business activity there is naturally restricted to the doughnut-shaped piece of land that constitutes the island's periphery. There is considerable specialization of labor on your island. People toil all day at their respective tasks and then take their evening meals at restaurants. People on your island lack the customary preference for culinary diversity. Instead, you and your neighbors prefer to eat baked potatoes and grilled beefsteak every night. Meals in any given restaurant are produced under increasing returns to scale—the more meals produced, the lower the average cost per meal.

How many restaurants should there be in this island nation? We are tempted to say only one, thereby keeping the cost per meal to a minimum. If the circumference of the island were, say, only 300 yards, this would almost surely be the correct answer. But for a much larger island, the direct cost of meals is not likely to be the only item of concern to you and your fellow residents. You will also care about the cost of getting to and from the nearest restaurant. If the island were 300 miles around, for example, the cost savings from having only a single restaurant could hardly begin to compensate for the travel costs incurred by those who live on the far side of the island.

---

[19]Models built on other interpretations are developed in the appendix (www.mhhe.com/economics/frank4).

The market for evening meals on this island is in one respect the same as the markets we have considered in earlier chapters: A single, standardized meal is served in every restaurant. But the type of food served is not the only important characteristic of a meal. Buyers care also about *where* the meal is served. When products differ along one or more important dimensions—location, size, flavor, quality, and so on—we immediately confront the general question of how much product diversity there should be. Should an economy have 5 different brands of cars, 10, or 50? How many different kinds of tennis racquets should there be?

To help fix ideas, suppose there are initially four restaurants evenly spaced around the periphery of the island, as represented by the heavy black squares in Figure 13-10. Suppose the circumference of the island is 1 mile. The distance between adjacent restaurants will then be $\frac{1}{4}$ mile, and no one can possibly live more than $\frac{1}{8}$ mile away from the nearest restaurant, the one-way trip length required for someone who lives exactly halfway between two restaurants.

To fill out the structure of the environment, suppose there are L consumers scattered uniformly about the circle, and suppose the cost of travel is t dollars per mile. Thus, for example, if t were equal to \$24/mile, the transportation cost incurred by someone who lives $d = \frac{1}{16}$ mile from the nearest restaurant would be the product of the round-trip distance ($2d$) and the unit travel cost (t)—$2td = 2(\frac{1}{16}$ mile)(\$24/mile) = \$3.

Suppose further that each consumer will eat exactly 1 meal/day at the restaurant for which the total price (which is the price charged for the meal plus transportation costs) is lowest. And suppose, finally, that each restaurant has a total cost curve given by

$$TC = F + MQ. \qquad (13.6)$$

FIGURE 13-10
Restaurants (heavy black squares) are the same except for their geographic location. Each person dines at the restaurant closest to home. If the circumference of the loop is 1 mile, this means that the distance between restaurants will be $\frac{1}{4}$ mile, giving rise to a maximum one-way trip length of $\frac{1}{8}$ mile.

AN INDUSTRY IN WHICH LOCATION IS THE IMPORTANT DIFFERENTIATING FEATURE

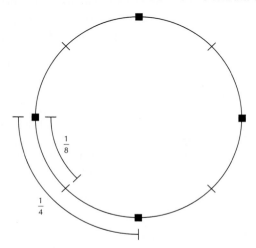

Recall from earlier chapters that the total cost curve in Equation 13.6 is one in which there is a fixed cost F and a constant marginal cost M. Here, F may be thought of as the sum of equipment rental fees, opportunity costs of invested capital, and other fixed costs associated with operating a restaurant; and M is the sum of the labor, raw material, and other variable costs incurred in producing an additional meal.

Recall also that average total cost (ATC) is simply total cost divided by output. With a total cost function given by $TC = F + MQ$, average total cost is thus equal to $F/Q + M$. This means that the more customers that are served in a given location, the lower the average total cost will be.

Suppose, for example, that each of our four restaurants has a total cost curve, measured in dollars per day, given by $TC = 50 + 5Q$, where Q is the number of meals it serves each day. If the population, L, is equal to 100 persons, each restaurant will serve $(100/4) = 25$ meals/day, and its total cost will be given by $TC = 50 + 5(25) = \$175$/day. Average total cost in each restaurant will be $TC/25 = (\$175/\text{day})/(25 \text{ meals/day}) = \$7$/meal. By comparison, if there were only two restaurants, each would serve 50 meals/day and have an average total cost of only $6/meal.

What will be the average cost of transportation when there are four restaurants? This cost will depend on unit transportation costs (t) and on how far apart the restaurants are. Recall that the distance between adjacent restaurants will be $\frac{1}{4}$ mile when there are four restaurants. Some people will live right next door to a restaurant, and for these people the transportation cost will be zero. With four restaurants, the farthest someone can live from a restaurant is $\frac{1}{8}$ mile, the one-way distance for a person who lives halfway between two adjacent restaurants. For this person, the round-trip will cover $\frac{1}{4}$ mile; and if t is again equal to $24/mile, the travel cost for this patron will be $(\$24/\text{mile})(\frac{1}{4} \text{ mile}) = \$6$. Since people are uniformly scattered about the loop, the average round-trip will be halfway between these two extremes; it will thus cover a distance of $\frac{1}{8}$ mile, and its cost will be $3.

The *overall average cost per meal* is the sum of average total cost ($7/meal in the four-restaurant example) and average transportation cost (here, $3/meal), which comes to $10/meal.

THE OPTIMAL NUMBER OF LOCATIONS

If unit transportation cost (t) were zero, it would then clearly be optimal to have only a single restaurant, because that would minimize the overall average cost per meal. But if transportation cost were sufficiently high, a single restaurant would not be optimal because the average patron would have to travel too great a distance. The optimal number of locations is thus the result of a tradeoff between the start-up and other fixed costs (F) of opening new locations, on the one hand, and the savings from lower transportation costs, on the other.

What is the best number of outlets to have? Our strategy for answering this question will be to ask whether the overall average cost per meal served (average total cost plus average transportation cost) would decline if we had one more restaurant than we have now. If so, we should add another restaurant and ask the same question again. Once the overall average cost stops declining, we will have reached the optimal number of restaurants.

To illustrate, suppose we increase the number of restaurants in our earlier example from four to five. How will this affect overall average cost? Again supposing that the restaurants are evenly spaced around the loop, each will now attract only one-fifth of the island's 100 inhabitants, which means that each will serve 20 meals/day. The ATC for each restaurant will thus be $[50 + 5(20)]/20 = \$7.50$/meal, up \$0.50/meal from the previous value. (Recall that ATC with four restaurants was \$7/meal.) The distance between adjacent restaurants is $\frac{1}{5}$ mile when there are five restaurants. This means that the average one-way trip with five restaurants is $\frac{1}{20}$ mile, which in turn means that the average round-trip length is $\frac{1}{10}$ mile. Average transportation cost is thus $(\frac{1}{10}$ mile)(\$24/mile) = \$2.40$. Note that this is \$0.60 less than the previous average transportation cost of \$3, reflecting the decline in average trip length. Adding average total cost and average transportation cost, we see that the overall average cost with five restaurants is \$7.50 + \$2.40 = \$9.90/meal.

EXERCISE 13-5

In the preceding example, what is the overall average cost per meal if we add a sixth restaurant around the loop?

Your calculation in Exercise 13-5 demonstrates that overall average cost per meal goes up when we increase the number of restaurants from five to six. And since the overall average cost declined when we moved from four to five, this means the optimal number of restaurants for our island nation is five.

We can make the preceding analysis more general by supposing that there are N outlets around the loop, as shown by the heavy black squares in Figure 13-11. Now the distance between adjacent outlets will be $1/N$, and the maximum one-way trip length will be half that, or $1/2N$. If we again suppose that people are uniformly distributed around the loop, it follows that the average one-way distance to the nearest outlet is $1/4N$ (which is halfway between 0, the distance of the person closest to a given outlet, and $1/2N$, the distance of the person farthest from it). The average round-trip distance is twice the average one-way distance, and is thus equal to $1/2N$.

Because the distance between restaurants declines as the number of restaurants grows, the total transportation cost, denoted C_{trans}, will be a decreasing function of the number of outlets. Since transportation cost is t dollars per per-

FIGURE 13-11
With N outlets, the distance between adjacent outlets will be $1/N$. The farthest a person can live from an outlet is $1/2N$. And the average one-way distance people must travel to reach the nearest outlet is $1/4N$. The average round-trip distance is $1/2N$.

DISTANCES WITH N OUTLETS

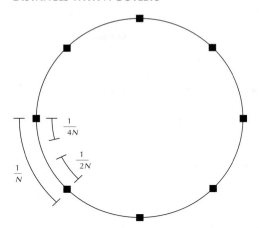

son per mile traveled, total transportation cost will be the product of the cost (L), and the average round-trip length:

$$C_{\text{trans}} = tL\frac{1}{2N}. \tag{13.7}$$

The total cost of meals served, denoted C_{meals}, also depends on both population and the number of outlets. It is given by

$$C_{\text{meals}} = LM + NF, \tag{13.8}$$

where the first term on the right reflects the fact that each of the L people eats a meal whose marginal cost is M, and the second term is the total fixed cost for N outlets. The object is to choose N to minimize the sum of the two types of costs, $C_{\text{trans}} + C_{\text{meals}}$.

The two cost functions and their sum are shown graphically in Figure 13-12, where N^* denotes the cost-minimizing number of outlets.[20]

The slope of C_{meals} curve is equal to F, which represents the cost of an additional outlet. The slope of the C_{trans} curve is equal to $-tL/2N^2$ and represents

---

[20]These functions are plotted as if N were a continuous variable, not an integer. For industries involving large numbers of firms, the continuous approximation will introduce only minimal error.

FIGURE 13-12
Total transportation cost (C_{trans}) declines with the number of outlets (N), while total cost of meals served (C_{meals}) increases with N. The optimal number of outlets (N^*) is the one that minimizes the sum of these costs.

THE OPTIMAL NUMBER OF OUTLETS

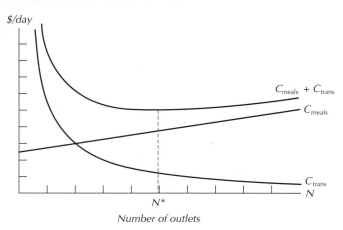

the savings in transportation cost from adding an additional outlet.[21] If the slope of C_{meals} is less than the absolute value of the slope of C_{trans}, the reduction in transportation cost from adding another outlet will more than compensate for the extra fixed cost from adding that outlet. The optimal number of outlets, N^*, is the one for which the slope of the C_{meals} curve is the same as the absolute value of the slope of the C_{trans} curve. N^* must thus satisfy

$$\frac{tL}{2N^{*2}} = F,$$ (13.9)

which yields

$$N^* = \sqrt{\frac{tL}{2F}}.$$ (13.10)

---

[21]This slope is found by taking the derivative

$$\frac{d(C_{trans})}{dN} = \frac{-tL}{2N^2},$$

again treating N as if it were continuously variable. Students who haven't had calculus can convince themselves that this expression is correct by letting ΔN be, say, 0.001 and then calculating the resulting change in C_{trans},

$$\Delta C_{trans} = \frac{tL}{2(N + 0.001)} - \frac{tL}{2N} = \frac{-0.001tL}{2N(N + 0.001)}.$$

The ratio $\Delta C_{trans}/\Delta N$ is thus

$$\Delta C_{trans} = \frac{tL}{2(N = 0.001)} - \frac{tL}{2N} \approx \frac{-0.001tL}{2N(N + 0.001)}.$$

This expression for the optimal number of outlets has a straightforward economic interpretation. Note first that if transportation cost rises, N^* will also rise. This makes sense because the whole point of adding additional outlets is to economize on transportation costs. Note that N^* also increases with population density, L. The more people there are who live on each segment of the loop, the more people there are who will benefit if the average distance to the nearest outlet becomes shorter. And note, finally, that N^* declines with F, the start-up cost of an additional outlet, which is also just as expected.

Applying Equation 13.11 to our restaurant example in which $L = 100$, $t = 24$, and $F = 50$, we get $N^* = \sqrt{(2400/100)} = 4.9$. Needless to say, it is impossible to have 4.9 restaurants, so we choose the integer nearest 4.9, namely, 5. And indeed, just as our earlier calculations indicated, having five restaurants results in a lower overall average cost than does having either four or six.

EXERCISE 13-6

How would N^* change in the preceding example if there were 400 people on the island instead of 100?

Will the independent actions of private, profit-seeking firms result in the optimal number of outlets around the loop? This question sounds very simple, but turns out to be exceedingly difficult to answer. We now know that under some conditions there will tend to be more than the optimal number, while under other conditions there will be fewer.[22] In the appendix to this chapter (www.mhhe.com/economics/frank4) you can examine the details of a specific spatial model in which there tends to be an excessive number of outlets. But for the moment let us note that the number of outlets that emerges from the independent actions of profit-seeking firms will in general be related to the optimal number of outlets in the following simple way: Any environmental change that leads to a change in the optimal number of outlets (here, any change in population density, transportation cost, or fixed cost) will lead to a change in the same direction in the equilibrium number of outlets. For example, a fall in transportation cost will tend to decrease both the optimal number of outlets and the number of outlets we actually observe in practice.

EXAMPLE 13-4 *Why are there so many fewer grocery stores in most cities now than there were in 1930? And why do residential neighborhoods in New York City have more grocery stores than residential neighborhoods in Los Angeles?*

---

[22]A detailed technical discussion of some of the relevant issues can be found in Avinash Dixit and Joseph Stiglitz, "Monopolistic Competition and Optimal Product Diversity," *American Economic Review*, 1977: 297–308; and A. Michael Spence, "Product Selection, Fixed Costs, and Monopolistic Competition" *Review of Economic Studies*, 1976: 217–235.

Grocery retailing, like other forms of retailing, is characterized by strong economies of scale. It thus confronts the usual tradeoff between direct production cost, on the one hand, and transportation cost, on the other. Throughout this century, changing patterns of automobile ownership have affected the pattern of grocery store size and location in the United States. In 1920, most families did not own cars and had to do their shopping on foot. In terms of our expression for the optimal number of outlets (Equation 13.10), this meant a high value of t, unit transportation cost. Today, of course, virtually every family has a car, which has led people to take advantage of the lower prices that are possible in larger stores. One exception to this general pattern is Manhattan. Even today, most Manhattan residents do not own cars. Moreover, population density is extremely high there, which means a high value of L in Equation 13.10. The combined effect of high values of L and t is that very few Manhattan residents have to walk more than two blocks to get to their nearest grocery store. The total population in Los Angeles is also very high, but it is spread out over a much larger area, and most families own at least one automobile. As a result, Los Angeles grocery stores are both larger and farther apart than their New York City counterparts.

THE ANALOGY TO PRODUCT CHARACTERISTICS

The power of the spatial interpretation of monopolistic competition is that it can be applied not only to geographic location, but also to a variety of other product characteristics. Consider, for example, the various airline flights between any two cities on a given day. People have different preferences for traveling at various times of day, just as they have different preferences about where to eat or shop. Figure 13-13 depicts an air-travel market (for example, Kansas City to Minneapolis) with four flights per day, scheduled at midnight, 6 A.M., noon, and 6 P.M. With the choice of an airline flight, just as with the choice of a place to dine, people will tend to select the alternative that lies closest to their most preferred option. Thus, a person who would most prefer to go at 7 P.M. will probably choose the 6 P.M. flight. In terms of our spatial model, having to wait for a flight is the analog of having to travel a certain distance in order to get to a store.

Why not have a flight leaving every 5 minutes, so that no one would be forced to travel at an inconvenient time? The answer again has to do with the tradeoff between cost and convenience. The larger an aircraft is, the lower its average cost per seat is. If people want frequent flights, airlines are forced to use smaller planes and charge higher fares. Conversely, if people didn't care when they traveled, the airline could use the largest possible aircraft (in today's fleet, the 450-seat Boeing 747) and fly at whatever interval was required to accumulate enough passengers to fill the plane. (In the Paducah, Kentucky–Klamath Falls, Oregon

FIGURE 13-13
In a market with
four flights per day,
there is no traveler
for whom there is
not a flight leaving
within 3 hours of his
most preferred de-
parture time.

A SPATIAL INTERPRETATION OF AIRLINE SCHEDULING

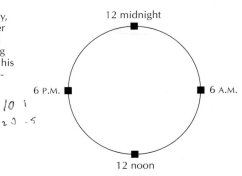

market, that would mean one flight every other February 29!) But most passengers have schedules to keep and are willing to pay a little extra for more conveniently timed flights. The result is the same sort of compromise we saw in the restaurant and grocery store examples.

Virtually every consumer product can be interpreted fruitfully within the context of the spatial model. In the automobile market, for example, the available permutations of turbo versus nonturbo, automatic versus standard, coupe versus convertible, sedan versus station wagon, two doors versus four doors, bucket seats versus bench seats, air conditioned versus not air conditioned, metallic indigo versus forest green, and so on, lead to an extraordinarily large number of possibilities. It would be considerably cheaper, of course, if we had only a single standard model. But people are willing to pay a little extra for variety, just as they are willing to pay a little extra for a more conveniently located store. In the parlance of the spatial model, car manufacturers are said to "locate" their models in a "produce space." Their aim is to see that few buyers are left without a choice that lies "close" to the car that would best suit them. Similar interpretations apply to cameras, stereos, vacations, bicycles, wristwatches, wedding bands, and virtually every other good for which people have a taste for variety. The appendix to this chapter (www.mhhe.com/economics/frank4), examines why the costs of variety tend to be borne largely by those customers who most demand it.

HISTORICAL NOTE: HOTELLING'S HOT DOG VENDORS

In Harold Hotelling's seminal paper on the spatial model of monopolistic competition,[23] he discussed the problem of two hot dog vendors who are free to position themselves wherever they wish along a stretch of beach. Suppose the beach

---

[23]Harold Hotelling, "Stability in Competition," *The Economic Journal, 39,* 1929: 41–57.

is 1 mile long and bounded at each end by some natural obstacle. Suppose also that the vendors charge the same price, customers are evenly distributed along the beach, and each customer buys one hot dog from the nearest vendor. If the vendors' goal is to sell as many hot dogs as possible, where should they position themselves?

Suppose, as in Figure 13-14, that vendor 1 stands at point A and vendor 2 stands at point B, where both A and B are $\frac{1}{4}$ mile from the midpoint of the beach located at C. In this configuration, all customers to the left of C are closest to vendor 1 and will buy from him, while those to the right of C will buy from vendor 2. Each vendor thus gets half the market. The greatest one-way distance any customer has to travel is $\frac{1}{4}$ mile, and the average one-way distance between customers and their nearest vendor is half that, or $\frac{1}{8}$ mile.

Mathematically inclined readers can verify that A and B are in fact the locations that minimize average travel distance for all consumers. And yet these locations are clearly not optimal from the perspective of either vendor. To see why, suppose vendor 1 were to move 10 steps toward B. The customers to the left of C would continue to find him the closest vendor. But now those customers less than 5 steps to the right of C—people who used to be closest to vendor 2—will suddenly find themselves switching to vendor 1. Moving farther to the right will increase vendor 1's sales still further. Vendor 1 will maximize his sales by positioning himself as close as he can get to vendor 2 on the side of vendor 2 that is closer to the center of the beach.

Vendor 2, of course, can reason in the same fashion, so his strategy will be perfectly symmetric: He will try to get as close to vendor 1 on the side of vendor 1 that is closest to the center. And when both vendors behave in this fashion, the only stable outcome is for each to locate at C, the center of the beach. At C, each gets half of the market, just as he did originally. But the average distance that customers must travel is now $\frac{1}{4}$ mile, twice what it was when the vendors were located at A and B.

Having both vendors at the middle of the beach is thus not optimal from the vantage point of customers, and yet neither vendor would be better off if he were to move unilaterally. The hot dog vendor location problem is thus not one of those cases in which Adam Smith's invisible hand guides resources so as to produce the greatest good for all.

FIGURE 13-14
Each hot dog vendor does best by positioning himself at the center of the beach, even though that location does not minimize the average distance that their customers must travel.

THE HOT DOG VENDOR LOCATION PROBLEM

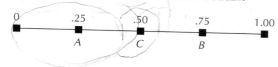

APPLICATION: A SPATIAL PERSPECTIVE ON POLITICAL COMPETITION

When former Alabama Governor George Corley Wallace ran for president as a third-party candidate in 1968, he often complained to his audiences that "there's not a dime's worth of difference between the Republican and Democratic candidates." Richard Nixon and Hubert Humphrey were those candidates, but Wallace preferred to call them "Tweedledum" and "Tweedledee." Although Wallace surely exaggerated the similarities between Nixon and Humphrey, his assessment nonetheless captures an essential truth about the American two-party political system, namely, that it tends to nominate presidential candidates whose positions on most major issues are remarkably similar.

This tendency is easily understood once we recognize the analogy between the political location problem and Hotelling's hot dog vendor location problem. Instead of having a beach, we now have a political spectrum ranging from left (liberal) to right (conservative) (see Figure 13-15). Voters to the left of the midpoint of the political spectrum classify themselves as liberal, increasingly so the farther left they are. Those to the right of the midpoint are increasingly conservative as we move farther to the right. To simplify discussion, suppose all voters to the left of the midpoint belong to the Democratic party, while all to the right are Republicans.

In an election involving only Democrats, a candidate positioned at A (the midpoint of the liberal half of the spectrum) would attract the greatest number of voters. Similarly, an election involving only Republicans would tend to favor a candidate positioned at B, the midpoint of the conservative half of the spectrum. Yet voters in each party know that their nominee must stand for general election before the voters of both parties. And so the most extreme members of each party have an incentive to set their own preferences aside in favor of a candidate located closer to the center of the overall political spectrum, someone like A' for the Democrats or B' for the Republicans.

In practice, the extent to which extremists in each party actually follow this prudent course varies from election to election. Occasionally the major parties do nominate candidates like Barry Goldwater or George McGovern, neither of whom would be mistaken for a centrist. Still, the location model's prediction that the nominees of the major parties will tend to be moderates corresponds remarkably well with the broad historical record.

FIGURE 13-15
A candidate positioned at A will be most attractive to Democrats, one at B most attractive to Republicans. But in a general election involving voters from both parties, the candidates standing closer to C will attract more voters.

A POLITICAL LOCATION PROBLEM

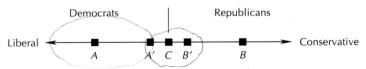

Consumer Preferences and Advertising

In perfectly competitive markets it would never pay a producer to advertise her product. Being only one of many producers of identical products, the firm that advertised would attract only an insignificant share of any resulting increase in demand. In monopolistically competitive and oligopolistic markets, the incentives are different. Because products are differentiated, producers can often shift their demand curves outward significantly by advertising.

How does advertising affect the efficiency with which markets allocate resources? In the description of the world offered by rational choice theory, producers are essentially agents of consumers. Consumers vote with their purchase dollars, and producers are quick to do their bidding. This description has been called the *traditional sequence,* and Harvard economist John Kenneth Galbraith is one of its most prominent critics. In its place, he proposed a *revised sequence* in which the producer, not the consumer, sits in the driver's seat. In Galbraith's scheme, the corporation decides which products are cheapest and most convenient to produce, and then uses advertising and other promotional devices to create a demand for them.

Galbraith's revised sequence recasts Adam Smith's invisible hand in an unflattering new light. Smith's story, recall, was that producers motivated only by self-interest would provide the products that best meet consumers' desires. Those who behaved otherwise would fail to attract customers and go out of business. If Galbraith is correct, however, this story is turned on its head: It is like saying the all-too-visible hand of Madison Avenue guides consumers to serve the interests of large corporations.

Galbraith's revised sequence is not without intuitive appeal. Many people are understandably skeptical, for example, when an economist says that the purpose of advertising is to make consumers better informed. The plain fact, after all, is that this is often anything but its intent. For example, the celebrity milk mustache is surely not part of a process whereby we become more knowledgeable about the nutritional merits of milk consumption.

But for all the obvious hype in advertising messages, the Galbraith view of the process overlooks something fundamental: It is easier to sell a good product than a bad one. All an advertisement can reasonably hope to accomplish is to induce the consumer to *try* the product. If it is one she tries and likes, she will probably buy it again and again. She will also recommend it to friends. If it is one she doesn't like, however, the process usually ends there. Even if a firm were to succeed in getting *everyone* to try it once, it still wouldn't be able to maintain a profitable, ongoing venture.

Imagine two alternative products, one that meets real human needs but is costly to produce, and another that meets no real need but is somewhat cheaper. Which of these two types would a profit-hungry producer do best to advertise? Given the importance of repeat business and word-of-mouth endorsements, the first will generally be more attractive, and by a compelling margin. The fact that it costs more to produce will not deter consumers unless its extra benefits do not justify those extra costs.

New products go through extensive market testing before they ever land on the shelves. Millions of dollars are spent analyzing test subjects' reactions to them. In the end, most products that enter this testing process never see the light of day. Only when a firm has concrete evidence that a product is likely to be well received does it dare to commit the millions of dollars required for an intensive national advertising campaign.

Firms that fail to adopt this posture often pay sharp penalties. The Lotus software company, for example, spent more than $10 million advertising *Jazz*, its spreadsheet program for the Apple Macintosh, even though it had clear evidence that the program lacked specific features that many users deemed vital. The Lotus ads were incredibly sophisticated, and no doubt succeeded in selling a fair number of programs. And yet *Jazz*'s main rival, Microsoft's *Excel*, a much better product, quickly captured the market with only a small fraction of Lotus' advertising outlays.

Advertising and other efforts to persuade consumers are best viewed as part of a pump-priming process. Given the enormous costs, it usually pays to promote only those products that consumers are likely to want to purchase repeatedly, or to speak well of to their friends. And in fact there is clear evidence that most firms follow precisely this strategy. Frozen-dinner producers advertise their fancy ethnic entrees, not their chicken pot pies. Publishers advertise books that seem likely to become best-sellers, not their titles with more limited appeal. Motion picture studios tout the movies they hope will become blockbusters, not their low-budget films.

Because producers have an incentive to advertise only those products that consumers are most likely to find satisfying, the so-called traditional sequence is more plausible than Galbraith and other critics make it out to be. True enough,

*"To paraphrase the great Vince **Lombardi**, packaging isn't everything, it's the only thing."*

where the quality differences between competing goods are small, advertising may have a significant influence on which brand a consumer chooses. But as a first approximation, it still makes sense to assume that consumers have reasonably well-defined notions of what they like, and that producers spend much effort on trying to cater to those notions.

This is not to say, however, that market incentives lead to the amount of advertising that is best from society's point of view. As we saw earlier in this chapter, strategic competition between rivals may sometimes lead firms to spend excessively on advertising.

Summary

The characteristic feature of oligopolistic markets is interdependence among firms. In the Cournot model, each firm takes the *quantities* produced by its rivals as given; in the Bertrand model, by contrast, each firm takes its rivals' *prices* as given. Although the behavioral orientation of firms sounds very much the same in these two cases, the results are strikingly different. The Cournot model yields a slightly lower price and a slightly higher quantity than we would see if the firms colluded to achieve the monopoly outcome. By contrast, the Bertrand model leads to essentially the same outcome we saw under perfect competition.

A slightly more sophisticated form of interdependence among firms is assumed in the Stackelberg model, in which one firm plays a leadership role and its rivals merely follow. This model is similar in structure to the Cournot model, except that where the Cournot firms took one another's quantities as given, the Stackelberg leader strategically manipulated the quantity decisions of its rivals.

The interdependencies among oligopolistic firms are often successfully analyzed using the mathematical theory of games. The three basic elements of any game are the players, the set of possible strategies, and the payoff matrix. A Nash equilibrium occurs when each player's strategy is optimal given the other player's choice of strategy. A strategy is called dominant if it is optimal no matter what strategy the other player chooses.

The incentives facing firms who attempt to collude are similar to the ones facing participants in the prisoner's dilemma. The difficulty in holding cartels together is that the dominant strategy for each member is to cheat on the agreement. Repeated interactions between a very small number of firms can support collusive behavior under circumstances in which strategies like tit-for-tat are effective.

Incumbent firms may sometimes act strategically to deter potential rivals from entering their markets. Often this involves incurring higher costs than would otherwise be necessary.

The basic idea of the theory of contestable markets is that when the cost of entry and exit is very low, the mere threat of entry can be sufficient to produce an allocation similar to the one we see under perfect competition. Critics of this theory have stressed that there are almost always nontrivial sunk costs associated with entry and exit, and that even small sunk costs leave considerable room for strategic entry deterrence.

Monopolistic competition is defined by two simple conditions: (1) the existence of numerous firms each producing a product that is a close, but imperfect, substitute for the products of other firms; and (2) free entry and exit of firms. In the spatial model of monopolistic competition, customers have particular locations or product characteristics they most prefer. The result is that firms tend to compete most intensively for the business of products most similar to their own.

A central feature of the spatial model of monopolistic competition is the trade-off between the desire for lower cost, on the one hand, and greater variety or locational convenience, on the other. The optimum degree of product diversity depends on several factors. Greater diversity is expected with greater population density and higher transportation costs (where, in the general case, "transportation costs" measure willingness to pay for desired product features). Optimal product diversity is negatively related to the start-up costs of adding new product characteristics or locations. The market metes out a certain rough justice in that the costs of additional variety tend to be borne most heavily by those to whom variety is most important.

An appendix to this chapter (see the "For the Instructor" section at our Web site www.mhhe.com/economics/frank4), discusses the Chamberlin model of monopolistic competition and presents a more in-depth mathematical treatment of the spatial model of monopolistic competition.

Questions for Review

1. What is the fundamental difference among the Cournot, Bertrand, and Stackelberg models of oligopoly?

2. How is the problem of oligopoly collusion similar in structure to the prisoner's dilemma?

3. What is the difficulty with the tit-for-tat strategy as a possible solution to the oligopoly collusion problem?

4. Does the equilibrium in the Cournot model satisfy the definition of a Nash equilibrium?

5. What role does the assumption of sunk costs play in the theory of contestable markets?

6. Describe the tradeoff between cost and variety.

7. How is the optimal degree of product variety related to population density? To transportation cost? To the fixed costs of offering new products?

Problems

1. The market demand curve for mineral water is given by $P = 15 - Q$. If there are two firms that produce mineral water, each with a constant marginal cost of 3 per unit,

fill in the entries for each of the four duopoly models indicated in the table. (In the Stackelberg model, assume that firm 1 is the leader.)

Model	Q_1	Q_2	$Q_1 + Q_2$	P	Π_1	Π_2	$\Pi_1 + \Pi_2$
Shared monopoly							
Cournot							
Bertrand							
Stackelberg							

2. The market demand curve for a pair of Cournot duopolists is given as $P = 36 - 3Q$, where $Q = Q_1 + Q_2$. The constant per unit marginal cost is 18 for each duopolist. Find the Cournot equilibrium price, quantity, and profits.

3. Solve the preceding problem for Bertrand duopolists.

4. The market demand curve for a pair of duopolists is given as $P = 36 - 3Q$, where $Q = Q_1 + Q_2$. The constant per unit marginal cost is 18 for each duopolist. Find the equilibrium price, quantity, and profit for each firm, assuming the firms act as a Stackelberg leader and follower, with firm 1 as the leader.

5. Because of their unique expertise with explosives, the Zambino brothers have long enjoyed a monopoly of the U.S. market for public fireworks displays for crowds above a quarter of a million. The annual demand for these fireworks displays is $P = 140 - Q$. The marginal cost of putting on a fireworks display is $20. A family dispute broke the firm in two. Alfredo Zambino now runs one firm and Luigi Zambino runs the other. They still have the same marginal costs, but now they are Cournot duopolists. How much profit has the family lost?

6. While grading a final exam a professor discovers that two students have virtually identical answers. He talks to each student separately and tells them that he is sure that they shared answers, but he cannot be sure who copied from whom. He offers each student a deal—if they both sign a statement admitting to the cheating, each will be given an F for the course. If only one signs the statement, he will be allowed to withdraw from the course and the other nonsigning student will be expelled from the university. Finally, if neither signs the statement they will both get a C for the course because the professor does not have enough evidence to prove that cheating has occurred. Assuming the students are not allowed to communicate with one another, set up the relevant payoff matrix. Does each student have a dominant strategy?

7. Suppose A and B know that they will interact in a prisoner's dilemma exactly four times. Explain why the tit-for-tat strategy will not be an effective means for assuring cooperation.

8. Firm 1 and firm 2 are automobile producers. Each has the option of producing either a big car or a small car. The payoffs to each of the four possible combinations of choices are as given in the following payoff matrix. Each firm must make its choice without knowing what the other has chosen.

	Firm 1	
	Big car	**Small car**

		Firm 1	
		Big car	**Small car**
Firm 2	**Big car**	$\Pi_1 = 400$ $\Pi_2 = 400$	$\Pi_2 = 800$ $\Pi_2 = 1000$
	Small car $\bullet$	$\Pi_1 = 1000$ $\Pi_2 = 800$	$\Pi_1 = 500$ $\Pi_2 = 500$

a. Does either firm have a dominant strategy?

b. There are two Nash equilibria for this game. Identify them.

9. Suppose we have the same payoff matrix as in Problem 8 except now firm 1 gets to move first and knows that firm 2 will see the results of this choice before deciding which type of car to build.

a. Draw the game tree for this sequential game.

b. What is the Nash equilibrium for this game?

10. The state has announced its plans to license two firms to serve a market whose demand curve is given by $P = 100 - Q$. The technology is such that each can produce any given level of output at zero cost, but once each firm's output is chosen, it cannot be altered.

a. What is the most you would be willing to pay for one of these licenses if you knew you would be able to choose your level of output first (assuming your choice was observable by the rival firm)?

b. How much would your rival be willing to pay for the right to choose second?

*11. Firm 1 and firm 2 are competing for a cable television franchise. The present value of the net revenues generated by the franchise is equal to R. Each firm's probability of winning the franchise is given by its proportion of the total spent by the two firms on lobbying the local government committee that awards the franchise. That is, if I_1 and I_2 represent the lobbying expenditures of firms 1 and 2, respectively, then firm 1's probability of winning is given by $I_1/(I_1 + I_2)$, while firm 2's probability of winning is $I_2/(I_1 + I_2)$. If each firm assumes that the other firm's spending is independent of its own, what is the equilibrium level of spending for each firm?

12. State whether true or false and briefly expain why. If a business owner is delighted to accept additional orders at the current price, he or she cannot have been a profit-maximizing, perfectly competitive producer.

13. A toll road commission is planning to locate garages for tow trucks along a 100-mile circular highway. Each garage has a fixed cost of $5000. Towing jobs are equally likely along any point of the highway and cost per mile towed is $50. If there were 5000 towing jobs per day, what number of garages would minimize the sum of the fixed costs and towing costs?

---

*This problem requires the use of calculus maximization techniques.

14. The 1000 residents of Great Donut Island are all fishermen. Every morning they go to the nearest port to launch their fishing boats and then return in the evening with their catch. The residents are evenly distributed along the 10-mile perimeter of the island. Each port has a fixed cost of $1000/day. If the optimal number of ports is 2, what must be the per mile travel cost?

Answers to In-Chapter Exercises

13-1.

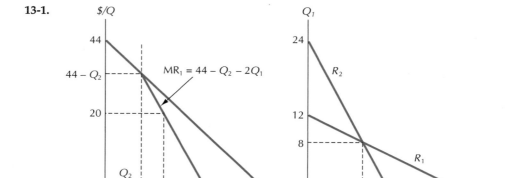

13-2. Price will settle at marginal cost, and so $P = 2$. The corresponding market demand, $Q = 8$, will be shared equally by the two firms: $Q_1 = Q_2 = 4$.

13-3. Firm 2's marginal revenue curve is given by $10 - Q_1 - 2Q_2$. Setting MR = MC = 2, we have firm 2's reaction function, $R_2(Q_1) = Q_2^* = 4 - (Q_1/2)$. Substituting into firm 1's demand function, we get $P_1 = 10 - Q_1 - 4 + (Q_1/2) = 6 - (Q_1/2)$, and the corresponding marginal review curve, $MR_1 = 6 - Q_1$. $MR_1 = MC = 2$ solves for $Q_1^* = 4$. This means that Q_2 will be 2 units, for a total market output of 6 units. The market price will be $10 - 6 = 4$.

13-4. Regardless of firm 1's strategy, firm 2 does best with a big research budget. The choice of a big research budget is thus a dominant strategy for firm 2. Firm 1 does not have a dominant strategy. If firm 2 chooses a low research budget, then firm 1 does best by choosing a low research budget. But if firm 2 chooses a high research budget, then firm 1 does best by choosing a high research budget. Since firm 1 can predict that firm 2 will choose a high research budget, firm 1's best strategy is to choose a high research budget. The combination of "High research budget—High research budget" is a Nash equilibrium.

13-5. With six restaurants the average round-trip distance is $\frac{1}{12}$ mile, which yields an average transportation cost of $2. On average, each restaurant will attract 100/6 people per day, which yields an ATC of $[50 + 5(100/6)]/(100/6) = \$8/day$. Overall average cost with six restaurants is thus $10/day.

13-6. N^* will now be $\sqrt{[(24)(400)/100]} \approx 9.8$, so there should now be 10 restaurants.

PART FOUR 4

Factor Markets

In these two chapters we examine the workings of markets for productive inputs. In Chapter 14 we see that although the labor market behaves like the market for ordinary goods and services in many respects, in other important ways it is very different. Chapter 15 discusses the markets for real and financial capital. One feature that sets capital apart from other inputs, we will see, is that while other inputs are usually hired on a period-by-period basis, capital equipment is often owned outright by the firm.

CHAPTER 14

Labor

During the 1931 season, Yankee slugger Babe Ruth was the highest-paid player in baseball at an annual salary of $85,000. Asked how he felt about earning more than President Herbert Hoover, Ruth responded with characteristic bravado that he deserved it. "I had a much better year than Hoover," he explained.

Productivity differences, however, are not always sufficient to account for pay differences among workers. For example, there is widespread movement of employees between the public and private sectors, and from watching what happens in these moves, we know that highly productive persons almost always earn dramatically less in the public sector. Thus, former Federal Reserve Board Chairman Paul Volcker, who occupied perhaps the most important post in the U.S. government, earned less than a tenth of the salary he used to command on Wall Street.

Why do people accept top positions in government at such a huge sacrifice in pay? By all accounts, the attraction for the high-level bureaucrat is the power and public attention such posts command. Volcker has now gone back to a top position on Wall Street, where he again earns many times what he earned in government. But his daily decisions no longer affect the lives of millions. The eager audience for his views and opinions evaporated overnight. Volcker took the Fed chairmanship, and the sharp reduction in pay that went with it, because the post carried benefits that no other employer could offer. The package, taken as a whole, was attractive to him.

Jobs that provide a high degree of public visibility do not always entail a cut in pay. San Francisco Giants outfielder Barry Bonds is in the news every day for at least 6 months of the year. No question, there is an eager audience for his views; and yet, with a salary of over $7 million a year, he hardly seems to have made a real economic sacrifice. There are plenty of people, including me, who would be willing to do Bonds' job for less. Indeed, Bonds himself would surely be willing to perform for a subsistence wage rather than work in lifelong obscurity in some anonymous job elsewhere in the private sector.

His lofty salary is the result of two important factors: (1) He can do valuable things that the rest of us can't; and (2) there is more than one employer who can provide Bonds with a place in the spotlight. Note that only the first of these factors applied in Paul Volcker's case. If you want to be Chairman of the Board of Governors of the Federal Reserve System of the United States, the U.S. government is the only employer you can work for. If you want to be a major league baseball player, however, 28 different teams can bid for your services. In Bonds' case, if the Giants didn't pay him such a high salary, some other team gladly would. Thousands of extra fans are drawn to the ballpark by the prospect of seeing perhaps the best all-around player in the game. The Giants management knows it could hire me for much less than it pays Bonds. But the Giants are smart enough also to know that, even for free, I would be a bad bargain.

Chapter Preview

Our goal in this chapter is to examine the economic forces that govern wages and other conditions of employment. Relatively simple models of the labor market shed light on a variety of interesting questions, such as: How much will a worker with a given set of skills earn? Why do working conditions differ from one occupation to another? What do unions do? And so on.

We begin by deriving the demand curve for labor in both the short run and long run. We then approach the supply side of the labor market from the standpoint of an individual worker trying to decide how much to work at a given wage rate.

Our next step is to take up the issue of compensating wage differentials, differences in wage payments that reflect differences in the environments in which people work. The general result is that the attractiveness of the overall compensation package—wages and environmental factors taken as a whole—tends to equalize across jobs that employ workers of a given skill level. As a further illustration of the concept of compensating differentials, we then examine the question of safety levels in the workplace.

We also apply the economic theory of labor markets to such topics as discrimination and minimum wage laws. We conclude, finally, by looking at why differences in pay sometimes seem to overstate differences in productivity while at other times seem to understate them.

The Perfectly Competitive Firm's Short-Run Demand for Labor

Consider a firm that produces output by the use of two inputs, capital (*K*) and labor (*L*). Suppose that in the short run, its capital stock is fixed. If this firm sells all its output in a perfectly competitive market at the going market price, and if it can hire any quantity of labor it wishes at a wage rate of $12/hr, how many units of labor should it hire?

If the manager of the firm is thinking like an economist, she will reason as follows: "The benefit of hiring an extra unit of labor will be the amount for which I can sell the extra output I will get. The cost will be the wage rate. Thus I should hire an extra unit of labor as long as the former exceeds the latter. If the latter exceeds the former, however, I should reduce the amount of labor I hire."

This reasoning is easily translated into a simple graphical hiring rule. Figure 14-1*a* shows the marginal product curve for the labor input when capital is fixed (see Chapter 9). The marginal product curve, recall, tells how much extra output the firm will get when it hires an extra unit of labor. For example, when there are 40 units of labor employed, hiring an extra unit will yield 8 units of output. The downward slope of the marginal product curve reflects the law of diminishing returns.

Figure 14-1*b* simply multiplies the marginal product curve by the price of output, here *P* = $2. The product of output price and marginal product, $P \times MP_L$, is called the ***value of the marginal product of labor***—denoted VMP_L, which is the extra revenue the firm will get by selling the extra output produced by the extra unit of labor. *The hiring rule for the firm is to choose that amount of labor for which the wage rate is equal to the* VMP_L. In Figure 14-1*b*, the rule thus tells the firm it should hire 80 units of labor when the wage rate is $12.

Value of marginal product (VMP) The value, at current market price, of the extra output produced by an additional unit of input.

To illustrate the logic of the rule, suppose that the firm had instead hired only 40 units of labor. At that level of employment, the value of extra output produced by an extra worker ($16) is greater than the cost of hiring the worker ($12),

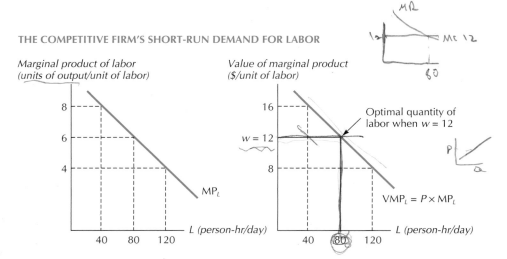

FIGURE 14-1
When the wage rate is $12/unit of labor (panel *b*), the perfectly competitive firm will hire 80 units of labor, the amount for which VMP_L and the wage rate are the same.

THE COMPETITIVE FIRM'S SHORT-RUN DEMAND FOR LABOR

Marginal product of labor (units of output/unit of labor)

Value of marginal product ($/unit of labor)

Optimal quantity of labor when *w* = 12

$VMP_L = P \times MP_L$

and so the firm can increase its profit by hiring more workers. Alternatively, suppose that the firm had hired 120 units of labor. VMP_L at $L = 120$ is only $8, which is less than the wage rate of $12, and so the firm can increase its profit by discharging workers. Only at $L = 80$ will the firm be unable to take additional steps to increase its profit.[1] Figure 14-1a is drawn for $MP_L = 10 - (\frac{1}{20})L$. When $P = 2$, the value of the marginal product of labor, depicted in Figure 14-1b, is

$$VMP_L = P(MP_L) = 2\left(10 - \tfrac{1}{20}L\right) = 20 - \tfrac{1}{10}L.$$

If the wage is $w = 12$, then the quantity of labor demanded by the firm will be

$$w = VMP_L \Rightarrow 12 = 20 - \tfrac{1}{10}L \Rightarrow 8 = \tfrac{1}{10}L \Rightarrow L^* = 80.$$

EXERCISE 14-1

> At a wage rate of $12/unit of labor, how many units of labor would the firm shown in Figure 14-1 hire if its product sold not for $2/unit but for $3/unit?

The Perfectly Competitive Firm's Long-Run Demand for Labor

In the short run, the only way for the firm to respond to a reduction in the wage rate is to hire more labor. In the long run, however, all inputs are completely variable. As we saw in Chapter 9, a reduction in the price of labor will cause the firm to substitute labor for capital, reducing its marginal cost still further. This additional cost reduction will cause an even greater expansion of output than before. It follows that the firm's long-run hiring response to a change in the wage rate will be larger than its short-run response. The relationship between the two labor demand curves is portrayed in Figure 14-2.

The firm's demand for labor will also tend to be more elastic the more elastic the demand is for its product. If a price reduction stimulates a large increase in the quantity of the product demanded, it will also stimulate a large increase in the amount of labor required to produce it. Finally, the firm's demand for labor

---

[1]There is one important limitation to the application of the $w = VMP_L$ rule. Suppose the wage rate were above the value of the average product of labor, which is the product of price and the average product of labor, denoted VAP_L. If the firm pays a wage higher than VAP_L, it will be paying out more than the total value of what workers produce, which means that it will earn a loss on each worker it hires. For values of w above VAP_L then, the perfectly competitive firm will demand no labor at all.

FIGURE 14-2
The demand for labor is more elastic in the long run because the firm has the opportunity to substitute labor for capital. In the short run, its only avenue of response is to increase output.

SHORT- AND LONG-RUN DEMAND CURVES FOR LABOR

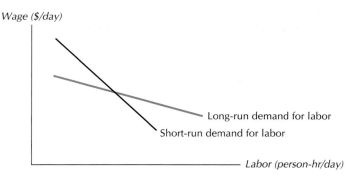

Wage ($/day)

Long-run demand for labor

Short-run demand for labor

Labor (person-hr/day)

will tend to be more elastic the more it is able to substitute the services of labor for those of other inputs. Other things equal, the firm with L-shaped isoquants will have the least elastic demand curve for labor.

The Market Demand Curve for Labor

Recall from Chapter 5 that the technique for deriving a market demand curve for a product is to add the individual consumer demand curves horizontally. The technique for generating the market demand curve for labor is similar except for one important difference. In Figure 14-3, the curve labeled $\Sigma VMP_L, P = P_1$ is the horizontal summation of the individual VMP_L curves when the output price is equal to P_1. At that value of the price of output, firms taken as a whole demand L_1 units of labor per time period when the wage rate is equal to w_1. Now let the

FIGURE 14-3
When the wage rate falls from w_1 to w_2, each firm hires more labor and produces more output. The increase in output causes output price to fall, which reduces the value of labor's marginal product. The market demand curve for labor is thus more steep than the horizontal summation of the individual demand curves.

THE MARKET DEMAND CURVE FOR LABOR

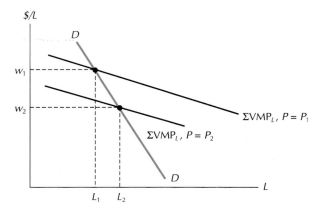

$/L

D

w_1

w_2

$\Sigma VMP_L, P = P_1$

$\Sigma VMP_L, P = P_2$

D

L_1 L_2

L

wage rate fall to w_2. Each firm will hire more labor, in the process moving downward along its own individual demand curve for labor. As each firm responds in this way, it offers more of its product for sale in the market. Such action by any one firm in a competitive market would leave the price of output unchanged. But the effect of all firms acting in concert is to produce a downward movement along the industry product demand curve.

This increase in output will necessarily involve a reduction in output price. And in turn this will cause the VMP_L curve for each firm to shift downward. If output price falls from P_1 to P_2, the aggregate demand for labor will be given by the point that corresponds to w_2 on the curve labeled ΣVMP_L, $P = P_2$. By this reasoning, we see that the market demand curve for labor (the curve labeled DD) will be steeper than the horizontal summation of the VMP_L curves.

The preceding discussion implicitly assumed that there is only one type of labor and that all of it is employed by a single competitive industry. In the real world, of course, matters are more complicated. There are almost countless categories of labor—carpenters, electricians, physicists, attorneys, high school teachers, and so on—and any one type finds employment in many different industries. Thus, electricians are employed in the residential construction, automobile, commercial office building, steel, computer, and fishing industries, to name but a small sample. The market demand curve for electricians is therefore made up of the individual demands of firms in not just one industry but many.

Suppose the payments to electricians by firms in each separate industry constitute only a small fraction—say, 0.1 percent—of their respective total costs. A small change—say, 10 percent—in the wage paid to electricians would then produce an all but imperceptible change—namely, 0.01 percent—in each industry's total costs, and hence no appreciable effect on their respective output prices. Under these circumstances, the demand for electricians will be closely approximated by the horizontal summation of the various individual firm demand curves, and the complication discussed in connection with Figure 14-3 may be ignored.

An Imperfect Competitor's Demand for Labor

Our discussion of the demand for labor has assumed that the firm faces a perfectly elastic demand for its product. Any additional output produced by additional workers could be sold at the same price as existing output. With an imperfect competitor, of course, this will not be so. Such firms face downward-sloping demand curves, and if they hire additional workers, they must cut their prices in order to sell the additional output.

Marginal revenue product (MRP) The amount by which total revenue increases with the employment of an additional unit of input.

We saw that with a perfect competitor, the value of the extra output obtained by hiring an extra worker is the product of price and the marginal product of labor. With an imperfect competitor, by contrast, it is the product of marginal revenue and marginal product. This product is called the *marginal revenue product of labor*, and is denoted MRP_L. In terms of the definitions of marginal revenue and marginal product, MRP_L is thus given by

$$MRP_L = \frac{\Delta Q}{\Delta L} \frac{\Delta TR}{\Delta Q}, \qquad (14.1)$$

which reduces to

$$MRP_L = \frac{\Delta TR}{\Delta L}. \qquad (14.2)$$

VMP_L and MRP_L are alike in that each represents the addition to total revenue that results from the addition of a unit of labor. The difference between them is that the MRP_L takes into account that the sale of additional output requires a cut in price for the imperfect competitor. VMP_L values the extra output at the existing product price, which is unaffected by variations in the perfect competitor's output. MRP_L values the additional output at its marginal revenue, which is less than its price.

How much labor will a firm hire if it faces a downward-sloping demand curve for its output? The answer is that it will hire that quantity for which the wage rate and MRP_L are equal. The argument for this claim is essentially similar to the one offered for the $w = VMP_L$ condition for the perfect competitor.

In the case of the perfectly competitive firm, the short-run demand for labor is downward sloping because of the law of diminishing returns. The more labor the firm hires, the lower the MP_L will be and hence the lower the VMP_L will be. For the monopolist, too, the law of diminishing returns causes the short-run demand curve for labor to be downward sloping. But there is an additional reason in the case of the monopolist, which is that its marginal revenue curve is also downward sloping.

For the same reasons discussed in the perfectly competitive case, the monopolist's long-run demand for labor will be more elastic than his short-run demand. But we need not make any additional adjustments to the MRP_L curve when moving from the firm to the industry demand curve, in either the long run or the short run. The monopolist's demand for labor *is* the industry demand for labor. It already takes account of the fact that extra output means a lower product price.

The Supply of Labor

For simplicity, let's again imagine that there is only one category of labor and that the choice confronting each worker is how many hours to work each day. The alternative to working is to spend time in "leisure activities," which here will include play, sleep, eating, and any other activity besides paid work in the labor market. If the worker will be paid at a constant rate of $10 for each hour he works, how many hours should he work?

On reflection, this turns out to be a simple consumer choice problem of the very same sort we took up in Chapter 3. The choice in this context is between two goods we may call "income" and "leisure." As in the standard consumer choice problem, the individual is assumed to have preferences over the two goods that can be summarized in the form of an indifference map. In Figure 14-4, the curves labeled I_1, I_2, and I_3 represent three such curves for a hypothetical worker.

The line labeled B in the same diagram represents the individual's budget constraint. If he spent the entire day in leisure activities, he would earn no income, which says that the point $(24, 0)$ must be the horizontal intercept of B. Alternatively, if he worked 24 hr/day at the wage rate of $w_0 = \$10/hr$, his daily income would be $24w_0 = \$240$, which tells us that the point $(0, 240)$ must be the vertical intercept of B. The remainder of B is the straight line that joins these two points. Its equation is $M = w(24 - h) = 10(24 - h) = 240 - 10h$, where M is daily income in dollars. The slope of B is simply the negative of the hourly wage rate, $-w_0 = -10$.

Given his preferences and budget constraint, the best this hypothetical consumer can do is to move to point A in Figure 14-4, the tangency between B and the indifference curve I_2. Here, the optimal bundle corresponds to spending $h^* = 15$ hr/day in leisure, the remaining $24 - h^* = 9$ hr in paid work. The consumer's daily income in dollars will be $(24 - h^*)w_0 = 90$. At A, the marginal rate of substitution between leisure and income is exactly w_0, the hourly wage rate. This means that at the optimal bundle, the marginal value of an extra hour of leisure is exactly equal to the opportunity cost of acquiring it—namely, the \$10 the consumer would have earned had he worked that extra hour.

EXERCISE 14-2

Suppose the wage is $w = \$20/hr$. Find the equation for the income/leisure budget constraint and graph it. Suppose that, facing this wage, an individual chooses $h = 14$ hr of leisure. Find the worker's income M per day for this amount of leisure.

To generate a worker's supply curve of labor, we simply ask how the optimal amount of paid work varies as the wage rate varies. Figure 14-5 looks at the optimal leisure choices for three different hourly wage rates, $w = \$4$, $w = \$10$, and $w = \$14$. The supply of labor corresponding to $w = \$4$ is $24 - h_1^* = 6$ hr; to $w = \$10$, $24 - h_2^* = 9$ hr; and to $w = \$14$, $24 - h_3^* = 7$ hr.

Figure 14-6 (page 496) plots the relationship between the wage rate and the hours of work supplied by the hypothetical worker whose indifference map is shown in Figure 14-5. Calling this person the ith worker of many, we see that his supply curve is the line denoted S_i. When compared with the other supply curves we have encountered, the salient feature of S_i is that it is not everywhere upward sloping.[2] In particular, it is "backward bending" for values of w larger

---

[2]Recall from Chapter 5 that we saw a similar supply curve in the case of savings.

FIGURE 14-4 THE OPTIMAL CHOICE OF LEISURE AND INCOME

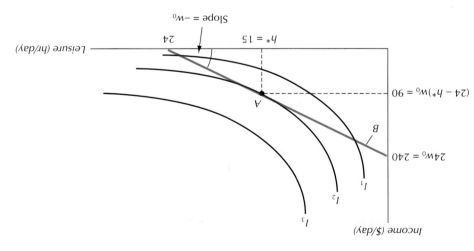

The optimal amount of leisure is $h^* = 15$ hr/day, which corresponds to a point of tangency between the budget constraint (B) and the indifference curve I_2. The corresponding amount of paid labor is $24 - h^* = 9$ hr/day, which yields a daily wage income of $(24 - h^*) w_0 = \$90$/day.

Income ($/day)

$24w_0 = 240$

$(24 - h^*)w_0 = 90$

A

B

I_3
I_2
I_1

Slope = $-w_0$

24

$h^* = 15$

Leisure (hr/day)

than \$10/hr, which is another way of saying that, in that region, higher wages lead to fewer hours of work supplied.

Colonialists who employed unskilled labor in less developed countries once thought it a sign of backwardness that their employees worked fewer hours whenever their wages rose. But as the following example makes clear, such behavior is consistent with the rational pursuit of a perfectly coherent objective.

FIGURE 14-5 OPTIMAL LEISURE CHOICES FOR DIFFERENT WAGE RATES

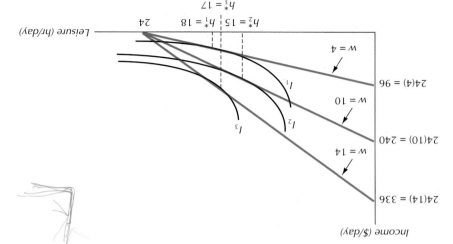

When the hourly wage rises from \$4 to \$10, the optimal amount of leisure falls from 18 to 15 hr/day. But when the wage rises still further to \$14, the optimal amount of leisure rises to 17 hr/day.

Income ($/day)

$24(14) = 336$

$24(10) = 240$

$24(4) = 96$

$w = 14$

$w = 10$

$w = 4$

I_3
I_2
I_1

$h_3^* = 17$
$h_2^* = 15$ $h_1^* = 18$
24

Leisure (hr/day)

FIGURE 14-6
For this worker, an increase in the wage elicits greater labor supply when the wage is less than $10/hr, but smaller labor supply when the wage is above $10/hr.

THE LABOR SUPPLY CURVE FOR THE ith WORKER

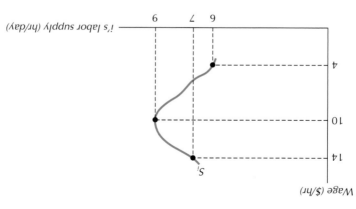

EXAMPLE 14-1 *Smith wants to earn $200/day because with that amount he can live comfortably and meet all his financial obligations. Graph Smith's labor supply curve.*

If L^S denotes the number of hours per day Smith chooses to work, it must satisfy $wL^S = 200$, where w is Smith's hourly wage rate in dollars. Smith's supply curve will thus be given by $L^S = 200/w$, which is shown in Figure 14-7.

Attempting to earn a target level of income is obviously not the only goal a rational person might pursue. But there is certainly nothing retrograde about it either. A person who holds this goal will always work less whenever the wage rate rises.

EXERCISE 14-3

Draw the labor supply curve for a person with a daily target income of $120.

Not all individuals exhibit backward-bending supply curves. An increase in the wage has both an income and a substitution effect on the quantity of leisure demanded. By making leisure more expensive, a wage increase leads people to consume less of it, and hence to work more—the substitution effect. But an increase in the wage also gives people more real purchasing power and, on the plausible assumption that leisure is a normal good, causes them to demand more of it—the income effect. If the income effect dominates the substitution effect over some range of wage rates, we see a backward-bending labor supply curve over that range. Otherwise, the labor supply curve will be everywhere upward sloping.

FIGURE 14-7
The higher his hourly wage rate, the fewer hours Smith has to work to earn his daily target of $200.

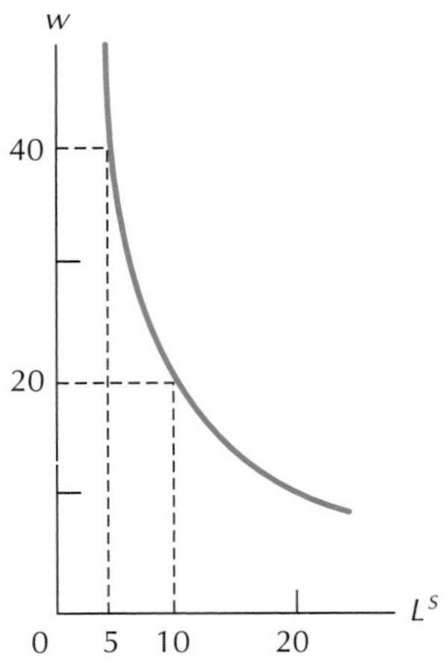

THE LABOR SUPPLY CURVE FOR A WORKER SEEKING A TARGET LEVEL OF INCOME

$$E_{XAMPLE} \ 14\text{-}2 \ \textit{Find the optimal leisure demand for wage } w = \$20/hr \textit{ for someone who views income and leisure as perfect complements in a 10-1 ratio (who requires 1 hr of leisure for every \$10 of income).}$$

The income/leisure budget constraint is

$$M = w(24 - h) = 20(24 - h) = 480 - 20h.$$

Since the individual requires 1 hr of leisure for every $10 of income, the consumption point must lie on the line $M = 10h$. The intersection of the budget constraint and this consumption line (see Figure 14-8) yields the leisure demand:

$$480 - 20h = 10h \Rightarrow 480 = 30h \Rightarrow h = 16 \text{ hr/day}.$$

FIGURE 14-8
If income and leisure are perfect complements in a 10-1 ratio, an individual will consume leisure at a point on the budget constraint that satisfies $M = 10h$.

WHEN LEISURE AND INCOME ARE PERFECT COMPLEMENTS

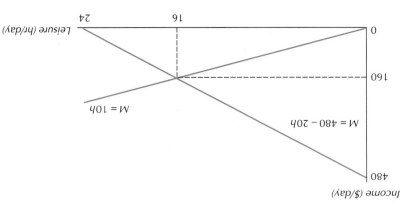

EXERCISE 14-4

Find the optimal leisure demand for wage $w = \$20$/hr for someone who views income and leisure as perfect substitutes in a 10-1 ratio (willing to sacrifice 1 hr of leisure for $10 of income). *Hint:* This person's indifference curves are straight lines $M = a - 10h$ for various values of a.

For many people, the wage rate varies with the number of hours they work, as in the case of a higher wage for overtime. Often we can judge whether a change in income possibilities leaves people better off or worse off without detailed information about their preferences. Knowing their two budget constraints, before and after, and their initial choice of leisure can suffice. If the initial choice of leisure lies on the new budget constraint but the wage at that point has changed, the individual must be better off. The individual can be no worse off since she can still afford the same leisure and income. Now, the worker can adjust leisure choice (more leisure if her wage fell, less leisure if her wage rose) to reach a higher indifference curve.

EXERCISE 14-5

Maynard can work as many hours as he chooses. In his current job, Maynard is paid $5/hr for the first 8 hours he works and $20 for each hour over 8. Faced with this payment schedule, Maynard chooses to work 12 hours a day. If Maynard is offered a new job that pays $10 for every hour he works, will he take the new job? Explain.

For the U.S. labor market taken as a whole, there has been a steady tendency for the average workweek to decline over time, while at the same time the real wages have been rising. The figures for manufacturing production workers for this century are displayed in Table 14-1. This negative correlation between wage rates and average hours naturally does not establish that rising wages are the sole cause of shorter workweeks. But given our theory of individual labor supply, it seems plausible to suppose that they have played an important role. This interpretation is reinforced by the observation that the recent declines in manufacturing wages have been accompanied by a small increase in average weekly hours.

The theory of labor supply plays a crucial role in the logic of welfare reform. The goal of welfare is to provide additional income to the poor. One concern, however, is that welfare assistance may weaken incentives to work. In this respect, the specific form taken by welfare assistance is important. As the

TABLE 14-1   AVERAGE WORKWEEK AND AVERAGE
HOURLY WAGES OF U.S. MANUFACTURING
PRODUCTION WORKERS

Year	Average weekly hours	Index of real hourly wages
1906	55.0	
1914	49.4	100
1920	47.4	126
1925	44.5	141
1930	42.1	151
1935	36.6	179
1940	38.1	214
1945	43.5	259
1950	40.5	273
1955	40.7	318
1960	39.7	348
1965	41.2	378
1970	39.8	396
1975	39.4	408
1980	39.7	403
1985	40.5	405
1992	41.0	373

SOURCE: Ronald Ehrenberg and Robert Smith, Modern
Labor Economics, New York: HarperCollins, 1994, p. 33.

following exercise shows, for example, lump sum transfers are more likely to reduce labor supply than wage subsidies, because transfers invoke a greater income effect relative to the substitution effect in labor supply.

EXERCISE 14-6

Consider the following two antipoverty programs: a payment of $24/day or a payment of 40 percent of wage income. Assuming that the poor people have the option of working at $5/hr, show how each program would affect the budget constraint of a representative poor worker. Which program would be most likely to reduce the number of hours worked?

Is Leisure a Giffen Good?

In the standard consumer choice problem considered in Chapter 3, we saw that the individual demand curve for a product is downward sloping except in the anomalous case of the Giffen good. Here we have seen that the supply curve of labor can be backward bending, which is just another way of saying that the demand curve for leisure can be upward sloping. Does this mean that in such cases leisure is a Giffen good? The answer is no because in the leisure demand case, a price increase (that is, a wage increase) is an increase that applies not only to something the consumer buys, but also to something he sells—namely, his labor. The income effect here thus works in the opposite direction from what we saw in the standard case.

The Noneconomist's Reaction to the Labor Supply Model

Seeing the economic model of labor supply for the first time, many noneconomists consider it a most unrealistic description of the way people actually allocate their time between labor and leisure. Most jobs, after all, offer little choice in the number of hours to work each day. One can of course choose between part-time and full-time work, but the jobs in the part-time category are often so unattractive that most workers view this as a choice not even worth considering.

In part, such criticism of the labor supply model is based on too narrow an understanding of it. The model does not say that people literally choose the number of hours they work each day. Critics are completely correct in pointing out that this is simply not a choice open to most workers. But over the span of several months or years, it is possible to have considerably more say over the amount of time spent at work. Law school graduates, for example, can go to work for fast-track law firms where associates routinely put in 14-hour days 7 days a week; or they can choose firms where everyone is out by 5 P.M. People can choose jobs, such as teaching, that offer summers off. They can moonlight. And they can change jobs frequently, taking time off in between.

Even allowing for all these possible sources of flexibility, however, it is still fair to say that the options for most people are limited. If firms could offer complete flexibility with no loss in productivity, it would be to their advantage to do so. But most firms hire groups of workers who must interact, and things begin to break down if people are not all on the premises during the same hours of the day. This still leaves the possibility of different firms having workdays of different lengths, which, as noted, we do see to some extent. But even here there are often limits. If the workers in one firm need to interact with those in other firms, even if only to exchange information over the telephone, there has to be a common span of time when people are reliably at their desks.

So for many people it is probably fair to say that the amount of time they work is more a result of the constraints imposed by employers than of any deliberate choices of their own. The need for coworker interaction explains the existence of a common workweek, but not why that workweek is 40 hours long instead of 30. This is the question that the economic model of labor supply really helps us to answer. The workweek is 40 hours long because, on the average, that's how long workers want it to be. If most people found an extra hour of leisure much more valuable than an extra hour's wage, profit-seeking employers would have an immediate incentive to reduce the length of the workweek. Here again we see the power of a simple theory to help explain what people do, even when they themselves correctly perceive that the proximate reasons for their actions are forces beyond their control.

The Market Supply Curve

The market supply curve for any given category of labor is obtained by horizontally adding the individual supply curves for the potential suppliers of labor in that category. Even though many individuals may have backward-bending supply curves—indeed, even though the nation as a whole may have a backward-bending supply curve—the supply curve for any particular category of labor is nonetheless almost certain to be upward sloping. The reason is that wage increases in one category of labor not only change the number of hours worked by people already in that category, but also lure people into that category from other categories. Just as an increase in the price of soybeans causes many cotton farmers to switch to soybeans, an increase in the wages of hairstylists causes file clerks, department store salespersons, and others to try their hand at cutting hair.

EXAMPLE 14-3 *Rising enrollments in MBA programs have increased the demand for economics faculty in business schools. If most economists are currently teaching in liberal arts schools, how will this increase in business school demands affect salaries and employment of economists in the two environments?*

The right panel in Figure 14-9 shows the market supply curve of economists as the line labeled S. It is upward sloping on the assumption that higher wage rates for economists will induce some people to choose economics over other professions. The demand curve for economists by liberal arts colleges is shown in the left panel. In the center panel, the original and new demand curves for economists by business schools are labeled D_{B1} and D_{B2}, respectively. Adding the liberal arts and business school demand curves horizontally (on the assumption that the salaries paid to economists are too small a share of total university costs to affect tuition significantly), we get both the original and new total demand curve for economists in the right panel, labeled $D_A + D_{B1}$ and $D_A + D_{B2}$, respectively.

FIGURE 14-9
The demand for economists to teach in business schools rises (center panel), causing the total market demand curve for economists to rise (right panel). Employment at the new higher wage is determined by consulting the respective demand curves of the liberal arts sector (left panel) and business school sector (center panel).

AN INCREASE IN DEMAND BY ONE CATEGORY OF EMPLOYER

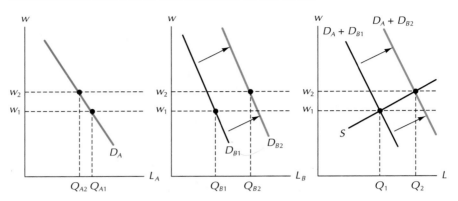

Note that the increased demand by business schools causes the wage rate for economists in both environments to rise from w_1 to w_2. To see how employment in the two environments is affected, we simply trace w_2 leftward to the respective demand curves. The increase in business school employment of economists is $Q_{B2} - Q_{B1}$, while the reduction in liberal arts employment is $Q_{A1} - Q_{A2}$. The gain in business school employment will be equal to the sum of the movements out of liberal arts positions ($Q_{A1} - Q_{A2}$) and the overall movement into the economics profession from the outside ($Q_2 - Q_1$).

This example illustrates two points of particular interest. First is the tendency of salaries for workers in a given occupation to equalize across sectors of the economy that employ that occupation. If the demand for carpenters goes up because of a boom in commercial construction projects, the homeowner who wants to add a recreation room in her basement soon finds herself paying more as well. The idea here is very simple: Unless the wages of carpenters employed in residential construction also rose, many of them would leave that sector for commercial construction. Provided that work in the two environments is in other respects equally desirable, the only stable outcome is for the wage to be the same in each.

The second point suggested by the example is that a small occupational subsector can experience a large proportional rise in demand without appreciably bidding up wages throughout the occupation. Because business schools employed only a small fraction of the total number of academic economists to begin with, these schools could increase their employment substantially without having to pay dramatically higher wages. The general rule is that the effective elasticity of supply to any small occupational subsector will be much higher than to the occupational market taken as a whole.

> As a strictly empirical matter, economists who teach in business schools earn about 20 percent higher salaries than those who teach in liberal arts colleges. This is a large enough difference to suggest that something must be missing from our theory that calls for equal wages in each sector. It is not sufficient merely to observe that business schools are "richer" and therefore can afford to pay more. The question is why they should have to pay more if the economist's only other alternative is to work at a liberal arts salary.
>
> The implicit assumption in our model most likely to be invalid is that economists regard the two working environments as being equally attractive. For reasons we will explore later in the chapter, it seems to be necessary to pay economists a premium to induce them to move from a liberal arts to a business school environment.

Monopsony

The classic illustration of a single-employer labor market is the so-called company town. Workers either cannot or will not leave the area, and new firms cannot enter. A firm in this position is called a *monopsonist*—for "sole buyer"—in its labor market. Does it follow that a monopsonist will exploit its workers by paying them too little and offering them too little safety?

Let's consider first the question of wages. A firm that hires labor in a perfectly competitive labor market faces a supply curve of labor that is a horizontal line at the market wage. Its own hiring decisions have essentially no effect on the market wage. For the monopsonist, by contrast, the labor supply curve is the market supply curve itself. Suppose, for the sake of discussion, that it is upward sloping, like the curve labeled *S* in Figure 14-10. *S* is also called the *average factor cost*, or *AFC*, curve, because it tells the average payment per worker necessary to achieve any given level of employment. The total cost of a given level of employment—called *total factor cost*, or *TFC*—is simply the product of that employment level and the corresponding value of AFC. Thus, the total factor cost of an employment level of 100 workers/hr in Figure 14-10 is equal to 100 × \$4 = \$400/hr.

Average factor cost (AFC) Another name for the supply curve for an input.

Total factor cost (TFC) The product of the employment level of an input and its average factor cost.

Marginal factor cost (MFC) The amount by which total factor cost changes with the employment of an additional unit of input.

Now suppose the firm already has 100 workers and is considering the cost of adding the 101st. To increase its employment by 1 unit, it must raise its wage by \$0.04/hr, not only for the additional unit of labor it hires, but for the current 100 units as well. The total factor cost of 101 workers is \$4.04 × 101 = \$408.04. The *marginal factor cost*, or *MFC*, of the 101st worker is the amount by which total factor cost changes as a result of hiring that worker:

$$\text{MFC} = \frac{\Delta \text{TFC}}{\Delta L}. \tag{14.3}$$

For the example given in Figure 14-10, we thus have MFC = \$408.04 − \$400 = \$8.04/hr. The MFC of the 101st worker is the sum of the \$4.04/hr he is paid

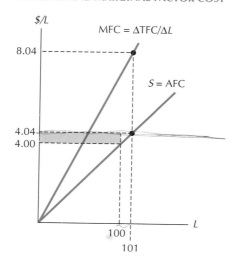

AVERAGE AND MARGINAL FACTOR COST

directly and the extra \$4/hr that must be divided among the existing 100 work-
ers. Because hiring an extra worker always means paying more to existing workers, the MFC curve will always lie above the corresponding AFC curve. If the
AFC curve is a straight line with the formula $AFC = a + bL$, then the corresponding MFC curve will be straight line with the same intercept and twice the
slope as the AFC curve: $MFC = a + 2bL$ (see footnote 3).

Figure 14-11 describes the equilibrium wage and employment levels for a
monopsonist. A monopsonist's demand curve for labor is constructed the same
way as any firm's. If it is a perfect competitor in its product market, its demand
for labor will be VMP_L. If its product demand curve is downward sloping, its
demand for labor will be MRP_L. Given its demand curve, its optimal level of
employment is the level for which MFC and the demand for labor intersect, L^*
in Figure 14-11. At that level of employment, it must pay a wage given by the
value on its supply curve, namely w^*.

The argument that L^* is the profit-maximizing level of employment takes
much the same form as the one we saw in the other labor market structures. The
demand curve for labor, recall, represents the increase in the firm's total revenue
that results from hiring an additional unit of labor, while the MFC curve represents the corresponding addition to its total costs. To the left of L^*, the former

---

[3]In calculus terms, MFC is defined as

$$MFC = \frac{d(TFC)}{dL}.$$

Thus, if $AFC = a + bL$, then $TFC = AFC \times L = aL + bL^2$, which yields $MFC = a + 2bL$.

THE PROFIT-MAXIMIZING WAGE AND EMPLOYMENT LEVELS FOR A MONOPSONIST

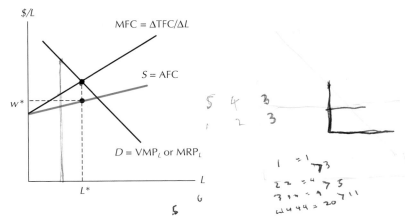

exceeds the latter, so the firm's profit will rise if it expands employment. To the right, the latter exceeds the former, so it will do better if it contracts.

EXERCISE 14-7

A monopsonist's demand for labor is given by $w = 12 - L$. If her AFC curve is given by $w = 2 + 2L$, with corresponding $MFC = 2 + 4L$, what wage rate will she offer and how much labor will she hire?

How do the wage and employment levels under monopsony compare with those in competitive labor markets? If the same overall demand were the result of hiring by not one but many firms, the level of employment would rise to L^{**}, the point at which demand intersects the supply curve in Figure 14-12. The wage rate, too, would rise, from w^* to w^{**}.

In comparison with this competitive norm, the monopsony equilibrium is inefficient in much the same sense that the monopoly equilibrium in the product market is inefficient—it does not exhaust all potential gains from trade. Note in Figure 14-12 that when the employment level is L^*, workers would be willing to supply an additional hour of labor for a payment of only w^*, whereas the extra revenue that would be produced by that extra unit is MFC^*. If the firm could somehow increase total employment by 1 unit without paying its existing workers more, both it and the extra worker would be better off. To the extent that such exchanges are blocked by the calculus of profit maximization, the monopsony structure is less efficient than the competitive ideal.

For the monopsony firm, then, wages will indeed be lower than under competition, lending force to the critics' claims of exploitation. What about other elements of compensation, such as safety equipment? Here, too, there will be a

FIGURE 14-12
Because the monopsonist takes into account the effect of employment expansions on wages paid to existing workers, it will employ less and pay less than the corresponding values under competition.

COMPARING MONOPSONY AND COMPETITION IN THE LABOR MARKET

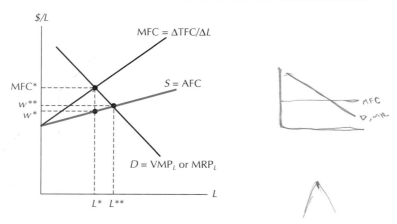

tendency for the monopsonist to offer less, for exactly parallel reasons. It does not follow, however, that employees of a monopsonist would be made better off by a regulation requiring additional safety equipment. The monopsonist's incentives cause it to offer a compensation package—consisting of wages, safety equipment, and other fringe benefits—that is worth less than the corresponding package under competition. But the monopsonist's incentives are to allocate the total amount spent on compensation within that package in exactly the way that workers would want. Suppose, for example, a safety device was worth $10/wk to each worker and cost only $9/wk per worker to install and operate. This device would meet the standard cost-benefit test, and the monopsonist would earn higher profits by installing it. Workers, after all, would tolerate up to a $10/wk pay cut rather than do without the device. Alternatively, suppose the device cost $11/wk. Then both the firm and the workers would do better by not installing it.

The firm's incentives regarding the distribution of total compensation are exactly the same as the workers'. A regulation requiring the firm to install the device will diminish wages even further. And if the monopsonist's wages are too low to begin with, workers will not necessarily regard this as an attractive solution.

How important is the problem of monopsony? Recall that the requirement for perfect competition in the labor market is that workers be freely mobile. Many workers, especially older ones, have commitments—networks of friends, mortgage payments, children in school, and so on—that make it difficult to move. It is far less clear, however, that this confers the power to exploit. At the entry level, most workers are relatively free to move, and most shop carefully for the jobs they ultimately accept. The late Stephen Marston estimated that between 1970 and 1978 alone, intercity migration flows exceeded 25 percent of the urban population.[4] No firm can survive for long without a steady inflow of new workers;

---

[4]See Stephen T. Marston, "Two Views of the Geographic Distribution of Unemployment," *Quarterly Journal of Economics*, 1985.

and without a competitive compensation package, it would be difficult to attract entry-level workers.

To this observation, critics often respond that firms offer competitive terms to entry-level workers but then cut wages and benefits (or have them grow insufficiently) once these workers have put down roots. But firms develop reputations in the labor market, much as they do in the product market. Other things the same, a firm with a reputation for paying competitive wages to all its workers will be able to lure the best entry-level workers away from firms with reputations for exploiting older workers.

But even if *no* workers were willing or able to move, firms might still not be able to exploit their workers in the long run. If firms in a labor market area paid much less than the value of what their workers produce, new firms could move into the area to compete for the services of those workers. Thus, many engineering firms moved to the Seattle area in the 1970s in the wake of the aerospace industry recession that had left thousands of technical employees out of work.

The most compelling argument against the allegation of widespread exploitation is that the profit rates we observe in practice are too low to be compatible with a significant degree of monopsony power. If we assume that the monopsonist holds wages down by only 10 percent of the level paid in competitive labor markets, it follows that the rate of return for the monopsonist will be roughly 50 percent higher than the competitive rate of return.[5] Yet few firms consistently earn profit rates as high as that.

---

[5]To illustrate this claim, consider the case of a firm that hires labor in a competitive market at an annual wage rate w, and that can borrow at an annual interest rate r. If L denotes this firm's employment level and K the size of its capital stock, and these are its only factors of production, then its total costs, TC, are given by

$$TC = wL + rK.$$

Suppose that $r = 0.10$ and that labor costs are 70 percent of total costs. Then

$$TC = 0.7TC + 0.1K,$$

from which it follows that $K = 3TC$ (in words, that the value of the firm's capital stock is three times its annual total production costs).

Now consider a firm identical to the one above except that its monopsony power in the labor market enables it to pay its workers only 90 percent of the competitive wage level. Let Π denote the excess profit it receives as a result of its monopsony power. To calculate Π, note first that the monopsonist's total revenue (which will be the same as the competitor's total costs, TC) will equal its total costs plus its extra-normal profit. Thus we solve

$$(0.9)(0.7)TC + (0.1)3TC + \Pi = TR = TC$$

for Π, which yields $\Pi = 0.07TC$. Suppose half of the firm's capital stock (1.5TC) is owned by stockholders; the other half is financed by loans. Its rate of return will then be the sum of the competitive return on capital ($0.10 \times 1.5TC = 0.15TC$) and the excess return ($0.07TC$) divided by the capital it owns (1.5TC), which yields $0.22TC/1.5TC \approx 0.147$, a 47 percent premium over the competitive rate of return.

More important, those industries that do have higher than average rates of return almost always turn out to be high-wage rather than low-wage industries. Empirical studies have repeatedly found that wage rates are positively, not negatively, influenced by profit rates.[6] To be sure, the West Virginia coal miner in a one-mine town earns a very low wage. But the mine that employs him probably exists on the margin of economic profitability. To say that exploitation is the cause of the miner's low wages seems strange if the consequence of paying higher wages would be to force the mine into bankruptcy.

The profitability argument does not say that firms never face upward-sloping supply curves for labor. But it does suggest that such conditions in the labor market are not an important mechanism whereby the owners of capital take unfair advantage of their workers. And it clearly does not provide a compelling justification for regulating safety procedures in the workplace.

Minimum Wage Laws

In 1938 Congress passed the Fair Labor Standards Act, one of whose provisions established a minimum wage for all covered employees. Coverage was initially limited to workers in large firms involved in interstate commerce but now has become almost universal. The intent of the legislation was to elevate the wages of unskilled workers sufficiently to lift them from poverty. Economists have long been skeptical, however, about the power of government to legislate the price of anything. And indeed the minimum wage laws seem to have had a variety of unintended, undesired consequences.

Figure 14-13 shows the demand and supply curves for unskilled labor, which intersect at an equilibrium real wage of w_0, at which employment is L_0. If the statutory minimum wage is set at w_m, the effect is to reduce employment to D_m, while increasing the quantity of labor supplied to S_m. The difference, $S_m - D_m$, is the unemployment that results from the minimum wage.

According to the simple model in Figure 14-13, there are both winners and losers from the imposition of the minimum wage. The unskilled workers who retain their jobs earn more as a result. Those who lose their jobs obviously earn less. Whether the net effect is to increase the amount of income earned by unskilled workers depends on the elasticity of demand for that category of labor. If it exceeds 1, earnings will fall; if it is less than 1, they will rise.

Proponents of the minimum wage implicitly assume that the demand curve for unskilled labor is nearly vertical. Opponents, by contrast, tend to describe it as highly elastic. Empirical estimates turn out to be highly variable, but for the most part lie slightly below 1, suggesting that the net effect is to increase wage

---

[6]See, for example, George J. Stigler, "The Economics of Minimum Wage Legislation," *American Economic Review, 36,* 1946: 358–365; Laurence Siedman, "The Return of the Profit Rate to the Wage Equation," *Review of Economics and Statistics, 61,* 1979: 139–142; and Alan Kreuger and Lawrence Summers, "Reflections on the Interindustry Wage Structure," *Econometrica,* 1987.

FIGURE 14-13
The effect of the minimum wage is to reduce employment of unskilled labor from L_0 to D_m, while increasing supply from L_0 to S_m. The resulting difference, $S_m - D_m$, is the unemployment attributable to the minimum wage.

A STATUTORY MINIMUM WAGE

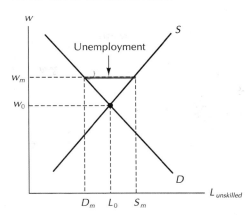

payments to unskilled labor.[7] Some recent studies even suggest that minimum wage laws may not raise overall unemployment at all.[8]

There is a strong consensus, however, that minimum wage legislation has sharply reduced the employment of teenagers. The size of any group's employment reduction will depend not only on the elasticity of demand, but also on the extent to which the minimum wage exceeds the market-clearing level. Teenagers as a group are much less productive than adults, if only because they have less education and experience, and so the statutory minimum creates a much larger employment gap for them than for other groups. There have been recent proposals in Congress to eliminate teenagers from minimum wage coverage altogether, or else to have a much lower "subminimum" wage apply to them. Opponents of these proposals fear that they will cause some firms to substitute teenagers for adult workers, but the proposals have nonetheless gained substantial support.

An interesting exception exists to the general proposition that minimum wages imply a reduction in employment. Figure 14-14 shows the case of a monopsony firm that without a minimum wage would hire L^* workers at a wage

[7]See, for example, Daniel Hamermesh, "Economic Studies of Labor Demand and Their Applications to Public Policy," *Journal of Human Resources,* Fall 1976: 507–525; Edward M. Gramlich, "Impact of Minimum Wages on Other Wages, Employment, and Family Incomes," *Brookings Papers on Economic Activity,* 2, 1976; Jacob Mincer, "Unemployment Effects of Minimum Wages," *Journal of Political Economy,* August 1976; Sar Levitan and Richard Belous, *More Than Subsistence: Minimum Wages for the Working Poor,* Baltimore: Johns Hopkins University Press, 1979; and Finis Welch, *Minimum Wages: Issues and Evidence,* Washington, DC: American Enterprise Institute, 1978. For a review, see Chapter 4 in Ronald Ehrenberg and Robert S. Smith, *Modern Labor Economics,* Glenview, IL: Scott, Foresman, 1982.

[8]See David Card, "Using Regional Variations in Wages to Measure the Effects of the Federal Minimum Wage," *Industrial and Labor Relations Review,* October 1992: 22–37.

FIGURE 14-14
The effect of a minimum wage at w_m is to make the monopsonist's MFC curve horizontal in the region from 0 to L_1, which increases employment from L^* to L_m.

THE MINIMUM WAGE LAW IN THE CASE OF MONOPSONY

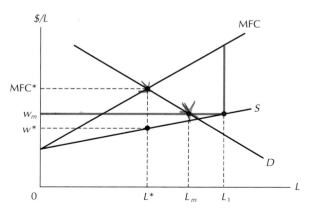

of w^*. Confronted with a minimum wage of w_m, its marginal factor cost curve suddenly becomes horizontal over the region from 0 to L_1. No matter how much labor it hires in that region, the marginal cost of an additional worker is constant at w_m. If it wants to expand employment beyond L_1, it must offer a higher wage than w_m, as indicated along the original supply curve. With the minimum wage in effect, the monopsonist's demand curve for labor intersects its new MPC curve at L_m. The effect of the law is thus to increase both the wage and the employment level for the monopsonist.

Minimum wages will not always increase employment in monopsony labor markets. If the minimum wage were set above MFC*, for example, the effect would be to reduce employment. And no matter where the minimum wage is set in the region above w^*, the effect will be to reduce the monopsonist's overall rate of return on investment. If the monopsonist's profit were close to normal to begin with, the long-run effect would thus be to induce him to leave the market. Needless to say, this too would result in a reduction of employment for unskilled workers.

Exercise 14-8

A monopsonist's demand curve for labor is given by $w = 12 - L$. If she originally faced an AFC curve given by $w = 2 + 2L$, with corresponding MFC $= 2 + 4L$, how will her wage and employment offers be affected by the passage of a law requiring $w \geq 8$? A law requiring $w \geq 10$?

Minimum wage legislation was once a much more hotly debated topic than it is today because inflation has so reduced the real value of the minimum wage that it is below the equilibrium wage level in many unskilled labor markets. In the Boston area, for example, entry-level employees in fast-food restaurants are paid roughly twice the minimum wage. Unless and until Congress enacts a substantial increase in the minimum wage, interest in the subject is likely to continue to wane.

Labor Unions

About one in six workers in the nonfarm sector of the U.S. economy is a member of a labor union. The primary difference between unionized and nonunionized employment is simple. Unionized workers bargain collectively over the terms and conditions of employment; to nonunionized workers, the firm simply announces its offer, which the workers can either accept or reject, by staying with or leaving the firm. Unions may also facilitate communication between labor and management.

For much of this century, economists focused almost exclusively on the collective bargaining aspect of union activity. The consensus in the profession was that unions were the labor market analog to cartels in the product market, serving only to enhance their members' interests at the expense of the general economic welfare. The basic argument in support of this claim is straightforward.

To illustrate, consider a simple economy with two sectors, one unionized, the other not. Suppose that the total supply of labor to the two sectors is fixed at S_0, and that the union and nonunion labor demand curves are as shown by D_U and D_N in the left and right panels of Figure 14-15, respectively. Without union bargaining, the same wage, w_0, would prevail in each sector, and employment levels in the two sectors would be L_{U0} and L_{N0}, respectively, where $L_{U0} + L_{N0} = S_0$.

Collective bargaining fixes the wage in the union sector at $w_U > w_0$. The demand for labor is downward sloping, and this causes firms in the union sector to reduce employment from L_{U0} to L_{U1}. The displaced workers in the union sector are then forced to seek employment in the nonunion sector, which drives the wage down to w_N in that sector.

FIGURE 14-15
Without collective bargaining, the same wage, w_0, prevails in each sector. With the union wage pegged at w_U, employment falls in the union sector. The displaced workers seek employment in the nonunion sector, driving wages down there. The result is a reduction in national output.

THE ALLOCATIVE EFFECTS OF COLLECTIVE BARGAINING

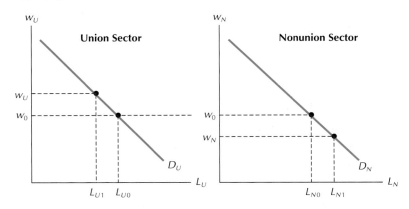

At first glance, the process resembles a zero-sum game, one in which the gains of the union workers are exactly offset by the losses of nonunion workers. On closer inspection, however, we see that the process actually reduces the value of total output. Recall from Chapter 9 that the condition for output maximization with two production processes is for the value of the marginal product of the resource to be the same in each process. With the wage set initially at w_0 in both sectors, that condition was satisfied. But with the divergence in wages caused by the collective bargaining process, the value of total output can no longer be at a maximum. Note that if a worker is taken out of the nonunion sector, the reduction in the value of output there will be only w_N, which is less than w_U, the gain in the value of output when that same worker is added to the union sector.

The economic distortion implied by the analysis in Figure 14-15 is exaggerated. If the union firm is required to pay a higher wage, it will attract an excess supply of workers. In practice, the skill levels of workers differ a great deal, and the natural response of the union firm will be to select the most qualified of its job applicants. The other side of the same coin is that nonunion firms will be left to hire workers who are less productive than average. Empirical studies have shown that the union premium not accounted for by differences in worker quality is only about 10 percent. This means that the gain from shifting workers from the nonunion to the union sector will be smaller than it first appeared.

Even if the union wage premium is only 10 percent, however, we should be puzzled about the ability of union firms to compete successfully against their nonunion counterparts. Of course, the nonunion firms sometimes do manage to drive the union firms out of business, as happened when the textile industry moved to the South to escape the burden of high union wages in New England. But much of the time union and nonunion firms compete head-to-head for extended periods. If their costs are significantly higher, how do the union firms manage to survive?

Researchers have begun to discover a variety of ways in which unions may actually boost productivity.[9] The revisionist view stresses their role in communicating worker preferences to management. When channels of communication between labor and management do not flow freely, the only option open to a dissatisfied worker is to leave the firm to search for a better situation. The union's role, in the revisionist account, is to offer the worker a voice as an alternative to leaving. The organization of formal grievance procedures, combined with the higher level of monetary compensation, boosts morale among union workers, which in turn leads to higher productivity. Quit rates in union firms, for example, are significantly lower than in nonunion firms, enabling them to economize on hiring and training costs. Recent empirical work suggests that union productivity may be sufficiently high, in fact, to compensate for the premium in

---

[9]See, in particular, Albert O. Hirschman, *Exit, Voice, and Loyalty*, Cambridge, MA: Harvard University Press, 1973; and Richard B. Freeman and James Medoff, *What Do Unions Do?*, New York: Basic Books, 1985.

union wages. That is to say, even though monetary wages are higher in union firms, labor costs per unit of output may not be. If this conclusion is correct, it resolves the paradox of how union firms survive in competition with their nonunion rivals.

But in so doing, it raises an even more troubling question: If unions lead to higher morale and increased wages, and don't raise unit labor costs, why don't all firms have unions? The trend in union membership in this country has been declining during the post–World War II era, precisely the opposite of what the revisionist theory would lead us to expect. From the record, it is tempting to conclude that unions may enhance productivity enough to offset wage increases in some industries but not in others. Much more research needs to be done, however, before we have a clear picture of just what unions do.

Discrimination in the Labor Market

One of the most emotionally volatile issues in all of economics is the phenomenon of discrimination in the labor market. Discussions of it almost always begin by noting the large disparities in earnings that exist between different groups in the labor force. For example, the average earnings of black males are roughly 70 percent of those for white males. The corresponding ratio for females and males is approximately the same.

Everyone recognizes that at least some components of these differentials have nothing to do with discrimination by employers. Part of the black-white differential, for example, reflects the fact that the median age of black males is almost a decade lower than for white males. Since earnings rise with experience, white males earn more in part simply because they are older. By the same token, part of the male-female differential reflects the historical pattern by which females' labor force participation was always much more intermittent than males'. Salaries increase most sharply when a worker follows the orderly career progression characteristic of male employment patterns. The female pattern has been to drop out of the labor force several times in connection with childrearing, which has often meant starting over each time at the bottom of the employment ladder.

Each effect is almost surely the result of *some* sort of discrimination against the affected groups. Median ages of black males are lower in part, for example, because blacks so often grow up in poverty, without the education or health care resources to achieve the same life expectancy as whites. No one denies that these conditions are rooted in society's history of discrimination against blacks. Nor do many people deny that the asymmetric distribution of child care responsibilities between the sexes is at least in part the result of discriminatory social attitudes about sex roles. For present purposes, however, it is important to emphasize that from any individual employer's point of view, such effects are examples of *nonmarket* discrimination—effects that lower productivity before job applicants even make contact with the employer. The wage differences for which nonmarket discrimination is responsible cannot logically be attributed to the employer's current hiring behavior. A completely nondiscriminatory employer would have to pay similar wage differentials on the basis of these effects, or else be forced out of business by competitors who did.

Our concern here is with that portion of the wage differentials that cannot be attributed to nonmarket discrimination. In particular, we are concerned with the case in which a firm pays a lower wage to a black, female, Hispanic, or other minority group member than it would to an equally productive white male (or, in the more extreme case, simply refuses to hire members of those groups). There have been numerous theories offered to explain why firms might behave in this fashion.

One theory is that the firm's customers do not wish to deal with minority employees. So-called *customer discrimination* has special force in the vivid examples of segregation in southern lunch counters before the mid-1960s. Any southern lunch counter operator who moved unilaterally to break the color barrier risked losing the bulk of his business to competitors who maintained the tradition of an all-white staff. The Civil Rights Act of 1964 made such discrimination illegal, which sought to ensure that no firm could maintain an advantage over its rivals by refusing to hire blacks.

When employment discrimination is the result of attitudes of the firm's customers, collective action through legislation is one logical way, perhaps even the only practical way, to end the impasse. The reason is that, without the legislation, discrimination may be the only strategy open to firms that is consistent with profit maximization, and hence with survival. Black staff may have been just as productive as white staff at preparing and serving food. But from the standpoint of a lunch counter's bottom line, blacks were less productive because of the racial bias of the customers.

Similar considerations may apply to a law firm's decision about whether to hire female lawyers. If clients, or even judges, are less likely to take advice from a female attorney seriously, the law firm's position is completely analogous to that of the southern lunch counter owner. The law firm might believe firmly that clients and judges would change their minds about female attorneys if given enough experience in dealing with them. But if it hires female attorneys while its competitors do not, its business may suffer in the short run. Here again, legislation requiring equal treatment in hiring may be the only effective way to end the impasse.

Customer discrimination is a powerful explanation of employment discrimination in cases such as these. But it cannot account for wage differentials in the cases of workers—such as manufacturing production workers—who never come in contact with customers. Wage differentials in such cases have sometimes been explained as the result of *coworker discrimination*. White workers who feel uneasy about working with blacks, for example, may prefer employment in firms that hire only white workers. Or the fragile egos of some males may be unable to deal with the idea of taking orders from a female supervisor.

Such preferences imply employment segregation, but not a pattern of wage differentials for equally productive workers. Blacks may work together in some firms or plants, while whites work together in others. Or males may tend to work in separate environments from females. Segregation of just this sort is sometimes observed, and this option makes it difficult for the coworker discrimination theory to explain any significant part of observed wage differentials. An employer in an all-black or all-female establishment who paid lower wages than were received by white males of the same productivity would have lower costs, and hence higher profits, than the all-white-male employers. This would provide an incentive for a new firm to bid for that employer's workers, an incentive that should persist until all wage differentials had been eliminated.

Employer discrimination is the term generally used to describe wage differentials that arise from an arbitrary preference by the employer for one group of worker over another. Since this is the type envisioned by popular accounts of discrimination in the labor market, let us examine it in some detail. To describe the process formally, let us suppose that there are two labor force groups, the Ms and the Fs, and that there are no productivity differences between them. More specifically, suppose that the values of their respective marginal products are the same:

$$\text{VMP}_F = \text{VMP}_M = V_0,\tag{14.4}$$

and that discriminating employers pay a wage of V_0 to Ms, but only $V_0 - d$ to Fs.

Labor costs for a discriminating employer will be a weighted average of $V_0 - d$, where the weights are the respective shares of the two groups in the employer's work force. Thus, the more Ms the employer hires, the higher his costs will be.

Apart from the isolated cases in which customer discrimination might be a relevant factor, a consumer will be unwilling to pay more for a product produced by an F. If product price is unaffected by the composition of the work force that produces the product, a firm's profit will be smaller the more Ms it employs. The most profitable firm will be one that employ only Fs.

Given our initial assumption that Ms are paid the value of their marginal product, firms that employ only Ms will earn a normal profit, while those that hire a mix will earn a positive economic profit. The initial wage differential provides an opportunity for employers who hire mostly Fs to grow at the expense of their rivals. Indeed, because such firms make an extra-normal profit on the sale of each unit of output, their incentive is to expand as rapidly as they possibly can. And to do that, they will naturally want to continue hiring only the Fs.

But as profit-seeking firms continue to pursue this strategy, the supply of Fs at the wage rate $V_0 - d$ will not be adequate for further expansion. The short-run solution is to offer the Fs a slightly higher wage. But this strategy works only if other firms do not pursue it. Once they too start offering a higher wage, the Fs will again be in short supply. In the end, of course, the only solution is for the wage of the Fs to be bid up all the way to V_0, thereby eliminating further opportunities for profitable expansion by hiring additional Fs.

Any employer who wants to voice a preference for hiring Ms must now do so by paying Ms a wage in excess of V_0. Employers can discriminate against Fs if they want to, but only if they are willing to pay premium wages to the Ms out of their own profits. Earlier we saw that if a monopsonist paid its workers 10 percent less than the going wage (or VMP_L), it would earn roughly 50 percent more than the competitive rate of return on investment. A parallel calculation reveals that a firm that paid its workers 10 percent more than the VMP_L would earn roughly 50 percent less than the competitive rate of return. Few firms could continue to attract capital for long at profit rates that much below normal.

The competitive labor market model suggests that the persistence of significant employer discrimination requires the owners of the firm to supply capital at a rate of return substantially below what they could earn by investing their money elsewhere. The theory of competitive labor markets tells us that unless we can come up with a plausible reason to suppose they might do so, we should concentrate our search for the sources of wage differentials on factors other than employer discrimination. Or else we should look for additional ways in which the theory of competitive labor markets provides an incomplete description of reality.

Statistical Discrimination

In Chapter 6 we saw how insurance companies employed data on average claims by various groups to arrive at differential rates for policyholders whose individual claim records were identical. A similar kind of statistical discrimination is pervasive in the labor market. The theory of competitive labor markets tells us that workers will be paid the values of their respective marginal products. But an employee's marginal product is not like a number tattooed on his forehead, there for everyone to observe at a glance. On the contrary, because people often work together in complicated team activities, it is often exceedingly difficult, even after many years on the job, to estimate what any one worker contributes. The problem of estimating the productivity of job applicants, with whom the employer has had no direct experience, is obviously even more difficult.

Still, the task is not hopeless. Just as insurance companies know from long experience that adolescent males are much more likely than other drivers to file accident claims, so too do employers know that applicants from certain groups are likely to be much more productive than others. The average college graduate, for example, will be more productive than the average high school graduate, even though many high school graduates are much more productive than their college counterparts.

In the insurance case, we saw that even when two people had identical driving records, competitive pressures led to different rates if they happened to belong to groups with differing accident records. We see closely analogous results in the labor market. Even when the employer's information indicates that two individuals have exactly the same productivity, there will be competitive pressure to pay higher wages to the person who belongs to the group with higher aver-

FIGURE 14-16
The productivity values for members of this group are uniformly distributed between $10/hr and $30/hr. This means that the VMP of a person chosen at random from the group is equally likely to be any number from $10/hr to $30/hr. The average VMP for members of this group is $20/hr.

A HYPOTHETICAL UNIFORM PRODUCTIVITY DISTRIBUTION

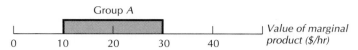

age productivity. The problem is, unless the employer's information about individual productivity is perfect, group membership conveys relevant information about likely productivity differences, information a firm can ignore only at its peril.

To illustrate how group membership influences the estimation of individual productivity, consider a labor market group—call it group *A*—the VMPs of whose members are *uniformly distributed* between $10/hr and $30/hr, as shown in Figure 14-16. This means that if we were to choose a person at random from group *A*, the value of his marginal product would be equally likely to be any number from $10/hr to $30/hr. If we knew nothing about this person other than that he was from group *A*, the expected value of his productivity would simply be the average for members of that group, which is $20/hr.

If there were no practical way to learn anything about a specific individual's productivity, and if the productivity distribution of his group were known, competitive pressures would require that members of group *A* be paid $20/hr (see footnote 10). Suppose an employer offered less—say, $15/hr—perhaps in the fear that he would be unlucky and hire the least productive member of group *A*. This employer would not be able to retain his workers because a competing firm could offer $16/hr and lure them away. And since group *A* workers are worth an average of $20/hr each, this competing firm would augment its expected profits by $4/hr for each worker it hired. But for the same reason, it too would eventually lose the workers to yet another competing firm.

Alternatively, consider a firm that paid $25/hr to workers from group *A*, perhaps because it felt bad about underpaying the more productive members of that group. This firm would lose an average of $5/hr for every worker from group *A* it hired, and unless it had some source of extra-normal profits, it would sooner or later be forced out of business.

If individual productivity values cannot be measured, the only competitively stable outcome is for members of group *A* to be paid $20/hr. Some of them will end up being paid much more than they are worth, others much less. But the firms that hire at this rate will cover all their costs, on the average, and can expect to remain in business. Any other policy will result in failure.

Now suppose that employers have a productivity test. This test is not perfect, but it does provide information about individual productivity values. To keep the analysis simple, suppose that the test is 100 percent accurate half of the time,

---

[10]This analysis ignores the complication of compensating wage differences for internal rank, discussed in the appendix to this chapter, which can be found in the "For the Instructor" section at our Web site www.mhhe.com/economics/frank4.

but has no value at all the other half of the time (that is, it yields a random number drawn from the group's productivity distribution); and suppose that employers have no way of knowing when the test is accurate.

Suppose further that this test is administered to a worker from group A and yields a value of \$24/hr. What is our best estimate of this worker's true productivity? The test is 100 percent accurate half of the time, and if we knew this was one of those times, the answer would, of course, be \$24. Alternatively, if we knew that this was one of the times the test was worthless, our best estimate would be the expected value of a random number drawn from the uniform distribution between \$10/hr and \$30/hr, namely, \$20/hr, the average productivity value for group A. The problem is that we don't know which particular mode this test result falls into. So the best we can do is to take a weighted average of the two results (where the weights are the respective probabilities of occurrence). Our best estimate of the VMP of a worker from group A with a test score of \$24/hr, denoted VMP(24), is thus given by

$$\text{VMP}(24) = (\tfrac{1}{2})(\$24/hr) + (\tfrac{1}{2})(\$20/hr) = \$22/hr \text{ (see footnote 11).} \quad (14.5)$$

This means that if we took a large number of persons from group A who happened to score \$24/hr on the test, their average productivity value would turn out to be \$22/hr.

Suppose instead that we had observed a test result of \$16/hr for a member of group A. Our best estimate of his VMP would then be

$$\text{VMP}(16) = (\tfrac{1}{2})(\$16/hr) + (\tfrac{1}{2})(\$20/hr) = \$18/hr. \quad (14.6)$$

This time note that the effect of the uncertainty in the test causes us to revise upward the estimate of the individual's productivity. *In general, the rule is that when a test is less than completely accurate, our best estimate of a worker's productivity will lie between his actual test score and the average productivity of the group to which he belongs.* And again, the prediction of competitive labor market theory is that any firm that did not pay its workers according to the best available estimates of their respective VMPs would eventually be driven from the market by the forces of competition.

EXERCISE 14-9

In the example above, what is the best available estimate of the VMP of a person with a test score of 12?

---

[11]Note the similarity of this adjustment procedure to the one discussed in Chapter 8, whereby we estimated the probability that a given shy person was a librarian.

Now suppose an employer confronts job applicants not only from group A, but also from group B. And suppose the VMP distribution for group B is uniform between \$20/hr and \$40/hr, as shown in Figure 14-17. Suppose, finally, that two applicants come in one morning, one from group A, the other from group B, and that each gets a score of 28 on the test (the same test as before). What are the employer's best estimates of their respective productivity values?

In both cases, the imperfection in the test calls for an adjustment toward the relevant group average. Specifically, the best estimate of the VMP for the worker from group A, denoted $\text{VMP}_A(28)$, is

$$\text{VMP}_A(28) = (\tfrac{1}{2})(\$28/\text{hr}) + (\tfrac{1}{2})(\$20/\text{hr}) = \$24/\text{hr}, \tag{14.7}$$

while the corresponding estimate for the worker from group B is

$$\text{VMP}_B(28) = (\tfrac{1}{2})(\$28/\text{hr}) + (\tfrac{1}{2})(\$30/\text{hr}) = \$29/\text{hr}. \tag{14.8}$$

Thus, even though the two workers earn exactly the same score on the test, the employer adjusts downward in one case, upward in the other. And again, note that if the firm fails to pay its workers according to the best available estimates of their VMPs, it is in danger of extinction. It is a cruel understatement to say that such competitive imperatives have caused great pain for both employees and employers. The many talented and productive members of group A cannot help but feel chagrined when their group identity causes them to be treated differently from the members of other groups. And surely there cannot be many employers who feel comfortable offering different salaries to people whose records look just the same.

Note carefully that statistical discrimination is the result, not the cause, of average productivity differences between groups. Its sole effect is to reduce wage variation within each group. If employers suddenly switched to a policy of setting wages strictly on the basis of individual-specific information, the average wage differential between groups would remain the same as before.

FIGURE 14-17
The VMP values of members of group A are uniformly distributed between \$10/hr and \$30/hr, while those of members of group B are uniformly distributed between \$20/hr and \$40/hr. If we know only the groups to which people belong, our best estimates of an individual's VMP would be the average VMP for his or her group—\$20/hr for group A, \$30/hr for group B.

PRODUCTIVITY DISTRIBUTIONS FOR TWO GROUPS

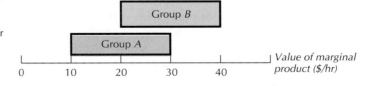

Winner-Take-All Markets

In this section we see that differences in rank sometimes cause small differences in ability to translate into large differences in the values of marginal products.[12] The essence of the idea is captured in the following simple example. Imagine that your company, General Motors, has been sued by Ford for $1 billion for patent infringement. On the merits, the case is so close that it is certain to be decided in favor of the side that hires the better lawyer. Suppose Belli and Bailey are the top two lawyers in the country, and that while they are almost equally talented in every respect, Bailey is just perceptibly better.

Naturally, both Ford and GM will want to hire Bailey, and so both start bidding vigorously for his services. How much will the winner have to pay him? On a moment's reflection, it should be clear that the answer must be $1 billion. If Ford offered only $999 million, it would be in GM's interest to bid still higher because the alternative is to lose the lawsuit. But then Ford will respond by raising its own bid, for its alternative too is to lose the lawsuit. Unless Ford and GM can collude successfully, the only stable outcome is for Bailey to be paid $1 billion. Belli's value, even though he is only a shade less talented, is exactly zero, for by assumption, the side that hires him will lose the lawsuit.

The example is a caricature, but it captures the flavor of what happens in a variety of labor market contexts. Consider, for example, the pay structure in professional tennis. Given the limited amount of time most people are willing to spend watching tennis matches on television, it is practical to see only a handful of players in action during any given year. And given a choice, most fans would be willing to pay a little extra to see the top-ranked players play. The result is that the demand for tennis players ranked in the top 10 is hundreds of times greater than for players ranked around 100. And yet the differences in playing ability between the two categories are often very small. Let the 101st-ranked player meet the 102nd-ranked player and fans will see almost as exciting a match as when the 1st-ranked player meets the 2nd-ranked player. The problem, from the perspective of the lower-ranked pair, is that most fans have time to watch only a single match and would naturally prefer to see the top-ranked pair. The result is that top-ranked players earn millions each year, while those in the second tier earn barely enough to cover their expenses on the tour.

Similar *superstar effects* are observed in virtually every professional sport, in the world of entertainment, and even in the ordinary workings of business. Three tenors earn the bulk of the royalties from the compact discs purchased by opera lovers. Regulated companies spend vast sums bidding for the services of a handful of expert witnesses. A small number of actors and actresses have their pick of all the best roles.

---

[12]The discussion in this section draws on R. Frank, "The Economics of Buying the Best," Cornell University Department of Economics Working Paper, 1978; Sherwin Rosen, "The Economics of Superstars," *American Economic Review,* September 1981; and R. Frank and P. Cook, *The Winner-Take-All Society,* New York: The Free Press, 1995.

For the superstar effect to occur, there must be a winner-take-all effect somewhere in the production process. In tennis it is that the top players capture virtually the entire viewing audience. In the lawsuit example, it was that the better lawyer wins the suit. For the superstar effect to be important, the stakes in the contest must be high, as they are in each of these examples.

The marginal productivity theory of pay determination has been criticized on the grounds that workers with nearly identical abilities are often paid vastly different amounts. At first glance, such observations do indeed seem to contradict the theory. But on a closer look, we see that here too the critics have been too hasty to condemn the model. The difficulty, as we have seen, is that small differences in ability sometimes translate into very large differences in the values of marginal products.

Summary

Our goal in this chapter was to examine the economic forces that govern wages and other conditions of employment. The perfectly competitive firm's hiring rule in the short run is to keep hiring until the value of what the last worker produces—the VMP_L—is exactly equal to the wage rate. In the long run, the firm's demand curve for labor is more elastic than in the short run, because the firm faces the additional possibility of substituting labor for capital.

To aggregate the individual firm demand curves into an industry demand curve for labor involves more than a simple horizontal summation of the individual firm demand curves. An adjustment has to be made for the fact that increasing industry output brings a lower product price.

The demand curve for labor for a monopolist in the product market is constructed by comparing the wage not with the value of the output the worker produces, but with the amount by which the worker's output will change total revenue—MRP_L. Unlike the perfectly competitive firm, monopolists must take into account that an increase in output requires them to sell existing output at a lower price.

We began our approach to the supply side of the labor market by considering the individual worker's decision of how much to work at a given wage rate. The more she works, the more she will earn, but the less time she will have available for other activities. The result is a standard consumer choice problem of the kind we examined in Chapter 3. In the consumer case, a price increase of a product is accompanied by a reduction in the quantity demanded (except in the case of the anomalous Giffen good). By contrast, in the labor supply context, it is not uncommon for people to supply fewer hours of labor when wage rates rise. To generate the market supply curve, we add the individual supply curves horizontally. The market supply and demand curves intersect to determine the industry wage level and total volume of industry employment.

The conventional view of labor unions is that they increase labor's bargaining power vis-à-vis management, thereby increasing labor's share of a fixed economic pie. Recent research, however, suggests that unions may actually improve the productivity of workers, thereby enlarging not only their slice of the economic pie but also management's.

Proponents of minimum wage laws say they are needed to protect workers from being exploited by employers with excessive market power. Whether the legislation actually serves this goal, however, turns out to be a difficult empirical question. There is a case, however, to be made on behalf of exempting teenagers from the minimum wage laws.

Critics claim that many firms pay members of certain groups—notably blacks and females—less than they pay white males with the same productivity. Such charges pose a fundamental challenge to the very core of microeconomic theory, for they imply that firms are passing up opportunities to enhance their profits. We saw several reasons, including discrimination by institutions other than firms, that people in the affected groups appear to earn lower salaries.

An apparent anomaly is the fact that people whose abilities differ only slightly sometimes earn vastly different salaries. This time the key to resolving the contradiction is to observe that in many contexts, the value of what someone produces depends not only on the absolute level of his or her skills, but on how those skills compare with others'. In arm wrestling, being just a little stronger than your opponent means you win just about every time. In the labor market as well, being just a little better than the competition sometimes means earning vastly more than they do.

An appendix to this chapter (see the "For the Instructor" section at our Web site www.mhhe.com/economics/frank4), examines how concerns about relative income affect decisions regarding workplace safety and the distribution of wages within firms.

Questions for Review

1. What is the difference between the perfect competitor's VMP_L curve and the imperfect competitor's MRP_L curve?

2. If a monopolist bought all the firms in a formerly competitive industry and acquired the legal right to exclude entry, how would the quantity of labor employed be affected?

3. Why might local employers pay workers the value of what they produce even if workers are unable or unwilling to move to another area to accept a better job?

4. Why does economic theory lead us to place more emphasis on discrimination by persons and institutions other than employers as a cause of wage differences that exceed productivity differences?

Problems

1. Given the information in the following table, fill in the value of the marginal product of labor for price $P = 4$. Find the perfectly competitive firm's optimal labor demand for a wage $w = \$4/hr$.

L	MP	VMP
0	4	
10	3	
20	2	
30	1	
40	0	

2. Given the information in the table below, graph the budget constraint (depicted for $w = \$6/hr$, where M is income per day). Find and graph the new budget constraint for $w = \$12/hr$. How do the slopes of the two budget constraints compare, and why?

h	M	M'
0	144	
6	108	
12	72	
18	36	
24	0	

3. Given the information in the accompanying table, find the monopsonist's optimal labor demand and wage paid.

L	AFC	TFC	MFC	VMP
0	0	0	0	16
10	2	20	4	12
20	4	80	8	8
30	6	180	12	4

4. A perfectly competitive firm has $MP_L = 22 - L$. Find and graph its value of the marginal product of labor at price $P = 5$. Find its optimal quantity demanded of labor at a wage of $w = \$10/hr$.

5. In his current job, Smith can work as many hours per day as he chooses, and he will be paid \$1/hr for the first 8 hours he works, \$2.50/hr for each hour over 8. Faced with this payment schedule, Smith chooses to work 12 hr/day. If Smith is offered a new job that pays \$1.50/hr for as many hours as he chooses to work, will he take it? Explain.

6. Consider the following two antipoverty programs: (1) A payment of $10/day is to be given this year to each person who was classified as poor last year; and (2) each person classified as poor will be given a benefit equal to 20 percent of the wage income he earns each day this year.

   a. Assuming that poor persons have the option of working at $4/hr, show how each program would affect the daily budget constraint of a representative poor worker during the current year.
   b. Which program would be most likely to reduce the number of hours worked?

7. A monopsonist's demand curve for labor is given by $w = 12 - 2L$, where w is the hourly wage rate and L is the number of person-hours hired.

   a. If the monopsonist's supply (AFC) curve is given by $w = 2L$, which gives rise to a marginal factor cost curve of MFC $= 4L$, how many units of labor will he employ and what wage will he pay?
   b. How would your answers to part (a) be different if the monopsonist were confronted with a minimum wage bill requiring him to pay at least $7/hr?
   c. How would your answers to parts (a) and (b) be different if the employer in question were not a monopsonist but a perfect competitor in the market for labor?

8. Acme is the sole supplier of security systems in the product market and the sole employer of locksmiths in the labor market. The demand curve for security systems is given by $P = 100 - Q$, where Q is the number of systems installed per week. The short-run production function for security systems is given by $Q = 4L$, where L is the number of full-time locksmiths employed per week. The supply curve for locksmiths is given by $W = 40 + 2L$, where W is the weekly wage for each locksmith. How many locksmiths will Acme hire, and what wage will it pay?

9. The demand curve for labor facing a monopsonist is given as $W = 35 - 6L$; the supply curve (AFC) for this monopsonist is $W = 3 + L$, with corresponding MFC $= 3 + 2L$, where W represents the hourly wage rate and L is the number of person-hours hired.

   a. Find the optimal quantity of labor and wage rate for this profit-maximizing monopsonist.
   b. Suppose a minimum wage law imposed a $17/hr minimum wage. How would this affect the quantity of labor demanded by this firm?

10. A monopolist can hire any quantity of labor for $10/hr. If his marginal product of labor is currently 2, and his current product price is $5/unit, should he increase or decrease the amount of labor hired?

11. The Ajax Coal Company is the only employer in its area. Its only variable input is labor, which has a constant marginal product equal to 5. Because it is the only employer in the area, the firm faces a supply curve for labor given by $W = 10 + L$, where W is the wage rate and L is the number of person-hours employed. This supply curve yields the marginal factor cost curve MFC $= 10 + 2L$. Suppose the firm can sell all it wishes at a constant price of 8.

    a. How much labor does the firm employ, how much output does it produce, and what is the wage?

b. Suppose now the firm sells a special kind of coal such that it faces a downward-sloping demand curve for its output. In particular, assume that Ajax faces the demand curve given by $P = 102 - 1.96Q$. How much labor does the firm employ, how much output does it produce, what price does it set for the output, and what is the wage?

c. Assume that Ajax still faces the demand curve $P = 102 - 1.96Q$, but now further assume that Ajax has five laborers under contract to produce coal at a wage of 15. If Ajax has the option of hiring additional laborers at a higher wage without increasing the wage to the five laborers already under hire, will Ajax increase its labor force? Explain.

12. Suppose vacation time comes in 1-week intervals, and that the total willingness to pay for total vacation time by younger and older workers in a competitive industry is as given in the following table:

	Total willingness to pay	
Total vacation time, weeks	**Younger workers**	**Older workers**
1	300	500
2	475	800
3	600	1050
4	700	1250
5	750	1400

Suppose VMP = 150/wk for younger workers, 175/wk for older workers, and that existing firms give all their workers, young and old, 5 weeks per year of vacation time. Can these firms be maximizing their profits? If so, explain why. If not, say what changes they should make, and how much extra profit will result.

13. Members of two groups, the blues and the greens, have productivity values that range from $5 to $15/hr. The average productivity of the blues is $6/hr and the corresponding average for the greens is $12/hr. A costless productivity test is known to have the property that it gives the correct productivity value with probability 1/3, and a random productivity value drawn from the relevant group distribution with probability 2/3.

    a. Assuming labor markets are competitive, how much will a blue with a test value of 9 be paid?

    b. How much will a green with the same test value be paid?

    c. Is it correct to say that statistical discrimination accounts for why the greens, as a group, are paid more than the blues?

14. A firm has a task to carry out that involves opportunities to shirk with little probability of detection. If it can hire a nonshirking employee for this task, it will make a lot of money. Its strategy for finding a nonshirker is to pay a very low wage at first, then increase the wage gradually each year so that, by the time the worker has been with the firm for 10 years, he will be earning more than he could elsewhere. The present value of the wage premiums in the later years is larger than the present value of the shortfall in the early years.

    a. Explain how this strategy helps to attract a nonshirking employee. Would the same strategy work if the probability of detecting shirking were zero?

    b. Explain why the ability of the firm to implement this strategy might depend to an extent on its own reputation in the labor market.

15. Consider a two-sector economy that employs a total of 80 units of a single input, labor. N_1 of these units are allocated to sector 1, where the wage is 100 for the top five workers in that sector and zero for all others. (Both the wage for the top workers and the number who receive that wage are invariant to changes in N_1.) The remaining $N_2 = 80 - N_1$ units of labor serve in sector 2, where every worker receives a wage of 10. All workers in sector 1 have an equal probability of being among the top five workers, $5/N_1$, and all workers are risk neutral.

    a. How many workers will work in sector 1?

    b. What will be the value of GNP for the economy?

    c. How would your answers differ if there were a 50 percent tax on the earnings of workers in sector 1?

*16. A firm produces output according to the production function $Q = K^{1/2}L^{1/2}$. If it sells its output in a perfectly competitive market at a price of 10, and if K is fixed at 4 units, what is this firm's short-run demand curve for labor?

*17. How would your answer to the preceding problem be different if the employer in question sold his product according to the demand schedule $P = 20 - Q$?

Answers to In-Chapter Exercises

14-1. When the product price rises to \$3, the VMP_L curve is as shown in panel *b* of the diagram below. The new quantity of labor demanded at $w = \$12$ is 120 units.

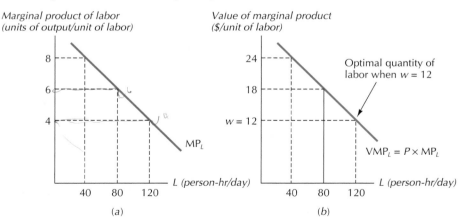

The value of the marginal product is

$$\text{VMP}_L = P(\text{MP}_L) = 3(10 - \tfrac{1}{20}L) = 30 - \tfrac{3}{20}L.$$

---

*This question requires the calculus definition of the marginal product of labor: $\text{MPL} = \partial Q/\partial L$.

The optimal hiring of labor is

$$w = \text{VMP}_L \Rightarrow 12 = 30 - \tfrac{3}{20}L \Rightarrow 18 = \tfrac{3}{20}L \Rightarrow L^* = 120.$$

14-2. With $w = \$20/\text{hr}$, the income/leisure budget constraint is

$$M = w(24 - h) = 20(24 - h) = 480 - 20h.$$

At leisure $h = 14$ hr/day, income per day is

$$M = 20(24 - h) = 20(24 - 14) = 20(10) = \$200.$$

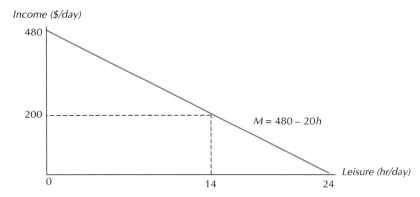

14-3.

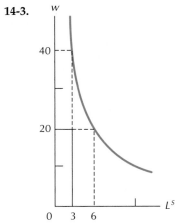

14-4. The budget constraint remains $M = 480 - 20h$. As the individual is willing to sacrifice 1 hour of leisure for \$10 of income, indifference curves are straight lines of the general form $M = a - 10h$ provided in the hint. The highest indifference curve that shares a point with the income/leisure constraint is $M = 480 - 10h$, with optimal leisure demand $h = 0$. This form of preferences exhibits extreme substitution effects (will consume no leisure for any $w > 10$ and all leisure for any $w < 10$).

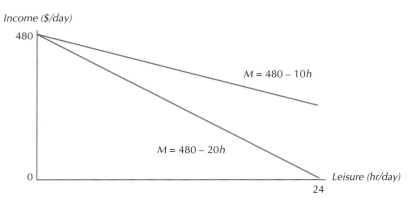

Income ($/day)

480

$M = 480 - 10h$

$M = 480 - 20h$

0

24

Leisure (hr/day)

14-5. Under his current job, Maynard's maximum income from working all 24 hours is the sum of 8 hours at $5/hr and the remaining 16 hours at $20/hr:

$$8(5) + 16(20) = 40 + 320 = \$360/\text{day}.$$

Each hour of leisure requires sacrifice of $20 up to $h = 16$ hr, but only $5 beyond 16 hr. Consuming $h = 16$ hr of leisure and working $24 - h = 24 - 16 = 8$ hr yields $8(5) = 40$ income (at the kink in the budget constraint). Maynard's original budget constraint is thus

$$M_1 = \begin{cases} 360 - 20h; \ 0 \le h \le 16 \\ 40 - 5h; \ 16 \le h \le 24 \end{cases}.$$

The budget constraint has two pieces reflecting the two wages (regular and overtime). If Maynard works 12 hours, then he enjoys $h_1 = 12$ hr of leisure per day, and thus with the original budget constraint earns income

$$M_1 = 360 - 20h = 360 - 20(12) = 360 - 240 = \$120/\text{day}.$$

Under his potential new job, Maynard's maximum income from working all 24 hours is $24(10) = 240$. An hour of leisure requires sacrifice of $10 income up to 24 hours. Maynard's new budget constraint is

$$M_2 = 240 - 10h.$$

Here the budget constraint is a simple straight line. Maynard's original optimal labor supply choice would still be feasible with the new budget constraint: Maynard could earn the same income with the same amount of leisure of time under the new budget constraint

$$M_2 \equiv 240 - 10h = 240 - 10(12) = 240 - 120 = \$120/\text{day}.$$

Thus, Maynard can be no worse off with the new budget constraint. However, Maynard will have an opportunity cost of leisure time of $w = 10$ with the new budget constraint rather than $w = 20$ with the old budget constraint. Therefore, Maynard must optimally adjust his labor supply toward more leisure. Maynard will be happier at his new optimal labor supply choice: He reaches a higher indifference curve (I_2) between income and leisure, so he will accept the new job.

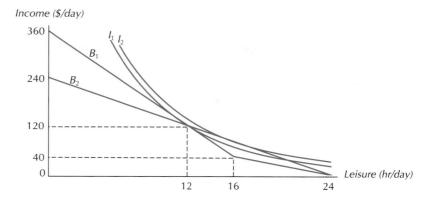

14-6. The original budget constraint is

$$M_0 = w(24 - h) = 5(24 - h) = 120 - 5h.$$

The first program yields a budget constraint

$$M_1 = S + w(24 - h) = 24 + 5(24 - h) = 144 - 5h.$$

The second program yields a budget constraint

$$M_2 = (1 + s)w(24 - h) = (1 + 0.4)5(24 - h)$$

$$= 7(24 - h) = 168 - 7h.$$

The first program is more likely to reduce hours worked because it increases income but leaves the opportunity cost of leisure unchanged: assuming leisure is a normal good, higher income leads to more leisure consumed. In contrast, the second program increases the opportunity cost of leisure: for low levels of wages, an increase in the wage generally increases labor supply as the substitution effect dominates the income effect. Thus, the poor will likely work less under the first program and more under the second program.

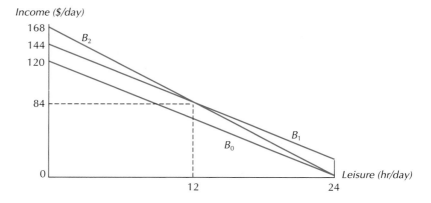

14-7. *Wage, MFC ($/unit of labor)*

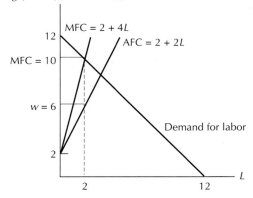

14-8. When the minimum wage is 8, the monopsonist's MFC curve is the heavy locus with the discontinuity at $L = 3$. The demand curve for labor passes through this discontinuity, which means that the monopsonist will hire 3 units of labor at a wage of 8. When the minimum wage is 10, the firm will pay $w = 10$ and hire 2 units of labor, the same quantity she would have hired in the absence of a minimum wage.

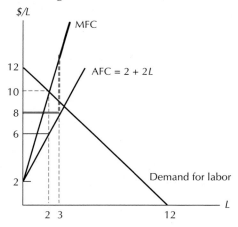

14-9. $\text{VMP}(12) = (\frac{1}{2})(\$12/\text{hr}) + (\frac{1}{2})(\$20/\text{hr}) = \$16/\text{hr}.$

CHAPTER
15

Capital

S everal years ago, *Fortune* magazine conducted a survey in which business leaders were asked to identify the "best managed companies in America." Respondents were requested not to name their own firms, and there was considerable overlap in the lists they submitted. Some firms, such as Procter & Gamble, appeared on virtually every list.

The people surveyed were probably the most knowledgeable observers to whom such a question could have been put, and there is every reason to believe that the companies they named are indeed among the most well managed. And yet a follow-up study discovered that people who bought stock in these companies after publication of the survey actually earned slightly less on their investments than the average return for the stock market taken as a whole.

We see a similar pattern with respect to the investment advice published in investment newsletters. These newsletters are compiled by the country's leading financial analysts, and often sell for several hundred dollars per year. Their subscription lists include some of the most sophisticated members of the investment community. And yet the stocks recommended in most of these newsletters perform no better, on the average, than the stocks picked by a monkey throwing darts at the financial page.

As anomalous as these patterns may appear at first glance, we will see that they are just what a careful analysis of the capital market would have predicted. Indeed, with investment newsletters, the real anomaly is not that the stocks they recommend do no better than others, but that people continue to pay such high prices for this kind of advice.

Chapter Preview

In this chapter we examine the market for services of capital inputs. In many respects, the results from our study of labor inputs will carry forward intact. One feature that often sets capital apart from other inputs is that whereas other inputs are usually hired on a period-by-period basis, capital equipment is often owned outright by the firm. In our first exercise we examine the factors that govern the firm's decision to buy a piece of capital equipment.

We then examine the distinction between real and nominal rates of interest. This distinction will help make clear why the interest rates banks and other lenders charge tend to rise hand in hand with the overall rate of inflation.

Next we see how interest rates are determined in the market for loanable funds. A topic of special focus is the market for stocks and bonds; we take up the apparent anomalies mentioned in the chapter introduction. Additional items on our agenda include economic rent and peak-load pricing.

Financial Capital and Real Capital

When people use the term "capital" they usually mean one of two very different things. They may have in mind *financial capital*, which essentially means money or some other form of paper asset that functions like money. Or they may mean *real capital* (or physical capital), which means a piece of productive equipment, such as a lathe or printing press, that generates a flow of productive services over time. When we refer to capital as a factor of production, we are almost always talking about real capital.[1] When people talk about the "capital market" they generally mean the market for financial capital, such as bank loans, corporate stocks, and bonds. Our direct concern in this chapter is with real capital, but because firms require financial capital to purchase real capital, we must consider markets for financial capital as well.

The Demand for Real Capital

Our theory of the individual firm's demand for labor developed in Chapter 14 applies without modification to the demand for other inputs. In the short run, if the firm can acquire the services of as much capital as it wishes at a constant rental rate of r/yr, it should employ capital up to the point at which its marginal revenue product (MRP_K) is exactly equal to the rental rate:

---

[1]The exception is what we call "working capital" money the firm keeps on hand to facilitate timely payment of debts when current revenues fall short. By allowing the firm to function more efficiently, this working capital is no less a factor of production than labor and machines are.

$$MRP_K = MR \times MP_K = r, \tag{15.1}$$

where MR is the firm's marginal revenue and MP_K is the marginal product of capital.

If the firm happens to be a perfect competitor in its product market, so that its marginal revenue is the same as its product price, then Equation 15.1 reduces to the simpler form:

$$VMP_K = P \times MP_K = r, \tag{15.2}$$

where VMP_K denotes the value of the marginal product of capital and P is the price of the firm's output.

For firms in a perfectly competitive industry, aggregation of individual firm demand curves into an industry demand curve for capital involves essentially the same complication we saw for labor. We must take into account that an expansion of industry output involves a reduction in the product price, with attendant moderations in the quantities of capital demanded. Again as before, this effect is already accounted for in the monopolist's demand curve for capital.

One salient difference between capital and labor markets is that whereas workers tend to specialize in particular types of activities, new sources of capital (financial capital) are almost completely fungible. Thus, a given sum of money can just as easily fund the construction of a machine to make soft ice cream as it can a printing press, or the production of an animated cartoon. Once financial capital has been used to purchase real capital, however, the firm's flexibility is significantly limited. Whereas labor can, at some expense, be retrained to perform new tasks when conditions change, it is much more difficult to transform a drill press into a sewing machine.

The Relationship Between the Rental Rate and the Interest Rate

Technological obsolescence
The process by which a good loses value not because of physical depreciation, but because improvements in technology make substitute products more attractive.

How is the rental price of a unit of real capital equipment related to the interest rate at which money can be borrowed? To answer this question, put yourself in the position of a firm whose business is to rent machines. Suppose the purchase price of a particular machine is $1000 and the interest rate at which money can be borrowed or loaned is 5 percent/yr. To cover just the opportunity cost of the $1000 you have tied up in the machine, you would have to charge $50/yr for it. But in general there will be additional costs as well. Suppose the machine requires $100/yr worth of maintenance. Your breakeven rental will then have risen to $150/yr. Finally, you must consider changes in the future price of the machine.

For simplicity, suppose that the overall level of prices in the economy is stable. (More below on what happens when we relax this assumption.) Even a well-maintained machine will lose some of its value each year. Indeed, if newer, more efficient machines are being designed each year, an existing machine may lose its economic value overnight, even though it continues to function exactly as it did when new. This phenomenon is called *technological obsolescence*. If the net result of these factors—physical wear and tear and technological obsolescence—is for the price of the machine in our example to fall by $100/yr, the total cost of supplying it will then be $250/yr —$50 in forgone interest, $100 in maintenance, and $100 in lost market value. Any additional costs you incur as a rental business—such as wages for your staff—would have to be added to that figure.

Let m stand for annual maintenance expenses, expressed as a fraction of the price of the capital good, and let ∂ stand for physical and technological depreciation, similarly expressed. If i denotes the market rate of interest, expressed in decimal form, then the annual rental price of capital, r, will be the sum of i, m, and ∂:

$$r = i + m + \partial. \tag{15.3}$$

Sometimes a machine will actually grow, rather than depreciate, in value over time. This can happen, for example, when a key input used in making the machine becomes more expensive. In such cases, the term ∂ in Equation 15.3 would be negative. For example, if the rental firm from our earlier example expected the price of a machine to go *up* by $100 in the year to come, it could break even at a rental fee of only $50, $200 lower than if the price of the machine went down by $100. Expectations of asset price increases appear to explain why, when housing prices are rising rapidly, rents are often lower than the corresponding mortgage payments.

EXERCISE 15-1

Suppose the purchase price of a Coke machine is $5000. If the annual interest rate is 0.08, the maintenance rate is 0.02, and the rate of physical and technological depreciation is 0.10, how much will the machine's annual rental fee be?

The Criterion for Buying a Capital Good

Another factor that sets capital apart from labor is that firms have the option of purchasing capital equipment. Professional athletes are sometimes bought and sold as if they were no different from machines, but even they cannot be forced to play for a team indefinitely against their wishes. Labor contracts in general permit workers to move whenever the terms of employment are no longer attractive, the primary reason being that it is impractical to make a disgruntled employee work effectively on the firm's behalf. The machine, of course, enjoys no such latitude. It goes to the highest bidder.

What factors govern a firm's decision about whether to buy a given piece of capital equipment? As always, the firm will wish to weigh the benefits of owning the machine against its costs. On the benefit side, the machine will bolster the firm's rate of production not only in the current period, but also in the future. Suppose the extra output made possible by the machine will enhance the firm's total revenue by R for each of the next N years. Suppose further that the machine costs M each year to maintain, and that at the end of N years it has a scrap value of S dollars. And suppose, finally, that the firm is given this machine and expects to operate it for N years, at which point it will sell it for scrap. How much will the present value of the firm's stream of profits go up?

To answer this question, we must translate net revenues the firm will receive in the future into an equivalent present value. As we saw in Chapter 6, the present value of a dollar to be received 1 year from now is $\$1/(1+i)$, where i denotes the market rate of interest. The net present value of the stream of returns produced by the machine, including the proceeds from sale for scrap, is therefore given by

$$PV = \frac{R-M}{1+i} + \frac{R-M}{(1+i)^2} + \cdots + \frac{R-M}{(1+i)^N} + \frac{S}{(1+i)^N}. \tag{15.4}$$

The cost of the machine is simply its purchase price, P_K. The firm's decision criterion should be to buy the machine if and only if PV is greater than or equal to P_K. We see from Equation 15.4 that PV is inversely related to the market rate of interest. Thus, as with the firm that rents its equipment, the firm that owns its capital will want to employ more of it the lower the market rate of interest is.

EXERCISE 15-2

Suppose a machine generates $121 worth of revenue at the end of each of the next 2 years, at which time it can be sold to a salvage company for $242. If the annual rate of interest is 0.10, what is the maximum amount a business would pay for this machine?

Interest Rate Determination

To recapitulate, a firm's demand for capital equipment depends on the rate of interest, the purchase price of capital, and the rates of technological and physical depreciation. Interest rates, in turn, are determined by the intersection of the supply and demand curves for loanable funds. Because financial capital is perfectly fungible, the market for loanable funds is an almost literal embodiment of the ideal of a perfectly homogeneous, standardized product. The result is a national—indeed international—market for loanable funds in which the interest rate charged to a given type of borrower is virtually the same everywhere.

How is the demand for loanable funds related to the demand for capital? A firm's demand for capital tells us how much capital it would like to employ at any given rental price of capital, r. If it is a firm that has already been in operation for some time, it presumably has already acquired much of the capital it needs.

For simplicity, let us assume that in the current year the firm wishes to bridge the entire gap between the amount of capital it has and the amount it would like to have. This gap then constitutes its demand for loanable funds. At the industry level, similarly, the demand for loanable funds is the difference between the amount of capital firms as a whole would like to have and the amount they already do have. The price that is used to ration money in the loanable funds market is the interest rate.

Firms are not the only borrowers in the loanable funds market. Consumers borrow to finance the purchase of houses and other goods. Governments borrow to build roads and schools, and, with increasing frequency, to finance general budget deficits. The demand curve for loanable funds is the horizontal summation of the demands from all these sources.

On the supply side, there are also multiple sources of loanable funds. Consumer savings supplement funds made available by firms out of profits. And of growing importance in recent years has been the active participation of foreign lenders in the American market for loanable funds. As we saw in Chapter 6, the theory of consumer behavior tells us that a rise in interest rates may either raise or lower consumer savings. The total effect is the net result of offsetting income and substitution effects, and theory alone does not tell us which will dominate. Empirical studies suggest that in fact the elasticity of consumer savings with respect to interest rates is sometimes positive, sometimes negative, but in any event almost certainly very small.

For savings by private firms, there is no analog to the income effect in the consumer case, so the quantity of loanable funds supplied by firms will respond positively to interest rates. Most foreign lenders are happy to supply funds to U.S. borrowers whenever the interest rate meets or exceeds what they can earn at home. Adding all sources of supply horizontally, we obtain the aggregate supply curve of loanable funds. The large size of foreign lending in recent years suggests that this source is responsible for most of the elasticity we see in the supply curve of loanable funds. The intersection of this curve with the aggregate demand curve for loanable funds, shown in Figure 15-1, determines both the market rate of interest, i^*, and the total volume of funds exchanged, LF*.

Real Versus Nominal Interest Rates

Suppose you borrow $1000 from a bank, which you agree to repay in a year's time at 5 percent interest. And suppose that once the year passes, the overall price level in the economy has risen by 10 percent (as, for example, would happen if each and every price rose by 10 percent). What has been the real cost to you of your loan?

FIGURE 15-1
The quantity of
loanable funds de-
manded at any inter-
est rate (*D*) is the
difference between
the desired stock of
capital at that inter-
est rate and the
amount of capital
stock already in
place. The supply of
loanable funds (*S*)
comes from con-
sumers, firms, and
international
lenders. The grow-
ing importance of
foreign lenders as-
sures that the supply
curve of loanable
funds will be up-
ward sloping.

EQUILIBRIUM IN THE MARKET FOR LOANABLE FUNDS

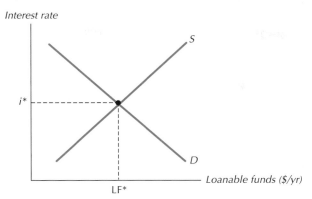

To answer this question, imagine that when you first borrowed the money, you used it to buy 100 oz of silver at $10/oz. Because the price of silver, like every other price, is assumed to be rising at 10 percent/yr, this means you can sell your silver for $11/oz when your loan comes due. The proceeds from this sale will be $1100, or $50 more than the $1050 you need to repay the bank. The real cost to you of the loan, measured in dollars on its due date, is therefore *minus* $50. Not only did it not cost you any real resources to borrow the money, but you actually came out $50 ahead. On the reciprocal end of this transaction, the bank that loaned you the money came out $50 behind.

Needless to say, a bank could hardly hope to remain in business if it contin-ued to loan money at such unfavorable terms. When banks expect the overall level of prices to rise, they will charge an interest premium to counteract the ero-sion of the real purchasing power of future loan payments. The actual number that appears on the bank loan contract is called the *nominal rate of interest*—5 per-cent in our example. If *n* denotes the nominal annual rate of interest, expressed as a fraction, and *q* denotes the annual rate of inflation, also expressed as a frac-tion, then the *real rate of interest* is given by

$$i = \frac{n - q}{1 + q}.\qquad(15.5)$$

Using the values from our hypothetical example, we have $i = (0.05 - 0.10)/\,1.10 = -0.0455$, or -4.55 percent. We can see from Equation 15.5 that when the rate of inflation is small, the real interest rate is approximately equal to the difference between the nominal rate of interest and the rate of inflation, $n - q$. In all our prior examples, the interest rate has been implicitly assumed to be the real inter-est rate. In its investment decisions, the firm wants to compare the real costs of capital against the real benefits, and proceed only if the latter exceeds the former.

The Market for Stocks and Bonds

One common method by which firms raise money for new investments is by issuing corporate bonds. A bond is essentially a promissory note issued by the firm. An investor gives the firm some money—say, $10,000—and in return the firm hands the investor a handsomely engraved certificate that promises to pay the investor a fixed rate of interest—say, 10 percent—for a specified time. The *face value* of the bond is the amount for which it was sold to the investor who bought it from the firm. The lifetimes of corporate bonds vary considerably. *Short-term bonds* often promise to return their face value in full within 90 days. Many *long-term bonds* reach maturity only after 30 years, and some have even longer lifetimes.

Once bought, a bond may be traded in the open market. If it is a short-term bond, its price will almost always be close to its face value. For longer-term bonds, however, the price fetched in the open market can differ substantially from face value.

To see why, suppose the market rate of interest is 10 percent when an investor buys a $10,000 bond from a corporation; the bond promises to pay her $1000/yr interest for the next 30 years and then return her $10,000 in full. As long as the interest rate remains 10 percent, the bond will continue to be "worth" $10,000 in the sense that its $1000 annual interest payment fully compensates the investor for the opportunity cost of doing without her money. But suppose the interest rate suddenly falls to 5 percent. Now the opportunity cost of doing without $10,000 suddenly falls from $1000/yr to only $500/yr. The investor who holds a bond that promises to give her $1000/yr would not be willing to sell it for only $10,000, because with the interest rate at 5 percent, she would need $20,000 in order to earn the $1000/yr interest she will get by keeping the bond.

The price of the bond in this example will not rise all the way to $20,000, however, because the new buyer knows that the bond will be worth only $10,000 when it reaches maturity. If the due date is imminent, the price will be close to $10,000 no matter what the interest rate is. But the farther away the maturity date of the bond is, the less its face value will affect its current market price. Indeed, there is a particular type of bond, called a *perpetual bond* or *consol,* for which the face value does not matter at all. A perpetual bond is a promise to pay its bearer a fixed sum of money each year forever. As a close approximation, the current market price of a consol is the amount of money that would be needed, at the current interest rate, to generate the same amount of interest as is paid by the consol. Thus, for example, a consol that promises to pay $1000/yr will be worth $10,000 when the interest rate is 10 percent, and $20,000 when the interest rate is 5 percent. More generally, if I represents the consol's annual payment and i is the market rate of interest, then the price of the consol, P_C, will be given by

$$P_C = \frac{I}{i}.$$ (15.6)

EXERCISE 15-3

Consider a perpetual bond that pays $120/yr to its owner. By how much would the price of this bond rise if the interest rate fell from 10 to 5 percent?

Corporations are not the only institutions that issue bonds. Governments at the federal, state, and local level do so as well. The examples discussed earlier implicitly assumed that there is a single, uniform market rate of interest at any moment, but in fact there are many different interest rates. The general rule is that the greater the risk is that a borrower will not repay a loan, the greater the interest rate that borrower will pay. United States government bonds carry the lowest risk of default available in the bond market, and the government therefore pays lower rates of interest than do the issuers of other bonds. Suppose, for example, that 30-year, $10,000 Chrysler Corporation bonds pay 11 percent annual interest, while the same type of bond issued by the federal government pays only 9 percent. The 2 percent interest rate differential is called a **risk premium**, and it compensates the investor for the fact that Chrysler has a higher likelihood of not repaying its loan than does the federal government.

Risk premium
A payment differential necessary to compensate the supplier of a good or service for having to endure risk.

Someone who owns a corporate bond does not have an ownership share in the corporation. The bondholder's financial position is similar to that of a bank that has issued the corporation a loan. The corporation's stockholders are the people who actually own it. A firm that wants to raise money to invest in capital equipment can hire a broker to arrange a new issue of stock certificates. The broker then prepares a description of the firm's investment proposal and, with the cooperation of a network of other brokers, offers the new stock for sale to the public.

If a firm sells 1,000,000 shares of stock, each share constitutes a claim against $\frac{1}{1,000,000}$ of the current and future profits of the firm. Profits may be distributed to shareholders directly in the form of dividends, or they may be reinvested in the company, which will increase the value of the company's future profits.

What price will each share of stock command? Suppose the present value of the current and future profits of our 1,000,000-share hypothetical company is known with certainty to be $500 million. Its stock should then trade at exactly $500/share. At a price any lower than that, investors could increase their wealth immediately by buying it. And at any price above $500, no one would have any economic incentive to own it.

Seldom, if ever, is a company's future profit stream known with certainty. The price people are willing to pay for shares depends on their best estimates of the firm's prospects. For new firms, or for firms that are moving into uncharted territory, the risk of low earnings can be very substantial indeed. If a genetic engineering company comes up with a way to clone a protein that destroys the AIDS virus, its profits will be virtually unbounded. But many companies are struggling to be first in that race, and the destiny of most of them is to fail.

In other areas of the economy, the economic prospects of a company are easier to predict. Hertz has been in the business of renting cars for many decades now, and no major surprises appear to be on the horizon. Hertz stands almost no chance of hitting a big jackpot. But by the same token, its odds of continuing to survive are relatively high.

Consider two firms with the same expected value of current and future profits. The present value of firm 1's profit stream is $100 million with certainty. The present value of firm 2's profit stream, by contrast, has a 50-50 chance of being either $200 million or zero. If the stock prices of the two firms were the same, which one would you prefer to buy? If you are like most investors, you are risk averse (see Chapter 6) and therefore prefer firm 1, the safer investment of the two.

Because most people have this preference, the stocks of firms with risky future earnings generally sell at lower prices, just as riskier bonds generally must pay higher interest rates. As an investor confronting the stock market, you face a budget constraint something like the curve labeled *BB* in Figure 15-2. Along *BB*, the safer the investment, the lower its expected return. Investors with relatively low marginal rates of substitution between return and safety will choose risky investments such as *A*, which offer relatively high expected returns. Those with higher marginal rates of substitution between return and safety will choose safer investments such as *C*. Virtually everyone would like to own stocks with high expected returns *and* high safety. But the terms available in the market force people to choose between these attributes.

THE EFFICIENT MARKETS HYPOTHESIS

Most economists believe that the stock market is efficient. By this we mean that the price of a stock embodies all available information that is relevant to its current and future earnings prospects. To illustrate, consider a hypothetical example involving Genentech, a highly successful genetic engineering company. Suppose that on the strength of its earnings prospects, the current value of a share of Genentech is $100. Now suppose that one of Genentech's researchers suddenly stumbles onto a miracle cure for cancer. The discovery is simple and easy to patent. The company is certain to win government approval for its

FIGURE 15-2
Because most investors are averse to risk, they will not buy a risky stock unless its expected return is greater than that of less risky stocks. Which type of stock to buy depends on the buyer's preferences. Relatively cautious investors will prefer safer stocks like *C*. Less cautious investors will give up some safety for the greater expected return on investments like *A*.

THE TRADEOFF BETWEEN SAFETY AND EXPECTED RETURN

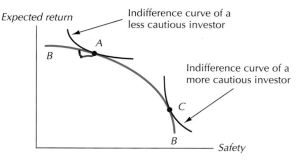

discovery, at which point its revenues will soar dramatically. But because of bureaucratic red tape, the approval process never takes less than 3 years. You read in *Newsweek* about Genentech's discovery and decide to buy stock in the company. Is this a shrewd move on your part?

The answer is almost certainly no, but not because the company does not have the rosy future that has been forecast for it. The difficulty, according to the efficient markets hypothesis, is that the value of the new discovery will be almost instantaneously bid into the market price of its stock. By the time you hear about it, the rise in price for which it is responsible will have long since occurred.

Critics of the efficient markets hypothesis often object that it refers to a frictionless ideal world. In the real world, they argue, it may take considerable time for new information to disseminate, and so its effect on stock prices may be gradual and protracted. Thus, they conclude, if the news of the Genentech discovery is only a few weeks old, there will still be plenty of room for stock prices to keep growing on the strength of it.

This view is almost certainly wrong. The difficulty is a confusion that arises because new information often comes not in the very sure form assumed in the example, but in highly uncertain form. In practice it would be much more common, for example, for the market to learn at first only that a Genentech researcher had a promising lead on a cure for cancer. This more limited information would justify a much smaller boost in the company's stock price, which would then be followed by further increases if the development continued to show promise. But it would be followed by a plunge in stock prices if the development were to fizzle. In either event, however, the full value of the information at hand would be reflected in the stock price of the moment. But because information about new profit opportunities usually emerges gradually, many observers erroneously conclude that the market's response to the new information is also gradual.

Unlike the conditions in our hypothetical example, in the real world it is usually hard to quantify exactly what information becomes available at specific times. Moreover, there is almost always latitude for differences in interpretation of any given piece of information. For these reasons, it is extremely difficult to verify the efficient markets hypothesis empirically. Nonetheless, most economists believe that it is correct. If the hypothesis is impossible to verify directly, what accounts for the strength of economists' commitment to it?

The answer is that the alternative hypothesis—namely that stock prices *don't* embody all the available information—leads to conclusions that we find so difficult to accept. To illustrate, consider our cancer cure example again, and suppose the market did not immediately bid up the price of the stock to reflect the higher future profits implied by the new discovery. Then you or I could simply pick up the phone and instruct our stockbrokers to buy as many shares in Genentech as we could afford. We could then sit back and wait for the market to bid up our shares to their full market value, reaping a substantial gain in the process.

The one belief that economists hold more deeply than any other is that the only way to reap such gains is by some combination of talent, hard work, and luck. But if we deny the efficient markets hypothesis, there can be examples like this one in which there is cash just sitting on the table for the taking. We need no talent; we needn't do any hard work; and because the information is certain, we don't even need to be lucky. We just call our brokers and wait for the money to roll in. There is an ample supply of people who would be delighted to earn their livings in this painless way. That it seems generally impossible to do so is all the confirmation most economists need for the efficient markets hypothesis.

Many people believe that it is better to buy stock in a highly profitable company than in one with only an average profit level. An important implication of the efficient markets hypothesis, however, is that this belief is wrong. To see why, consider two firms identical in all respects except that one is a monopoly and earns twice the profit earned by the other. If the prices of the two stocks were the same, everyone would naturally want to own stock in the monopoly. But for that very reason, the prices of the two stocks cannot be the same. The excess profit of the monopoly will result in its stock selling for twice the price of the other firm's stock. From the perspective of the person buying the stock, therefore, the rate of return will be exactly the same for the two firms. True enough, the monopoly is twice as profitable, but its stock will cost twice as much to acquire.

This observation helps us explain one of the apparent anomalies mentioned at the outset of the chapter. Recall that shares in the best-managed companies performed no better than the stock market taken as a whole. Indeed, they even performed slightly worse. We can now see that this does not mean that the best-managed companies are no more profitable than others (although this may be so). If they do have higher profits because they are better managed, and if investors already know that, then their stock prices will have been high to begin with. There is no reason to expect them to grow more rapidly than the stock prices of other firms.

THE ANOMALY OF THE INVESTMENT NEWSLETTER

I am always amused at how often I am asked to give or receive expert advice on the stock market. For example, when people at parties first learn that I am an economist, they often ask me which stocks they should buy. I tell them that if I knew the answer to that question, I wouldn't have to work for a living.

Stockbrokers who don't know that I am an economist often get my name from various mailing lists and then have their assistants call me to ask whether I would like to receive investment advice from their bosses. Here again, I am forced to decline, and certainly not because I already know which stocks will do well.

Because of their faith in the efficient markets hypothesis, most economists believe that it is generally fruitless to act on investment advice. The one important exception to this general rule occurs when the advice is based on information not available to other investors. Suppose, for example, that your brother was the Genentech researcher who came up with the miracle cure for cancer. You know that he has been working on this problem in his office in the house you share, and you can tell by the spring in his step that he has just solved it. And because you have learned this before anyone else did, you can be sure of making a lot of money by buying Genentech stock. But note that even this example does not violate the rule that substantial gains require talent, hard work, or luck. Here, it is simply your good fortune to have learned of the discovery before anyone else could act on it.

But generally the information we get about new profit opportunities is days, weeks, or even months old. It is very hard to see how information of that vintage could have any residual economic value. And yet ostensibly sophisticated investors frequently behave as if old news is worth acting upon.

One of the most puzzling examples of such behavior is the investment newsletter. Most major stock brokerages employ analysts to keep abreast of industry developments. The findings of these analysts are periodically distilled into investment newsletters that are then mailed to subscribers. Typically, subscriptions to these newsletters, which come out as infrequently as once a month, cost several hundred dollars a year. To economists, the disturbing question is why anyone would think the advice that comes in these newsletters could be worth acting on.

To illustrate the problem, consider an analyst who on June 1 discovers in his research that faulty accounting procedures have understated the profits of some company. Because investors thought the company was less profitable than in fact it was, its stock sold for too low a price. The analyst discusses this finding with his colleagues and superiors, who do some additional digging and confirm his conclusion. On June 15, the researcher writes up his findings in an article for the company's newsletter. The newsletter goes to the typesetter on June 22, and comes back for proofreading by July 6. Errors are corrected, and the printer returns the finished copies by July 20. The staff prepares the newsletters for mailing, and they are in subscribers' hands by the first of August.

During the nearly 2 months that have elapsed between the initial discovery of the information and the time it reaches subscribers, numerous people are in a position to act on it. The entire staff of the brokerage house, for example, has nearly 60 days in which to purchase shares of the undervalued stock. With the ample pools of resources into which large brokerages can tap, 60 minutes would be sufficient to capitalize fully on the discovery. Of course, many newsletters come out more frequently than once a month, but even with a daily newsletter the problem remains essentially the same. Even on the instantaneous Internet, you are unlikely to be the first upon an update; after all, someone had to write the Web page.

Why would anyone think it possible to make money from information in a newsletter? And why, therefore, would anyone part with several hundred dollars a year to buy a subscription to this kind of information? Perhaps many investors buy the newsletters not for investment advice but in order to keep themselves informed of industry developments. The buying and selling of assets in the capital markets involves transactions among real people. In the social and business gatherings that take place in the investment industry, people naturally find it advantageous to appear well informed, and the newsletters may help them achieve this goal. But it is difficult to see how anyone could make money following their investment advice.

SOUND ADVICE FOR INVESTORS

The preceding discussion may make it appear that investment advisers serve no purpose. On the contrary, there is a clear role for professional investment advice, only of a different sort than many investors hope for. The efficient markets hypothesis suggests that investment advisers will not be able to tell you how to pick stocks that do better than the market as a whole. But they can tell you how to select the kinds of stocks that best suit your investment objectives. More specifically, they can help you decide intelligently about what combination of risk and expected return best suits your purposes. If you are a young person trying to save for retirement, it will usually make sense for you to acquire a portfolio of riskier stocks with higher than average returns. They may perform poorly during some periods, but if your real concern is to obtain the highest growth over the long run, this is the best mix for you.

If, by contrast, you are a person nearing retirement, a competent adviser will probably tell you to choose stocks that are safer but have lower expected returns because in this situation your primary concern is not to obtain long-term growth but to make sure your savings are protected against a large drop in value.

When you go out in the world, you will receive calls from stockbrokers who will tell you they can help you beat the market. Politely decline their services and seek out an adviser with a more realistic sense of what can be accomplished.

Tax Policy and the Capital Market

The government's tax policy toward the income earned from investments often has strong effects on how people allocate their resources. One example is the exemption from federal income tax that applies to the interest earned by holders of municipal bonds. A municipal bond is in most respects like a corporate bond, except that it is issued by a local government, not a corporation. An investor gives the government some money—say, $10,000—and the city pays the investor a fixed rate of interest—say, 7 percent—for a specified period, often 10 years, and then returns the $10,000.

To make it easier for local governments to raise money, Congress has exempted the interest earned on municipal bonds from the federal income tax. The holder of the bond in the example would thus receive $700 of tax-free interest each year. The interest earned on federal government bonds, by contrast, is fully taxable, as is the interest on bonds issued by corporations.

Hearing about this government policy for the first time, you may wonder why anyone ever buys any kind of bond other than a municipal bond. Why buy a federal or corporate bond and pay tax on the interest? People would indeed purchase only municipal bonds if the terms they offered were in other respects the same as those of federal or corporate bonds. Naturally, however, their terms will not be the same. In particular, local governments quickly discovered that they didn't have to pay as high an interest rate as the issuers of other bonds. Thus, a 10-year Treasury bill (a common federal bond) might pay 9 percent interest, while a 10-year Iowa City bond pays only 7 percent.

Which kind of bond you should buy depends on the marginal rate at which your income is taxed. Suppose you are taxed at the 33 percent rate on any extra income you earn. A federal bond that pays $900/yr interest will leave you with only $600/yr of interest after taxes. You would do better to purchase the municipal bond with its smaller, but tax-free, interest of $700/yr. Alternatively, suppose you pay tax at the marginal rate of only 10 percent. Your after-tax earnings for the federal bond ($810) would then be higher than for the municipal bond (again, $700).

Tax policy also affects the firm's decision of whether to buy or lease its capital equipment. Under federal tax law, firms are granted a depreciation allowance for all capital equipment they own. The details of this allowance are complex, but a simple example will help make the essential point. If a firm owns a machine with, say, a 10-year life span, it is permitted to deduct 10 percent of the purchase price of the machine from its corporate profit each year in reflection of the machine's depreciation in value. By so doing, it avoids having to pay tax on that portion of its profit. This makes good economic sense because wear and tear on equipment is a legitimate operating expense for the firm. It should no more have to pay tax on such an expense than on its expenses for labor, paper, or any other input.

The depreciation allowance reduces the firm's income tax only if it has to pay income tax in the first place. If a firm experiences not a profit but a loss, or if it is a nonprofit firm, then it owes no tax to the federal government, and its depreciation allowance essentially goes unclaimed. This fact has opened up an opportunity for entrepreneurs who start companies to lease capital equipment to firms that owe little or no corporate income tax. Because the leasing company can claim the full value of the depreciation allowance, it can essentially supply capital to its clients more cheaply than they can supply it to themselves. From the point of view of society as a whole, however, there is no savings in resources. What the companies save under this arrangement, the government loses in tax revenue. Indeed, the net effect is almost certainly to reduce the total value of output, since additional resources are expended to organize the leasing companies.

Corporations expend real resources in a variety of other ways to reduce their corporate income taxes. This waste could be eliminated if the tax on corporate profits were simply eliminated. The effect would be for more income to be transferred to the shareholders of corporations, where it could be taxed at whatever rate the government saw fit.

As a final example of how tax policy influences investment behavior, let us consider the government's treatment of income earned from capital gains. A capital gain is income earned by the sale of an asset—such as a stock or a piece of real estate—that has gone up in price during the time it was held. Someone who bought stock in a company for $10,000 in 1980 and sold it for $20,000 in 1985 would experience a capital gain of $10,000 in the 1985 tax year. Until the tax reform act of 1986, income from capital gains was taxed at less than half the rate that applied to income earned from other sources.

This differential treatment created a strong incentive for firms not to pay dividends to their stockholders. If a firm paid a shareholder $1000 in dividends, for example, that income would be taxed at the same rate as ordinary income, which for a wealthy person in 1985 was approximately 50 percent. If the firm instead reinvested that $1000, causing its stock price to appreciate by a like amount, the shareholder could sell his more valuable stock for a capital gain of $1000 on which he would be taxed at the rate of only 20 percent. Proposals have been made each year since 1986 to return to the differential tax treatment of dividends and capital gains. But there would be real economic costs of restoring this incentive for firms not to pay dividends.

Economic Rent

Economic rent
The difference between what a factor of production is paid and the minimum amount necessary to induce it to remain in its current use.

In everyday usage, the term "rent" refers to the payment received by a landlord, a rental car company, or some other owner in return for the use of a real economic asset. In economic analysis, however, the term has taken on a slightly different definition. *Economic rent* is the difference between the payment actually received by the owner of a factor of production and his reservation price (the minimum amount necessary to induce him to employ it in its current use). For example, if a landlord would rather see his land lie fallow than let someone else farm it for a payment of less than $100/mo, then only $150 of the $250 monthly payment he currently gets for his land is economic rent.

If an input is supplied perfectly inelastically (that is, if its owner would supply it no matter how low the price), then the entire payment to the owner is economic rent. This situation is shown in Figure 15-3a. Suppose, however, that the owner of an input has an upward-sloping supply curve, which intersects the demand curve for the input at a price of r_1^*, as shown in Figure 15-3b. If buyers of the input could collude and make the owner a take-it-or-leave-it offer for K_1^* units of the input, the lowest amount the owner would accept is equal to the area under the supply curve up to K_1^* (the lower shaded area in panel b). But if buyers do not collude, the owner receives a price of r_1^* on each unit sold, and thus receives more than this minimum amount. His economic rent is the shaded area above the supply curve.

Economic rent is the factor market analog of producer surplus in the goods market. Producer surplus, recall, is the revenue in excess of the minimum required to call forth a given supply of output in the goods market. As with producer surplus, economic rent will be greater, other things equal, the more inelastic the supply curve of the product.

Whether the payment to a factor of production constitutes an economic rent depends in part on the vantage point from which the transaction is viewed. Consider, for example, the parcel of land on which the McGraw-Hill Companies headquarters sits. From the landowner's point of view, no portion of McGraw-Hill's monthly payment for the site is an economic rent. After all, if the company paid any less than it did for the site, the landowner could rent it for the same amount to some other company. In this sense, McGraw-Hill is not paying a penny more than necessary. But if we view the same transaction from the point of view of the economy as a whole, virtually the entire payment is an economic rent, because the owner of that land will offer it to *someone*, no matter how low the price falls.

FIGURE 15-3
(a) When an input is supplied perfectly inelastically, the entire payment it receives is an economic rent. (b) The economic rent received by an input with an upward-sloping supply curve is the shaded area above the supply curve.

ECONOMIC RENT

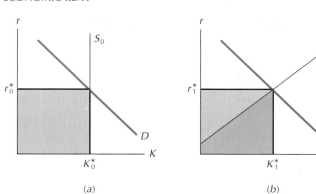

(a)   (b)

Though rent is strongly associated in the public mind with payments to the owners of capital inputs, economic rents are often of even greater importance in the labor market. Recall, in particular, our discussion of the economics of winner-take-all markets in Chapter 14. People of rare talent or ability often command exceptionally high salaries, even though, in many instances, they would be willing to perform their services for next to nothing. The multimillion-dollar salaries of top entertainers and professional athletes, for example, are for the most part economic rent, not compensation for the inconvenience of sacrificing leisure.

Peak-Load Pricing

A firm's demand for capital will depend not only on the rental rate of capital, but also on how it apportions the costs of its capital equipment among the buyers of its product. To illustrate the nature of this relationship, and at the same time to help shed light on an extremely important policy issue, let us consider the case of an electric utility whose demands differ sharply at different hours of the day. The historical pattern has been for such companies to be regulated by the state, which has instructed them to charge a single, uniform price for electricity sold at different times of the day or year. This price was generally pegged at a level sufficient to enable the company to cover its labor, equipment, fuel, and other costs, plus a normal return on its investment.

Recently, however, regulatory commissions have begun to alter this policy, implementing rate structures in which prices are directly related to the intensity of overall usage at the time of consumption. For example, a company whose loads are heaviest during business hours may be instructed to charge a higher price for electricity used between 8 A.M. and 8 P.M. than for electricity used during other hours. Such rate structures are commonly referred to as *peak-load pricing*.

Peak-load pricing The practice whereby higher prices are charged for goods or services during the periods in which they are consumed most intensively.

To illustrate the effects of peak-load pricing, consider an electric utility that uses only two inputs, generators and fuel. Suppose that customer demands for electricity in the short run vary by time of day according to the pattern shown in Figure 15-4. The demand curve during business hours is labeled "Peak demand."

FIGURE 15-4
By charging higher prices during the peak hours ($P = 12$) and lower prices during the off-peak hours ($P = 5$), utilities give their customers an incentive to shift consumption onto off-peak hours. The resulting fall in peak-period usage enables the utility to serve its customers with a significantly smaller stock of generating equipment.

THE EFFECT OF PEAK-LOAD PRICING

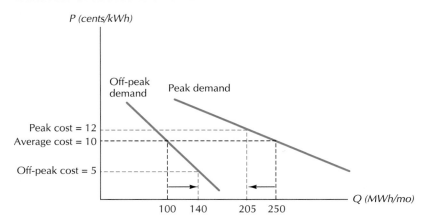

The demand curve during the rest of the day is labeled "Off-peak demand." Suppose the company initially sells all its power at the same rate, 10 cents/kWh, and that its revenues at that rate exactly cover all its costs. Note in the diagram that when all power sells for 10 cents/kWh, peak demand is 250 MWh/mo.

If the average cost of production is 10 cents/kWh, we know that the marginal cost of serving off-peak users must be less than 10 cents/kWh, while the marginal cost of serving peak users must be more. This follows because we can serve an extra off-peak user without having to add any more generating equipment, whereas we must add new generators to serve additional peak users. The only cost of serving an off-peak user will be the extra fuel required to run some of the generating capacity that would otherwise be idle during that period. Suppose this off-peak marginal cost is 5 cents/kWh. The extra cost during the peak period will include not only the cost of fuel, but also the cost of the required extra capital. For purposes of illustration, suppose that these peak-period costs add to 12 cents/kWh.

And suppose, finally, that the utility charges 12 cents/kWh to peak-period users and only 5 cents/kWh to off-peak users. Note in Figure 15-4 that the effect is to reduce peak-period consumption by 45 MWh/mo, most of which shifts to the off-peak period. The shift is achieved in a variety of ways. For example, people may buy timers that operate water heaters, air conditioners, and space heaters only during off-peak hours. Similarly, they may avoid using dishwashers, washing machines, and clothes dryers during the peak period. The net result of such consumption shifts is that a utility can serve its customers with much smaller generating capacity. The resulting cost savings represent a real increase in customer living standards.

Peak-load pricing is by no means limited to the electric utility industry. Airlines employ peak-load pricing, canceling some or all of their discount seats during heavy travel periods. Many ski areas have higher lift prices on major holiday weekends. Seasonal price differences are a common practice among resort hotels. And as noted in Chapter 12, many movie theaters charge lower prices during the dinner hour. Experience with these pricing practices tells us that when capital costs are assigned to the users responsible for their incurrence, the overall level of capital required can be reduced significantly.

Summary

Our task in this chapter was to examine the market for services of capital inputs. Many of the results from our study of labor inputs apply to capital as well. Thus, for example, a firm's demand for the services of a capital input is the marginal revenue product of that input—which, in the case of the perfectly competitive firm, is the same as the value of capital's marginal product.

One feature that often sets capital apart from other inputs is that while other inputs are usually hired on a period-by-period basis, capital equipment is often owned outright by the firm. In considering whether to purchase a machine, the firm must ask how much its output will increase not only in the current period, but also in future periods. The firm's decision rule is to acquire the machine if and only if the present value of the current and future increases in revenue made possible by the machine exceeds its purchase price. This rule illustrates the factors that determine the rental rate of capital. These include the interest rate, or opportunity cost, of borrowed funds, the rates of physical and technological depreciation, and expected future movements in the price of the capital.

• The real rate of interest measures interest in terms of equivalent quantities of real goods or services. If, for example, a bank lends 100 oz of gold and requires a repayment of 105 oz after 1 yr, the real interest rate would be 5 percent. When the rate of inflation is small, the nominal rate of interest is approximately equal to the real rate of interest plus the rate of inflation. This relationship helps make clear why the interest rates charged by banks and other lenders tend to rise hand in hand with the overall rate of inflation.

A firm's demand for borrowed money depends on how the amount of capital equipment it would like to have compares with the amount it actually does have. The supply of loanable funds is highly responsive to interest rates because of the importance of foreign lenders in this market. The market interest rate and equilibrium level of borrowing are determined by the intersection of the supply and demand curves for loanable funds.

The market for stocks and bonds is one of the principal sources of funds to finance new capital equipment. A corporate bond is essentially a loan from the purchaser of the bond to the corporation. As a bond nears maturity, its price must converge to its face value. But for bonds that are far from maturity, there will be a significant inverse relationship between current interest rates and the price of the bond. The price of a given stock is the present value, suitably discounted for risk, of the current and future profits to which it provides claim.

The "efficient markets hypothesis" says that, holding risk constant, all available information about current and future earnings of a firm is immediately incorporated into the price of its stock. The implication is that an investor should do equally well no matter which stocks he or she purchases. The efficient markets hypothesis thus helps explain why the investment tips of "experts" are of little or no value.

Tax policy has numerous effects on capital market decisions. The fact that municipal bonds are tax-free helps explain why their interest rates are generally lower than for bonds with taxable interest. Tax policy also sometimes induces firms to lease, rather than buy, their capital equipment. And tax policy in the past provided an incentive for firms to reinvest their profits, rather than pay them directly to shareholders as dividends.

The term "rent" as used by economists has a somewhat different meaning from the one familiar from everyday usage. It is the payment to a factor of production in excess of the minimum value required to keep that factor in its current use. A significant share of the payments received by owners of capital constitutes economic rent under this definition. Rents often constitute a large share of incomes generated in the labor market as well.

In peak-load pricing schemes, firms and regulatory agencies must decide how much to charge for the use of capital equipment when the intensity of demand varies greatly. As ever, the rule for efficient allocation is to set prices on the basis of marginal cost. Peak-load pricing enables firms to serve their markets while using significantly smaller amounts of capital equipment.

An appendix to this chapter (see the "For the Instructor" section at our Web site www.mhhe.com/economics/frank4), discusses the use of natural resources, both renewable and exhaustible, as inputs in production.

Questions for Review

1. What is the difference between real capital and financial capital? Why does concern with one type of capital invariably involve concern with the other?

2. Explain why depreciation is an economic cost just like any other.

3. Why do higher interest rates make future events economically less important?

4. Why do nominal interest rates rise approximately 1-for-1 with increases in inflation?

5. Why are bond prices and interest rates inversely related?

6. Why is published investment advice unlikely to be worth very much?

7. Give three examples of peak-load pricing used in your community.

8. Who will typically achieve a higher expected return on their investments: young investors or older investors with more immediate need for retirement income?

Problems

1. You are deciding which of two computers to purchase. The interest rate is 0.09 and the maintenance rate of both machines is 0.01. The first computer costs $4000 and has a

rate of physical and technological depreciation of 0.10. The second computer, on the verge of obsolescence, has a rate of physical and technological depreciation of 0.30. If the annual rental rate for the two computers is the same, how much must the purchase price of the second computer be?

2. A machine that costs 100 will yield returns of 30 at the end of each of the next 3 years, at which time it will be sold as scrap for 30. If the interest rate facing this firm is 10 percent, should it purchase this machine?

3. Suppose a perpetual bond pays $3000/yr to its owner. What is the price of the bond at 5 percent interest? At 6 percent?

4. If everyone's marginal tax rate is 50 percent and if the interest rate on taxable government bonds is 8 percent, what will be the interest rate on nontaxable government bonds?

5. If the interest rate on taxable government consols is 10 percent, what will happen to the price of an existing tax-exempt government consol if the government reduces everyone's marginal tax rate from 50 to 30 percent?

6. Suppose a majority of investors do not care whether the companies whose stock they own do business in South Africa. How, if at all, will the rate of return on stocks that do business in South Africa differ from the rate of return on stocks that do not?

7. Tony's barbershop has four chairs and four barbers. Most of the time at least one barber is idle, except on Saturday mornings when all four are continuously booked. Explain, in terms a noneconomist could understand, why the cost of providing a haircut on Saturday morning is higher than at other times of the week.

8. Around 1890 the vineyards in Bordeaux were infected by Phylloxera, a louse that attacks the vine's roots. To preserve the original grape varieties, the Bordeaux vines were grafted onto roots taken from American grape plants. Since 1890 all Bordeaux wines have been made with vines grafted onto American roots. These wines do not taste the same as the wines made before the Phylloxera infection. A bottle of Bordeaux wine that was made before the infection sells for thousands of dollars. Suppose you had a bottle of pre-Phylloxera Bordeaux that you could sell today for $2000 and you were interested only in its value as an investment. To make it worthwhile for you to hold on to your investment, what must be the expected price of the bottle in n years if the market rate of interest is i?

Answers to In-Chapter Exercises

15-1. Since $r = i + m + \partial$, we have $r = 0.08 + 0.02 + 0.10 = 0.20$. So the annual rental payment will be $r(\$5000) = \$1000$.

15-2. $PV = (121/1.1) + (121/1.1^2) + (242/1.1^2) = 110 + 100 + 200 = \$410$.

15-3. The price at 10 percent is $\$120/0.10 = \$1200$. At 5 percent the price will be $\$120/0.05 = \$2400$, so the rise in price is $\$1200$.

15-4. $(\Delta B/\Delta t)/B = (40/\sqrt{t})/80\sqrt{t} = 1/2t = 0.02$, which solves for $t = 25$ years.

PART FIVE

General Equilibrium and Welfare

This part of the text examines in greater detail the conditions under which unregulated markets tend to produce efficient outcomes. Chapter 16 uses the theory of consumer and firm behavior to help identify these conditions and also offers an assessment of when these conditions are not likely to be satisfied in practice. Chapter 17 examines the role of a well-defined system of property rights in the functioning of markets and the consequences of externalities, both positive and negative. Chapter 18 concludes by examining what microeconomic theory tells us about the role of government.

CHAPTER 16

General Equilibrium and Market Efficiency

General equilibrium analysis The study of how conditions in each market in a set of related markets affect equilibrium outcomes in other markets in that set.

*B*arbers earn more today than they did 50 years ago, not because they cut hair any faster than they did then but because productivity has grown so rapidly in the other occupations they could have chosen. By the same token, computer paper now sells in much greater quantities, not because we have discovered a cheaper way to produce it but because so many more people now own their own computers. And we know that when a frost kills half the coffee crop in Brazil, the price of tea grown in Darjeeling usually rises substantially.

In the preceding chapters we saw occasional glimpses of the rich linkages between markets in the real world. But for the most part, we ignored these linkages in favor of what economists call *partial equilibrium analysis*—the study of how individual markets function in isolation. One of our tasks in this chapter is to investigate the properties of an interconnected system of markets. This is called *general equilibrium analysis,* and its focus is to make explicit the links that exist between individual markets. It takes into account, for example, the fact that inputs supplied to one market are unavailable for any other and that an increase in demand in one market implies a reduction in demand in others.

Chapter Preview

We begin with one of the simplest possible general equilibrium models, a pure exchange economy with only two consumers and two goods. We will see that for any given initial allocation of the two goods between the two consumers, a competitive exchange process will always exhaust all possible mutually beneficial gains from trade.

Next we add the possibility of production, again using one of the simplest possible models, one with only two inputs whose total supply is fixed. We will see that here too competitive trading exploits all mutually beneficial gains from exchange.

We then add the possibility of international trade, assuming that prices are given externally in world markets. We will see that even though trade leaves domestic production possibilities unchanged, its immediate effect is to increase the value of goods available for domestic consumption.

From trade, we move to the question of how taxes affect the allocation of resources. We conclude with a brief discussion of factors that interfere with the efficient allocation of resources.

A Simple Exchange Economy

Imagine a simple economy in which there are only two consumers—Ann and Bill—and two goods, food and clothing. Food and clothing are not produced in this economy. Rather, they arrive in fixed quantities in each time period, just like manna from heaven. To help fix ideas, suppose there is a total of 100 units of food each time period and a total of 200 units of clothing. An *allocation* is defined as an assignment of these total amounts between Ann and Bill. An example is the allocation in which Ann receives 70 units of clothing and 75 units of food, with the remaining 130 units of clothing and 25 units of food going to Bill. In general, if Ann receives F_A units of food and C_A units of clothing, then Bill will get $100 - F_A$ units of food and $200 - C_A$ units of clothing. The amounts of the two goods with which Ann and Bill begin each time period are called their *initial endowments*.

In the next section we'll have more to say about where these initial endowments come from, but for now let's take them as externally determined. The question before us here is "What will Ann and Bill do with their initial endowments?" One possibility is that they might simply consume them, but only in rare circumstances will that be the best option available. To see why, it is helpful to begin by portraying the initial endowments diagrammatically. Consider again the case in which Ann receives 70 units of clothing and 75 units of food, with the remaining 130 units of clothing and 25 units of food going to Bill. From earlier chapters, we know how to represent these initial endowments as bundles in two separate food-clothing diagrams. The same allocation can also be represented as a point in a single rectangular diagram—namely, point R in Figure 16-1.

FIGURE 16-1

A's quantity of food at any point is measured by how far the point lies above O^A. A's clothing is measured by how far the point lies to the right of O^A. B's clothing is measured leftward from O^B, and his food downward from O^B. At any point within the Edgeworth box, the individual quantities of food and clothing sum to the total amounts available.

AN EDGEWORTH EXCHANGE BOX

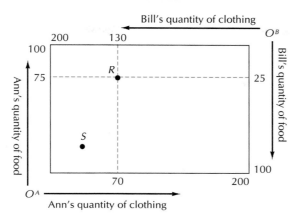

The height of the rectangle corresponds to the total amount of food available per time period, 100 units. Its width is equal to the total amount of clothing, 200 units. O^A is the origin for Ann, and the left and bottom sides of the rectangle are the axes that measure her quantities of food and clothing, respectively. O^B is the origin for Bill, and movements to the left from O^B correspond to increases in his amount of clothing. Downward movements from O^B correspond to increases in Bill's amount of food.

Because of the special way the rectangle is constructed, every point that lies within it corresponds to an allocation that exactly exhausts the total quantities of food and clothing available. Thus, point R is 70 units to the right of O^A and 130 units to the left of O^B, which means 70 units of clothing for Ann and 130 units for Bill, for a total of 200. R also lies 75 units above O^A and 25 units below O^B, which means 75 units of food for Ann and 25 for Bill, for a total of 100. The rectangular diagram in Figure 16-1 is often referred to as an *Edgeworth exchange box*, after the British economist Francis Y. Edgeworth, who introduced it.

Edgeworth exchange box A diagram used to analyze the general equilibrium of an exchange economy.

EXERCISE 16-1

Suppose point S in Figure 16-1 lies 25 units above O^A and 25 units to the right of O^A. Verify that Bill's initial endowment at S is 75 units of food and 175 units of clothing.

If Ann and Bill have the initial endowments represented by R, what will they do with them? Their possibilities are either to consume what they already have or to engage in exchange with one another. Exchange is purely voluntary, so trades can take place only if they make both parties better off.

Our criterion for saying an exchange makes someone better off is very simple: It must place him on a higher indifference curve. In the Edgeworth box in Figure 16-2, Ann's indifference map has the conventional orientation, while Bill's is rotated 180°. Thus the curves labeled I_{A1}, I_{A2}, and I_{A3} are representative curves from Ann's indifference map, while I_{B1}, I_{B2}, and I_{B3} play the corresponding role for Bill. Ann's satisfaction increases as we move to the northeast in the box; Bill's as we move to the southwest.

Because we assume that preference orderings are complete, we know that each party will have an indifference curve passing through the initial endowment point R. In Figure 16-2 these curves are labeled I_{A2} and I_{B2}. Note that Ann's MRS between food and clothing at R (that is, the slope of her indifference curve) is much larger than Bill's (where the MRS for Bill is measured with respect to his own food and clothing axes). Suppose, for example, that Ann requires 2 units of food in order to be willing to part with a unit of clothing, while Bill requires only $\frac{1}{2}$ unit of food to make the same exchange. Both parties will then be better off if Ann gives Bill a unit of food in exchange for a unit of clothing. Indeed, any point in the lens-shaped shaded region in Figure 16-2 is one for which each party lies on a higher indifference curve than at R. Point T, at which Ann has 65 units of food and 85 units of clothing, is one such point. The two parties can move from R to T by having Ann give Bill 10 units of food in exchange for 15 units of clothing.

But the movement from R to T does not exhaust all possible gains from exchange. Note in Figure 16-3 that there is an additional, albeit smaller, lens-shaped region enclosed by the indifference curves that pass through T by both parties.

Through a process of repeated exchange, Ann and Bill will finally reach a

FIGURE 16-2
By moving from R to T, each party attains a higher indifference curve.

GAINS FROM EXCHANGE

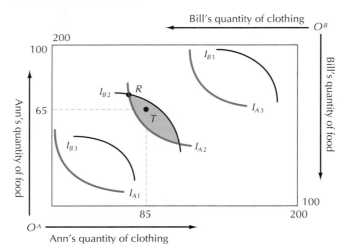

FIGURE 16-3
Any point in the
shaded region lies
on a higher indiffer-
ence curve for both
parties than the ones
that pass through *T*.

FURTHER GAINS FROM EXCHANGE

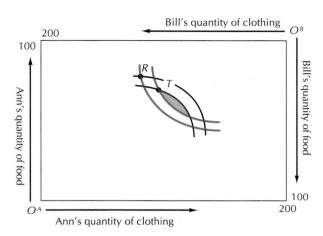

point at which further mutual gains from trade are no longer possible. The indifference curves for the two parties that pass through any such point will necessarily be tangent to one another, as at point *M* in Figure 16-4. (If they were not
tangent, they would necessarily enclose yet another lens-shaped region in which
further gains from exchange would be possible.) Note that at *M* the marginal
rates of substitution of Ann and Bill are exactly the same. It was a difference in
these rates that provided the original basis for exchange, and once they are the
same, all voluntary trading will cease.

FIGURE 16-4
At the allocation *M*,
no further mutually
beneficial exchange
is possible. The mar-
ginal rate of substi-
tution of food for
clothing is the same
for both parties at
M.

A PARETO-OPTIMAL ALLOCATION

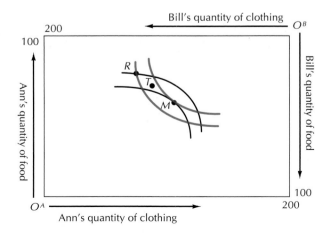

Pareto superior allocation
An allocation that at least one individual prefers and others like at least as well.

Pareto optimal
The term used to describe situations in which it is impossible to make one person better off without making at least some others worse off.

One allocation is said to be *Pareto preferred* or **Pareto superior** to another if at least one party prefers it and the other party likes it at least as well. Allocations like the one at *M* are called **Pareto optimal.** A Pareto-optimal allocation is one for which there is no other feasible reallocation that is preferred by one party and liked at least equally well by the other party. The concept of Pareto optimality was introduced by the nineteenth-century Italian economist Vilfredo Pareto. Pareto-optimal allocations are essentially ones from which further mutually beneficial moves are impossible.

*E*XERCISE 16-2

> Suppose Ann has an initial allocation of 50 units of food and 100 units of clothing in Figure 16-3. She regards food and clothing as perfect, 1-for-1 substitutes. Bill regards them as perfect, 1-for-1 complements, always wanting to consume 1 unit of clothing for every unit of food. Describe the set of allocations that are Pareto preferred to the initial allocation.

Contract curve
A curve along which all final, voluntary contracts must lie.

In any Edgeworth exchange box, there will be not one but an infinite number of mutual tangencies, as illustrated in Figure 16-5. The locus of these tangencies is called the **contract curve**, a name that was chosen because it describes where all final, voluntary contracts between rational, well-informed persons must lie. Put another way, the contract curve identifies all the efficient ways of dividing the two goods between the two consumers.

Where Ann and Bill end up on the contract curve naturally depends on the initial endowments with which they start. Suppose they start with the one labeled *F* in Figure 16-6. We can then say that they will end up somewhere on

FIGURE 16-5
The locus of mutual tangencies in the Edgeworth exchange box is called the contract curve. Any point that does not lie on the contract curve cannot be the final outcome of a voluntary exchange because both parties will always prefer a move from that point in the direction of the contract curve.

THE CONTRACT CURVE

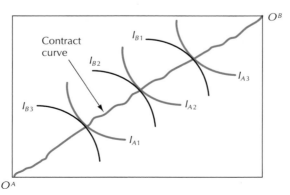

the contract curve between points *U* and *V*. Given that they are starting from *F*, the best possible outcome from Ann's point of view is to end up at *V*. Bill, of course, would most prefer *U*. Whether they end up closer to *U* or to *V* depends on the relative bargaining skills of the two traders. Had they instead started at the allocation *G*, they would have ended up between *W* and *Z* on the contract curve.

The uses and limitations of the two Pareto criteria—Pareto preferred and Pareto optimal—can be seen by an examination of some of the points in Figure 16-6. Note, for example, that both *W* and *Z* are Pareto preferred to the original allocation *G*. This follows because *W* is better than *G* from Bill's point of view and no worse from Ann's; and similarly, *Z* is better from Ann's point of view and no worse from Bill's. Note that both points are also Pareto optimal. The two Pareto criteria are essentially relative in nature. Thus, when we say that *U* is Pareto preferred to *F*, or even when we say that *U* is Pareto optimal, we are not saying that *U* is good in any absolute sense. On the contrary, Ann is hardly likely to find *U* very attractive, and it is certainly much worse, from her standpoint, than an allocation like *G*, which is neither Pareto optimal nor even Pareto preferred to *U*. If Ann is starving to death in a tattered coat at *U*, she will not take much comfort in being told that *U* is Pareto optimal.

The Pareto criteria thus have force only in relation to the allocation with which the two players begin. Rather than remain at an initial allocation, both will always agree to move to one that is Pareto preferred and, indeed, to keep on moving until they reach one that is Pareto optimal.

In the simple, two-person economy described above, exchange took place through a process of personal bargaining. In market economies, by contrast, most exchanges have a much more impersonal character. People have given endowments and face given prices, and then decide how much of the various goods and services they want to buy and sell. We can introduce market-type exchange into our simple economy by the simple expedient of assuming that there is a third person

FIGURE 16-6
Starting from *F*, traders will move to a point on the contract curve between *U* and *V*. They will land closer to *V* the better Ann's bargaining skills are relative to Bill's. If they start at *G*, they will end up between *W* and *Z* on the contract curve.

INITIAL ENDOWMENTS CONSTRAIN FINAL OUTCOMES

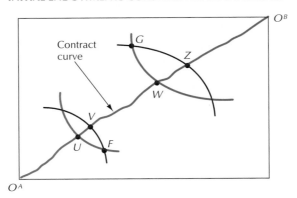

who plays the role of an auctioneer. His function is to keep adjusting relative prices until the quantities demanded of each good match the quantities supplied.

Suppose Ann and Bill start with the allocation at E in Figure 16-7, in which each has 50 units of food and 100 units of clothing. Suppose also that the ratio of food to clothing prices announced by the auctioneer is $P_{C0}/P_{F0} = 1$, meaning that food and clothing both sell for the same price. When the prices of the two goods are the same, the auctioneer stands ready to exchange 1 unit of clothing for 1 unit of food. (More generally, he will exchange clothing for food at the rate of P_{C0}/P_{F0} units of food for each unit of clothing.) Note that with the given initial endowments, this rate of exchange uniquely determines the budget constraints for both Ann and Bill. We know that E has to be a point on each person's budget constraint because each has the option of simply consuming all of his or her initial endowment. But suppose that Ann wants to sell some food and use the proceeds to buy more clothing. She can do this by moving downward from E along the line labeled HH'. Alternatively, if she wants to sell clothing to buy more food, she can move upward along HH'. The same HH', seen from Bill's point of view, constitutes the budget constraint for Bill.

Given their budget constraints and preferences, Ann and Bill face a simple choice problem of the sort we discussed in Chapter 3. The optimal bundle for Ann on the budget HH' is the one labeled A_0^* in Figure 16-7, in which she consumes 30 units of food and 120 units of clothing. The corresponding bundle for Bill is labeled B_0^*, and it too contains 30 units of food and 120 units of clothing. Note that by choosing A_0^*, Ann indicates that she wants to sell 20 units of her initial endowment of food in order to buy 20 units of additional clothing. Simi-

FIGURE 16-7
At the price ratio $P_{C0}/P_{F0} = 1$, both Ann and Bill want to sell 20 units of food and buy 20 more units of clothing. But in general equilibrium, the amount sold by one party must equal the amount bought by the other. Both the food and clothing markets are out of equilibrium here.

A DISEQUILIBRIUM RELATIVE PRICE RATIO

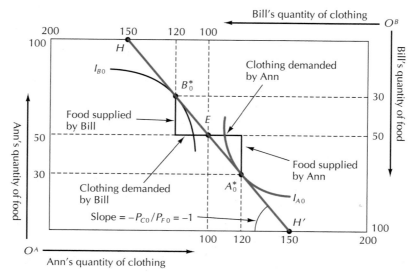

larly, by choosing B_0^*, Bill indicates that he too wants to sell 20 units of food and buy 20 more units of clothing.

This creates a problem, however. There are only 200 units of clothing to begin with, and the initial endowments of clothing at E add to precisely that amount. It is thus mathematically impossible for each person to have more clothing. By the same token, it is not possible for each person to sell food. The auctioneer in this exercise is a figment, a hypothetical person who calls out relative prices in the hope of stimulating mutually beneficial exchange. He acts as a middleman, arranging for clothing to be exchanged for an equivalent value of food. But if *everyone* wants to sell food and buy clothing, there is no such exchange he can arrange.

At the price ratio $P_{C0}/P_{F0} = 1$, there is excess demand for clothing and excess supply of food. At this price ratio the markets are not in general equilibrium. The solution to this problem is straightforward: The auctioneer simply calls out a new price ratio in which the price of clothing relative to food is higher than before. If there is still excess demand for clothing, he calls out a still higher price ratio, and so on, until the excess demand in each market is exactly zero.[1] Starting with the allocation at E, the price ratio $(P_C/P_F)^*$ that produces general equilibrium is shown in Figure 16-8. On the budget line through E with slope $(P_C/P_F)^*$, the highest attainable indifference curves for Ann and Bill are tangent. In order to move from E to the bundle A^*, Ann must purchase exactly the quantity of food (12 units) that Bill wishes to sell. And for Bill to move from E to the bundle B^*, he must purchase exactly the quantity of clothing (10 units) that Ann wishes to sell. In this illustration, excess demands for both products are exactly equal to zero at the price ratio $(P_C/P_F)^* = \frac{6}{5}$.

ONLY RELATIVE PRICES ARE DETERMINED

From the information given in our simple exchange model, note that we are able to determine only the *ratio* of clothing to food prices, not the actual value of individual prices. If, for example, $P_C = 6$ and $P_F = 5$ produce a budget constraint with the slope shown in Figure 16-8, then so will the prices $P_C = 12$ and $P_F = 10$, or indeed any other pair of prices whose ratio is $\frac{6}{5}$. Doubling or halving all prices will double or halve the dollar value of each consumer's initial endowment. In real terms, such price movements leave budget constraints unchanged.

THE INVISIBLE HAND THEOREM

We are now in a position to consider one of the most celebrated claims in intellectual history, namely, Adam Smith's *theorem of the invisible hand*. In the context of our simple exchange economy, the theorem can be stated as follows:

> An equilibrium produced by competitive markets will exhaust all possible gains from exchange.

---

[1]In advanced courses, we show that a competitive equilibrium will exist in a simple exchange economy if the sum of all individual excess demands is a continuous function of relative prices. This will always happen whenever individual indifference curves have the conventional convex shape.

FIGURE 16-8

A simple exchange economy is in equilibrium when excess demands for both products are exactly equal to zero. At the price ratio $(P_C/P_F)^* = \frac{6}{5}$, Ann wants to buy 12 units of food, which is exactly the amount Bill wants to sell; also, Ann wants to sell 10 units of clothing, which is exactly the amount Bill wants to buy.

GENERAL EQUILIBRIUM

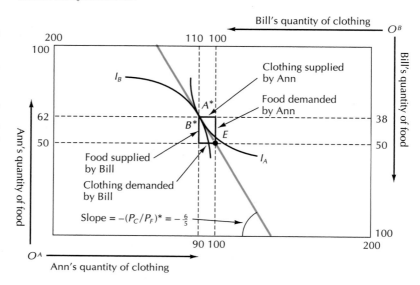

The invisible hand theorem is also known as the *first theorem of welfare economics,* and an alternative way of stating it is that *equilibrium in competitive markets is Pareto optimal.* To see why this must be so, recall that at the general equilibrium allocation, the optimizing indifference curves are tangent to one another. The possible allocations that Ann regards as better than the equilibrium allocation all lie beyond her budget constraint, and the same is true for Bill. And since the two budget constraints coincide in the Edgeworth box, this means that there is no allocation that both prefer to the equilibrium allocation, which is just another way of saying that the equilibrium allocation is Pareto optimal.

The invisible hand theorem tells us that every competitive equilibrium allocation—like D in Figure 16-9—is efficient. But suppose you are a social critic and don't like that particular allocation; you feel that Bill gets too much of each good and Ann too little. The problem, in your view, was that the initial endowment point—*J* in the diagram—is unjustly favorable to Bill. Suppose there is some other allocation on the contract curve—such as E—that you find much more equitable. Is there a set of initial endowments and relative prices for which E will be a competitive equilibrium? The *second theorem of welfare economics* says that, under relatively unrestrictive conditions:

Any allocation on the contract curve can be sustained as a competitive equilibrium.

The basic condition that assures this result is that consumer indifference curves be convex when viewed from the origin. We know that an allocation like

FIGURE 16-9
If indifference curves are convex, any efficient allocation can be sustained through a suitable choice of initial endowments and relative prices. To sustain *E*, for example, we announce a relative price ratio equal to the slope of *HH'*, the mutual tangent to *I*$_{A2}$ and *I*$_{B2}$, and give consumers an initial endowment bundle that lies anywhere on *HH'*, such as *M*.

SUSTAINING EFFICIENT ALLOCATIONS

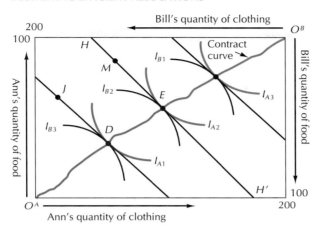

E, or any other efficient allocation, lies at a point of tangency between indifference curves. In Figure 16-9, the locus *HH'* is the mutual tangent between *I*$_{A2}$ and *I*$_{B2}$. If the difference curves are convex, any initial endowment along *HH'*—such as *M*—will lead to a competitive equilibrium at *E*. If we redistribute the initial endowments from *J* to *M*, and announce a price ratio equal to the slope of *HH'*, Ann and Bill will then be led by the invisible hand to *E*. Indeed, any point along the contract curve can be reached in this fashion by a suitable choice of initial endowments and relative prices.

In the context of this simple, two-good, two-person exchange economy, it may not seem like a major accomplishment to be able to sustain all efficient allocations in the manner described by the second welfare theorem. After all, if we are free to redistribute initial endowments, why not simply redistribute them so as to achieve the desired final outcome directly? Why even bother with the intermediate steps of announcing prices and allowing people to make trades? If we are free to move from *J* to *M* in Figure 16-9, then we ought to be able to move directly to *E* and cut out the intervening steps.

The difficulty in practice is that the social institutions responsible for redistributing income have little idea of the shapes and locations of individual consumer indifference curves. People know their own preferences much better than governments do. And for an initial endowment of given value, they will generally achieve a much better result if they are free to make their own purchase decisions. *The significance of the second welfare theorem is that the issue of equity in distribution is logically separable from the issue of efficiency in allocation.* As the nineteenth-century British economist John Stuart Mill saw clearly, society can redistribute incomes in accordance with whatever norms of justice it deems fitting, at the same time relying on market forces to assure that those incomes are spent to achieve the most good.

Efficiency in Production

In our simple exchange model, the total supply of each good was given externally. In practice, however, the product mix in the economy is the result of purposeful decisions about the allocation of productive inputs. Suppose we now add a productive sector to our exchange economy, one with two firms, each of which employs two inputs—capital (K) and labor (L)—to produce either of two products, food (F) or clothing (C). Suppose firm C produces clothing and firm F produces food. In order to keep the model simple, suppose that the total quantities of the two inputs are fixed at $K = 50$ and $L = 100$, respectively. Suppose, finally, that the production processes employed by the two firms give rise to conventional, convex-shaped isoquants.

Just as the Edgeworth exchange box provided a convenient way to summarize the conditions required for efficiency in consumption, a similar analysis serves an analogous purpose in the case of production. Figure 16-10 is called an *Edgeworth production box*. O^C represents the origin of the clothing firm's isoquant map, O^F the origin of the food firm's. Any point within the box represents an allocation of the total inputs to firm C and firm F. Firm C's isoquants correspond to increasing quantities of clothing as we move to the northeast in the box; firm F's correspond to increasing quantities of food as we move to the southwest.

Suppose the initial allocation of inputs is at point R in Figure 16-10. We know that this allocation cannot be efficient because we can move to any point within the shaded lens-shaped region and obtain both more food and more clothing. As in the consumption case, the contract curve is the locus of efficient allocations, which here is the locus of tangencies between isoquants. Recalling from Chapter 9 that the slope of an isoquant at any point is called the marginal rate of technical substitution (MRTS) at that point, it is the ratio at which labor can be exchanged for capital without altering the total amount of output. Note that the MRTS between K and L must be the same for both firms at every point along the contract curve.

Suppose the equilibrium food and clothing prices are P_F^* and P_C^*, respectively. Suppose also that the two firms hire labor and capital in perfectly competitive markets at the hourly rates of w and r, respectively. If the firms maximize their profits, is there any reason to suppose that the resulting general equilibrium will satisfy the requirements of efficiency in production? That is, is there any reason to suppose that the MRTS between capital and labor will be the same for each firm? If both firms have conventional, convex-shaped isoquants, the answer is yes.

To see why, first note that a firm that maximizes its profits must also be minimizing its costs. Recall from Chapter 10 that the following conditions must be satisfied if the firms are minimizing costs:

FIGURE 16-10 Firm *C*'s quantity of capital at any point is measured by how far the point lies above O^C. Firm *C*'s quantity of labor is measured by how far the point lies to the right of O^C. The corresponding values of firm *F*'s inputs are measured downward and leftward, respectively, from O^F. At any point within the Edgeworth production box, the separate input allocations to the two firms add up to the total amounts available, $K = 50$ for capital, $L = 100$ for labor. The contract curve is the locus of tangencies between isoquants.

AN EDGEWORTH PRODUCTION BOX

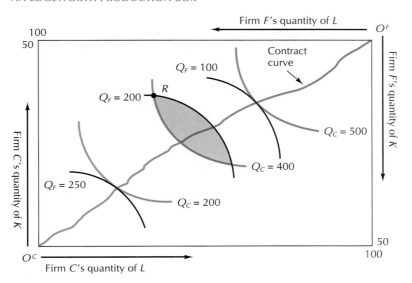

where MPL_C and MPK_C are the marginal products of labor and capital in clothing production and MPL_F and MPK_F are the corresponding marginal products in food production. Recall, too, that the ratio of marginal products of the two inputs is equal to the marginal rate of technical substitution. Since both firms pay the same prices for labor and capital, Equations 16.1 and 16.2 tell us that the marginal rates of technical substitution for the two firms will be equal in competitive equilibrium. And this tells us, finally, that competitive general equilibrium is efficient, not only in the allocation of a given endowment of consumption goods, but also in the allocation of the factors used to produce those goods.

$$\frac{MPL_C}{MPK_C} = \frac{w}{r} \qquad (16.1)$$

and

$$\frac{MPL_F}{MPK_F} = \frac{w}{r}, \qquad (16.2)$$

EXERCISE 16-3

For an economy like the one described above, suppose the price per unit of labor and the price per unit of capital are both equal to \$4/hr. Suppose also that in clothing production we have $\text{MPL}_C/\text{MPK}_C = 2$ and that in food production we have $\text{MPL}_F/\text{MPK}_F = \frac{1}{2}$. Is this economy efficient in production? If not, how should it reallocate its inputs?

Efficiency in Product Mix

Production possibilities frontier The set of all possible output combinations that can be produced with a given endowment of factor inputs.

An economy could be efficient in production and at the same time efficient in consumption and yet do a poor job of satisfying the wants of its members. This could happen if, for example, the economy for some reason devoted almost all its resources to producing clothing, almost none to food. The tiny quantity of food that resulted could be allocated efficiently. And the inputs could be allocated efficiently in the production of this lopsided product mix. But everyone would be happier if there were less clothing and more food. There is thus one additional efficiency criterion of concern, namely, whether the economy has an efficient mix of the two products.

To define an efficient product mix, it is helpful first to translate the contract curve from the Edgeworth production box into a ***production possibilities frontier***, the set of all possible output combinations that can be produced with given quantities of capital and labor. Every point along the contract curve gives rise to specific quantities of clothing and food. Suppose $F_C(K, L)$ and $F_F(K, L)$ denote the production functions for clothing (firm C) and food (firm F), respectively. Point O^C in the top panel in Figure 16-11 represents what happens when we allocate all the inputs (50 units of capital, 100 units of labor) to food production and none to clothing. If $F_F(50, 100) = 275$, then the product mix to which this allocation gives rise has zero units of clothing and 275 units of food, and is shown by point O^C in the bottom panel. Point O^F in the top panel in Figure 16-11 represents what happens when we allocate all the inputs to clothing production and none to food. If $F_C(50, 100) = 575$, then the product mix to which this allocation gives rise has 575 units of clothing and zero units of food, and is shown by point O^F in the bottom panel. The product mix corresponding to point E in the top panel has $F_C(14, 30) = 200$ units of clothing and $F_F(36, 70) = 250$ units of food, and is shown by point E in the bottom panel. Similarly, the product mix at F in the top panel has $F_C(22, 53) = 400$ units of clothing and $F_F(28, 47) = 200$ units of food, and corresponds to F in the bottom panel. Likewise, G in the top panel has $F_C(38, 76) = 500$ units of clothing and $F_F(12, 24) = 100$ units of food, and corresponds to G in the bottom panel. By plotting other correspondences in like fashion, we can generate the entire production possibilities frontier shown in the bottom panel.

FIGURE 16-11
Each point on the contract curve in the Edgeworth production box (top panel) gives rise to specific quantities of food and clothing production. The food-clothing pairs that lie along the contract curve are plotted in the bottom panel, and their locus is called the production possibilities frontier. Movements to the northeast along the contract curve correspond to movements downward along the production possibilities frontier.

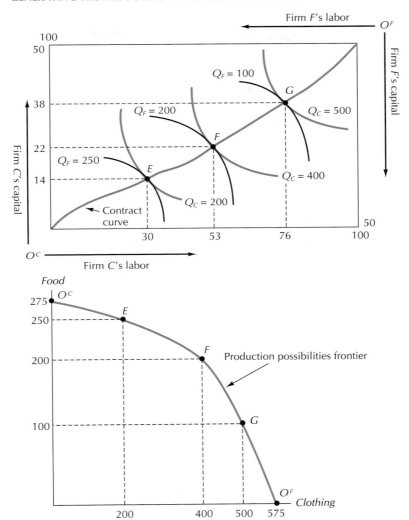

GENERATING THE PRODUCTION POSSIBILITIES FRONTIER

*E*XERCISE 16-4

In the economy shown in Figure 16-11, suppose that a technical change occurs in the clothing industry that makes any given combination of labor and capital yield twice as much clothing as before. Show the effect of this change on the production possibilities frontier.

Marginal rate of transformation (MRT) The rate at which one output can be exchanged for another at a point along the production possibilities frontier.

As we move downward along the production possibilities frontier, we give up food for additional clothing. The slope of the production possibilities frontier at any point is called the *marginal rate of transformation* (MRT) at that point, and it measures the opportunity cost of clothing in terms of food. For the economy shown, the production possibilities frontier bows out from the origin, which means that the MRT increases as we move to the right. As long as both production functions have constant or decreasing returns to scale, the production possibilities frontier cannot bow in toward the origin.

In order for an economy to be efficient in terms of its product mix, it is necessary that the marginal rate of substitution for every consumer be equal to the marginal rate of transformation. To see why, consider a product mix for which some consumer's MRS is greater or less than the corresponding MRT. The product mix Z in panel *a* in Figure 16-12, for instance, has an MRT of 1, while Ann's consumption bundle at W in panel *b* shows that her MRS is 2. This means that Ann is willing to give up 2 units of food in order to obtain an additional unit of clothing, but that an additional unit of clothing can be produced at a cost of only 1 unit of food. With the capital and labor saved by producing 2 fewer units of food for Ann, we can produce 2 additional units of clothing. We can give 1.5 units of this extra clothing to Ann and the remaining 0.5 unit to Bill, making both parties better off. It follows that the original product mix cannot have been efficient (where, again, efficient means Pareto optimal).

We are now in a position to ask, finally, whether a market in general competitive equilibrium will be efficient in terms of its product mix. Here, too, the answer turns out to be yes, provided the production possibilities frontier bows out from the origin. Let P_F^* and P_C^* again denote competitive equilibrium prices for clothing and food. As we have already seen in the case of the simple exchange economy, the MRS of every consumer in equilibrium will be equal to the ratio of these prices, P_C^*/P_F^*. What we must show is that the MRT will also be equal to P_C^*/P_F^*.

FIGURE 16-12
At the product mix Z (panel *a*) the MRT is smaller than Ann's MRS at W (panel *b*). By producing 2 fewer units of food, we can produce 2 additional units of clothing. If we give 1.5 of these extra units to Ann and the remaining 0.5 unit to Bill, both parties will be better off. Efficiency requires that every consumer's MRS be exactly equal to the economy's MRT.

AN INEFFICIENT PRODUCT MIX

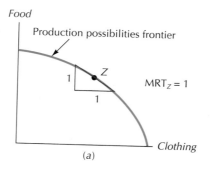

(a)

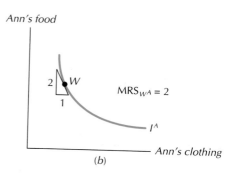

(b)

FIGURE 16-13
At Z, to produce an extra unit of clothing requires MC_C worth of labor and capital. Each unit less of food we produce at Z frees up MC_F worth of labor and capital. To get an extra unit of C, we must give up MC_C/MC_F units of food, and so the marginal rate of transformation is equal to MC_C/MC_F.

MRT EQUALS THE RATIO OF MARGINAL COSTS

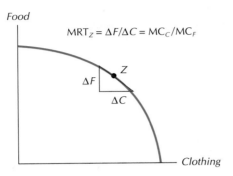

To do this, note first that the MRT at any point along the production possibilities frontier is equal to the ratio of the marginal cost of clothing (MC_C) to the marginal cost of food (MC_F). Suppose, for example, that MC_C at point Z in Figure 16-13 is \$100/unit of clothing and that MC_F is \$50/unit of food. The marginal rate of transformation at Z is $\Delta F/\Delta C$, the amount of food we have to give up to get an extra unit of clothing. Since MC_C is \$100, we need \$100 worth of extra labor and capital to produce an extra unit of clothing. And since MC_F is \$50, we have to produce 2 fewer units of food in order to free up \$100 worth of labor and capital. MRT at Z is therefore equal to 2, which is exactly the ratio of MC_C to MC_F:

$$\text{MRT} = \frac{MC_C}{MC_F}. \tag{16.3}$$

We also know that the equilibrium condition for competitive food and clothing producers is that product prices be equal to the corresponding values of marginal cost:

$$P_F^* = MC_F \tag{16.4}$$

and

$$P_C^* = MC_C. \tag{16.5}$$

Dividing Equation 16.5 by Equation 16.4, we have

$$\frac{P_C^*}{P_F^*} = \frac{MC_C}{MC_F}, \tag{16.6}$$

which establishes that the equilibrium product price ratio is indeed equal to the marginal rate of transformation.

To summarize, we have now established that an economy in competitive general equilibrium will, under certain conditions, be simultaneously efficient (Pareto optimal) in consumption, in production, and in the choice of product mix. As we have already seen, a society with a Pareto-optimal allocation of resources is not necessarily a good society. The final equilibrium in the marketplace depends very strongly on the distribution of initial endowments, and if this distribution isn't fair, we have no reason to expect the competitive equilibrium to be fair. Even so, it is truly remarkable to be able to claim, as Adam Smith did, that each person, merely by pursuing his own interests, is "led by an invisible hand to promote an end which was no part of his intention"—namely, the exploitation of all gains from exchange possible under given initial endowments.

Gains from International Trade

In our simple model of exchange and production, we saw why efficiency requires that every consumer's MRS be equal to the economy's MRT. This same requirement must be satisfied even for an economy that is free to engage in foreign trade. To illustrate, consider an economy just like the one we discussed, and suppose that its competitive general equilibrium in the absence of international trade occurs at point V in Figure 16-14. Now suppose that country opens its borders to international trade. If the country is small relative to the rest of the world, output prices will no longer be determined in its own internal markets, but in the much larger international markets. Suppose, in particular, that world prices for food and clothing are P_F^w and P_C^w, respectively. The best option available to this economy will no longer be to produce and consume at V. On the contrary,

FIGURE 16-14
Without international trade, the economy's competitive equilibrium was at V. With the possibility of buying or selling in world markets, the economy maximizes the total value of its output by producing at Z, where its MRT is equal to the international price ratio, P_C^w/P_F^w. Along BB', the international budget constraint, it then chooses the consumption allocation for which every consumer's MRS is equal to P_C^w/P_F^w. If this occurs at T, the country will export $C^* - C^{**}$ units of clothing and import $F^{**} - F^*$ units of food.

GAINS FROM INTERNATIONAL TRADE

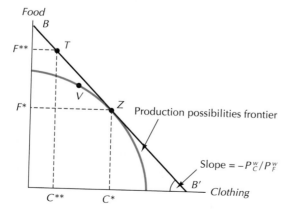

it should now produce at Z, the point on its production possibilities frontier at which the MRT is exactly equal to the international price ratio, P_C^w/P_F^w. Z is the point that maximizes the value of its output in world markets. Having produced at Z, the country is then free to choose any point along its "international budget constraint," BB'. Since the original competitive equilibrium point, V, lies within BB', we know that it is now possible for every person in the economy to have more of each good than before.

Which of the infinitely many bundles along BB' should be chosen? The best outcome is the one for which P_C^w/P_F^w is equal to every consumer's MRS. We know that without international trade the common value of MRS was equal to the MRT at V, which is smaller than the MRT at Z. Since there is more clothing and less food at Z than at V, it follows that the MRS at Z will be smaller than the MRT at V. This means that people will be better off moving to the northwest from BB'. Suppose T is the combination of food and clothing that equates everyone's MRS to P_C^w/P_F^w. This economy will then do best by exporting $C^* - C^{**}$ units of clothing and using the proceeds to import $F^{**} - F^*$ units of food.

As noted, the fact that the international budget constraint contains the original competitive equilibrium point means that it is possible to make everyone better off than before. But the impersonal workings of international trading markets provide no guarantee that every single person will in fact be made better off by trade. In the illustration given, international trading possibilities led the economy to produce more clothing and less food than it used to. The effect will be to increase the demand for factors of production used in clothing production and to reduce the demand for those used in food production. If factors of production are used with equal intensity in the two production processes, there will be no change in the intensity of demand for each factor. But suppose that food production is relatively intensive in the use of labor and that clothing production is relatively intensive in the use of capital. Depending on the specific magnitudes involved, the shift in product mix might then drive up the price of capital and drive down the price of labor. In this case, the primary beneficiaries from trade would be the owners of capital. People whose incomes come exclusively from the sale of their own labor would actually do worse than before, even though the value of total output is higher. What our general equilibrium analysis shows is that trade makes it *possible* to give everyone more of everything. It does not prove that everyone necessarily *will* get more.

Example 16-1 *You are the president of a small island nation that has never engaged in trade with any other nation. You are considering the possibility of opening the economy to international trade. The chief economist of the island's only labor union, to which every worker belongs, tells you that free trade will reduce the real purchasing power of labor, and you have no reason to doubt him. You are determined to remain in office and need the union's support in order to do so. The union will never support a candidate whose policies adversely affect the welfare of its members. Does this mean you should keep the island closed to trade?*

The answer is yes only if there is no way to redistribute the gains that trade will produce. Our general equilibrium analysis establishes that trade will increase the total value of output, which makes it possible for everyone to do better. If the alternative is for the island to remain closed, the owners of capital should readily agree to transfer some of their gains to labor. The only president who would fail to open the island's economy is one who is too lazy or unimaginative to negotiate an agreement under which every party ends up with more of everything than before.

Much has been written about the agonizing tradeoff between equity and efficiency, the notion that greater distributional fairness requires some sacrifice in efficiency. The lesson in Example 16-1 is that when people are able to negotiate costlessly with one another, there is in fact no conflict between equity and efficiency. When the total size of the economic pie grows larger, it is always possible for everyone to have a larger slice than before. Efficiency is achieved when we have made the economic pie as large as possible. Having done that, we are then free to discuss what constitutes a fair division of the pie.

Taxes in General Equilibrium

Suppose we are back in our simple production economy without the added complication of international trading opportunities. The economy is in competitive general equilibrium at point V in Figure 16-15, where the marginal rate of transformation is equal to the competitive equilibrium product price ratio, P_C^*/P_F^*. Now suppose the government decides to raise revenue by taxing food at the rate

FIGURE 16-15
A tax on food causes a shift away from food toward clothing consumption. If the original allocation was Pareto optimal, the new one will not be. The marginal rate of transformation will exceed the marginal rate of substitution. There will be too much clothing and too little food.

TAXES AFFECT PRODUCT MIX

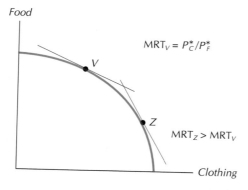

of t/dollar. Every time a producer sells a unit of food for P_F^*, she gets to keep only $(1 - t)P_F^*$. How will such a tax affect resource allocation?

The immediate effect of the tax is to raise the relative price ratio, as seen by producers, from P_C^*/P_F^* to $P_C^*/(1 - t)P_F^*$. Producers who were once content to produce at V on the production possibilities frontier will now find that they can increase their profits (or reduce their losses) by producing more clothing and less food than before. Suppose that, in the end, the effect is to cause producers to relocate at point Z along the production possibilities frontier. Recall that the MRT at V was equal to the common value of MRS at V. Since Z has more clothing and less food than V, the MRS at Z will be smaller than at V. It follows that the MRT will be higher than the MRS at Z, which means that the economy will no longer have an efficient product mix. The original allocation at V was Pareto optimal. The new allocation has too much clothing, too little food.

Note that a tax on food does not alter the fact that consumers will all have a common value of MRS in equilibrium. Nor does it alter the fact that producers will all have a common value of MRTS. Even with such a tax, the economy remains efficient in consumption and production. The real problem created by the tax is that it causes producers to see a different price ratio from the one seen by consumers. Consumption decisions are based on *gross prices*—that is, on prices inclusive of taxes. Production decisions, by contrast, are guided by *net prices*—the amount producers get to keep after the tax has been paid. When producers confront a different price ratio from the one that guides consumers, the MRS can never be equal to the MRT in equilibrium. By driving a wedge between the price ratios seen by producers and consumers, the tax leads to an inefficient product mix.

Subsidies, like taxes, upset the conditions required for efficiency. The problem with a taxed product is that it appears too cheap to its producer. By contrast, the problem with a subsidized product is that it appears too expensive. In general equilibrium, we get too much of the subsidized product and too little of the unsubsidized one.

The distortionary effects of taxes and subsidies identified by our simple general equilibrium analysis form the cornerstone of the so-called supply-side school of economic policy. As supply-siders are ever ready to testify, taxes almost always lead to some sort of inefficiency in the allocation of resources.

Does it then follow that the world would be better off if we simply *abolished* all taxes? Hardly, for in such a world there could be no goods or services provided by government, and as we will presently see, there are many valuable goods and services that are unlikely to be provided in any other way. The practical message of general equilibrium analysis is that care should be taken to design taxes that keep distortions to a minimum. Note that in our simple model, the problem would have been eliminated had we taxed not just food but also clothing at the same rate t. Relative prices would then have stayed the same, and producers and consumers would again be motivated by a consistent set of price signals.

In more realistic general equilibrium models, however, even a general commodity tax would have distortionary effects. A tax on all commodities is essentially the same as a tax on income, including the income earned from the sale of one's own labor. In our simple model, the supply of labor was assumed to be fixed, but in practice it may be sensitive to the real, after-tax wage rate. In a fuller model that included this relationship, a general commodity tax might thus lead to a distortion in decisions about the allocation of time between labor and leisure—for example, people might work too little and consume too much leisure.

From the standpoint of efficiency, a better tax would be a *head tax* (also called a *lump-sum tax*), one that is levied on each person irrespective of his or her labor supply decisions. The problem with this kind of tax is that many object to it on equity grounds. If we levied the same tax on every person, the burden of taxation would fall much more heavily on the poor than it does under our current system, which collects taxes roughly in proportion to individual income. On efficiency grounds, the very best tax of all is one levied on activities of which there would otherwise be too much. And as we will see below and in the next chapter, there are many such activities—more than enough to raise all the tax revenue we need.

Other Sources of Inefficiency

MONOPOLY

Taxes are but one of many factors that stand in the way of achieving Pareto optimality in the allocation of resources. One other source of inefficiency is monopoly. The general equilibrium effects of monopoly are closely analogous to those of a commodity tax. Consider again our simple production economy with two goods, and suppose that food is produced by a monopolist, clothing by a price taker. The competitive producer selects an output level for which marginal cost is equal to the price of clothing; the monopolist, as we saw in Chapter 12, selects one for which marginal cost is equal to marginal revenue. Because price always exceeds marginal revenue along a downward-sloping demand curve, this means that price will exceed marginal cost for the monopolist.

From the standpoint of efficiency, this wedge between price and marginal cost functions exactly like a tax on the monopolist's product. The marginal rate of transformation, which is the ratio of the marginal cost of clothing to the marginal cost of food, will no longer be equal to the ratio of product prices. Producers will be responding to one set of relative prices, consumers to another. The result is that too few of the economy's resources will be devoted to the production of food (the monopolized product) and too many to the production of clothing (the competitive product).

The general equilibrium analysis of the effect of monopoly adds an important dimension to our partial equilibrium analysis from Chapter 12. The partial analysis called our attention to the fact that there would be too little output produced by the monopolist. The general equilibrium analysis forcefully reminds us that there is another side of this coin, which is that the resources not used by the monopolist will be employed by the competitive sector of the economy. Thus, if monopoly output is too small, competitive output is too big. The additional competitive output does not undo the damage caused by monopoly, but it partially compensates for it. Viewed within the framework of general equilibrium analysis, the welfare costs of monopoly are thus smaller than they appeared from our partial equilibrium analysis.

EXTERNALITIES

Externality
Either a benefit or a cost of an action that accrues to someone other than the people directly involved in the action.

Another source of inefficiency occurs when production or consumption activities involve benefits or costs that fall on people not directly involved in the activities. Such benefits and costs are usually referred to as *externalities.* A standard example of a *negative externality* is the case of pollution, in which a production activity results in emissions that adversely affect people other than those who consume the product. The planting of additional apple trees, whose blossoms augment the output of honey in nearby beehives, is an example of a *positive externality.* And so is the case of the beekeeper who adds bees to his hive, unmindful of the higher pollination rates they will produce in nearby apple orchards.

Externalities are both widespread and important. We will discuss them in great detail in Chapter 17. For now, let us note that the problem they create for efficiency stems from the fact that, like taxes, they cause producers and consumers to respond to different sets of relative prices. When the orchard owner decides how many trees to plant, he looks only at the price of apples, not at the price of honey. By the same token, when the consumer decides how much honey to buy, he ignores the effects of his purchases on the quantity and price of apples.

In the case of negative externalities in production, the effect on efficiency is much the same as that of a subsidy. In deciding what quantity of the product to produce, the producer equates price and his own private marginal cost. The problem is that the negative externalities impose additional costs on others, and these are ignored by the producer. As with the subsidized product, we end up with too much of the product with negative externalities and too little of all other products. With positive externalities, the reverse occurs. We end up with too little of such products and too much of others.

TAXES AS A SOLUTION TO EXTERNALITIES AND MONOPOLY

As noted earlier, the best tax from an efficiency standpoint is one levied on an activity there would otherwise be too much of. This suggests that the welfare losses from monopoly can be mitigated by placing an excise tax on the good produced in the competitive sector. Properly chosen, such a tax could exactly off-set the wedge that is created by the disparity between the monopolist's price and marginal cost.

In the case of negative externalities, the difficulty is that individuals regard the product as being cheaper than it really is from the standpoint of society as a whole. By taxing the product with negative externalities at a suitable rate, the efficiency loss can be undone. For products accompanied by positive externali-ties, the corresponding solution is a subsidy.

PUBLIC GOODS

One additional factor that stands in the way of achieving efficient allocations through private markets is the existence of *public goods*. A pure public good is one with two specific properties: (1) *nondiminishability*, which means that one per-son's use of the good does not diminish the amount of it available for others; and (2) *nonexcludability*, which means that it is either impossible or prohibitively costly to exclude people who do not pay from using the good. In the days before the invention of channel scramblers, broadcast television signals were an exam-ple of a pure public good. My tuning in to a movie on channel 11, for example, does not make that movie less available to anyone else. And before the advent of scramblers and cable TV, there was no practical way to exclude anyone from making use of a television signal once it was broadcast. National defense is another example of a pure public good. The fact that Smith enjoys the benefits of national defense does not make those benefits any less available to Jones. And it is exceedingly difficult for the government to protect some of its citizens from foreign attack while denying the same protection to others.

There is no reason to presume that private markets will supply optimal quan-tities of pure public goods. Indeed, if it is impossible to exclude people from using the good, it might seem impossible for a profit-seeking firm to supply any quantity of it at all. But profit-seeking firms often show great ingenuity in devis-ing schemes for providing pure public goods. Commercial broadcast television, for example, covers its costs by charging advertisers for access to the audience it attracts with its programming. But even in these cases, there is no reason to suppose that the amount and kind of television programming we get under this arrangement is economically efficient. (More on this specific issue in Chapter 18.)

The problem is less acute in the case of goods that have the nondiminishability but not the nonexcludability property. Once every household is wired for cable TV, for example, it will be possible to prevent people from watching any given program if they do not pay for it. But even here, there are likely to be ineffi-ciencies. Once a TV program has been produced, it costs society nothing to let an extra person see it. If there is a positive price for watching the program, however, all those who value seeing it at less than that price will not tune in. It is inefficient to exclude these viewers, since their viewing the program would not diminish its usefulness for anyone else.

Summary

One of the simplest possible general equilibrium models is a pure exchange economy with only two consumers and two goods. For any given initial allocation of the two goods between the two consumers in this model, a competitive exchange process will always exhaust all possible mutually beneficial gains from trade. This result is known as the invisible hand theorem and is also called the first theorem of welfare economics.

If consumers have convex indifference curves, any efficient allocation can be sustained as a competitive equilibrium. This result is known as the second theorem of welfare economics. Its significance is that it demonstrates that the issues of efficiency and distributional equity are logically distinct. Society can redistribute initial endowments according to accepted norms of distributive justice, and then rely on markets to assure that endowments are used efficiently.

An economy is efficient in production if the marginal rate of technical substitution is the same for all producers. In the input market, too, competitive trading exploits all mutually beneficial gains from exchange.

Even though international trade leaves domestic production possibilities unchanged, its immediate effect is to increase the value of goods available for domestic consumption. With a suitable redistribution of initial endowments, a free trade economy will always be Pareto superior to a non-free trade economy.

Taxes often interfere with efficient resource allocation, usually because they cause consumers and producers to respond to different price ratios. The practical significance of this result is to guide us in the search for taxes that minimize distortions. The best tax, from an efficiency standpoint, is one levied on an activity that would otherwise be pursued too intensively.

Monopoly, externalities, and public goods are three other factors that interfere with the efficient allocation of resources.

Questions for Review

1. Why does efficiency in consumption require the MRS of all consumers to be the same?

2. Distinguish among the terms "Pareto superior," "Pareto preferred," and "Pareto optimal."

3. Why might voters in a country choose a non-Pareto-optimal allocation over another that is Pareto optimal?

4. How do the initial endowments constrain where we end up on the contract curve?

5. In general equilibrium, can there be excess demand for every good?

6. How might a social critic respond to the claim that governmental involvement in the economy is unjustified because of the invisible hand theorem?

7. Why is the slope of the production possibilities frontier equal to the ratio of marginal production costs?

8. How might a critic respond to the claim that taxes always make the allocation of resources less efficient?

Problems

1. Bert has an initial endowment consisting of 10 units of food and 10 units of clothing. Ernie's initial endowment consists of 10 units of food and 20 units of clothing. Represent these initial endowments in an Edgeworth exchange box.

2. Bert regards food and clothing as perfect 1-for-1 substitutes. Ernie regards them as perfect complements, always wanting to consume 3 units of clothing for every 2 units of food.

   a. Describe the set of allocations that are Pareto preferred to the one given in Problem 1.
   b. Describe the contract curve for that allocation.
   c. What price ratio will be required to sustain an allocation on the contract curve?

3. How will your answers to Problem 2 differ if 5 units of Ernie's clothing endowment are given to Bert?

4. Consider a simple economy with two goods, food and clothing, and two consumers, A and B. For a given initial endowment, when the ratio of food to clothing prices in an economy is 3/1, A wants to buy 6 units of clothing while B wants to sell 2 units of food. Is $P_F/P_C = 3$ an equilibrium price ratio? If so, explain why. If not, state in which direction it will tend to change.

5. How will your answer to Problem 4 change if A wants to sell 3 units of clothing and B wants to sell 2 units of food?

6. Suppose Sarah has an endowment of 2 units of X and 4 units of Y and has indifference curves that satisfy our four basic assumptions (see Chapter 3). Suppose Brian has an endowment of 4 units of X and 2 units of Y, and has preferences given by the utility function $U(X, Y) = \min \{X, Y\}$, where

$$\min(X, Y) = \begin{cases} X & \text{if } X \leq Y \\ Y & \text{if } Y \leq X \end{cases}.$$

On an Edgeworth box diagram, indicate the set of Pareto-superior bundles.

7. A simple economy produces two goods, food and clothing, with two inputs, capital and labor. Given the current allocation of capital and labor between the two industries, the marginal rate of technical substitution between capital and labor in food production is 4, while the corresponding MRTS in clothing production is 2. Is this economy efficient in production? If so, explain why. If not, describe a reallocation that will lead to a Pareto improvement.

8. Given the current allocation of productive inputs, the marginal rate of transformation of food for clothing in a simple two-good economy is equal to 2. At the current allocation of consumption goods, each consumer's marginal rate of substitution between food and clothing is 1.5. Is this economy efficient in terms of its product mix? If so, explain why. If not, describe a reallocation that will lead to a Pareto improvement.

9. Crusoe can make 5 units of food per day if he devotes all his time to food production. He can make 10 units of clothing if he spends the whole day at clothing production. If he divides his time between the two activities, his output of each good will be proportional to the time spent on each. The corresponding figures for Friday are 10 units of food and 15 units of clothing. Describe the production possibilities frontier for their economy.

10. If Crusoe and Friday regard food and clothing as perfect 1-for-1 substitutes, what should each produce?

11. Now suppose a trading ship visits the island each day and offers to buy or sell food and clothing at the prices $P_F = 4$, $P_C = 1$. How, if at all, will the presence of this ship alter the production and consumption decisions of Crusoe and Friday?

12. How will your answers to Problems 9, 10, and 11 differ if Friday's maximum production figures change to 20 units of food and 50 units of clothing?

13. There are two industries in a simple economy, each of which faces the same marginal cost of production. One of the industries is perfectly competitive, the other a pure monopoly. Describe a reallocation of resources that will lead to a Pareto improvement for this economy.

14. Suppose capital and labor are perfect substitutes in production for clothing: 2 units of capital *or* 2 units of labor produce 1 unit of clothing. Suppose capital and labor are perfect complements in production for food: 1 unit of capital *and* 1 unit of labor produce 1 unit of food. Suppose the economy has an endowment of 100 units of capital and 200 units of labor. Describe the set of efficient allocations of the factors to the two sectors (determine the contract curve in an Edgeworth production box).

15. Construct the production possibilities frontier for the economy described in Problem 14. What is the opportunity cost of food in terms of clothing?

16. Construct the production possibilities frontier for an economy just like the one described in Problem 14, except that its endowment of capital is 200 units.

Answers to In-Chapter Exercises

16-1. Bill's endowment of food = 100 − Ann's endowment = 75. Bill's endowment of clothing = 200 − Ann's endowment = 175.

16-2. Let M denote the initial allocation. Ann's indifference curve through M is a straight line with slope = −1. Bill's indifference curve through M is right-angled, as shown in the following diagram. The set of Pareto-superior allocations is indicated by the shaded triangle.

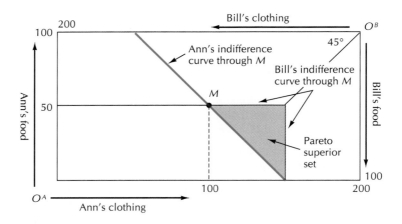

16-3. Here, $P_L/P_K = 1$, which is half as big as $\text{MPL}_C/\text{MPK}_C$:

$$\frac{P_L}{P_K} = \frac{1}{2}\frac{\text{MPL}_C}{\text{MPK}_C},$$

from which it follows that

$$\frac{\text{MPK}_C}{P_K} = \frac{1}{2}\frac{\text{MPL}_C}{P_L}.$$

In words, this says that the last dollar spent on capital in clothing production produces only half as much extra output as does the last dollar spent on labor in clothing production. It follows that clothing producers can get more output for the same cost by hiring less capital and more labor. Parallel reasoning tells us that food producers can increase food production at no extra cost by hiring less labor and more capital.

16-4. Only when these producers have reached a cost-minimizing input mix characteristic of a competitive equilibrium will efficiency in production be achieved.

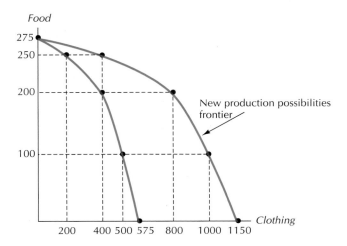

CHAPTER
17

Externalities, Property Rights, and the Coase Theorem

At the corner of 22nd and M Streets, NW, in Washington, D.C., stands a venerable restaurant called Blackie's House of Beef. During the real estate boom of the 1970s, this location emerged as a prime site for the construction of high-rise commercial buildings. With the passage of each month, the opportunity cost of continuing to operate a one-story restaurant on that site continued to soar. And yet the owners of Blackie's were of no mind to abandon their location. The restaurant had been the family business for many years, and the family was determined to see it continue.

Eventually they came up with a creative solution. They negotiated a multi-million-dollar agreement whereby, without disturbing a single brick in the restaurant, a high-rise structure would be constructed on stilts *above* the restaurant. Blackie's is still open for business, a quaint, old-world country inn nestled beneath a high-rise Marriott Hotel. In a similar multimillion-dollar transaction, a developer purchased the rights to build a new skyscraper astraddle the Museum of Modern Art in midtown Manhattan.

In most jurisdictions, owning a piece of property confers the right to exclude anyone from constructing a building in the airspace above it. But a similar right does not extend to all other forms of activity in the same airspace. For example, hundreds of thousands of American houses are located beneath commercial flight paths between major cities, and each day thousands of airliners use the airspace above these houses without paying a penny. This pattern of rights is not a matter of historical accident. It has emerged, as we will see, as a means of making the most efficient use of property when it is difficult to negotiate agreements on a case-by-case basis.

Chapter Preview

Our subjects in this chapter are externalities and property rights. We begin with a series of examples illustrating what happens when an action by one party harms another and the parties are able to negotiate costlessly with one another. Next we consider a related set of examples in which negotiation is costly. We then apply the principles that emerge from these examples to a variety of questions regarding the design of property rights. Should the owner of a dock be allowed to exclude a boater from tying up during a storm? When should a person be allowed to exclude others from walking across his land? Or from blocking his view? Should pastureland be owned privately or in common? Should a developer be allowed to construct an office building over someone else's property without her consent? Should airplanes be allowed to fly over houses? The answers to such questions, we will see, depend on the kinds of accommodations people would reach among themselves if they were free to negotiate costlessly with one another.

Next we apply the theory of property rights and externalities to the topic of contests for relative position. We conclude this chapter with an examination of taxation as a possible solution to the problem of negative externalities.

The Reciprocal Nature of Externalities

In the first edition of this text, I began this section with the following sentence:

> One of the great injustices of academic life is that Ronald H. Coase[1] has never been awarded the Nobel Prize in economics.

I was thus delighted when I learned that Coase was at last awarded the prize in 1992. Now an emeritus professor at the University of Chicago Law School, Coase is the author of the most influential and widely cited economics paper of the postwar era. Titled "The Problem of Social Cost,"[2] this paper profoundly changed the way economists, legal scholars, political philosophers, and others think about externalities and the legal and social institutions that have evolved to deal with them.

---

[1] Rhymes with "dose."

[2] *Journal of Law and Economics,* 3, 1960: 144–171.

Coase began with an example involving a doctor whose ability to examine patients was disrupted by the noise of machinery operated by a confectioner (candy maker) in an adjacent building. Historically, the economic and legal view toward such a situation was simple and clear: The confectioner's noise was harming the doctor and it ought to be restrained. Coase's seminal insight was that this view completely overlooks the reciprocal nature of the problem. True enough, the confectioner's noise does harm the doctor. *But if we prevent the noise, we harm the confectioner.* After all, the confectioner makes the noise, not for the purpose of harming the doctor, but in pursuit of his own livelihood. In such situations, there will be harm to *someone,* no matter what happens. Whether the harm caused to the doctor by the noise is greater than the harm that would be caused to the confectioner if he were prohibited from making it is strictly an empirical question. The common interest of each party, Coase recognized, is to avoid the larger of these two unpleasant outcomes.

The earlier, one-sided view of externalities led to a legal tradition in which the confectioner was generally held liable for any damage his noise caused to the doctor. Coase pointed out, however, that if the doctor and the confectioner were able to negotiate costlessly with one another, the most efficient outcome would occur regardless of whether the confectioner was liable. His simple and elegant argument in support of this claim is illustrated in the following series of numerical examples.

*E*XAMPLE *17-1* *Suppose the benefit to the confectioner of continuing to make noise is 40, while the cost of the noise to the doctor is 60 (see footnote 3). If the confectioner's only alternative to making the noise is to produce nothing, what will happen if he is made liable for the noise damage? (To be liable for the damage means being required to compensate the doctor for any damage caused by the noise.)*

The confectioner will examine his two options—shutting down or compensating the doctor—and choose the one that makes him best off. If he stays open, he will earn 40, but will have to pay 60 to the doctor, for a net loss of 20. If he shuts down, his net gain is 0, and since this is clearly better than losing 20, he will discontinue operation.

Alternatively, suppose the confectioner had not been liable for noise damage. That is, suppose the law grants him the right to continue operating without compensation to the doctor. Coase argued that in this case the doctor will pay the confectioner to shut down. If the confectioner stays open, he will gain only 40 while the doctor will lose

---

[3]The numerical cost and benefit values used in this and in the following examples represent the present values of all current and future costs and benefits to the parties in question.

60. But the doctor can compensate the confectioner for the loss of shutting down and still have enough left over to be better off than if the confectioner had stayed open. Suppose, for example, the doctor pays the confectioner 50 to shut down. The confectioner's net gain will now be 10 more than if he had stayed open. And the doctor's net gain of 10 is 10 more than if the noise had continued.

If P denotes the payment the doctor makes to the confectioner to compensate him for shutting down, we know that P must be at least 40 (what the confectioner would get by staying open) and no larger than 60 (what the doctor would get if there were no noise). The net results under the two legal regimes (confectioner liable versus confectioner not liable) are summarized in Table 17-1.

Note that because the gain to the confectioner of operating his machinery (40) is smaller than the noise damage it imposes on the doctor (60), the most efficient outcome is for the confectioner to shut down. Example 17-1 makes clear that if both the doctor and confectioner are rational and can negotiate costlessly with one another, this will happen regardless of whether the confectioner is liable for noise damage. On efficiency grounds, the legal regime is thus a matter of complete indifference here. On distributional grounds, however, the parties will be anything but neutral about liability. If the confectioner is not liable, his gain is $P \geq 40$, whereas he will be forced to shut down and earn nothing if he is liable. The doctor's net gain will be 60 if the confectioner is liable, but only $60 - P$ if the confectioner is not liable.

EXAMPLE 17-2 *Same as Example 17-1, except now the benefit to the <u>confectioner</u> of operating is 60, the benefit to the doctor in a noise-free environment only 40. Assume that the doctor must shut down if the noise continues.*

The gain to the confectioner from operating is 40. The loss to the doctor from the noise is 60. The efficient outcome is for the confectioner to shut down, and this happens under both legal regimes.

TABLE 17-1 OUTCOME AND PAYOFF SUMMARY FOR EXAMPLE 17-1

Legal regime	Outcome	Net benefit		
		Doctor	Confectioner	Total
Liable	Confectioner shuts down to avoid liability payment	60	0	60
Not liable	Doctor pays confectioner P to shut down, $40 \leq P \leq 60$	$60 - P$	P	60

The gain to the confectioner from operating is 60. The loss to the doctor from the confectioner's noise is 40. The efficient outcome is for the confectioner to continue operating, and this happens under both legal regimes.

TABLE 17-2 OUTCOME AND PAYOFF SUMMARY FOR EXAMPLE 17-2

Legal regime	Outcome	Net benefit		
		Doctor	Confectioner	Total
Liable	Confectioner stays open and pays doctor 40	40	20	60
Not liable	Confectioner stays open; doctor shuts down	0	60	60

This time the efficient outcome is for the confectioner to continue operating, since his gain exceeds the cost he imposes on the doctor. If he is not liable for noise damages, the confectioner will stay open and the doctor's best option will be to shut down. Alternatively, if the confectioner is liable for noise damage, he will again continue to operate and pay the doctor 40 to compensate him for his losses. The net results for this example are summarized in Table 17-2. Note that, as in Example 17-1, both legal regimes lead to the most efficient outcome, but have very different distributional consequences.

The preceding examples assumed that the only alternatives open to two parties were either to continue operations in the current form or to shut down entirely. In practice, however, one or both parties often face a broader range of alternatives. As the following examples will illustrate, here too the ability to negotiate costlessly leads to efficient outcomes.

EXAMPLE 17-3 *Same as Example 17-1, except now the confectioner has access to a soundproofing device that will completely eliminate the noise from his machines. The cost of the device is 20, which means that if he installs it his net gain from operating will fall from 40 to 20. As in Example 17-1, the doctor will gain 60 if there is no noise, 0 if there is noise.*

If the confectioner is liable for noise damage, his best option will be to install the soundproofing. His alternatives are either to shut down or to pay the doctor 60 in noise damages, and each of these is clearly worse. If the confectioner is not liable, it will be in the doctor's interest to pay the confectioner to install the soundproofing. His alternative, after all, is to shut down or to endure the noise damage. The minimum payment that would be acceptable to the confectioner to install the soundproofing is 20, its cost. The most the doctor would be willing to pay for him to install it is 60, the amount the doctor would lose if it weren't installed. Again letting P denote the payment from the doctor to the confectioner, the outcomes and payoffs for the two legal regimes are as summarized in Table 17-3.

The gain to the confectioner from operating without soundproofing is 40. Soundproofing costs 20. The loss to the doctor from the confectioner's noise is 60. The efficient outcome is for the confectioner to install soundproofing and to continue operating, and this happens under both legal regimes.

TABLE 17-3 OUTCOME AND PAYOFF SUMMARY FOR EXAMPLE 17-3

| Legal regime | Outcome | Net benefit | | |
		Doctor	Confectioner	Total
Liable	Confectioner installs soundproofing at own expense	60	20	80
Not liable	Doctor pays confectioner P to install soundproofing, $20 \leq P \leq 60$	$60 - P$	$20 + P$	80

Let us now consider what happens when the doctor too has some adjustment he can make to escape the damage caused by the confectioner's noise.

EXAMPLE 17-4 Same as Example 17-3, except now the doctor can escape the noise damage by moving his examination room to the other side of his office. The noisy room in which he now examines patients could then be used for storage. The cost to the doctor of this rearrangement is 18.

With this new option available, the doctor is the one who is able to eliminate the noise damage at the lowest possible cost. If the confectioner is liable for noise damage, he will offer the doctor a payment P to compensate him for rearranging his office. The payment must be at least 18, or else the doctor would not make the accommodation. (Recall that, with the confectioner liable, the doctor has the option of being fully compensated for any noise damage.) And the payment cannot exceed 20, or else the confectioner could install soundproofing and solve the problem on his own. If the confectioner is not liable for noise damage, the doctor will rearrange his office at his own expense. The outcomes and payoffs for this example are summarized in Table 17-4. Note that we again get the efficient outcome no matter which legal regime we choose. Note also that the choice of legal regime again affects the distribution of costs and benefits, only this time by a much smaller margin than in Example 17-3. The difference is that each party now has a relatively inexpensive method for solving the noise problem unilaterally. In Example 17-3, the doctor lacked such an alternative, making the confectioner's bargaining power very strong when he was not liable for noise damage. In this example, by contrast, the confectioner cannot extract a large payment from the doctor for keeping quiet because the doctor can solve the noise problem on his own.

The gain to the confectioner from operating without soundproofing is 40. Soundproofing costs 20. The loss to the doctor from the confectioner's noise is 60. The doctor can rearrange his office to eliminate the noise problem at a cost of 18. The efficient outcome is for the doctor to rearrange his office, and this happens under both legal regimes.

TABLE 17-4 OUTCOME AND PAYOFF SUMMARY FOR EXAMPLE 17-4

Legal regime	Outcome	Net benefit		
		Doctor	Confectioner	Total
Liable	Confectioner pays doctor P to rearrange his office, $18 \leq P \leq 20$	$42 + P$	$40 - P$	82
Not liable	Doctor rearranges his office at his own expense	42	40	82

The patterns revealed in the preceding examples may be stated formally as:

The Coase Theorem: *When the parties affected by externalities can negotiate costlessly with one another, an efficient outcome results no matter how the law assigns responsibility for damages.*

In the wake of its publication, Coase's classic paper became a subject of great controversy. Many took him to be saying that there is no real role for government in solving problems related to pollution, noise, and other externalities. By this interpretation, Coase's message seemed to be that if government stays out of the way, people will always come up with efficient solutions on their own. And yet Coase stated clearly that this conclusion holds only for a world in which parties can negotiate with one another at relatively low cost. He recognized that there are many important externalities for which this assumption is not satisfied. At the simplest level, time and energy are required for negotiation, and when the potential benefits are small, it may simply not be worth it. Alternatively, there are situations in which a single polluter causes damage to a large number of people. Negotiating with large groups is inherently difficult and costly, and each person in the group faces strong incentives to escape these costs. Another serious barrier to negotiation is the problem of how to divide the surplus. Recall from Example 17-3 that the efficient outcome was for the doctor to pay the confectioner to install soundproofing. The minimum payment acceptable to the confectioner was 20, the cost of the soundproofing. The most the confectioner could hope to extract from the doctor was 60, the value to the doctor of eliminating the noise. The doctor would naturally like to pay only 20, and the confectioner would like to get 60. If each takes a hard line in the discussion, animosities may emerge and the possibility of a deal may break down altogether. For these and a host of other reasons, negotiations are often costly. When they are, it matters very much indeed which legal regime we choose, as the following examples will illustrate.

EXAMPLE 17-5 *As in Example 17-2, suppose that the gain to the doctor in a noise-free environment is 40, while the gain to the confectioner from unfettered operations is 60. Suppose also that the confectioner has access to a soundproofing device that eliminates all noise damage at a cost of 20. And suppose, finally, that it costs the doctor and confectioner 25 to negotiate a private agreement between themselves. For negotiation to be a worthwhile alternative, they must be able to share this cost in some way that makes each of them better off than if they did not negotiate.*

If the confectioner is made liable for noise damage, he will install the soundproofing. His next-best alternative, after all, is to pay the doctor 40 in noise damages,[4] and the installation of soundproofing costs him only 20. Because being liable gives the confectioner an incentive to install the soundproofing on his own, there is no need for him to negotiate an agreement with the doctor, and thus no need to incur the cost of negotiation.

But now suppose that the confectioner is not liable for noise damage. If there were no costs of negotiation, the doctor would pay the confectioner P, where $20 \leq P \leq 40$, to install soundproofing. If it costs 25 to negotiate an agreement, however, then it is no longer possible for the doctor to compensate the confectioner for installing soundproofing. The soundproofing makes it possible for the doctor to gain 40, which is insufficient to cover both the cost of the soundproofing (20) and the cost of negotiating the agreement (25), which total 45. When it is costly to negotiate, we no longer get the most efficient outcome irrespective of which legal regime we choose. In this example, for which the relevant data are summarized in Table 17-5, we get the most efficient result only if the confectioner is liable.

The gain to the confectioner from operating without soundproofing is 60. Soundproofing costs 20. The loss to the doctor from the confectioner's noise is 40. The cost of negotiating a private agreement is 25. The efficient outcome is for the confectioner to install soundproofing, but this happens only when he is made liable for noise damage.

TABLE 17-5 OUTCOME AND PAYOFF SUMMARY FOR EXAMPLE 17-5

| | | Net benefit | | |
Legal regime	Outcome	Doctor	Confectioner	Total
Liable	Confectioner installs soundproofing at his own expense	40	40	80
Not liable	Confectioner does not install soundproofing; doctor shuts down	0	60	60

[4]For the confectioner to operate and pay noise damages to the doctor, it is not necessary for them to incur the cost of negotiating a private agreement.

In Example 17-5, the total gain for society as a whole is 80 if the confectioner is liable, only 60 if he is not liable. But as the following example will illustrate, the existence of barriers to negotiation does not guarantee that we will always get a more efficient outcome by making parties liable for the damage caused by external effects.

EXAMPLE 17-6 *Same as Example 17-5, except the confectioner no longer has a soundproofing option; instead, the doctor has the option of avoiding the noise by rearranging his office, which will cost him 18.*

If the confectioner is not liable for noise damage, this is exactly what the doctor will do. But if the confectioner is liable, the cost of negotiation now stands in the way of his paying the doctor to rearrange his office. The sum of negotiating costs (25) and rearrangement costs (18) comes to 43, which is 3 more than the 40 that will be saved by avoiding the noise. So if he is liable, the best option available to the confectioner is simply to continue operating and pay the doctor 40 for the noise damage.[5] Here, unlike Example 17-5, we get the most efficient outcome when the confectioner is not liable. The data for Example 17-6 are summarized in Table 17-6.

EXERCISE 17-1

How would the entries in Table 17-6 be affected if the cost of negotiation were 20 instead of 25?

APPLICATION: EXTERNAL EFFECTS FROM NUCLEAR POWER PLANTS

Although Austria itself has had a law banning nuclear power plants since 1978, it is surrounded by countries that operate a total of 41 such plants. Two of these plants, located just 35 miles from the Austrian border with Slovakia, share important design features with the ill-fated Chernobyl plant that in 1986 experienced the worst nuclear accident in history. Thus the citizens of Austria were understandably concerned about their vulnerability to a similar mishap.

In a remarkably bold application of the reasoning Coase suggested, Austrian officials offered in January 1991 to provide Slovakia (then part of Czechoslovakia) with free electric power as an inducement to shut down the two Soviet-designed

---

[5]Again, making a liability payment does not require the parties to incur the costs of negotiation.

The gain to the confectioner from operating is 60. The loss to the doctor from the confectioner's noise is 40. The doctor can escape the noise by rearranging his office at a cost of 18. The cost of negotiating a private agreement is 25. The efficient outcome is for the doctor to rearrange his office, but this happens only when the confectioner is not liable for noise damage.

TABLE 17-6 OUTCOME AND PAYOFF SUMMARY FOR EXAMPLE 17-6

Legal regime	Outcome	Net benefit		
		Doctor	Confectioner	Total
Liable	Confectioner operates and pays doctor 40 for noise damage	40	20	80
Not liable	Doctor rearranges his office at his own expense	22	60	82

reactors.[6] Austrian Economics Minister Wolfgang Scheussel estimated that the cost of the replacement power would be about $350 million annually.

Czech Premier Marian Calfa expressed interest in the Austrian offer and pledged that a working group would study it. In the years since the proposal was initially made, however, no agreement has been reached to implement it. As this experience illustrates, the costs of negotiation sometimes stand in the way even of agreements that would substantially benefit both parties.

Coase's observation that people will reach the most efficient outcomes when they can negotiate costlessly has widespread application. In many situations, after all, the costs of negotiation are small relative to the benefits of reaching agreements about externalities. But the more far-reaching implications of Coase's work lie in the pattern illustrated in Examples 17-5 and 17-6, where we find the seeds of a very powerful theory of law and social institutions. Boiled down to its essence, the theory can be stated as the following rule:

> *The most efficient laws and social institutions are the ones that place the burden of adjustment to externalities on those who can accomplish it at least cost.*

One of the immediate implications of this rule is that the best laws regarding harmful effects cannot be identified unless we know something about how much it costs different parties to avoid harmful effects. If, as in Example 17-5, the emitter of noise has lower costs, we get a more efficient outcome by making him liable for damages. But if the person adversely affected by the noise has a lower cost of avoidance, as in Example 17-6, we do better by not making the noise-maker liable.

The efficiency rule finds application in a rich variety of situations, several of which we examine in the sections that follow.

---

[6]See Michael Z. Wise, "Prague Offered Payoff to Shut Nuclear Plant," *The Washington Post*, January 30, 1991.

Property Rights

USE OF THE AIRSPACE

Think back to the examples with which we began this chapter, the ones involving the rights to use airspace over various parcels of land. For a developer to build a hotel in the airspace above my land, he must first secure my permission, which I will grant only in return for a substantial payment. But the law permits commercial airliners to fly over my land without payment whenever they choose. Why this distinction?

Note first that each case involves an externality—the visual blight and inconvenience of having a hotel overhead in the first case, the noise and possible danger from the airplanes in the second. The cost to me of the first externality is much larger than the second, but that alone cannot account for why we treat the two cases differently, since the benefits to the developer from erecting a building over my land are also likely to be great. The crucial distinction is that individual negotiation is much more practical in the case of the developer than in the case of the airlines. In the former case, there are only two parties involved, and the benefits from an efficient outcome are likely to be large enough to justify the costs of negotiation. So in this case, we can feel confident of achieving an efficient outcome most of the time if we define property rights to exclude developers from building in the airspace above our houses. In the airline case, by contrast, the benefits of flying over any single house are small, and in any event, the cost of negotiating with all the potentially affected parties would be prohibitive. Because the total benefits of overflight are large relative to the total costs imposed on homeowners, we get a more efficient outcome here if property rights do not permit landowners to exclude planes from flying overhead.

There are exceptions to this general principle, however, and these too provide an illuminating illustration of the Coasian efficiency rule. The most conspicuous exception involves approach and takeoff lanes to and from airports near major metropolitan areas. Jets fly low to the ground just after takeoff and just before landing, and the noise that reaches property below is often deafening. In these situations, local ordinances commonly prohibit landings and takeoffs during the hours when it is most costly (difficult) for property owners to adjust to noise—namely, the hours when most of them are sleeping. Here again, negotiation on an individual basis is impractical, and the best we can do is to define rights to achieve the lowest cost of accommodation.

THE LAW OF TRESPASS

In many cultures of the world, people regard a stranger walking across their land as an intrusion. The trespasser, in the economist's parlance, confers a negative externality on the property owner. Such externalities might be dealt with in a variety of ways. Most of my neighbors, for example, have built fences across their yards to prevent people from taking shortcuts across their property. Some even post signs saying to beware of violent dogs. In most jurisdictions, it is perfectly lawful to take such steps to exclude others from using your property. And yet the laws of my community do not afford the same rights to people who own cottages on the shore of nearby Cayuga Lake. On the contrary, they explicitly permit any citizen to walk across any parcel of land located along the lakeshore.

This distinction exists not because the owners of lakeshore property value their privacy any less than others do. Rather, it is because the cost of not being able to cross a person's land along the lakeshore is so much higher than it is elsewhere. To illustrate, suppose that A, B, and C in Figure 17-1 are three lakeshore properties and that someone at A wants to visit someone at C. Access to lakeshore properties by road involves travel from the main highway down long, steep, often treacherous driveways. Lacking the ability to cross B's property, A would have to ascend his driveway out to the main road, travel to C's driveway, and then make the trip down it. Because the costs of this circuitous routing are so much larger than the costs of the direct path along the lakeshore, the law of trespass makes an exception for these properties. Their owners consider an occasional unwelcome disturbance a small price to pay for the additional convenience of being able to travel freely along the lakeshore.

By contrast, the right to cross someone's property in my neighborhood would be worth relatively little. The streets are all close together, so there is always a relatively easy way to get where you want to go without having to take shortcuts. With respect to potential trespass on both the lakeshore and other properties, negotiation is prohibitively costly on a case-by-case basis. So the law of property defines rights of access in the way that, on average, leads to the most efficient outcome. It gives most property owners the right to exclude, but withholds that right from the owners of lakeshore property.

FIGURE 17-1
The cost of getting from A to C without crossing B's property is much higher than by the direct route along the lakeshore. For this reason, the law does not allow lakeshore homeowners to exclude people from walking across their property.

LAKESHORE PROPERTY AND THE LAW OF TRESPASS

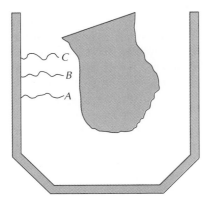

SAFE HARBOR IN A STORM

On the 13th day of November 1804, the Ploof family went sailing on Vermont's Lake Champlain. A sudden violent storm came up, making it impossible for them to get back to their home port. In desperation, they took refuge by tying up at a dock on an island in the lake. The dock was owned by a Mr. Putnam, who sent his servant down to order the Ploofs off of his property. The Ploofs cast off into the storm, and shortly thereafter their sloop was destroyed, injuring several family members. The Ploofs later filed a successful damage suit against Putnam. The court decided that although Putnam would ordinarily have the right to exclude people from using his dock, the circumstances of the storm created an exception. Note that in deciding the case this way, the Vermont court was mimicking the result that dock owners and boat owners would generally reach for themselves if it were possible to negotiate costlessly and dispassionately during a storm. The value of the dock to a boater in distress is almost certainly higher than the value to the owner of being able to exclude him, and the Vermont court chose to define the state's laws of property with this observation in mind.

THE RIGHT TO AN UNOBSTRUCTED VIEW

Consider the situation pictured in Figure 17-2. Resident A owns a house on a hillside overlooking the sea and places high value on being able to watch the sunset from his living room window. Now B purchases the property below A and is considering which of two houses to build. The first is a one-story house that would leave A's view intact. The second is a two-story design that would completely block A's view. Suppose the gain to A from an unobstructed view is 100, the gain to B from having a one-story house is 200, and the gain to B from a two-story house is 280. If the laws of property let people build houses of any height they chose, and if negotiation between property owners were costless, which of the two houses would B build?

To answer this question, first note that the increase in B's gain from having the taller house is 80, which is 20 less than the cost to A from the loss of his view. The efficient outcome is thus for B to build the one-story house. And that is exactly what would happen if the two parties could negotiate costlessly. Rather than see B build the taller house, it will be in A's interest to compensate B for choosing the shorter version. To do so, he will have to give B at least 80, for that is what B gives up by not having the two-story house. The most A would be willing to give B is 100, since that is all the view is worth to A. For some payment P, where $80 \leq P \leq 100$, A will get to keep his view.

Suppose, however, that negotiations between the two parties were impractical. B would then go ahead with the two-story house, since that is the version he values most. By comparison with the one-story design, B would gain 80, but A would lose 100. The optimal structure of property rights in this particular example would be to prohibit any building that blocks a neighbor's view.

THE VALUE OF AN UNOBSTRUCTED VIEW

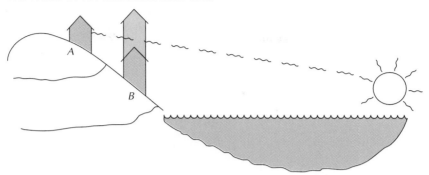

Of course, if the valuations assigned by the parties were different, a different conclusion might follow. If, for example, *B* valued the two-story house at 300 and *A*'s view were again worth 100, the optimal structure of property rights would be to allow people to build to whatever height they choose. In either case, the optimal structure of property rights is the one that places the burden of adjustment (either the loss of a view or the loss of a preferred building design) on the party that can accomplish it at the lowest cost.

As a practical matter, the laws of property in many jurisdictions often embody precisely this principle. In cities like San Francisco, where the views of the ocean and bay are breathtakingly beautiful, strict zoning laws regulate construction that blocks an existing building's line of sight. Zoning laws in cities where there is less to look at are generally much more liberal in the kinds of buildings they permit. But even in cities that have no special view to protect, zoning laws generally limit the fraction of the lot that can be occupied by man-made structures. Most people value access to at least some sunlight, and ordinances of this sort make it possible for them to get it.

Most people who grow up in market economies like the United States take the institution of private property rights for granted. But as the preceding examples made clear, the details of our various property laws have a great deal of economic structure. They embody sophisticated, if often implicit, calculations about how to reach the most efficient solutions to practical problems involving externalities. Indeed, as the following section illustrates, the very existence of private property may be traced to early attempts to deal with externalities.

THE TRAGEDY OF THE COMMONS

To explore the origins of the institution of private property, it is instructive to consider, as in the next example, what would happen in a society that lacked a well-developed institution of property rights.

*E*XAMPLE *17-7* *A village has six residents, each of whom has wealth of 100. Each resident may either invest his money in a government bond, which pays 12 percent per year, or use it to buy a year-old steer, which will graze on the village commons (there being no individually owned grazing land in this village). Year-old steers and government bonds each cost exactly 100. Steers require no effort to tend and can be sold for a price that depends on the amount of weight they gain during the year. Yearly weight gain, in turn, depends on the number of steers that graze on the commons. The prices of 2-year-old steers are given in Table 17-7 as a function of the total number of steers. If village residents make their investment decisions independently, how many steers will graze on the commons?*

As long as each villager cannot control access to the commons by cattle owned by others, the income-maximizing strategy will be to send an extra steer out onto the commons if and only if its price next year will be at least 112. (At that price, the gain from owning a steer is equal to the gain from buying a bond.) By this reckoning, there will be 3 steers sent onto the commons, and the rest of the villagers' money will be invested in government bonds. With this pattern of investment, village income from investment will be 14 from each of the 3 steers and 12 from each of the 3 bonds, for a total of 78.

Notice, however, that this is not the largest possible income the villagers could have earned. From the point of view of the village as a whole, the investment rule for steers should be: Send an extra steer onto the commons if and only if its marginal contribution to the value of the total herd after 1 year is greater than or equal to 112. Sending the third steer onto the commons resulted in a total herd worth $3 \times 114 = 342$, which is only 106 more than the value of a herd with only 2 steers ($2 \times 118 = 236$). Total village income is maximized by buying 4 bonds and sending 2 steers onto the commons. This pattern results in an income of 48 from bonds and 36 from steers, for a total of 84.

As more steers graze on the commons, each steer gains less weight, resulting in a lower price per steer.

TABLE 17-7   STEER PRICES AS A FUNCTION OF GRAZING DENSITY

Number of steers	Price per 2-year-old steer
1	120
2	118
3	114
4	111
5	108
6	105

The reason that the invisible hand failed to produce the best social result here is that individual villagers ignored an important externality. Their criterion for deciding to send another steer was to look only at the price increase that would occur for that particular steer. They took no account of the fact that sending an extra steer would cause existing cattle to gain less weight. Pastureland is a scarce resource in this example, and the villagers failed to allocate it efficiently because they were allowed to use it for free.

The problem would be solved if individual villagers could own pastureland and exclude others from using it. Suppose, for example, the village government decided to put the pastureland up for auction. What price would it fetch? Anyone who buys the pastureland has the right to restrict the number of steers to 2, which is the income-maximizing amount. We saw that, if used in this way, the land will generate an annual income of 36 from an annual investment of 200 (the price of two steers). Had the 200 instead been used to purchase government bonds, only 24 would have been earned. Having control over the commons thus yields a surplus of 12/yr over the income available to a person able to buy only government bonds. It follows that the price of the pastureland at auction will be 100 (the price of a bond that pays an income of 12/yr). If the price of pastureland were any less than 100, all investors would want to buy it instead of buying government bonds. If it sold for more than 100, every investor could do better by buying government bonds. The village government could take the 100 raised from the auction of its pastureland and distribute it among the 6 villagers, for an average payment of $\frac{100}{6}$.

EXERCISE 17-2

What grazing fee would solve the commons problem discussed in Example 17-7?

In early societies, it was a general practice for important resources such as pastureland and fisheries to be owned in common. The difficulty with such ownership schemes is that they lead to overexploitation of the resource. Figure 17-3 illustrates the problem of individual villagers who have the option of working in a factory at a wage of W/day, or of keeping all the fish they can catch from the village lake. The curve labeled AP shows how the average catch per fisherman varies with the number of fishermen, while MP shows the change in the total catch as a function of the number of fishermen. If fishermen get to keep whatever they catch, their decision rule will be to fish up to X', the point where AP = W. At X', the value of the total catch is exactly equal to the total income that the villagers who fished could have earned by working in the factory.

The socially optimal allocation is to fish only up to X^* in Figure 17-3, the point at which W = MP, and for all remaining villagers to work in the factory. At this allocation, the villagers who fish will earn a total of S^* (the shaded area) more than they could have earned by working in the factory.

If villagers are given free access to fish in the lake, the allocation that sends X^* out to fish will not be stable. Because each fisherman will be earning more than the villagers who work in the factory, factory workers will have an incentive to switch to fishing. Switching will stop only when X' have gone out to fish, making earnings in the two alternatives the same. As in the earlier pastureland example, the additional fishermen ignore the externality they impose on the existing fishermen. Each looks only at the size of his own catch, ignoring the fact that his presence makes everyone else's catch smaller.

In order to sustain the efficient allocation, something must be done to limit access to the lake. The simplest approach is to charge people for the right to go fishing. If the fishing fee were set at $AP^* - W$ (see Figure 17-3), the optimal allocation would result automatically from the income-maximizing decisions of individual villagers. Here, as in the pasture example, the problem was that individuals overutilized a productive resource they were allowed to use for free. The invisible hand mechanism can function properly only when all resources sell for prices that reflect their true economic value.

One of the continuing sources of inefficiency in modern economies involves the allocation of resources that no single nation's property laws can govern. For instance, several species of whales have been hunted to near extinction because no international laws of property exist to restrain individual incentives to kill whales. And the Mediterranean Sea has long had serious problems with pollution because none of the many nations that border it has an economic incentive to consider the effects of its discharges on other countries. As the world's population continues to grow, the absence of an effective system of international property rights will become an economic problem of increasing significance.

FIGURE 17-3
When a resource, such as a fishery or a pasture, is owned in common, each user gets to keep the average product of his own productive inputs he applies to the resource. Privately owned inputs will be applied to the resource until X', the point at which their average product equals their opportunity cost, W, resulting in an economic surplus of zero. The socially optimal allocation is X^*, the level of input for which W is equal to the marginal product of privately owned inputs, and results in an economic surplus of S^*.

THE TRAGEDY OF THE COMMONS

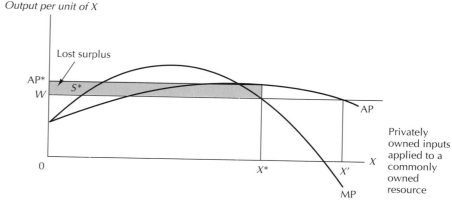

Externalities, Efficiency, and Free Speech

As the following discussion illustrates, the Coasian principles of efficiency apply not only to the design of property rights but also to the design of constitutions. In particular, they shed light on the extent to which society has an interest in protecting the right to free speech.

The First Amendment to the U.S. Constitution protects most forms of speech and expression, even those that cause intensely painful effects on others. A man once wrote to a newspaper advice columnist to confess to a cruel act he had committed decades earlier, during his senior year in high school. He and his friends had leafed through the school yearbook and picked out the photograph of the girl they agreed was the ugliest in their class. The letter writer had then called the girl on the telephone to congratulate her on her selection. During the ensuing years, he had never been able to forget her anguished groan in response. He would give anything, he said, if he could turn back the clock and recant that phone call.

Given the choice between receiving such a telephone call and being hit sharply on the arm with a stick, many people would immediately choose the latter. Had the boys hit the girl with a stick, they could have been put in jail. And yet they were perfectly within their First Amendment rights to make that phone call.

Why does our Constitution prohibit one form of harm but not the other? In the Coasian framework, the first thing to recognize is that it is highly impractical to negotiate solutions case by case to either type of harmful effect. We just cannot imagine the boys and the girl dickering about what she would be willing to pay to avoid hearing a painful remark or, for that matter, to avoid being struck with a stick. The structure of the law must therefore be guided by a judgment about which structure of rights will generate the best outcome where case-by-case negotiation is impractical.

Most people would surely agree that the world would be better if speech like the telephone prank could be prohibited. The practical question is whether it is possible to frame a law that would prevent such speech without preventing other speech that we value highly. Sadly, the answer seems to be no. Any law that prevented people from making cruel remarks to others would almost surely prohibit a great deal of highly valuable speech as well. The fear of criticism keeps many an otherwise wayward person in line, much to society's benefit. If it were practical to write a law that would permit justified criticism but prohibit criticism that is unwarranted, or even merely unkind, we might be seriously tempted to implement it. But so far, no one has come up with such a law.

Even so, the First Amendment's protection of free speech is far from absolute. For example, it does not protect a person's right to yell "Fire" in a crowded theater. Nor does it permit people to shout profanities on public street corners. Nor are we permitted to advocate the overthrow of the government by violent means. In such cases, we seem willing to say that the benefits of free speech are too small to justify its external costs.

Smoking Rules, Public and Private

Research studies show that exposure to cigarette smoke exhaled by others can be harmful to one's health. Such findings have lent considerable support to the recent trend toward laws that ban smoking in public places. On the plausible assumptions that (1) negotiating with strangers in public places is generally impractical and (2) the harm to nonsmokers from undesired exposure to smoke is more important than the harm to smokers from not being able to smoke in public places, such laws make good sense in the Coasian framework.

Thus far, however, no law has been proposed that would disallow smoking in private dwellings. The result is that sometimes people are exposed to smoke from their roommates. On the plausible assumption that the costs of negotiation with prospective roommates is relatively low, the following example illustrates that the lack of such laws is not likely to lead to an undesirable outcome.

EXAMPLE 17-8 *Smith and Jones are trying to decide whether to share a two-bedroom apartment or to live separately in one-bedroom apartments. The rental fees are $300/mo for one-bedroom and $420/mo—or $210/mo per person—for two-bedroom apartments. Smith is a smoker and would be willing to give up $250/mo rather than give up being able to smoke at home. Jones, however, is a nonsmoker and would sacrifice up to $150/mo rather than live with a smoker. Apart from the issues of smoking and rent, the two find joint living neither more nor less attractive than living alone. Neither has an alternative roommate available. Will they live together or separately?*

If they live separately, each can have things the way he wants on the smoking issue. The downside is that it is more costly to live alone. If they live together, they will save on rent, but one of them will have to compromise. Either Smith will have to give up smoking, or Jones will have to tolerate Smith's smoke. If a compromise is to be made at all, it will be made by Jones, since he is willing to pay less than Smith is to have his way. By living together, each party saves $90/mo in rent. If we ignore the possibility of negotiation, they will not live together because this savings is less than the cost to Jones of having to live with a smoker.

But suppose they are able to negotiate costlessly. The practical question then becomes whether the *total* savings in rent justifies the cost of the compromise to Jones. The total savings in rent is $180/mo, which is the difference between the $600/mo total they would pay if they lived alone and the $420 they will pay living together. And since this savings exceeds the cost to Jones by $30/mo, it should be possible to negotiate an agreement whereby the two will prefer to live together. Smith will have to give some of his $90/mo savings to Jones.

Let X denote the amount Smith gives to Jones. Since the cost to Jones of living with a smoker is $150/mo, and his savings in rent is only $90/mo, X must be at least $60/mo. Because Smith gets to continue smoking in the shared living arrangement, his $90/mo rent savings is pure gain, which means that $90/mo is the largest possible value for X. The relevant details for this example are summarized in Table 17-8.

Example 17-8 drives home the point that external effects are completely reciprocal. Smith's smoking harms Jones, just as traditional discussions of the issue emphasize. But denying Smith the opportunity to smoke will harm him, at least as he sees it. When it comes to the question of sharing living quarters, the smoke problem is a quintessentially shared problem. Because people are free to make whatever living arrangements they find mutually agreeable, Jones cannot be forced to endure smoke against his wishes. And by the same token, Smith cannot be forced to give up smoking. If they are to reap the savings from living together, one party must compromise on the smoke issue, and the other must compromise financially. Unless the terms of their agreement represent a clear improvement for both parties over the alternative of living alone, there will simply be no agreement.

EXERCISE 17-3

How would the entries in Table 17-8 be different if there were an exhaust system that completely eliminated the damage from smoke at a cost of $60/mo?

The cost to Smith of not smoking is $250/mo. The cost to Jones of living with a smoker is $150/mo. The total savings in rent from living together is $600/mo −$420/mo = $180/mo, which is $30/mo more than the least costly compromise required by shared living quarters, which is the $150/mo it costs Jones to live with a smoker.

TABLE 17-8 PAYOFF SUMMARY FOR EXAMPLE 17-8

	Net rental payment ($/mo)		Net gain ($/mo)		
	Jones	Smith	Jones	Smith	Total
Live separately	300	300	—	—	—
Live together; Smith pays Jones X to compensate for smoke, $60 \leq X \leq 90$	$210 - X$	$210 + X$	$X - 60$	$90 - X$	30

Positive Externalities

The Coase theorem applies not only to negative externalities but also to positive ones. Recall from Chapter 16 the example of the beekeeper and the owner of the apple orchard. The activities of each confer positive externalities on the other, which, if ignored, will result in suboptimally small levels of both apple and honey production. But if negotiation between them is costless, the beekeeper can offer to subsidize the orchard owner for planting more trees. The orchard owner, likewise, can offer payments to induce the beekeeper to enlarge his apiary. With either positive or negative externalities, inefficiencies result only if it is costly or otherwise impractical to negotiate agreements about how to correct them.

Positional Externalities

In many areas of endeavor, rewards are determined not by our absolute performance, but by how we perform relative to others. To be a champion swimmer, for example, what counts is not how fast you swim in absolute terms, but how your times compare with others'. As noted before, Mark Spitz won seven gold medals in the 1972 Olympics, and yet his winning times would not even have qualified him for the 1996 American men's swimming team.

Situations in which rewards are determined by relative performance are often called contests. In virtually every contest, each contestant will take a variety of actions in an attempt to enhance his or her probability of winning. Indeed, to take such actions is the essence of what it means to be in a contest. Some of these actions entail only minimal costs. Swimmers, for example, sometimes shave the hair from their heads and bodies in order to glide more smoothly through the water.

But in every contest where something important is at stake, competitors almost always take much more costly steps to win. In the race for national political office, contestants spend millions on advertising. In the race for military supremacy, nations invest billions developing and building new weapons.

Because the rewards in contests are distributed according to relative position, the laws of simple arithmetic tell us that any action that increases one contestant's chances of winning must necessarily reduce the chances of others. With this observation in mind, it is instructive to think of performance-enhancing actions as giving rise to *positional externalities*. If A and B are competing for a prize that only one of them can attain, anything that helps A will necessarily harm B.

The result is that when the stakes are high, unregulated contests almost always lead to costly *positional arms races*. In the absence of effective drug regulations, for example, many linemen in the National Football League apparently now feel compelled to enhance their size and strength by using anabolic steroids. It is easy to see why. In an arena where sheer physical bulk plays a central role, failure to use these dangerous hormones might obviously jeopardize a player's position on his team.

Like so many other arms races, however, the race to grow bigger and stronger yields few real benefits for the group of contestants as a whole. After all, the contest at the line of scrimmage can have only one winner, whether each team's linemen average 300 pounds or 240. At the same time, the race imposes substantial costs. Anabolic steroids have been linked to cancer of the liver and other serious health problems.

In hockey it is standard procedure for defensemen to throw their bodies to the ice to prevent an opponent's shot from going into the net. In NCAA hockey contests, this practice seldom causes serious injury anymore, because players are now required to wear helmets with heavy wire cages over the face openings. But before the appearance of these helmets, it was a risky proposition indeed. When a hockey puck traveling at more than 100 miles/hr makes contact with a human face, the results are ugly. On objective grounds, it seems utter folly for a player to risk mutilation by throwing his face in the path of the puck. And yet few players ever hesitated to do so when the chance arose. The urge to win—to do well in relative terms—is a powerful force of human nature. In situations where the material payoffs from winning are very large, this is hardly surprising. But even when the stakes are ostensibly low—as, for example, in a nonleague high school hockey game in upstate New York—people go to extreme lengths to enhance their chances.

Given what is at stake, voluntary restraint is rarely an effective solution to positional arms races. And so governing bodies in many sports now require strict drug testing of all competing athletes. The NCAA's helmet rule, similarly, has been a face-saving solution, both literally and figuratively; without it, few players would have dared to wear a face cage on their own. (In the National Hockey League, which has no similar requirement, helmets with face cages are rarer than defensemen's front teeth.)

As a further illustration of collective restraint of positional externalities, consider the ancient practice of dueling. A gentleman once felt compelled to defend his honor by challenging the offending party to a duel with pistols at sunrise. Duelists, and the people who cared about them, soon recognized the unfettered duel as an unacceptably costly practice. Over time, rules evolved that reduced the mortality rate. For example, the distance at which the pistols were fired grew steadily longer. And pistols with spiral-grooved barrels were forbidden. (Such grooves impart a spin to the bullet, making its trajectory much more true.) With these restrictions in place, only 1 in 6 duelists was actually struck by a bullet, and only 1 in 14 died. This was still a steep price to pay, of course, and it eventually led to an outright prohibition against dueling. With firm legal sanctions in place, we are now able to maintain our honor in a variety of much less injurious ways.

One of the most important contests people face in life is the task of making sure their children enter the labor market with a good education. This task is a contest because a "good" education, like an "effective" lineman, is an inescapably *relative* concept. If an effective lineman is one who is bigger, stronger, and faster than most other linemen, a good education is one that is *better than the education that most others receive.* This relativistic aspect of our objective is what makes us vulnerable to a positional arms race of the sort we see elsewhere.

In the education context, what form does this arms race take? Because public schools are funded largely by local property taxes, educational quality and neighborhood quality are closely linked in our public school systems. Competition for position thus often involves trying to move to the best possible neighborhoods. It is common for families to endure many hardships—working long hours, accepting risky jobs, going without vacations, skimping on savings, and so on— in order to scrape together the cash needed to move into a better school district. Again, however, the laws of simple arithmetic remind us that it is not possible for *everyone* in society to move forward in relative terms. Only 10 percent of our children can occupy the top tenth of our school seats, no matter how valiantly everyone strives.

Even in contests with very low stakes, we have seen that people often accept considerable sacrifice and risk to enhance their chances of winning. The contest to launch our children well in life is a contest whose stakes are high. Any one family's efforts to move forward in relative terms impose a negative externality on others. In a variety of other contexts, we have seen that social institutions evolve to promote efficient solutions to externalities. Armed with this view, we can gain similar new insights into a variety of social institutions that restrain the positional arms race among families. The traditional explanations for many of these institutions, we will see, often raise more questions than they answer.

LIMITING THE WORKWEEK

The Fair Labor Standards Act requires, among other things, that employers pay a 50 percent wage premium whenever people work more than 8 hours a day or 40 hours a week. This regulation sharply discourages overtime work, and has been defended on the grounds that, without it, monopsony employers would require workers to work unacceptably long hours.

Critics of overtime laws respond that if workers disliked working long hours, competition would result in an overtime premium even without a regulation. Alternatively, if workers wanted to work long hours, why would they support a law that discourages employers from having them do so? In the eyes of its detractors, the overtime law is either irrelevant or harmful.

Positional externalities provide a much more plausible rationale for hours regulation. If someone stays a few extra hours at work, she will increase her earnings, both in absolute and in relative terms. One result is that she will be able to afford a house in a better school district. But again, the problem is that one family's forward movement in relative terms means a backward movement for others. Rather than see their families fall behind, others will feel pressure to work longer hours themselves. In the end, these efforts are largely offsetting. As before, only 10 percent of our children can occupy seats in top-decile school districts.

By working until 8 P.M. each day, we can produce more and enjoy larger incomes than if we work only until 5 P.M. But in the process, we have less time to spend with our families and friends. It is easy to see why people might prefer to live in communities where everyone quits work at 5 P.M. And it is equally easy to see why there might be few such communities in the absence of overtime laws.

SAVINGS

Many observers complain, correctly, that the Social Security system prevents them from deciding for themselves when and how much to save for retirement. On the traditional view that having more options is better than having fewer, it would appear better for participation in Social Security to be purely voluntary. Yet most societies have mandatory programs to supplement retirement incomes. Positional externalities again help us to understand why.

The argument is essentially the same as in the case of hours regulation. A parent has the choice of saving some of her current income for retirement or spending that income now on a house in a better school district. As before, many parents find the second option compelling.

The aggregate effects of such choices, however, turn out to be far from what parents intend. When everyone spends more on a house in a better school district, the result is merely to bid up the prices of those houses. In the process, no one moves forward in the educational hierarchy, and yet parents end up having too little savings for retirement. Acting as individuals, however, their only real alternative is to send their children to less desirable schools.

The Social Security system mitigates this dilemma by making a portion of each person's income unavailable for spending. It helps solve a related set of positional externalities as well. A job seeker, for example, is well advised to look as good as he or she possibly can for job interviews. Looking good, however, is not a simple matter of wearing clothes that are clean and mended. Like a good education, a tasteful appearance is a relative concept. To look good means to look better than others, and the most practical way to do that is to spend more than most others do on clothing. The rub is that this same calculus operates for everyone. In the end, we get a fruitless escalation in the amount a person has to spend on clothing merely to avoid looking shabby. Viewed from the perspective of the population as a whole, it would make sense to save more and spend less on clothing. But it would not pay any individual, acting alone, to take this step. The Social Security system, by sheltering a portion of our incomes, keeps people from spending too much in this and a variety of other analogous situations.

WORKPLACE SAFETY

As a final illustration of positional externalities, consider the case of safety regulations in the workplace. As in the case of hours regulations, proponents of safety regulations often defend them by saying that monopsonists would otherwise force their workers to labor under unacceptably risky conditions. But as we saw in Chapter 14, this argument seriously underestimates the pressures of competition in the labor market. With these pressures in mind, critics of safety regulation say that it deprives workers of the right to decide for themselves how much safety they want to purchase in the workplace.

Once we take positional externalities into account, however, the institution of safety regulation begins to appear much less puzzling. One worker's choice of a riskier job makes it difficult for other workers to bid as effectively as before for houses in the best school districts. Feeling this pressure, they too are more likely to opt for riskier jobs. In positional terms, of course, these movements largely offset one another. People may prefer to neutralize this arms race by adopting laws that set minimum standards for workplace safety.[7]

Taxing Externalities

Before the appearance of Coase's 1960 paper, the economics profession was wedded to the view, pioneered by the British economist A. C. Pigou, that the best solution to negative externalities is to tax them. The idea is simple. If *A* carries out an activity that imposes a cost on *B*, then taxing *A* by the amount of that cost will provide him with the proper incentive to consider the externality in his production decisions. As the following example makes clear, however, such taxes sometimes make matters worse than if we did nothing at all.

EXAMPLE 17-9 Consider again the doctor and confectioner from Examples 17-1 to 17-6. Suppose that the doctor gains 60 by operating in a noise-free environment, and that the confectioner gains 40 by operating his noisy equipment. Suppose also that the doctor can eliminate the noise problem by rearranging his office at a cost of 18. And suppose, finally, that negotiation between the doctor and confectioner is prohibitively costly. The tax approach calls for a tax on the confectioner equal to the damage his activity would cause, which, in the absence of a response by the doctor, means a tax of 60. How will the outcome under such a tax compare with what would have happened in its absence?

> If there were costless negotiation, the confectioner could pay the doctor to rearrange his office and then operate without paying the tax, since his operation would cause no noise damage. But since negotiation is impractical, the doctor has no reason to incur this cost on his own. He knows that by doing nothing, the confectioner will face a tax of 60 if he operates, which in turn means that the confectioner's best option is to shut down. After all, his operation generates a gain of

---

[7]Whether such standards achieve their stated goal of making the workplace safer is strictly an empirical question. Some authors have argued that the bureaucratic inefficiencies of safety regulation have actually led to *reduced* safety levels. See Albert Nichols and Richard Zeckhauser, "Government Comes to the Workplace: An Assessment of OSHA," *The Public Interest*, 49, 1977: 39–69.

only 40 to begin with. With the confectioner no longer in operation, the doctor will gain 60 and the confectioner 0.

With no tax, however, the confectioner would have continued operations, for a gain of 40. The doctor's best response would have been to rearrange his office at a cost of 18, leaving him with a net gain of 42. Without the tax, we thus get the most efficient outcome, whereas the total gain with the tax is considerably smaller. The relevant data for this example are summarized in Table 17-9.

As Example 17-9 amply demonstrates, a tax on pollution can leave us in a worse position than if there were no tax at all. This is not surprising once we recognize that a tax on pollution has essentially the same effect as making the polluter liable for pollution damages. But this same recognition implies that taxation will not *always* be inefficient. It happened to be inefficient in Example 17-9 because the doctor happened to be the party who was best able to deal with the noise problem and the tax removed all incentive for him to do so. Suppose, to the contrary, the doctor had not had some inexpensive means of escaping the noise damage. The tax still would have led the confectioner to shut down, but this would now be the most efficient outcome. (See Example 17-1.)

Alternatively, suppose the confectioner had had some inexpensive means of eliminating the noise problem. Suppose, for example, that he could have installed soundproofing for a cost of 10. Here, too, the tax would have led to the most efficient outcome. The confectioner would have installed the soundproofing to escape the tax, and the doctor would have operated without disturbance.

Whether it is efficient to tax pollution thus depends on the particular circumstances at hand. If negotiation is costless, taxing will always lead to an efficient outcome. (But so, for that matter, will not taxing.) If negotiation is impractical, taxing pollution will still lead to an efficient outcome if the polluter has the least

The gain to the confectioner from operating is 40. The loss to the doctor from the confectioner's noise is 60. The doctor can rearrange his office to eliminate the noise problem at a cost of 18. The efficient outcome is for the doctor to rearrange his office, and this happens only when there is no tax on the confectioner.

TABLE 17-9 OUTCOME AND PAYOFF SUMMARY FOR EXAMPLE 17-9

Legal regime	Outcome	Net benefit		
		Doctor	Confectioner	Total
Tax of 60 on confectioner	Confectioner shuts down	60	0	60
No tax or liability	Doctor rearranges his office at his own expense	42	40	82

costly way of reducing pollution damage. Only if negotiation is impractical and the victim has the least costly means of avoiding damage will taxing pollution lead to an inefficient outcome. Taxing and not taxing will yield essentially the same outcomes if the costs of limiting pollution damage are roughly the same for both polluter and victim.

Suppose society has reached the judgment that the producers of pollution are in fact the ones who can mitigate its damages at the lowest cost. Society must then choose a policy that provides an incentive for the polluter to take action. One option is to set direct limits on the amount of pollution discharged. Alternatively, we could adopt a pollution tax, which means to charge polluters a fee for each unit of pollution they discharge. As the following example will demonstrate, the tax option offers a compelling advantage over the option of direct regulation.

EXAMPLE 17-10   *Two firms, X and Y, have access to five different production processes, each one of which has a different cost and gives off a different amount of pollution. The daily costs of the processes and the corresponding number of tons of smoke are listed in Table 17-10. If pollution is unregulated, and negotiation between the firms and their victims is impossible, each firm will use A, the least costly of the five processes, and each will emit 4 tons of pollution per day, for a total pollution of 8 tons/day. The city council wants to cut smoke emissions by half. To accomplish this, they are considering two options. The first is to require each firm to curtail its emissions by half. The alternative is to set a tax of T on each ton of smoke emitted each day. How large would T have to be in order to curtail emissions by half? And how would the total costs to society compare under the two alternatives?*

If each firm is required to cut pollution by half, each must switch from process A to process C. The result will be 2 tons/day of pollution for each firm. The cost of the switch for firm X will be 600/day − 100/day = 500/day. The cost to Y will be 140/day − 50/day = 90/day, which means a total cost for the two firms of 590/day.

How will each firm respond to a tax of T per ton of pollution? First it will ask itself whether switching from process A to B will increase its costs by more or less than T/day. If by less, it will pay to switch, because process B, which yields 1 ton less smoke, will save the firm T/day in taxes. If process B's costs exceed A's by more than T, however, the firm will not switch. It will be cheaper to stick with A and pay the extra T in taxes. If the switch from B to C pays, the firm will then ask the same question about the switch from B to C. It will keep switching until the extra costs of the next process are no longer smaller than T.

To illustrate, suppose a tax of 50/ton were levied. Firm X would stick with process A because it costs 90/day less than process B and produces only 1 ton/day of extra smoke, and thus 50/day in extra taxes. Firm Y, by contrast, will switch to process B because it costs only 30/day more and will save 50/day in taxes. But firm Y will not continue on to C because it costs 60/day more than B and will save only an additional 50/day in taxes. With firm X staying with A and firm Y switching to B, we get a total pollution reduction of 1 ton/day. A tax of 50/ton thus does not produce the desired 50 percent reduction in pollution.

The solution is to keep increasing the tax until we get the desired result. Consider what happens with a tax of 91/ton. This tax will lead firm X to adopt process B, firm Y to adopt process D. Total emissions will be the desired 4 tons/day. The cost to firm X will be 190/day − 100/day = 90/day, and the cost to firm Y will be 230/day − 50/day = 180/day. The total cost for both firms is thus only 270/day, or 320/day less than the cost of having each firm cut pollution by half. Note that the taxes paid by the firm are not included in our reckoning of the social costs of the tax alternative, because this money is not lost to society. It can be used to reduce whatever taxes would otherwise have to be levied on citizens.

The advantage of the tax approach is that it concentrates pollution reduction in the hands of the firms that can accomplish it in the least costly way. The direct regulatory approach of requiring each firm to cut by half took no account of the fact that firm Y can reduce pollution much more cheaply than firm X can. Under the tax approach, note that the cost of the last ton of smoke removed is the same for each firm.

More generally, suppose that there are two producers, firm X and firm Y, whose marginal costs of smoke removal are shown by the curves labeled MC_X and MC_Y, respectively, in Figure 17-4. If the goal is to reduce total smoke emissions by $Q = Q_X^* + Q_Y^*$ tons/day, a tax of T^* will accomplish that goal in the

Each firm has access to five alternative production processes, A–E, which vary both in cost and in the amount of pollution they produce.

TABLE 17-10 COST AND EMISSIONS FOR FIVE PRODUCTION PROCESSES

Process (smoke)	*A* (4 tons/day)	*B* (3 tons/day)	*C* (2 tons/day)	*D* (1 ton/day)	*E* (0 tons/day)
Cost to firm X	100	190	600	1200	2000
Cost to firm Y	50	80	140	230	325

FIGURE 17-4
MC_X and MC_Y represent the marginal cost of smoke reduction for firms X and Y, respectively. When pollution is taxed at a fixed rate, each firm reduces its emissions up to the point where the marginal cost of further reduction is exactly equal to the tax. The result is the least costly way of achieving the corresponding aggregate pollution reduction.

THE TAX APPROACH TO POLLUTION REDUCTION

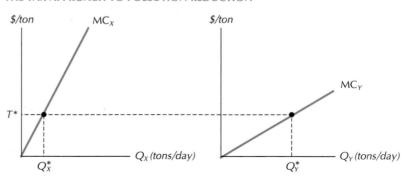

least costly way. The characteristic feature of this solution is that the marginal cost of pollution reduction would be exactly the same for all firms. If that were not the case, it would always be possible to reallocate the pollution reduction in such a way as to reduce total costs.

The direct regulatory approach (telling each firm how much to reduce pollution) could also achieve any given total pollution reduction at minimum costs if regulators knew each firm's marginal cost of reduction curve. They could then simply assign reduction quotas in such a way as to equate marginal reduction costs across firms. The difficulty is that regulatory officials will generally not have even the vaguest idea of what these curves look like. The compelling advantage of the tax approach is that it achieves efficiency without requiring any such knowledge on the part of regulators.

Recall from Chapter 16 our discussion of the efficiency losses generally caused by taxation. Another important advantage of taxing negative externalities is that it provides a means of raising government revenue that does not entail such efficiency losses. On the contrary, we have seen that the taxation of negative externalities can actually *increase* efficiency. Whether taxing negative externalities would yield enough revenue for government to carry out all its activities is an empirical question. If it would, then concerns about inefficiencies from taxation would no longer be a subject of concern.

TAXING POSITIONAL EXTERNALITIES

There is considerable evidence in support of the proposition that the utility that people get from consumption depends not only on absolute consumption levels, but on relative consumption levels as well. No one in the nineteenth century felt disadvantaged by not owning an automobile or a television set, and yet people who lack these items today are apt to feel strongly dissatisfied indeed. And their dissatisfaction is not merely a matter of envying the possessions of their neighbors. If no one owned a car, then I would not be required to have one to meet the minimal demands of social existence. But because almost everyone has a car today, it is extremely difficult to get along without one.

If relative consumption is important, it follows logically that each person's consumption imposes negative externalities on others. When any one person increases his consumption, he raises, perhaps imperceptibly, the consumption standard for others. As the British economist Richard Layard once stated, "In a poor society a man proves to his wife that he loves her by giving her a rose, but in a rich society he must give a dozen roses."

The fact that many forms of consumption generate negative externalities has important implications for tax policy. To illustrate, consider a young man's decision about how big a diamond to give his fiancée. Because the function of this gift is to serve as a token of commitment, the one he buys must necessarily cost enough to hurt. His jeweler will tell him that the custom in this country is to pay 2 months' salary for a stone and setting. If he makes $36,000/yr, he will have to come up with $6000 or else feel like a cheapskate.

From the perspective of the economy as a whole, the outcome would be better if there were a 500 percent tax on jewelry. The after-tax price of what is now only a $1000 diamond would then rise to $6000. In buying this smaller diamond, the young man would incur the same economic hardship as before. And since this is the essence of the gift's function, his goal would not really be compromised by the tax. Nor would the young man's fiancée suffer any real loss. Because *everyone* would now be buying smaller diamonds, the smaller stone would provide much the same satisfaction as the larger one would have. On the plus side, the government gets an additional $5000 to finance its expenditures. The only loser is the deBeers diamond cartel of South Africa, which would earn $5000 less than before the tax.

The standards that define acceptable schools, houses, wardrobes, cars, vacations, and a host of other important budget items are inextricably linked to the amounts other people spend on them. Because individual consumers ignore positional externalities in their choices, the result is that such commodities appear much more attractive to individuals than to society as a whole. For the same reasons that it is often efficient to tax pollution, it will be efficient to tax many of these forms of consumption. On efficiency grounds, such taxes would be an attractive substitute for existing taxes that interfere with efficient resource allocation.

Summary

When an action by one party harms another and the parties are able to negotiate costlessly with one another, the negative externalities are dealt with efficiently regardless of whether the law makes people liable for the harmful effects of their actions. This result is known as the Coase theorem.

When negotiation is costly, it does matter how liability is assigned. In general, the most efficient outcome occurs when the law places the burden of avoiding harmful effects on the party that can accomplish it at the lowest cost.

This general principle sheds light on a variety of questions regarding the design of property rights. It helps explain: why the owner of a dock may not legally exclude a boater from tying up during a storm; when people are allowed to exclude others from walking across their land or from blocking their view; why pastureland is more productive if owned privately rather than in common; why airplanes are allowed to fly over someone's property, while developers cannot build above it without permission. In each case, the laws of property are set up to mimic as closely as possible the kinds of accommodations people would reach for themselves if they were free to negotiate costlessly with one another.

Similar principles apply to a variety of other governmental restraints on behavior. In the case of free speech and other constitutional liberties, the best legal solutions turn out to be the ones that most closely resemble the solutions people would have negotiated among themselves, had it been practical to do so.

Similar conclusions apply in situations that involve positive externalities. If negotiation is costless, people will forge agreements that result in efficient outcomes, even in cases where one party's activities create indirect benefits to the other. And where negotiation is costly, institutions tend to evolve that encourage activities with positive external effects.

In contests for relative position, as in all other contests, the efforts by one contestant confer a negative externality on other contestants: anything that increases one party's odds of winning necessarily reduces the odds of others. The effect is almost always to induce some form of arms race among contestants, in which the efforts of each party serve largely to offset one another. The theory of externalities and property rights sheds a great deal of light on the laws by which citizens of modern societies restrict such arms races.

Taxation is one solution to the problem of negative externalities. Although it is not always an ideal answer, it does offer several important advantages over direct regulation in many situations. Taxation of negative externalities provides a source of governmental revenue that is largely exempt from the allocative inefficiencies we encountered in Chapter 16.

Questions for Review

1. When negotiation costs are negligible, why is the assignment of liability for externalities irrelevant for efficiency?

2. Does the assignment of liability matter for distributional reasons?

3. Suppose you are the party who can avoid a particular external effect at the lowest cost. Why might you favor a general rule that assigns liability to whichever party can avoid damage at the lowest cost?

4. Why do we permit airplanes but not real estate developers to use the airspace over private homes without prior consent?

5. Why do most property laws limit private coastal property to the waterline at high tide?

6. Give three examples of the tragedy of the commons on your campus.

7. How does the widespread existence of negative externalities alter the claim (see Chapter 16) that taxing goods lowers economic efficiency?

Problems

1. Every November, Smith and Jones each face the choice between burning their leaves or stuffing them into garbage bags. Burning the leaves is much easier but produces noxious smoke. The utility values for each person, measured in utils, are listed in the table for each of the four possible combinations of actions:

	Smith	
	Burn	**Bag**
Burn	Jones: 4	Jones: 8
	Smith: 4	Smith: 2
Jones		
Bag	Jones: 2	Jones: 6
	Smith: 8	Smith: 6

a. If Smith and Jones are utility maximizers and make their decisions individually, what will they do?

b. How will your answer to part (a) differ, if at all, if Smith and Jones can make binding agreements with each other?

Now suppose the payoff matrix is as follows:

	Smith	
	Burn	**Bag**
Burn	Jones: 6	Jones: 8
	Smith: 6	Smith: 2
Jones		
Bag	Jones: 2	Jones: 4
	Smith: 8	Smith: 4

c. What will they do this time if they can make binding agreements?

2. Smith can produce with or without a filter on his smokestack. Production without a filter results in greater smoke damage to Jones. The relevant gains and losses for the two individuals are listed in the table below:

	With filter	Without filter
Gains to Smith	$200/wk	$245/wk
Damage to Jones	$35/wk	$85/wk

a. If Smith is not liable for smoke damage and there are no negotiation costs, will he install a filter? Explain carefully.
b. How, if at all, would the outcome be different if Smith were liable for all smoke damage and the cost of the filter were $10/wk higher than indicated in the table? Explain carefully.

3. Smith can operate his sawmill with or without soundproofing. Operation without soundproofing results in noise damage to his neighbor Jones. The relevant gains and losses for Smith and Jones are listed in the table:

	Without soundproofing	With soundproofing
Gains to Smith	$150/wk	$34/wk
Damage to Jones	$125/wk	$6/wk

a. If Smith is not liable for noise damage and there are no negotiation costs, will he install soundproofing? Explain.
b. How, if at all, would your answer differ if the negotiation costs of maintaining an agreement were $4/wk? Explain.
c. Now suppose Jones can escape the noise damage by moving to a new location, which will cost him $120/wk. With negotiation costs again assumed to be zero, how, if at all, will your answer to part (a) differ? Explain.

4. Smith and Jones are trying to decide whether to share an apartment. To live separately, each would have to pay $300/mo in rent. An apartment large enough to share can be rented for $450/mo. Costs aside, they are indifferent between living together and living separately except for these two problems: Smith likes to play his stereo late at night, which disturbs Jones's sleep; and Jones likes to sing in the shower at 6 A.M., which awakens Smith. Jones would sacrifice up to $80/mo rather than stop singing in the shower, and Smith would sacrifice up to $155/mo rather than stop playing his stereo late at night. Smith would tolerate Jones's singing and Jones would tolerate Smith's stereo in return for compensation payments not less than $75/mo and $80/mo, respectively.

a. Should they live together? If so, indicate how they can split the rent so that each does better than by living alone. If not, explain why no such arrangement is feasible.

b. Now suppose Smith wins a free pair of stereo headphones. If he wears them late at night, Jones's sleep is not disturbed. Smith likes the headphones well enough, but would be willing to pay $40/mo to keep on listening to late-night music through his speakers. How, if at all, does the existence of this new option affect your answer to part (a)? Explain carefully.

5. A and B can live separately at a rent of $400/mo each, or together at a rent of $600. Each would be willing to give up $30/mo to avoid having to give up his privacy. In addition to the loss of privacy, joint living produces two other conflicts, namely, each has a particular behavior the other finds offensive: B is a trumpet player, and A smokes cigarettes. B would be willing to pay $60/mo rather than tolerate smoking in his house and $120/mo to continue playing his trumpet. A, for his part, would pay up to $100/mo to continue smoking and up to $90/mo to avoid listening to trumpet music. Will they live together? Explain carefully. Would your answer be different if A didn't mind giving up his privacy?

6. A and B live on adjacent plots of land. Each has two potential uses for her land, the present values of each of which depend on the use adopted by the other, as summarized in the table. All the values in the table are known to both parties.

		A	
		Apple growing	**Pig farming**
Rental housing		A: $200	A: $450
		B: $700	B: $400
B			
	Bee keeping	A: $400	A: $450
		B: $650	B: $500

a. If there are no negotiation costs, what activities will the two pursue on their land?

b. If there are negotiation costs of $150, what activities will the two pursue on their land?

c. What is the maximum net income A can earn in parts (a) and (b) above?

7. A village has six residents, each of whom has $1000. Each resident may either invest his money in a government bond, which pays 11 percent/yr, or use it to buy a year-old steer, which will graze on the village commons. Year-old steers and government bonds each cost exactly $1000. Steers require no effort to tend and can be sold for a price that depends on the amount of weight they gain during the year. Yearly weight gain, in turn, depends on the number of steers that graze on the commons. The prices of 2-yr-old steers are given in the table as a function of the total number of steers:

Number of steers	Price per 2-year-old steer
1	$1200
2	1175
3	1150
4	1125
5	1100
6	1075

a. If village residents make their investment decisions independently, how many steers will graze on the commons?

b. How many steers would graze on the commons if investment decisions were made collectively?

c. What grazing fee per steer would result in the socially optimal number of steers?

8. A competitive fishing industry consists of five independently owned and operated fishing boats working out of the port of Ithaca. Assume that no other fishermen fish Cayuga Lake, and that the MC of operating a boat for 1 day is equivalent to 70 pounds of fish. (A boat left idle generates no costs.) The total catch per shoreline, in pounds, is given in the following table as a function of the number of boats fishing the east and west shores of the lake:

	Total catch	
Number of boats per side	East shore	West shore
1	100	85
2	180	150
3	255	210
4	320	260
5	350	300

a. If each boat owner decides independently which side of the lake to fish and all boats are in plain view of each other, how many boats would you expect to find fishing each shore on any given day? What is the net catch (that is, the total catch from both shores, less operating costs)?

b. Is this distribution of fishing craft optimal from the social point of view? If so, explain why. If not, what is the socially optimal distribution and the corresponding net catch?

9. Two firms, X and Y, have access to five different production processes, each one of which gives off a different amount of pollution. The daily costs of the processes and the corresponding number of tons of smoke are listed in the table:

Process (smoke)	A (4 tons/day)	B (3 tons/day)	C (2 tons/day)	D (1 ton/day)	E (0 tons/day)
Cost to firm X	100	120	140	170	220
Cost to firm Y	60	100	150	255	375

   a. If pollution is unregulated, which process will each firm use, and what will be the total daily smoke emissions?
   b. The city council wants to cut smoke emissions by half. To accomplish this, it requires a municipal permit for each ton of smoke emitted and limits the number of permits to the desired level of emissions. The permits are then auctioned off to the highest bidders. If X and Y are the only polluters, how much will each permit cost? How many permits will X buy? How many will Y buy?
   c. Compare the total cost to society of this permit auction procedure to the total cost of having each firm reduce emissions by half.

10. Suppose the government attempts to restrict pollution by mandating a maximum amount that each firm can pollute. In general, this will result in a higher cost for pollution control than is necessary. Explain why.

*11. A small village has six people. Each can either fish in a nearby lagoon or work in a factory. Wages in the factory are $4/day. Fish sell in competitive markets for $1 apiece. If L persons fish the lagoon, the total number of fish caught is given by $F = 8L - 2L^2$. People prefer to fish unless they expect to make more money working in the factory.

   a. If people decide individually whether to fish or work in the factory, how many will fish? What will be the total earnings for the village?
   b. What is the socially optimal number of fishermen? With that number, what will the total earnings of the village be?
   c. Why is there a difference between the equilibrium and socially optimal numbers of fishermen?

12. Once a week Smith purchases a six-pack of cola and puts it in his refrigerator for his two children to drink later. He invariably discovers that all six cans get drunk the first day. Jones also purchases a six-pack of cola once a week for his two children, but unlike Smith, he tells them that each may drink no more than three cans. Explain why the cola lasts much longer at Jones's house than at Smith's.

---

*This problem is most easily solved by making use of the calculus definition of marginal product given in the appendix to Chapter 9, which can be found in the "For the Instructor" section at our Web site www.mhhe.com/economics/frank4.

13. Suppose Smith owns and works in a bakery located next to an outdoor cafe owned by Jones. The patrons of the outdoor cafe like the smell that emanates from the bakery. When Smith leaves his windows open, the cafe faces the demand curve $P_C = 30 - 0.2Q_C$, while when the windows are closed, demand is given by $P_C = 25 - 0.2Q_C$. However, Smith doesn't like the street noise he hears when his windows are open, and in particular, the disutility he receives has a monetary value of 5. Assume that the cafe has a constant marginal cost of 10, and that integration (merger) is not a possibility because each owner greatly enjoys owning and operating his own establishment.

   a. In the absence of a contract between the parties, do the firms behave in an efficient fashion? If not, describe the range of contracts that might emerge in response to the externality problem present in the environment. In answering this question, assume Smith understands how the bakery odor affects demand at the cafe, and Jones knows how much Smith dislikes street noise.

   b. Suppose now everything is the same as above, except that given the current seating arrangement in the cafe, the cafe does not face a higher demand when the bakery windows are open. To realize this higher demand, Jones needs to make a sunk investment of 50, which moves the tables closer to the bakery. Is it wise for Jones to make this investment prior to Smith and Jones signing a contract? Explain.

   c. Go back to the initial setup, but now assume that Smith's disutility from street noise equals 50 rather than 5. Further, suppose that prior to the parties agreeing on a contract Jones becomes the mayor and grants to himself the property rights concerning whether the bakery windows are left open or closed. Does this have an effect on whether the parties reach an efficient outcome? Explain.

14. Smith and Jones face the choice of driving to work early or late. If they both drive to work at the same time, each gets in the way of the other on the road, and so their daily commute takes longer and is more irritating. The monetary payoffs for each person are listed in the table below for each of the four possible combinations of actions:

		Smith	
		Early	Late
Jones	Early	Jones: 30 Smith: 30	Jones: 50 Smith: 20
	Late	Jones: 20 Smith: 50	Jones: 10 Smith: 10

a. If Smith and Jones are payoff maximizers and make their decisions individually, what will they do?

b. If Smith and Jones can make binding agreements with each other, what will they do?

15. Same as Problem 14, except now the payoff values of each person are

		Smith	
		Early	**Late**
Jones	**Early**	Jones: 30 Smith: 30	Jones: 50 Smith: 20
	Late	Jones: 20 Smith: 60	Jones: 10 Smith: 10

a. If Smith and Jones are payoff maximizers and make their decisions individually, what will they do?

b. If Smith and Jones can make binding agreements with each other, what will they do?

c. How do your answers differ from Problem 14 and why?

16. Smith loves dogs and has a pair of West Highland terriers. Jones has an incredible fear of dogs and cannot stand to be within sight of them. Smith and Jones are deciding whether to live in Arlington or Bexley. If they end up living in the same part of town, Jones will run into Smith out walking the Westies and get frightened. Thus, Jones prefers to be physically separated from Smith. The payoffs for each person are listed in the table below for each of the four possible combinations of actions:

		Smith	
		Arlington	**Bexley**
Jones	**Arlington**	Jones: 0 Smith: 800	Jones: 500 Smith: 900
	Bexley	Jones: 800 Smith: 800	Jones: 0 Smith: 900

a. If Smith and Jones are payoff maximizers and make their decisions individually, what will they do?

b. If Smith and Jones can make binding agreements with each other, what will they do?

17. Same as Problem 16, except now payoff values of each person are

		Smith	
		Arlington	**Bexley**
Jones	**Arlington**	Jones: 0 Smith: 800	Jones: 500 Smith: 1000
	Bexley	Jones: 600 Smith: 800	Jones: 0 Smith: 1000

- **a.** If Smith and Jones are payoff maximizers and make their decisions individually, what will they do?
- **b.** If Smith and Jones can make binding agreements with each other, what will they do?
- **c.** How do your answers differ from Problem 17 and why?

Answers to In-Chapter Exercises

17-1. With a negotiation cost of only 20, it is now practical for the confectioner to pay the doctor to rearrange his office when the confectioner is liable. But note in the table below that it is still more efficient for the confectioner not to be liable:

			Net benefit	
Legal regime	**Outcome**	**Doctor**	**Confectioner**	**Total**
Liable	Confectioner operates and pays doctor $18 \leq P \leq 20$ to rearrange office	$22 + P$	$40 - P$	62
Not liable	Doctor rearranges his office at his own expense	22	60	82

17-2. Recall that the optimal number of steers is two. The grazing fee must be more than 2 to prevent a third steer from being sent out to graze. The fee cannot be more than 6 without keeping the second steer from being sent out.

17-3. Now the cost of accommodating to the smoke problem is 60, which is again less than the joint savings in rent. Let X represent Jones's contribution to the cost of the exhaust system, which means that Smith's contribution is $60 - X$. X cannot exceed 90, or else Jones will live separately; and X cannot be less than -30, or else Smith will live separately. The total gain is $180 - 60 = 120$.

	Net rental payment ($/mo)		Net gain ($/mo)		
	Jones	Smith	Jones	Smith	Total
Live separately	300	300	—	—	—
Live together and install exhaust system smoke, $-30 \leq X \leq 90$	$210 + X$	$270 - X$	$90 - X$	$30 + X$	*120*

CHAPTER
18

Government

ocal telephone companies are regulated monopolies, and so governmental regulators must rule on all their charges to the public. Historically, regulatory agencies prevented charges for directory assistance calls in the belief that such charges would "diminish the value of a vital public communications network." This conclusion, needless to say, seemed hopelessly vague to most economists. Directory assistance calls cost the phone company (and hence society) a lot of money to provide, and the economist's immediate fear is that people will be uneconomical in their use of this or any other resource for which they do not have to pay.

Some years ago, Alfred Kahn, then chairman of the New York State Public Service Commission (which regulates New York telephone companies), proposed that the companies begin charging 10 cents for every call made to directory assistance. Kahn was on leave from his post as an economics professor at Cornell, and earned cheers from his colleagues for his sensible proposal to give people an incentive to look numbers up for themselves in the phone book.

But his proposal drew a much different response from consumer advocates. These groups hired sociologists and other expert witnesses, who testified that the social fabric would deteriorate sharply if people were penalized for attempting to get in touch with one another. Other witnesses complained that the charges would impose an unacceptable burden on the poor.

The proposal seemed doomed when Kahn made a brilliant amendment, one that would preserve its efficiency gains while at the same time eliminating any adverse effects on the poor. The amendment was that every telephone subscriber would be given a 30-cent credit on his or her monthly telephone bill in reflection of the costs saved on directory assistance calls. For example, someone who made one directory assistance call per month would be charged 10 cents, which, when combined with the credit, would make his monthly bill 20 cents less than before. Someone who made three directory assistance calls per month would break even, someone with four would pay 10 cents more than before, and so on. On the plausible assumption that a charge of 10 cents per call would be more likely to induce a low-income person than a high-income person to cut down on directory assistance calls, the net effect of the amended proposal was actually to increase the real purchasing power of the poor.

Chapter Preview

The directory assistance episode illustrates two critically important points about government economic policy: (1) that distributional concerns permeate discussion of even the most seemingly trivial policies; and (2) that the most efficient solution to a public policy problem is one that enables both rich and poor alike to do better than before. Our task in this chapter is to explore two important functions of government: the provision of public goods and the direct redistribution of income. Concerns about both fairness and efficiency, we will see, are inextricably linked in both of these areas.

We will also see that the mere fact that a good has the characteristics of a public good does not mean that it must necessarily be provided by government. We will examine a variety of ingenious schemes, ranging from free commercial television to highly structured collective legal contracts, whereby public goods are provided with virtually no involvement by government.

We will also see that problems similar to those that arise in connection with public goods are encountered whenever there are significant indivisibilities or economies of scale in the production of private consumption goods.

Next we take up the question of how societies make choices between competing public projects, with particular focus on cost-benefit analysis as an alternative to majority voting schemes.

Our next topic is a problem that plagues all mechanisms of public decision making, namely, that self-interested parties have an incentive to influence outcomes in their own favor. This problem goes by the name of rent seeking and has become an increasingly serious threat to our social welfare.

From the problems of public choice, which themselves have important distributional overtones, we next turn our attention to the topic of direct income transfer programs. Here our focus is on how such transfers might be accomplished without undermining incentives to work and take risks.

Public Goods

As noted in Chapter 16, public goods are those goods or services that possess, in varying degrees, the properties of *nondiminishability* and *nonexcludability*. The nondiminishability property, again, says that any one person's consumption of a public good has no effect on the amount of it available for others. Nonexcludability means that it is either impossible or prohibitively costly to exclude nonpayers from consuming the good.

Pure public good
A good that has a high degree of nondiminishability and nonexcludability.

Collective good
A good that is excludable but has a high degree of only nondiminishability.

Goods that have high degrees of both of these properties are often called **pure public goods,** the classic example of which is national defense. Goods that have only the nondiminishability property are sometimes referred to as **collective goods.** Collective goods are sometimes provided by government, sometimes by private companies. Most pure public goods are provided by government, but even here there are exceptional cases in which profit-seeking companies have devised schemes for providing them.

Let's begin our analysis with the case of a government trying to decide what quantity to provide of some pure public good—say, public television programming. For simplicity, imagine that there are only two citizens, A and B, and that each assigns a different value to any given quantity of the public good. In Figure 18-1, the horizontal axis measures the quantity of programming. The curve labeled *AA'* represents the amount *A* would be willing to pay for an additional unit of programming, and *BB'* represents the corresponding curve for B. Thus, at a level of 4 units of programming, *A* would be willing to pay $9/wk for an additional unit, while *B* would be willing to pay only $6/wk. The fact that the two willingness-to-pay curves are downward sloping reflects the fact that the more programming there already is, the less valuable an additional unit will be.

FIGURE 18-1
AA' and *BB'* represent the respective amounts that *A* and *B* are willing to pay for an additional unit of the public good. The aggregate willingness-to-pay curve is the vertical summation of the individual willingness-to-pay curves, the curve labeled *DD'A'*.

THE AGGREGATE WILLINGNESS-TO-PAY CURVE FOR A PUBLIC GOOD

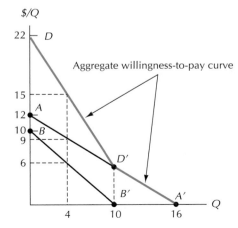

The central fact about providing any pure public good is that each person must consume the same amount of it. In markets for private goods, by contrast, each person can consume whatever amount she chooses at the prevailing price. To obtain the market demand curve for a private good, we simply added the individual demand curves horizontally. In the case of public goods, the analog to the market demand curve is the aggregate willingness-to-pay curve. It is obtained by adding the individual willingness-to-pay curves not horizontally but vertically. At $Q = 4$ units of programming in Figure 18-1, for example, A and B together are willing to pay a total of $9 + 6 = \$15/wk$ for an additional unit of programming. The curve labeled $DD'A'$ represents the vertical summation of the two individual willingness-to-pay curves.

EXERCISE 18-1

Ten homogeneous consumers all have individual willingness to pay curves $P = 12 - \frac{1}{5}Q$ for a public good—say, a concert in an open park (where P is measured in dollars and Q is measured in minutes). Construct and graph the aggregate willingness to pay curve. For a 30-minute concert, what is the maximum each individual would be willing to pay?

THE ANALOGY TO JOINT PRODUCTION

In passing, let's note the striking similarity between the procedure for generating the aggregate willingness-to-pay curve for a public good and the procedure whereby the demand curve for a product like chicken is generated from the demand curves for the various parts of a chicken. For simplicity, suppose chickens are composed of only two parts, wings and drumsticks, the demand curves for which are given by the curves labeled WW' and DD' in Figure 18-2. The horizontal axis in Figure 18-2 measures three things simultaneously: total pairs of drumsticks, total pairs of wings, and total number of chickens—because any given number of chickens will give rise to that same number of pairs of wings and drumsticks. On the simplifying assumption that wings and drumsticks are the only two chicken parts, we get the market demand curve for chickens by adding the demand curve for wings and the demand curve for drumsticks vertically. The curve labeled $CC'D'$ in Figure 18-2 represents this vertical summation.

The curve labeled SS' in Figure 18-2 is the supply curve for chickens. Assuming the chicken industry is competitive, it is the horizontal summation of the marginal cost curves of the individual chicken producers. As in any other competitive market, equilibrium in the market for chickens occurs at the intersection

FIGURE 18-2

FIGURE 18-2

DD' is the demand curve for pairs of drumsticks; *WW'* the demand curve for pairs of wings. Their vertical sum, *CC'D'*, is the market demand curve for chickens. The equilibrium price and quantity of chickens are determined by the intersection of this demand curve and the market supply curve.

EQUILIBRIUM IN A MARKET FOR JOINTLY PRODUCED PRODUCTS

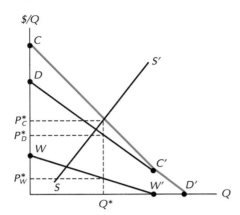

of the supply and demand curves. The equilibrium quantity of chickens will be Q^*, and that quantity will give rise to Q^* pairs of drumsticks and Q^* pairs of wings. The market-clearing prices for drumsticks and wings will be P_D^* and P_W^*, respectively. These two prices sum to the equilibrium price of chickens, P_C^*.

There are several important points to note about the equilibrium in the market for jointly produced goods. First note that the equilibrium quantities of wings, drumsticks, and chicken are efficient in the Pareto sense. At Q^* the cost to society of producing another chicken is P_C^*, and this is exactly the total value that consumers place on its component parts. Any other quantity of chickens would leave open the possibility of mutual gains from exchange. Note also that the price of each chicken part cannot be determined from cost information alone, even if we know exactly the marginal cost of raising another chicken. There is simply no scientific basis for apportioning the cost of the entire bird among each of its constituent parts. Drumsticks and wings sell for their respective prices because those are the prices necessary to clear the markets for each. In a precisely analogous way, there is no correspondence between the amount that any one individual is willing to pay for a public good and its marginal cost of production.

THE OPTIMAL QUANTITY OF A PUBLIC GOOD

Let's return again to our example of public television programming. Given the aggregate willingness-to-pay curve, what is the optimal quantity of programming? The answer is determined in much the same way as in the market for chickens. In Figure 18-3, the curve labeled *DD'A'* again represents the aggregate willingness-to-pay curve for public television programming. The curve labeled MC represents the marginal cost of television programming as a function of its quantity. The intersection of these two curves establishes $Q^* = 4$, the optimal level of public television programming. At $Q^* = 4$, the amounts that A and B

FIGURE 18-3
The optimal level of
the public good is
$Q^* = 4$, the level for
which aggregate
marginal willingness
to pay for the good
is exactly equal to
its marginal cost.

OPTIMAL PROVISION OF A PUBLIC GOOD

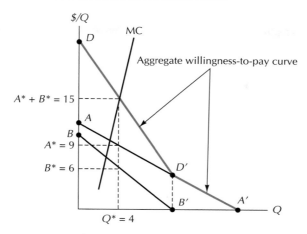

would be willing to pay for another unit of programming add to exactly the cost
($15/wk) of producing another unit. If this equality did not hold, we could eas-
ily show that society would be better off by either expanding or contracting the
amount of programming.

EXERCISE 18-2

> Consider the scenario described in Exercise 18-1, but now suppose that
> the marginal cost of providing the concert is MC = $2Q$. Determine the
> optimal length of the concert.

PAYING FOR Q^*

We must make a slight qualification to the claim that Q^* is the optimal level
of the public good in Figure 18-3. The statement is true subject to the provision that the *total* cost of Q^* does not exceed the total amount that the public
would be willing to pay for it. The total willingness to pay for Q^* is the area
under the aggregate willingness-to-pay curve up to Q^*. The total cost is the
area under the marginal cost curve up to Q^*, plus any fixed costs. Provided
that the total cost is smaller than the total willingness to pay, Q^* is the optimal
level of the public good. This qualification is similar to the requirement that a
profit-maximizing firm produce where MR = MC, subject to the proviso that
total revenues cover total costs (total variable costs in the short run, all costs
in the long run).

If the government is to produce Q^* units of a public good, it must somehow raise sufficient tax revenue to cover the total production costs of that amount. Suppose, for the sake of discussion, that the government's tax structure requires the collection of equal tax payments from all citizens. In the example in Figure 18-3, B's willingness to pay for the public good is smaller than A's. It follows that B will vote for the provision of Q^* only if the total cost of Q^* is less than twice the area under BB' up to Q^*. For example, if the total cost of the good is 100, and each party must be taxed equally, B will vote for it only if his total willingness to pay exceeds 50. If the amount B is willing to pay for the public good is only, say, 40, this condition will not be satisfied, and so the project will not win approval.

And yet we know that this public good is one whose benefits to all citizens add up to more than its costs. Compared with the alternative in which the public good is not provided, both A and B can be made better off by providing Q^* of it and then taxing A more heavily than B in order to pay for it. It follows that a tax structure that levies the same tax on all citizens cannot in general be Pareto efficient.

The situation here is analogous to the case in which the incomes of two spouses differ substantially. Suppose Julie earns \$100,000/yr while her husband, Bruce, earns only \$15,000. Given her income, Julie as an individual would want to spend much more than Bruce would on housing, travel, entertainment, and the many other items they consume in common. But suppose the couple adopted a rule that each had to contribute an equal share toward the purchase of such items. The result would be to constrain the couple to live in a small house, to take only inexpensive vacations, to skimp on entertainment and dining out, and so on. And so it is easy to imagine that Julie would find it attractive to pay considerably more than 50 percent for jointly consumed goods, thereby enabling both of them to consume in the manner their combined income affords.

As in the case of private goods, the willingness to pay for public goods is generally an increasing function of income. The rich, on the average, assign greater value to public goods than the poor do, not because they have different tastes but because they have more money. A tax system that taxed the poor just as heavily as the rich would result in the rich getting smaller amounts of public goods than they want. Rather than see that happen, the rich would gladly agree to a tax system that assigns them a larger share of the tax burden. It would be missing the point to criticize such a system by saying that the system is unfair because it enables the poor to enjoy the services of public goods for a smaller price. It does have this property, to be sure; but from the viewpoint of the rich, its terms are still attractive because the tax payments of the poor, though small, mean the rich end up paying less than if they had to finance public goods all by themselves.

PRIVATE PROVISION OF PUBLIC GOODS

Governments are not the exclusive providers of public goods in any society. Substantial quantities of such goods are routinely provided through a variety of private channels. If it is impractical to exclude people from consuming a public good, the pressing question is how can the good be paid for, if not by mandatory taxes?

Funding by Donation.   One method for funding public goods is through voluntary donations. People donate great artworks to museums; they make contributions to listener-supported radio stations, to fund animal shelters, to research on debilitating diseases, and so on. Motives for such donations are as varied as the projects they support. Some see charitable giving as a means to achieve respect and admiration in the community.[1] Others may feel pressure to give in order to avoid social ostracism. These motives are really two sides of the same coin—social reward in the first case and social penalty in the second. Where such social forces are effective, they are a practical way of excluding nonpayers from full enjoyment of the public good.

Alternatively, people may donate because the increment to the public good that their contribution will finance is simply worth that much money to them. This motive is most likely to be important in situations where one person's action can significantly affect the scale of the public good. Someone who lives at the end of a short dirt road in a rural area, for example, may find it worthwhile to pave the entire road at his own expense. He would naturally be happier if everyone who lived on the road chipped in. But rather than do without the road altogether, it may be worthwhile for him to pave it himself. Similarly, a person who plants a flower garden in front of her house provides a public good for neighbors to enjoy. If her own personal enjoyment from the garden exceeds its cost, pure self-interest is a sufficient motive for her to plant it.

But self-interested motives do not seem sufficient to explain why people make anonymous donations that will have no appreciable effect on the benefits they themselves receive. In the case of listener-supported radio stations, no single person's contribution will make a perceptible difference in the nature or quality of programming. The station will either continue to operate in its current form, or else improve, or else get worse—irrespective of what any one person does.

Free riding
Choosing not to donate to a cause but still benefiting from the donations of others.

In such situations, the logic of pure self-interest seems to dictate *free riding*—abstaining in the hope that others will contribute. And yet millions of people contribute to such enterprises each year. For many of these people, the satisfaction of giving—of having contributed to the common good—is an end in itself. And as we saw in Chapter 7, there may well be important material advantages in being such a person.

The fact that public goods are often supported through voluntary contributions does not necessarily mean, however, that they are supported at socially optimal levels. Residents might be perfectly willing to pay sufficient taxes to build the socially optimal road. And yet, in the absence of taxes, the road that actually gets built is likely to be considerably smaller. Similarly, many people

---

[1]To achieve the social benefit of charitable giving, the gift must become public knowledge. Most charitable organizations publicize their list of donors.

might strongly want society to invest more in public television programming. But these same people might be reluctant to give voluntarily as much as they would be willing to pay in taxes.

Sale of By-Products.   Free-rider problems are sometimes solved by devising novel means to finance the public good. One such way is the sale of an important by-product of the public good. In the case of commercial television, for example, financing comes from sponsors, generally private corporations, who pay for the right to beam advertising messages to the audience attracted by the broadcast. The captive viewing audience is a by-product of the broadcast, and sponsors are willing to pay a lot for access to it. As the following example makes clear, however, this system does not always assure an optimal allocation of broadcast resources.

EXAMPLE 18-1   *In a given time slot, a television network faces the alternative of broadcasting either the Jerry Springer Show or Masterpiece Theater. If it chooses Springer, it will win 20 percent of the viewing audience, but only 18 percent if it chooses Masterpiece Theater. Suppose those who would choose Springer would collectively be willing to pay $10 million for the right to see that program, while those who choose Masterpiece Theater would be willing to pay $30 million. And suppose, finally, that the time slot is to be financed by a detergent company. Which program will the network choose? Which program would be socially optimal?*

> The sponsor cares primarily about the number of people who will see its advertisements, and will thus choose the program that will attract the largest audience—here, the *Jerry Springer Show*. The fact that those who prefer *Masterpiece Theater* would be willing to pay a lot more to see it is of little concern to the sponsor. But this difference in willingness to pay is critical when it comes to determining the optimal result from society's point of view. Because the people who prefer *Masterpiece Theater* could more than compensate the *Springer* viewers for relinquishing the time slot, *Masterpiece Theater* is a Pareto-superior outcome. But unless its supporters happen to buy more soap in total than the *Springer* viewers, *Springer* will prevail. The difficulty with reliance on advertising and other indirect mechanisms for financing public goods is that there is no assurance that they will reflect the relevant benefits to society.

Development of New Means to Exclude Nonpayers.   Another way to finance public goods privately is to devise cheap new ways of excluding people who do not pay for the good. In broadcast television, it was once impossible to prevent any household from tuning in to a program once it was sent out over the airwaves. With the advent of cable TV, however, households are now simple to exclude. With the ability to charge for specific programs, it is no longer necessary to make programming decisions on the basis of which program will garner the largest audience. In our *Jerry Springer* versus *Masterpiece Theater* example, a broadcasting company that can exclude nonpayers would have every incentive to show *Masterpiece Theater,* because its proponents now have a practical means of translating their greater willingness to pay into profits for the producer.

But note that whereas the outcome of pay-per-view TV is more efficient in the sense of selecting the programs the public most values, it is less efficient in one other important respect. By charging each household a fee for viewing, it discourages some households from tuning in. And since the marginal social cost of an additional household watching a program is exactly zero, it is inefficient to limit the audience in this way. Which of the two inefficiencies is more important—free TV's inefficiency in choosing between programs or pay TV's inefficiency in excluding potential beneficiaries—is an empirical question.

Private Contracts.   Legal contracts among private individuals offer yet another means for overcoming some of the difficulties associated with the free-rider problem. Consider, for example, the public good consisting of residential maintenance and beautification. As neighborhoods are customarily organized, it is impractical to exclude your neighbors from the benefits they will reap if you keep your house well painted and your yard neatly trimmed. Nor would it be efficient to exclude them, because their consumption of these benefits does not diminish their value to you and others in any way. In this respect, home maintenance and beautification satisfy the definition of a pure public good and, for this reason, will generally be undersupplied by private individuals.

We saw in Chapter 17 that if transactions were costless, your neighbors could subsidize your investments in home maintenance and beautification, and you could do likewise for them. Set at the proper levels, subsidies of this sort would result in the optimal levels of investment by every homeowner. But in general it is very costly to negotiate such subsidies on a case-by-case basis, and so the level of investment in home maintenance often ends up being well below optimal.

The organizers of condominiums, cooperatives, and other forms of legal residential associations have come up with an effective solution to this problem. The condominium contract requires each owner to contribute a specified sum each month toward maintenance and beautification. This payment functions much like a tax in the sense that it is mandatory for all parties to the contract. The advantage is that it is less coercive than a tax in one important respect: People who wish to spend less on home maintenance are free to live elsewhere.

Similar selection may occur between neighborhoods in different school districts. One district may choose higher spending levels on schools (and higher taxes to fund them) than another district nearby. Households then self-select: Families with children choose to live in the high-tax area, and singles and retirees choose to live in the other district.[2]

---

[2]See also the subsequent discussion of local public goods.

The Economics of Clubs.   A pure public good has the property that an additional person's consumption of the good does not limit the amount of it available to others. Stated another way, the marginal cost of additional consumption of the public good is exactly zero. Many privately produced goods have the property that marginal cost, although not zero, declines sharply with the number of users accommodated. The swimming pool is a case in point. The number of swimmers it can accommodate rises in proportion to its surface area, but its cost rises much more slowly. The difference between such goods and goods that satisfy the nondiminishability criterion perfectly is thus one of degree rather than of kind.

When the marginal cost of expanding the capacity of a private good is low relative to its average cost, consumers face an economic incentive to share the purchase and use of the good. In the swimming pool example, the cost to each of 20 families of a pool large enough for all to share will be much smaller than the cost of a pool large enough to serve the needs of only a single family. Indeed, the same statement is true of virtually any good that is not kept in continuous use by a single user. For example, most homeowners use extension ladders only once or twice a year, making it possible for several families to cut costs by sharing a single ladder.

The disadvantage of sharing, besides the fact that it requires someone to take the initiative to organize the arrangement, is that it limits both privacy and flexibility of access to the good. Thus, a homeowner might want to use the ladder on a particular Saturday afternoon, only to find it already in use by one of its other co-owners. Sometimes such inconveniences are trivial in relation to the cost savings; other times they will not be.

Opportunities for shared ownership thus confront the consumer with a variant of the standard consumer choice problem. To illustrate, consider again the choice between a privately owned pool and a shared pool. If we measure privacy and flexibility in the use of a pool on a scale from 0 to 1.0, a private pool would take the value 1.0, representing maximal privacy and flexibility. The limiting case at the other extreme is a large pool shared by infinitely many other people; the flexibility index for such a pool takes the value 0, representing virtually no privacy or flexibility.

The vertical axis in Figure 18-4 measures the amount the consumer spends on all other goods besides pools. If she buys her own private pool, at a cost of $Y' - Y_0$, she will achieve a privacy and flexibility index of 1.0. The other extreme represents a completely crowded pool, at a cost of 0 and a flexibility index of 0. Pools of intermediate size and crowdedness are represented by intermediate points on the budget constraint BB' in Figure 18-4. The consumer's best option is (F^*, Y^*), the point for which this budget constraint is tangent to an indifference curve (IC^*).

On the plausible assumption that the demand for privacy increases with income, we would predict that high-income consumers would be more likely to purchase their own pools than low-income consumers. But even consumers with very high incomes will find it attractive to participate in sharing arrangements

FIGURE 18-4
When the marginal cost of accommodating an extra user of a consumption good is less than the average cost, consumers can save money by forming clubs that share ownership of such goods. The optimal club for members with the same tastes is one for which the marginal rate of substitution between all other goods and privacy is exactly equal to the cost of additional privacy.

THE TRADEOFF BETWEEN PRIVACY AND COST

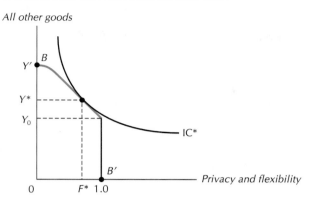

for extremely costly consumption goods. Rather than maintain exclusive rights to operate an airplane that would sit idle on the tarmac most hours of the week, for example, even wealthy amateur pilots often choose to become members of flying clubs, the use of whose aircraft is shared with other members.

In the case of very inexpensive goods, by contrast, we would expect the demand for privacy to take precedence over the lure of cost savings even for consumers of relatively modest means. A privately owned toothbrush, like a privately owned airplane or swimming pool, is destined to remain idle for most hours of the day. Its cost per owner could be lowered substantially if it were shared by the members of a toothbrushing club. But the savings from such a transaction would be far too small to justify the sacrifice in privacy. Virtually everyone, even the poorest citizen, finds it worthwhile to maintain exclusive access to his personal toothbrush.

Public Choice

Whether public goods are provided by governments, charitable organizations, or private clubs, decisions must be made about the types and quantities to provide. The budget constraint confronting the group is often clear enough. The much more difficult aspect of the problem is to devise some means for translating the diverse preferences of the group's members into a single voice.

MAJORITY VOTING

One method of discerning group preferences is the majority vote. By this standard, projects favored by a majority—in either a direct referendum or a vote taken by elected representatives—are adopted and all others are abandoned. In recent years, much attention has been given to the fact that majority voting often leads to intransitivities in the ranking of alternatives. To illustrate, consider a group with three members—McCain, Biden, and Schumer—each of whom has a well-ordered ranking of three alternative projects: a new missile, a medical research project, and more aid to the poor. McCain likes the missile best, medical research next best, and aid to the poor last. Biden likes medical research best, aid to the poor next best, and the new missile last. Schumer, finally, likes aid to the poor best, a new missile next best, and medical research last. These rankings are summarized in Table 18-1.

Given these rankings, note what happens when each of the three pairs of alternatives is put to a vote. In deciding which of any pair of alternatives to vote for, each voter will naturally choose the one he prefers to the other. Thus, in a vote between a new missile and medical research, the missile will get 2 votes (McCain and Schumer); the research only 1 (Biden). In a vote between research and aid to the poor, research gets 2 votes (McCain and Biden); aid only 1 (Schumer). And finally, in a vote between aid and the missile, aid gets 2 votes (Schumer and Biden); the missile only 1 (McCain). Thus the missile defeats the research program and the research program defeats aid to the poor, and yet aid to the poor defeats the missile program! Such intransitivities were assumed not to occur in individual preference orderings, but can easily happen if social choice takes place by successive majority votes between pairs of alternatives.

Agenda Manipulation.   The possibility of intransitivities in majority voting makes the order in which alternatives are considered by the electorate critically important. Suppose, for example, that McCain is in charge of setting the agenda for voting. His first priority will be to avoid a direct confrontation between the missile (his most favored project) and the aid project (which he knows will defeat the missile in a majority vote). He can ensure the missile's success by first conducting a vote between the aid project and the research project, followed by a vote between the winner of that election and the missile. The research project will win the first vote and will then be defeated by the missile in the second. Given power to set the agenda, either Biden or Schumer could have taken similar steps to ensure victory for either the research project or the aid project.

In a majority vote, the missile defeats the research program, which in turn defeats aid to the poor. And yet aid to the poor wins when paired against the missile. Majority voting schemes can lead to intransitivities even when individual preference orderings are transitive.

TABLE 18-1   **PREFERENCES THAT PRODUCE INTRANSITIVE CHOICES IN MAJORITY VOTING**

	McCain	Biden	Schumer
Best	Missile	Research	Aid
Second	Research	Aid	Missile
Third	Aid	Missile	Research

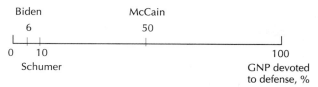

FIGURE 18-5
The most preferred options for Biden, Schumer, and McCain are 6, 10, and 50 percent, respectively, making Schumer the median voter. No matter what pair of proposed percentages for defense is put to a vote, the one closest to Schumer's most preferred option will win.

The Median Voter Theorem.   Intransitive rankings do not always result when alternatives are considered pairwise in a majority voting system. For example, we will get no intransitivities when the alternatives represent different quantities of a given public good and each voter ranks each according to how close it is to what, for her, is the optimal amount of the good. To illustrate, suppose our three voters are now considering what percentage of GNP to devote to national defense; and suppose that, as shown in Figure 18-5, the ideal percentages for McCain, Biden, and Schumer are 50, 6, and 10, respectively. Suppose, finally, that the percentages being considered for adoption are 5, 8, 11, 20, 40, and 60.

Does the power to set the order in which pairs of alternatives are considered confer the power to choose the ultimate outcome? This time the answer is no. In any pair of alternatives put to a vote, the winner will always be the one preferred by Schumer. Suppose, for instance, that 5 and 8 are put to a vote. McCain and Schumer will vote for 8 and Biden for 5, making Schumer's choice the winner. If the alternatives are 20 and 60, Biden and Schumer will vote for 20 and McCain for 60, and Schumer's choice again wins. Because Schumer's most preferred outcome lies between the most preferred choices of the other two, he is the so-called *median voter* in this situation, and his vote will always prevail. The *median voter theorem* states that whenever alternatives can be ranked according to their closeness to each voter's ideal outcome, majority voting will always select the alternative most preferred by the median voter.

Median voter
The voter whose ideal outcome lies above the ideal outcomes of half the voters.

EXERCISE 18-3

Given that the percentages of GNP under consideration for spending on national defense are again 5, 8, 11, 20, 40, and 60, which outcome will be chosen if the most preferred percentages of Biden, Schumer, and McCain are 11, 25, and 40, respectively?

Single-peaked preferences
Preferences that exhibit a single most-preferred outcome, with other outcomes ranked lower as their distances from their most-preferred outcome increases.

The technical feature of preferences that eliminates intransitivities in the defense spending example is called *single-peakedness*. To have single-peaked preferences with respect to the share of GNP spent on defense means to have a uniquely most preferred outcome and to rank all other outcomes in terms of their distance from it. Such preferences rule out liking 10 percent most and then ranking 30 percent better than 20 percent.

In contexts like the defense example, it seems plausible to assume that preferences are indeed single-peaked. But in other contexts, such as the missile-aid-research example, preferences need not have this property. Numerous important examples occur in practice in which majority voting leads to intransitive rankings, making the power to set the agenda tantamount to the power to choose the final outcome.

COST-BENEFIT ANALYSIS

The difficulty of public choice by majority voting is not just that it sometimes leads to intransitivities. An even more serious problem is that it almost completely obscures important differences in the intensity with which different voters hold their preferences. Suppose, for example, that there are two alternatives put to a vote: (1) to allow smoking in public buildings and (2) to prohibit smoking in public buildings. If 51 percent of the voters prefer the first alternative and only 49 percent the second, the result will be to allow smoking in public buildings. But suppose the 49 percent who favor a prohibition feel very strongly about it and collectively would be willing to pay $100 million/yr in order to have it. And suppose the opponents of the prohibition are only mildly opposed; they know it will cause them some short-term inconvenience, but most of them want to quit or cut down on their smoking anyway, and they realize the ordinance will help them to do that. Collectively, the most they would be willing to pay in order to continue smoking in public buildings is only $1 million/yr. Under these circumstances, there is a simple transfer payment that makes the outcome chosen by the majority clearly Pareto inferior to the prohibition on smoking in public buildings. If the prohibitionists give the smokers $10 million/yr in exchange for agreeing to the ban, both groups will be better off than if smoking continues—the smokers by $9 million/yr, the nonsmokers by $90 million/yr.

Cost-benefit analysis is an alternative to majority voting that attempts to take explicit account of how strongly people feel about each of the alternatives under consideration. Its method for measuring intensity of preference is to estimate how much people would be willing to pay in order to have the various alternatives. In the smoking example, it would immediately rule in favor of the prohibition because its benefits to its supporters (as measured by what they would be willing to pay to have it) strongly outweigh its costs to its opponents (as measured by what they would be willing to pay to avoid it).

Another advantage of cost-benefit analysis is that it would also avoid the intransitivities that often arise under majority voting. To illustrate, let's consider how it would deal with the missile-aid-research decision we discussed earlier. Table 18-2 displays hypothetical valuations assigned by McCain, Biden, and Schumer to each of the three alternatives. Positive entries in the table represent the amounts each person would pay to have a program he likes. Negative entries represent what someone would pay to avoid a program he dislikes. The entries

Cost-benefit analysis chooses the project with the largest surplus of benefits over costs. If each project costs 100, the surplus will be 20 for the missile, 65 for the research program, and 35 for the aid program. The cost-benefit test will therefore choose the research program.

TABLE 18-2   WILLINGNESS TO PAY FOR THREE PROJECTS

	McCain	Biden	Schumer	Total
Missile	100	−25	45	120
Research	35	90	40	165
Aid	−20	60	95	135

in the first column of the table, for instance, indicate that McCain would pay 100 to have the missile, 35 to have the medical research program, and 20 to avoid the aid program for the poor. Note that each person's ranking of the alternatives is the same in Table 18-2 as it was in Table 18-1.

To keep the discussion simple, suppose that the cost of each program is 100, but that because of budgetary shortages, only one of the three programs can be undertaken. How will cost-benefit analysis choose among them? It will pick the one for which the surplus of total benefit over cost is greatest. Again for simplicity, assume that the amounts the three voters would pay for each program accurately capture all relevant benefits. The total benefit of each program will then be the sum of what each voter would pay to have (or avoid) it. These totals are listed in the last column of Table 18-2 and reveal that the research program is the clear winner.

Note also that the research program would not have won if McCain had been able to set the agenda for a majority voting session. He would first pit the research program against the aid program, defeating it 2 to 1. And McCain's favored missile project would then defeat the research program by the same margin. Schumer, through similar agenda manipulation, could arrange for his favored aid program to emerge the winner in a majority voting sequence.

Note, finally, that if the research program did *not* get adopted, it would always be possible to construct a Pareto-preferred switch to the research program. Suppose, for example, that McCain set the agenda in a majority voting sequence, with the result that the missile was chosen. This outcome yields a loss of 25 for Biden. By contrast, had the research program been chosen, Biden would have had a gain of 90, a net improvement of 115 for him. This improvement is big enough to enable Biden to compensate both McCain and Schumer for the losses they would suffer by switching from the missile to the research program. Suppose, for example, that Biden gives McCain 70 and Schumer 10 for switching. Then the net benefits to McCain and Schumer will be 105 and 50, respectively, a gain of 5 each over their positions with the missile. A similar Pareto-improving move could be constructed if we had begun with the aid program. Indeed, the cost-benefit test will in general lead to a Pareto-efficient outcome.

If cost-benefit analysis satisfies the Pareto criterion while majority voting does not (at least, not always), why do we so often use majority voting for making collective choices? One objection to cost-benefit analysis is that because it measures benefits by what people are willing to pay, it gives insufficient weight to the interests of people with little money. On this view, the poor may feel very strongly about an issue, and yet their feelings will not count for much in cost-benefit analysis since they don't translate into large willingness-to-pay values. This sounds at first like a serious objection, but as the following example clearly demonstrates, it does not survive close scrutiny.

*E*XAMPLE 18-2 *Suppose there are only two people, R (who is rich) and P (who is poor). And suppose that R favors a public project that P opposes. In purely psychological terms, their intensity of feeling is the same. But because R has much more money, he would be willing to pay 100 to have the project, while P would be willing to pay only 10 to avoid it. If each could choose which method to use for deciding on public projects, which would each favor, cost-benefit analysis or majority rule?*

> At first glance, majority rule sounds attractive to *P* because it gives him veto power over any project he does not favor. But the first step *P* would take if he were given that veto power would be to yield it in exchange for a compensation payment. If *R* values the project at 100 and *P* would pay only 10 to avoid it, the most efficient outcome here is to go ahead with the project. If *R* gives *P* a compensation payment of *X*, where $10 \leq X \leq 100$, then each party will be better off than if *P* had insisted on exercising his veto. By *P*'s own reckoning, the inconvenience of the project is less than the value to him of the compensation payment. The fact that the cost-benefit test always leads to the greatest economic surplus means that it will always be in the interests of *R* and *P* alike to use it.

Critics of cost-benefit analysis sometimes concede that it would lead to Pareto-optimal outcomes in every case if it were practical to make the needed compensation payments. But they go on to argue that such compensation payments usually are not practical on a case-by-case basis. And so, they conclude, it is unfair to make decisions on the basis of cost-benefit analysis.

This argument also fails on close examination. First, note that in most societies literally thousands of decisions are taken each year with respect to public goods and programs. Each one, if adopted, would help some people and hurt others. Almost always the individual magnitudes of the gains and losses in any one decision are extremely small, much less than 1 percent of even a poor person's annual earnings. If projects are decided by the cost-benefit criterion, the amount that winners gain on any adopted project will necessarily outweigh the amount that losers lose. Where small projects are concerned, then, the cost-benefit test is like flipping a coin that is biased in your favor. On each flip of the coin you might either win or lose, but the probability of winning exceeds the probability of losing. If both the gains and losses are small and randomly distributed among individuals, and if the coin is to be flipped thousands of times, this makes for a very attractive gamble indeed. The law of large numbers (see Chapter 6) tells us that it is virtually certain that everyone will come out a winner in the end.

But suppose that the gains and losses from each outcome are not random; that, on the contrary, the poor usually come out on the losing side of the cost-benefit test because of their inability to back up their favored programs with high willingness-to-pay values. Even if it is impractical to compensate the poor on an issue-by-issue basis, it is *still* possible to achieve a better outcome for everyone by relying on the cost-benefit criterion. The reason is that the poor can be compensated on an ongoing basis through the tax system. If the alternative is to rely on majority voting, which would allow the poor to block projects whose benefits exceed their cost, the cost-benefit criterion, together with compensation through the tax system, will deliver a preferred outcome for every party.

The only telling argument in favor of majority voting is its simplicity. It is much easier to take a majority vote than to gather detailed information about what different individuals would be willing to pay for their preferred alternatives. Much progress has been made in recent years in the design of mechanisms that induce people to reveal truthfully what their valuations are. But these mechanisms remain cumbersome, and it is a lot easier to allow people to reveal their preferences by their votes. And in many situations, of course, majority voting and cost-benefit analysis will lead to the same outcome anyway.

LOCAL PUBLIC GOODS AND THE TIEBOUT MODEL

Even with a perfect mechanism for choosing between alternative public goods, it is difficult to escape the need for painful compromise. One group will sincerely believe that it is society's duty to provide complete health care for every citizen; another will believe with equal sincerity that it is each individual's responsibility to provide for his own health care. Given heterogeneous preferences of this sort, the result is often some form of compromise—partial public support for health care—that pleases neither group of voters.

With respect to public goods provided at the local level, Professor Charles Tiebout suggested that at least some of these compromises can be avoided if people are free to form communities with others of similar tastes.[3] Those who favor high levels of public goods can group together in communities in which they willingly accept the high tax rates necessary to finance these levels. And others who favor a more limited menu of public goods and services can form groups of their own and have lower tax rates.

As an empirical matter, local governments do differ widely with respect to the level of public goods they provide. Even so, there are practical difficulties with the notion of trying to tailor a local environment to precisely one's own preferences. Consider, for example, the issue of public support for the poor. People

---

[3]Charles Tiebout, "The Pure Theory of Local Expenditure," *Journal of Political Economy*, October 1956: 416–424.

have legitimate differences over what this level of support should be. But those who favor high levels of support often take on more than they bargained for when they enact generous welfare policies at the local level. The difficulty is that such policies attract new low-income beneficiaries from other jurisdictions with lower benefits. This, in turn, makes it necessary to raise tax rates, which leads some upper-income taxpayers to leave, further exacerbating the fiscal imbalance. The ability to form local communities of like-minded voters softens the need to compromise in some areas, but by no means eliminates it.

RENT SEEKING

As a practical matter, the gains from public choices are often large and concentrated in the hands of a few, whereas the costs, while also large, are spread among many. The difficulty such situations create for the public is clear. The prospective beneficiaries of a public program have powerful incentives to lobby government in favor of it, while each of the prospective losers has too little at stake to bother about. The result, all too frequently, is that projects are approved even when their benefits do not exceed their costs.

A related difficulty arises in the case of similar projects whose benefits do exceed their costs. Because there are large gains to be had from the project, private parties are willing to spend large sums in order to enhance their odds of being chosen as its beneficiaries. Pursuit of these gains goes by the name of *rent seeking*. One consequence of rent seeking is that the expected gains from government projects are often squandered by the competition among potential beneficiaries.

Consider, for example, a local government faced with the task of awarding the local cable TV franchise. Unless the government is prepared to engage in strict rate-of-return regulation, which most local governments are not, the franchisee can expect to earn substantial monopoly profits. The likelihood of any applicant being awarded the franchise is an increasing function of the amount of money it spends lobbying local legislators. The lure of the franchise's expected profits thus causes applicants to engage in a lobbying war to win the franchise. And as the following example illustrates, such lobbying wars tend to dissipate much of the gains made possible by the project.

*E*XAMPLE 18-3 *Three firms have met the deadline for applying for the franchise to operate the cable TV system for Cedar Rapids during the coming year. The annual cost of operating the system is 25, and the demand curve for its services is given by P = 50 − Q, where P is the price per subscriber per year and Q is the number of subscribers. The franchise lasts for exactly 1 year and permits the franchisee to charge whatever price it chooses. The city council will choose the applicant that spends the most money lobbying city council members. If the applicants cannot collude, how much will each spend on lobbying?*

The winner will set the monopoly price for the service, which is the price that corresponds to the quantity at which marginal revenue equals marginal cost. Marginal revenue for the cable system is given by MR = 50 − 2Q, and marginal cost is zero by assumption. The profit-maximizing quantity will thus be 25, which gives rise to a price of 25. Total revenue will be 25(25) = 625, which makes for a profit of 625 − 25 = 600. If any applicant spends more on lobbying than the other two spend, it will win the franchise. If all three spend the same, each applicant will have a 1-in-3 chance of earning 600 in profit, which means an expected profit of 200. If the lobbyists could collude, each would agree to spend the same small, token amount on lobbying. But in the absence of a binding agreement, each will be strongly tempted to try to outspend the others. If each firm's spending reaches 200, each will have expected profits of zero (a one-third chance to earn 600, minus the 200 spent on lobbying). At this point, it might seem foolish to bid any further, because higher spending levels would mean an expected loss. And yet if any one of the three spent 201, while the other two stayed at 200, it would get the franchise for sure and earn a net profit of 399. The losers would each have losses of 200. Rather than face a sure loss of 200, the losers may well find it attractive to bid 201 themselves. Where this process will stop is anyone's guess.[4] The one thing that seems certain is that it will dissipate some or all of the gains that could have been had from the project. From the viewpoint of any individual firm, it is perfectly rational to lobby in this fashion for a chance to win government benefits. From the standpoint of society as a whole, however, such activity is almost completely wasteful. The efficient government is one that takes every feasible step to discourage rent seeking—for example, by selecting contractors on the basis of the price they promise to charge, not on the amount they lobby.

---

[4]The following experiment provides some relevant evidence. A $1 bill is auctioned off subject to the following rules. The bill goes to the highest bidder, who must pay the auctioneer the amount he bid. The second-highest bidder gets nothing, but must also pay the auctioneer the amount he bid. In a typical trial of this auction, the bids slowly approach 50 cents, at which point there is a pause. Then the second bidder offers more than 50 cents and the bids quickly escalate to $1. There is another pause at $1, whereafter the second bidder bids more than $1, and the bids again quickly escalate. It is not uncommon for the winning bid to exceed several dollars.

Income Distribution

In market economies, the main means of earning income is by selling factors of production. Some people, by far the minority, earn a significant portion of their income from the ownership of stocks, bonds, and other financial instruments. Most people depend primarily on the proceeds from the sale of their own labor.

This system of distributing incomes is far from perfect, but it does have several attractive properties. First, it leads to a determinate outcome: The theory of competitive factor markets tells us that each factor will be paid the value of its marginal product, and that in long-run competitive equilibrium, these payments will add up to exactly the total product available for distribution.[5] Given the obvious potential for claims to exceed available output in any system, the fact that the marginal productivity scheme clearly identifies a feasible payment for every party is no small advantage. A second attractive feature of the marginal productivity system is that it rewards initiative, effort, and risk taking. The harder, longer, and more effectively a person works, the more she will be paid. And if she risks her capital on a venture that happens to succeed, she will reap a handsome dividend.

THE RAWLSIAN CRITICISM OF THE MARGINAL PRODUCTIVITY SYSTEM

The marginal productivity system is not without flaws, however. The most common criticism is that it often generates a high degree of inequality. Those who do well in the marketplace end up with vastly more than they can spend, while those who fail often cannot meet even their basic needs. Such inequality might be easier to accept if it were strictly the result of differences in effort. But it is not. Talent plays an important role in most endeavors, and although it can be nurtured and developed if you have it, whether you have it in the first place is essentially a matter of luck.

Even having abundant talent is no guarantee of doing well. It is also necessary to have the *right* talent. Being able to hit a baseball 400 feet with consistency will earn you millions annually, while being the best fourth-grade teacher in the nation will earn you little; and being the best handball player in the world will earn you virtually nothing. The baseball star earns so much more, not because he works harder or has more talent, but because he is lucky enough to be good at something people are willing to pay a lot for.

John Rawls, a Harvard moral philosopher, constructed a cogent ethical critique of the marginal productivity system, one based heavily on the microeconomic theory of choice itself. The question he asked was "What constitutes a just dis-

---

[5]Recall that long-run competitive equilibrium occurs at the minimum point of every firm's long-run average cost curve; at that point there are constant returns in production. It is a property of production functions with constant returns that $F(K, L) = K\partial F/\partial K + L\partial F/\partial L$, which says that paying each factor its marginal product will exactly exhaust the total product available.

tribution of income?" To answer it, he proposed the following thought experiment. Imagine that you and the other citizens of some country have been thrown together in a meeting to choose the rules for distributing income. This meeting takes place behind a "veil of ignorance," which conceals from each person any knowledge of what talents and abilities he and others have. No individual knows whether he is smart or dull, strong or weak, fast or slow, and so on—which means that no one knows which particular rules of distribution would work to his own advantage. Rawls argued that the rules people would choose in such a state of ignorance would necessarily be fair; and if the rules are fair, it follows that the distribution to which they give rise will also be fair.

What rules would people choose from behind a veil of ignorance? If the national income to be distributed were a fixed amount every year, it is likely that most would choose to give everyone an equal share. This is likely, Rawls argued, because most people are strongly risk averse. Since an unequal distribution would involve not only a chance of doing well, but also a chance of doing poorly, most people would prefer to eliminate the risk by choosing an equal distribution.

The difficulty, however, is that the total amount of income available for distribution is *not* a fixed amount every year. Rather, it depends on how hard people work, how much initiative and risk they take, and so on. If everyone were guaranteed an equal share of the national income at the outset, why would anyone work hard or take risks? Without rewards for hard work and risk taking, national income would be dramatically smaller than if such rewards existed. Of course, material rewards for effort and risk taking necessarily lead to inequality. But Rawls argues that people would be willing to accept a certain degree of inequality as long as these rewards produced a sufficiently large increase in the total amount of output available for distribution.

How much inequality? Much less than the amount produced by purely competitive factor markets, Rawls argued. The idea is that each person behind the veil of ignorance would rationally fear being in a disadvantaged position, and so each would choose distributional rules that would maximize the income of the poorest citizen. That is, additional inequality would be considered justified as long as it had the effect of raising the income of each and every citizen. Rawls's own critics responded that his proposal was unrealistically conservative—that most people would allow additional inequality if the effect, say, were to increase *most* incomes. But Rawls's basic point was that people behind a veil of ignorance would choose rules that would produce a more equal distribution of income than we get under the marginal productivity system. And since these choices define what constitutes a just distribution of income, he argued, fairness requires at least some attempt to reduce the inequality produced by the marginal productivity system.

PRACTICAL REASONS FOR REDISTRIBUTION

The moral argument Rawls outlined has obvious force. But there are also compelling practical reasons for limiting inequality. We saw, for example, that an equal tax levied on every citizen will in general result in an inefficient level of public goods. To the extent that willingness to pay for public goods increases with income, high-income citizens will have every selfish reason to support a tax structure in which they carry a much larger share of the tax burden than the poor do. And to the extent that the public goods financed under such a tax system are equally available to persons of different income levels, the effect will be to reduce inequality.

Forces analogous to the ones that shape pay distributions within firms suggest another practical reason for income redistribution at the society level. Recall from Chapter 14 that within any single firm the tendency is for the most productive employees to be paid less than the values of their marginal products, and for the least productive employees to be paid more. The difference between a worker's wage and the value of her marginal product may be interpreted as a compensating differential that reflects her rank within the firm. Heterogeneous collections of workers will remain together in a firm only if those who hold positions of low rank are adequately compensated by those who hold high rank.

These forces in the firm are reflected at the societal level as well. It is obviously advantageous to occupy a position in the upper portion of society's income distribution. Such positions exist, however, only if there are others willing to occupy positions in the lower portion of the income distribution. Society has a clear interest in forging terms on which all members will view it as in their interests to remain part of society. If experience is any guide, social cohesion may simply not be possible without some attempt to compensate people for the implicit burden of occupying low positions in the overall distribution of income.

FAIRNESS AND EFFICIENCY

We saw that efforts to reduce inequality may be justified on the basis of both moral and practical arguments. Some mix of such arguments has apparently been found compelling, for no modern economy leaves income distribution entirely to the marketplace. This underlying commitment to norms of equality is strong and plays a pivotal role in almost every debate on public policy.

The economist's natural advantage lies in answering questions related to efficiency. For this reason, many economists are reluctant even to discuss issues related to equity. Yet virtually every policy change will affect not only efficiency, but also the distribution of income. And we know that most societies seem prepared to reject efficient allocations if they do not pass muster on grounds of fairness. The result is that unless economists are prepared to work within social constraints on inequality, there will be little or no audience for their policy recommendations.

During a supply interruption of some important commodity, for example, economists are almost always quick to recommend letting the price rise to market-clearing levels. We know, after all, that this policy will lead to an efficient allocation of the scarce good. The social complaint, however, is that sharply rising prices will impose an unacceptable burden on the poor. And so, in the wake of shortages, governments often reject the free market path in favor of rationing, queues, and other, more cumbersome, methods of distribution.

The unfortunate irony in this response is that inefficient solutions make the economic pie smaller for everyone, rich and poor alike. Contrary to popular impressions, the goals of fairness and efficiency need not be in conflict at all. We saw in Chapter 16 that distribution and efficiency are separable issues. Given a suitable choice of initial endowments, *any* Pareto-efficient allocation is sustainable as a competitive equilibrium. When economists recommend a policy on grounds of efficiency, they must also be prepared to explain how its distributional consequences can be altered to meet social constraints.

A case in point is the episode with which we began this chapter. The issue, recall, was whether local telephone companies should be permitted to charge for calls to directory assistance. Alfred Kahn's proposal that they should was greeted by complaints that this policy would impose unacceptable hardships on the poor. Kahn salvaged the proposal by amending it to require that every telephone subscriber be given a 30-cent credit on his telephone bill in reflection of the costs saved from having fewer directory assistance calls.

Let's examine how this amended proposal works. In Figure 18-6, the horizontal axis measures directory assistance calls per month and the vertical axis measures expenditure on all other goods. The horizontal line labeled B_2 represents the budget constraint for a consumer with a monthly income of Y_0 in the event that there is no charge for directory assistance calls. B_1 represents the same person's budget when there is a 10 cent charge for such calls. And B_3 is the budget constraint when there is a 30 cent monthly credit in addition to the 10 cent charge per call. I_1, I_2, and I_3 are indifference curves. They have the conventional shape, except that beyond some number of calls each month they turn upward,

FIGURE 18-6
When directory assistance calls are free, the consumer makes C_3 of them each month. Charging 10 cents each for them cuts down on the volume of these calls substantially, enough to finance a 30 cent per month credit for every customer. The new system is more efficient than the old and places more purchasing power in the hands of the typical customer.

CHARGING FOR DIRECTORY ASSISTANCE

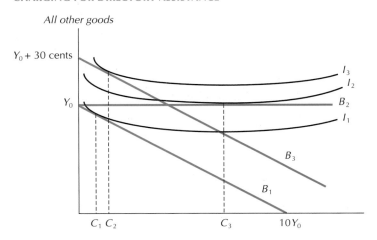

reflecting the fact that most people would not choose to make an unlimited number of calls to directory assistance even if those calls were free. For the consumer shown, failure to charge for directory assistance calls results in C_3 calls/mo. A simple 10 cent charge results in C_1 calls/mo, a sharply lower number. The 10 cent charge with 30 cent credit results in C_2 calls/mo. On the plausible assumption that 30 cents/mo is a trivial amount of income even for a poor person, C_2 and C_1 should be almost the same. The 30 cent credit is financed by the cost savings that result when the number of calls falls from C_3 to C_2. This reduction in calls enables the telephone company to run its operations with fewer switchboards and operators—resources that are freed up to do something more useful.

A social scientist from another planet might find it hard to believe that the trivial hardship of paying for directory assistance calls would have dissuaded a regulatory commission from approving the charge. Yet such is the strength of distributional concerns in public policy debate. By taking care to share the cost savings with ratepayers in the form of a conspicuous 30 cent monthly credit, an otherwise doomed policy reform was salvaged.

In many other markets, such as those for gasoline and natural gas, the distributional consequences of charging prices based on cost are much more pronounced than in the case of directory assistance calls. In such situations, of course, the distributional issue is all the more salient. The efficiency gains from charging prices that reflect costs are also much larger in these cases, and with sufficient attention to the distribution of these gains, it should be possible to reach political agreement on how to achieve them.

METHODS OF REDISTRIBUTION

The methods by which society redistributes income are subject to the same kinds of analysis that economists bring to bear on other programs and institutions. Our principal concern here is that poorly designed redistributive programs can easily undo the very efficiency gains they were created to facilitate.

Our Current Welfare Programs.   Abba Lerner, one of my former professors in graduate school, once remarked that the main problem the poor confront is that they have too little income. The solution, in his view, was disarmingly simple. We should give them some money. Traditional welfare programs, however, are much more complicated. We have food stamps, rent stamps, energy stamps, day care subsidies, aid to families with dependent children, and a host of other separate programs, each with its own administrative bureaucracy. The end result is that it takes approximately 7 tax dollars to get 1 additional dollar of income into the hands of a poor person.

High as they are, these costs are not the major problem from an efficiency standpoint. Of potentially far greater concern is the effect current programs have on work incentives. To illustrate the difficulty, it is necessary first to describe some of the administrative details of the programs. Each program has a full benefit level that all persons who earn less than some threshold income level are

FIGURE 18-7
Persons who earn below $4000/yr receive the full benefit level of $1000/yr. For each dollar earned above $4000, benefits go down by 50 cents. Once a person's income reaches $6000/yr, all benefits cease.

BENEFITS VERSUS INCOME FOR A TYPICAL WELFARE PROGRAM

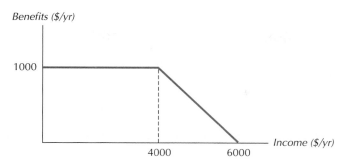

eligible to receive. Once a beneficiary begins to earn more than that threshold, his benefits are reduced by some fraction of each additional dollar earned. This fraction is called the *marginal benefit reduction rate.* Figure 18-7 shows how benefits vary with income for a program with a full benefit level of $1000/yr, a threshold income level of $4000/yr, and a marginal benefit reduction rate of 50 percent.

The real problem comes when a person participates in several welfare programs at once, as is common under our current system. Consider, for example, a person enrolled in four programs like the one shown in Figure 18-7. Once his income reaches $4000/yr, he will lose $2 in benefits (50 cents from each of the four programs) for every additional dollar he earns. Needless to say, these terms are hardly conducive to the expenditure of effort. The adverse effects on labor supply decisions are one of the most serious costs of our current welfare system.

The Negative Income Tax. Milton Friedman calculated that for the cost of our current programs, every man, woman, and child now classified as poor in the United States could be given a payment of more than $8000/yr. This calculation, together with his concern about adverse effects on work incentives, led Friedman to propose a radical reform in which our entire array of current programs would be replaced by a single program he called the *negative income tax (NIT).*

Friedman's version of the NIT starts out by giving every man, woman, and child—rich or poor—an income tax credit that is large enough to sustain a minimally adequate standard of living. Someone who earned no income would receive this credit in cash. People with earned income would then be taxed on their income at some rate less than 100 percent. The initial credit and the tax rate combine to determine a breakeven income level at which each person's tax liability exactly offsets his initial tax credit. People earning below that level would receive a net benefit payment from the government, while those earning more would make a net tax payment.

Figure 18-8 shows how the program would work with a tax credit of $4000/yr and a tax rate of 50 percent. The breakeven income level for these program values is $8000/yr. Someone earning $4000/yr would receive a net benefit payment of $2000/yr, while someone earning $12,000/yr would make a tax payment of $2000/yr.

EXERCISE 18-4

Find the breakeven income level for a program whose tax credit is $6000 and whose tax rate is 40 percent. What is the net benefit received by a person who earns $4000/yr from paid employment?

The NIT would be administered in much the same way as our current income tax is administered. One strong advantage of the NIT is thus its promise to eliminate the costly overlapping bureaucracies of our current programs. But the main attraction of the NIT to economists is that it has a much less perverse effect on work incentives than current programs do. Because the marginal tax rate confronting poor people would never exceed 100 percent under the NIT, people would be assured of having more after-tax income if they worked longer hours.

Although the incentive problem is less severe under the NIT than under our current welfare programs, it remains a serious difficulty. If the NIT is to be the *sole* means of insulating people against poverty, its payment to people with no earned income must be at least as large as the poverty threshold. And if the payment is large enough to live on, it will inevitably induce many people to stop

FIGURE 18-8
This NIT starts each person out with a tax credit of $4000/yr. People who earn no income receive that amount in cash. All earned income is then taxed, here at the rate of 50 percent, resulting in a breakeven income level of $8000/yr. People who earn less than that amount receive a net benefit payment from the government; people who earn more make a net tax payment.

A NEGATIVE INCOME TAX PROGRAM

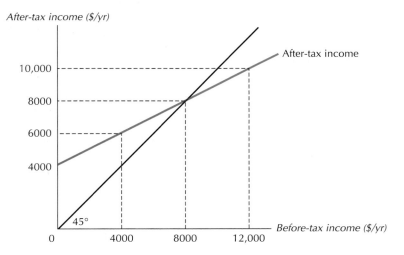

working. The importance of this problem was confirmed by federal experiments with the NIT during the 1970s. Although the labor force withdrawals observed in these experiments were smaller than predicted by the NIT's fiercest critics, they were nonetheless substantial.

But even if the NIT induced only a handful of people to pursue lives of leisure at taxpayer expense, critics would find these people, and there would be an eager audience for reports of their doings on the nightly news. Both liberals and conservatives alike would be chagrined at the sight of NIT recipients practicing their guitars and playing volleyball on Monday mornings. In the face of such images, an NIT with a grant large enough to support able-bodied people who chose not to work would be politically unsustainable.

Public Employment for the Poor.   Like the NIT, proposals for public jobs for the disadvantaged (JOBS) received much attention during the early days of the war on poverty. These proposals had the obvious appeal of not providing handouts for people who could support themselves. In the language of program advocates, the government would serve as the "employer of last resort," the guarantor of "decent employment at a decent wage" to all who were unable to find such work in the private sector.

As the sole mechanism for lifting the poor from poverty, the public jobs idea fell victim to several criticisms. Perhaps the most important was that guaranteed public employment would cause people to desert the private sector in droves. This claim was based on evidence that unskilled workers find government jobs much more attractive than private jobs with similar wages. Thousands of applicants line up when openings for menial government jobs are posted; at the same time want ads for kitchen help in the private sector go unanswered. With the prospect of a large-scale employment migration clearly in mind, policymakers concluded that resources simply would not permit an open-ended offer of government employment at wages comparable to those in the private sector.

A second criticism was that public jobs for the disadvantaged would inevitably be make-work tasks, no more useful than Keynes' call for people to dig holes and fill them up. This criticism struck a resonant chord in the United States, where the predisposition has often been to view *all* government jobs as make-work. This attitude alone would probably have killed the JOBS proposals, even if they could somehow have been made economically feasible.

A Combination of NIT and JOBS.   With a few simple changes, however, the JOBS and NIT programs can be combined in a way that eliminates many of the difficulties we encounter when each is viewed as the sole weapon against poverty.

With JOBS, for example, the government could solicit bids from private contractors to hire unskilled workers at subminimum wages to perform a variety of specified tasks. (More on these tasks in a moment.) With the wage set much lower than for private jobs, there would be no reason to fear a massive exodus from the private sector.

Having public jobs for the poor administered by private contractors chosen through competitive bidding would do much to eliminate the inefficient management that so often plagues government operations. As noted in Chapter 12, many cities have found that their costs go down by more than half, with no reductions in quality, when they provide services like fire protection and trash removal through private contractors. If the administration of JOBS were subjected to the ruthless cost-cutting pressures of private markets, there would be every reason to expect efficient performance here as well.

There is general agreement that, given competent management, many useful tasks can be performed by people who lack extensive experience and training. What city would not be pleased to have additional landscaping and maintenance in its parks? With proper supervision, unskilled persons can carry out such tasks. And they can transport the elderly and handicapped in specially equipped vans; fill potholes in city streets; replace burned-out street lamps; transplant seedlings in erosion control projects; remove graffiti from public places; paint government buildings; and recycle newspapers and aluminum and glass containers.

These and countless other socially useful tasks remain to be done, and could be done by people who lack the skills necessary to find employment in the private sector. Even single parents with small children could participate, by helping to staff day care centers in which their own children were enrolled.

A simple design change would also eliminate the major difficulties associated with the traditional NIT. This change would be to limit the maximum NIT payment to a figure that, like the JOBS salary, is well below the annual earnings equivalent of full-time employment at the minimum wage. With the payment held below that level, it would not be possible for people to drop out of the labor market to live at taxpayer expense. Yet when combined with earnings from the JOBS program—or, better still, with earnings from a private job—the NIT grant would lift a person above the poverty threshold (see Figure 18-9). Neither program alone can accomplish this goal without creating unacceptable side effects. But the two programs together can.

Indirect Benefits of the Combined Program. The JOBS-NIT combination would not be cheap. But neither is our current system. In addition to their direct costs and perverse work incentives, current programs impose innumerable indirect costs. Many of these take the form of regulations designed to help the poor. Because current programs cannot transfer extra income directly to the poor without undermining work incentives even further, policymakers constantly face pressure to interfere with private markets to shield the poor from price increases. As discussed in Chapter 2, for example, bureaucrats designed a Byzantine system of regulations in order to prevent gasoline price increases during the oil supply interruption of 1979. It was common to see lines at gas stations wrap around several city blocks, and several motorists were killed or injured in disputes over who stood where in those queues.

With a combination of NIT and JOBS in place of our current welfare programs, policymakers could have transferred extra income directly to the poor in the

FIGURE 18-9
An NIT with a cash grant far too small to live on would not encourage people to drop out of the labor force. Nor would a government-sponsored job at subminimum wages lure productively employed workers out of private-sector jobs. But the combined income from both programs would be sufficient to lift people above the poverty threshold. And because of the low pay in public jobs, participants would have strong incentives to continue searching for jobs in the private sector.

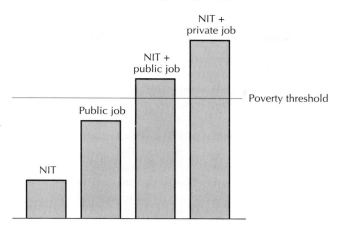

INCOME SOURCES IN THE NIT-JOBS PROGRAM

NIT + private job

NIT + public job

Poverty threshold

Public job

NIT

wake of the oil shocks of 1979. And this, in turn, would have permitted us to allocate oil in the most sensible and efficient way—by the price mechanism.

Many cities have similarly adopted rent controls in the name of their concerns about the poor. Yet as any intermediate microeconomics student can readily explain, these controls cost us many dollars for every dollar they save the poor. Low-income housing deteriorates; lawyers prosper from otherwise pointless condominium conversions; couples whose children have left home continue living in eight-room apartments; desperate tenants bribe superintendents to get on waiting lists; and so on. With a combination of JOBS and NIT programs, people's incomes could be augmented directly, thereby circumventing the need for wasteful stopgap measures like rent controls.

An Objection to JOBS. Many people who think of themselves as friends of the poor will find it unpalatable to require that people perform services in return for public assistance. Some would liken this policy to forced servitude and object that it deprives poor people of their dignity.

Such objections stem from a refusal to acknowledge our true menu of policy choices. In an ideal world, liberals and conservatives alike might agree to provide generous unconditional assistance to those who cannot fend for themselves, and no assistance at all for others. In the world we live in, however, there is no reliable scheme for separating the members of these two groups. Lacking such a scheme, we are hardly in a position to offer one group benefits while denying them to the other. And no one pretends that it is possible to offer generous unconditional assistance to *everyone*. Our practical alternatives, in plain view for everyone to see, are: (1) to offer very limited unconditional assistance to everyone (roughly, our current scheme) or (2) to offer more generous assistance conditional on the performance of useful tasks.

As a college student, you are unlikely to be desperately poor. But try for a moment to imagine that you are not only poor but unlucky. There are private jobs out there somewhere that pay a decent wage, but your luck is so bad that you have despaired of ever landing one. Policymakers in Washington are trying to decide what to do about you. You and they know that the choices are limited to the two alternatives mentioned. Which would *you* prefer?

Suppose you prefer the second—to perform a useful task in exchange for a living wage. That way, you reason, you can afford to live in an apartment in which your children do not eat flakes of leaded paint off the walls and door-frames. You also know that working in a government job might help you acquire skills that would enable you to get the high-wage job you really want. Finally, despite what you have heard to the contrary, you do not feel that performing a socially useful task demeans you in any way. How would you then feel if your "friends" in high places lobbied vigorously against your chosen alternative, saying that it would "rob you of your dignity"?

Liberals and conservatives have a shared interest—both moral and practical—in redistributing income in ways that do not undermine efficiency. Our current redistributive programs are for the most part both costly and ineffective. Micro-economic analysis has as much to teach us about the reform of these programs as it does about the many other important policy issues we've examined throughout this text.

Summary

Public goods are like other goods in that their value can be measured by what people would be willing to pay to have more of them. But whereas the aggre-gate demand curve for a private good is formed by adding the individual demand curves horizontally, the aggregate willingness-to-pay curve for a public good is the vertical summation of the corresponding individual curves. This dif-ference arose because the quantity of a public good must be the same for every consumer. In the private case, by contrast, the price is the same for different buy-ers, who then select different quantities.

There is a clear analogy between the demand for public goods and the demand for jointly produced private goods. To produce additional chicken wings, it is necessary to produce additional drumsticks. Just as the quantity of a public good must be the same for all consumers, so must the quantity of chicken wings consumed be exactly equal to the quantity of drumsticks con-sumed. And just as the price one person is willing to pay for a given quantity of a public good can differ from what another is willing to pay, so will the price of drumsticks generally be different from the price of wings.

As with private goods, the supply curve of a public good is simply the mar-ginal cost of producing it. The optimal quantity of a public good is the level for which the aggregate willingness-to-pay curve intersects the supply curve. In order to pay for the optimal quantities of public goods it will generally be necessary for individual tax payments to vary directly with the amounts that individuals are willing to pay for public goods. To the extent that people with higher incomes demand higher quantities of public goods, the result is that both rich and poor will favor a tax system that places a larger share of the total tax burden on the rich.

The mere fact that a good has the characteristics of a public good does not mean that it must necessarily be provided by government. There are many ingenious schemes, ranging from free commercial television to highly structured collective legal contracts, whereby public goods are provided with virtually no involvement by government.

Problems similar to those that arise in connection with public goods are encountered whenever there are significant indivisibilities or economies of scale in the production of private consumption goods. In such situations, we saw, it is common for clubs to form in which members share the costs of important consumption goods. The tradeoff confronting a potential member of such a club is between cost savings and reduced privacy in the use of the good.

Majority voting sometimes produces intransitive rankings among projects. When it does, the power to choose the order in which different pairs of alternatives are considered is often tantamount to the power to determine the final outcome. There is a special class of issues in which majority voting is not vulnerable to agenda manipulation. With respect to single issues in which each voter ranks every alternative in terms of its distance from his ideal choice, the final outcome will be the one most preferred by the median voter, no matter what order the votes are taken in. This result is known as the median voter theorem.

Cost-benefit analysis is a simple but very powerful alternative to majority voting. Applied in the proper way to a sufficiently large number of small decisions, it almost always satisfies the Pareto criterion.

Even with a perfect mechanism for revealing public sentiments about the relative desirability of different public goods, there will still be difficult choices about which goods to produce. The problem is that the types of public goods strongly favored by some groups are often strongly opposed by others. If heterogeneous voters are forced to coexist in a single jurisdiction, the frequent result is a painful compromise that satisfies no one. But the need for such compromises is greatly reduced if voters are able to group themselves into communities with relatively homogeneous tastes.

A problem that plagues all mechanisms of public decision making is that self-interested parties have an incentive to influence outcomes in their own favor. This problem goes by the name of rent seeking and has become an increasingly serious threat to our social welfare.

The primary mechanism for distributing income in market economies is the factor market. People sell their labor in return for a payment equal to the value of its marginal product. And they invest their savings at interest rates that are similarly linked to the marginal productivity of capital. This method of income distribution has several desirable properties on efficiency grounds—in particular, it rewards effort and the willingness to incur risk. But critics, notably John Rawls, have argued that people would never voluntarily choose to live under a process that yields such highly unequal outcomes as we see in untempered factor markets.

In addition to the moral argument Rawls offered, there are at least two practical reasons for income redistribution. First, the rich would favor paying more than an equal share of the total tax burden because otherwise they would end up with an inefficiently small provision of public goods. And second, redistribution may be necessary to maintain a voluntary sense of social cohesion, something as much in the interests of the rich as of the poor.

Our current array of welfare programs is costly, not only because of bureaucratic duplication, but also because of its indirect effects on work incentives and on public policies with respect to private markets. A combination of a small negative income tax, supplemented by subminimum-wage public jobs, could transfer income to the poor without many of the unintended side effects of our current programs.

Questions for Review

1. Why are the individual willingness-to-pay curves added vertically, not horizontally, to get the aggregate willingness-to-pay curve for a public good?

2. How are jointly produced private goods analogous to public goods?

3. Why would even rich citizens be likely to oppose having equal tax payments by rich and poor alike?

4. In what way does a private good produced under conditions of increasing returns to scale resemble a public good? Describe the tradeoff between flexibility and cost that confronts users of such goods.

5. How does majority voting lead to intransitive social rankings?

6. Describe two forms of inefficiency associated with rent seeking.

7. Why is a negative income tax, by itself, unable to solve the redistribution problem?

Problems

1. A government is trying to decide how much of a public good to provide. The willingness-to-pay curves for each of its two citizens are as given in the diagram. The marginal cost curve for the public good is given by $MC = Q/2$, where Q is the quan-

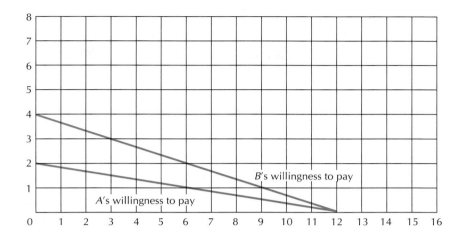

tity of the good. There is also a fixed cost of 10 associated with production of the good.

    a. What is the optimal quantity of the public good?

    b. If both citizens must be taxed equally to provide the good, will it receive a majority vote?

2. On the assumption that the public good described in Problem 1 is provided at the optimal level, how much should the state charge each citizen each time he or she uses the public good?

3. Ten identical consumers all have individual willingness to pay curves $P = 5 - \frac{1}{20}Q$ for a public good—say, local parks (where P is measured in hundreds of dollars and Q is measured in acres). Construct and graph the aggregate willingness to pay curve. For 50 acres of parks, what is the maximum each individual would be willing to pay?

4. Consider the scenario described in Problem 3, but now consider that the marginal cost of providing parks measured in hundreds of dollars is MC $= \frac{1}{2}Q$. Determine the optimal size of local parks.

5. Chicken wings and chicken drumsticks are jointly produced private goods. The introduction of Buffalo wings—the fast-food sensation—has led to a sharp increase in the demand for chicken wings. Show how this affects the equilibrium price and quantity of drumsticks.

6. Lumber and sawdust are joint products, whose demand functions are D_L and D_S, as shown in the diagram on the next page. The quantity axis measures the number of trees. Points on the demand schedules indicate demands for the lumber or sawdust equivalents of a given quantity of trees.

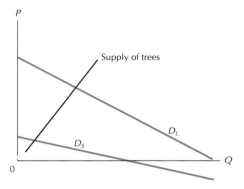

a. Provide an economic interpretation of the fact that the demand schedule for sawdust extends below the horizontal axis.

b. If the supply schedule for trees is as given in the diagram, show the equilibrium prices and quantities of sawdust and lumber on a graph.

7. Viewer-supported television stations often give contributors "free" gifts for making contributions at various levels. ("Two handsome *News Hour* coffee mugs for a donation of $120.") Based on what you know about the psychology of framing decisions (see Chapter 8), explain why this practice might help stations raise more money.

8. Colleges and universities commonly name buildings and business or medical schools after substantial donors (witness Ohio State's Max Fisher School of Business and Schottenstein Center/Value City Arena). Meanwhile, few donors care to earmark their gifts for routine maintenance of university buildings. How might the social benefits of charitable giving explain these observations?

9. *True or false:* Because the issues at stake in national presidential elections are much more important than those at stake in a small village mayoral election, rational choice theory says a much larger proportion of voters will turn out in the former than in the latter. Explain.

10. *True or false:* The fact that the voter turnout is significantly greater in close presidential elections than in one-sided ones provides clear support for the proposition that voters are rational. Explain.

11. A fraternity consisting of 20 sophomores, 20 juniors, and 20 seniors is about to elect its next president. Arnold, Bo, and Chuck are the three candidates. Members of each class have the ranking schemes given in the table:

Class	Best	Next best	Last
Seniors	Arnold	Bo	Chuck
Juniors	Bo	Chuck	Arnold
Sophs	Chuck	Arnold	Bo

The tradition in the fraternity is to pit two candidates against each other and then pit the winner of that contest against the third candidate. If you were a sophomore, whom would you pair off in the preliminary round? If you were a senior?

12. Smith is a hardhearted person who favors giving the poor only sufficient aid to keep them from going hungry. Assuming everyone else in Smith's community feels the same way he does, why might Smith nonetheless be opposed to a proposal to let each community set its own level of welfare support?

13. A. Smith, who is currently unemployed, is a participant in four welfare programs that offer daily benefits of $10 each to people with no earned income. Each program then curtails its benefits by 50 cents for every dollar of income a recipient earns. A. Smith's identical twin brother, B. Smith, is enrolled in an experimental negative income tax program that gives him $40/day in benefits and then taxes him at the rate of 50 percent on each dollar of earned income. Now suppose A. Smith is offered a job that pays $4/hr, the same wage his brother earns.

    a. Draw the budget constraint for each twin.
    b. How many hours would they have to work before A. Smith ends up with more net cash and benefits than his brother?

Answers to In-Chapter Exercises

18-1. The aggregate willingness to pay curve would be $P = 120 - 2Q$, the vertical summation of the individual willingness to pay curves (see graph). For $Q = 30$ minutes, each individual would be willing to pay up to $P = 12 - \frac{1}{5}Q = 12 - \frac{1}{5}(30) = \$6$, for a total of $60 from 10 consumers.

18-2. To find the optimal duration of the concert, equate the aggregate willingness to pay $P = 120 - 2Q$ and the marginal cost $MC = 2Q$ to find $Q = 30$ minutes.

18-3. Again, Schumer is the median voter. The alternative closest to his ideal percentage is 20, and this will win a majority in a vote on any pair of alternatives.

18-4. Let Y^* denote the breakeven income level. To calculate Y^*, we solve $6000 + (1 - 0.4)Y^* = Y^*$, which yields $Y^* = \$15,000/\text{yr}$. A person who earns $4000/yr would pay $0.4(\$4000) = \$1600/\text{yr}$ in taxes, and would thus receive a net annual benefit of $6000 - \$1600 = \$4400$.

INDEX